State and Society
in the Philippines

State and Society
in the Philippines

Second Edition

Patricio N. Abinales and
Donna J. Amoroso

ROWMAN & LITTLEFIELD
Lanham • Boulder • New York • London

Published by Rowman & Littlefield
A wholly owned subsidiary of The Rowman & Littlefield Publishing Group, Inc.
4501 Forbes Boulevard, Suite 200, Lanham, Maryland 20706
www.rowman.com

Unit A, Whitacre Mews, 26-34 Stannary Street, London SE11 4AB, United Kingdom

British Library Cataloguing in Publication Information Available

Library of Congress Cataloging-in-Publication Data

Names: Abinales, P. N., author. | Amoroso, Donna J., 1960–2011, author.
Title: State and society in the Philippines / Patricio N. Abinales and Donna J. Amoroso.
Description: Second edition. | Lanham: Rowman & Littlefield, [2017] | Series: State and
    society in East Asia | Includes bibliographical references and index.
Identifiers: LCCN 2017006076 (print) | LCCN 2017007297 (ebook) | ISBN
    9781538103937 (cloth : alk. paper) | ISBN 9781538103944 (pbk. : alk. paper) | ISBN
    9781538103951 (electronic)
Subjects: LCSH: Philippines—Politics and government. | Philippines—Social conditions.
Classification: LCC DS672.8 .A25 2017 (print) | LCC DS672.8 (ebook) | DDC
    306.09599—dc23
LC record available at https://lccn.loc.gov/2017006076

Printed in the United States of America

To Angela Marie Amoroso Abinales,
in memory of her mother, Donna J. Amoroso

Contents

Boxes

Foreword: The History Textbook as a Story of Generations

Lisandro Claudio

Every generation has its history book. Gregorio Zaide, who wrote in the immediate postwar period, was a historian appreciative of colonial legacies. His numerous textbooks reflected the strength of a "Filipino-American friendship" forged in a war against Imperial Japan. If our historians loved America, it was because Filipinos also loved America.

In the 1960s and 1970s, Teodoro Agoncillo's *History of the Filipino People* (*HFP*) decolonized history, presenting events from the perspective of the common Filipino *tao* (people). *HFP* was more than a textbook. Its radical reinterpretation of history anchored the militant nationalism of the Marcos years. Using the book, activists discovered the colonial and postcolonial sins of "American Empire," with Agoncillo serving as one of the Left's first helmsman. Although he belonged to a generation older than baby-boomer activists, Agoncillo connected with youth concerns in a way that other older historians could not. My father still remembers his first encounter with *HFP* after years of reading Zaide in high school. For him, an anticolonial, nationalist textbook was a breath of fresh air.

After fifty years, *HFP* is still in print, and it is still widely used in classrooms across the Philippines. Which is unfortunate. *HFP*, an important historical document, should now *become* history rather than *impart* history. I say this not because I think the book is bad, but because scholarship moves on. Moreover, the concerns of students change. In the 1970s, students grappled with the contradictions of coloniality; now students are concerned with globality. Your average Filipino college student no longer rants about the "U.S.-Rodrigo Duterte" dictatorship. Rather, he or she lives in a Philippines impacted by the ruptures induced by migration, the revolution in information technology, and other phenomena associated with a contracting globe.

Globalization changes the historical questions we need to ask. Instead of asking, "How have Spain and the United States oppressed *us*?" it becomes more productive to ask, "How did the Philippines enter the global economy?" Or, at a time of accelerated ASEAN (Association of Southeast Asian Nations) integration, we may wish to ask, "How does the history of state formation in the Philippines compare with those of other Southeast Asian states?"

This proposed shift is not an attempt to deny the violence of colonialism. Instead, it is an injunction to make history more relevant to those who read it. Too often, the Philippine historian's concern with colonialism has narrowed the ambit of scholarship. Many American-Filipino scholars, for example, obsess over the "U.S. Empire in the Philippines" as a means to connect their or their parents' homeland's story with that of multicultural America. The result of such endeavors has been parochial work about the Philippines told through the lens of a simplified notion of America.

The Philippines of the twenty-first century must be represented in its own terms, through an examination of its distinct sociopolitical development in the context of Southeast Asia and the globe.

This book transcends the parochialism of Philippine nationalist historiography, without losing sight of the specificity of the country's experiences. It is both local and cosmopolitan. And for this reason, *State and Society in the Philippines* (now revised and updated) should be *the* history textbook of the current generation of Filipino students, who must be weaned from historical navel-gazing. It should also be the first introduction of non-Filipinos to the country's history. Apart from being succinct yet comprehensive, the book's focus on state-formation will allow non-Filipinos to compare the history of the Philippine nation-state with theirs. American readers, for example, will be fascinated with a book that dares compare Filipino politicos (caciques) with the bosses of New York's Tammany Hall.

In the same way that the older Agoncillo spoke to the baby boomers, baby boomers Patricio Abinales and Donna Amoroso are now speaking to millennials. The authors wrote this book for their American and Filipino nieces and nephews, and in this edition for their American-Filipina daughter, to see whether students from both sides of the Pacific could be drawn to a single text. They also wrote it for young historians like me, almost as a cheat sheet that provides an overview of the latest scholarship in Philippine history (the bibliography of this book is itself an achievement). The result is a work that introduces the reader to the uneven, contradiction-ridden story we call Philippine history. More important, the result is an invitation to discover what others have written and to see what else can be written, both through words and political praxis.

The fruits of intergenerational conversations are hard to predict. Teachers impart lessons with little foresight of what students will do with the knowledge. But the best teachers are open to surprises. Abinales, who hails from Ozamiz City in the southern Philippine island of Mindanao and revels in his own marginality, probably does not expect to impact a generation's thinking through one book. After all, he claims that most of his writing is addressed to his barber. But my gut tells me this book will have a lasting effect on the very "national" scholarship that the "provincial" Abinales, our preeminent scholar of Mindanao, often critiques.

Regretfully, Donna passed away in 2011 and was only able to see the initial ripples of *State and Society in the Philippines*. Their daughter, Angela, however, is lucky, because her mother left her this book. Through it, her mother will sustain a conversation with her and others like her in the years to come. And when this book has run its course, when its contents no longer speak to young people, the only way to honor the legacy of a fine scholar and a humble woman will be to let this work go. But that will be many years from now. For the foreseeable future, *State and Society in the Philippines* will remain the definitive Philippine history textbook.

—Lisandro Claudio, Department of History,
De La Salle University, Philippines

Preface to the Second Edition

The genesis of *State and Society in the Philippines* (*SSP*) dates back to the March 2003 annual conference of the Association for Asian Studies, when Susan McEachern, Rowman & Littlefield's editorial director for International Studies, invited Donna to contribute to the publisher's new "State and Society in East Asia" series, edited by Elizabeth J. Perry. Donna said she liked the idea and proposed writing about the Philippines with me as coauthor. Susan thought it was a splendid idea, so when Donna returned to Japan, we began discussing how to go about writing the book.

We explored ideas and themes with the help of our friend and colleague Carol Hau, who shared her insights on state-society relations, the centrality of marginal groups like the Filipino-Chinese and the Muslims, and the need to revise the political timeline. Our discussions with Carol yielded fruit, and we came up with the following goals:

First, the book should address a broad and young audience, and thus must be written as a text that examines Philippine political development from a state-in-society framework.

Second, the book should be able to draw the attention of readers from both sides of the Pacific as well as other parts of the world. Our reason was relatively straightforward: Donna was American, I am Filipino, and we have nephews and nieces at both ends of the Pacific whom we hoped would read something that their aunt and uncle wrote.

Third, the book should rely as much as possible on Philippine sources. We wanted to show the wealth of primary and secondary sources that can be found in the country as well as the best analytical pieces on Philippine political development written by Filipinos.

The final reason was academic and personal. Donna and I wanted to know whether two scholars who both schooled in Cornell University's Southeast

Asia Program, who were married to each other, but trained in different disciplines (Donna in history; I in government) and studying countries with different historical trajectories and political systems, could write a book together. This was the most difficult part of the process; it was also the most fun.

We finished a draft in mid-2004, which we showed to several friends, colleagues, and our academic mentors while Susan sent the manuscript for external review. Both groups sent us extremely helpful comments, and we completed the revised version at year's end while in Bangkok, Thailand.

Rowman & Littlefield published *SSP* in mid-2005. The book did not attract much attention in the first months after its publication (it was low on the Amazon list of books read when compared to books on Indonesia and Thailand that came out at about the same time). But a year later, the winds began to change. We received news from American colleagues and friends that *SSP* was being added to the list of readings in classes on Philippine and Southeast Asian politics. Then the American Library Association surprised us by choosing the book as one of its Choice Outstanding Academic Titles for 2006. At the other end, young Filipino historians like Lisandro Claudio (who has graciously written the foreword to this edition) were using *SSP* as their classes' official textbook. Anvil also reported a fast turnover and reprinting of the book.

All this good news, however, was bittersweet. On January 22, 2011, Donna passed away. A few months before this fateful date, while she was painfully recovering from the ravages of chemotherapy and radiation, we thought of asking Susan if Rowman & Littlefield would be interested in an updated edition. Sadly, this did not happen. A few years later, Karina encouraged me to think about expanding the book "to honor Donna's memory." I agreed and completed three draft chapters in 2016. Rowman & Littlefield published the U.S. edition, while Ateneo de Manila University Press put out the Philippine edition.

What has been changed and added? A new chapter 10 evaluates the record of President Gloria Arroyo's "Strong Republic" project and explains why she was never able to accomplish the goals she set out at the start of her term. After Arroyo, the pendulum swung away from strengthening state institutions to the personalized presidency of Benigno Aquino III. This is the focus of chapter 11. Finally, this edition closes with a short chapter 12 that discusses the first six months or so of President Rodrigo Duterte's administration. While I am aware that Duterte's presidency is still evolving, I was also confident that there are now patterns that are quite noticeable even this early in his term that are worth investigating. Whether these reflections are correct or not will be left to other scholars to evaluate.

Honolulu, Hawaii

Preface to the First Edition

This book took some time to write. First, there were frequent debates over how to frame and interpret state–society relations in different historical periods and, throughout, the challenge of adjusting to each other's writing style and work pace. Our response to the substantive and detailed commentary of an encouraging anonymous reviewer—to whom we owe many thanks—took much longer than anticipated. Finally, we waited for the slow canvassing of votes to determine the winner of the crucial May 2004 Philippine presidential election and its aftermath.

At last finished, we offer an immediate disclaimer. All too aware that many issues are not discussed in the depth they deserve, we nevertheless considered this an acceptable trade-off in our decision to attempt a sustained analysis of state formation over the course of a millennium. As a result, the book is not meant to be an exhaustive treatment, but an evolving framework for understanding Philippine state–society relations over time.

Here we wish to express our appreciation to colleagues and friends for egging us on. We are, foremost, grateful to Caroline Sy Hau, for early discussions exploring alternative perspectives on Philippine political history and for encouraging us to devote attention to important "outsiders" in the story. When we began drafting the book in Ithaca, New York, we benefited from much-needed advice and friendship from Audrey Kahin, Ben Anderson, Ben Abel, Eveline Ferretti, Vince Boudreau, and Toinette Raquiza. We are also grateful to Cornell University's Southeast Asia Program for welcoming us back, and especially for our friendly reception by Nancy Loncto and Teresa Palmer.

The revisions were carried out—and carried around—from Kyoto to Bangkok, Cebu to New Jersey. In residence in Bangkok for six months, we bounced around ideas with Coeli Barry, Thanet Aphornsuvan, and Alan

Feinstein, and we imposed our stories on Pasuk Pongphaichit, Chris Baker, and Viengrat Nethipo. We value their friendship, suggestions, and gracious assistance.

In the Philippines, we enjoyed stimulating discussions with Alvin Batalla, Maricor Baytion, Karina Bolasco, Sheila Coronel, Tesa Encarnacion, Glenda Gloria, Ronald Holmes, Edna Labra-Hutchcroft, Paul Hutchcroft, Popo Lotilla, Resil Mojares, Ambeth Ocampo, Nancy Pe-Rodrigo, Raul Rodrigo, Ed Tadem, Lisandro Claudio, and Marites Vitug. We appreciate their insights, comments, and criticisms. The staff of the Philippine National Historical Institute, the Lopez Museum, the Philippine Center for Investigative Journalism, and *Newsbreak* magazine gladly helped us find appropriate photos, and Kiyoko Yamaguchi drew us a wonderful sketch. Finally, we express our gratitude to Susan McEachern of Rowman & Littlefield for not giving up on us, and thanks to Becki Perna, Jenn Nemec, Rebeccah Shumaker, Alden Perkins, and the production staff.

We dedicate this work to our nephews and nieces on both sides of the Pacific—Carlo, Charisse, Honey, Myki, and Mia Abinales in Misamis Occidental; and Colin and Devon Amoroso in Florida.

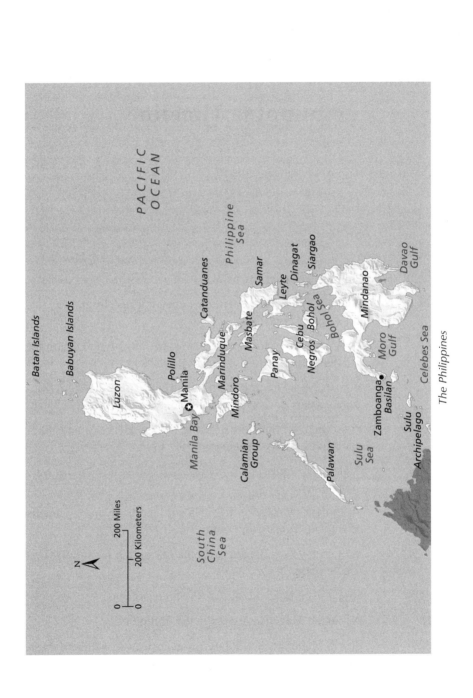

The Philippines

Philippine Timeline

618–906   Philippine contact begins with China during the Tang dynasty.

900   Political and social hierarchies are indicated by the Laguna copperplate inscription.

982   Ma-i, probably Mindoro, brings goods directly to Canton for the first time.

1001   Butuan, a gold mining and trading center in northeastern Mindanao, sends its first tribute mission to Sung-dynasty China.

c.1100   First Malays from Borneo settle in Manila/Tondo and intermarry with native Tagalogs.

c.1275   Arab missionaries and Chinese traders bring Islam to the Sulu archipelago.

1277–1368   Yuan-dynasty trade proliferates with the Visayan settlements of Butuan, Tanjay, and Cebu.

1368–1424   Sulu sends six missions to China during the period of Ming tribute trade.

c.1450   Sayyid Abu Bakr establishes the Sulu sultanate.

1521   Ferdinand Magellan arrives in the Philippines.

c.1525   Sharif Muhammad Kabungsuwan arrives in southern Mindanao and converts the Magindanao and Buayan ruling families to Islam.

1542	A Spanish expedition to the archipelago bestows the name "Felipinas" in honor of Prince (later King) Philip II of Spain.
1568	Philip II empowers Miguel Lopez de Legazpi to establish cities and towns and grant his followers *encomiendas*.
1571	Legazpi conquers Maynilad, an outpost of the Brunei sultanate. King Philip grants the new settlement, Manila, the royal title of city.
1572	The galleon trade begins between Mexico and China, with Manila as the transshipment point.
1578	A papal bull of Pope Gregory XIII formalizes the establishment of diocesan authority in Manila and the construction of Manila Cathedral. The first Franciscan missionaries arrive.
1581	The first Jesuit missionaries arrive.
1591	The first tensions arise between civil officials and the religious orders. Charges and countercharges of abusing the natives are exchanged.
1594	Philip II partitions the Philippines among the religious orders.
1595	Philip II decrees Manila the capital of the Philippine Islands.
1596	The first expedition is launched to pacify Mindanao, mobilizing 50 ships, 200 Spaniards, and 1,500 indios.
1599	Magindanao datus, with 50 vessels and 3,000 warriors, attack the central Philippines and return to southern Mindanao with 800 captives.
1600	The Spanish fleet battles Dutch warships near Manila, losing a flagship and 300 men, but forcing the Dutch to withdraw.
1603	The first mass uprising by Chinese follows the misinterpretation of Spanish war preparations. After Spanish reprisals, total casualties are estimated at 15,000–20,000.
1609	The *polos y servicios* (conscript labor) edict is decreed to ensure manpower for public works projects and naval battles against the Dutch, which continue up to 1648.
1611	The Universidad de Santo Tomás is founded.
1619–1671	Sultan Kudarat rules Maguindanao.

1621   Revolts occur in the Visayas.

1622   King Philip IV prohibits Dominican friars from interfering in colonial affairs.

1635   The first military garrison is established in Zamboanga in southwestern Mindanao to deter Muslim raids and Dutch forays.

1637–1639   Spanish forces defeat the Magindanaos and expeditions are launched into the Lanao region, Sulu archipelago, and Brunei.

1639   A Chinese revolt rocks Manila, led by Christian converts who protest the conscript labor policy. Revolt spreads to areas south of Manila.

1642   Sultan Kudarat defeats a Spanish force and captures its leader.

1645   A peace treaty is signed between Sultan Kudarat and the Spanish. The Dutch aid Sulu in attacking the Spanish garrison.

1648   The Spanish sign a peace treaty with the Dutch at Westphalia, recognizing Dutch independence and ending all attacks on the Philippines.

1649   Another major revolt spreads to the Visayan islands of Leyte, Masbate, Cebu, and Bohol and to Camarines and Albay in southern Luzon.

1656–1658   Sultan Kudarat declares war against the Spanish and seeks support from Sulu, Ternate, Brunei, and Makassar. Muslim raids on the central Visayas prompt a Spanish counterattack.

1660–1661   Revolts erupt in the provinces north of Manila to protest abuse of conscript labor.

1662–1663   Spain abandons the Zamboanga garrison and moves troops to Manila to await attack by the Chinese "pirate" Koxinga. He never arrives, but an uprising and massacre of the Chinese occurs.

1697   Tensions escalate between bishops and religious orders over parish visitation (inspection by diocesan officials). King Charles II temporarily proscribes the practice.

1700   The Sulu and Magindanao sultanates fight to control trade in the region.

1719	The Zamboanga garrison is reoccupied. A friar-led mob executes reformist Governor-General Fernando Bustamante.
1737	Spain signs a peace treaty with the sultan of Sulu.
1739	The first viable road system from Manila to northern Luzon opens.
1743	The British step up attacks on Spanish galleons plying the Acapulco–Manila route.
1744	Francisco Dagohoy leads a revolt in Bohol after Jesuits refuse to give his brother a Christian burial. It would be quelled only in 1829.
1745	An early revolt over access and control of hacienda lands occurs in Cavite municipality and Batangas province.
1747–1756	Spanish bombardment of Jolo in 1752 leads to the defeat of Sulu and the imprisonment of the sultan. A peace treaty favoring the Spanish is signed; the sultan is exiled from Jolo until 1764.
1754	King Ferdinand VI decrees the compulsory teaching of Spanish in all schools to boys and girls.
1755	Governor-General Manuel de Arandia orders unconverted Chinese to leave the Philippines.
1757	Iranun and Maranao Muslims increase attacks on Spanish camps in Mindanao and launch raids on the Visayas.
1762	The British invade Manila. Their occupation sparks revolts in Pampanga, Pangasinan, and Ilocos Sur provinces north of Manila, including an uprising by 900 Pampanga Chinese allied with Manila Chinese. Diego Silang leads a revolt in Ilocos Sur in alliance with the British.
1763	Spain and England sign a peace treaty returning the Philippines to Spain the following year.
1764	The Spanish retaliate against the rebels.
1766	Chinese who sided with the British are expelled.
1768	The Jesuits are expelled from the Spanish empire. The archbishop of Manila supports the secularization of parishes (transfer from religious order to diocesan control) and the

	ordination of indio priests. The Ordinances of Good Government are issued by Madrid.
1771	Governor-General Simon de Anda encounters resistance from the religious orders and uses troops to enforce secularization.
1774	King Charles III reaffirms secularization policy by a royal decree ordering the secularization of parishes as they fall vacant.
1777	A royal decree orders indios to engage in the production of cotton and other fibers.
1781	Governor-General Basco y Vargas implements the tobacco monopoly, limiting production to areas designated by the government.
1784	The Philippines remits 150,000 pesos to Madrid, the first remittance since the establishment of Spanish rule. The first shipment of indigo is sent to Europe.
1785	The Royal Company of the Philippines is established to promote economic development. The office of cabeza de barangay becomes elective.
1786	A customhouse is established in Manila by royal decree. It is privatized in 1805.
1789	The office of cabeza de barangay is placed under the authority of the alcalde mayor to reduce the influence of the friars.
1796	The *Astrea*, the first U.S. ship to trade in the Philippines, loads indigo, hemp, spices, and sugar for export.
1803	A royal decree orders the secularization of more parishes.
1805	The governor of Zamboanga signs a peace treaty with the sultan of Sulu, giving the governor the right to vet foreign residents in the archipelago.
1807	Spanish deserters revolt in Ilocos to protest the government wine monopoly and prohibition on the production of *basi* (rice wine).
1810	Spanish revolutionaries establish the Cortes and grant colonies the right to representation.
1811	The colony's first newspaper, the government-owned *Del Superior Gobierno*, begins publication. The Philippines sends a delegate to the Cortes.

1813	The Liberal Constitution of Cadiz is implemented in Manila with provisions including individual liberties.
1814	King Ferdinand VII abrogates the Constitution and dissolves the Cortes.
1815	The galleon trade ends.
1820	Ferdinand VII reestablishes the Cortes and restores the 1812 Constitution. Three Philippine representatives are sent to Madrid in 1822.
1824	Spain attacks Jolo. King Ferdinand again defeats the Spanish liberals and restores absolutist rule.
1826	A monarchist counteroffensive ends further secularization of parishes.
1827	A Spanish attack on Jolo is repulsed.
1829	Spanish raiding parties establish a presence in the Gran Cordillera.
1834	The Royal Company of the Philippines is abolished. Americans establish two commercial houses in Manila. A royal decree declares Manila open to international trade.
1835	Constitutionalist forces win in Spain and restore Philippine representation to the Cortes.
1836	Spain signs a commercial treaty with the sultan of Sulu.
1837	Philippine representation to the Cortes is revoked by the 1837 Constitution, which mandates that overseas possessions be governed under special laws. Tariff regulations are implemented for the first time.
1844	Alcaldes mayors lose the right to trade while in office.
1847	A second newspaper, *La Estrella de Manila* (The Star of Manila), begins publication, followed by the *Diario de Manila* (Manila Newspaper), whose workers would be instrumental in founding the Katipunan. The office of gobernadorcillo becomes elective.
1848–1851	The Spanish attack Balangigi in the Sulu archipelago to free 300 captives. The Sulu sultanate signs an agreement recognizing Spanish authority.

1849–1850	Governor-General Narciso Claveria decrees that indios be given Spanish surnames. The first steam-engine war vessel arrives in Manila.
1853	The British firm Smith, Bell and Company is established in Manila and becomes a major trader of sugar and hemp.
1856	A British consul arrives in Iloilo, Negros, and his thirteen-year residence helps transform the island into a major sugar-producing area.
1859	The Jesuits return to the Philippines and accept missions in Muslim areas.
1861	Separation of executive and judicial functions is mandated at the alcalde mayor and governor-general levels.
1863	The Educational Decree mandates the establishment of a public school system.
1864	Father José Burgos publishes a "Manifesto Addressed by the Loyal Filipinos to the Noble Spanish Nation," criticizing Spanish discrimination against secular priests.
1865	The Jesuits establish the Escuela Normal (Normal School) and the secondary school Ateneo Municipal de Manila.
1868	The Guardia Civil is established to suppress crime and insurrections.
1872	In the aftermath of a mutiny at the Cavite naval arsenal, Fathers José Burgos, Mariano Gomez, and Jacinto Zamora are executed.
1873	More Philippine ports are opened to world trade.
1876	Combined Spanish and indio forces overrun Jolo.
1877	England and Germany recognize Spain's sovereignty over Sulu.
1878	Sultan Jamal ul-Azam of Sulu signs a treaty of peace and capitulation with Spain, the last treaty signed between the two.
1880	The tobacco monopoly is abolished.
1882	*Diariong Tagalog* (Tagalog Newspaper), the first Spanish-Tagalog newspaper, begins publication. José Rizal leaves for Europe.

1883	Spanish forces invade Sulu and set up a naval station and garrison. Sultan Bada ud-Din II sends a letter of protest to the British, calling the invasion a violation of the 1877 agreement.
1887	Rizal publishes *Noli Me Tangere*. A three-man committee reports to the archbishop of Manila that the novel is "heretical, impious and scandalous . . . anti-patriotic, subversive of public order and offensive to the government of Spain."
1888	Germany, Britain, and Spain sign a new protocol reiterating recognition of Spanish sovereignty over Sulu and guaranteeing freedom of navigation and trade in the region.
1888	The Spanish Civil Code is applied to the Philippines. Filipino expatriates in Spain establish La Solidaridad and issue their first fortnightly newspaper the following year.
1891	Rizal publishes *El Filibusterismo*. His family is removed from the friar estates they lease. Magindanao datus of Cotabato recognize Spanish authority after Governor-General Valeriano Weyler's military success in adjoining Lanao.
1892	A railroad line connects Manila with Pangasinan province for the first time. Rizal returns to Manila, organizes La Liga Filipina, and is exiled to northern Mindanao. Andres Bonifacio establishes the Katipunan.
1894	Municipal government is reorganized, separating executive and judicial functions.
1895	The Katipunan network expands and elects Bonifacio its supremo. *La Solidaridad* newspaper closes due to lack of funds.
1895	Cuba launches a revolution against Spain.
1896	The Katipunan is discovered and begins an uprising. Rizal is executed on December 30.
1897	Emilio Aguinaldo replaces Bonifacio as president of the Katipunan; Bonifacio is arrested and executed. In December, Aguinaldo and his leadership go into exile in Hong Kong, but the revolution continues.
1898	The United States declares war on Spain. Aguinaldo returns to the Philippines and declares independence on June 12. The

United States signs a peace treaty with Spain on December 10, purchasing the Philippines for $20 million. President William McKinley issues the "Benevolent Assimilation Proclamation."

1899	Aguinaldo proclaims the Philippine Republic in January and is sworn in as president. The Philippine–American War begins. The first Philippine Commission arrives in Manila.

1900	War continues and the Aguinaldo government begins to unravel. Former members surrender to the Americans and form the Federal party in support of American rule.

1901	Aguinaldo is captured and Filipinos shift to guerrilla warfare. McKinley declares a civil government in the Philippines with William H. Taft as the first governor-general.

1902	The U.S. Congress passes the Philippine Bill of 1902, delineating the structure of the colonial state. President Theodore Roosevelt declares the Philippine "insurrection" over.

1903	The Philippine Commission establishes a Moro province to govern Muslim Mindanao under the U.S. Army. General Simeon Ola surrenders to American forces in Albay province.

1905	Americans arrest Macario Sakay and members of the New Katipunan. The first national convention of provincial governors is held in Manila and Nacionalista party members Manuel L. Quezon and Sergio Osmeña enter the national political arena.

1907	Elections to the first Philippine Assembly are held, beginning Nacionalista party dominance. Sakay is hanged on charges of sedition and banditry.

1908	The University of the Philippines is established.

1909	The U.S. Congress passes the Payne-Aldrich Act, allowing partial free trade between the Philippines and the United States. General elections are held for delegates to the second Philippine Assembly.

1911	The American-dominated Philippine Commission and Filipino-controlled Philippine Assembly clash repeatedly over appointments.

1912–1915	Democrat Woodrow Wilson is elected president and appoints Francis Burton Harrison governor-general of the Philippines. Harrison vows to hasten Filipinization of the colonial state.
1916	Wilson signs the Jones Law, granting Philippine independence "as soon as a stable government is established." The Philippine Commission is replaced by a Senate and a House of Representatives.
1917	The Partido Democrata is formed as the main opposition party to the dominant Nacionalista party.
1918	Governor Harrison sets up the Council of State, which includes Quezon, Osmeña, and the heads of different departments.
1919	The first "Philippine independence mission" is sent to the United States to negotiate with U.S. officials on the terms of independence.
1921	General Leonard Wood, former governor of Moro province, replaces Harrison, vowing to roll back Filipinization.
1922	Tensions between Quezon and Osmeña lead to a split in the Nacionalista party.
1923	Conflict between Filipino leaders and Governor Wood reaches a high point. Both houses issue a resolution calling for Wood's recall and a mission is sent to the United States, but President Calvin Coolidge supports Wood.
1924	The Colorums, a millenarian movement in the central Philippines, attack Constabulary units. Osmeña and Quezon end factional battles and reunite the Nacionalista party.
1926	The Nacionalista and Democrata parties form a Supreme National Council to coordinate a "campaign for independence." Wood abolishes the Board of Controls, a supervisory body of state corporations used by Filipino politicians to control the Manila Railroad Company and the Philippine National Bank.
1927	Wood dies in surgery. Henry Stimson replaces him a year later.
1930	The Sakdal movement accuses Filipino politicians of misgovernance and compromising independence. The Partido Komunista ng Pilipinas (PKP) is established.

1931   Filipinos send another independence mission to Washington under the leadership of Osmeña and House Speaker Manuel Roxas.

1934   The Tydings-McDuffie Law approves independence after a ten-year transition. Filipinos elect representatives to a convention to draft a constitution.

1935   The new constitution is approved by President Franklin D. Roosevelt and by the Filipino people in a plebiscite. Quezon is elected president and Osmeña vice president of the Commonwealth of the Philippines.

1937   Women are granted suffrage in a plebiscite.

1938   The PKP merges with the Philippine Socialist party.

1939   The National Assembly creates a Department of National Defense in response to the expansion of Japanese military power.

1941   Quezon and Osmeña are reelected just as war breaks out. Japanese forces invade the Philippines and defeat American and Filipino military units of the United States Armed Forces in the Far East.

1942   Japanese forces enter Manila and General Homma Masaharu declares the end of the American occupation. PKP organizes the Hukbong Bayan laban sa Hapon (People's Anti-Japanese Army, or Hukbalahap).

1943   The Japan-sponsored Philippine Republic is inaugurated with José P. Laurel as president. In U.S. exile, Quezon takes the oath of office as reelected Commonwealth president.

1944   Quezon dies in New York from tuberculosis as U.S. forces return to the Philippines and defeat the Japanese. Manila is destroyed.

1945   General Douglas MacArthur turns the government over to President Osmeña, and the Philippine Congress creates a People's Court to try collaborators. Roxas splits from the Nacionalistas and creates the Liberal party.

1946   The United States grants Philippine independence but imposes a number of unequal economic and military treaties: The Bell Trade Act grants U.S. businesses "parity rights" to

Philippine land ownership and natural resource exploitation, and a Military Bases Agreement grants the United States the right to maintain bases in the country. Roxas defeats Osmeña to become the first president of the (third) republic.

1947   The treaties are ratified by plebiscite.

1948   President Roxas issues a blanket pardon of all who collaborated with the Japanese but declares the Huks and associated peasant organizations illegal. He dies of a heart attack and is succeeded by Elpidio Quirino, who issues a general amnesty to the Huks.

1949   The Central Bank of the Philippines is established as the government imposes import and exchange controls to halt the drain of foreign reserves. Quirino is elected president as the Huks launch an offensive.

1950   President Harry Truman's economic mission recommends diversification and improved production to raise incomes. Lieutenant Colonel (and CIA agent) Edward Lansdale arrives to oversee the anti-Huk campaign.

1951   The Huk offensive is stopped. The National Movement for Free Elections (NAMFREL) is established.

1952   Land reform specialist Robert Hardie recommends a comprehensive and radical land reform program. His report is met with resistance from Congress.

1953   Ramon Magsaysay defects from the Liberal party, joins the Nacionalistas, and is elected president with CIA assistance.

1954   Huk supreme commander Luis Taruc surrenders. The Laurel-Langley trade agreement with the United States allows the Philippines to unpeg the peso from the U.S. dollar and impose export tariffs, but gives U.S. companies full access to all sectors of the Philippine economy. The Philippines is a founding member of the Southeast Asia Treaty Organization (SEATO).

1956   The Philippine Congress makes the teaching of José Rizal's life and works compulsory at the college and university levels.

1957   President Magsaysay dies in a plane crash. Vice President Carlos P. Garcia serves out his term and wins the subsequent election. Congress passes the Anti-Subversion Law, outlawing the PKP and the Huks.

1958   President Garcia launches import-substitution industrialization with the Filipino First policy.

1959   The Philippines and the United States renegotiate the military bases agreement, reducing the 99-year lease to 25 years subject to renewal or termination.

1960   The International Rice Research Institute (IRRI) is established with funding from the Ford and Rockefeller Foundations, with a mission to develop high-yielding varieties of rice.

1961   Diosdado Macapagal defeats Garcia in the November presidential election.

1962   President Macapagal lifts import and exchange controls. He changes Independence Day from July 4 to June 12.

1963   The Philippines, the Federation of Malaya, and Indonesia sign the Manila Accord to assert their common "racial heritage." Macapagal signs into law the Agricultural Land Reform Code, which abolishes share tenancy and replaces it with the leasehold system.

1964   PKP leaders revive the party and recruit students from the University of the Philippines and the Lyceum of the Philippines.

1965   Ferdinand Marcos defeats Macapagal to become the sixth president of the republic.

1966   The Asian Development Bank sets up headquarters in Manila. President Marcos dispatches a military engineering battalion to Vietnam in violation of a campaign pledge.

1967   Government troops massacre members of a peasant religious sect as they approach the presidential palace. Nationalists, civil libertarians, and radicals form the Movement for the Advancement of Nationalism to protest American intervention in Vietnam. The Philippines becomes a founding member of the Association of Southeast Asian Nations (ASEAN).

1968   The killing of twenty-eight Muslim trainees in a secret camp exposes a government plan to infiltrate the Malaysian state of Sabah in support of the Philippines' claim of ownership. Jose

Maria Sison forms the Communist Party of the Philippines (CPP).

1969   Marcos becomes the first postwar president to win a second term in an election marred by massive cheating and looting of the national treasury. The CPP establishes the New People's Army (NPA).

1970   Radicalized students battle police in the streets of Manila in the "First Quarter Storm." Lieutenant Victor Corpuz, a young Constabulary officer, raids the Philippine Military Academy and defects to the CPP-NPA.

1971   A grenade is thrown at a campaign rally of the anti-Marcos Liberal party, killing nine and wounding most of the candidates; Marcos blames the Communists and suspends the writ of habeas corpus.

1972   Nur Misuari establishes the Moro National Liberation Front (MNLF), which calls for the separation of Mindanao, Palawan, and the Sulu archipelago from the Philippines and the creation of a Bangsa Moro Republic. Marcos declares martial law "to save the Republic and reform society." MNLF forces engage the military in conventional warfare in southern Mindanao.

1973   A new constitution is "ratified" by "citizens' assemblies." The CPP-NPA forms the Preparatory Commission of the National Democratic Front to create a broad "anti-fascist, anti-imperialist, anti-feudal" force against the Marcos dictatorship.

1974   The Laurel-Langley trade agreement expires. The Catholic Bishops Conference of the Philippines petitions Marcos to end martial law.

1975   Marcos's jailed political opponent, Benigno Aquino Jr., begins a hunger strike to protest military jurisdiction over his case. The Philippines and the People's Republic of China formalize diplomatic relations.

1976   The CPP-NPA suffers a setback with the arrest of its two top military commanders. The Philippine government and the MNLF sign a cease-fire agreement and open discussions on Muslim autonomy.

1977   CPP-NPA chairman Sison is captured. A military commission finds Aquino and the CPP-NPA commanders guilty of subversion and sentences them to death. The first urban protests against martial law are led by students, workers, nuns, and priests.

1978   Elections for an interim National Assembly are held, the first since 1972. From prison, Aquino leads an opposition party that loses to Marcos's Kilusang Bagong Lipunan (New Society Movement).

1979   The military bases agreement is amended, requiring U.S. bases to fly the Philippine flag in recognition of Philippine sovereignty. Noncommunist anti-Marcos groups bomb selected sites in Manila to destabilize the dictatorship.

1980   The CPP-NPA establishes the Kilusang Mayo Uno (May First Movement) in urban areas and launches "people's strikes" and "mass uprisings" in the provinces. Aquino is released from prison and flown to the United States for heart bypass surgery.

1981   Marcos formally lifts martial law and is "elected" to another six-year term. Businessman Dewey Dee flees the Philippines, leaving a $100 million debt; cracks in the economy become ever more apparent.

1982   Anti-Marcos politicians form the United Nationalist Democratic Opposition. The first open opposition newspapers, *We Forum* and *Malaya* (Freedom), are ordered closed by the government.

1983   Aquino is assassinated upon his return to the Philippines. His death sparks massive protests, and the Catholic Church becomes more vocal in its criticism of the dictatorship.

1984   Business and professional groups revive NAMFREL, while anti-Marcos politicians win 53 of the 183 seats in the National Assembly. The commission investigating the Aquino assassination concludes that it was a military conspiracy and indicts Armed Forces of the Philippines (AFP) chief of staff and close Marcos aide General Fabian Ver.

1985   Junior officers organize the Reform the AFP Movement (RAM). Late in the year, to everyone's surprise, Marcos calls for a "snap" presidential election; Corazon Aquino declares her candidacy.

1986   The CPP-NPA announces it will boycott the election. Marcos "wins" the February 7 poll through fraud and intimidation. RAM launches a coup that is saved by "people power," a massive mobilization leading to the downfall of Marcos and the ascension of Aquino to the presidency.

1987   Aquino's government is buffeted by RAM coup attempts and renewed confrontation with the CPP-NPA. Filipinos overwhelmingly approve a new constitution that restores a bicameral legislature; in the ensuing election, President Aquino's allies win control of Congress and many local and provincial governments.

1988   The CPP-NPA is weakened by internal dissension. The Moro Islamic Liberation Front (MILF) replaces the MNLF as the advocate of Islamic separatism. Negotiations with the United States begin over a new military bases treaty.

1989   Marcos dies in exile. The discovery of mass graves in Mindanao and southern Luzon provides evidence that the CPP-NPA killed its own cadres and guerrilla fighters as suspected military spies. A RAM coup on the verge of success is thwarted by the flyover of American fighter jets over Manila.

1990   In the aftermath of the 1989 RAM coup attempt, the economy "sputter[s] almost to a halt." The bases negotiations continue as the United States withdraws its Peace Corps personnel and upgrades base security against increased CPP-NPA attacks.

1991   The June 15 eruption of Mount Pinatubo effectively closes the U.S. air base at Clark Field. The Philippine Senate rejects the new military bases treaty that would have extended the U.S. presence for another ten years.

1992   Fidel Ramos succeeds Aquino as president. Ramos mends fences with "Marcos loyalists," signs a peace agreement with RAM, and opens indirect channels to the CPP-NPA. The repeal of the Anti-Subversion Law allows CPP participation in electoral politics. The kidnapping of wealthy Chinese-Filipinos becomes alarmingly frequent.

1993   President Ramos achieves a number of breakthroughs, in-
            cluding anticorruption reforms in the police force, a popula-
            tion control program (despite opposition from the Catholic
            Church), and deregulation of the strategic communications
            and travel industries. Ramos strengthens ties with ASEAN
            and the economy shows signs of a major turnaround.

1994   The total ransom paid to kidnappers since 1992 reaches 189
            million pesos.

1995   Overseas Filipino worker (OFW) Flor Contemplacion is
            convicted of murder and sentenced to death in Singapore.
            National anger over her execution leads to a diplomatic row
            with the Singaporean government. The Abu Sayyaf Group
            joins forces with breakaway factions of the MILF to attack a
            town in southwestern Mindanao, while kidnappings continue
            to afflict major urban centers.

1996   The government signs a peace pact with the MNLF and ap-
            points its chairman as governor of the Autonomous Region in
            Muslim Mindanao (ARMM) and chair of the Southern Philip-
            pines Development Authority (SPDA).

1997   The Asian financial crisis ends Ramos's dream of making the
            Philippines the next "tiger economy." His attempt at constitu-
            tional reform to gain a second term fails in the face of popu-
            lar opposition. The MILF displays the force of its reputedly
            million-strong military, while the CPP-NPA shows signs of
            recovery.

1998   Former movie star-turned-politician and "man of the poor"
            Joseph Estrada becomes president of the republic in a land-
            slide election.

1999   The first annual U.S.-Philippine joint military exercises are
            held in the Philippines.

2000   The Abu Sayyaf Group kidnaps twenty-one tourists at a Ma-
            laysian resort in Borneo. The revelation that President Estrada
            received payoffs from a nationwide illegal lottery leads to his
            impeachment (the first of a Philippine president), but convic-
            tion is blocked by his allies in the Senate.

2001   Another "people power" mobilization unseats Estrada, but
            a subsequent lower-class revolt by his supporters unsettles
            Vice President Gloria Arroyo's succession to the presidency.

Malaysia agrees to host peace talks between the government and the MILF.

2002 President Arroyo pledges support for the U.S. war on terror, struggles to establish the legitimacy of her government, and declares her commitment to build a "Strong Republic."

The United States extends its "Global War on Terrorism" to the Philippines and American troops return to the Philippines in February and President Gloria Arroyo pledges support for the U.S. war on terror.

The *Balikatan* (Shoulder-to-Shoulder) 02-01 joint military exercises between U.S. and Philippine troops begin and American troops are deployed in Basilan and Zamboanga cities in Mindanao.

AFP launches operations to rescue the American couple kidnapped by the Abu Sayyaf. The husband is killed.

2003 Fernando Poe Jr., an action-movie star and friend of deposed president Estrada, announces his candidacy for president. Arroyo issues an executive order approving a "visiting forces agreement" with the United States. Junior officers from the different military services stage a coup in Makati, the country's prime business district, accusing the government of corruption. The coup fails.

2004 Arroyo wins a full term in the May election after a protracted tabulation process. The U.S military continues to train and advise the Philippine military in the pursuit of Abu Sayyaf militants in southern Mindanao.

2005 The Philippine Center for Investigative Journalism releases an audio recording of a phone conversation between Arroyo and a senior member of the Commission on Elections (COMELEC) over the alleged rigging of the 2004 elections and sparks a crisis. Seven cabinet secretaries and three government agency heads resign while members of the minority coalition in the House of Representatives pass a resolution to impeach Arroyo, which is blocked by her supporters. Arroyo ally, Zaldy Ampatuan, wins as governor in the ARMM elections. Four U.S. marines are charged with raping a Filipina, jeopardizing the future of U.S.-Philippine military collaboration.

2006   Arroyo declares "a state of emergency" in February after another failed coup attempt and massive demonstrations over revelations that she cheated in the 2004 polls. She lifts this a month later but also issues an order preventing senior military officers and cabinet members from testifying in congressional hearings; the Supreme Court subsequently declares this unconstitutional. Arroyo signs the repeal of the death penalty law.

2006   U.S. Lance Corporal Marine Daniel Smith is found guilty of raping a Filipina; the three others are acquitted of the crime. Smith however is placed under U.S. embassy custody instead of in a Philippine jail. Implementation of revised Value-Added Tax (VAT) causes prices to go up.

2007   Estrada is found guilty of plunder and perjury and sentenced to life in prison, but Arroyo pardons him. Fourteen Philippine marines are killed and beheaded by Islamic rebels in Basilan island. A car bomb kills a Muslim congressman in front of the House of Representatives.

2007   ASEAN leaders vow to forge closer ties in the Association's twelfth meeting, held in Cebu. The National Economic and Development Authority (NEDA) announces that the country's gross domestic product at year's end rose to 7.3 per cent, while the gross national product increased by 7.8%, the highest since 1977

2008   The Arroyo government and the MILF sign a Memorandum of Agreement on Ancestral Domain but the Supreme Court rules it unconstitutional. A group of MILF fighters also reject the agreement, break away from the MILF, and form the Bangsamoro Islamic Freedom Fighters (BIFF). The BIFF launches several attacks on settler communities but are repulsed.

An official of the Department of Environment and Natural Resources reveals in Senate testimony that a former COMELEC chairman offered P200 million in bribe money so that the NEDA chief would approve a broadband network contract.

Imelda Marcos is acquitted by a Manila court in relation to a charge of 32 counts of illegal money transfer.

The Supreme court rules that the Senate cannot compel the head of the National Economic Development Authority to reveal what he and President Arroyo discussed in relation to the contract.

The Abu Sayyaf kidnaps the news anchor of a major television station.

An American court hears oral arguments on a petition by the Philippine government to invoke sovereign immunity in connection with the enforcement of a civil judgment in the United States against the estate of former president Marcos in favor of 9,500 human rights victims during the authoritarian period.

2009   Former president Cory Aquino dies of lung cancer; thousands attend her funeral.

An armed group led by the son and nephew of the most powerful and brutal warlord family in Muslim Mindanao kills fifty-eight people, including thirty-one journalists. Arroyo places the province of Maguindanao under martial law and arrests the warlord and his sons.

Benigno Aquino III, son of Cory Aquino, is elected president in first automated elections in Philippine history.

2010   President Benigno Aquino III signs the P1.645 trillion national budget. The Supreme Court declares "unconstitutional" Aquino's executive order no. 1, creating a Truth Commission tasked to investigate graft and corruption under the Arroyo government.

A hostage taking involving Chinese tourists strains Philippine-Hong Kong relations.

2011   In February a Senate hearing reveals massive corruption inside AFP beginning with senior officers receiving P50 million as "retirement gift." AFP Chief of Staff commits suicide as a former auditor of the Commission on Audit reveals more instances of corruption inside the military.

Vice President Jejomar Binay visits China to appeal the case of three Filipinos sentenced to death in China for drug trafficking. The Hong Kong government also sentences a member of the Philippine House of Representatives for bringing in 6.67 grams of pure cocaine.

In March, the House of Representatives votes to impeach the Ombudsman, who proceeds to resign.

In November, former president Gloria Arroyo is arrested for allegedly sabotaging the 2004 elections. Arroyo, feigning sickness, is allowed to be detained at a government hospital.

In December, the House of Representatives signs the impeachment complaint against the Chief Justice of the Supreme Court for "betrayal of public trust." The complaint is sent to the Senate, which convenes itself as an impeachment court.

2012   President Aquino signs the Cybercrime Prevention Act in September and a controversial Reproductive Health Bill into law in December. The Supreme Court declares the first law constitution in February 2014.

An April standoff between Philippine and Chinese ships in the Scarborough Shoal in the west creates more tensions between the two countries.

Impeachment proceedings against the Chief Justice of the Supreme Court lead to a May 2013 decision declaring him guilty and stating that he should therefore be removed from office.

Former president Arroyo is released from hospital arrest after posting bail.

The Philippine government and the Moro Islamic Liberation Front sign a "Framework Agreement on the *Bangsamoro* (Moro nation)" that would lead to the creation of a "new political entity" that will replace the Autonomous Region in Muslim Mindanao (ARMM). In December, the two sides agree to a power-sharing arrangement once the "new political entity" is established.

2013   In February President Aquino signs into law the Human Rights Victims Reparation and Recognition Act compensating victims of human rights violations during the Marcos dictatorship.

An armed group claiming to represent the "royal army" of the Sultan of Sulu attacks the town of Lahad Datu in Sabah, testing Malaysian-Philippine relations.

Nationwide protest over the plunder of the government's Priority Development Assistance Fund (PDAF) by politicians. A million people demonstrate in the Luneta Park in Manila in August.

In September, MNLF fighters occupy a section of Zamboanga City, leading to heavy clashes with government troops.

In November, a businesswoman is accused of being the mastermind of a scam that lost the government over P10 billion pesos (US$ 439 million).

Typhoon Haiyan devastates the central Philippines.

2014   In January, the Philippine government and the Moro Islamic Liberation Front sign the fourth and last annex of the "Framework Agreement on the Bangsamoro" creating the *Bangsamoro* to replace the ARMM, while government troops launch offensives against the Bangsamoro Islamic Freedom Fighters, an MILF breakaway group. A comprehensive agreement is signed in March.

The government recovers P1.3 billion pesos (US$ 58.3 million) from the secret Swiss account of former president Ferdinand Marcos after a Singapore court rules it belongs to the Philippine National Bank.

Communist Party of the Philippines chairman Benito Tiamson and his wife Wilma, who is also secretary-general of the New People's Army, are arrested in Cebu in March.

The Philippines submits a 10-volume plea to the International Tribunal for the Law of the Sea to resolve a territorial feud with China over the West Philippine Sea.

In April, a Senate committee recommends filing of plunder chargers against four senators involved in the looting of PDAF funds with the assistance of a businesswoman.

In May, the Philippines and the United States sign an "Enhanced Defense Cooperation Agreement" (EDCA) allowing U.S. military forces access to Philippine military bases, hours before the official visit of American president Barack Obama. The 30th *Balikatan* (Shoulder-to-Shoulder) joint military exercises between the Philippines and the United States commence.

The ombudsman (state prosecutor) clears former president Gloria Arroyo of being involved in a P728 million pesos (US$ 3.8 million) fertilizer scam. The vice president, several members of Congress, and senior AFP officials are investigated for graft and corruption. Philippine protest Chinese construction activities in a reef in the disputed Spratlys Islands in the West Philippine Sea.

In June, Senators implicated in PDAF funds scam surrender to the police.

In July, the Supreme Court declares the government's "acts and practices" in connection to the distribution of its Disbursement Acceleration Program (DAP) unconstitutional.

2015   The Supreme Court declares the Priority Development Assistance Fund (PDAF) and the Disbursement Acceleration Program unconstitutional.

On January 25, forty-four members of the Philippine National Police Special Action Force (SAF), seventeen MILF fighters, and five civilians are killed after a fierce long battle in Mamapasano village, Maguindanao Province. SAF units were sent to the area to capture a Malaysian bomb maker but were surprised by the MILF as well as members of the BIFF. The "Mamapasano massacre" ends any possibility of congressional approval of a proposed Bangsamoro Basic Law bill.

A United States Marine is found guilty for the murder of a transgender Filipina

On November 27, Davao City mayor Rodrigo Duterte announces his candidacy for the presidency of the Philippines. Duterte, who was mayor of Davao for twenty-two years, is sworn in as the 16th president of the country on June 30, 2016.

2016   The Philippine government files diplomatic protests over Chinese test flights in the West Philippine Sea. The Supreme Court upholds the legality of the Enhanced Defense Cooperation Agreement between the United States and the Philippines. Japan donates defense and surveillance equipment to the Philippines.

The *Bangsamoro Basic Law* that was supposed to be the constitutional framework to establish autonomy in the Muslim areas of Mindanao island fails to pass the first reading the House of Representatives. Congress also does not allow President Aquino's Anti-Dynasty, Anti-Discrimination and Freedom of Information bills to pass.

El Nino continues to devastate large parts of southwestern Mindanao and the government has to declare a state of calamity to deal with food shortages in the area. A farmers' protest against the slowness of the government response ends in violence.

The Office of the Ombudsman files several corruption cases against two mayors, 2 city councilors, and 7 members of the House of Representatives. It finds "probable cause" to file charges against a police general and a Secretary of Health. On July 19, however, the Supreme Court acquits former president Gloria M. Arroyo from her plunder case.

National and local elections are held on May 9, and on May 30, Congress proclaims Rodrigo Duterte and Leni Robredo president and vice president, respectively. Both formally assume their respective offices on June 30.

The Permanent Court of Arbitration decides in favor of the Philippine government which has challenged the legality of China's claim over the South China Sea (a.k.a. West Philippine Sea). China refuses to recognize the ruling on the grounds that the proceedings were illegal.

In his first State of the Nation address, President Duterte promises to implement the Responsible Parenthood and Reproductive Health Law

Duterte announces his antidrug campaign in a July 5 speech during a Philippine Air Force ceremony, orders the Philippine National Police Special Action Force to take over the management of the national penitentiary, and presents a list of 150 government officials, including lawmakers, mayors, judges, and police officers, who are allegedly involved in the drug trade. A mayor's son suspected of being involved in drugs and six of his aides is killed in a shootout with police.

Duterte reopens peace talks with the Communist Party of the Philippines in August 20 and releases senior communist leaders as sign of goodwill. The Senate Committee on Justice and Human Rights beings hearings on extrajudicial killings associated with President Duterte's antidrug campaign. Duterte allies take control of the hearings and try to undercut the testimony of a former member of the antidrug "death squad" that Duterte formed when he was mayor of Davao City.

Also in August, Duterte insults the United States ambassador with a homophobic slur after the latter discusses concerns over the elections, and then raises the stakes in September by calling President Barack Obama a "son of a whore" and telling the United States to "go to hell." In October, during his state visit to China, Duterte suspends some of the joint military operations between the Philippines and the United States and declares his intention "to separate" from the United States. He proposes an alternative alliance with China and possibly Russia.

Former president Ferdinand Marcos's body is transferred from his hometown and buried at the Heroes' Cemetery in Manila amidst protests.

At the end of the year police records show that over 6,000 people have been killed since President Duterte launched his antidrug war.

2017   President Duterte suspends antidrug campaign after several police officers are discovered to have used the campaign to kidnap and demand ransom for a South Korean businessman, whom they killed and burned his body inside the headquarters of the national police. Police arrest Senator Leila de Lima, a vocal critic of President Duterte, charging her with violating the Dangerous Drugs Act of 2002 (Republic Act 9165).

President Duterte changes his position and signs the Paris Agreement on Climate Change.

As of March 22, 2017, over 7,000 have been killed in antidrug police operations and/or vigilante-style assassinations of suspected drug addicts and pushers.

Chapter One

Introducing Philippine Politics

In her 2002 State of the Nation address, Philippine President Gloria Arroyo committed herself to building a "strong Republic" with two "essential features."

> The first is independence from class and sectoral interests so that it stands for the *interests of the people* rather than a powerful minority. The second is the capacity, represented through *strong institutions and a strong bureaucracy*, to execute good policy and deliver essential services—the things that only government can do. [emphasis added]

Such a republic would deliver "faster economic development and social reform"; it would be "the bedrock of the victory we seek over poverty within the decade."[1]

This was not the first time a president promised Filipinos a government strong enough to address their needs. For a century and more, Filipinos have invoked the state as the embodiment of strength and unity moving the country forward. Some presidents have emphasized the power of the state to invigorate society and economy—Ferdinand Marcos promised, "This nation can be great again." Others, like Ramon Magsaysay and Corazon Aquino, sought to repair the state's democratic foundations to better serve the people.

The thread running through these presidential pledges is the recurring dilemma of state–society relations in the Philippines. One horn of the dilemma is the persistent inability of the state to provide basic services, guarantee peace and order, and foster economic development. State weakness is manifest in uncollected taxes and uncontrolled crime, bloated bureaucracies and denuded forests, low teacher salaries, and high emigration rates. Society regularly calls for better governance—business leaders for consistent policy

1

implementation, urbanites for clean and affordable water, the middle class for professionalism and honesty, and the poor majority for a government that represents *them*.

State weakness is due in part to a history of state capture by sectoral interests. The rural poor demand land reform—indeed, improving the country's productive capacity depends upon it—but powerful landed elites oppose it, and so it happens only very slowly. Such elites, along with political clans and opportunistic politicians who use government office as a source of booty, constitute a small but powerful minority. They are popularly denigrated as *trapo* (a pun on *tra*ditional *po*litician, literally "dishrag" in Filipino); a state independent of class and sectoral interests would not be in *their* interest.

Some Philippine leaders—technocrats, police chiefs, presidents—have proposed to overcome special interests and root out corruption through tighter supervision of local agencies, hard-nosed law enforcement, or executive dominance over the legislature. But here we encounter the other horn of the dilemma—Filipinos' equally enduring suspicion of a strong state. Despite Arroyo's statement that a strong republic would stand for "the interests of the people," her appeal for "strong institutions" evoked President Marcos's martial law regime of the 1970s and 1980s. Marcos's extreme centralization of state power spawned two armed rebellions. It cost thousands of lives in repression and billions of dollars in corruption. It set the nation back years in economic development and exacerbated suspicion of the state. Today, everyone wants law and order, but no one trusts the police.

Together, those who *use* a weak state and those who *fear* a strong one may constitute a majority coalition of sorts. Yet the call for good governance does not abate, for Filipinos are neither complacent nor quiescent. They vote, run for office, organize social movements. A truly representative and effective state should be able to mobilize and be legitimized by a new majority that would include many state actors and ordinary citizens and the voluntary associations citizens join to express their values and further their social goals, such as sectoral peoples' organizations (POs), issue-oriented nongovernmental organizations (NGOs), professional organizations, and lay religious groups. Why has this mobilization not happened? "How," in the words of one close observer, "could a country with so many gifted, so many nice people, end up in such a mess?"[2]

This dilemma of state–society relations is the concern of our book. We engage it through a historical treatment of state formation and the corresponding conflicts and collaborations between state leaders and social forces. We examine the long history of institutional state weakness in the Philippines and the efforts made to overcome the state's structural fragility and strengthen its bond with society. While these efforts have fallen short of their goals, we believe it would be a mistake to ignore them, for the chance of a successful political and economic turnaround depends greatly on awareness of precedents.

Along the way, we hope to stimulate thinking about the puzzle of state resilience: How has this "weak state" maintained the territorial integrity of the Philippines in the postwar period in the face of two major rebellions and an armed separatist movement, corruption, mismanagement, intractable poverty, weak sovereignty, and an often chaotic electoral system? Why does the inability to collect taxes, secure citizens' lives and property, and maintain economic infrastructure not result in state failure? We will look for answers by focusing on how the state has shaped and been shaped by its interaction with social forces, especially in the rituals of popular mobilization that have produced such surprising and diverse results.

THE BOOK'S APPROACH

In presenting the general contours of Philippine state formation and state–society relations, we will situate the Philippines in a global context, tracing its development in the world of maritime Asia in the age of commerce, the Spanish empire of missionaries and galleons, the American Century of state building and democracy, the postcolonial Cold War, and beyond. This approach is essential to understanding the distinctive attributes of the Philippine nation-state. It is a society twice colonized—by Spain in the sixteenth century and the United States at the turn of the twentieth—and the first nation in Asia to establish a republic (1898) through anticolonial nationalist revolution. It is the most Catholic of Asian countries (currently almost 83 percent), but one in which the institutional Church confronts radical reinterpretations of religion and the polity has not resolved how to integrate members of preexisting religions. It is a society that strongly identifies with liberal democracy, but which endured fifteen years of dictatorship and cannot end one of the last communist insurgencies in the post–Cold War era.

These elements are better understood if the precolonial and Spanish colonial periods are presented within the context of regional developments, for despite its unique qualities, the Philippines did not develop in isolation. In the American era, too, awareness of the nature and priorities of U.S. domestic politics illuminates features of Philippine colonial politics. Attentiveness to the broader world helps us see why Filipino leaders were attracted to fascism and Stalinism as well as liberal democracy, or how Marcos could present martial law as a "constitutional dictatorship" combining American constitutionalism with East and Southeast Asian one-party developmentalism (state-led capitalist economic development). Finally, state formation in the Philippines is worth a closer look because today we see the indications of Philippine-style political dilemmas emerging in neighboring countries.

Recognition of the country's "comparability" arising from its global context and the distinctiveness of its specific political experiences persuaded us to reconsider the narrative of Philippine political development. The standard narrative adheres closely to the conventional historical periodization: "pre-Hispanic"; Spanish; revolutionary; American; Commonwealth; Japanese; and, in the Republican era, by presidential administration. Instead, we have organized the book in a manner that acknowledges the Southeast Asian connections of the Philippines and the changing rhythm of state and social formation across time and regimes.

- Chapter 2 (The Philippines in Maritime Asia to the Fourteenth Century) positions the archipelago analytically within the world of maritime Asia, emphasizing regional commonalities in the political, economic, and social practices of the pre- and early historical periods. We discuss the connections its polities had with each other and with regional state formations such as the Chinese empire and the larger maritime Southeast Asian polities.
- Chapter 3 (New States and Reorientations, 1368–1764) examines dramatic changes occurring in the early modern period as new religions—Islam and Christianity—and new state forms entered the maritime world. We explain the relationship between religion and state in the southern sultanates from 1450 and in the areas of Spanish conquest from 1571. We identify the origins of territorial definition and the weak state in Spanish conversion and governance practices and trace the development of internal social and geographic delineations between Muslim and non-Muslim, Christian and non-Christian, native and Chinese.
- Chapter 4 (State and Societies, 1764–1898) tracks Spanish efforts to modernize the political economy of the colony to cope with changing international conditions, particularly the loss of the profitable American colonies and competition from industrializing nations. Economic reforms resulted in a new export economy that relied little on Spanish expertise or capital, while Spain's domestic inability to reach political consensus hindered efforts to rationalize and centralize the state in the Philippines. We show how the economic and social changes of the nineteenth century resulted in a major reconstitution of ethnic and class categories and the gradual emergence of a new "Filipino" identity.
- Chapter 5 (Nation and States, 1872–1913) examines how different Philippine social groups tried to "speak" to the Spanish colonial state, created their own state through revolution, and dealt with the imposition of a new American colonial state. Filipino nationalism is presented in the two major

articulations that provide the framework for twentieth-century political development: elite constitutionalism and radical lower-class "brotherhood." Here we also suggest that state formation—primed by Spanish state reforms, debated by educated revolutionaries, and consolidated by American colonialism—was a continuous development underlying the revolution, war, and regime change of the period.

- Chapter 6 (The Filipino Colonial State, 1902–1946) moves from the American-controlled executive structures of the previous chapter to the electoral framework established to create a Philippine legislature. We explore the connection between American practices of electoral democracy—especially patronage party politics—and the effort of Filipino politicians to take control of the colonial state from within. At the height of this era, Filipino leaders commenced an ambitious process of state centralization that was interrupted by World War II.
- Chapter 7 (All Politics Is Local, 1946–1964) shows how the political center of gravity in the independent Republic of the Philippines moved from the central to the local level with the rise of new provincial elites and the development of a two-party system. We identify some "islands of state strength in an ocean of weakness," but explain why most centralizing efforts in this period failed.[3] In an era of moderate industrial growth but stagnant agriculture, we track the resurgence of nationalism among rural tenants and urban workers and show this to be a period in which a few wealthy insiders controlled the constitutional system, and many—peasants, workers, Muslims, Chinese—remained outsiders.
- Chapter 8 (Marcos, 1965–1986) is devoted to the constitutional presidency and subsequent dictatorship of President Ferdinand Marcos. We discuss how Marcos made extensive use of executive agencies to bypass the power of Congress and how his reelection began a process of political polarization that allowed him to declare martial law in 1972. We trace the militarized state's initial success and later decline, examining its mechanisms of control, economic programs, and degree of autonomy from class and sectoral interests. Then we turn to social forces, going back to highlight the Muslim secessionist and communist revolutionary movements. Finally, we bring state and social forces together to understand Marcos's downfall through "people power."
- Chapter 9 (Democratization, 1986–2004) discusses President Corazon Aquino's restoration of constitutional democracy and surveys elements of the economic liberalization program championed by her successor Fidel V. Ramos. Both presidencies claimed to further "people empowerment," but the 1997 Asian financial crisis also exposed the fragility of the left-to-right coalitions that have replaced functional political parties. We then

explore the populist surge that led to the brief presidency of President Joseph Estrada, and the efforts of his successor, Gloria M. Arroyo, to mix technocratic governance and the spoils system to keep her in power as well as to grow the economy.

- Chapter 10 (Cacique Democracy Personalized) is a preliminary assessment of the presidency of Benigno Aquino III and his attempts to stop the spread of institutional corruption caused by his predecessor's effort to mix patronage politics into governance and improve state capacity. Aquino's crusade, however, had its limits: it only applied to political enemies and not to allies. This selective reformism allowed the economy to grow faster, but it was not enough for Aquino to leave an enduring positive legacy. Instead, he lost a lot of political capital at the end of his term and providing an opening for an antipodal candidate to succeed him.
- Chapter 11 (Neo-Authoritarianism?) looks at the first seven months of Rodrigo R. Duterte's presidency and suggesting that his unusual way of governing is not a deviation from the norm. It is, in fact, the inevitable nationalization of local power and its attributes: absence of diplomatic language, a personalization of political authority, and the use of violence. It closes with a discussion of how Duterte's War on Drugs has become more and more a war against the poor, and whether if this will, in the long run, brings down his widespread popularity.

CONCEPTUAL TOOLS

The State

Our historical narrative of state formation and state–society relations is informed by scholarship attempting to explain why some states in Asia, Africa, Latin America, and the Middle East have grown in strength, while others are weak. The concept of "state" we find most useful in discussing these postcolonial situations is that presented by political scientist Crawford Young in *The African Colonial State in Comparative Perspective.* Young starts in a standard place—philosopher Max Weber's definition of the state as "an agency of domination" that "bounds a civil society."[4] He then outlines what he considers the eight main attributes of a modern state: territoriality, exercise of power, jurisdiction over a population, sovereignty, legal personality, role as an international actor, close association with the nation, and compelling ideological appeal.[5]

The modern state is "a territorial entity" whose principal concern is to accumulate and effectively exercise power over a "spatial domain . . . with precise boundary demarcations." Boundaries may be well defined, however, but still not stable; the history of states shows many "fluctuations" at their peripheries. These and other problems may be caused by the way states exercise power over the "human subjects resident within [their] sphere of territorial jurisdiction." When, for whatever reason, people defy the "formal legal classifications" states assign them to define rights and responsibilities, they become subject to state coercion and may be imprisoned, exiled, or even executed. What is most important is that without a population to rule, the state "ceases to exist."

The state's domestic sovereignty—its right to exercise power within its borders—possesses no inherent limits. Young describes what a state can do:

> Land without an owner belongs to the state; property without an heir escheats the state. A helpless individual is a ward of the state. The state may conscript labor for its projects or personnel for its armies. The possessions of the individual are subject to taxation; behavior is open to regulation through law.

But domestic sovereignty exercised without limit would rely too much on coercion. So, limits are inscribed in a "legal compact" between state and society. All the language that mediates this relationship—whether trouble-free or conflict-ridden—is legal. Laws are used by states to exercise power and by individuals and groups to limit state intrusiveness and procure accountability. State power can also be limited by institutionalized popular representation and "tamed by its dispersal among several branches of government." The effectiveness of state power, therefore, lies not so much in its coercive resources—armies, police, weapons, prisons—but in its ability to impose "a single body of law" and a "unified judicial system."

Through these mechanisms, state and society "become full partners in the exercise of sovereignty." It is a partnership that restrains the inherent tendency of the state to exercise "limitless, total, indivisible power" and legitimizes the state as an "international legal person" with a right to independence and security within a "world system of states."

The partnership of state and society brings us to the state's "momentous marriage with the idea of nationalism." Today, it is impossible to think of the state without the nation—so much so that Benedict Anderson reminds us of the tendency to "read *nation* as merely a convenient shorthand expression for *nation-state*, and thereby to overlook the fact that a tiny hyphen links two different entities with distinct histories, constituents, and 'interests.'"[6] This union has proved of great benefit to the modern state. According to Young, the "warm, vibrant, profoundly emotive notion of nation invests the more arid, abstract, jurisprudential concept of state with a capacity for eliciting passionate attachment." The most important state honors are given to those who defend the national interest on the battlefield or other arenas where nations compete. The worst political label is "traitor," one who betrays the nation. States can also lose legitimacy if they fail to protect the nation.

Finally, the state is an "ensemble of affective orientations, images and expectations imprinted in the minds of its subjects." Those who control state power take seriously the task of embellishing the state with a host of "symbolic splendors" ranging from "the monumental architecture of their capital cities" to "anthems, pledges of allegiance, oaths of office." In the era of "democratization," even elections become more than tabulated expressions of the popular will, rising to ideological validations of the democratic nature of the state (however democracy may be defined). All these images, emotions, and expectations are deployed to inspire loyalty or deference, instill fear, or pro-ject a sense of the power of the state.

To Crawford Young's definition, we would like to add a final element—people. Not people as subjects, but people as part of the state—the men and women who carry out its missions, defend its interests, and act on its behalf. In his study of the colonial origins of the modern Indonesian state, Anderson asserts that "the state has to be understood as an *institution*, of the same species as the church, the university, and the modern corporation."

> Like them, it ingests and excretes personnel in a continuous, steady process, often over long periods of time. It is characteristic of such institutions that "they" have precise rules for entry—at least age, often sex, education, and so forth—and, no less important, for exit—most notably, mandatory retirement. No more impressive sign exists of these institutions' inner workings than the steady rotation *out* of their top leaders (corporate presidents, senior prelates, distinguished academicians, high civil servants, and so on).[7]

Some political leaders like to identify themselves with the state in the mode of Louis XIV—"I *am* the state." More common are bureaucrats who resist pressure to reform in the name of defending the institution, or military men who seize power to protect the state from "weak" or corrupt civilian leaders. This warns us not to treat the state as wholly discrete from society. Even as the state rules society, society flows into and out of the state—shaping, enhancing, limiting what the state can do and be.

In addition to state, the concept of "regime" will be used in the text. Regime can be used in two ways. One is the somewhat common use as synonymous with "government of the day." In this sense, it carries a connotation of illegitimacy and is often used to disparage, as by opponents of "the Marcos regime." We use regime in the sense defined by Young as "a given formula for the organization and exercise of state power."[8] In this sense, regime describes the kind of "institutional arrangements" that emerge out of a country's history and the "dominant ideas" that legitimize the arrangements. The simplest categorization of twentieth-century regimes was into two types, "democratic" and "communist." With the end of the Cold War, more complicated classifications have arisen. Dietrich Rueschemeyer, Evelyne Huber Stephens, and John D. Stephens, for example, provide a classification of five major regime types: constitutional oligarchic, authoritarian, restricted democratic, fully democratic, and bureaucratic authoritarian.[9] In many countries of Asia, Africa, Latin America, and recently the Middle East, "regime change" may occur more than once in a lifetime. Such is the case in the Philippines, where the "given formula for the organization and exercise of state power" has changed several times in a little more than one hundred years.

Social Forces

Governance is a continual process in which a state imposes authority and society responds to that imposition with collaboration, resistance, or something in between. Society does not act as one, of course, but in differentiated groups we call "social forces." In *State Power and Social Forces*, Joel Migdal defines social forces as "powerful mechanisms for associative behavior."

> These forces encompass informal organizations (such as Senegal's patron–client networks, or friendship groups and old-boy networks in other societies) as well as formal organizations (such as businesses and churches). They can also be social movements, including those held together by common, strongly motivating sets of ideas (even where organizational ties are absent).[10]

In the Philippines, the concept of "sector" is also commonly used to refer to large segments of society (women, workers, peasants) or classes (middle class, rural poor). If organized, even loosely, into social movements with political goals, the sectors can also constitute social forces.

Social forces compete with one another "over symbolic and material interests" in their effort to dominate social and political "arenas." The winners are those that can establish coalitions and forge alliances through accommodation and struggle (peaceful or violent) with other forces inside and outside the state. The cohesiveness and resources of a social group and its leadership and the ability to deploy "pervasive and powerful symbols" are important factors in determining success.[11]

Our understanding of "social forces" can be sharpened if we contrast it with "civil society forces," a term used recently to describe the movements and voluntary associations that have engaged the Philippine state.[12] This new category has gained widespread acceptance, but we find "social forces" to be a more accurate representation of reality. While "civil society" would seem to encompass "social forces" in its description as "an arena of friendship, clubs, churches, business associations, unions and other voluntary associations that mediate the vast expanse of social life between the household and the state," it has been further and rather benignly defined as "the place where citizens learn habits of free assembly, dialogue and social initiative . . . to bring about that delicate balance of private interests and public concern vital for a vibrant democracy."[13] In reality, however, the place where social forces contend is often violence-prone and quite unbalanced even *among* private interests; it does not always teach good habits. Not just the state but social forces themselves sometimes embody antidemocratic practices.[14]

Further, "*civil* society forces" carries the implicit notion that these movements and voluntary associations remain outside the state. In the Philippines and elsewhere, however, such groups often cross the divide to become part of the state. The powerful and excluded alike seek representation and employment in the state; radical social forces aspire to *seize* the state. We find there to be incessant movement not only within society but also between state and society. Analytically, "social forces" allows the possibility of such movement, while "civil society forces" does not. Social forces are therefore movements and voluntary associations with political agendas that contend with each other and the state. They try to achieve their goals through coalition or accommodation with or defeat of other groups or the state, are willing to move into the state, or may endeavor to take over the state.

In our discussion of Philippine politics, we will keep these features of state and social forces in mind as we evaluate the extent to which the state is able to achieve its key attributes and social forces are able to affect the state. Before proceeding into that story, we will present some essential information about the country.

BASIC INFORMATION ABOUT THE PHILIPPINES

Location and Geography

The Philippines is one of the largest island groups in the world. It is an archipelago of 7,107 islands with a land area of about 300,000 square kilometers (more than 115,000 square miles) surrounded by three major bodies of water: the Pacific Ocean to the east, the South China Sea to the west, and the Celebes Sea to the south.

The country is comprised of three major regions—the largest island, Luzon (pronounced loo-ZONE), in the north; the Visayas (vee-SIGH-uhs), an island group in the center; and Mindanao (MIN-da-now), the second-largest island,

and the Sulu (soo-loo) archipelago in the south. Because these zones correspond to social, political, and, to a certain extent, linguistic divisions, we will refer to them often. The capital is Manila in Luzon. Other important cities are Cebu (in the Visayas); Davao, Cotabato, and Zamboanga (in Mindanao); and Jolo (in Sulu).

Luzon and Mindanao, as well as the larger of the Visayan Islands, are characterized by irregular shorelines, alluvial plains, narrow valleys, mountains, and rolling hills. The total forest cover of what was once a lush tropical island system has been reduced to only 19.4 percent.[15] Rapid deforestation has caused major ecological damage in many provinces and has threatened almost a third of all mammal species identified in the Philippines (49 out of 153) and more than 20 percent of the bird species (86 out of 395). Despite straddling three seas, Philippine maritime resources—including once-rich mangrove zones on the coasts of most islands—are threatened by overfishing and pollution, including the use of cyanide and dynamite to increase the catch.

From the standpoint of international politics, the Philippines is part of Southeast Asia and an original member of the Association of Southeast Asian Nations (ASEAN). Until the 1990s, however, the relationship between the Philippines and its neighbors was not close, largely because Filipino political leaders considered links with the United States to be more important. Pro-American sentiment earned the Philippines suspicion from such neighbors as Malaysia and Indonesia, and—through the years of U.S. intervention in Indochina—the animosity of Vietnam, Laos, and Cambodia. This orientation changed in 1991, when the Philippine Senate declined to renew the bases treaty that had allowed the United States to maintain two large and more than twenty smaller military facilities in the country. The end of the long security relationship with the United States compelled the Philippines to turn its attention to Southeast Asia and become meaningfully involved in the diplomatic, economic, and political activities of ASEAN. Although the current government of President Gloria Arroyo has become an active partner in the American "war on terror," it is unlikely that links with Southeast Asia will be neglected.

People and Practices

Filipinos are distinguished by ethnolinguistic groups originally corresponding to geographical areas. Although 78 languages and 500 dialects have been identified, the eight major language groups are Tagalog, Visayan, Ilocano, Hiligaynon (also known as Ilonggo), Bicol, Waray, Pampango, and Pangasinense. The politically dominant language over the last century has been Tagalog (ta-GAH-lug), the language of Manila and the surrounding provinces.

Visayan has the most native speakers; its major dialect is Cebuano (see-BWA-no). "Filipino," one of two official languages (the other is English), is based on Tagalog. In the past, speakers of other languages complained of "Tagalog linguistic imperialism," but as more non-Tagalogs are exposed to Filipino-language news and entertainment on national television, this opposition has lessened. Increased mobility has also enhanced linguistic mixing; a visitor will hear "Taglish" (a blend of Tagalog and English) in Manila or "Davao-Tagalog" (Tagalog, English, and Cebuano) in southeastern Mindanao.

Filipinos are also differentiated by religious affiliation: Roman Catholic (82.9 percent), various Protestant denominations (5.4 percent), Islam (4.6 percent), Philippine Independent Church (2.6 percent), Iglesia ni Kristo (2.3 percent), and others (2.2 percent), including animist. The two independent Christian churches were established as a result of differences with the Roman Catholic Church. In the 1890s, Filipino priests broke with the Spanish-controlled Church in order to better serve the needs of the Revolution through the Philippine Independent Church. The Iglesia ni Kristo (founded in 1913) is based on the idea that the principal tenets of Christianity have not been well taught in the Philippines. The Iglesia ni Kristo, with an estimated three million members, has become an important force in Philippine politics, rivaling the Catholic Church.

Excluding members of the two independent churches and those belonging to fundamentalist Catholic, Protestant, and Islamic groups, Filipinos are not regarded as religiously doctrinaire. While Catholics diligently participate in rituals like Sunday Mass, many observers note the dominance of "folk Catholicism," often described as the reinterpretation of Catholic beliefs and practices to fit the local worldview. A crucifix or a prayer book may simultaneously serve as a Christian symbol and an *anting-anting* (amulet) to ward off evil or even a policeman's bullet. The teachings of Jesus Christ have spiritually instructed Filipinos and also provided them justification for revolt against colonial masters and oppressive landlords. Even Filipino communists tap into the peasants' millenarian worldview—the belief in a coming heaven on earth—to encourage revolutionary action. A similar "folk Islam" combines Islamic teaching with pre-Muslim animist practice among the Maguindanaos, the dominant Muslim ethnolinguistic group. Both are the result of the "localization" of new belief systems according to preexisting social needs. But neither precludes movement toward a more "universal" practice of these two world religions.

Whatever the substance of practiced religion, a distinct characteristic of Philippine politics is the strong presence of religious themes. Two major political movements in the country's history—the 1896 Revolution and the 1986 uprising against Marcos—depended on religious mobilization. During election campaigns, politicians are sure to be seen at church, mosque, or religious shrine, kissing the hand of the archbishop of Manila, greeting an *imam* (Muslim prayer leader), or embracing the head of the Iglesia ni Kristo. Religious actors are among the most powerful social forces in the Philippines and have at times also been part of the state.

Political Administration and Political Power

The Philippines is divided into 17 regions, 79 provinces, 115 cities, 1,499 municipalities, and 41,969 *barangays* (the smallest political unit). (See box 1.1.) Metropolitan Manila is a massive urban sprawl that includes thirteen cities and four municipalities.

Box 1.1. Regions and Provinces of the Philippines

Cordillera Administrative Region
  Abra
  Apayao
  Benguet
  Ifugao
  Kalinga
  Mountatin Province

Region I (Ilocos Region)
  Ilocos Norte
  Ilocos Sur
  La Union
  Pangasinan

Region II (Cagayan Valley)
  Batanes
  Cagayan
  Isabela
  Nueva Vizcaya
  Quirino

Region III
  Aurora
  Bataan
  Bulacan
  Nueva Ecija
  Pampanga
  Tarlac
  Zambales

Region IV-A (Calabarzon)
  Batangas
  Cavite
  Laguna
  Quezon
  Rizal

Region IV-B (Mimaropa)
  Marinduque
  Occidental Mindoro
  Oriental Mindoro
  Palawan
  Romblon

Region V (Bicol Region)
  Albay
  Camarines Norte
  Camarines Sur
  Catanduanes
  Masbate
  Sorsogon

Region VI (Western Visayas)
  Aklan
  Antique
  Capiz
  Guimaras
  Iloilo
  Negros Occidental

(continued)

Region VII (Central Visayas)	Region XI (Davao Region)
Bohol	Compostela Valley
Cebu	Davao del Norte
Negros Oriental	Davao del Sur
Siquijor	Davao Oriental
Region VIII (Eastern Visayas)	Region XII (Soccsksargen)
Biliran	Cotabato (North Cotabato)
Eastern Samar	Sarangani
Leyte	South Cotabato
Northern Samar	Sultan Kudarat
Samar (Western Samar)	
Southern Leyte	Region XIII (Caraga)
	Agusan del Norte
Region IX (Zamboanga Peninsula)	Agusan del Sur
Zamboanga del Norte	Surigao del Norte
Zamboanga del Sur	Surigao del Sur
Zamboanga Sibugay	
	ARMM (Autonomous Region in Muslim
Region X (Northern Mindanao)	Mindanao)
Bukidnon	Basilan
Camiguin	Lanao del Sur
Lanao del Norte	Maguindanao
Misamis Occidental	Sulu
Misamis Oriental	Tawi-Tawi

Source: National Statistical Coordination Board, http://www.nscb.gov.ph/activestats/psgc/listprov.asp

The country is governed by a constitutional democracy (fully democratic in the Rueschemeyer, Stephens, and Stephens rubric) that adopted some of its structures and political rituals from the United States. For example, the three branches of government—executive, legislative, and judiciary—are equal in principle and perform specific functions as outlined by the Constitution. Unlike the United States, however, the fifteen justices of the Supreme Court are appointed by the president and not subject to legislative scrutiny and approval. The popularly elected bicameral legislature consists of a Senate, whose twenty-four at-large members serve six-year terms, and a House of Representatives comprised of 206 district-based congressmen and twenty at-large representatives of sectoral party-list organizations ("small parties and marginalized and underrepresented sectors").[16] Members of the lower house are elected to three-year terms, and the president can appoint additional members up to the constitutionally mandated limit of 250 members.

The president is elected to a single six-year term, a tenure increased from four years to allow sufficient time for economic and political achievement, given the prohibition on reelection. These were among the changes made in 1987, when a new constitution replaced the one that had been gutted by presidential decrees during the Marcos dictatorship. The 1987 Constitution has weakened the president's ability to keep the country under martial law (or in a state of emergency) for any length of time. But the executive still oversees all departments and agencies of the state, releases funds appropriated by Congress, and acts as commander-in-chief of the Armed Forces of the Philippines (AFP). All Philippine presidents have used the enormous resources of this administrative reach to win the support of Congress and local officials.

If the presidency has the central state to serve its purposes, congressional power is based on a combination of institutional authority granted by the Constitution and an extensive network of allies, supporters, and relatives at the local level. Congress has authority over the national budget, officially proclaims the president and vice president, determines promotions in the military, and conducts investigations into the performance of executive offices. Under opposition control, Congress can derail a president's economic development program as well as undermine his or her legitimacy. In recent years, this kind of institutional combat has been increasing. The May 2004 election featured the slowest tabulation of votes for the presidency and vice presidency in the country's history.

The major locus of congressional power, however, is at the local level—to paraphrase the late U.S. congressman "Tip" O'Neill, all politics in the Philippines is local. Members of the House of Representatives are elected through adept handling of a local network often centered on the family (or political clan) and extended through their district by alliances and patronage. Incumbents have a tremendous advantage in building and protecting networks through their control of "pork barrel," discretionary funds allotted to each representative and senator (and released at the discretion of the president). Political party affiliation is subordinate to the patronage network; if party affiliation threatens patronage funds or networks, politicians don't hesitate to switch parties.

Presidential, vice presidential, and senatorial candidates, who all compete in national elections, must tap into these vast networks of local power to be elected. Money flows from the candidates' coffers to the local political clans to ensure loyalty and delivery of votes. Loyalty is critical because as election day approaches, local officials like to open a bidding game in which the national candidate making the highest offer wins the votes of the city, province, or region. In areas where patronage is insufficient and political competition intense, congressional candidates and political clans invest in private armies to enforce their will. Elections in the Philippines have therefore been described as representing "guns, goons, and gold" as much as the will of the people.

Despite such shortcomings, voter turnout has been consistently above 60 percent since the 1950s. Filipinos enthusiastically participate in elections, believing that their votes can put good leaders into government. But alongside this penchant for voting is a willingness to "take to the streets." A failed rural rebellion in the 1950s yielded to an urban- and rural-based Communist party in the 1960s that has waged "people's war" ever since. Two popular uprisings in the last eighteen years have toppled a dictator and a president, and a third undermined the ability of another president to govern. These extraconstitutional acts of popular mobilization—dubbed "people power"—are becoming habitual, spurring debate about the practice of democracy in the Philippines.

Economic Changes[17]

With a population of 103.4 million, Filipinos now constitute 1.38 percent of the world total population. From the crisis periods of early 2000, the country's economy has undergone a dramatic turn-around in 2012, its gross domestic product (GDP) now averaging 6.6 percent. GDP for the first part of 2017 is estimated at $348.6 billion.

The main driver of this growth remains the remittances of overseas Filipino workers (OFWs), which totaled $28 billion in 2016. Coming in second is a "new" industry: Business Process Outsourcing (BPOs) revenues reached $25 billion in 2016. BPOs have boosted the service sector's share of the GDP (59.8 percent), with industry coming second (30.5 percent) and agriculture last (9.7 percent).

As a result, the poverty incidence among Filipinos shrank to 21.6 percent beginning in 2015, and the unemployment rate is now 5.7 percent, down from 8 percent in 2010. However, the income gap remains a problem In 2009, the lowest 10 percent controlled 2.6 percent of the national income, while the top 10 percent owned 33.6 percent. The economic decline has stopped, but this cannot be said of the country's politics, as the last two chapters suggest.

NOTES

1. Gloria Macapagal-Arroyo, "Towards a Strong Philippine Republic," State of the Nation address at the opening of the 2nd Regular Session of the 12th Congress, July 22, 2002.

2. Benedict Anderson, personal communication, January 25, 2003.

3. The phrase is from Kenneth Finegold and Theda Skocpol, "State Capacity and Economic Intervention in the Early New Deal," *Political Science Quarterly* 97 (1982): 271.

4. Crawford Young, *The African Colonial State in Comparative Perspective* (New Haven and London: Yale University Press, 1994), 6.

5. Quotations in the following paragraphs, except where noted, are from Young, *African Colonial State,* 25–34.

6. Benedict Anderson, "Old State, New Society: Indonesia's New Order in Comparative Historical Perspective," in *Language and Power: Exploring Political Cultures in Indonesia* (Ithaca, N.Y.: Cornell University Press, 1990), 94.

7. Anderson, "Old State, New Society," 95.

8. Young, *African Colonial State*, 40.

9. Dietrich Rueschemeyer, Evelyne Huber Stephens, and John D. Stephens, *Capitalist Development and Democracy* (Chicago: University of Chicago Press, 1992), 161–62.

10. Joel S. Migdal, "The State in Society: An Approach to Struggles for Domination," in *State Power and Social Forces: Domination and Transformation in the Third World*, ed. Joel S. Migdal, Atul Kohli, and Vivienne Shue (Cambridge: Cambridge University Press, 1994), 20.

11. Migdal, "State in Society," 21–22.

12. See Isagani R. Serrano, *On Civil Society* (Quezon City: Philippine Rural Reconstruction Movement, 1993); G. Sidney Silliman and Lela Garner Noble, eds., *Organizing for Democracy: NGOs, Civil Society, and the Philippine State* (Honolulu: University of Hawai'i Press; Quezon City: Ateneo de Manila University Press, 1998); Caucus of Development NGOs, *Civil Society: Creative Responses to the Challenge of Globalization, 3–5 September 1996 Proceedings* (Quezon City: Center for Alternative Development Initiatives, 1998); and *Philippine Civil Society and International Solidarity Partners: Strengthening Local and Global Advocacy Initiatives: Conference Proceedings* (Quezon City: Bayanihan International Solidarity Conference, 2001).

13. Robert W. Hefner, "Civil Society and Democracy," *Journal: Civnet's Journal for Civil Society* 2, no. 3 (May/June 1998), 3–4.

14. Vincent Boudreau, *Grass Roots and Cadre in the Protest Movement* (Quezon City: Ateneo de Manila University Press, 2001).

15. United Nations Food and Agriculture Organization, *The State of the World's Forests* (New York: UNFAO, 2003).

16. Republic of the Philippines, "A Guide to the Election of Party-List Representatives through the Party List System," Republic Act no. 7941 (1998).

17. Sources for this section include: "The Philippines GDP and Economic Data," *Global Finance,* March 26, 2017, https://www.gfmag.com/global-data/country-data/the-philippines-gdp-country-report (last accessed March 17, 2017); Kristian Javier, "OFW remittances seen to reach 'all-time high' $28B in 2016," *PhilStar Global*, December 21, 2016, http://www.philstar.com/business/2016/12/21/1655597/ofw-remittances-seen-reach-all-time-high-28b-2016 (last accessed March 17, 2017); Karin Raslan, "How outsourcing transformed the Philippine middle class," *This Week in Asia,* December 29, 2016, http://www.scmp.com/week-asia/business/article/2057901/how-outsourcing-transformed-philippine-middle-class (last accessed

March 17, 2017); Philippine Statistics Authority, "Poverty Incidence among Filipinos registered at 21.6 in 2015 – PSA," October 27, 2016, https://psa.gov.ph/poverty-press-releases (last accessed March 17, 2017); and Philippine Statistics Authority, "Labor force survey," n.d., https://psa.gov.ph/poverty-press-releases (last accessed March 17, 2017).

Chapter Two

The Philippines in Maritime Asia to the Fourteenth Century

EARLY SOUTHEAST ASIAN POLITIES

A central paradox in discussing the Philippine past is that "the Philippines" did not exist as such in the tenth century, or even in the sixteenth century when the archipelago received this name from colonizing Spaniards. In fact, present-day Filipinos might have a hard time recognizing themselves in their tenth-century predecessors. There were some familiar social features, such as the importance of family ties and a reliance on the sea for food. Less-familiar traits included body tattooing to mark achievement in battle and slave raiding. But while early communities in the archipelago did not constitute a single and recognizable Philippine polity, they did contain elements of social organization, material life, and interisland contacts that would contribute to the present nation-state. It should be kept in mind, however, that neither commonalities found within the archipelago nor continuities observed through time are exclusive characteristics of the Philippines or Filipinos. Many are shared with other Southeast Asian societies and constitute a kind of sociocultural milieu out of which the Philippines and other modern nations of the region developed.

Localities and Leadership

What were the characteristics of early Southeast Asia? Most languages in the maritime region (the archipelagos, islands, and peninsula jutting out from the Asian mainland) belong to the Austronesian family of languages. Numbering in the thousands, some major examples of Austronesian languages today are the national languages of Indonesia and Malaysia, along with the widely spoken

Tagalog and Visayan of the Philippines. This linguistic affinity stems from the probable dispersal through the region more than 4,000 years ago of people from today's southern China who became the ancestors of most Southeast Asians. (A separate group populated mainland Southeast Asia, speaking languages of the Austroasiatic family.) These early migrants were not yet Sinicized, or culturally Chinese, but their movement south points to the important fact that "in these early times southern China was culturally and environmentally a part of Southeast Asia."[1] As we will see, that link continues to be important to the region as a whole and to the Philippines in particular ways.

Another characteristic of the region from early times was the widespread practice of cognatic kinship, in which families trace descent through both the male and female lines. In practical terms, this means that both sons and daughters may have inheritance rights and that neither "disappears" from the family tree upon marriage. (Contrast this with the strictly patrilineal descent of the Chinese.) Where cognatic kinship is practiced in Southeast Asia, it has had immense significance socially and politically. Children grow up and marry but continue to be part of their natal family, and sibling relationships are significant throughout life. People who are not biologically related can make new claims on each other through fictive kinship, which creates ritual brothers, godmothers, and godfathers. And political alliances are typically confirmed through marriage, creating larger family networks. Where family relations proliferated so readily, kinship became the way most social ties were expressed, "the idiom of social organization."[2]

Family also played an important part in religious life. The earliest religions in Southeast Asia, as elsewhere, were animistic, seeing and worshipping divinity in the surrounding environment, which had the power to give life (e.g., a good harvest, a successful hunt) or bring harm (death in childbirth, a shipwreck). To navigate through this world and into the next, people made offerings to the divinities of nature and to relatives who had already passed on. Ancestor worship was a spiritual expression of kinship ties that were relied upon and imposed duties in daily life.

Finally, interaction between people and the geography they inhabited led to distinctive settlement patterns through most of Southeast Asia. With the exception of certain large plains, such as the Red River delta in northern Vietnam and the central plain of Java, the region features central mountain ranges that were once thickly forested. Natural resources were abundant, especially from the sea, but travel over land was often difficult; rivers running from mountain to coastline were separated by difficult terrain. These factors, combined with a low population density, yielded a patchwork of human settlements, often along rivers and initially isolated from one another, rather than concentrated population centers. Even when settlements grew into networks that traded and competed, a local mindset persisted—people felt strongly attached to their own locality and didn't feel it to be less important than other larger or more powerful settlements. Historian Oliver Wolters described this multicentrality of early Southeast Asia: "Every center was a center in its own right as far as its inhabitants were concerned, and it was surrounded by its own groups of neighbours."[3]

What type of state arose in these conditions? We need to examine the question itself before beginning to answer it. The question has been shaped by scholarship on the development of Western European states, on the one hand, and by the Chinese sources that provide some of the earliest evidence about Southeast Asia, on the other. Through the Weberian lens, an early state would emerge from and exist above a growing population engaging in trade and other economic activities. The classical Chinese-defined state would feature dynastic succession within defined territorial boundaries. But we find neither in early Southeast Asia, particularly in the Philippines, so should we conclude that there was no state? Or can we look instead for early state formation in the engagement of social forces—in the spiritual life, social and economic hierarchies, and cultural practices of a society? (See box 2.1.) To find this picture of "state" in early Southeast Asia, we should take a closer look at the early river-based settlements.

As a source of water and food, rivers were logical settlement sites. They also provided channels of transportation, so that communities at the mouth of a river could trade with those upriver. This trade was an important feature of early Southeast Asian societies, for to sustain life, upriver settlements needed salt and protein (seafood) from the coast. In exchange, they traded rice and forest products that coastal dwellers needed for food and external

---

Box 2.1. Looking for States in Early Southeast Asia

"The two sets of signifiers—Western and Chinese—have precise meaning only in cultural contexts outside Southeast Asia. . . . In other words, the criteria for incipient and fully-fledged states are established by an arbitrary vocabulary drawn from an archaeology with an economic bias and from Chinese conventions transferred to a part of the world which was virtually unknown to them. The result is that one is in danger of looking for what could never be there in either prehistoric or protohistoric times. If, however, we think simply of 'political systems'—a neutral expression—the way is open for considering other cultural phenomena such as religious and social behavior that can be expected to affect political and economic activities in both prehistory and protohistory."

—O. W. Wolters, *History, Culture, and Region in Southeast Asian Perspectives*, rev. ed. (Ithaca, N.Y.: Cornell Southeast Asia Program, in cooperation with the Institute of Southeast Asian Studies, Singapore, 1999), 24–25

trade. Settlements at river mouths were particularly strategic, having the potential to control the entry of upriver goods into the trading system. But realizing such potential required social organization through the mobilization of kinship ties to establish one settlement's dominance within a network of similar settlements.

The person capable of mobilizing people to achieve these goals has been described in various ways: "chief" or "big man" in anthropological studies, "charismatic leader" in Weberian political scholarship, and "man of prowess" in Southeast Asia. This person exhibited unusual achievement in warfare and trade, an indication of spiritual power that could enhance community well-being. His achievements and charisma enabled him to command the personal loyalty of an extended kinship group and continually increase the number of his followers, including slaves. Such a man of prowess was often called *datu*, a title common throughout the maritime region. During his life, he was subject to frequent challenge and could keep his position only through continuous success. After his death, he might be worshipped as a revered ancestor by those who hoped to succeed him. These successors were not necessarily biological offspring; dynasties were difficult to establish because a son was not guaranteed to inherit the prowess of his father. The power conveyed by ancestors could be claimed by anyone with talent.

While the phrase "man of prowess" signifies male leadership, there are indications that women were central to community life as well. These are most obvious in the origin myths that feature women and highlight the complementarity of male and female roles. We cannot rule out the existence of female datus, but women were more likely to be prominent as ritual specialists with power to access and influence the spirits existing in nature. The sources that historians rely on, however, are very scarce for the early historical period. Later periods, for which sources are more abundant, already feature the male-centered political and cultural hierarchies that obscure women in the historical record. Nor can we make firm generalizations, given the importance of local context in Southeast Asian cultures. However, "gender regimes"—the assignment of attributes, roles, and power to male and female human beings as part of the "wider social order"—are vitally important to the state's relationship with and control of society.[4] (See box 2.2.)

As we have stressed above, each locality felt itself to be central. So was each datu convinced of his own superior stature, putting him in endless competition with his counterparts and requiring diplomatic skills and constant knowledge of what his rivals were doing. Trade via the region's waterways was vital to this competition. Busy harbors enriched and empowered the coastal datu in several ways. As the biggest local merchant, he profited directly from the trade. As the one who maintained the port—providing safety,

---

Box 2.2.   Gender, Family, and the State in Southeast Asia

"Although interpretations of the 'state' in Southeast Asia are constantly debated, there is a growing realization that indigenous governance grew out of cultural understandings of the obligations and responsibilities embedded in family relationships. Because enforcement of any overarching authority often relied on the metaphor of family hierarchies, ruling elites became deeply committed to 'gender regimes' that both reflected and influenced the wider social order. Regardless of military or territorial strength, the dynamics of gender in Southeast Asia is intimately connected with the rise of states and their efforts to redefine and regulate appropriate roles for men and women in the society at large."

—Barbara Watson Andaya, "Introduction," in *Other Pasts: Women, Gender, and History in Early Modern Southeast Asia*, ed. Barbara Watson Andaya (Honolulu: Center for Southeast Asian Studies, University of Hawai'i at Manoa, 2000), 21

---

facilities, and provisions to traders—he collected harbor fees. And as the political leader, he demanded tribute from visiting merchants and enforced his authority through armed force. The latter was necessary to deter piracy and prevent visiting foreign ships from bypassing his port to trade in competitors' ports. Regional producers with items to trade (typically rice, spices, aromatics such as sandalwood, and other forest products) were obliged to feed goods into his port, which in turn attracted rich foreign merchants, resulting in a cosmopolitan entrepôt—a center of trade and transshipment of goods. These developments enabled some datus to style themselves as royalty, maintaining a court and richly rewarding followers.

Whether large entrepôts or subregional centers, the polities created by datu leadership were not centrally ruled or based on abstract principles or institutions. They were networks of personal loyalties and marriage alliances that were held together by personal achievement and diplomatic skill. The alliances were hierarchical; one datu was the acknowledged superior to whom others owed regular tribute (usually a portion of the local product) and manpower for warfare or the maintenance of infrastructure. But the polity was quite fluid and impermanent, because subordinate datus (or vassals) were always on the lookout for better alliances, more reliable protectors, and more profitable opportunities. Warfare was a frequent part of this jockeying for position, but it usually took the form of raids to seize people, who were in short supply, not the conquest of land, which was plentiful. In any case, men of prowess did not have the institutional capacity to rule large areas. The key characteristic of premodern polities in Southeast Asia was that political community was defined and space was organized by personal relationships, not territorial boundaries.

Localization and the Growth of Regional Networks

As sea trade between India and China increased in the first millennium of the common era (C.E.), coastal Southeast Asian polities had more and more contact with other peoples, cultures, and ideas. We have already sketched the basic logic of how trade facilitated political hierarchy and datuship. The expanding Asian trade routes multiplied that effect by bringing knowledge of new belief systems and ways of governing. From this time on, Southeast Asia could be characterized as a crossroads, a place where local and foreign ideas, goods, and people interact to produce cultural and social change. Until recently, some people felt the "crossroads" characterization implied a lack of identity, suggesting that Southeast Asians were easily shaped by foreign influence. But this negative interpretation has been eclipsed by two ideas. First is the acknowledgment that all societies change through contact with outsiders; Southeast Asia's geography simply exposed it to much more contact than most other places. Perhaps as a result, fluidity continued to characterize local polities, and "outsiders" relatively easily became "insiders" through marriage, commerce, or possession of useful expertise.

The second idea concerns how societies change. Many scholars now argue that foreign ideas and practices adopted by Southeast Asians were precisely those that enhanced their existing values and institutions, rather than radically transforming them overnight. We feel that this view of change—a "localization" of new elements—is broadly correct. But we should remember that as societies became differentiated hierarchically, values and institutions were differentiated as well, serving the interests of some more than others. The relatively benign view of how new social, religious, and trade practices are adopted should not obscure competition between social forces or the occurrence of coercion and violence.

The first transformative localization in Southeast Asian statecraft occurred when Indian merchants and Brahmans (priests) began to frequent Southeast Asian ports with textiles to trade for local and Chinese products. With the Indian textiles came Hindu religious beliefs and political practices that enabled local rulers to enhance both their spiritual power and political authority. Adopting Hindu modes of worship, a Southeast Asian ruler gained in stature by association with a particular god and participation in his divinity. Economically valuable gifts the ruler presented to court officials and local datus became spiritually precious because they were imbued with the ruler's new divinity; this in turn enhanced the recipients' power in their own communities. Likewise, titles adopted from Sanskrit (such as *rajah*) enabled the most powerful datus to distinguish themselves and their kin groups as royalty and nobility—classes with an enhanced capacity to transfer political power to their descendants. These cultural assets represented a measurable increase in the benefits a ruler could provide to his followers and resulted in a greater concentration of political power.

Localizing Indian cultural practices linked the ruler to a powerful "universal" religion, which did not displace but joined the local divinities people already worshipped. The divine ruler made his stature clear to the populace by building religious monuments and temples proclaiming his devotion to the deities and instructing the people in their duty and place in the cosmos. At the same time, localization domesticated the foreign system, filtering out elements that did not resonate with the local culture. In short, the localization of Indian beliefs and practices did not replace the old culture, but added new meanings and utilities to it.

Politically, the stakes became higher in the endless datu competition as Hindu, and later Buddhist, religio-political practices made possible large-scale polities. By late in the first millennium, for example, Java and Cambodia were home to land-based kingdoms ruled by divine kings supported by large populations engaged in wet-rice agriculture. These kingdoms left behind the magnificent monuments of Borobudur and Angkor Wat, which testify to the spiritual and political prowess of their rulers. Divine kingship did not obliterate the smaller centers, however; it enabled the growth of wider networks of personal loyalties called *mandala*s (circles of kings) with one king at the center acknowledged as the universal ruler.

Angkor (in present-day Cambodia) is a classic example of a durable land-based mandala of the Hindu-Buddhist era, and Srivijaya (centered in present-day Indonesia) was its rough contemporary in the maritime region. Srivijaya was a trade-based mandala that dominated east–west commerce through the Strait of Malacca for four hundred years (c.700–1100 C.E.). From its center in Sumatra, its powerful navy suppressed piracy in the strait, provided safe passage to foreign ships, and downgraded competing entrepôts into collection centers for Southeast Asian products forwarded to Srivijaya's harbors for transshipment and export to international markets. The kingdom's initial military force of twenty thousand included sea nomads, people whose mobility allowed them to remain outside the hierarchy of datus and who constituted the king's loyal personal following. His military forces eventually grew to include the followings of rival, subjugated datus. Finally, and crucially, Srivijaya was able to dominate shipping through the strait because China recognized how well it ordered trade and granted preferential status to ships arriving from Srivijayan ports.

Commercially, Srivijaya oversaw commerce in Western manufactured goods (Indian cottons and beads, Middle Eastern glassware), local goods (mostly jungle produce such as ivory, rhinoceros horn, tin, camphor, sandalwood, and spices), and superior Chinese silk and porcelain. Culturally, it became an important stopover and center of Buddhist learning for religious pilgrims traveling between India and China. Because foreign ships sailed with the seasonal monsoon winds, they stayed in port for many months, during which Srivijaya provided safe berth for ships, cargos, and crews, as well as food for all these diverse people. Food imports included rice, which indicates that Srivijaya was not self-sufficient and needed to maintain hegemony over regional production centers.

But such large polities, stable over the decades and capable of mobilizing many people, were still held together by personal connections. And while they sometimes left a visible heritage in monuments and temples—Srivijaya, for one, did not—these large polities were not the norm in early Southeast Asia. More common were the small trading centers that enjoyed a combination of one or two local products in regional demand, decent harbors, and a location along a trade route. There were many of these whose prosperity allowed the formation of an elite class, and they rose and fell in power as they competed with one another and responded to fluctuations in the fortunes of the larger centers. All such polities were dependent on networks of personal loyalty and characterized by a local mindset, with each center under its own ruler. It is this underlying pattern that best represents the Philippine experience.

Unfortunately, Filipinos and foreign observers searching for evidence of an early state have often looked for authoritative law codes, centralized political rule, and temple complexes. This way of looking at the Philippines began with Spanish rule in the sixteenth century. The Spaniards themselves were organized under a highly centralized, autocratic kingship, and when they encountered datus, they initially assumed they were seeing kings in the European sense. They soon realized, however, that a typical datu had only a local following and that there were many datus competing within a small area. Then they often erred in the other direction, seeing "no kings or rulers worthy of mention."[5] In seeking to impose its own state structure and universal moral code, discussed in the next chapter, Spanish rule nearly succeeded in obscuring the cultural and political links of the Philippine archipelago with the rest of maritime Asia.

But through recent advances in archaeology, as well as new studies in philology and anthropology, we can say with increasing certainty that the Philippines was indeed part of the maritime Asian trading network. It was a sparsely populated archipelago of local communities that spoke different languages but shared many of the cultural traits, values, and practices outlined above. As another Spaniard with more local knowledge would observe, they were "governed by kings in the manner of the Malays"—the ethnic group from the western end of the Indonesian archipelago whose language was the lingua franca of regional trade.[6] In this part of the world, history happened in many centers, and many of those were in the Philippines.

EARLY COMMUNITIES IN THE PHILIPPINE ARCHIPELAGO

Spatial and Spiritual Arrangement

An early settlement in the Philippines was referred to as *barangay*, a Tagalog word originally meaning "boat," referring to a boatload of related people, their dependents, and their slaves. These kinship groups were led by a datu, hence "barangay" also meant the following of a datu, a political community defined by personal attachment, not territorial location. The barangay settled together in a community ranging from thirty to one hundred households, and through subdivision, many were still that size when the Spanish arrived in the sixteenth century.

Settlements were arranged along rivers, as in other parts of Southeast Asia. Those at the river's mouth were oriented toward the sea, where they obtained most of their protein and had the potential to grow into trading ports in contact with foreign merchants. But they were intimately connected with upriver settlements that grew rice and had access to the forest. Permanently settled upriver farmers practiced swidden cultivation, in which parts of the forest were cut down and cultivated and then allowed to lie fallow to regenerate secondary growth while alternate sites were sown—a system that did not cause environmental degradation. In these settlements, the products of the land, but not the land itself, could be owned and sold, enabling coastal communities to buy mountain-grown rice and cotton, root crops, medicinal herbs, and other forest products. In exchange, people upriver obtained fish and salt from the sea and manufactures such as pottery and cloth. There was often raiding between upriver and coastal settlements, but this only underscores their interdependence.

Power and spirituality in the archipelago were interwoven in an animistic world permeated with religious belief. Visayans (of the central Philippines) had a pantheon of divinities, which they referred to with the Malay-Sanskrit word *diwata*. Tagalogs (of central and southern Luzon) called these *anito* and had a principle deity among them, Bathala, whose name derived from the Sanskrit "noble lord," variations of which appeared as titles in the southern Philippines, Borneo, and Java. Everywhere in the islands, divinities resided all around people in nature and were appealed to and appeased regularly. Divinity was found in the sun and the moon, the rain and the fields, in very old trees, and in crocodiles, an ever-present danger which was appeased with a bit of food when people went out on the river. A Spanish missionary would later ask, "What more did they adore? the very stones, cliffs, and reefs, and the headlands of the shores of the seas or the rivers." Perhaps most important were ancestors, especially "those who distinguished themselves through valiant deeds," objects of veneration who were thought to offer personal protection if their names were invoked at feasts and upon leaving the house.[7] These potentially helpful divinities lived alongside evil spirits, which were avoided, and evil omens, which were respected.

Offerings, sacrifices, ceremonies, and feasting were the modes of worship. Offerings were made routinely and individually to *diwata* or *anito* (the words here refer to the painted wooden figures that represented divinities) in household shrines or on passing a locality inhabited by a god. With the help of a paid spirit ritualist—someone with power to intercede in the spirit world—ceremonies were held to heal the sick, bless a marriage, or ensure safe childbirth. At crucial times in the agricultural cycle, or before commencing a voyage or raid, the datu would sponsor a feast, an event that demonstrated the obligations and exercise of power in early Philippine societies. The feast would be held in a temporary shelter built beside the datu's house or at the entrance to the village, and the spirit ritualist would make offerings of cooked food, live poultry, and hogs. Later, the community ate the food and drank quite a lot of alcohol. Both serious and fun, feasting had the underlying purpose of fulfilling both society's duty to its divinities and the datu's obligation to share his wealth with the community.

The spirit ritualist, *baylan* in Visayan and *catalonan* in Tagalog, was typically an elderly woman of high status or a male transvestite (therefore female by gender), who learned her profession from her mother or other female relatives. She cultivated contacts among the friendlier spirits who possessed her in a trance as she interceded for the community, family, or individual who sought her services. In many cases, spirit power itself was gendered female, as with the Visayan divinity Laon, who was worshipped at harvest time.[8]

Social Stratification: A Web of Interdependence

Datus were part of a hereditary class (*maginoo* in Tagalog) that married endogamously. Datuship was also a political office that included military, judicial, religious, and entrepreneurial roles (see box 2.3). Success and power always depended on an individual's charisma and valor, a combination of diplomacy and military prowess resulting in wealth that was used to attract and support more followers. A further skill possessed by powerful datus was noticed by Antonio Pigafetta, the chronicler of the first Spanish voyage to the archipelago in 1521: "Kings know more languages than the other people."

Box 2.3. Two Faces of Datu Power

"A datu was expected to govern his people, settle their disputes, protect them from enemies, and lead them into battle. He was assisted by a considerable staff. His chief minister or privy counselor was *atubang sa datu*—literally, 'facing the datu'—and his steward or majordomo was *paragahin*, dispenser, who collected and recorded tribute and crops. . . . His sheriff or constable was *bilanggo*, whose own house served as a jail. . . . A kind of town crier, *paratawag*, . . . was a slave. He announced proclamations, *mantala*, either by shouting them out from the top of a tall tree, or by delivering them to the persons concerned—for example, timawa being summoned for a hunt or sea raid. [These] served as the datu's military forces, armed at their own expense."

* * * * *

"A powerful datu's power was enhanced by popular fear of his arcane knowledge of black magic, sometimes reputed to be handed down from one generation to another. *Ropok* was a charm which caused the one who received it to obey like a slave. *Panlus* was a spear or G-string which caused leg pains or swelling in the victim as soon as he stepped over it. *Bosong* caused intestinal swelling in those who crossed the datu. *Hokhok* was to kill simply with a breath or the touch of a hand, and *kaykay* was to pierce somebody through just by pointing a finger at him from a distance. A reputation for such powers no doubt both facilitated a datu's effective control over his subjects, and arose from it."

—William Henry Scott, *Barangay: Sixteenth-Century Philippine Culture and Society*
(Manila: Ateneo de Manila University Press, 1994), 130, 83

Another observer remarked upon the extent to which datus were self-made men: "There is no superior who gives him authority or title, beyond his own efforts and power." Those who especially distinguished themselves attributed their success to divine forces and after their death became ancestors who were the focus of "adoration and deification."[9]

Datus were distinguished by the way they lived, looked, and dressed. The datu's large entourage and the many dependents in his household (a sign of his power) were partly self-supporting and partly supported by tribute paid by the people under his control and protection. In the Visayas, where tattooing was practiced by both men and women, datus added a tattoo with each military victory. The most powerful were painted from head to toe. Datus wore gold, fine cotton, and silk, in contrast to ordinary clothing woven from tree bark fiber. They sponsored the feasts that validated their status and led the season's raiding parties on local enemies.

Below the datu class in social rank were the warrior-supporters: the people who formed the datu's entourage, served him as aides and bodyguards, fought with him as warriors and oarsmen, and surrounded him at feasts. They were quite often related to the datu and included the offspring of his various wives.

This created a bond between the two upper classes that broadly separated them from commoners. In the Visayas, this class was called *timawa* and never did common agricultural labor. In the Tagalog region, wet-rice agriculture was becoming important and social stratification was more advanced. Here this class was subdivided into the lower-status timawa, who did labor in the datu's fields and waters, and the higher-status *maharlika*, who were more likely to do military service, although they too could be called upon to labor in the field or pay tribute in agricultural goods. Like everyone else outside the datu class, timawa could not bequeath wealth to their children because everything formally belonged to the datu. But great wealth did not guarantee power nor did its absence preclude it. A man of timawa birth might rise to datuship if he had the right qualities and opportunities; likewise, he could fall in status through indebtedness or capture.

The mass of society was the *tao* (common people)—farmers, fishers, and artisans—who owed tribute to the datu and service in general to the upper classes. Many of these people spent some portion of their lives in servitude. This is the most complex and least understood aspect of early Philippine society, largely because the details were recorded only after the society was under stress and in transition, just before and during Spanish colonization. The Spanish called many of those in servitude "slaves" (*esclavo*), though there was no such single word in any Philippine language for the many degrees of labor obligation that existed. What follows is a brief discussion highlighting how people moved into and out of servitude and its role in society.[10]

One route into bondage was to be convicted of a crime. The judicial system consisted solely of the datu, who heard witnesses, rendered judgment, and handed down punishment. Most crimes, including theft and often murder, were punished with a fine, often a heavy one inflicted on the criminal's whole family. If unable to pay, all responsible parties owed labor to the wronged party (or to the money lender they borrowed from) until the debt was paid off. People could also be purchased—there was a large regional trade in human labor—or captured in warfare. This kind of slaving, whether in periodic raids on neighboring villages or on the sea, occurred well into the early modern period when Europeans in the region both practiced and fell victim to it themselves. Anyone could become a slave in this way, though a captured datu was usually ransomed by his family.

Indebtedness was perhaps the most common way people fell into servitude. A family that borrowed rice, for example, was given a whole agricultural cycle to repay the debt in kind, but an unpaid debt doubled every year. If ultimately unable to pay, the whole family became debt slaves to their creditor. Hoping for good treatment in the not unlikely event of this happening, people chose their creditors carefully. During famines, they tended to go to wealthy "relatives and surrender themselves to them as slaves—in order to be fed."[11] This was a kind of voluntary bondage, broadly understood as dependency within another's household, survival at the price of social status.

But bondage was not a static or monolithic condition. Upward and downward mobility on complex and regionally varied social ladders was common. The lowest in status were akin to the chattel slaves of the West: These were "hearth slaves" who lived in the master's home; children born to them automatically belonged to the master. But where male hearth slaves were allowed to marry and start their own household, they could rise in status. Most "householders"—slaves who maintained their own residence—were debtors who were allowed to work a few days a week for themselves and the rest for their creditors. While a whole household was liable for one member's debt, their creditor was obliged to release them once the debt was repaid. A child born to one slave parent and one free parent inherited her parents' status in equal measure and owed half her labor to the master. If she, in turn, had a child with a fully free person, that child would owe one-fourth of his labor, and so forth. A slave who accompanied his chief on a raid might distinguish himself in battle and so begin a rise from bondage to leadership. There were even "rich and respectable slaves" who themselves had slaves.[12]

These carefully calculated degrees of dependency and status, as well as the widespread vulnerability to bondage, are a clue to the nature of slavery in the premodern Philippines and Southeast Asia generally. It was not an indelible status attached to a particular ethnic group, but a way of controlling and mobilizing labor in a society with an abundance of natural resources and a shortage of human resources. Some Spanish observers thought slavery in the Philippines was "mild" compared to that practiced by Europeans, but the fact that it was so widespread was more significant. Control over people was the attribute of power in this system and the imperative to accumulate dependents operated at all levels. It was part of a system of interdependence marked by mutual obligations up and down the social ladder.

TRADE, TRIBUTE, AND WARFARE IN A REGIONAL CONTEXT

Relations between Settlements

In this locally focused world, attachment to one's own group and village was strong. This can be seen in the attitude toward outsiders. At the beginning of the tilling season, no strangers were allowed in a village while ceremonies were conducted for a productive harvest. Likewise, a family engaged in harvesting rice would allow no outsiders into the house, lest the fields yield nothing but straw. Upon pain of death, strangers were warned away during the funeral of a datu. Further evidence is found in the differential treatment of slaves from within the community and those from outside. Slaves born within a household were considered part of the family and were rarely sold. On the other hand, when a life was to be sacrificed—for instance, when a slave was to be buried with a great datu to serve him in the afterlife—someone captured in war or purchased from outside would be chosen.

But evidence of early shipbuilding indicates that communities were not insular. Travel for the purpose of trade was common and had an impact on the growth of settlements and the way they were governed. An archaeological site in Tanjay, Negros Oriental (in the Visayas), shows a settlement's evolution from before the tenth century to the sixteenth century. In its earliest form, this coastal community at the mouth of a large river covered less than seven hectares (around fifteen acres). The excavation of Chinese porcelain from the twelfth century is a sign of early trade, but doesn't prove direct contact with China. By the sixteenth century, when the settlement engaged in metal production, it covered thirty to fifty hectares (roughly one hundred acres). Houses by then varied in type and size and included one with fortifications—all signs of growing social stratification.

As more goods were imported into coastal settlements, those who controlled the trade grew in material wealth and status. Not surprisingly, these were the datus who controlled harbors, collected trade duties, and imported goods. As a class, they were distinguished by their possession of larger-than-average, well-constructed, sometimes stockaded houses filled with such foreign prestige goods as Chinese porcelains, gold ornaments, musical instruments, wood carvings, and fine silks and cottons.

This evolving elite did not merely siphon off wealth in the form of duties; it also created wealth. There is some evidence from the Tanjay site that the datu himself was a producer of various grades of pottery (and that his workforce was probably female). The everyday ceramics would have been sold to commoners and the high-quality decorated ceramics given as gifts to allies and high-status followers. But even where datus were not themselves producers, they did finance production, create a market for high-end goods, and facilitate both interisland and foreign trade. Increased commerce, in turn, attracted more people to the settlement and stimulated cottage industries to supply and equip the traders. Iron- and woodworking, the building trades, shipbuilding and repair, and food supply were all areas that thrived.

As some settlements grew large through trade or manufacturing, their datus sought to project power beyond their immediate settlement, often through warfare. According to a late sixteenth-century Spanish account, "There were many chiefs who dominated others less powerful. As there were many without much power, there was no security from the continual wars that were waged between them."[13] Common reasons for going to war included avenging a killing, mistreatment, or abduction; there were also customary times of year to plunder and capture slaves. But although the situation was fluid, it was not as chaotic as it appeared to the Spanish. Alliances were made, often through marriage, for friendship and help against mutual enemies. These alliances yielded hierarchies of chiefs who paid tribute to those above—at once a system of trade and a way to reinforce the hierarchy (see box 2.4). Alliances were always sensitive to the relative strength of the partners, as is the case in international diplomacy still, and were liable to be tested by warfare. But warfare was episodic, not continual, ending quickly with the seizure of goods and people. The end of hostilities usually saw the withdrawal of the victorious forces and the payment of heavy tribute by the defeated datu. Each locality remained under its own datu, although of course a datu was liable to fall to an externally sponsored rival if unsuccessful in war.

Box 2.4.   Prestige Goods and Datu Alliances

"Ethnohistorical analyses indicate that for . . . Philippine chiefs, gifts of prestige goods were the primary material means of cementing strategic alliances with other elites and rewarding the loyalty of subordinates. In a society in which political coalitions are not automatically defined by territory or unilineal descent groups, personalized alliance networks were, by necessity, built through intermarriage and the circulation of prestige goods. Archeological evidence . . . suggests that, before the early-second-millennium beginnings of the Chinese porcelain trade, chiefs and other elites circulated locally manufactured 'fancy' earthenware and either locally made or trade-obtained metal implements and glass beads both within a polity and between island chiefdoms. The growth of the chiefly political systems in the first millennium A.D. created the conditions for an ever-increasing demand for valuable and exotic prestige goods. The expansion of trading networks to encompass extra-archipelagic trade for Chinese porcelains and other status goods may be a reflection of this intensifying desire for sumptuary goods to validate positions of status and authority. At the same time, competition for access to foreign prestige goods may have transformed these internal alliance and prestige goods exchange systems. The desire of foreign traders for interior forest products and other local exports would have enhanced the need for extensive internal alliance and exchange systems cemented by prestige goods redistribution."

—Laura Lee Junker, *Raiding, Trading, and Feasting: The Political Economy of Philippine Chiefdom* (Honolulu: University of Hawai'i Press, 1999), 311–12

Connections within and beyond the Archipelago

The standard textbook long used in Philippine classrooms, Gregorio Zaide's *Philippine Political and Cultural History*, held that the Philippines was once ruled by Srivijaya's maritime empire. Later scholarship discounted this view, citing lack of evidence of Hindu/Buddhist beliefs, statecraft, and monuments in the Philippines. A more recent textbook suggests that because the archipelago lay at the end of the "long route from Arabia and India, any cultural push from those cultural centers would have petered out before reaching it"; mainland Southeast Asia is also said to have "served as a protective screen" against China.[14] In this perspective, "great traditions" become diluted as they move away from their source and are reduced to a "trickle" of "influence." Both Zaide's view and its correction are flawed. The first reflects a conception of empire that did not pertain to early Southeast Asia's mandalas. The second ignores the dynamics of localization and the multicenteredness of Southeast Asia, as well as Luzon's geographical proximity to China. Further, it misinterprets a large centralized polity like Hinduized Angkor as a normative political structure from which the Philippines deviated. This leads to the erroneous conclusion that the archipelago was "isolated from the rest of Southeast Asia . . . [and] largely unaffected by foreign influences."[15]

But the archipelago was not isolated; we have increasing evidence of its economic, linguistic, and political connections within maritime Asia. Inhabitants of the archipelago were capable of oceangoing trade from at least the fourth century, judging from a boat relic dated to 320 C.E. that was found in northeastern Mindanao. And ceramic tradeware from China, Siam (Thailand), and Vietnam dated several centuries earlier has been excavated from Philippine sites, though we don't know if these arrived through direct trade.[16]

There is also the important evidence of the Malay-Sanskrit titles powerful coastal datus gave themselves—"Rajah (Ruler), Batara (Noble Lord), . . . [and] Salipada, Sipad, and Paduka, [which are variations of] the Sanskrit Sri Paduka . . . (His Highness)."[17] These titles were common throughout maritime Southeast Asia. Rather than seeing the absence of a large state as evidence of the Philippines' marginality to the main cultural currents of the region, we could see the communities of the archipelago participating according to their economic and geographical opportunities and priorities, as did all local centers in the region. This included the adoption of foreign practices as they were encountered, if they were compelling and useful, and a role in the region's networks of trade and political alliance. These, in turn, were given order by tribute relations with China.

From the Tang dynasty (618–907) through the Qing dynasty (1644–1911), relations between China and the "barbarian states" that surrounded it were based on China's view of itself as the "middle kingdom"—the moral center to which tribute was due on account of its superior virtue backed by military power. Like the vassals who owed tribute to superior datus in Southeast Asia, tributary states throughout maritime Asia acknowledged China's supremacy. This reinforced a hierarchical order among the rulers of the region because only those recognized by the Chinese emperor were permitted to send the tribute missions that formed the basis of regional trade (see box 2.5). Subordinate rulers became part of a network of vassals; their trade moved along feeder routes into the recognized ports. Sending a tribute mission was thus a sign of political independence and an achievement in itself, requiring the organization, resources, and power to command ships and assemble valuable goods.

Philippine contact with China almost certainly began during the Tang dynasty. Chinese currency and porcelains from this period have been found from Ilocos in the north to the Sulu archipelago in the south. Chinese records refer to "Ma-i," probably Mindoro, which brought goods directly to Canton for the first time in 982. By this time, China's Sung government (960–1279) had established the office of superintendent of maritime trade in various coastal cities. One was assigned to handle "all Arab, Achen, Java, Borneo, Ma-i, and Palembang barbarians, whose trade passed through there." These

---

Box 2.5. Tribute Relations and Trade

"Tribute was the only way to trade legally and safely with China, and it proved extremely lucrative to rulers as well as to those who arranged the missions. The language of tribute to a faraway emperor, expressed in an alien language, did not appear to trouble Southeast Asian rulers. . . . Within the East Asian world of exchanges in written Chinese, trade was legitimate only as an aspect of the formal relations among rulers.

"Within Southeast Asia there were replications of this kind of 'tribute,' often little more than an opportunity to trade at a larger port in return for a symbolic acceptance of its primacy. States in Borneo, South Sumatra, and the Lesser Sundas frequently offered such tribute to Java, while those in the Malayan Peninsula offered the 'golden flowers' (*bunga emas*) of fealty to the court of Siam. In the 1680s even faraway Jambi (Sumatra) was sending the golden flowers to Siam with a 'return gift' of pepper for the China trade, in response to the Siamese king's 'gift' of saltpetre and sulphur. Only when a neighbouring state was conquered by force of arms did tribute become a one-way flow of goods and manpower to the capital."

—Anthony Reid, *Southeast Asia in the Age of Commerce, 1450–1680*, vol. 2, *Expansion and Crisis* (New Haven, Conn.: Yale University Press, 1993), 234

traders sold "aromatics, rhinoceros horn and ivory, coral, amber, pearls, fine steel, sea-turtle leather, tortoise shell, carnelians and agate, carriage wheel rims, crystal, foreign cloth, ebony, sapan wood, and such things."[18] Pearls were a signature Philippine product, and other sea and forest products could have been among Ma-i's trade goods.

Another Philippine place name appearing in Sung trade records is that of Butuan, a gold-mining and trading center in northeastern Mindanao that sent its first tribute mission to China in 1001. From the tenth to the thirteenth centuries, Butuan was known for manufacturing metal tools and weaponry (blades, knives, and projectiles), musical instruments (bells, cymbals, and gongs), and gold jewelry (earrings, buckles, and rings). Though probably the earliest major trading center in the Philippine archipelago, Butuan did not send tribute missions of the same level as those of Champa, a coastal power in what is now southern Vietnam. The Sung trade history records Butuan trade as part of Champa's, indicating the latter's superior power and importance, but also providing evidence of Butuan's regional links.

A significant change in the pattern of trade occurred in the twelfth century when Chinese trading vessels began sailing directly to Southeast Asian producers, thus eliminating the need for a major entrepôt to gather merchandise for export. This caused Srivijaya's decline, boosted the importance of smaller trading centers like Butuan, and gave Chinese merchants dominance in regional shipping. During the following period, the Yuan dynasty (1279–1368), Chinese contacts with Philippine trade centers proliferated, especially with Visayan settlements such as Butuan, Tanjay, and Cebu. The last had grown from a fishing village into a manufacturing center specializing in metallurgy and shipbuilding. Even before it began to be visited by international merchants around the 900s, it was already a center of interisland trade and a "society with developing technologies and a settled existence."[19] In the Yuan period, it entered the international network directly.

Meanwhile, newer power centers had begun to expand their reach through trade and settlement. In the eleventh or twelfth century, Malays from Brunei, a north Borneo port, first settled in Tondo (part of present-day metropolitan Manila) and intermarried with the local population. These developments stimulated an expansion in agriculture, industry, and coastal population centers, as well as the emergence of prosperous elites who adopted new ideas and fashions from their cosmopolitan connections. In Tondo, for example, the native Tagalogs adopted Malay social customs and Malay words. Around this time, a new religion—Islam—was beginning to spread through the trading and ruling networks of other parts of Southeast Asia, but had not yet reached the Philippine archipelago.

By the time the first Spaniards arrived in 1521, their chronicler could give the following description of a Butuan chief that testifies to his ruling status, access to foreign and manufactured goods, and military achievement: "According to their customs he was very grandly decked out, and the finest looking man that we saw among those people. His hair was exceedingly black, and hung to his shoulders. He had a covering of silk on his head, and wore two large golden earrings fastened to his ears. He wore a cotton cloth all embroidered with silk, which covered him from the waist to the knees. At his side hung a dagger, the haft of which was somewhat long and all of gold, and its scabbard of carved wood. He had three spots of gold on every tooth, and his teeth appeared as if bound with gold. He was perfumed with storax and benzoin. He was tawny and painted [tattooed] all over."[20]

An Early Legal Document

In 1986, an inscribed copperplate measuring about 8 × 12 inches was found in Laguna province near Manila. It was later carbon-dated to 900 C.E., making it the oldest document found in the Philippines to date. We close this chapter with a discussion of the Laguna Copperplate Inscription because of what it contributes to and confirms of our knowledge about early Philippine political structure.[21] (See the text of the inscription in box 2.6.)

First, we can see in this document—which resembles thousands found in Indonesia—the centrality of debt and servitude in early Philippine society.

Box 2.6. The Laguna Copperplate Inscription

"Hail! In the Saka-year 822 [900 C.E.] in the month of March–April, the 4th day of the dark half of the moon, on Monday, Lady Angkatan together with her relative, Bukah, the child of His Honor Namwran, was given, as a special favor, a document of full acquittal by Jayadewa, Chief and Commander of Tundun, to the effect that His Honor Namwran was totally cleared of a debt to the amount of 1 *kati* and 8 *suwarna*, in the presence of His Honor Kasumuran, the Leader of Puliran; His Honor Ganasakti, the Leader of Pailah; and His Honor Bisruta, the Leader of Binwangan. And on orders of the Chief of Dewata representing the Chief of Mdang: because of his loyalty as a subject of the Chief, all the descendants of His Honor Namwran have been cleared of the whole debt that His Honor owed the Chief of Dewata. This document is issued in case there is someone, whosoever, some time in the future who will state that the debt is not yet acquitted of His Honor. . . ."

E. P. Patanñe, *The Philippines in the Sixth to Sixteenth Centuries* (Manila: LSA Press, 1996), 85; based on the translation by Anton Postma

We can tell that the debtor in question, Namwran, was a man of status ("His Honor") who had become a "subject" (debt slave or servant) to the chief of Dewata. Because of Namwran's absence from these proceedings, where he is represented by Lady Angkatan (his wife?) and his child, we can surmise that he had died and his relatives were seeking release from the obligation they would otherwise inherit. On the basis of Namwran's loyalty to the chief, their request is granted, and his relatives will have this document to prove their free status.

Second, the document demonstrates political hierarchy and networks. Jayadewa, the chief and commander of Tundun (Tondo), is the authority who summons the vassal chiefs of Puliran, Pailah, and Binwangan to witness the acquittal of Namwran's debt. Jayadewa invokes the authority of the chief of Dewata, who in turn represents the chief of Mdang. Through the document's language and place names, scholars have tried to reconstruct the political connections mentioned here. Jayadewa and many of the other chiefs' names are Sanskrit and most of the document is written in Old Malay, which had absorbed much from Sanskrit and was the lingua franca of commerce throughout the region dominated by Srivijaya. Jayadewa's title is given in Javanese, suggesting political links there as well.

Place names help fill in the picture. Tondo is in present-day Manila. Its commander's loyalty is to the chief of Dewata (present-day Mt. Diwata), near Butuan, discussed above. Mdang seems to refer to a temple complex in Java, where the kingdom of Mataram was emerging as a rival to Srivijaya. According to E. P. Patanñe, "This relationship is unclear but a possible explanation is that the chief of Dewata wanted it to be known that he had a royal connection in Java. The picture [of Jayadewa] that emerges is that of a Srivijayan subordinate of a vassal chief . . . in Dewata [who is] appointed [as] a chief and commander in Tundun . . . to take charge of a vital trading center in the Tondo-Manila-Bulacan area."[22]

To summarize the claims of this chapter: The Philippines in early times had less-populated and less-centralized polities than did other parts of Southeast Asia, but was of the same cultural and political realm, sharing the hierarchical, yet fluid, ruling practices of the region and contacts organized through the Chinese tribute trade. Small barangays were often linked through networks of datus, while retaining a high sense of locality and resolute independence. Despite the lack of "supra-barangay" political institutions, we can see state formation in kinship practices, religious beliefs, and systems of socioeconomic status and dependency. Increasing trade from the twelfth century on resulted in growing populations, social stratification, political innovation, and the concentration of political power. These developments would greatly accelerate starting in the fourteenth century, a subject to be taken up in the next chapter.

NOTES

1. Mary Somers Heidhues, *Southeast Asia: A Concise History* (New York: Thames and Hudson, 2001), 16.

2. O. W. Wolters, *History, Culture, and Region in Southeast Asian Perspectives*, rev. ed. (Ithaca, N.Y.: Cornell Southeast Asia Program, in cooperation with The Institute of Southeast Asian Studies, Singapore, 1999), 18.

3. Wolters, *History, Culture, and Region*, 17.

4. Barbara Watson Andaya, ed., *Other Pasts: Women, Gender, and History in Early Modern Southeast Asia* (Honolulu: Center for Southeast Asian Studies, University of Hawai'i at Manoa, 2000), 21.

5. Seventeenth-century Spanish missionary Francisco Colin, in F. Landa Jocano, ed., *The Philippines at the Spanish Contact: Some Major Accounts of Early Filipino Society and Culture* (Manila: MCS Enterprises, 1975), 175.

6. Quoted in William Henry Scott, *Looking for the Prehispanic Filipino and Other Essays in Philippine History* (Quezon City: New Day Publishers, 1992), 59 n. 3.

7. Father Pedro Chirino, writing around the turn of the seventeenth century, in Jocano, *Philippines at the Spanish Contact*, 142–43.

8. Filomeno V. Aguilar Jr.'s *Clash of Spirits: The History of Power and Sugar Planter Hegemony on a Visayan Island* (Honolulu: University of Hawai'i Press, 1998) is an excellent account of power and its spiritual dimensions in the precolonial and colonial Philippines.

9. Antonio Pigafetta, Colin, and Chirino, in Jocano, *Philippines at the Spanish Contact*, 44, 178, 142.

10. Based on Scott's "*Oripun* and *Alipin* in the Sixteenth-Century Philippines," in *Looking for the Prehispanic Filipino*, 84–103.

11. Spanish chronicler Miguel Lopez de Loarca, writing in 1582, in Jocano, *Philippines at the Spanish Contact*, 92.

12. Loarca, in Jocano, *Philippines at the Spanish Contact*, 97.

13. Colin, in Jocano, *Philippines at the Spanish Contact*, 176.

14. Rosario Mendoza Cortes, Celestina Puyal Boncan, and Ricardo Trota Jose, *The Filipino Saga: History as Social Change* (Quezon City: New Day Publishers, 2000), 1–2.

15. Cortes, Boncan, and Jose, *The Filipino Saga*, 14.

16. The following discussion is based on E. P. Patanñe, *The Philippines in the Sixth to Sixteenth Centuries* (Manila: LSA Press, 1996).

17. William Henry Scott, *Barangay: Sixteenth-Century Philippine Culture and Society* (Manila: Ateneo de Manila University Press, 1994), 128–29.

18. *Sung Shih* (Sung History) Monographs, 1345, chap. 139, quoted in William Henry Scott, *Prehispanic Source Materials for the Study of Philippine History*, rev. ed. (Quezon City: New Day Publishers, 1984), 65.

19. Patanñe, *Philippines in the Sixth to Sixteenth Centuries*, 134.

20. Pigafetta, in Jocano, *Philippines at the Spanish Contact*, 50.

21. See Patanñe's discussion of Anton Postma's conclusions and other scholar-ship on early inscriptions and linguistic history; *Philippines in the Sixth to Sixteenth Centuries*, 83–96.

22. Patanñe, *Philippines in the Sixth to Sixteenth Centuries*, 95.

Chapter Three

New States and Reorientations, 1368–1764

TRANSFORMATIONS IN COMMERCE AND RELIGION

The first emperor of China's Ming dynasty (1368–1644) declared a new policy in 1368: Maritime trade would henceforth be a government monopoly. Only countries recognized as tribute-paying vassals would be permitted to trade with China, and private trade would no longer be allowed. This new definition of the tribute trade refocused Southeast Asian polities both economically and politically. The Chinese emperor welcomed tribute missions bringing goods, information, and affirmations of loyalty; Southeast Asian port-polities with the organizational and financial resources took advantage of the opportunity. These included at least twenty-two places in the Philippines: For example, "Luzon" sent missions in 1372, 1405, and 1410, and the rising southern port of Sulu sent six missions between 1370 and 1424. Some rulers traveled to China to pay fealty in person, and when one Sulu ruler died at the Chinese court, he was given a respectful funeral attended by the emperor. Official Chinese ships paid return visits to recognize their vassals—Admiral Zheng He's seven expeditions from 1405 to 1443 included one or two visits to Sulu. The number of Ming ceramics found in Philippine archaeological sites and shipwrecks confirm the high level of trade in the Ming period.

These parameters for the tribute trade lasted only about a century before Chinese emperors abandoned state trading. But it was long enough to stimulate the development of powerful port-states throughout the region. On the mainland, Ayutthaya (in Thailand), Champa (southern Vietnam), and Cambodia and, in island Southeast Asia, Brunei, Java, and Melaka all benefited from Chinese engagement. Melaka was established about 1400 by a prince in exile from Srivijaya. On the west coast of the Malay Peninsula facing the strait that came to bear its name, Melaka (Malacca) was in a position to control maritime trade between India and China. The Ming trade edict offered the first rulers of this new port-state a timely opportunity, and they made several personal appearances at the Chinese capital to secure the emperor's backing.

The port-state polities that grew during the Ming tribute trade were urban and cosmopolitan. Their populations reached 100,000 or more, comprised of the diverse groups who traded in the region—Chinese and Southeast Asians, Indians, Arabs, Turks, and Armenians. After the Chinese emperors lost interest in the southern trade, these port-states continued to dominate the region as political, commercial, and cultural centers until the end of the sixteenth century. They played a particularly important role in the diffusion of Islam as a faith and political system.

At this juncture—with the Philippine archipelago on the brink of historic reorientations in religion and governance—it is worth considering again its place in Southeast Asia. To some people, the conversion of most of the population to Hispanic Catholicism over the sixteenth and seventeenth centuries confirms a sense of cultural apartness; some Filipinos even see it as diversion from an "authentic" identity. When viewed from a wider lens, however, we see that the whole region was undergoing tremendous change at this time, much of which served to differentiate one area from another. Anthony Reid, a historian who has written extensively on early modern Southeast Asia, argues that religious change often occurs during upheavals and disruptions of the old order that highlight inadequacies in the old belief system: "The period 1550–1650 was such a period of dislocation in Southeast Asia as a whole . . . one that stimulated a remarkable period of conversion toward both Sunni Islam and Catholic Christianity."[1] For the Philippine and eastern Indonesian archipelagos, which became targets of commercial and territorial conquest and competing missionary pressure, this period certainly represented a disruption of the old order. In this sense, the Philippines was well within the regional mainstream of religious change. And like religions already practiced in Southeast Asia, Islam and Christianity closely linked spirituality to governance.

Islam

Islam had first entered Southeast Asia in the thirteenth century through Indian and Arab traders and missionaries who converted port rulers on the coasts of Sumatra and Java. By the fourteenth century, the Mongol-ruled Yuan dynasty of China had conquered Muslim regions as far west as Baghdad, facilitating the flow of Muslim scholars, preachers, and traders into East and Southeast Asia. The Ming tribute trade beginning in 1368 brought even more traffic, including Chinese Muslim merchants and Arab and Indian missionaries. The first important commercial center in Southeast Asia to convert to Islam was Melaka, heir to Hindu-Buddhist Srivijaya's geographical reach and cultural pull. Srivijaya's court style—based on loyalty to the ruler, hierarchy, marriage alliances, and the proceeds of thriving trade—did not disappear with Melaka's conversion, but was gradually imbued with Islamic traits, beliefs, and practices. The court language of Malay, widely used throughout the maritime region, began to be written in Arabic script, and the Arabic language itself replaced Sanskrit as the source of new terminologies of governance. As Melaka's power and commercial success grew, so did the moral, military, and commercial momentum of the new faith among port rulers seeking advantage against rivals.

A Muslim ruler found that Islam helped him build and centralize political power, which rested on three bases: material reward, coercion, and spiritual power. Conversion strengthened a datu's commercial advantages through favored access to growing Muslim trade networks. Greater wealth led to more armed troops and slaves, which in turn increased the ability to collect tribute and make alliances. The third element of power was more complicated. Certain aspects of Islam—equality of all believers before God, the importance of religious officials, a body of learning external to the realm—challenged older forms of spiritual power. The Muslim ruler was not divine, but "God's shadow on earth" and defender of the faith. Yet a royal ruler—a *sultan*—was imbued with a charge of spiritual power (*daulat*) that had clear antecedents in pre-Islamic culture. So the surrounding religious experts, rather than competing with his spiritual power, worked in its service to "overrule" local spirits and local datus alike. The faith also lent the ruler moral justification for conquering rivals and final authority in appointing religious officials and adjudicating disputes.

Sultans commissioned royal genealogies and claimed the right to bequeath power to their heirs, a significant institutionalization of political power. Subordinate datus benefited too, with higher status and titles—especially those in charge of the palace and the port. The datu class as a whole took advantage of greater social stratification by distinguishing itself as "nobility." This "sanctified inequality" justified exaction of tribute from commoners and made datuship hereditary in fact as well as in name.[2]

Sulu, the island group near northeast Borneo, was home to the first sultanate and supra-barangay state in the Philippine archipelago. Sulu appeared in Chinese records beginning in 1349 and sent several tribute missions during the early Ming dynasty. According to historian Cesar Majul, Sulu was visited by Chinese Muslim traders and Arab missionaries who began to spread the faith in the late fourteenth century. Paduka Batara, the Sulu ruler who died in

Figure 3.1.   The Mosque at Tawi-Tawi: Said to be the first in the Philippines (courtesy of the Philippine National Historical Institute)

China, left two sons to be raised among Chinese Muslims. But Sulu did not have a Muslim ruler until about 1450, when Rajah Baginda (a Minangkabau prince) and Sayyid Abu Bakr (*sayyid* signifies descent from the Prophet Muhammad) fled Sumatra after its defeat by non-Muslim Javanese. Baginda arrived in Sulu with a group of wealthy merchants and married locally, but lacked the spiritual credentials to become more than a paramount datu. Abu Bakr, with his prestigious lineage, had the necessary stature. He allied with Baginda by marrying his daughter and became Sultan Sharif ul-Hashim.

Majul tells us that Abu Bakr introduced "not Islam as such but Islam as a form of state religion with its attendant political and social institutions" modeled on those of Melaka.[3] The sultanate spread its religion and authority from the port of Jolo to the interior of Sulu and neighboring islands, claiming ownership of land and rights over all subject peoples. Authority was established through missionary activity and the creation of political districts. Each district was administered by a *panglima*, an official one rank lower than a datu, who collected taxes, adjudicated disputes, organized conscripted labor, and announced royal decrees. A later observer confirmed the centralization of Muslim polities, noting that laws were enacted by "the greatest chief, whom all the rest obeyed."[4] Sulu's diverse population was incorporated into the authority of the sultanate through the assignment of panglima posts to leading members of each resident community, including the Chinese, Tausug, and Sama-Bajaw ethnic groups.[5] The Tausug were the dominant local group, with whom the new rulers intermarried; their language began to borrow heavily from Malay and to be written in the Arabic script.

As rulers converted to Islam, their subjects followed. Contemporary Arab and European observers noted, however, how little their lifestyles changed with conversion, sometimes entailing only abstention from eating pork. Ignorance of the Koran, arbitrary application of Islamic law, and marriage with nonbelievers frequently persisted. This is an example of localization—Islam being incorporated gradually into existing beliefs and practices, as it continues to be today. Groups that did not accept Islam were proselytized, but generally not forcibly converted as long as they accepted the political authority of the sultanate. Nevertheless, they were clearly set apart from the community, and were henceforth treated differently from Muslims (see box 3.1).

The important new division between believers and nonbelievers—those inside and those outside the community—is reflected in the practice of slavery. Among Muslims, who were considered equal before God, slaves were no longer taken except in debt bondage; chattel slaves who accepted Islam were usually freed. Henceforth, non-Muslims became the targets of slave-raiding expeditions, allowing the perpetuation of a trade/slave/plunder economy. The insider–outsider division had an important effect *within* the community as well. Thomas McKenna discusses the "amalgam of armed force, material remuneration, and cultural commitment" that maintained the social order in Muslim Mindanao. According to McKenna: "The presence of disdained aliens may have worked to sustain the stratification system largely through its psychological effect on subordinates, who were inclined to draw the most meaningful social dividing line below rather than above themselves and identify with insider Muslims as opposed to outsider pagans and Christians."[6]

Christianity

Only decades before traveling to the Philippines, Spanish Catholics had ended almost eight hundred years of Muslim political rule over much of the Iberian Peninsula (711–1492) and expelled Spanish and North African Muslims and Jews from their realm. In all their endeavors, Spanish religious zeal—the spirit of *reconquista*—was particularly acute. But the Spanish were also driven by the desire for wealth and profit, something they had in common with Muslim traders in Southeast Asia. Despite the protests of missionaries on board, the five Spanish expeditions to the Philippines in the sixteenth century frequently traded in commodities and slaves with Muslims. Without this trade, they would not have survived.

Box 3.1. Conversion Stories

Sulu

"The hill people were still unconverted. The coast people said, 'Let's fight the hill people and convert them to Islam.' But Abubakar would not allow it, and instead told the people to pound rice and make cakes and clothing. Then the coast people marched inland to a place now called Pahayan. Abubakar sent word to the head man that he was an Arabian who could be spoken to by writing on paper. The head man, called in those days 'Tomoai,' said that he did not want to see him for he did not want to change the customs of his ancestors. So Abubakar approached and threw cakes and clothing into the houses of the [hill people]. The children ate the cakes, but the older people thought them poison and gave them to the dogs. The dogs were not killed and the children went out to the camp of Abubakar where they were treated kindly. The two tribes came to an understanding. That night Abubakar slept in the house of the chief. The chief had a dream that he was living in a large house with beautiful decorations. Abubakar interpreted the dream saying that the house was the new religion and the decorations its benefits. The news spread and after much difficulty the people were converted."

—Haji Buto, "Traditions, Customs, and Commerce of the Sulu Moros,"
Mindanao Herald, February 3, 1909, quoted in Cesar Adib Majul, *Muslims in the Philippines*, 2d ed. (Quezon City: University of the Philippines Press), 57–58

Mindanao

"Sherif Kabungsuwan sailed from Mecca with many [ships] filled with warriors and their women and children.

"After many months of travel and much fighting on both sea and land, he arrived and disembarked with part of his people at Malabang. Others of his people went on eastward to Parang-Parang, and others again went still further, to the lower Rio Grande, where they built the town of Cotabato. So were the people of Kabungsuwan divided; but he was still the ruler over all.

"After a time . . . [he found that] many of the people [in Cotabato] had ceased to regard the teachings of the Koran and had fallen into evil ways. . . . Kabungsuwan with a portion of his warriors went from Malabang to Cotabato and . . . assembled together all the people. Those of them who had done evilly and disregarded the teachings of the Koran and would not swear to repent, live in the fear of God and obey the Koran thenceforth, he drove out of the town into the hills, with their wives and children.

"These wicked ones who were thus cast out were the beginnings of the tribes of the Tirurais and Manobos, who live to the east of Cotabato in the country into which their evil forefathers were driven. And even to this day they worship not God; neither do they obey the teachings of the Koran. . . . But the people of Kabungsuwan, who regarded the teachings of the Koran and lived in fear of God, prospered and increased, and we Moros of today are their descendants."

—Samuel Lyon, "A Moro Fundamentalist: Some Teachings of Oudin,
a Mahommedan Priest of Mindanao," *Asia*, February 1927,
quoted in Majul, *Muslims in the Philippines*, 66–67

The object of the Spaniards, as of the Portuguese before them and the Dutch soon to follow, was to capture and monopolize the highly profitable spice trade that stretched from a group of islands called the Moluccas (now Maluku in eastern Indonesia) to European markets. Europe was rebuilding its population and prosperity after the disastrous, plague-ridden fourteenth century and experiencing a rising demand for exotic Eastern goods that sharply spiked from 1550 to 1620.[7] The extremely high price of spices made them among the first items of conspicuous consumption in early modern Europe. Pepper, cloves, nutmeg, and cinnamon were the fashion of the day on the tables of the rich, where "prepared foods were virtually buried under spices" and they were "passed around on a gold or silver tray—the spice platter— during the meal or just after it."[8]

Before Europeans entered the trade directly, these spices were collected from local producers by Southeast Asian traders and delivered to the Muslim entrepôts of Melaka and Aceh on the Strait of Malacca. Through the Indian Ocean, around the Indian subcontinent, and through the Persian Gulf, they were carried on Indian, Arab, or Turkish ships. Across the desert at the Mediterranean ports, the Egyptian ruler took his cut. Finally, Venetian sailors completed the last leg of the journey, bringing the now highly expensive product to European ports. Wresting this trade from Muslim control was a dream first realized—though briefly, incompletely, and quite destructively—by the Portuguese. In 1499, they began capturing seaports along the route and destroying their Muslim rivals to monopolize the trade through superior military power. In 1511, they captured Melaka, forcing the sultanate into exile.

The goal in this navigational race—by this time the Spanish were involved—was direct access to the primary producers of Maluku. Competition between the two Catholic powers was mediated by the pope, who drew a line of demarcation based on incomplete geographic knowledge and added the condition that conquered lands had to be Christianized. It was in this context that the Spanish crown, sponsoring the Italian Christopher Columbus, sought a better route, stumbled on the Western Hemisphere, and built an empire based in Mexico that enriched Spain with silver. In 1520, Ferdinand Magellan, a Portuguese sailor who defected to the Spanish king, sailed from Spain across the Atlantic, around South America, and over the Pacific to chart the western route to Maluku, "discovering" the Philippines along the way. In fact, Magellan may have heard about the archipelago when he was previously in Melaka, where a community of non-Muslim "Luzones," who had been loyal to the exiled sultan, still lived. A powerful indication of how cosmopolitan a world it was that the Europeans were entering was that Magellan's expedition had little trouble finding interpreters (usually slaves) who spoke languages ranging from Spanish and Arabic to Malay and Tagalog.[9]

Magellan landed in the central Philippines in 1521. He and the Visayans immediately began to trade and exchange gifts. From the Spanish side came hats, knives, mirrors, combs, bells, and ivory. The Visayans brought fish, poultry, palm wine, bananas and coconuts, ginger, and gold. One of the first datus encountered by the expedition was the "king" of Butuan, who "was very grandly decked out" and ate off gold dishes.[10] He and Magellan became "brothers." Magellan demonstrated his military power by firing mortars and displaying a fully armed and armored soldier.

After a few weeks of friendly meetings, eating, and drinking, the Spaniards held Easter Mass in the settlement. Two datus joined in the worship, kissing the cross but not making an offering nor taking communion. Before the expedition moved on, Magellan's men erected a cross on the highest summit "for their benefit." If they followed his admonition to "adore it" every morning, he said, nothing would harm them. In this first encounter, the Spanish clearly associated religious belief with military prowess in a way that was locally comprehensible.

This association continued when the expedition landed on Cebu Island, which Magellan had been told in Butuan was the largest settlement with the most trade. As a manufacturing center producing iron weaponry, copper and gold jewelry, cloth, and boats, Cebu depended on trade for its food and had been trading in foreign goods since at least the thirteenth century. So when Magellan arrived in 1521, Rajah Humabon welcomed him as a matter of course and tried to collect tribute from him, as he had from a recently departed Siamese vessel. Magellan refused, asserting the superiority of his own king and again demonstrating his weaponry. Upon this display of power and the whispered (but erroneous) information from a Muslim trader that these were the same people who had conquered Melaka, the rajah offered to pay tribute to Magellan's king. Magellan responded that he sought not tribute, but trade and conversion to his religion.

Magellan made it clear that his only enemies would be "those who hate our faith," while those who became Christian of their own free will "would be better regarded and treated than the others." He added that as a Christian, Rajah Humabon could more easily defeat his enemies. Thereupon the rajah and his subordinate chiefs expressed interest in learning about the religion. In the next week, about eight hundred people in Cebu and some surrounding islands were baptized, taught to adore the cross daily on their knees, and asked to burn their diwatas. Not many were willing to take the last step. Adopting a new faith was within their cultural experience—especially with a powerful foreign missionary in their midst—but giving up access to local divinities was not. Magellan eventually convinced some by healing a sick man, and he began the process of localization when he baptized Humabon's "queen" and gave her a carved wooden child Jesus to take the place of her "idols." Known as the Santo Niño, the baby Jesus image was later widely adopted by Filipino Christians. Historian Zeus Salazar traces this to "the early identification of the Christian image in Cebu (1521–1565) as the representation (*likha*) of an *anito* (divinity) connected with the sun, the sea and agriculture."[11]

Magellan also tried to reorient the existing power structure toward Spain by having all the datus pledge loyalty to Rajah Humabon and Humabon himself to the king of Spain. But not all were prepared to follow Humabon into alliance with the newly arrived power. One village on the neighboring island of Mactan was burned for refusing to convert and Mactan's powerful chief, Lapulapu, took this opportunity to move against Cebu's rajah, who was probably his brother-in-law. On his own initiative, Magellan went into battle to punish the disobedient vassal of the one whom he had declared paramount. Recklessly, he refused Humabon's offer of reinforcements, aiming to show the power of the vastly outnumbered Christians against the assembled forces of Lapulapu. The result was a rout in which Magellan himself was killed and his body never recovered. Having failed to see the divine backing in warfare that Magellan had promised, Humabon hastily tried to recover his position by turning on the Spanish survivors. The Santo Niño was hidden away by the Visayans, and the survivors of the expedition spent several months haplessly searching for Maluku—seizing and ransoming those who crossed their path—before sailing back to Spain to complete the first circumnavigation of the globe.

Conquest and Division

Over the next fifty years, Spain sent four more expeditions, including one that first used the name "Felipinas" (after King Philip II) for some of the islands. These culminated in the expedition of Miguel Lopez de Legazpi, which returned to seize Cebu in 1565 and after three years succeeded in converting the rajahs of the Visayas to Christianity. He was aided by his recovery of the Santo Niño (which had acquired divine status in connection with Magellan's unavenged death), key defections to his side, and the interest of local traders in doing business with the silver-rich Spaniards. According to historian William Henry Scott, "All these sellers swore allegiance to the Spanish Crown: the tribute which was required for doing business with customers who paid in hard specie and offered military protection." This was, in other words, "no more than an ordinary example of . . . interisland politics."[12]

Legazpi's position in the Visayas was tenuous, however. He faced food shortages and attacks from the Portuguese. Another problem became apparent when "seven or eight Luzon natives came to see the Spaniards and asked for permission to come there and trade. . . . The[ir] ships were laden with . . . iron, tin, ceramics, scarves, light wool cloth, glossy and fine tafettas and other Chinese goods, spices and other miscellaneous things."[13] Legazpi reported to the viceroy of Mexico that Maynilad (Manila) on the northern island of Luzon would be a superior base because of its direct access to the China trade, which did not come to Cebu. In 1571, the fledgling state followed the trade as Legazpi mounted a military expedition to the north.

Maynilad in the sixteenth century was an emerging center within the orbit of Brunei, a sultanate on the north coast of Borneo that was a powerful rival of Sulu. Chinese sources tell us that at its height Brunei had a fleet of more than one hundred war vessels; its ruler traveled with an entourage of five hundred armed men and in a raid on Sulu acquired two large pearls and the daughter of the ruler in marriage.[14] Brunei's power extended east from the island of Borneo to the Sulu archipelago and north to Palawan and into Luzon. Maynilad's rulers were Brunei aristocrats intermarried with Tagalog elites. The Maynilad ruling class was bilingual in Malay and Tagalog, and the latter was rapidly absorbing Malay vocabulary in the fields of commerce, material culture, and religion. Unlike the Visayans, who seem not to have had writing when the Spaniards arrived, many Tagalogs were literate in their local script. But unlike the Tausugs in Sulu and Malays in Melaka and Brunei, their language was not yet written in the Arabic script. They were observed to have only rudimentary knowledge of Islam, which was not widespread in the area.

The ruler of Maynilad was the son of a Luzon datu and grandson of a Brunei king; Brunei Malays also ruled Tondo and other settlements around Manila Bay. In the absence of strongly centralized authority, however, they were unable to mount an effective defense against the Spanish. One datu who signed a treaty with Legazpi told him, "There is no king and no sole authority in this land; but everyone holds his own view and opinion, and does as he prefers."[15] With the help of six hundred Visayan troops, Legazpi conquered Maynilad and surrounding settlements and renamed it Manila.

With Legazpi's victory in 1571, the Spanish establishment of Manila set out to redefine the archipelago internally and resituate it in relation to the Asian trade. The enormity of the endeavor cannot be overstated. Like their Muslim rivals, the Spanish sought to replace "pagan" beliefs with a religion of the book. Moreover, they tried to bring all the islands under a single political and religious authority for the first time. This process was neither unopposed nor completely successful. Among the islands Spain claimed were Maluku and Mindanao. For a period in the seventeenth century, when the Spanish and Portuguese crowns were united, Spain did control Maluku, but the Dutch eventually proved stronger. Mindanao remained beyond Spain's control until almost the end of its three-hundred-year colonial tenure and was never administered internally. Maluku is now part of Indonesia and Mindanao is a (contested) part of the Philippines. It could have been otherwise; the geo-body we now call "the Philippines" was not yet determined.

The extension of Spanish rule through lowland Luzon and the Visayas took many decades of combined military and missionary action. Like other colonial powers, the Spanish did not have much manpower and relied on a combination of local alliances and superior firepower. Inducements offered to datus to accept the new authority included gifts, housing, medical treatment, protection from soldiers, and the ritual and pageantry of Catholic practice. If this failed, settlements were razed and conquered populations controlled by militias. But the primary agents of *conquista espiritual* (spiritual conquest) were Spanish friars—Augustinian, Franciscan, Jesuit, Dominican, and Augustinian Recollect missionaries. Because Spain's "right" to the Philippines had been granted by the pope on condition of Christianizing its inhabitants, these religious orders were official agents of the colonial state assigned to different parts of the archipelago.

The mission to convert was inseparable from the goal of political pacification. Missionary friars became parish priests, learning local languages and living among their converts in an effort to "translate" Christianity into local cultures and stamp out worship of local spirits. Under their leadership, everyday life was framed and regulated by church teachings and guidelines. The friar was everywhere—mobilizing people for state and church work, cajoling their support through sermons, and punishing the sins they revealed in confession. For the friar, religion was a tool of both liberation and subordination. Imbued with a deep sense of righteousness and moral ascendancy, the friar hoped the conversion of the "heathens" would bring about their salvation. At the same time, the threat of eternal damnation helped ensure loyalty to the church and colonial state.

As acculturation to Christianity progressed, important continuities and underlying patterns persisted, as they did in Islamized areas. Converts adopted Christian teachings and rituals creatively, blending them with pre-Spanish norms and practices to create a "folk Catholicism" unique to the Philippines.[16] Typical examples were the adoption of Catholic icons to correspond to the waning power of specific anito and diwata and the worship of revered ancestors along with the new Catholic saints (who were seen, reasonably enough, as revered ancestors of the Spanish). Filomeno Aguilar argues that local animism and Hispanic Catholicism of the time were fundamentally alike: "The *indio* [native] and the Spaniard shared an intrinsically similar worldview founded upon a solid belief in a nonmaterial yet palpable reality . . . populated by spirit-beings with power to affect and even determine worldly affairs. With that spiritual realm humans communicated through words and actions performed by individuals possessing specialized sacral knowledge, hence the mediating role of priests and shamans [baylan]."[17] This similarity greatly aided in the conquest of the Philippines: Just as datu power had an important spiritual component, so would the power of the colonial state rely heavily on spiritual conquest.

Another important component of conquista espiritual was hostility to Islam, which complemented the Muslim distinction between believers and nonbelievers. Because Muslims were highly resistant to missionary efforts, Spaniards saw them as qualitatively different from the "heathens" they were Christianizing. The Spanish referred to the new Christians of Luzon and the Visayas, who would eventually comprise the majority population of the Philippines, as *indios* or *naturales* (natives). They called the Muslims "Moros" after the hated Moors of Islamic Spain, and they described Islam as a noxious weed that "had taken root in [Brunei] before we took possession of the Philippines; and from that island they had come to preach it in Manila, where they had begun to teach it publicly when our people arrived and tore it up by the roots."[18] Once Manila was secure, the Spanish sent military expeditions against Brunei, cutting its political and economic links with the archipelago.

The proximity of Spanish power caused Brunei to go into decline, concentrated anti-Spanish Muslims in Sulu, and encouraged the spread of Islam in the south.[19] This created a lasting new division within the territory that would become the Philippines and undercut the Spanish attempt to rule the entire archipelago. Earlier divisions of language and local polity now became religio-political, with the rival states oriented to different universal centers, legal systems, and moral codes. Language and naming was especially sensitive to the localization process, as seen in the titles earlier adopted from Malay-Sanskrit. Now, in an era of mass conversion, the names of ordinary individuals became markers of identity tied to a larger Catholic or Muslim world: Baptized Christians took Hispanic Christian names, while converts to Islam adopted Arabic Muslim names.

From this time on, Christian communities feared Moro slave raids (as well as attacks from mountain communities who resisted Christian conversion). Disarmed and forbidden to retaliate, Christians quickly forgot that they themselves had recently engaged in such raids; they and the Spanish alike condemned Moro "barbarians." Meanwhile, Islam spread through southern Mindanao from the port city of Cotabato, and Muslim political practice continued in the usual way: "When they find themselves beset by the troops from Filipinas, they make an alliance and help one another."[20]

SPANISH RULE: SOCIAL, SPATIAL, AND SPIRITUAL REDEFINITION

Reducción and Friar Power

From thirteen missionary friars in 1576, the population of Spanish "religious" (members of missionary orders) in the islands grew to 269 by 1594. This was still insufficient to control and Christianize perhaps 750,000 people living in scattered, independent settlements. Conquista espiritual was therefore accompanied by resettlement. In a process called *reducción*, barangays were coaxed or coerced into towns (*cabeceras*) organized around a newly built church with resident friar. Reducción was a long process, as whole barangays fled to the mountains to avoid conquest or families slipped away after the soldiers left the area. Most reluctant converts were gradually brought into *visitas*, small outlying settlements equipped with a chapel to receive a visiting friar. Reducción eventually achieved the remapping of Philippine settlement patterns into today's *cabaceras* (district capitals), *poblaciones* (towns), *barrios* or barangays (villages), and *sitios* (hamlets). The object of reducción was to bring all indios into Christian communities *bajo de la campana* (under the church bells) and to accurately count the population in order to collect the tribute—the combined goals of church and state carried out under friar supervision.

The new political and spiritual order was reflected spatially in town planning. Even when sited on an older settlement, the cabecera departed from "organic" indigenous organization—houses arranged linearly along a river or next to kin—to follow "rational" lines derived from classical Western theory. These included open spaces, a nearby body of water, and an orderly grid in which the rank of persons and institutions was clearly visible. There was some variation between coastal and inland towns, and not all achieved the ideal, but in the basic plan, a quadrilateral *plaza mayor* (open square) housed the church and *convento* (friar's residence), civic buildings, and homes of prominent Spaniards and indios.[21] The church was the most impressive building and a visible representation of Spanish power. It was the first to be constructed of stone—built with tribute and unpaid labor—and towered above native and civic structures. In coastal towns, the church faced the sea, where its bell tower, an adjacent structure, served also as a watchtower against Muslim raids. In commercial towns, including Manila, certain sections were fortified against invasion, a new manifestation of the insider–outsider dynamic seen in precolonial and Islamized communities. Inside the walls (an area called "Intramuros" in Manila) resided Spaniards, leading indios, and important institutions of church and state. Outside lived non-Christians, common indios,

Figure 3.2. Contemporary drawing of the Argao church, Cebu Province (Kiyoko Yamaguchi)

dispossessed datus at odds with the new order, and Chinese and other foreign communities. (See box 3.2.)

Throughout lowland Luzon and the Visayas, the structure of administrative authority that evolved after pacification reflected two fundamental conditions of the conquest period. First was a pressing need to mobilize labor and collect tributes, a major source of revenue for the early colonial state. The second condition was a shortage of civilian officials in this far-flung outpost of empire. In contrast, there was a relative abundance of soldiers serving in the conquest and the Muslim and Dutch wars of the following years who expected material reward. To solve both problems, King Philip II granted *encomiendas*, the administrative right to collect tribute and draft labor from among the inhabitants of a defined geographical area, along with the responsibility to protect them and provide religious instruction. One encomienda might cover a portion of a población or the whole town. From the late sixteenth century, the tribute was set at ten reales per adult male (eight reales equaled one Mexican peso), of which two went to the state and eight to the *encomendero*; two reales of his share were owed to the church in fulfillment of his religious responsibilities.

Friar and encomendero—the two representatives of the Spanish state— quickly became rivals as friars began to report abuse in the collection of tribute. Because the uprooted and resettled barangays had little surplus and no access to currency, tribute was paid "in kind"—local produce such as unhulled rice, "salt, chickens, eggs, venison, other game meat, swine, and native liquor or wine."[22] Encomenderos arbitrarily assigned low value to the tribute products and sold them at higher market prices in Manila; they used underweight scales to cheat tribute-payers; their soldiers brutally exacted payment even when crops failed; and they accepted the substitution of labor for payment, a kind of debt slavery. The first bishop of Manila was outspoken in his letters to the king, declaring that encomenderos hurt the cause of Christ through their brutality and greed. In the long run, the encomendero was no match for the friar—largely because until the mid-eighteenth century colonial law prohibited nonofficial, nonclerical Spaniards from residing outside the cities, to prevent the abuses that decimated local populations in Spanish America. Based in Manila, encomenderos turned their attention to overseas trade, and as they and their heirs died or left the Philippines, the encomiendas were allowed to revert to royal authority. By 1700, the encomienda system was largely replaced by administrative provinces, each headed by an *alcalde mayor* (provincial governor).

What was the effect of the new order on the political economy, evolving class structure, and gender regime of indigenous Philippine societies? Datus survived, but datu power as such was severely attenuated and transformed.

Box 3.2. Colonial Manila

"From a small Muslim community of only 2,000 Filipinos and a handful of Chinese sojourners, Manila in several generations became a flourishing multiracial city of more than 40,000 inhabitants. . . . During the early period of commercial florescence and rapid urban growth in the decades immediately before and after 1600, the Spanish quarter of Manila was metamorphosed from a mere cluster of impermanent and highly flammable *caña y nipa* [bamboo and palm thatch] structures into a carefully planned and walled city [Intramuros] of substantial stone, brick, and tile buildings fashioned in Western architectural style. Among the most distinctive morphological elements of the Philippine colonial capital were its grid form, a monumental Catholic cathedral, many stately public buildings, a nuclear *plaza mayor*, several smaller squares, five large monastic complexes, and about 600 handsome two-story houses occupied by Spaniards and their dependents. Additionally, the authorities replaced the flimsy wooden palisades of precolonial Manila with massive walls of stone and brick which encircled the entire district of Intramuros. These were further supplemented by a deep moat and a strong fort located at the point where the Pasig River entered Manila Bay. Before the end of the sixteenth century, Intramuros through its morphology served to confirm and emblematize the power and permanence of Hispanic colonialism.

"Even as wealth derived from international commerce made possible the infrastructural improvements and architectural embellishments of the Spanish quarter, so did the galleon trade generate forces which contributed to the development of Manila's extramural area and to the ethnic and occupational differentiation of the *arrabales* [embryonic suburbs]. Throughout the period of unrestricted commercial exchange, Manila was visited by a myriad of foreign merchants and seamen, most of whom moved on to other Asian ports following a sojourn of several months in the Philippines. But two groups—the Japanese and the Chinese—remained in sufficient numbers during the year to warrant separate residential quarters amidst the growing population of urbanized Filipinos. A sizable body of Japanese, which had reached 3,000 by the 1620s, lived immediately southeast of Intramuros in the suburb of Dilao and for several decades maintained their own unique culture. By far the largest alien community consisted of the Chinese, who through their labors as traders, sailors, and artisans made possible the galleon trade. From a tiny band of forty persons who lived in pre-Hispanic Manila, the Sangley [Chinese] population grew to more than 20,000 people by 1600 and, despite continuing racial conflict and periodic massacres, fluctuated between 5,000 and 30,000 individuals throughout the seventeenth century. Not only was Chinese labor and organizational skill essential to efficient commercial operations, but they also dominated almost all crafts and services within the Spanish colonial capital. Because of their great numbers, the Spaniards as early as 1581 inaugurated a policy of residential segregation by assigning the Sangleys to a large extramural quarter—the Parian. In addition to this district, which was carefully situated beneath the guns of Intramuros, a substantial Chinese area later developed north of the Pasig in Binondo. Through countless informal relationships and religiously sanctioned marriages between Sangley immigrants and Filipinas, Binondo in time became the home of a large community of Christianized and Hispanicized Chinese *mestizos* [offspring of indio-Chinese unions]. These three *arrabales*, whose inhabitants preserved for several generations many elements of culture from their respective homelands, were thus fashioned by Spanish authorities late in the sixteenth century in order to guarantee the effective supervision of potentially rebellious alien Asians whose labor and skills proved essential to the developing urban economy."

—Robert Reed, *Colonial Manila: The Context of Hispanic Urbanism and Process of Morphogenesis* (Berkeley: University of California Press, 1978), 68–69

When the Spanish put an end to raiding and bondage, the datu had no way to reward his timawa and maharlika and no need for their military service. Further, the requirement for everyone to engage in agricultural production resulted in social leveling, leaving the warrior class with little to distinguish itself from commoners.[23] Datus, on the other hand, played an important role in reducción and this helped them retain status. Datus who brought their people voluntarily into cabeceras were rewarded with positions in the new state as a *gobernadorcillo* ("little governor") or a lower-ranked *cabeza de barangay* (village head). Constituting a new class called the *principalia*, ex-datus and their descendents lived prominently on or near the plaza mayor. They became responsible for collecting and remitting tributes and other contributions to the encomendero and church, and in return, they and their eldest sons were exempt from tribute and labor service. Although they were not entitled to keep a share of the tribute, their position allowed them to engage in various tactics of enrichment, such as demanding excess payment and reviving debt slavery.

The principalia also took advantage of confusion over the Spanish concept of land ownership to expand their landholdings and rebuild their economic power. The first governors of the Philippines made small land grants—in the name of the king—to individual Spaniards who raised cattle from China to satisfy the colonists' appetite for meat. Eventually these *haciendas* (landed estates) would be devoted to agricultural production, but first the owners needed to enlarge them. In the precolonial Philippines, it was only the product of the land, not the land itself, that could be owned and sold. But the principalia, encountering the new land tenure concept, found it easy to claim as "private property" land earlier cultivated by their barangays, under the pretext that it was land granted to them by the Spanish monarchy.[24] Despite Spanish policy not to dispossess indios, officials often looked the other way when their local allies sold common land to hacienda owners. Even the religious orders, forbidden to engage in commercial or land transactions, soon began to accumulate property to convert to agricultural production. The principalia solidified ties with the orders by selling or donating land to so-called friar estates. As the nationalist historian Renato Constantino noted, accommodation with the Spanish "provided these chiefs with opportunities to further entrench themselves in positions of dominance within the native community . . . accelerat[ing] the process of stratification which had already begun operating in pre-conquest society."[25]

Yet, despite the reemergence of the datu class as principalia under Spanish rule, the basis of their status was quite altered—firmly hereditary, yet stripped of spiritual prowess and subordinated to the friars. In his historical study of political economy and culture in Negros, Aguilar argues that "the colonial state transformed the preconquest elites into a fixed institution characterized by hereditary succession but bereft of their preconquest prestige and magic. . . . [S]eparated from personal accomplishment and extraordinary feats as a sign of favor from the spirits, [their position] was thoroughly corrupted." Essentially, the cabeza was "a mere tribute gatherer" who answered to the friar and depended on his protection from the arbitrary demands and not infrequent cruelty of the encomendero's soldiers and the alcalde mayor. Having forfeited his spiritual authority to the friar, he had no means of controlling followers who rejected the new order.[26] (See box 3.3.)

For the baylan and catalonan—female ritual specialists of animist practice—the introduction of Christianity by male Spanish priests brought a more catastrophic loss of power and status. Such women had earned respect, authority, and their livelihood by conducting public ceremonies, making diwata and anito,

---

Box 3.3. Friar Power

"Organized as political families, the native elite continually had to court the local friar to earn his favor, which they did by providing services and monetary contributions to the local church. In return, they enjoyed prominent roles in Catholic ceremonies and rituals. It also became easy for them to obtain from the priest a favorable letter of reference, required by the central government at Manila in the appointment of town magistrates. The friar became the native elite's protector against the felt abuses of civilian administrators. The markers of colonial prestige and protection, which the elite constantly had to seek and augment, seemed like signs of approval from the dominant power realm personified by the friar. . . .

"At the same time, because the colonial state retained the preconquest chiefship, at least in its outward form, as a means of indirect rule, native elites were compelled to contrive a system of affirmation of their continuing legitimacy as local leaders. One mechanism was the largesse that flowed through their sponsorship of the feast of the town's patron saint, a shift in the flow of resources given that . . . the *datu*'s control of the surplus had been eroded and taken over by the friar. Not predisposed to recognizing their leadership, however, were the rebel segments of indigenous society. The latter, who contested colonial authority using their otherworldly prowess, could easily terrorize the native elites who, though nominally Catholics, were awed and frightened by magic [even in] the late nineteenth century."

—Filomeno V. Aguilar Jr., *Clash of Spirits: The History of Power and Sugar Planter Hegemony on a Visayan Island* (Honolulu: University of Hawai'i Press, 1998), 58

treating the sick and dying, and attending women in childbirth. All these activities came under attack by friars in what Carolyn Brewer terms "holy confrontation." Beginning with the arrival of Magellan, the friars relentlessly pursued the destruction—and sometimes desecration—of anito in their effort to displace the old religion and its practitioners. Brewer refutes the conventional picture of peaceful transition from indigenous religion to Catholicism by highlighting the violence of this process. When anito and other ritual instruments were broken, dragged through villages, burned, or defecated upon by young boys, as encouraged by parish priests, it had the effect of "depowering, dishonoring and defiling the religion of the ancestors."[27]

Baylan were similarly pushed out of the business of midwifery, healing, preparing bodies for burial, and performing mourning rituals, although they did not give up without a fight. Some attempted to incorporate Catholic prayer and images into their ritual, but the friars rejected syncretism when it did not submit to their own authority. In one instance, a group of baylan convinced the local population to come to them secretly without directly challenging the friar's healing power. This compromise was successful for a time, for people didn't see the old spirits and the Christian spirits as mutually exclusive, as did the missionary priest. Two years passed before someone in the village informed the friar, at which point he forced the "worthless band of women" to convert and the whole community to bring their anito, including images of their ancestors, to be destroyed.[28]

The friars rooted out, humiliated, punished, and exiled the baylan not only to discredit and eliminate competitors but also to reorder gender relations to conform to Hispanic Catholic norms. New models of nothing less than male and female personhood were being taught, imposed if necessary. For women, their new model entailed greater modesty and humility, celibacy outside of marriage and fidelity within, and subordination to male authority—husband, priest, and god. New religious roles were devised for spiritually inclined women in "tertiaries or confraternities" that worked under the authority of the orders to instruct others in the "demeanor of 'good' Christian women."[29] There was no room for compromise with autonomous women who did not accept the mediation of the male priest to approach divinity.

Spirit ritualism nevertheless lived on in "folk Catholicism," which mixed elements of the two belief systems. The icon of this fusion is the *anting-anting*, an amulet or potion said to give special powers to its possessor, who was now frequently male, "in imitation of the Spanish friarship."[30] Reynaldo Ileto describes how anting-anting were obtained:

[One] way . . . was to go to the cemetery on midnight on Holy Wednesday or Thursday and place bowls of food, a glass of wine and two lighted candles on a tomb. Before the candles burned out, the food and drink would have been consumed by spirits who would leave a white stone in one of the empty vessels. A struggle for possession of this anting-anting would then ensue between the aspirant and earth-spirit called *lamang lupa*. Only extraordinarily brave or daring men used this method; these were the ones, it is said, who usually became rebel or bandit chiefs.[31]

Mixing the religion of the powerful friar—signified by holy days, wine, and candles—with anito of the indigenous spirits—the white stone and *lamang lupa* (literally, land spirit)—is an example of localization in communities struggling with Spanish domination. (See box 3.4.)

Reshaping the Economy to Pay for Colonization

Uprooting and resettling hundreds of thousands of people constituted a major socioeconomic rupture with the past in a relatively short time. "By the 1590s," Spanish historian Luis Alonso says, "the breakup of the indigenous economy of the barangays was completed."[32] Effects included population decline, the abandonment of cleared and cultivated fields, and the disruption

---

Box 3.4.   Millenarian Revolts

"Between 1620 and 1820, discord emanated from a variety of sources. Some outbreaks were stimulated by economic policies. Others were generated by inept local administration. Regardless of their secular origin, however, many militant movements took on sacred characteristics. . . . [P]opular redeemers usually claimed miraculous powers. They won and retained supporters by portraying themselves as prophets or deities in regular communication with a 'supernatural pseudo-community.' They also expanded the ranks of their adherents through apocalyptic pronouncements linked to assurances of collective vulnerability. Sooner or later, leaders and followers alike experienced delusions of limitless power. At that juncture, they frequently attacked available symbols—usually clerical—of Spanish authority. Village violence in turn provoked metropolitan vengeance. Sorely outnumbered Spaniards, in fact, tended to overreact to challenges from scattered segments of the population. The repetitive pattern—religious insurgency followed by Spanish repression—produced a series of miniature Armageddons in Luzon and the Visayas. Iberian churchmen and administrators, however, never grasped the significance of the rhythmic phenomena. More importantly, they refused to accept the upheavals as manifestations of profound cultural stress or deep-seated social tension. Instead, they regarded them as outlandish examples of provincial perversity. Devotees of native messiahs, moreover, were dismissed as naïve and superstitious 'fanaticos' deserving neither curiosity nor compassion."

—David R. Sturtevant, *Popular Uprisings in the Philippines, 1840–1940*
(Ithaca, N.Y.: Cornell University Press, 1976), 81–82

of interisland trade. Yet the new state, as described above, was determined to collect tributes, now owed to the Spanish king in compensation for the conquest, conversion, and rule of the Philippines. More practically speaking, the influx into the cities of foreign soldiers, missionaries, officials, and traders put greater demand on food production. Resettlement therefore included a new land-tenure and land-use system.

Each family was assigned a lot for a house in town and a parcel of land for cultivation on the outskirts. Several elements of the new system differed from past practice. First, although it was not apparent to the cultivators, they had no customary rights (as before) or legal rights to the land they were assigned and passed down to their children, for it all belonged to the king of Spain. The importance of this fundamental principle will be discussed in the next chapter. Second, socioreligious control and increased agricultural production demanded a sedentary population—indios were henceforth forbidden to leave town without the friar's permission. This introduced an element of European feudalism that had not been present in the mobile preconquest societies of the archipelago. Cultivators tied to land they did not own lost the ability to trade with other communities and could not easily evade onerous taxation.

The third and fourth changes were designed to increase food production through more intensive land use. In addition to cultivating their fields, indios were required to raise chickens and pigs and plant fruit trees on their household plots, a pattern still visible today. The productivity of the fields themselves was increased through technology—a Chinese plow pulled by a domesticated *carabao* (water buffalo). Training in the new techniques was done by the friars. Dissemination took many decades, but slowly raised the productivity of the land. The recovery of agriculture also allowed the production of goods once traded and now offered for tribute:

> mats, jars and pottery, various cloths from plain homespun cotton for sheets and blankets to table cloths and elaborate embroidered altar cloth; coconut oil for lighting, wax from the forest for church candles; abaca fiber and rope for rigging and tackle for ships, *brea* (pitch) and coconut husk or coir for caulking; and the famed Ilocos *mantas*, heavy cotton sailcloth for the trading boats, [for] the craft in the wars against the Muslims, and for the galleons in the Manila–Acapulco trade.[33]

Several other types of taxation were imposed to support Spanish colonization, trade, and conversion efforts. Until about 1650, Spain engaged in frequent wars with Muslims and with the Dutch. To finance these wars or simply to enrich encomenderos, the state periodically requisitioned food and other goods at lower-than-market prices. Indios called the system *vandala* (feeling vandalized), for these purchases were often not paid for.

In 1572, a monopoly trade between Spanish America, the Philippines, and China was institutionalized that made the fortune of Spanish individuals and institutions. The "galleon trade" was named for the huge ships that carried cargo on the dangerous but highly lucrative voyages. Europe had insatiable demand for Chinese silk and other Asian luxury goods; Spain had the Mexican silver necessary to buy them. Manila became the transshipment point for this trade, and Spanish residents were awarded a cargo quota on the ships. The Philippine state government was somewhat disadvantaged in obtaining revenue from this trade because the Mexican viceroys controlled the galleons, prevented other New World traders from sailing to Manila, and collected customs duties in Acapulco on incoming Chinese merchandise and outgoing Mexican silver. Manila's share of this revenue was supposed to be remitted on the following galleon, but was chronically late and incomplete.

Indigenous trade with China was largely shut out of the galleon trade. Local goods from Luzon, Butuan, Cebu, or Sulu could only be smuggled aboard in small quantities. A more serious hardship was the forced labor that went into building the huge ships. Such labor was mobilized by the cabeza de barangay through the *polos y servicios*, the compulsory forty days labor per year owed by tribute payers to the state. Servicio was performed by men and women and consisted largely of domestic service in churches and conventos. The polo was hard labor performed by men—constructing government buildings and churches, rowing and fighting in military expeditions, and the dreaded *cortes de madera*, cutting and hauling trees and building galleons and warships (see box 3.5). The forty-day limit was frequently ignored for cortes duty, causing agricultural disruption back home and threatening the ability to pay the following year's tribute. Men worked for rations under inhumane conditions; there were frequent deaths and uprisings. As a Spanish observer wrote to the king in 1619, "The shipbuilding carried on in these islands on your Majesty's account is the total ruin and death of these natives."[34]

Finally, there were religious contributions. The church automatically received two reales per tribute (that is, per family) per year, but the friar, in a position of ultimate authority locally, solicited contributions in kind and in service throughout the year. Fees—once paid to baylan for rituals—were now paid to the local church for baptisms, marriages, and funerals.

In sum, residents of the Philippines paid for their own colonization and religious instruction, as well as subsidizing Spain's wars and its China trade. The economic foundations of the state—tribute, vandala, polos, and church contributions—weighed heavily on the population. By draining surplus from peasant production, these exactions and the loss of trade removed any incentive to improve agriculture. They also produced uprisings

Box 3.5.   Construction of the Galleons

"Though probably not so large as the legend created by the tales of English raiders made them, . . . [s]ome of the great galleons used against the Dutch and the Portuguese were of over 2000 tons. . . . The galleons had the high forecastle and poop characteristic of their class. The apparent topheaviness of ships whose ends stood so high out of the water was partly offset by their unusual breadth of beam. Their half-moon appearance was thus very different from the straighter lines of their predessesor [sic], the oared galleass of the Mediterranean, and of their successors, the frigates. It was their unwieldy and lumbering aspect that led Thomas Carlyle to call the heavy coach in which Louis XVI and Marie Antoinnette [sic] attempted to flee from France an 'Acapulco Ship.' . . .

"Most of the galleons of the line were built in the yards at Cavite on the Bay of Manila, where a great force of Chinese and Malay [indio] workmen carried on the work of construction and repairs. However, many were built in other parts of the northern islands, where there were found together the three requisites of a safe port and a plentiful supply of good timber and of native labor. . . .

"The hard woods of the islands were very well adapted for shipbuilding. Casimiro Díaz considered them 'the best that can be found in the universe,' and added 'if it were not for the great strength of the galleons and the quality of their timbers that so dangerous voyage could not be performed.' The framework was often made of teak. . . . For the ribs and knees, the keel and rudder, and inside work the hard Philippine *molave* was generally employed. The sheathing outside the ribs was usually of *lanang*, a wood of great toughness, but of such peculiar nature that small cannon balls remained embedded in it, while larger shot rebounded from a hull made of this timber. Excellent courage for the rigging was obtained from the *abaca* or Manila hemp. Sail cloth was produced in the province of Ilocos, while the metal necessary was mostly bought from China, Japan, Macao, or even from India and worked up by Chinese smiths. . . .

"The labor of cutting the timber in the mountains and transporting it to the coast was performed by great gangs of natives. While the more skilled work of construction was performed by Chinese carpenters, the islanders were used in large numbers for the rough work in the yards. These Filipinos were generally impressed under a sort of corveé or *repartimiento* system, and their condition probably represented the most oppressive phase of the Spanish domination in the islands. Sometimes the natives were drafted as punishment for some local sedition or insurrection, while their harsh treatment by Spanish or Moro foremen was in itself a source of riots and more serious commotions. . . . Writing in 1676, Fernández Navarrete tells of the suffering of the natives from 'the infernal fury of some Spaniards,' and three years later the king ordered Governor Vargas to see that the native workmen were treated with 'benignity.'"

—William Lytle Schurz, *The Manila Galleon*
(Manila: Historical Conservation Society, 1985), 162–64

and flight from cabeceras throughout Spanish-controlled territory. Most uprisings were abortive or short-lived—a friar learned of the plan in confession, inter-barangay rivalry hampered cooperation, or the Spanish crushed it with soldiers (often from Pampanga, a province near Manila that became prosperous under Spanish rule). But underlying conditions were a constant provocation.

From 1565 to 1591, conquest, forced labor, excessive tributes, the shift to sedentary agriculture, military campaigns, famine, and epidemics led to rapid population decline. The first census of 1591 counted only 166,903 tribute payers (heads of household) from an estimated preconquest population of 750,000. The population stabilized and grew again by the end of the century, but another decline in the 1600s was caused by forced military service, food shortages, and disease. Certain areas of Luzon experienced a 40 percent drop from 1591 to 1655.[35] From the mid-1600s, the population began to recover again and by 1766, there were 200,000 tribute payers, or roughly 800,000 Christians living under Spanish control. Furthermore, this number did not represent the total population of the islands, but only those living in the lowland areas of Luzon, the bigger of the Visayan islands, and northern Mindanao.

The Chinese: Essential Outsiders

We have discussed Chinese–Philippine political and economic contact in the several centuries preceding the Spanish conquest, and there is evidence of at least temporary Chinese residence in port towns. The Spanish chose Manila for their capital precisely because the presence of 150 Chinese there raised hopes of trade and missionary access to China. Yet almost from the start, the two groups fell into an ambivalent relationship characterized by mutual profit, suspicion, and intermittent violence. The silver brought in on the galleon attracted a quick influx of Chinese merchants importing all the things the colonists desired—sugar, butter, flour, and walnuts; oranges, chestnuts, plums, and pears; silk woven into satin, brocade, and damask; salt pork, ham, and especially beef.[36] Many artisans and laborers—mostly from the southern Chinese province of Fujian—also came to Manila, and within a few years they numbered in the thousands, far higher than the Spanish population. The Spanish became suspicious of the influence of hard-to-convert Chinese on the indios, however, and thought of them in the same terms as the economically active and culturally different Moors and Jews back home, on whom they had imposed policies of "segregation, hispanization, and expulsion." Then, in 1574, the Chinese pirate Limahong attacked Manila and some resident Chinese fought alongside him; others attacked friars, churches, and Spanish residents. When it was over, "relations between the Chinese and the Spaniards fell into a pattern of distrust and latent hostility." Both necessary and seemingly so different, the Chinese, stereotyped as *sangley* (from "traveling merchant"), became "a despised cultural minority."[37]

The China trade obviously could not be halted, for the sake of both everyday needs and the investments of Spanish officials and religious orders. And Chinese settlers proved just as important to the internal working of the colony. Their experience trading with river and harbor ports, the destruction of indigenous interisland trade, and the Spanish focus on the galleon trade encouraged the Chinese to fill a niche in the economy. Moving through the country by permit, they became wholesalers, distributors, and shopkeepers keeping Manila provisioned. In this capacity they had good relations with alcaldes mayores and lay administrators of friar estates. Yet the Spanish felt wary and insecure. Their response was to extract maximum resources and labor from the Chinese, discourage them from settling in the colony, and control and segregate Chinese settlers from Christianized indios. These were policies based on Spain's own weaknesses, and they contributed to cycles of exploitation, revolt, massacre, and expulsion, followed by repopulation and the rebuilding of tension.

In 1581, Chinese traders were forced to live in the *Parián*, a restricted quarter built outside the fortified walls of Manila. Here officials could more easily collect taxes and restrict trade. Chinese who settled were required to pay a yearly license fee, tribute, and house tax totaling eighty-one reales (compared to the indios' ten), render unpaid labor, and pay occasional arbitrary taxes. Theirs was the highest level of taxation in the colony, but it was the arbitrary demands that caused Chinese hostility to flow back to the Spanish. In 1593, when four hundred Chinese were forcibly drafted to row vessels in a military expedition against Maluku, they mutinied and killed the governor of the colony. In the aftermath, half the Chinese population was deported and the rest placed under guard.[38] Other revolts occurred when the mutual suspicions of Spaniards and Chinese were provoked. In 1603, the Spanish began to fortify Manila against a phantom Chinese invasion; residents of the Parián, fearing a preemptive massacre, rose in revolt, and the Spanish killed nearly the whole community of twenty thousand. Sixty years later, Spanish fear of the Chinese warlord Koxinga ended in a tragic replay.

Frequent expulsions during the first two centuries of Spanish rule—usually following revolts—determined the size and composition of the Chinese population, not actually reducing it to the mandated six thousand, but usually holding it close to twenty thousand.[39] In 1589, all Chinese except farmers, carpenters, and mechanics were expelled. Those who remained generally converted to Christianity with the encouragement of the Spanish, who hoped it would make them loyal and open up China to missionary efforts. But since Catholic Chinese enjoyed more freedom to move about the colony, the Spanish came to see their conversion as a business tactic. The Chinese were also encouraged to become farmers, especially to provide labor on the royal and friar haciendas that supplied the tables of Manila. Again, the result was not the compliance the Spanish hoped for. A wave of agrarian resistance began in 1639 when Chinese tenants of a royal hacienda protested the death of some three hundred of their number clearing land for cultivation under grueling conditions.

More significant than conversion was the tendency of domiciled Chinese to marry indias (female indios) in the absence of Chinese women. Salazar notes:

> Chinese revolts in the 17th century . . . tended not only towards the expulsion of the Chinese but likewise their more rapid absorption into the native population. Escapees from Spanish repression were generally accepted into Filipino families in Laguna and Batangas, if they had not already been in close contact with them beforehand. In any case, the [adoptions of Chinese kinship terms into Tagalog] point to very early intermarriages among Chinese and Filipinos.[40]

Thus an unintended effect of Spanish policy was to increase the integration of Chinese into indio society. Although intermarriage alone did not assimilate the Chinese, it produced offspring who comprised a new social category—*mestizos*. When their number was small, mestizos tended to identify with the Chinese. When their numbers grew larger (especially during periods of Chinese expulsion), they became distinct communities, self-governing and loyal to the Spanish state.[41] Meanwhile, the continuing pattern of suspicion and expulsion reinforced the status of Chinese as "essential outsiders"[42] in the Philippines.

ORIGINS OF THE WEAK STATE

Balance of Power in the Clerical-Secular State

Order was maintained in the colonial Philippines by the interdependence of secular and clerical state officials, who together administered body and soul. But it was neither a cooperative nor equal division—the secular state was weak in personnel, its power did not flow evenly through the territory it claimed, and it remained extremely dependent upon the friars for its most basic functions.

Part of the reason for this weakness was the shortage of lay Spaniards willing to serve in the new colony. Those in top positions were royal appointees who expected to reap a fortune, but soldiers and petty bureaucrats were quite reluctant. From 1624 to 1634, for example, only sixty nonclerical Spaniards were present in the whole country outside Manila and Cebu. In 1677, the crown offered a full pardon to criminals in Spanish America who would enlist for service in the Philippines. There were few takers. We have also noted that nonofficial, nonclerical Spaniards were banned from residence in the countryside. Combined, these factors created in effect two Philippine worlds: cosmopolitan Manila—home to indio artisans, Chinese and other foreign traders, secular and religious officials, and private Spanish residents—and the vast linguistically and geographically segmented countryside. In the latter, the local friar acting as parish priest was frequently the only Spaniard indios ever saw. He spoke their language, heard their confessions, enforced collection of the tribute, and provided some protection from excessive taxation. In much of the Philippines, the friars *were* the state.

Theoretically, the governor of the colony held tremendous executive, legislative, and judicial power. As captain-general, he commanded the armed forces; as crown representative, he controlled the assignment of priests to indio parishes. But the religious orders whose personnel filled these positions simply refused to submit to his authority. Their power in local areas was based on intimate knowledge and influence, and they were also members of international religious organizations financially and administratively independent of the secular state in Manila and even Madrid. When occasionally a governor tried to enforce his authority, the orders' threat to desert the parishes en masse exposed the state's dependence and ended the attempt. The religious also successfully resisted "visitation"—inspection by bishops answerable to Rome via Madrid—thus avoiding correction of friar abuses such as overcharging for weddings, baptisms, and funerals, demanding excessive contributions and menial labor from parishioners, engaging in moneymaking activities, and violating clerical celibacy. Yet another indication of friar power was the expansion of haciendas. Politically, friar estates were not towns and had no secular authority in residence. They were managed by lay administrators of the order in a setting in which church and local government were fully meshed.

Friar power in the countryside was reflected in church influence in Manila, where buildings of the religious orders occupied a third of Intramuros. Officials complained that friars were haughty and demanded extreme deference from all laypersons, including the governor himself. On the other hand, the many useful functions they performed for the state—from maintaining order and guaranteeing tributes to acting as policy advisers and foreign envoys—relieved state officials of the need to develop these capacities, allowing them to concentrate on galleon profits. Throughout this period, the secular state remained weak and underdeveloped in administrative structure.

Territorial Stalemate

In its first two hundred years in the Philippines, Spain claimed formal possession of the whole archipelago, but lacked full administrative and military control. This was due to factors arising from both Spanish and Philippine sources. On the one hand, Spain focused its military resources on the defense of Manila, coastal areas, and the galleon trade. On the other hand, two indigenous reactions to Spanish colonialism helped determine the reach of the state: upland retreat from colonial intrusion and rival state building in the south.

The policy of reducción reflected the importance of settling the population in controllable, Christianized zones near rivers and coasts. Its corollary was the role of the mountains and the deep countryside, where unrepentant baylan were banished and reluctant Christians fled to re-create the order and meaning of preconquest life or simply to escape taxation. In addition to these *remontados* (those who return to the mountains) were preconquest mountain settlements in the Gran Cordillera of northern Luzon and the interiors of other islands. Together they were able to resist missionaries and tribute collectors into the eighteenth and nineteenth centuries because the terrain gave them a tactical edge, while lowland revolts and external threats commanded the state's scarce military resources. (See box 3.6.)

The longevity of the Cordillera's independence was not due to indigenous political organization, however; disunity and recurring friction remained the

---

Box 3.6. Remontados

"In these forests and hills live many people of different tribes mixed together, Christians and pagans. Some are there because they are attracted to the mountains from which they came. Others are fugitives from justice. Many likewise go there to live at their ease and be free from paying tribute and from the fulfillment of the other obligations laid on them. Finally many are there because it is the territory where they were born as pagans. Living mixed together like this with pagans intermarrying with Christians, they mix together a thousand superstitions with the law of Jesus Christ. The result is a monster, more fierce and difficult to overcome than that famous one with which Hercules fought. For the apostates, being entirely corrupted, are the most difficult to reduce to settled life again, and they by their corruption, their persuasion, and their evil customs, pervert to a great extent the simplicity of the pagans."

—Antonio Mozo, *Noticia histórico-natural de los gloriosos triumphos y felices adelantamientos conseguidos en el presente siglo por los religiosos del orden de N.P.S. Augustín en las missiones que tienen a su cargo en las Islas Philipinas* (Madrid, 1763), 117–19, in John N. Schumacher, *Readings in Philippine Church History*, 2d ed. (Quezon City: Loyola School of Theology, Ateneo de Manila University, 1987), 190

rule among the mountain communities. "Pagan" barangays resisted not only Spanish religious and economic impositions but also the increased social stratification that accompanied state formation, retaining a datu-led social structure in defiance of political developments in the lowlands. Contact was never completely severed between coastal and upland populations, despite friars' attempts to insulate the Christian populations. But as political and cultural differences widened, animosity became manifest in pagan raids on lowland towns, the need for a "defensive perimeter along the Christian frontier,"[43] and the development of Christian cultural distain similar to that felt toward Muslims. But precisely because the mountains lay outside Christian control, they could also serve as a refuge and base of resistance for people pressed too hard by the church and state. The term *remontado* even today "embraces people on the run from Spanish friars, Spanish taxes, Japanese concentration camps, American suppression of peasant rebellions, lowland crop failures, local vendettas and the modern Philippine Constabulary."[44]

In the Muslim zone, Spanish attacks on Brunei in the late sixteenth century eliminated Bornean influence from Luzon, and early seventeenth-century battles pushed Mindanao Muslims out of the Visayas. Thereafter, prioritizing the galleon trade and resettling barangays under church supervision severed economic links between the Muslim south and the rest of the archipelago outside Manila. In their effort to defeat the sultanates politically, convert the Moros to Christianity, and claim full control over the archipelago, the Spanish launched intermittent military assaults on Muslim areas in 1578–1596, the 1630s–1650s, 1718–1762, and the second half of the nineteenth century. In these wars, both the sultanates and the Spanish used devastating tactics, burning villages and taking prisoners. But the results were inconclusive—in the 1640s Spain signed peace treaties with the strongest sultanates, Sulu and Maguindanao, recognizing their de facto independence. At other times, Spain simply abandoned its forts—in 1663 to defend Manila against the Chinese warlord Koxinga and in 1762 when the British attacked Manila. Each time the Spanish established a fort (principally at Zamboanga) and a zone of military control, the Jesuits began missionary activity. But they had little success among the Muslims, and when the forts were abandoned, most converts shrugged off Christianity.

Because the Spanish never fully controlled Mindanao and Sulu, Muslim state building proceeded. Thomas McKenna explains that this process cannot be understood in isolation from ongoing economic and military engagements with Spain and other European powers in the region, especially the Dutch.[45] As Spain consolidated its control over lowland Luzon and the Visayas, the Sulu sultanate developed commercial and political ties with the wider Muslim world of insular Southeast Asia. On the island of Mindanao, Spanish pressure and Sulu's strength to the west accelerated the Islamization of the Pulangi River basin and southern Mindanao. There the Maguindanao sultanate, based at the port of Cotabato, competed with the upriver Buayan sultanate for dominance of Mindanao. The slave economy continued to operate in the sultanates and slaves constituted the most important source of a sultan's wealth. They were both a sign and a means of access to resources outside his own community. They supported the maintenance of armed forces that, along with spiritual legitimacy, helped him collect tribute from his datu allies. And they supplied him with rice for subsistence and interisland trade. Forest products for the China trade—tobacco, rattan, beeswax, and hardwoods—came from uphill "client" groups, outside Maguindanao society but under its control.

The strength of the Maguindanao sultanate peaked during the long reign of Sultan Kudarat (c.1619–1671). The Muslim rituals of daily prayer, circumcision, abstention from pork, and fasting during Ramadan were observed more evenly, schools taught the Koran, and the Arabic script was adopted. Kudarat also engaged in international politics: He sought an alliance with the Dutch trading company VOC and sold it rice and slaves; he tried to play the Dutch off against the Spanish; he allied with Sulu to conduct joint raids on the Visayas; and he fought, signed treaties, and traded with the Spanish themselves. By the late 1700s, however, Spanish blockades cut off Cotabato from direct participation in international trade. Thereafter, Sulu became the strongest sultanate in the Philippines, and on Mindanao Island, the upriver Buayan asserted dominance over Maguindanao.

The sultanates existed as rival states to the one based in Manila—they represented spiritual and political independence from Spain. As maritime states, Maguindanao and Sulu pursued their own commerce and diplomacy. But as McKenna argues, intersultanate rivalry was just as important as hostility to the Spanish. And most of the seventeenth and eighteenth centuries was marked by stalemate with Manila, as the Spanish lacked the ability to take over the south and the sultanates prioritized trade and the economic benefits of slave raids undertaken by Muslim client groups.[46] As the sultans' territory was encroached upon and, conversely, they came to rely on Philippine towns for slave labor, the south was drawn into the conceptual and geographical entity called "the Philippines." Yet like those areas outside the walled forts, beyond the church bells, and in the mountains, the Muslim south represented a space *inside* the territory claimed by the Spanish that was *outside* the control of the state.

The British Occupation

The Philippines was of limited importance to the Spanish empire, whose center remained its American possessions. While Spain's ambition to control the spice trade was an initial reason for retaining the Philippines, its navy lacked the ability to operate in so distant a region and the Dutch won control of Maluku. What kept the Spaniards in the Philippines was the value of Manila as a staging post for religious missions, especially to China and Japan, and as a transshipment point for the galleon trade. As a strategic outpost, however, the Philippines remained a liability, open to attack by rival European powers and slave raiders.

Spain's growing military weakness was matched by its economic position. Lacking valuable southern Philippine commodities (for example, pearls) or attractive manufactures (such as those the British produced) to exchange for Chinese goods, the Spanish watched silver drain from their empire. They tried to protect their position by banning other Europeans from participating in the galleon trade, but such mercantilist policies were losing ground to the "free trade" philosophy of British traders. The British also wanted access to China, specifically to Chinese tea, without spending their own hard currency. To accomplish this, they inserted themselves into existing networks, trading arms to Sulu to obtain marine and forest products China wanted. They also intruded on the galleon trade, buying Mexican silver with Indian textiles through Asian middlemen and loading their own goods onto the Acapulco-bound galleon. Manila's administrative weakness became apparent as state officials accepted bribes to permit this illicit trade.

Some members of the English East India Company and the British military sought to do away with even this slight impediment, and in 1762 an opportunity was afforded by the Seven Years War to attack and occupy Manila. Although the British force was small, the Spanish offered no real resistance and the occupation lasted until a 1764 negotiated withdrawal.[47] British control never reached much past Manila, but the circumstances of the assault and occupation offer an opportunity to assess state and social cohesion. Militarily, defenses were wholly inadequate and the weakness of the clerical-secular state was in full view. The Philippines' governor-general had died in office, and until his successor arrived—the colony had been waiting three years already—the archbishop of Manila was the legal civil and military commander. Receiving prior warning of the attack, Archbishop Rojo made no preparations; worse, he agreed neither to surrender nor to take military action. The city was therefore subject to looting and violence.

But the British were surprised that the indios did not desert the city as their troops prepared to take Intramuros. Instead of watching the natives panic along with the Spanish, the British came under attack by a unit of 1,900 Pampangans, forces loyal to the state who were accustomed to putting down revolts (see box 3.7). Only after the Pampangans were defeated did the indios flee the city. On the other hand, many indio revolts occurred throughout

---

Box 3.7.   The Defense of Manila

"Had their Skill or Weapons been equal to their Strength and Ferocity, it might have cost us dear. Although Armed chiefly with Bows, Arrows, and Lances, they advanced up to the very muzzles of our Pieces, repeated their Assaults, and died like wild Beasts, Gnawing the Bayonets."

—Journal of Colonel William Draper, quoted in Nicholas Tracy,
Manila Ransomed: The British Assault on Manila in the Seven Years War
(Exeter, Devon, England: University of Exeter Press, 1995), 47

---

the colony during the occupation against the authority of alcaldes mayores and parish friars. When the Pampanga-based Spanish government-in-exile ordered a preemptive massacre of the Chinese of Manila, most of whom were Catholic, this population sent an armed force of five thousand against the Spanish. In the aftermath, the last expulsion order (in 1766) reduced the numbers of Chinese once again. But the next century would bring many more foreigners into the Philippines as the colony's economic engagement with the world underwent a great transformation.

NOTES

1. Anthony Reid, "Islamization and Christianization in Southeast Asia: The Critical Phase, 1550–1650," in *Southeast Asia in the Early Modern Era: Trade, Power, and Belief*, ed. Anthony Reid (Ithaca, N.Y.: Cornell University Press, 1993), 152.

2. Thomas M. McKenna, *Muslim Rulers and Rebels: Everyday Politics and Armed Separatism in the Southern Philippines* (Berkeley: University of California Press, 1998).

3. Cesar Adib Majul, *Muslims in the Philippines,* 2d ed. (Quezon City: University of the Philippines Press, 1973), 57.

4. Miguel Lopez de Loarca, in F. Landa Jocano, ed., *The Philippines at the Spanish Contact: Some Major Accounts of Early Filipino Society and Culture* (Manila: MCS Enterprises, 1975), 103.

5. E. P. Patanñe, *The Philippines in the Sixth to Sixteenth Centuries* (Manila: LSA Press, 1996), 158–60.

6. McKenna, *Muslim Rulers and Rebels,* 66.

7. Anthony Reid, *Southeast Asia in the Age of Commerce, 1450–1680*, vol. 2, *Expansion and Crisis* (New Haven, Conn.: Yale University Press, 1993), chap. 1.

8. Wolfgang Schivelbusch, *Tastes of Paradise: A Social History of Spices, Stimulants, and Intoxicants*, trans. David Jacobson (New York: Vintage Books, 1993), 5.

9. See the essays in William Henry Scott, *Looking for the Prehispanic Filipino and Other Essays in Philippine History* (Quezon City: New Day Publishers, 1992), especially "The Mediterranean Connection."

10. Antonio Pigafetta, in Jocano, *Philippines at the Spanish Contact*, 50.

11. Zeus A. Salazar, *The Malayan Connection: Ang Pilipinas sa Dunia Melayu* (Lunsod Quezon, The Philippines: Palimbagan ng Lahi, 1998), 61.

12. Scott, "Why Did Tupas Betray Dagami?" in *Looking for the Prehispanic Filipino*, 56.

13. Ch'en Ching-ho, *The Chinese Community in the Sixteenth-Century Philippines* (Tokyo: Centre for East Asian Cultural Studies, 1968), 27.

14. Patanñe, *Philippines in the Sixth to Sixteenth Centuries*, 185.

15. Hernando Riquel, "News from the Western Islands" (1573), quoted in Reid, *Southeast Asia in the Age of Commerce*, 252.

16. Vicente Rafael, *Contracting Colonialism: Translation and Christian Conversion in Tagalog Society under Early Spanish Rule* (Ithaca, N.Y.: Cornell University Press, 1988).

17. Filomeno V. Aguilar Jr., *Clash of Spirits: The History of Power and Sugar Planter Hegemony on a Visayan Island* (Honolulu: University of Hawai'i Press, 1998), 36.

18. Pedro Chirino, in Jocano, *Philippines at the Spanish Contact*, 127.

19. Reid, *Southeast Asia in the Age of Commerce*, 2:252.

20. Francisco Colin, in Jocano, *Philippines at the Spanish Contact*, 150.

21. See René B. Javellana, "The Colonial Townscape," in *Kasaysayan: The Story of the Filipino People*, vol. 3, *The Spanish Conquest*, ed. José S. Arcilla (Manila: Asia Publishing Co., 1998), 66–67.

22. O. D. Corpuz, *An Economic History of the Philippines* (Quezon City: University of the Philippines Press, 1997), 32.

23. William Henry Scott, *Barangay: Sixteenth-Century Philippine Culture and Society* (Manila: Ateneo de Manila University Press, 1994), 132.

24. Corpuz, *Economic History*, 27.

25. Renato Constantino and Letizia R. Constantino, *The Philippines: A Past Revisited* (Manila: Tala Pub. Services, 1975), 62.

26. Aguilar, *Clash of Spirits*, 57–59.

27. Carolyn Brewer, "From Animist 'Priestess' to Catholic Priest: The Re/gendering of Religious Roles in the Philippines, 1521–1685," in *Other Pasts: Women, Gender, and History in Early Modern Southeast Asia*, ed. Barbara Watson Andaya (Honolulu: Center for Southeast Asian Studies, University of Hawai'i at Manoa, 2000), 69, 74–75.

28. Chirino, in Jocano, *Philippines at the Spanish Contact*, 137.

29. Brewer, "From Animist 'Priestess,'" 84.

30. Aguilar, *Clash of Spirits*, 50.

31. Reynaldo Clemeña Ileto, *Pasyon and Revolution: Popular Movements in the Philippines, 1840–1910* (Quezon City: Ateneo de Manila University Press, 1979), 22–23.

32. Luis Alonso, "Financing the Empire: The Nature of the Tax System in the Philippines, 1565–1804," *Philippine Studies* 51, no. 1 (2003): 68.

33. Corpuz, *Economic History*, 32.

34. Quoted in Corpuz, *Economic History*, 35.

35. Linda Newsom, "Old World Diseases in Early Colonial Philippines and Spanish America," in *Population and History: The Demographic Origins of Modern Philippines*, ed. Daniel F. Doeppers and Peter Xenos (Quezon City: Ateneo de Manila University Press, 1998), 26.

36. Ch'en, *The Chinese Community*, 74–75, 77.

37. Edgar Wickberg, *The Chinese in Philippine Life, 1850–1898* (New Haven, Conn.: Yale University Press, 1965), 9.

38. Ch'en, *The Chinese Community*, 126–46.

39. Wickberg, *The Chinese in Philippine Life*, 11.

40. Salazar, *The Malayan Connection*, 64.

41. Wickberg, *The Chinese in Philippine Life*, 20.

42. Daniel Chirot and Anthony Reid, eds., *Essential Outsiders: Chinese and Jews in the Modern Transformation of Southeast Asia and Central Europe* (Seattle: University of Washington Press, 1997).

43. Robert Ronald Reed, *Hispanic Urbanism in the Philippines: A Study of the Impact of Church and State* (Manila: University of Manila, 1967), 51.

44. Fenella Cannell, *Power and Intimacy in the Christian Philippines* (Quezon City: Ateneo de Manila Press, 1999), 4.

45. McKenna, *Muslim Rulers and Rebels*, chap. 4.

46. McKenna, *Muslim Rulers and Rebels*, 83.

47. Nicholas Tracy, *Manila Ransomed: The British Assault on Manila in the Seven Years War* (Exeter, Devon, England: University of Exeter Press, 1995).

Chapter Four

State and Societies, 1764–1898

THE IMPERATIVE TO REFORM

In the late eighteenth century, Spain was compelled to reconsider the way it ruled the Philippines, as external realities intruded on the isolated life of the colony. Most dramatically, the rise of British power and temporary loss of Manila exposed the state's weakness in defense and control of the population. More fundamental still was economic change. The galleon trade had begun losing money as European merchants and smugglers used the maritime peace enforced by Britain's navy to trade directly with China. British rule then opened the Philippines to world trade, and the Spanish state was unable to reverse this trend or stop the illegal entry of commodities into the colony.

After almost 250 years, the galleon trade ended with the last eastbound ship leaving the Philippines in 1811, the last westbound ship in 1815. In the next ten years, Mexican revolutionaries won independence and Spain's American empire dwindled to a few Caribbean islands. The Philippines lost both customs revenue and its commercial raison d'être and was forced to make administrative and economic changes to survive. Exiles from Spanish America complicated this process, competing for jobs and influence with Philippine-born Spaniards. Ironically, the challenge of creating a modern colonial state and economy was faced in the imperial periphery just as much of the empire was lost.

But Spain's decline was offset by economic growth and industrialization in the wider world that created new markets for raw materials. The development of Philippine agricultural and mineral resources was therefore the logical replacement for the galleon trade. This development would make land—hitherto underexploited—a more important resource, and Manila and other port cities would become commercial, managerial, and professional centers. The object was to create a unified colonial economy out of the separate indio, Chinese, and Spanish sectors and to modernize the state in order to promote and benefit from these changes.

THE NEW ECONOMY

Export Agriculture

The reorientation of the colonial economy began with the arrival in 1778 of Governor-General José de Basco y Vargas, who saw the futility of the galleon trade and the potential for large-scale production of cash crops for export. He encouraged Spaniards to invest in the cultivation of spice plants; of silk, cotton, indigo, and hemp; of fruit trees, sugarcane, cacao, and coconut. He tried to spur local manufacturing to limit the silver drain. And he established the Royal Company of the Philippines in 1785 to finance these projects and handle the new trade he envisioned with Europe, other Spanish colonies, and the rest of Asia.[1] Unfortunately, his proposals met with "profound and general silence."[2] Resistance came from friars who opposed changes in the labor force and from others with vested interests in the galleon trade. Although the Royal Company did promotional work and started pilot projects, it failed to introduce the new skills and scientific knowledge lacking in the friar-dominated educational curriculum.[3]

Basco was able to accomplish a few things, however: He repealed the ban on Chinese merchants, which helped bring internal trade back to life; he began to open Manila to foreign traders, both Asian and non-Asian; and he established the tobacco monopoly. This last enterprise was a "tax farm"—a government-auctioned right to produce, sell, and/or operate a monopoly. Later examples included liquor, meat-slaughtering, municipal tax collection, and cockfighting. (For colonial governments in the eighteenth and nineteenth centuries, tax farming was a common source of revenue that spared them the expense of developing state capacity in revenue collection.) The tobacco monopoly was successful in several ways. First, the state, paid in advance on a yearly basis, was able to remit revenues to Spain. Second, the cultivation of tobacco led to the production of cigars, which became the Philippines' only major manufactured export in the nineteenth century. And finally, the clearing of forested land for tobacco pioneered the way for other commercial crops—especially abaca and sugar—to be cultivated in interior and mountainous regions of the colony.[4]

Change came more rapidly with the end of the galleon trade, which was a money-losing business in its last two decades. When it ended, the Spanish lost all remaining control of the Philippines' foreign trade, for the Royal Company had been reduced to a shambles by mismanagement, friar opposition, and waning interest on the part of Manila merchants.[5] In 1834, the company was abolished, and Manila was officially opened for trade and residence to merchants of any nationality coming from any foreign port. At the same time, discrimination against Chinese ships trading at Manila ended; henceforth all ships were subject to the same taxes and procedures.[6] In the following decade, the trading privileges of alcaldes mayores (provincial governors) and military governors were abolished in order to stimulate private trade. This opportunity, though meant for Spaniards coming to the Philippines looking for work, was taken up by Chinese immigrants who played an important role in the development of cash cropping.

When Basco allowed the Chinese to return in 1778, their numbers were officially limited to a "necessary" four thousand, the Parián was reestablished, and a capitation (head) tax was imposed. As priorities shifted to economic development from the 1830s, however, policy changed to encourage immigration and eliminate restrictions on movement. The new immigrants fanned out beyond the urban Spanish settlements of previous generations to the places where export crops were being produced. They initially faced competition from Chinese mestizos who had taken up wholesaling and provisioning urban areas during the previous century. But the new immigrants were able to reclaim their role and expand it—linking provincial producers to the world market—through a combination of well-placed agents and credit from Western commercial firms. The latter were British and some American trading companies that advanced imported goods on credit, allowing Chinese businesses to operate with little of their own capital.[7] In the absence of government direction, the firms also conveyed demand information from foreign markets, guiding producers' planting decisions—a key factor in the development of sugar plantations.[8]

So Basco's ideas were eventually realized. In the first decade of the nineteenth century—the last of the galleon trade—exports of Philippine origin accounted for less than 10 percent of the value of total exports, and many of these were harvested forest or sea products such as bird's nest, mother-of-pearl, tortoise shell, sea cucumber, and timber.[9] By the 1840s, though, almost 90 percent of total export revenue came from six Philippine-grown cash crops: sugar, tobacco, abaca (hemp) fiber and cordage, indigo, coffee, and cotton.[10] Throughout the colony, the cash economy replaced trade in kind, and by the 1830s only three provinces still paid tribute in rice. In the 1850s and 1860s, the ports of Iloilo and Cebu opened to foreign shipping, stimulating trade and agriculture in the Visayas.[11] Soon new tracts of forestland on Negros Island were cleared for sugar.

Figure 4.1. Douane de Manille (Customs of Manila), 1852 lithograph by A. N. Vaillant (Gallery of Prints, Makati City, Metro Manila)

As exports rose, economic life became more complex and "metropolitan Manila"—Intramuros and its growing suburbs—grew into a real commercial center (see box 4.1). The city's opening to foreign traders made it a port of call for ships from India, China, and as far away as the east coast of the United States. It contained people enjoying more diverse jobs, more money transactions, and more cultural diversions. Manila's population increased from 100,000 in 1822 to about 150,000 by mid-century. (There was no strict enumeration until 1903, so all population estimates are based on tribute lists and parish records of births and deaths.) Most of this population growth came from migration to the city. According to demographer Daniel F. Doeppers, "Manila's population in the early 1890s was primarily derived from two zones of intense interaction facilitated by water transportation—from around Manila Bay and the short Pasig River . . . and across the South China Sea from the coastal core of riverine southern Fujian . . . [both] long-standing patterns of circulation."[12]

The steady stream of internal migrants in the nineteenth century came mainly from the nearby Tagalog-speaking provinces that had long supplied Manila with its basic necessities. People migrated to the city for a variety of reasons—some found increased economic and educational opportunities, others were driven by loss of livelihood caused by the importation of cheap manufactured textiles from Britain. Both Chinese and internal migrants were

---

Box 4.1.　Nineteenth-Century Manila

"Foreign visitors around the middle of the nineteenth century found Intramuros, where the Spanish elite tried to make life as much as possible like life in Spain, dull and monotonous, with few social activities and frequent religious processions. Across the Pasig River, Binondo, the commercial center was a much livelier place.

"Binondo was where the rich merchants—foreign, Chinese mestizos and natives—resided, in the newest, most elegant houses along the Pasig River. Escolta and Rosario were the principal streets in the district, where most of the Chinese shops could be found. In the district could be found all the large working establishments of Manila. Binondo's importance as commercial capital can be seen from the average daily traffic in its main thoroughfares in 1858; over the *Puente Grande* (great bridge), 1,256 carriages passed; through the largest square, the Plaza de San Gabriel, 979 and through the main street, 915. On the *Calzada*, the great promenade of the capital, 499 carriages were counted, representing the aristocracy of Manila. . . . Manila's development as a cosmopolitan center brought modern amenities. Tramway lines with horse-drawn cars were running through the city and its suburbs by the last quarter of the nineteenth century. In 1884, the government constructed a waterworks system for Manila and its suburbs with funds bequeathed by a Spanish philanthropist. Steam tramways were introduced in 1888. The gas lamps of Manila's streets were replaced with electric lights in 1893. The first news-sheet was published in 1822. By the end of the Spanish regime, there were five dailies and a biweekly paper, subject to strict censorship (jointly exercised by a priest and a layman).

"Foreign travellers found more variety in Manila's cultural life from the middle of the nineteenth century onwards. By the 1880s, there were four theaters in Manila, a bull ring, a Spanish comedy company, and occasional visits by foreign performers such as a circus or an Italian Opera Company to entertain the public in the city. The first big hotel was opened in Binondo in January 1889 with 83 rooms and stabling for 25 horses. It ranked with the best hotels in the East."

—Manuel A. Caoili, *The Origins of Metropolitan Manila: A Political and Social Analysis* (Quezon City: University of the Philippines Press, 1999), 40–41

---

subject to push-and-pull factors, but while Chinese (as well as Spanish) migrants were overwhelmingly male, Doeppers argues from individual registration data that many indias were part of the migrant stream:

> Certainly there is an important record of employment and subsistence opportunities for Filipino women in the city dating from at least the mid-nineteenth century. A long history of cash-wage employment in the cigar industry, petty commerce, and social complementarity with some of the more than 25,000 unaccompanied Chinese and Spanish sojourners, in particular, offer powerful rationales for female migration in the absence of cultural rules to the contrary and against a background of disruptive rural economic change.[13]

But while internal male migrants had higher-than-average literacy rates—suggesting sons of the elite pursuing higher education—female migrants tended to be illiterate and poor. Two points should be noted here: First, despite the relative "backwardness" of Spain and its colonial administration that will become apparent in this chapter, forces of modernization were felt in the Philippines well before the twentieth century. And second, insofar as those forces were often not benign, we can trace a gender disparity in their impact upon individual lives.

Many Spaniards also migrated to the Philippines, especially after the opening of the Suez Canal in 1869 dramatically decreased travel time from Europe. But they did not have much involvement in the export economy beyond the collection of customs duties for the state. British and Chinese domination of imports, exports, and distribution left little scope for Spaniards bereft of managerial experience or capital, and the country became known informally as an "Anglo-Chinese colony." This 1849 observation by the Belgian consul conveys the marginality of Spaniards to economic life:

> The Spanish firms established in Manila have for the most part only very limited capital and many of them, in order to maintain themselves or to undertake any ventures, have to resort to the funds of the religious corporations . . . which they borrow at 5 percent annually.[14]

Spanish wealth, like Spanish power, resided in the religious orders. These maintained formal control over old friar estates that covered "nearly 40 percent of the surface area in the four Tagalog-speaking provinces" surrounding Manila and supplied the city with rice, fruit, and vegetables.[15] Much more significant in the production of export crops were the accumulated small plots in outlying provinces controlled by indio and mestizo elites, the new producers of wealth.

The Importance of Land

The transition to an export economy had a major impact on land tenure and social stratification in the Philippine countryside. Before the nineteenth century, most families living in rural towns tilling family farms grew rice and vegetables for their own consumption and produced little surplus. Their earnings depended on middlemen and markets, and their few cash expenses included church contributions, the tribute, and payments to tax farmers for entertainment such as cockfights. Gradually, however, farmers faced an increasing need for money. Birth, marriage, illness, and death all came to require cash as the economy modernized. This led many small farmers into export crop production, which in turn made them dependent upon purchased rice to feed their families. At the same time, population growth—rising from perhaps 2.2 million in 1820 to 4 million in 1846 and 6.5 million in 1898[16]—

caused the successive subdivision of family farm plots. Combined, these forces led to significant turnover in agrarian holdings—land loss on the part of many families and accumulation on the part of others.

When they had a pressing need for money, peasants turned for a loan to those with capital to spare—usually an indio or mestizo member of the principalia, who was sometimes a relative. In a system called *pacto de retroventa* (agreement of repurchase), the land was "sold" to the lender, who agreed to sell it back at the same price within a specified period of time. The borrower continued to have usufruct rights on the land, but was now seriously indebted. Pacto de retroventa loans were difficult to repay and were usually renewed and increased until the amount owed was far more than the plot of land was worth. Eventually dispossessed of their land, most families stayed on as sharecroppers or tenants. In this way, the evolving colonial elite used the capital earned in retail trade to accumulate the best land for export crops and a labor force to which it was "linked by kinship or by networks of personal relationships."[17] (See box 4.2.)

Accumulation also occurred through land grabbing, often by the powerful religious orders. To expand their vast holdings, friar estates simply demanded rent on land they wanted or conducted fraudulent land surveys. Cultivators again stayed on the land as tenant labor, but didn't deal directly with friar owners or lay managers. Instead, large tracts were rented to principalia *inquilinos* (renter-lessors), who sublet the small parcels to peasant cultivators and

---

Box 4.2. Dependency circa the Nineteenth Century

"One factor kept village views of the elite from deteriorating to the point of outright hostility. For the most part, class relations retained personalistic qualities. Social distance grew, but physical and psychological proximity survived. Since production for export required close supervision to assure maximum output, many landowners maintained houses in the barrios. Regular visits enabled them to oversee tenant labor and keep in touch with village affairs. Peasant families who experienced misfortune took advantage of such occasions to request succor and sympathy, both of which were usually granted. In the final analysis, paternalism held the system together. Prominent men regarded their dependents as children and treated them accordingly, while tenants looked upon the landowner as a potential benefactor and usually addressed him as elder brother or father. In a changing world, the intimate nature of the unequal relationship gave villagers an illusion of permanence and a false sense of security. Face-to-face interactions, however, did not persist everywhere. Absentee ownership—which prevailed on many church estates, and appeared on some private holdings—destroyed the last vestiges of sentiment and compassion. Its emergence signaled the death of social reciprocity and the simultaneous birth of class antipathy."

—David R. Sturtevant, *Popular Uprisings in the Philippines, 1840–1940*
(Ithaca, N.Y.: Cornell University Press, 1976), 40

managed production. In this three-tiered system, the friars were the ultimate economic, spiritual, and political rulers of the countryside. The indio-mestizo elite gained earned considerable wealth—"without doing a stroke of work, they make more than the estate owners themselves."[18] And the cultivators descended into precarious, hand-to-mouth existence. As the population increased faster than land was opened for new cultivation, debt or inability to pay rent forced many families off land they had worked for generations. The dispossessed became seasonal wage laborers in export crop production, migrated to cities, or made their way into hill communities or banditry, a process generating new outsiders.

If the transition to commercial cropping was relatively swift, stagnant production methods constrained agrarian development. Collection and distribution networks evolved and landholders accumulated wealth, but planting, harvesting, and processing methods remained crude and no investment in technical improvement was forthcoming. According to economic historian O. D. Corpuz, agriculture "lagged behind all sectors, although it accounted for the major part of total output by value, land under cultivation, and labor force and number of families covered." This was true for both staple and cash crops: "The foreign trade demand for unprocessed agricultural produce went hand in hand with little utilization of modern technology, and helped arrest progress in manufacturing and industry."[19]

Underlying these problems was the fact that up until the end of the Spanish colonial era, the land was not *legally* owned by the producers. Unchanged since the conquest, all land in the Philippines, except the minority expressly granted by the king, still technically belonged to the Spanish crown or state. The government did not seriously attempt to rationalize land ownership and systematically issue land titles until 1880 (when the reform proposal was successfully opposed by the friars) and again in 1894.[20] This meant that no land transactions, real estate, or production from the land was subject to taxation, an anomaly that had consequences for state, economy, and society. First, the only significant new sources of state revenue were the tobacco monopoly and customs paid on largely unprocessed agricultural exports. By not updating its laws to accord with the reality of land alienation, the state effectively cut itself off from a growing revenue source. Second, lack of land title removed any incentive to invest in land improvement, and undertaxation of the export sector meant "little pressure to attain optimum efficiency through technology."[21] Third, the state's reliance on a regressive head tax, rather than an earnings or property tax, taxed the peasantry disproportionately, contributing to increasing social stratification between the mass of poor indios and the indio-mestizo elite.

The uneven impact of these economic changes devastated rural populations. In the northern Luzon provinces supplying the tobacco monopoly, the government's strict prohibition on growing any other crop sparked revolts and population flight. The central plains of Luzon were transformed from a forested area into a rice-producing zone in a process that concentrated land ownership in the hands of the few and dispossessed original homesteaders.[22] In the western Visayas, the weaving industry collapsed after British firms imported cheap cotton, pushing the industry's female labor force into indebtedness and poverty. And though the shift to sugar production on the "Negros plantation frontier" absorbed these displaced workers, it didn't improve their lives. For the sugar industry grew by "depressing wages and constantly acquiring new land, rather than by investing capital in new technology for more intensive and efficient cultivation of existing plantations."[23] The end-of-century revolution against Spanish rule would have a strong basis in the woeful conditions accompanying economic transformation.

Over the course of the century, then, a new economy took shape that utilized the Philippines' least exploited resource—land—to sell agricultural commodities on the world market. Was it the unified colonial economy that Governor-General Basco y Vargas tried to initiate one hundred years earlier? It did reward concentration of land ownership within the country and provided increased revenues to the colonial state. But it was an economy that had strikingly little connection to Spain itself. According to economic historian Benito Legarda, it was "never economically complementary to Spain and in this specific sense was not a colonial economy." From the middle of the century, the Philippines sent its primary exports, sugar and abaca, overwhelmingly to the United States and United Kingdom; only in leaf tobacco exports was Spain an important customer.[24]

More importantly, it was far from being "a unitary economy." Historian Alfred McCoy argues that the archipelago "emerged as a series of separate societies that entered the world economic system at different times, under different terms of trade, and with different systems of production." McCoy attributes this fragmentation largely to the fact that individual foreign firms drove the transition to commercial agriculture. The Spanish supplied neither private capital for export production nor legal infrastructure to manage the key resource. As a result, different regions of the colony "developed separate ties to global markets through local branches of Anglo-American merchant houses [that] tolerated diversity in local production systems and made no attempt . . . to regularize patterns of production."[25]

In short, the new economy unified the colony only in the formal sense that it produced Philippine products. In substance, this "patchwork of diversity" prevented communities from finding unity based on shared exposure to the global capitalist market. Instead, regional or language group consciousness persisted, to which was added increasing class tension between growing rural poor and emergent rural elites, as well as general resentment toward Spanish arrogance and economic parasitism.

Would administrative reforms fare any better?

REFORMING THE STATE

System-Wide Reform

In the aftermath of the British invasion, Spain pursued reform throughout its empire to remove trade restrictions, improve revenue collection, and reorganize government administration.[26] We have seen that the colony was opened commercially and that revenues increased through the tobacco monopoly. To improve administrative performance, the state was to be centralized in accordance with the "Ordinances of Good Government" issued in 1768. In his study of the nineteenth-century Philippines, Eliodoro Robles explains that strengthening the central agencies of the state was considered the only way to improve governance, given the following liabilities and demands on local government:

1. the lack of technical and qualified personnel . . . ,
2. the inability of many communities and provinces isolated by geographical features to raise their own funds . . . ,
3. the unbridled use of power on the part of local officials, resulting in rampant abuse and miscarriage of justice . . . ,
4. the rise of brigandage and social restlessness (not to mention Muslim piracy) rendering local police ineffective . . . ,
5. the inadequacy of public improvements and general services . . . ,
6. the rationality of balancing ecclesiastical power . . . and of secularizing public instruction (including the teaching of Spanish) to make it more functional rather than dogmatic,
7. the need for more economy in administration,
8. the necessity of extending effective authority and control over "frontier" areas . . . , [and]
9. the need for promoting agriculture [and] industry. . . .[27]

In short, the arbitrary rule of friars and systematic corruption of alcaldes mayores, gobernadorcillos, and cabezas was to be replaced by state objectives defined from above. This called for financial accountability through oversight and the separation of executive from judicial, not to mention secular from clerical, functions—an enormous undertaking. Unfortunately, almost none of it was attempted until the governorship (1801–1806) of Rafael Maria de Aguilar, who republished the Ordinances and began implementing some of their provisions.

The most urgent problems facing reformers were social unrest rising from corruption in administration of the tribute, the polos, and justice; escalating Muslim raids, which destabilized communities and disrupted trade; and a government debt of 5.6 million pesos. In response, Aguilar attempted to institute accounting procedures for both secular and parish administration, improve local defenses, and develop provincial road links and public works to stimulate the economy. He faced serious opposition from the religious orders, however, especially in attempting to establish civil oversight of parish affairs. As long as the local priest was the sole Spaniard in most Philippine towns, progress would be slow. And as late as 1810, there were only four thousand Spaniards in the whole colony, including religious, in relation to a Christian population of almost 2.4 million.[28]

As with economic measures, the pace of reform quickened as the century progressed. But unlike the economy, governance in the Philippines closely followed political events in Spain. In his work on Africa, Crawford Young discusses how modern state formation in colonies often paralleled developments in the colonial metropole.[29] In this case, a century of Spanish instability was reflected in its governance of the Philippines. In 1808, Napoleon invaded Spain, deposed the "enlightened despot" Fernando VII, and installed his own brother as king. As in other French-occupied territories in Europe, the ensuing war of independence gave voice to liberal opponents of absolutist monarchical rule and church power over civic life. Nineteenth-century liberalism, emerging from the Enlightenment ideals of rationality and progress, called for freedom in thought, politics, economics, and religion. Economic liberalism was exemplified by Britain's free trade ideology, and political liberalism began to transform the world with the French Revolution and Napoleonic wars. Liberalism quickly developed moderate, radical-democratic, and socialist variants, while the reaction against it was upheld by monarchy, church, and aristocracy.[30] In Spain in 1810, liberal revolutionaries established the Cortes, the country's first representative body, and declared the Constitution of Cádiz in 1812. These were abrogated by the return in 1814 of Fernando, who ruled absolutely until 1820 and again from 1823 to 1833. The rest of the century saw a succession of absolutist, military, and constitutional governments, punctuated by the liberal apotheosis of the Glorious Revolution and a brief republic in the years 1868 to 1873.

The appointment of twenty-four Philippine governors between 1800 and 1860 reflected the alternating factions in power in Madrid. When reformers

ruled, they hastily mandated changes in the colonies, often without considering local conditions. Officials in the Philippines then attempted to implement
the changes in the same spirit. According to Robles, "the rather strict manner
in which the laws were enforced by fearful and overzealous subordinates . . .
[often] resulted in undue hardships on the part of the governed so as to render
the laws oppressive and unpopular." They were also "complicated, and far
advanced of the available administrative machinery."[31] Box 4.3 lists some
of the significant reforms enacted, though the gap between enactment and
implementation was often considerable.

A complicating factor was the increasing number of Spaniards arriving in
the colony. Often in flight from changes at home, few of these *peninsulares*
(born on the Iberian Peninsula) had commercial experience or administrative
ability, yet their status entitled them to favorable positions. This pressure
alone caused the central state to expand because local government posts were
reserved for the principalia. An 1876 count found 13,264 peninsulares in
Manila, and their numbers continued to rise until the end of the century. In
appointments and politics, tension and competition increased between these
Spaniards and the *criollos*, or creoles—Spaniards born in the Philippines or
Americas. Spanish creoles in the Philippines were known through most of
the century as "Filipinos"—just as Englishmen and women born in Britain's
American colonies had called themselves "American"—and they resented
the assumed superiority of the come-lately peninsulares. Creoles tended to

---

Box 4.3.   Selected Reforms of the Spanish Colonial Government, 1786–1894

1786   Office of cabeza de barangay made elective (by principalia voters)
1806   Bureau of Vaccination created to supervise efforts against smallpox
1836   Primary schools mandated at town level
1837   Postal services reorganized
1842   Office of General Administration of the Tribute created to oversee tax collec-
       tion and tabulation of statistics
1844   Trading privileges of alcaldes mayores abolished
1847   Trading privileges of military governors abolished; office of gobernadorcillo
       made elective
1851   Tributary age lowered and amount of tribute raised
1860   Politico-military districts created for the Visayas and Mindanao
1861   Executive and judicial functions separated at the provincial and capital level
       (not fully implemented until 1885)
1863   Overseas Ministry created in Madrid to govern colonies
1863   Free primary education mandated at village level
1868   Guardia Civil established to suppress crime and insurrections
1884   Tribute replaced by cédula personal tax
1894   Executive and judicial functions separated at the local level

favor liberal governments in Spain and sometimes resisted the reimposition of monarchist governments, as in the 1823 and 1828 military mutinies led by Mexican-born and Philippine-born Spanish officers.

Reform efforts peaked from the 1860s to the 1880s. A Council of Administration was established as a cabinet for the governor-general. It also acted to check his power by representing the interests of the administration, treasury, judiciary, church, military, and commerce within the executive. Among other reforms, the Treasury was reorganized to separate the functions of finance, accounting, and auditing. A General Inspector of Public Works was appointed to supervise the polos y servicios. And a Board of Civil Administration was given extensive powers over everything related to local government, including education, the appointment of local officials, permits and patents, the subdivision and naming of towns, the authorization of local expenditures, statistics, prisons, public lighting, and emergency relief (though in practice, the board's personnel lacked technical expertise to carry out such extensive responsibilities).[32]

The trend of these and other efforts was toward both accountability and centralization—through these measures it was expected that abuse of power would decline and the capacity to effect progress would increase. But centralized power and accountability are not natural bedfellows. One of the two most important obstacles to accountability was the simultaneous possession of executive and judicial authority in the same office, from governor-general down to gobernadorcillo. This transgression of the liberal principle of separation of powers was addressed in 1861, when the governor-general and provincial governors were divested of judicial responsibility. But the change was not fully implemented until the 1880s at the provincial level and was not applied locally until the 1890s. The other major impediment to accountable government was the power of the clergy at all levels. In Manila, the civil authorities tried to tame the friars and gain control of the justice system by incorporating the church into a judicial agency with two branches—one for clerical and one for civil affairs. But this reform was wholly unsuccessful because the church rejected limits on its judicial role and the state soon abandoned the attempt.

The overall aim of reform was to improve conditions in the country in order to forestall further social unrest. But this goal was often undercut by the autocratic imposition of new policy—a hazard of centrally imposed reform. The layers of authority that develop in a state each have their own interests (both public and private) and their own relationship with various social forces. Accommodation between two levels may be reached because of shared interests or orientations. Madrid and Manila, for example, when governed by reformers, shared an interest in centralizing and rationalizing power in order to increase revenue and improve the standing of the state. Even though their implementation lacked continuity and their exchange of information was faulty, momentum toward these goals was discernable and backed by many criollos. But in the provinces, towns, and barrios, Manila's intermittent reform efforts were met by friar power, which dominated local state and society alike.

Provincial and Municipal Government

The highest provincial officeholder was the Spanish alcalde mayor (or a military governor in the case of unpacified territories, discussed below). In the early nineteenth century, there was much room for improvement in the quality of Spaniards appointed to provincial positions. Spanish historian Tomas Comyn wrote in 1820 that it was "common enough to see a hairdresser or a lackey converted into a governor; a sailor or a deserter, transformed into a district magistrate, a collector, or military commander of a populous province." According to Comyn, these officials were rapacious, using their appointments to "become chief consumers, purchasers, and exporters of everything produced and manufactured within the districts under their command, thus converting their licenses to trade in[to] a positive monopoly." Such an official often acted "with unbounded sway, without dread, and almost without risk, of his tyranny ever being denounced to the superior tribunals."[33]

In the mid-nineteenth century, minimum qualifications for the post of alcalde mayor were introduced (lawyer with two years' experience) and then increased (judge with experience as lieutenant governor). From the 1850s, promotion to the highest rank required passing an examination in Tagalog. To liberalize the economy, Spanish provincial officials lost the right to use their office for commercial purposes in 1844, and as part of the separation of executive and judicial functions in the 1860s, the office of alcalde mayor was divided into a judicial alcalde and a civil executive. As noted above, however, implementation of this important reform was slow. Many provincial governors in the 1880s were still performing both executive and judicial functions, and miscarriages of justice were common.

Nevertheless, new parameters of governance had been articulated that spoke to changing economic and social realities, such as the sharp increase in crime in the 1830s. Provincial governments were expected to initiate public works and promote the local economy, issue permits for logging and mining, oversee public education and the election of local officials, and see to the overall moral and civic condition of the province. Their staffs gradually took on professionals in administration, customs, finance, security, and language interpretation. But while the performance of some governors stood out in public works and agricultural development, most were considered successful as long as they excelled in revenue collection.[34] This was imperative, as the Philippines was expected to help the royal treasury recover from the ongoing instability of Spain's domestic politics. In practice, increased collection and stricter accounting of revenue were the highest reform priorities.

Tribute remained the paramount source of state revenue and polos labor the means of carrying out public works. These functions were in the hands of principalia officials—the cabeza de barangay collected the tribute and the gobernadorcillo mobilized villagers for polos y servicios. Collection of these taxes was the touchstone of interaction between state and society, yet the local officials who carried it out were no more accountable to society than they had been at the time of reducción. When the office of cabeza became "elective" in the 1780s and that of gobernadorcillo in 1847, the voting public consisted of the principalia alone—in the strict sense of current and former gobernadorcillos and cabezas. These men drew lots (only thirteen voting at any one time) to "write the names of their first and second choices for the office on their ballots." This was done under the supervision of the provincial governor and parish priest, who did not hesitate to make their own preferences clear. From the result of the balloting, a list of three names was compiled for the provincial governor's final decision. As Glenn May writes, "The thirteen voters were not so much electing the gobernadorcillo as they were drawing up a short list for the post."[35]

Gobernadorcillos and cabezas were exempt from the tribute and labor service themselves and were known to extract "surplus" in the form of excessive tribute and bribes. On the other hand, they were *personally* liable for remitting the full amount of the official tribute, upon pain of imprisonment (see box 4.4). It is no exaggeration to say that in this realm of governance, the Spanish state functioned very badly. Further, the effort to maximize revenue collection exposed various dilemmas that aggravated state–society tensions.

First was the classification scheme on which the tax system was based: ethnoreligious categories devised in the period of the conquest, when the state squeezed maximum revenue out of distrusted non-Christian Chinese merchants and taxed indios at a rate befitting sedentary peasants with little surplus. Socioeconomic transformations since that time—urbanization, the rise of a wealthy indio principalia, a growing Christian mestizo population, and the influx of new Chinese immigrants—made this classification scheme obsolete. The state started to adjust to new realities with an 1828 decree classifying Chinese residents according to occupation rather than religion. Mestizos (perhaps half a million by mid-century) were taxed less than the Chinese but twice as much as "rich, urbanized indios [who] were still paying a mild tribute as their only tax, as if they had never left the villages."[36]

Box 4.4.   The Burdens of Office

"In the first place, there was the risk of financial ruin because the collection of taxes was becoming more and more difficult, due primarily to the continuously rising hatred of the masses against the tribute. This was intensified by the reform of 1851, which not only reduced the tributary ages but also raised the amount of tribute itself. Other immediate causes of the difficulty were the increasing geographic mobility of the people and number of mixed marriages, making census enumeration difficult and jurisdiction oftentimes conflicting. These conditions were a real difficulty for the *cabezas* but only superficial for the Superior Government, as represented in practice by the *alcalde mayor*, who, as a rule, was not interested in the reasons for failure to collect. Indeed, what was important was for the *cabeza* to fill his quota—it did not matter how—for otherwise, his own properties and goods might be confiscated. Moreover, as a debtor to the Royal Treasury, a *cabeza* was liable for imprisonment. Thus, in addition to financial ruin, there was the risk of degradation.

"The position of the *gobernadorcillo* was no better; in fact, it was worse. The tribute, as we noted, was payable in money or in kind. Such being the case, the *gobernadorcillo* often found himself with loads of goods to transport to the capital, including poultry and livestock. Since the law did not provide for the expenses in storage, packing, and transportation of the goods, he had to shoulder these burdens. . . . [There was also] the maintenance of prisoners [and] the *Casa Tribunal* itself, both as a government building and a lodging house, to look after. Although the law . . . did not intend that these burdens should be borne solely by the *gobernadorcillos* and *cabezas* . . . government appropriations were very inadequate. Moreover, a lot of documentation and formal details were required with which even Spanish officialdom found it difficult to comply. Because of these conditions, many native officials, either through limited administrative training or other causes—including honesty—found themselves actually emptying their own pockets in order to square accounts with the treasury, or provide for expenses necessary to maintain the [town]. In many instances, *gobernadorcillos* and *cabezas*, unless they were smart enough, were imprisoned for alleged debts to the treasury. Against this background, it is therefore not strange that internal abuses continued."

—Eliodoro Robles, *The Philippines in the Nineteenth Century*
(Quezon City: Malaya Books, 1969), 84–86

Second, the tribute lists upon which the collection was based were increasingly unreliable. Despite the evident importance of enumerating the growing population (estimated as exceeding 1.7 percent growth per annum),[37] it was not until 1887 that the Spanish attempted to conduct the first census of the population. The suggestion of a population count twenty-six years earlier nearly caused a panic in Manila, with rumors circulating that it would be used to conscript men for war in Africa or to send women to Spain. In the provinces, the announcement caused people to flee to the mountains. Tribute lists therefore continued to be prepared by cabezas and were made to conform to lists kept by parish friars. Names were entered when a person reached tribute-paying age and crossed off (or perhaps not) upon Christian burial. As society became more mobile, the lists became less reliable. The cabeza could not cross off people who had died or moved away without the approval of the friar. But the friar might object because the church received its percentage based on the official number of tributes.

Some people managed to evade being listed by moving from their parish of birth, while others were listed twice, an occurrence caused by the prevalence of nicknames in addition to baptismal names. In 1849, Governor Narciso Claveria, determined to eliminate "confusion" caused by "the general lack of individual surnames" in "the administration of justice, government, finance and public order," decreed that Filipinos be assigned permanent family names.[38] The government then issued the Catalogo de Apellidos (Catalogue of Family Names), from which names were assigned in the following peculiar manner:

> A town would choose the names of one letter of the alphabet, a second chose the names of another letter, and so on. Until recently, one could tell the hometown of an individual by his or her surname. This was true, for example, in Albay province. Those with family names beginning with "R" were almost certainly from the town of Oas, those with "O" from Guinobatan, and those with "B" from Tiwi. This also explains why many Filipinos today bear Spanish family names although they may not have Spanish blood.[39]

The assignment of surnames, an ambitious directive of the central state, was carried out fairly quickly and thoroughly in the settled parts of the country. How was this possible, given the weak capacity of local state offices? Simply put, the civil state did not even attempt it; the governor-general entrusted the task to the parish friars. It is telling that this seminal episode in state building *and* state–society relations should depend entirely on the mediation of the clergy. The full range of tasks the parish priest supervised by the end of the century speaks to the continuing weakness of the local state (see box 4.5).

Unfortunately, surnames alone could not rationalize the tax system. This was only begun in 1884, when the tribute was replaced by a new tax levied equally on all, based upon the issuance of a *cédula personal* (identification card) to every adult. It was accompanied by a *contribución industrial* (tax on earnings), with which the state finally began to capture some of the colony's economic growth. But even a rationalized drive for revenues caught office-holders between increasing responsibilities and inadequate infrastructure for their implementation, a situation that promoted rather than curbed corruption.

The failure of reform to penetrate to the local level had two consequences. Weak local officials were still dominated by the clergy in all areas of governance and even relied on their interpretation of the complicated regulations

---

Box 4.5.   The Parish Priest at the Turn of the Century

"He was inspector of primary schools; president of the health board and board of charities; president of the board of urban taxation . . . ; inspector of taxation; previously he was the actual president, but lately the honorary president of the board of public works.

"He certified to the correctness of the cedulas [taxpayer identity papers], seeing that they conformed to the entries in the parish books. They did not have civil registration here, and so they had to depend upon the books of the parish priests. These books were sent in for the purpose of this cedula taxation, but were not received by the authorities unless vised [stamped] by the priest.

". . . Under the Spanish law every man had to be furnished with a certificate of character. If a man was imprisoned and he was from another town, they would send to that other town for his antecedents, and the court would examine whether they were good or bad. They would not be received, however, unless the parish priest had his vise on them. The priest also certified as to the civil status of persons. Every year they drew lots for those who were to serve in the army, every fifth man drawn being taken. The parish priest would certify to that man's condition. . . .

"By law the priest had to be present when there were elections for municipal duties. . . . He was the censor of the municipal budgets before they were sent to the provincial governor.

"He was the president of the prison board and inspector (in turn) of the food provided by the prisoners. He was a member of the provincial board. . . . Before the provincial board came all matters relating to public works and other cognate matters. All estimates for public buildings in the municipalities were submitted to this board.

"He was also a member of the board for partitioning Crown lands. . . . In some cases the parish priests in the capitals of the provinces would act as auditors. . . . He was also counselor for the municipal council when that body met. . . . The priest was the supervisor of the election of the police force. He was the examiner of the scholars attending the first and second grades in the public schools. He was the censor of the plays, comedies, and dramas in the language of the country, deciding whether they were against the public peace or the public morals."

—Testimony of Father Juan Villegas, provincial of the Franciscan Order,
before the Philippine Commission of 1900, in *Report of the Philippine Commission*
(Washington, D.C.: GPO, 1900), 25–26

---

and legislation handed down in Spanish. Second, the alienation of well-off principalia from government service led them to search for other avenues of social advancement.

Education

The state's interest in educating the population was left to the religious orders until very late in the colonial period. Primary education, where it existed, was overseen by parish friars, who tolerated only religious topics to be taught. They were especially hostile to indios learning to speak and read Spanish, an ability that would give them access to the same body of knowledge the friar had. Secular education was wholly neglected; even Manila in 1830 had but one public primary school. A royal decree of 1714 creating a secular university was never implemented, and a 1702 decree creating seminaries for natives was implemented only in 1772.

In 1836, government policy called for all towns to have primary schools and to teach Spanish, but a lack of qualified teachers with Spanish language skills and the opposition of local priests made this impossible. In the 1840s, it was still common Spanish opinion that the indios should be kept ignorant. As a consequence, "prayer schools" rather than secular primary schools were the norm, and only diocesan capitals had seminaries where sons of the elite studied Spanish to prepare for higher education in Manila.[40]

The participation of the Philippines in the global economy naturally demanded that all this change in order to produce a trained workforce for the public and private bureaucracies, supporting industries, and professions. It was necessary to expand the school system with institutions in Manila and the provinces, to bring women into the educational system, and to modernize curricula that were excessively religion-focused. An 1863 decree, with backing from the central state, mandated free primary education at the village level. The comprehensive reforms called for a primary curriculum that introduced secular topics and Spanish, but was still heavily religious. The decree also called for the creation of a men's normal school (teacher training academy) to produce teachers of Spanish. The Escuela Normal was duly established in 1865 by the Jesuits, an order that did not share the hostility of the other orders to this mission. Two years later, literacy became a requirement for officeholders.[41] By 1886, there were 2,143 primary schools throughout the country.[42] By the 1890s, public secondary schools were opening outside of Manila, including ten normal schools for women.

Like other government reforms, these were strongly opposed by the religious orders, which viewed them as infringements on their monopoly of education. In 1868, for example, a review of colonial education conducted by the revolutionary government in Spain resulted in an order for Intramuros's Universidad de Santo Tomas—established by the Dominicans in 1611—to be secularized and renamed the University of the Philippines. This order was successfully resisted until it became moot with the restoration of the monarchy.[43] Reformist pressures nevertheless forced the university to revise an antiquated curriculum centered on theology, canon law, and scholastic philosophy. In 1870, university officials added medicine, pharmacy, midwifery, and surgical medicine, although as Peter Stanley notes, they "still ignored sciences, technology, engineering, business and civil administration"—crucial disciplines needed by the new economy.[44] (See box 4.6.) The Jesuits, however, did embrace reform in their schools, introducing a comprehensive program that included Spanish,

---

Box 4.6.   The Physics Laboratory: A Satire of the Universidad Santo Tomas de Manila

"The classroom was a broad rectangular space with large grilled windows which gave abundant access to air and light. Along the walls could be seen three wide seats of stone covered with wood, filled with students arranged in alphabetical order. At the end, opposite the entrance under a portrait of Saint Thomas of Aquinas, rose the chair of the professor, elevated, with a small stairway on each side. Except for a beautiful narra-framed blackboard hardly used, since on it still remained written the *viva* which appeared on the first day, nothing was to be seen there by way of furniture, useful or useless. The walls, painted white and protected in part by glazed tiles to prevent abrasions, were totally bare; not a sketch, not an engraving, not even a diagram of an instrument of Physics.

"The students had no need for more; no one missed the practical instruction of a science eminently experimental. For years and years, it had been taught that way, and the Philippines was not disturbed; on the contrary it continued as always. Now and then, a little instrument would drop from heaven which would be shown to the class from afar, like the Holy Sacrament to the prostrated faithful: look at me and touch me not. From time to time, when some professor wanted to please, a day of the year was set aside to visit the mysterious laboratory and to admire from outside the enigmatic apparatuses placed inside the cabinets; no one could complain; on that day could be seen much brass, much glass, many tubes, discs, wheels, bells, etc.; and the bazaar did not go beyond that, nor was the Philippines disturbed. Besides, the students were convinced that those instruments had not been bought for them; the friars would be real fools. The laboratory had been set up to be shown to the guests and the high officials who came from the Peninsula, so that upon seeing it they could shake their heads with satisfaction while he who guided them smiled as if to say:

"'You thought that you were going to encounter some backward monks, eh? Well, we are on top of the century, we have a laboratory!'"

—José Rizal, *El Filibusterismo*, trans. Ma. Soledad Lacson-Locsin
(Manila: Bookmark, 1996), 98–99

Latin, Greek, basic mathematics, literature, history, rhetoric, and philosophy, in addition to Christian teachings.

It would be noted by American colonizers at the turn of the century that instruction in village primary schools remained poor and that little of the mandated curriculum was actually taught. Education conducted by the state still aimed to "produce good wards, both for the colonial and church regimes, and not to develop learned minds."[45] But government schools had in any case ceased to be the most important sites of learning from the 1860s onward. Sparked by mandated reforms and social frustration, a flood of private institutions began to open—trade schools, night schools, art schools, schools of commerce. In the 1860s and 1870s, Philippine society essentially educated itself.

It was not only the elite that benefited from greater access to education. In 1900, U.S. officials counted 1,914 teachers (almost half of whom were women) in a population of 6,709,810—a ratio of one teacher per 3,500 inhabitants. This is very low, of course, but literacy—the basic ability to read and write in one's native language—was considered "comparatively common" (in Spanish, only 2 percent).[46] By comparison, in mid-1920s French-ruled Vietnam, only about 5 percent of the population "could read a newspaper, proclamation or letter in any language"; in Dutch-ruled Indonesia, the 1930 "literacy rate for adult Indonesians throughout the archipelago was only 7.4 per cent" (in Dutch, 0.32 percent); and in about 1950, only 30 percent of Malays in British Malaya were literate in any language (in English, 2 percent).[47]

Mapping the Peripheries

Like administrative reforms, military modernization must be judged a mixed success. The army, which had fared badly against British invaders and Muslim raiders, expanded and modernized quite a bit in the nineteenth century, and Manila's fortifications were somewhat improved. In the first half of the century, though, the expansion of state authority into the Gran Cordilleras still depended on the religious orders, which sent missions to convert "mountain tribes" to Christianity and settled agrarian life. They had more success than in past centuries, but a British observer in the 1850s noted that "there were still at large in the island of Luzon alone, some 200,000 inhabitants, who, like the Muslims, absolutely refused to be subjected under Spanish authorities."[48]

An increased French and British presence in the southern waters also worried the Spanish, who had occupied and Christianized only the coasts of Mindanao and Sulu. In fact, the initiative was rather the other way around, with incessant Muslim "slave raids" haunting the colony. (The Sulu sultanate was a major supplier of slaves in the declining Southeast Asian maritime trade.) Spain's slow-moving warships were no match for fast-moving Muslim raiding vessels, and the efficacy of Spanish forts in protecting strategic coastal towns was uneven.

By the second half of the century, centralizing reforms and technology gave the state's coercive agencies more backbone. The military's presence on the governor-general's Council of Administration increased its influence and the colonial state's determination to make state power coterminous with state boundaries. One method of accomplishing this goal combined bureaucratic and military means—the creation of new provinces. The state began to surround the Gran Cordillera with special military provinces and to launch continuous punitive expeditions against areas that resisted its authority. The military took advantage of recurring internal rivalries within the mountain communities to weaken their opposition and was aided greatly by missionary friars who turned converted communities against defiant ones. While some new provinces represented territory the Spanish had not previously commanded, population growth also encouraged administrative subdivision for purposes of greater control. The number of provinces increased from twenty-seven in 1810 to fifty in 1859, of which thirty-one were military. In 1860, two major administrative districts were put under the authority of military governors, one in the Visayas and one in Mindanao, in order to increase central authority.[49]

In Muslim Mindanao, the acquisition of steam-powered gunboats in the 1840s gave the Spanish, like other colonial powers, an edge over unconquered polities. Over the next thirty years, the sultanates were repeatedly attacked by Spanish forces, beginning with the destruction of Sulu's major trading towns, Balangiga and Jolo, in major engagements in the late 1840s and early 1850s. As the Sulu sultanate's power fragmented, the Maguindanao sultanate went into terminal decline. Long blocked by the Spanish navy from direct international access, it had depended on Sulu as a conduit of trade. By the end of the century, the Spanish had destroyed nearly all Muslim shipping in the Sulu archipelago, in parallel development with British and Dutch domination of Malay shipping and piracy in the region. Spain finally won "capitulation" from Sulu on the question of sovereignty in 1878 (see box 4.7). Still, there was little conversion and local Muslim control of the hinterlands was not eliminated, due to Spain's inability to penetrate the interior, especially of Mindanao. The further incorporation of the "outsider" Muslims would have to await the next state incarnation.

As a complement to the army, a paramilitary police was established in 1868 to replace a variety of provincial and local militias. The Guardia Civil, with Spanish officers and locally recruited troops, had the authority to operate throughout the Philippines suppressing "banditry," rebellion, criminality, and petty civil indiscretions. Its presence and brutality in civilian settings became a major grievance against Spanish rule and "created a collective Filipino memory of military abuse that inspired a later commitment to civil supremacy."[50] The unified and relatively pacified archipelago the Spanish long envisioned had finally become a reality, but, according to Robles, "It was difficult to determine to what extent Spain realized that centralization would engender Filipino unity, which could endanger her sovereignty—particularly if conditions in the Philippines were not sufficiently improved."[51]

SOCIAL FORMATION AND STATE RESPONSE

Philippine "Societies"

The Philippine polity at the beginning of the nineteenth century was based upon the many rural communities ruled by Spanish friars with assistance by

Box 4.7. The Subjugation of Sulu

Excerpts from the Treaty of Peace and Commerce between Spain and Sulu
Signed at Sulu, 23 September 1836

Art. I. The Captain-General doth assure to the most Excellent Sultan and the Dattos of Joló . . . Peace on the part of the Spaniards, and of the Natives of all the Islands subject to the Crown of Spain, with the Tributaries in the Lands subject to the Sultan and his Dattos; and he offers the protection of his Government and Naval and Military assistance . . . against the enemies who may attack him, or in order to subject the Towns which may revolt in any of the Islands situated within the limits of the Spanish jurisdiction. . . .

   The Sultan of Joló . . . engages also to preserve peace with all the subjects of Her Catholic Majesty, and to consider as Enemies all those who may henceforward be such to the Spanish Nation, and to concur with armed forces for the wars which may arise, in the same manner as if they were Spaniards.

Art. II. . . . Joloan ships may sail and trade freely in the open Ports of Mañila and Zamboanga, and the Spanish in that of Joló. . . . Joloanos who carry a cargo of goods from those Islands, are to pay in Mañila and Zamboanga less than Foreign ships, and the Spaniards are not to pay in Joló so much as is exacted from the vessels of other Nations.

Excerpts from the Bases of Peace and Capitulation
Signed at Jolo, 22 July 1878

Art. I. We [the Sultan of Sulu] declare as beyond discussion the sovereignty of Spain over all the Archipelago of Sulu and the dependencies thereof. . . .

Art. III. Spain assumes the right to occupy such points of the Sulu Archipelago and its dependencies as she may desire. . . .

Art. VIII. We shall endeavour to put a stop to the evil doings of pirates and malefactors. . . .

Art. IX. We shall be allowed the free exercise of our religion and customs; Catholic missionaries will have the liberty to reside in and visit any point of Sulu and its dependencies. . . .

Raphael Perpetuo M. Lotilla, ed., *The Philippine National Territory: A Collection of Related Documents* (Quezon City: Institute of International Legal Studies, University of the Philippines Law Center and Foreign Service Institute, Department of Foreign Affairs, 1995), 1–2, 27–28.

indio and mestizo principalia, who collected taxes and mobilized labor for the needs of the colonial state and church. In Manila and a few other cities, Chinese and Chinese mestizos were organized into self-governing municipal corporations under the rule of a provincial governor. These communities remained segmented by language, distance, and lack of mobility. The limited nature of the state–"societies" relationship had been adequate for much of the colonial era. As long as tributes were collected, the galleon trade was profitable, and retail networks of "necessary" Chinese provisioned the cities, there was no perceived need to create a more unified society, nor for residents to be touched by more representatives of the state.

As we have seen in this chapter, however, over the course of the nineteenth century the economy was transformed and the state was reformed, albeit in fits and starts and against the bitter opposition of the religious orders. These developments had a profound effect on the composition of colonial society, as commerce, land ownership, and professional status slowly supplanted religion and ethnicity as the basis of social identity. The importance of Chinese mestizos to this process cannot be underestimated: A foreign observer in Manila described them as "rich, active and intelligent."[52] By 1876, they "comprised about 23 percent of the combined total of Malay Filipinos [indios] and mestizos."[53] These two groups intermarried, and the old structure of local government weakened as they spurned political office and moved beyond the influence of the local friar. Their rise was a major challenge to the colonial state.

Meanwhile, newer Chinese immigrants were more identifiable as outsiders and were easily associated with foreign capital. They attracted a rising indio hostility that, in combination with overseas Chinese nationalism, slowed their assimilation and intermarriage. Instead, this community turned inward, tried to "reclaim" its mestizo children, and established its own newspapers, schools, cemeteries, and hospitals. Such separateness was problematic in a society where the Chinese were so economically prominent. In addition to their traditional roles as wholesalers and retailers, they were producers of abaca and tobacco; processors of rice, sugar, and timber; urban artisans; rural laborers; and monopoly contractors.

Spaniards—a late addition to the social mix—were no longer restricted to Manila or the few garrison cities. Inevitably, they mixed with the local and Chinese population, creating another mestizo population. (Earlier Spanish mestizos in the countryside were illicit offspring of friars and were absorbed into indio communities. Many Filipino families today claim a friar on their family tree.) Confusingly, Spanish mestizos often referred to themselves as criollos, wanting to claim "pure" Spanish blood and fearing descent on the colonial social ladder. But their status would never again rise on the prestige of the old empire; they tended to be as striving as the principalia and Chinese mestizos and thus constituted competition for the ruling Spaniards.

In short, the old socioeconomic network of "Spanish" at the top and "indios" at the base with "Chinese" providing an economic link between the two was steadily displaced by a more dynamic social hierarchy.

Filipinos

The economy's new wealth was mainly land-related, and the income derived allowed the indio-mestizo principalia to expand its cultural wealth as well.

After obtaining basic education, sons were sent to Manila and often to Europe to acquire professional training and a cultural patina rivaling the peninsulares. In contrast to earlier hispanization in the rural areas, which was mediated through friars and further localized as "folk Catholicism," this urban flowering of "filipinized Hispanic culture" was "a more sophisticated version of Spanish culture than any hitherto available in the Philippines."[54] And it was available strictly on the basis of wealth, not ethnicity (or "race," the increasingly common way of expressing ethnic difference).

With wealth and higher education came a quest for social recognition. In town, elites were proud to display their prosperity, purchasing huge houses, sponsoring church activities, demanding more say in local decision making, and flaunting "European tastes" they had acquired in travel abroad. By the last decade of the century, ethnic distinctions between Chinese and Spanish mestizos and indio elites had become anachronistic and were replaced by class-, culture-, and profession-based identities. The three groups gravitated toward a common identity and found it in the evolving meaning of "Filipino," a term appropriated from Spanish criollos by those with new claims to leadership. Although small relative to the mass of rural peasantry, the new Filipino elite had a budding internal class structure. Below the *caciques* (mostly absentee landlords residing in Manila) and a middle stratum of inquilinos and merchants was an "urban wing" of professionals (doctors, lawyers, journalists, priests) and workers (accountants and clerks, factory workers and stevedores). From this urban wing emerged intellectuals who would articulate the demands of the Filipinos for social recognition and a place in society.

But the colonial state—both secular and clerical—regarded the new elites as threats, calling them "brutes laden with gold." The reforms they had introduced to cope with economic and social change had not been total failures, but were increasingly inadequate to maintain Spain's hold on the Philippines as a "colony." In fact, where reform most succeeded—as in the economy and education—it seemed only to highlight Spanish lack of leadership and dynamism. After a period of reform, the Spanish closed ranks rather than admit the new groups and retreated behind friar power.

NOTES

1. Benito J. Legarda, *After the Galleons: Foreign Trade, Economic Change, and Entrepreneurship in the Nineteenth-Century Philippines* (Quezon City: Ateneo de Manila University Press, 1999), 77–88.

2. Basco y Vargas, quoted in O. D. Corpuz, *An Economic History of the Philippines* (Quezon City: University of the Philippines Press, 1997), 91.

3. Legarda, *After the Galleons*, 82–83.

4. Luis Alonso, "Financing the Empire: The Nature of the Tax System in the Philippines, 1565–1804," *Philippine Studies* 51, no. 1 (2003): 88.

5. Legarda, *After the Galleons*, 99.

6. Edgar Wickberg, *The Chinese in Philippine Life, 1850–1898* (New Haven, Conn.: Yale University Press, 1965), 48.

7. Wickberg, *The Chinese in Philippine Life*, 47–49, 62–63, 70–71.

8. Corpuz, *Economic History*, 108.

9. Corpuz, *Economic History*, 132.

10. Legarda, *After the Galleons*, 101–45; Corpuz, *Economic History*, 109–11.

11. See Alfred W. McCoy, "A Queen Dies Slowly: The Rise and Decline of Iloilo City," 307–26, and Michael Cullinane, "The Changing Nature of the Cebu Urban Elite in the Nineteenth Century," 271–76, both in *Philippine Social History: Global Trade and Local Transformations*, ed. Alfred W. McCoy and Ed. C. de Jesus (Quezon City: Ateneo de Manila University Press, 1982).

12. Daniel F. Doeppers, "Migration to Manila: Changing Gender Representation, Migration Field, and Urban Structure," in *Population and History: The Demographic Origins of the Modern Philippines*, ed. Daniel F. Doeppers and Peter Xenos (Quezon City: Ateneo de Manila University Press, 1998), 169.

13. Doeppers, "Migration to Manila," 171.

14. Quoted in Legarda, *After the Galleons*, 100.

15. Dennis Morrow Roth, "Church Lands in the Agrarian History of the Tagalog Regions," in McCoy and Jesus, *Philippine Social History*, 131.

16. Estimates of the population under Spain's control in the Philippines. See the appendix to vol. 1 of O. D. Corpuz's *The Roots of the Filipino Nation* (Quezon City: Aklahi Foundation, 1989) for an analysis of population estimates during Spanish colonial rule.

17. Corpuz, *Economic History*, 112.

18. Joaquin Martinez de Zuniga, *Historia de las Islas Pilipinas* (1803), in Horacio de la Costa, *Readings in Philippine History: Selected Historical Texts Presented with a Commentary by H. de la Costa* (Makati City: Bookmark, 1992), 112–13.

19. Corpuz, *Economic History*, 197–98.

20. Marshall S. McLennan, "Changing Human Ecology on the Central Luzon Plain: Nueva Ecija, 1705–1939," in McCoy and Jesus, *Philippine Social History*, 70.

21. Corpuz, *Economic History*, 195.

22. Ed. C. de Jesus, "Control and Compromise in the Cagayan Valley," in McCoy and Jesus, *Philippine Social History*, 28–29; McLennan, "Changing Human Ecology," 77.

23. McCoy, "A Queen Dies Slowly," 311.

24. Legarda, *After the Galleons*, 4, 126–35.

25. Alfred W. McCoy, "The Social History of an Archipelago: Introduction," in McCoy and Jesus, *Philippine Social History*, 8.

26. Alonso, "Financing the Empire," 87.

27. Eliodoro Robles, *The Philippines in the Nineteenth Century* (Quezon City: Malaya Books, 1969), 290.

28. Robles, *Philippines in the Nineteenth Century*, 31–33.

29. Crawford Young, *The African Colonial State in Comparative Perspective* (New Haven, Conn.: Yale University Press, 1994).

30. Eric Hobsbawm, *The Age of Revolution, 1789–1848* (New York: Vintage Books, 1996), 112–13.

31. Robles, *Philippines in the Nineteenth Century*, 292.

32. Robles, *Philippines in the Nineteenth Century*, chap. 8.

33. Tomas Comyn, *Estado de las Islas Filipinas en 1810* (1820), quoted in Robles, *Philippines in the Nineteenth Century*, 111–12.

34. Robles, *Philippines in the Nineteenth Century*, 103–4, 121–22, 125–27.

35. Glenn Anthony May, "Civic Ritual and Political Reality: Municipal Elections in the Late Nineteenth Century," in *Philippine Colonial Democracy*, ed. Ruby R. Paredes (Quezon City: Ateneo de Manila University Press, 1989), 16–17.

36. Wickberg, *The Chinese in Philippine Life*, 140–41.

37. Daniel F. Doeppers and Peter Xenos, "A Demographic Frame for Philippine History," in Doeppers and Xenos, *Population and History*, 4.

38. Michael Cullinane, "Accounting for Souls: Ecclesiastical Sources for the Study of Philippine Demographic History," in Doeppers and Xenos, *Population and History*, 296.

39. Jose S. Arcilla, ed., *Kasaysayan: The Story of the Filipino People*, vol. 3, *The Spanish Conquest* (Manila: Asia Publishing Company Ltd., 1998), 71.

40. Corpuz, *Economic History*, 125.

41. Onofre D. Corpuz, *Education and Socioeconomic Change in the Philippines, 1870–1960s* (Quezon City: University of the Philippines Press, 1967), 203.

42. Arcilla, *Kasaysayan*; Corpuz, *Education*, 204.

43. Arcilla, *Kasaysayan*.

44. Peter W. Stanley, *A Nation in the Making: The Philippines and the United States, 1899–1921* (Cambridge, Mass.: Harvard University Press, 1974), 33.

45. Corpuz, *Education*, 208–9.

46. Robles, *Philippines in the Nineteenth Century*, 228.

47. David G. Marr, *Vietnamese Tradition on Trial, 1920–1945* (Berkeley: University of California Press, 1981), 34; M. C. Ricklefs, *A History of Modern Indonesia* (London: Macmillan, 1981), 152; T. N. Harper, *The End of Empire and the Making of Malaya* (Cambridge: Cambridge University Press, 1999), 277.

48. John Bowring, *A Visit to the Philippine Islands* (London: Smith, Elder and Co., 1859), 71, quoted in Robles, *Philippines in the Nineteenth Century*, 49.

49. Robles, *Philippines in the Nineteenth Century*, 187–88.

50. Alfred W. McCoy, *Closer than Brothers: Manhood at the Philippine Military Academy* (New Haven, Conn.: Yale University Press, 1999), 15.

51. Robles, *Philippines in the Nineteenth Century*, 289.

52. Corpuz, *Roots of the Filipino Nation*, 1:554.

53. Daniel F. Doeppers, "Evidence from the Grave: The Changing Social Composition of the Populations of Metropolitan Manila and Molo, Iloilo, during the Later Nineteenth Century," in Doeppers and Xenos, *Population and History*, 266.

54. Wickberg, *The Chinese in Philippine Life*, 129.

Chapter Five

Nation and States, 1872–1913

THE FINAL YEARS OF SPANISH RULE

We have seen how liberalizing the Philippine economy and attempting to centralize its administrative structure could not reverse Spain's weakening grasp on its colony. Economic growth led to domination by British capital, Chinese distribution networks, and Filipino-led export agriculture. Political reforms were undercut by lack of continuity, uneven tax burdens, and corruption. Socially, the greatest challenges to the state were an impoverished and discontented peasantry and a wealthy but disgruntled elite. The problems of the first could not be addressed without confronting the interests of the religious orders and the new elite itself. The challenge of the second might have been lessened by strategic concessions to demands we will discuss in this chapter.

The profound socioeconomic changes of the century began to find political expression in the 1870s. In this decade, the Philippines felt the mixed results of increased integration into the global marketplace. An economy tied to global trade was vulnerable to trade fluctuations, and during the long global recession of the 1870s and 1880s, declining exports could not always compensate for rising import costs—the Philippines' first modern trade deficit.

The combination of demographic change, rural poverty, new wealth, and the failure (on balance) of liberal reform produced a seminal moment in 1872. An indio mutiny in the Cavite naval arsenal near Manila that flared briefly and was contained quickly nevertheless provided a pretext for the arrest, conviction, and public execution of three Filipino (one criollo and two mestizo) priests: Fathers José Burgos, Jacinto Zamora, and Mariano Gomez. Burgos had written critically about the government, but none of the three was involved in the uprising. They were, however, representative of social groups exerting mounting pressure on peninsulare privilege, especially within the country's most powerful institution.

Conflict within the Church

In the 1770s, a royal decree had ordered the secularization of Philippine parishes. This meant the transfer of parish posts from friars of the religious orders to "secular clergy" of the dioceses (territories under the jurisdiction of bishops, from which the religious orders were autonomous). The lack of Spanish secular clergy in the years after the conquest had given the missionary orders control of the parishes. But by the late eighteenth century, the Jesuits had left the Philippines, and diocesan leaders saw an opportunity to further reduce the influence of the orders by transferring their vacated local parishes to secular jurisdiction. Newly opened seminaries welcomed the sons of indio and mestizo families into the secular priesthood, and liberal governors also attacked friar abuses directly.[1] O. D. Corpuz relates one instance:

> An observer sent from Spain to Filipinas reported in 1842 that "during the last years" officials newly arrived in Manila issued anti-friar measures. One of these forbade the friars' practice of whipping their parishioners for not religiously observing church requirements. The friars petitioned to be allowed to continue the practice, explaining that the lashing would be done in front of the church door. The governor-general not only dismissed the petition but also circulated his decision among the natives. This caused "the greatest grief to the parish priests."[2]

The secularization of the parishes was stalled several times during the nineteenth century by political reaction in Spain, but not before principalia families began to gravitate toward the church for careers more rewarding than service as a cabeza and gobernadorcillo. The priesthood was influential both morally and politically, and secular Filipino priests agitated for appointment to the parishes. Tensions heightened as the bishops renewed their insistence on "visitation" to inspect the state of religious education, always resisted by parish friars but not secular priests.

In the ensuing battle, the seculars were used as pawns, assigned by the bishops to subordinate posts in order-controlled parishes where they became targets of friar anger. Spaniards were accustomed to treating indios and mestizos as inferiors, regarding them as spiritually and intellectually deficient. By the late nineteenth century, however, Filipino priests were among the most intellectually able men of the colony, while Spanish friars in the Philippines were mainly poor provincials of limited education and experience. Working as subordinates to them gave the Filipinos an opportunity to observe closely, and as a result, "the friars ceased to be the representatives of a ruling race and were seen as they were—men with faults and errors."[3]

Never had the religious orders been so besieged. To friars' eyes, liberal government undermined the foundations of Spanish power in the Philippines—indio impiety increased, attendance at Mass declined, subversive literature circulated, and fraternization with non-Spanish foreigners encouraged heretical views. To the secular clergy, liberal policies merely leveled the playing field and gave them evidence to make their own accusations. Filipino priests were incensed by the orders' concern with profits at the expense of spiritual responsibilities—a questioning of the "moral qualifications of the regime itself." Airing their views with their families and parishioners marked them as culprits behind the increasing "anti-Spanish" sentiment in the country. The tide turned against them as the orders wrested back control of many secular parishes. The Jesuits returned to the Philippines in 1859 and were followed by several new orders, which claimed parishes among the growing population.[4] By 1898, the total Catholic population was about 6.5 million, but less than one million were under the pastoral care of secular Filipino priests.[5]

This confrontation was the context for the executions of Gomez, Burgos, and Zamora. Striking out with self-defeating rage, conservative officials also persecuted elite families who had supported Spain's Glorious Revolution in the 1860s. Hundreds were detained and deported to the Visayas and Mindanao, the Marianas Islands (also under the Spanish flag), and Spain. But instead of instilling fear, the executions in particular only galvanized elite opposition under the slowly broadening identity of "Filipino." Fathers Gomez, Burgos, and Zamora became martyrs, and their deaths made the push for social and political change in the colony irresistible.

Struggle against Church and State

Tensions rose simultaneously in other spheres where the interests of the elite and friars met. The higher value of land planted in commercial crops prompted the religious orders to raise land rents and leasehold fees, hurting the income of inquilinos who leased and sublet the estates. Already grumbling about taxes, church contributions, and corruption, they saw the increase as another sign of Spanish parasitism. Conflict over parishes and rents spilled over into social tension when friars derided the talents and intellect of Filipinos.

The principal site of social conflict was higher education, where the orders clung to reactionary curricula and resisted making the Spanish language intrinsic to Philippine learning. From this conflict—and the consequent outflow to Europe for higher education—emerged a group of self-proclaimed *ilustra-*

Figure 5.1. Garroting: The usual method of public execution in the Spanish Philippines (courtesy of the Philippine National Historical Institute)

dos (enlightened ones). The most valuable education they got abroad was not in universities, however, but in seeing the relative backwardness of Spain in relation to its European peers. This added self-confidence to the ilustrados' public stance. Their most illustrious member described it as a class "whose number is gradually increasing, is in constant communication with the rest of the Islands, and if today, it constitutes only the brains of the country, in a few years, it will constitute its whole nervous system and will manifest its existence in all the acts of the country."[6]

Frustration with the Catholic Church in the Philippines and Spain led many ilustrados to abandon it for the anticlerical Freemasons, an international fraternal order that originated in Europe and first appeared in the Philippines in the 1880s. One attraction of Masonry was that its lodges (local branches) did not practice racial discrimination. Another was its tradition of secrecy, so well suited to the need to develop ideas outside the hearing of friars. In Masonry they found a structure to help forge a new "life of association; in the midst of that brotherhood we have communicated to one another our impressions, our thoughts, our aspirations, and we have made ourselves apt to unite our desires and acts."[7] (See box 5.1.)

The ilustrado effort to shape the future was embodied in the Propaganda Movement waged in Manila and Europe by the organization La Solidaridad.

Box 5.1.   The Role of Masonic Lodges in the Reform Movement

". . . to study problems of political organization of our country, of economic, of military organization, etc., and especially the better development of the new municipal governments. For Masonry is the brain, called on to think out what people are to do. Suppose Spain should grant us tomorrow the intervention which we have been asking for in the government of the State? What positive and concrete solutions do we have to put into practice? What reforms have we thought out to improve the situation of the country, to develop its sources of wealth, etc., etc.? This is what I would like the lodges to be thinking about; let each one speak out his ideas, let them give conferences on the subjects they have competence in: the businessman on business, the farmer on farming, the military man on military affairs, etc. etc., and that variety of studies will be fruitful for all. Thus will Masonry be useful."

—Marcelo del Pilar, quoted in John N. Schumacher, *The Propaganda Movement,*
1880–1895: The Creators of a Filipino Consciousness, The Makers of Revolution
(Quezon City: Ateneo de Manila University Press, 1997), 180

The movement wrote and lobbied in Spain about the poor condition of the colony and the need for reform. The Propagandist program was comprehensive: "administrative reform, eradication of corruption in the government, recognition of Filipino rights as loyal Spaniards, extension of Spanish laws to the Philippines, curtailment of the excessive power of the friars in the life of the country, and assertion of the dignity of the Filipino." Graciano Lopez-Jaena, a boisterous orator, called for direct taxation to replace tribute and forced labor.[8] This was a call for Filipino self-government as an integral part of Spain, with full representation in the Spanish Cortes. Pedro Sanciangco, one of the first Propagandists, declared:

> If, then, the Philippines is considered part of the Spanish nation and is therefore a Spanish province and not a tributary colony; if her sons are born Spanish just as are those of the Peninsula; if, finally, *recognizing in the peninsulars the rights of citizenship, one must equally recognize it in the Filipinos*; no tribute in the proper sense of the word can be imposed on them, but a tax proportioned to their resources, larger or smaller in amount, according to the larger or smaller services which the State renders them for the security of their persons and interests.[9]

A central leader of the Propagandists was Marcelo del Pilar; he was born in Malolos, Bulacan province, an important commercial town in the network of markets connected by roads and bridges to Manila. Growing rice and sugarcane, Malolos had three steam-powered sugar mills by the late 1880s; processed coconut oil, rice, indigo, and fish; and manufactured baskets, cloth, and candles. By the end of the century, with a population of 13,250, Malolos was an exemplar of export-oriented development. Wealth had made it "a highly urbanized town with its center now, ironically, in the very midst of the Pariancillo [small parián], the place for 'outsiders.'"[10] Malolos was exemplary in another way—as a hub of principalia political and antifriar activity.

Del Pilar studied law at the Universidad de Santo Tomas until 1870, when he withdrew after quarreling with a friar over the fee for a baptism at which he stood as godfather. Del Pilar went back to the university in 1878 and received his licentiate in law in 1880. Soon he joined the staff of the Malolos *Diariong Tagalog* (Tagalog newspaper), the first bilingual newspaper in the Philippines, as editor of the Tagalog section. After the paper folded, del Pilar devoted himself to practicing law and "spreading nationalist and antifriar ideas, both in Manila among the students and in the towns of Bulacan wherever he could gather a crowd, be it a barrio baptismal party or a local cockpit."[11]

In the early 1880s, the Malolos activists outmaneuvered the friars to elect their candidate as gobernadorcillo. The friars tried to enlist government support in 1885 when the Bulacan principalia refused to reconcile their tax list with the parish list, but del Pilar's liberal Spanish allies—the provincial governor and some officers in the Guardia Civil—allowed the antifriar campaign to continue. The climate changed, however, in 1887–1888, when the colony's governor-general was replaced by the conservative Valeriano Weyler, who backed the church, removed liberal Spanish officials, and moved against the antifriar principalia. As one of the most well known, del Pilar was declared "filibustero y anti-español" (subversive and anti-Spanish), and under threat of arrest, he left the country for Spain.[12] In the more repressive conditions that followed, the reform movement pressed on in other ways. When the governor-general visited Malolos, a group of women belonging to the town's "four big mestizo-sangley clans" petitioned Weyler for permission to open a night school to learn Spanish. Their demand drew the attention of Propagandists, who wrote extensively about them and their campaign in Europe. These wealthy "Women of Malolos" were at the center of the town's activism for years, secretly hosting reform meetings and publicly spurning church attendance.[13]

The most famous Propagandist was José Rizal—highly accomplished, well traveled (to Spain, Germany, France, Japan, and America, among other places), and best known for writing two incomparable novels expressing the absurdities of life in the colony (see box 4.6 for an excerpt). As a university student, Rizal witnessed the religious authorities' dogged resistance to modernization. His mestizo family experienced direct conflict with the state and religious bureaucracy when his brother Paciano, a student of Burgos, was caught up in the post–Cavite Mutiny reaction. Afterward, while Rizal was traveling and writing in Europe, the people of his hometown became embroiled in a land dispute that led to the deportation of Paciano and two brothers-in-law and the imprisonment of his mother for two years. (See box 5.2.)

Box 5.2. José Rizal, the First Filipino

"The central figure in the revolutionary generation was José Rizal, poet, novelist, oph-
thalmologist, historian, doctor, polemical essayist, moralist, and political dreamer. He
was born in 1861 into a well-to-do family of mixed Chinese, Japanese, Spanish, and
Tagalog descent; five years after Freud, four years after Conrad, one year after Chekov,
the same year as Tagore, three years before Max Weber, five before Sun Yat-sen,
eight before Gandhi, and nine before Lenin. Thirty-five years later he was arrested on
false charges of inciting Andres Bonifacio's uprising of August 1896, and executed
by a firing squad composed of native soldiers led by Spanish officers. . . . At the time
of Rizal's death, Lenin had just been sentenced to exile in Siberia, Sun Yat-sen had
begun organizing for Chinese nationalism outside China, and Gandhi was conducting
his early experiments in anticolonial resistance in South Africa.

"Rizal had the best education then available in the colony, provided exclusively by
the religious Orders, notably the Dominicans and Jesuits. It was an education that he
later satirized mercilessly, but it gave him a command of Latin (and some Hebrew),
a solid knowledge of classical antiquity, and an introduction to western philosophy
and even to medical science. It is . . . vertiginous to compare what benighted Spain
offered with what the enlightened, advanced imperial powers provided in the same
Southeast Asian region: no real universities in French Indochina, the Dutch East
Indies, or British Malaya and Singapore till after World War II. From very early on,
Rizal exhibited remarkable literary abilities. At the age of nineteen he entered an
open literary competition, and won first prize, defeating Spanish rivals writing in
their native tongue."

—Benedict Anderson, "The First Filipino," in *The Spectre of Comparison:
Nationalism, Southeast Asia, and the World* (London: Verso, 1998), 227–29

Rizal's writings, particularly his novels *Noli Me Tangere* (Touch Me Not)
and *El Filibusterismo* (The Subversive), went beyond simply detailing the
travails of his own class and became a general indictment of colonial society.
They put into words—and the minds of his readers—a vision of the soon-to-
arise Filipino nation. Written in Spanish, published in Germany, smuggled
into the Philippines, translated and circulated clandestinely, *Noli Me Tangere*
was the first of its kind in Asia—an anticolonial novel that imagined a new
social entity. A sense of Rizal's accomplishment is conveyed by Benedict
Anderson:

> The two most astonishing features of *Noli Me Tangere* are its scale and its style.
> Its characters come from every stratum of late colonial society. . . . Its pages
> are crowded with Dominicans, shady lawyers, abused acolytes, corrupt police-
> men, Jesuits, small-town caciques, mestiza schoolgirls, ignorant peninsular
> carpetbaggers, hired thugs, despairing intellectuals, social-climbing *dévotes*,
> dishonest journalists, actresses, nuns, gravediggers, artisans, gamblers, peas-
> ants, market-women, and so on. . . . Yet the geographical space of the novel
> is strictly confined to the immediate environs of the colonial capital, Manila.

The Spain from which so many of the characters have at one time or another arrived is always off stage. This restriction made it clear to Rizal's first readers that "The Philippines" was a society in itself, even though those who lived in it had as yet no common name. That he was the first to imagine this social whole explains why he is remembered today as the First Filipino.[14]

For his new articulation of the Philippines, Rizal was declared an enemy of the state and the church. But his novels and essays—del Pilar's translation of "The Love of Country," for example—made it possible for fellow Propagandists and organic intellectuals of the urban classes to imagine themselves "subjects of history"—people with a past to learn from, a present to act in, and a future to shape. Rizal's literary, political, and historical writings provided intellectual and ideological validation for the new classes to intervene in political life—to make history.

Despite Rizal's growing fame in the Philippines and in Europe, the Propaganda Movement was unable to sustain itself. Differences over the aims of the movement and its inability to effect change in Madrid led Rizal away from La Solidaridad. The reform movement was thereafter plagued by financial difficulties, defections, and propaganda counterattacks by opponents in Spain. Because the authorities in Madrid ignored ilustrado recommendations, sympathizers in the Philippines also withdrew support. The deaths of both del Pilar and his collaborator Lopez-Jaena in 1896 closed the chapter on the reform movement.[15]

A more radical path was shortly initiated, but the reformists had articulated and circulated the foundational ideas of the dominant stream of Filipino nationalism. Later asked why the Filipinos rose against Spain, Apolinario Mabini explained:

> The reason can be condensed into the following: the popular desire to have a government which will assure the Filipinos the freedom of thought, conscience, and association; the right to life, the inviolability of the home and the freedom of communication; a popular assembly that will make the laws of the country and decide the kinds of taxation; equality of opportunity to hold public offices and equality in the share of public benefits; respect for law and property; and the progressive development of the country by modern methods.[16]

THE PHILIPPINE REVOLUTION AND THE FIRST REPUBLIC

The Katipunan

Although written to appeal to Spain, Propagandist writing was enthusiastically read and reinterpreted by unintended audiences—self-made intellectuals and struggling lower-class students in Manila, peasant leaders disenchanted with friar Catholicism, and minor elites in the provinces. These groups were inspired by the ilustrados but found the reformism of the Propaganda Movement inadequate. So when Rizal returned to Manila in 1892 and established La Liga Filipina to pursue reform at home, urban workers and students joined the organization and formed a militant wing. Rizal was subsequently arrested and sent into exile in Dapitan, in northern Mindanao. His exile stopped La Liga in its tracks, but the radical wing, led by Andres Bonifacio, went on to form the Kataastaasan Kagalang-galang na Katipunan ng mga Anak ng Bayan (Highest and Most Honorable Society of the Sons of the Country)—Katipunan for short.

The Katipunan (kah-tee-poo-nahn) was a secret society committed to overthrowing Spanish rule. In the change from Rizal's Spanish to Bonifacio's Tagalog, we can see the movement shift from elite reformism to lower-class radicalism. Bonifacio was born to poor parents in Tondo, in metropolitan Manila, received only primary schooling, and was orphaned and left responsible for five younger siblings as a young man. He supported his family as a craftsman (making canes, paper fans, and business posters), as a clerk-messenger, and as a commercial agent. He had real drive and in his spare moments taught himself Spanish, perfected his native Tagalog, and acted in a drama club. He read about the French Revolution, the lives of American presidents, and of course, the works of Rizal, some of which he translated into Tagalog. We should not imagine a complete intellectual divide, therefore, between elite ilustrados and this young urban worker. Bonifacio was also anti-friar and a Mason, for example, and he imported Masonic rituals into the Katipunan, combining the blood compacts familiar to Filipinos with the rhetoric of independence.[17]

The Katipunan was unable to remain underground for long. Spanish knowledge of its existence prompted Bonifacio to launch a preemptive rebellion in the working-class districts of Manila in 1896. The uprising spread to nearby provinces and emboldened communities to form their own chapters of the Katipunan. Tenants and smallholders rallied to the revolution in reaction to persistent friar abuse and economic hardship. If Rizal's class suffered direct persecution and the frustration of blocked advancement, it was precisely because it was benefiting from the new economy. The growing peasantry was taking the brunt of the country's economic transformation, and the Katipunan tapped its social resentments.[18]

Although their interests did not always coincide, the peasantry also "owned" Rizal and interpreted his ideas and the man himself through a peasant worldview heavily infused with a folk interpretation of Spanish Catholicism. When Rizal was accused of instigating the Katipunan revolt and was executed by firing squad in late 1896, he attained a popular status akin to Jesus Christ. Thereafter, his life was frequently integrated into local tellings of the *pasyon*—biblical stories including the life, death, and resurrection of Christ. The ideas of freedom (*kalayaan*) and nation (*bayan*) associated with Rizal were redefined to fit the millenarian peasant quest for salvation and heaven on earth. In this nationalism, Spanish rule was understood as the oppression of a Pharisee-like clergy and the corruption of a Roman-like officialdom; resistance was an attempt to overcome the darkness of false religion, the obstacle to the nation.[19] (See box 5.3.) Rizal himself, a Mason and writer in the Enlightenment tradition, would be elevated into the Trinity of the Father, Son, and Holy Spirit by Rizalista cults throughout the country.[20]

The charismatic Bonifacio was able to combine and embody the ideas of the elite and the aspirations of the masses. Influenced by Rizal, he also articulated the millenarian themes of the peasantry through his facility with poetic Tagalog. The popular imagination was inspired by "religious tracts and metrical romances," of which the most popular was the pasyon, with

---

Box 5.3. The Pasyon

"[The] masses' experience of Holy Week fundamentally shaped the style of peasant brotherhoods and uprisings during the Spanish and early American periods. Instead of glorifying the ancient rituals of the *babaylanes* (native priests) as evocative of the true native spirit, the fact has to be accepted that the majority of lowland Filipinos were converted to Spanish Catholicism. But like other regions of Southeast Asia which 'domesticated' Hindu, Buddhist, Confucian and Islamic influences, the Philippines, despite the fact that Catholicism was more often than not imposed on it by Spanish missionaries, creatively evolved its own brand of folk Christianity from which was drawn much of the language of anticolonialism in the late nineteenth century. The various rituals of Holy Week, particularly the reading and dramatization of the story of Jesus Christ, had in fact two quite contradictory functions in society. First . . . they were used by the Spanish colonizers to inculcate among the *Indios* loyalty to Spain and Church; moreover, they encouraged resignation to things as they were and instilled preoccupation with morality and the afterlife rather than with conditions in this world. The second function, which probably was not intended by the missionaries, was to provide lowland Philippine society with a language for articulating its own values, ideals, and even hopes of liberation. After the destruction or decline of native epic traditions in the sixteenth and seventeenth centuries, Filipinos nevertheless continued to maintain a coherent image of the world and their place in it through their familiarity with the *pasyon*, an epic that appears to be alien in content, but upon closer examination in a historical context, reveals the vitality of the Filipino mind."

—Reynaldo Clemeña Ileto, *Pasyon and Revolution:*
Popular Movements in the Philippines, 1840–1910
(Quezon City: Ateneo de Manila University Press, 1979), 11–12

which Bonifacio closely identified. According to historian Reynaldo Ileto, long after his death he continued to be a symbol of the independence movement, because he understood "the world of awit [sung] poetry."[21]

Spanish military forces easily routed the revolutionaries. Yet outside Manila one community after another declared independence, and military victories could not undo what the Katipunan had done—transform political conditions despite military defeat. But Bonifacio himself became open to challenge. At a meeting in Cavite province, where he had retreated, the local elite denigrated his leadership ability and lack of education and engineered his ouster as supremo in favor of Emilio Aguinaldo. Bonifacio, who refused to acknowledge Aguinaldo's leadership, was arrested on charges of undermining the revolution and secretly executed. Until his own death in 1945, Aguinaldo denied a role in this miscarriage of justice, but with Bonifacio's death, leadership of the revolution passed to him.[22] The change at the top more broadly signaled the transfer of power from lower-class leaders to provincial elites and ilustrados. The latter joined the ongoing revolution for reasons ranging from sincere belief in political change to the strategic attempt to protect their wealth.[23] Undeniably, they brought ability to the revolution— Aguinaldo was a skillful general—but their fear of Bonifacio represented a wider gap in interests and ideals within the nation. (See box 5.4.)

Aguinaldo's military could not stop the Spanish counteroffensive and his revolutionary forces were pushed toward the mountains. But most of Spain's military was tied up fighting revolutionaries in Cuba, so the government pursued a truce. With war and negotiation ongoing, Aguinaldo declared the "Biak-na-Bato Republic" on November 1, 1897. The new republic was to

---

Box 5.4. Two Military Ideals

"As a lower-class radical, Bonifacio had a populist ideal of the army as a brotherhood of patriots that made decisions democratically. When the fighting began, he assembled three hundred troops at a camp near Manila and told them to elect a commanding officer and deputy. After a voice vote, Bonifacio nodded his approval and the troops shouted in unison, 'Long live the newly elected generals!'

"By contrast, his rival, General Aguinaldo, was inspired by the Spanish ideal of the heroic commander to mobilize an army of gentry officers and peasant conscripts. In the revolution's first weeks, he promised local landholders that anyone who 'offered his services together with a hundred or so of his tenants . . . would be appointed a lieutenant or captain.' . . . For these landlord officers, the revolution was a chance for elite males to recover the authority denied them under Spain and its suffocating, emasculating rule."

—Alfred W. McCoy, *Closer than Brothers: Manhood at the Philippine Military Academy* (New Haven, Conn.: Yale University Press, 1999), 15–16

have a constitution (borrowed from Cuba), supreme council, and centralized government, but instead, the revolutionary leadership accepted a truce and exile in Hong Kong. Whether this retreat was tactical or opportunistic is still debated, but it did not end the resistance. More and more communities rallied to the cause of independence—not only in the Tagalog provinces but also in northern Luzon (excluding the Cordilleras), southern Luzon, the Visayas, and northern Mindanao—and military clashes continued.[24]

The Malolos Republic

On February 15, 1898, the United States declared war on Spain, and the Philippine Revolution became embroiled in the Spanish–American War. Aguinaldo returned to the Philippines with U.S. assistance to reclaim leadership of the revolution, and the U.S. Pacific Fleet soon destroyed the Spanish defenses of Manila. When Spain surrendered to the United States on August 13, neither combatant recognized the legitimacy of the Filipino revolutionaries who had declared independence on June 12. Given their disparate identities and interests—U.S. power rising in an imperialist world and the Philippines staging the first anticolonial revolution in Asia—the "anti-Spanish alliance" between Americans and Filipinos could not last long. In the Treaty of Paris signed in December 1898, the United States "purchased" the colony from Spain for $20 million and the Philippines came under a second colonial power.

U.S. colonization was quite different from Spain's long-ago conquest. "The Philippines" had achieved a measure of corporeality beyond mere geographic description. It existed as a state—despite institutional weakness and less-than-total territorial coverage, the state had shaped society over the centuries in ways ranging from religion, gender norms, and family naming to the spatial definition of civic life and economic livelihood. It also existed as a nation—one that tried to speak to the colonial state through the reform movement but ultimately rejected it in a radical revolution of self-definition. Filipino reaction to the new colonizers was therefore not a continuation of the revolution against Spain. It was the reaction of an emerging nation-state in defense of its imagined community. On January 23, 1899, this community was realized in the Constitutional Republic of the Philippines, commonly called the Malolos Republic, after its capital. Within a month, the republic was at war with the United States. (See box 5.5.)

In retrospect, we can see little chance of Filipino military success once the United States determined to stay in the Philippines. The war is important, however, because it initiated Filipino nationhood and was the context for the revolutionaries to articulate the powers and obligations of the state

Box 5.5. The Malolos Republic

President Emilio Aguinaldo's Proclamation of the Constitutional Republic of the Philippines
January 23, 1899

"Great is this day, glorious this date, and forever memorable this moment in which our beloved people is raised to the apotheosis of Independence. Hereafter, January 23 will be in the Philippines a national holiday, as July 4 is to the American nation; and, as in the past century God helped a weak America when she fought against powerful Albion for the conquest of her liberty and independence, so to-day He will help us also in an identical enterprise for the manifestations of divine justice are immutably the same in rectitude and wisdom."

Excerpts from the Manifesto of President Emilio Aguinaldo Declaring War against the United States
February 5, 1899

"In my edict dated yesterday, I gave public notice of the opening of hostilities between the Filipino and the American forces of occupation in Manila, provoked by the latter in an unexpected and unjust manner. . . .

"I know that war is always productive of great losses. I know that the Filipino people, not yet fully recuperated from sacrifices in the past, are not in the best condition to bear such losses. But I know also from experience how bitter is slavery, and from experience I feel that we should sacrifice our all for the sake of our national honor and integrity so unjustly attacked.

"I have done everything possible to avoid armed conflict, in the hope of securing our independence through peaceful means and without entailing the costliest sacrifice. But all my attempts have proved vain in the face of the unmeasured pride of the American Government and its representatives in these Islands, who have insisted in considering me a rebel because I defend the sacred interests of my country, and I refuse to be a party to their foul intentions.

"Campaigns in the past must have convinced you that a people is always strong when it wills to be strong; without arms we have driven away from our beloved land the old conquerors, and without arms we can repulse the alien invasion, if we so purpose. Providence always has strength and instant aid in readiness for the defense of the weak, that they not be annihilated by the strong, and that they may share the justice and the progress of humanity.

"Do not be discouraged; we have watered our independence with the blood of your martyrs; what blood will be shed in the future will serve to make it blossom anew and become sweeter. Nature is never prodigal of generous sacrifices.

"But you should remember that in order that our efforts may not be in vain, that our counsels may be heard, and our hopes realized, it is indispensable that we harmonize our acts with the principles of right and justice, by learning to triumph over our enemies and yet to still our evil passions."

Quoted in Teodoro M. Kalaw, *The Philippine Revolution* (Kawilihan: Jorge B. Vargas Filipiniana Foundation, 1969), 146, 166–67.

they struggled to establish. The newly drafted Malolos Constitution provided for a representative form of government, a detailed Bill of Rights,
the separation of church and state, and the dominance of a single-chamber
legislative branch over the executive and judiciary. These features, argues
historian Cesar Majul, "reflect the aspirations of Filipinos based on their
past experiences with oppression from a colonial government."[25] But they
also reflect the attempt of that colonial state during the nineteenth century
to check executive power through the separation of functions. The revolutionary Philippine government inherited these conflicting goals—protection
against abuse by power-holders versus centralized, effective governance.
Their dilemma was framed by war, meditated by politics, and filtered
through the emerging class structure of a nation born with competing internal interests.

The most important protection against abuse of power was the guarantee
of rule of law, applied from the largest landholder to the smallest peasant.
Yet the constitution's articles on property rights, consistent with nineteenth-
century liberalism, were designed to protect what was owned after a century
of land accumulation, not what the dispossessed might claim by moral right.
We should note, too, that legislative preeminence was not a democratic ges-
ture. While the constitution did not specify voting rights, the June Decrees
of the revolutionary government limited the franchise to men of high social
standing and education.[26] Felipe Calderon, whose constitutional draft was adopted by the Revolutionary Congress, later explained single-chamber legislative supremacy as a defense against tyranny by an insurgent army consisting
of "the most ignorant classes."

> Being fully convinced, therefore, that in case of obtaining our independence, we
> were for a long time to have a really oligarchic republic in which the military el-
> ement, which was ignorant in almost its entirety, would predominate, I preferred
> to see that oligarchy neutralized by the oligarchy of intelligence, seeing that the
> Congress would be composed of the most intelligent elements of the nation.[27]

Behind this ilustrado rhetoric lies the reality of social stratification and the
fact that many members of Congress had not been among the antifriar principalia, had initially fought with the Spanish against the Katipuñeros, and were
already considering conciliatory approaches to the Americans. For these conservative members, even General, then President, Aguinaldo, a rather minor
elite, was suspect.

But it is also fair to consider the international context, in which nineteenth-
century liberalism was yielding only grudgingly to popular democracy. Britain's franchise of 29 percent of the adult male population (after the Reform

Bill of 1883) was offset by a hereditary upper house. Meiji Japan introduced representation in 1890 that was similarly restricted by property and education. France, Germany, and the United States had ostensibly universal male suffrage, but lower-class and/or racial minority voting was minimized through district gerrymandering, open balloting, and outright intimidation.[28] Despite its obvious limitations, it is well to remember that the Philippines established the first republic in Asia.

Aguinaldo's ilustrado cabinet leader and adviser Apolinario Mabini opposed legislative power over the executive. He argued that the conduct of the war demanded a strong president, even a "politico-military dictator." The Congress rejected Mabini's argument and the contending factions agreed provisionally on a separation of powers and a Bill of Rights. Mabini then proposed amendments to give the president various "emergency" powers to legislate when Congress was not in session, to arrest members who acted against the state, to veto bills approved by even two-thirds of the legislature, and to dissolve Congress in the event of disagreement between the Congress and cabinet. Not surprisingly, a congressional committee headed by Calderon rejected these amendments and called for Mabini's resignation, which shortly followed. Interestingly, the grounds for rejection was that Congress's power was more representative than that of the presidency.[29] This debate remained unresolved, but it prefigured future contests over the most effective way to govern Philippine society, especially at times of crisis when the state was battered by rebellion or imminent invasion.

The debate between executive and legislative dominance also had a dimension of central state versus local power. While the nature of the presidency beyond the revolutionary period remained unclear, the national legislature would represent the interests of the provinces, or those who held power in the provinces. In this dimension, it mirrored political battles in American domestic politics. At the turn of the century in the United States, the state-based, Congress-centered political parties engaged in institutional and electoral combat with the Progressive Movement, whose supporters advocated the power of the federal government over the states. The political parties opposed strengthening the federal government on the grounds of "states' rights" and autonomy; Progressives viewed "sectionalism" and "machine politics" as hampering the implementation of electoral reform and the professionalization of the national military and bureaucracy.[30] This battle, too, ended in a draw, with signs of a "national state" emerging as America embarked on its imperial adventure, but the power of Congress to restrain it still dominant.[31] Parallels would continue in the course of Philippine state formation under the United States.

The Philippine–American War

The United States joined the ranks of colonial powers in Asia with support from American expansionists (including Progressives) and Protestant missionaries, but over the objections of domestic tobacco and sugar producers. Strategic interests proved most decisive in the age of Alfred Thayer Mahan's treatise on the necessity of naval power. The United States was pursuing an "Open Door" policy in China, and the possession of coaling stations was imperative to a would-be Pacific power. Yet imperialism was difficult to square with the country's republican tradition, as the noisy Anti-Imperialist League kept reminding Americans. Finally, U.S. leaders had to contend with the likes of Mabini and other ilustrados, despite the prevailing lens of racism that tended to see Filipinos as "uncivilized" or "savage." (See box 5.6.) This difficult reality compelled the new colonizers to demonstrate that their rule would be better than Spain's or that of any other European power. The result was President William McKinley's policy of "benevolent assimilation"—the American promise to train Filipinos in democratic governance until they were "ready" to govern themselves. But the first order of business was to achieve control over the country.

The Philippine–American War has been described as the United States' first Vietnam War because of its brutality and severity.[32] Historians have cited conflicting figures, but according to the Philippine–American War Centennial Initiative (PAWCI), an organization dedicated to compiling information on the conflict, roughly twenty-two thousand Philippine soldiers and half a million civilians were killed between 1899 and 1902 in Luzon and the Visayan Islands, while one hundred thousand Muslims were killed in Mindanao.[33] The war devastated the Philippines in several ways, and bullets were not the cause of most deaths. Provinces already weakened from famine during the war against Spain were less able to withstand the hardship of a second war.[34] Disease claimed hundreds of thousands of lives; in 1902 alone, a cholera epidemic killed 137,505.[35] While the determined but poorly organized Filipino forces under President Aguinaldo were defeated by superior American military arms, the Filipino people's commitment to national independence was slowly drained by disease and hunger.[36]

To this was added the breakdown of the revolutionary leadership. Once provincial elites understood that the United States was offering them the opportunity to run a state free from friar control—all that many had asked of Spain—there was little to hold them to the goal of independence. President McKinley dispatched a Philippine Commission to Manila in 1900 to meet with educated Filipinos and determine a form of government for the colony. Many "men of substance" testified before the committee on the need for

---

Box 5.6.   Apolinario Mabini Debates William Howard Taft

**Apolinario Mabini's account of his meeting with the
Philippine Commission headed by William Howard Taft on August 1, 1900**

"When the meeting began I said: I have been a prisoner since last December [1899] and I shall not be set free unless I swear allegiance to American sovereignty. The word 'allegiance' in international law has no precise and exact definition. . . . My efforts in behalf of my country have no other object than the institution of an enduring guarantee for the rights and prerogatives of the Filipinos; if, therefore, American sovereignty offers, more or less, the same guarantee as would be offered by a government of our own, I shall have no hesitation to swear allegiance for the sake of peace. I ended saying that I asked for the conference in order to know in what degree American sovereignty would limit what naturally belongs to the Filipino people.

"After listening to the remarks of his companions, Mr. Taft replied: 'American sovereignty has no purpose other than to institute for the Filipinos a good government; the sovereignty which the United States of America will impose is the same as that which Russia and Turkey would impose, if they were to occupy the Philippines, only with the difference that the exercise of that sovereignty will be in consonance with the spirit of the Constitution of the United States. Inspired by that Constitution, the Commission would attempt to establish in the Philippine Islands a popular government, patterned after that which was recently adopted for Porto Rico.'

"To this I replied that the principles upon which the American Constitution rests declare that sovereignty belongs to the nations by natural right; that the American Government, in not remaining contented with limiting the sovereignty of the Filipino people, but annulling it completely, commits an injustice which, sooner or later, will demand retribution; that there can be no popular government when the people are denied real and effective participation in the organization and administration of that government.

"They rejoined, saying that they were not authorized to discuss abstract questions, for they had orders to impose their opinions even through the use of force, after hearing the opinions of the Filipinos. I remarked, therefore, that I presumed the conference terminated as I considered it idle to discuss with force and to express my opinions to one who refuses to listen to the voice of reason.

"Mr. Taft asked me if I would not help them in the study of taxes which they might impose on the people; to which I replied that, considering unjust all taxes imposed without the intervention of those who would have to pay them, I could not help in that study without the representation and mandate of the people."

Quoted in Teodoro M. Kalaw, *The Philippine Revolution* (Kawilihan: Jorge B. Vargas Filipiniana Foundation, 1969), 245–46

"American sovereignty in this country for the good of these ignorant and uncivilized people."[37] This first group of collaborators soon formed a political party that positioned itself as pragmatically nationalist (discussed below).

Emilio Aguinaldo was captured in March 1901, turning the tide against the revolutionaries. Newly inaugurated president Theodore Roosevelt proclaimed the end of the "Philippine insurrection" in July 1902, and although sporadic guerrilla resistance persisted, it was clear that America would stay in the archipelago. By the middle of the decade, the United States was able to cut its forces from 108,800 to 72,000, and by the end of the decade to 13,000. This reduction was due in part to pressure from the U.S. Congress, which was suspicious of maintaining a large standing army, and in part to the success of American-officered Filipino troops, the Philippine Scouts, in counterguerrilla operations. Warfare finally subsided after 1906, and the Philippine Constabulary (discussed below) assumed most "police" functions from the U.S. Army.[38]

THE EARLY YEARS OF AMERICAN RULE

State Building

While still debating whether tutelary government would culminate in autonomy or independence,[39] the new governors of the Philippines continued the rationalization and strengthening of the colonial state begun by the Spanish. They particularly focused on increasing capacity and infrastructure and consolidating control throughout the territory. The United States departed from Spanish practice, however, in quickly expanding Filipino participation in governance and building a universal educational system in the metropolitan language.

The institutional pillars of colonial state building included a professional civil service, public education to unify the country and build capacity, and the formation and training of a Philippine Constabulary to keep the peace. American supervision of these and other key agencies was tight, with few Filipinos in executive positions, though many were recruited onto their staffs. While there was no shortage of Filipino applicants, Americans were quite critical of their quality, especially in public education and municipal-level "public improvements."[40] The Pampango military units that fought with the United States against the Malolos Republic also needed further training to ensure their loyalty to the new regime.[41]

The Bureau of Civil Service was established on November 31, 1900, with the mandate that the "greatest care should be taken in the selection of officials for civil administration." To head the various executive and line agencies, the Philippine Commission preferred American civilians or military men who had been honorably discharged. All recruits, both American and Filipino, were to be "men of the highest character and fitness" who could conduct their duties unaffected by "partisan politics."[42] To attract them, William Howard Taft, the first American governor-general, granted the right to engage in private business while on active service[43]—a surprising echo of

Spanish policy during the conquest! Two goals are discernable in the Commission's attitude toward colonial administration. First was an eagerness to distinguish American rule from that of the Spanish era, when "the bureaucrat groveled in formal self-abasement in introducing his official correspondence [and was] dominated by the bishop's miter and cleric's gown." The Americans promised a new civil service that would be "the product of a daring adventure in ideas."[44]

Second, the Commission was determined that politics not undermine bureaucratic development. Filipino leaders also acknowledged the need for a professional apparatus to implement programs created by the executive and future legislature. Thus in its early phase, the civil service was "a regime of law, and not of men"; while there were cases of abuse of authority, overall this agency of roughly 2,500 Americans, 4,600 Filipinos, and 1,500 Spaniards (in 1906) performed well. O. D. Corpuz calls this phase "a steady but rather plodding process, unmarked by basic structural alteration or dramatic innovation in the service itself."[45]

Free public education at the elementary and secondary levels was aimed at achieving mass literacy, regarded as an important foundation for a democratic polity. Top U.S. officials were contemptuous of the Spanish educational system. Cameron Forbes, Philippine governor-general from 1909 to 1913, wrote that his predecessors "had not encouraged the general learning of Spanish, perhaps from a fear that general education and a common language would give the Filipinos too much cohesion." Forbes also criticized the state of higher education, noting that since 1865 the Jesuits' normal school had "graduated only 1900, of whom less than half had pursued a career of teaching in the public schools."[46]

Although directed to conduct primary schooling in the local vernaculars, the Philippine Commission decreed English as the "common medium of instruction" in order to equip Filipinos with a "common language with which they could communicate readily with each other. This was regarded as an essential step in making them capable of nationality." In neglecting the value of education in what they called "local dialects," the Americans were in tune with the European colonial powers, which also associated higher learning and political advancement with their own languages. But these powers, the British in Malaya and the Dutch in Indonesia, for example, severely restricted such education.

Schooling in English began immediately, with soldiers in the classroom until civilian teachers arrived from the United States. By the end of the first year of civil government (1902), more than two hundred thousand students were enrolled in primary school, with an attendance rate of about 65 percent. An additional twenty-five thousand students were enrolled in night school

Figure 5.2.   School for Moro children in Zamboanga: Learning English with an officer-teacher (courtesy of the Lopez Memorial Museum, Philippines)

programs, and almost twenty thousand in secondary schools. Those enrolled at the secondary level were given special attention because they would be the first generation of American-trained Filipino teachers. This rapid expansion of English education outstripped the supply of teachers, so while Forbes and other Americans felt "there were no Filipinos properly trained according to American standards," they were compelled to increase their intake. By the end of 1902, supervision of the student population was in the hands of about four thousand teachers, of whom only 926 were American.[47] Educational policy and overall supervision remained in American hands, however.

As with the civil service, educational policy met with the broad approval of Filipino political leaders. Obviously, the Spanish-trained faced a linguistic transition, but advancement in the civil service was a powerful incentive to learn English. At the same time, other Filipinos were exploring the need for a common language. The press favored Tagalog. According to Andrew Gonzalez's study of language and nationalism, "reviews, weeklies, biweeklies, and newspapers" were predominantly in the language of Manila and environs: "While there was no lack of other vernacular publications . . . those in non-Tagalog languages were significantly fewer, not the multiple titles one finds in the Tagalog area. And where there were trilingual or even quadrilingual editions, Tagalog was always one of the languages."[48] Organizations were formed to discuss a future "national language," with the early emergence of two options, Tagalog or a "fusion." But almost until the end of colonial rule,

Americans retained control of the system of public education and vetoed a switch to vernaculars at the primary level. Nevertheless, Gonzalez and others observe that English education was a popular choice. Because the overwhelming number of teachers were Filipino, "the unescapable conclusion is that it was the Filipinos themselves who were mostly responsible for the dissemination of English in this country."[49]

A third essential institution was the Philippine Constabulary, established in 1901, an insular police force that replaced the irredeemable Guardia Civil. Led by Americans, with some junior Filipino officers, the Constabulary recruited among Christians, Muslims, and northern Philippine "non-Christian groups." The constabulary had the power to regulate the use of firearms, take the lead in health emergencies (typically cholera epidemics), and expand the telegraph and postal systems throughout the archipelago. Regarded as "peace officers," constabulary units were also charged to "prevent and suppress brigandage, insurrection, unlawful assemblies, and breaches of the peace."

The constabulary supervised municipal police forces to improve professionalism and thwart politicization by elected local officials. Here reform-minded central state actors (mostly American) came into contact with local state actors (Filipino). As Forbes put it delicately: "The work of those officers often interfered with practices which local magnates had come to regard as perquisites of high place . . . [so] it was not surprising that abuses of various sorts occurred; the remarkable thing was that these were so few."[50] As we will discuss in chapter 6, some Constabulary officers entered into political alliances with local Filipino politicians.

Not every aspect of state building was successful—two important failures were in land and tax policy. In 1903, the United States announced the purchase of 165,922 hectares (640 square miles) of friar estates for $7.2 million. Planning to sell the land to cultivators, Taft hoped to remove a cause of countless revolts in the Spanish era and also to consolidate his relationship with Filipino elites.[51] He accomplished half his goal. Peasants working village plots within the purchased estates immediately received parcels, but the 80,937 hectares that were still virgin forest were not transferred to landless peasants. Instead, the Department of Interior sold or leased them to American and Filipino business interests. This early "land reform" program was implemented with no support mechanisms to ensure its success—no credit, cooperatives, or technology. Farmers "were given a tantalizing glimpse of freedom and [then] abandoned to find their own way out of the agrarian wilderness."[52] Predictably, many fell back into tenancy, now to wealthy Filipino hacenderos who later purchased or expropriated the land when tenants failed to pay debts.

Efforts to simplify the archaic and complex Spanish tax system were likewise unsuccessful. The Americans removed the clergy's role in tax collection, but did not fulfill the promise of more *equitable* taxation. The head tax (cédula) was retained despite its very regressive nature—one peso being more costly to the poor peasant than thirty-five pesos to the rich landowner—while a proposal to tax inheritances and corporations was withdrawn in 1904 in "an obvious concession to the landed elite." According to Harry Luton, U.S. officials "showed a surprising lack of real commitment to equity in taxation, even in their own terms, especially in view of their professed aim of uplifting the 'whole Filipino people.'"[53]

Parallel State Building in the Special Provinces

Constabulary units joined the army to help govern two military-controlled special provinces—the Moro province and the Mountain province. The classification of regular and special provinces corresponded to the late Spanish-era civil and military provinces. The populations of the latter, only recently and incompletely colonized by the Spanish, were considered backward and "uncivilized" in contrast to the lowland, Christian, "civilized" Filipinos. There was resistance from these communities to the initial American incursion, especially among the Muslims. In two major military encounters in the first decade, American forces killed hundreds of Muslim men, women, and children in actions that were widely condemned in both the United States and the Philippines.[54] These were the only major engagements the U.S. Army faced in Mindanao. Smaller, intermittent revolts occurred during the period of direct army rule, but they were disorganized and easily suppressed. In the Cordilleras, as in the past, conflict between the various communities precluded the emergence of a unified resistance.

Both provinces were soon under effective military control, due in part to the active collaboration of Muslim and Cordilleran elites who saw an opportunity in the new order to shelter their trading activities and local resources from Christian Filipino control.[55] Muslim elites also hoped that through "alliance" with the powerful Americans, they could recover their position in the Southeast Asian trading network. By 1906, Moro province governor General Leonard Wood declared, "There need to be no apprehension of a general Moro uprising or of concerted effort among them," while his colleagues in the Mountain province mentioned no serious threat in their sector.[56]

The military's legacy in these newly bounded peripheries was ambiguous. On the one hand, military power effectively ended the relative autonomy enjoyed through most of the Spanish period. Roads and to a lesser extent railroads made the state's territorial boundaries a reality on the ground and all its inhabitants more accessible to the colonial state.[57] On the other hand,

American racial classification and state structures perpetuated the outsider status of Muslims and other non-Christians.

A new state agency, the Bureau of Non-Christian Tribes, signaled the shift from religious to ethnoracial understandings of human diversity. It accepted the broad population categories of the Spanish state, but grafted onto them the racialized language of "tribes" and contemporary notions of civilizational hierarchy. The census of 1903, for example, portrayed colonial society as "a collection of many tribes speaking different languages" and declared the term *Filipino* to be "properly applicable to the Christian peoples only."[58] It helped consolidate Filipino identity by doing away with "Spanish-Filipino" and "Chinese-Filipino" census categories.[59] This also served to highlight "Chinese" as an ethnic minority.

The Bureau acknowledged the ethnolinguistic diversity of Muslim Mindanao, rejecting the long-standing demonization and homogenization of "Moros." But neither this recognition nor the debunking of other misconceptions rooted in religious prejudice changed the fundamental stance of the state.[60] Muslims and other non-Christians in Mindanao were described as "uncivilized races." Continuing military rule was recommended both to protect them from Filipino abuse *and* to effect their eventual integration with the rest of the colony. Officers in the Cordillera promised their "tribal wards" the same kind of patronizing security and contradictory goals.

Army and constabulary officers accepted their administrative role with alacrity, sharing their wards' antipathy toward Manila. The military distrusted its civilian superiors and their Filipino counterparts and assumed that integration with the regular provinces was at least two generations away. As a consequence, military rule preserved these communities' political distinctiveness from the rest of the Philippines instead of moving rapidly toward similar state structures. For example, there were no elected governments in the special provinces throughout the period of special rule, in contrast to the speedy development of representative institutions in the rest of the colony (see below and chapter 6). In Mindanao, most Muslim datus acquiesced in military rule because the military assured them protection from Filipino inroads. When Manila's civilian officials tried to assert central authority, especially in Mindanao, they were rebuffed by officers who warned that Moro pacification could not be guaranteed if Muslim communities were forced to submit to Filipinos. Army and constabulary officials insisted that cultural difference dictated special rule of long duration because Muslims knew little about "our form of representative government" and saw no reason to unite with Filipinos.[61] In 1908, Muslim leaders and American officers and settlers even called for the separation of Mindanao from the rest of the colony.

Army and constabulary officers were seriously at odds with developments in Manila, where neither American civilian officials nor Filipino politicians intended to allow military rule to continue indefinitely. They interfered with the budget allocation of the Moro province and pushed senior officials to end military rule in the special provinces. Eventually, the army lost this battle because of two internal weaknesses. First, military rotation and promotion prevented the continuity of personnel necessary for state building in the Moro and Mountain provinces. The constabulary could replace the army, but with a regular force of only 150 per province, the additional responsibility of governing would strain its resources. In any case, Filipinos were encroaching on the leadership of the constabulary as well. Second, decision-making authority over these provinces lay ultimately with the U.S. Congress, which distrusted the maintenance of a large standing army. Even during the campaigns against Aguinaldo, this body was committed to reducing troop numbers and replacing the army with police and constabulary forces. At the end of 1913, the army was forced to relinquish power in the special provinces to civilian leaders in Manila.

The relatively short duration of parallel state building should not obscure its legacy—it was under U.S. colonial rule that the Philippine "geo-body" was fully realized. American military power was able to achieve a substance of governance that the Spanish state and the Malolos Republic were not. The modern Philippines, in short, was a colonial state creation as well as a nationalist imagining. But while the insider–outsider *territorial* relationship of the past was settled, it left unresolved problems of *political* exclusion. By the time the U.S. Army withdrew from the special provinces, these populations were more firmly inside, yet now defined more intractably as minority outsiders. This consolidation of the administrative grid in combination with political exclusion would have a paradoxical result. Although outsider sentiments became stronger, the political form they would eventually assume was determined by the grid—the "Bangsa Moro" (Moro Nation) for which armed Islamic movements now fight is based on the map produced by American colonial governance.

Conservative Nationalism

The United States, like Spain, could not draw the best and brightest of its countrymen to the Philippines, because most American leaders were indifferent to the new "possessions."[62] This apathy created problems for colonial officials faced with perpetual shortages of personnel; they were ultimately compelled to set aside racist assumptions about Filipino capability and speed up "tutelage training." Even when guerrilla warfare still raged in many parts of the archipelago, the Philippine Commission established the election of municipal officials and provincial governments, to be followed by election of representatives to a Philippine Assembly, the legislative arm of the new regime.

This peculiar consolidation of colonial rule through "democratic means" hastened the conversion of Filipino elites to the American side. Once they had judged the war a lost cause, they looked for a way to come out of it with their wealth and status intact. One clear way was to take up the American offer to help govern. Many landowners, merchants, and professionals had had a taste of governance in the late Spanish regime, when, in addition to gobernadorcillo and cabeza, electoral posts included deputy mayor, chief of police, livestock officer, and plantation officer. Furthermore, the electoral system proposed by the new American state would heavily favor them. In 1901, the Philippine Commission created the basic civil law for municipal and provincial government, and posts up to the level of provincial governor became elective as early as 1902.[63] The civil law set the following terms for the franchise:

> It required that qualified electors: (1) be males; (2) be aged 23 years and above; (3) reside in the municipality where they were to vote for a period of six months immediately preceding the elections; and (4) belong to any of the following three classes: individuals who speak, read and write English/Spanish, own real property worth at least P500, or have held local government positions prior to the occupation of the country in 1899.[64]

The first generation of Filipino leaders under the American regime—the established elites who turned away from the revolution—formed the Partido Federal (Federalist party) in 1900. The Federalistas were publicly committed to Philippine autonomy under the American colonial mantle, although most of its leaders privately hoped for the Philippines' annexation to the United States. The prominence they gave publicly to political autonomy showed their sensitivity to the legacy of the Malolos Republic and the fact that many Filipinos still favored independence. By charting a middle road, the Federalistas hoped to show that they remained true to the spirit of the revolution, but realistic in the face of American power—that the only practical route was collaboration with the new colonizers and "tutelage training." This political pragmatism became the foundation of conservative Filipino nationalism.

The Federalistas were the first to outline this political alternative to revolution and resistance, but their opponents ultimately perfected it. When restrictions on nationalist expression were relaxed, a bevy of revolutionary veterans, former Katipuñeros, intellectuals, and members of the urban middle classes and "lower strata" reentered political life and began to form *nacionalista* (nationalist) parties. In the early years, nacionalistas were weaker than their rivals: They were subject to constant harassment and imprisonment for "seditious" activity and, more importantly, had no access to American patrons. Things began to change when a new generation of elected provincial governors and appointed local judges took on the "nacionalista" label. Some had been well placed in the late Spanish period and switched allegiance as their areas were pacified; others entered politics with American sponsorship.[65] What did these aspiring provincial and municipal leaders have in common with ex-revolutionaries and urban workers? They were all either excluded from or hampered by the Federalistas' emerging monopoly on power and patronage.

These forces joined in coalition for the 1907 elections to the first Philippine Assembly, winning a majority of seats, and soon formed a Partido Nacionalista (Nationalist party), which publicly advocated eventual "independence under the protectorate of the United States of America."[66] Through this slogan and the network of supporters created during their incumbency as provincial governors, the Partido Nacionalista successfully established itself as heir to the 1896 Revolution and the Malolos Republic. While it conceded power to the Americans, it differentiated itself from the Federalistas by its commitment to work for eventual Philippine independence.[67]

Having abandoned armed resistance, the new generation of Filipino leaders mastered the rules of the new colonial game to take advantage of the "rights" and "powers" available under American "tutelage training." This allowed the consolidation of their own political interests and the possibility of broadening Filipino influence in the colonial state. They detached the idea of "Philippine independence" from its radical moorings by accepting American rule and, according to historian Frank Golay, "envisaged independence as a culmination of successive stages of increasing Filipino autonomy, which would convince Americans that the Filipinos were ready for independence and at the same time reduce American interest in retaining the colony to a size the American people would be willing to forfeit."[68]

They had reason to do this quickly—in the countryside, sporadic armed resistance against American colonial rule continued. While these revolts were no military threat to the colonial state, their persistence created a political dilemma for the Americans and their Filipino allies. It suggested that the radicalism of the anti-Spanish revolution and the Philippine–American War remained popular: "Notwithstanding the defeat of the revolutionary armies, the hundreds of thousands of lives lost and the desolation of the countryside, the image of *kalayaan* [independence] continued to pervade the consciousness particularly of the poorer and less-educated classes."[69]

The Continuing Revolutionary Tradition

The defeat of Aguinaldo's army corresponded with an expansion of religio-political groups, an attempt by former General Macario Sakay to revive Bonifacio's Katipunan, and an effort by veterans to form a radical wing of the Partido Nacionalista. Millenarian themes of salvation had rallied the poor to the original Katipunan; these reemerged in Sakay's movement and that of "Pope" Felipe Salvador. In the provinces adjoining and north of Manila, American and Filipino forces had their hands full suppressing the growth of "fanatical sects" and "bandit bands" led by self-proclaimed "popes" promising heaven and national independence.[70] Not all resistance had this religious element; many "were simply ex-Katipuñeros, veterans of the revolution."[71]

What concerned colonial authorities was that the radical invocation of kalayaan was a critique of *both* the Malolos Republic *and* the emerging colonial aspiration of independence. Reynaldo Ileto describes the difference between the radical and elite visions:

> In the Malolos Republic . . . an emphasis on the appearance of unity to attain world recognition as a sovereign state had all but suppressed the Katipunan idea of releasing the potentialities of *loob*—love, compassion, virtue—in the act of participating in the redemption of Mother Filipinas. Independence had come to be defined in a static sense as autonomy, and unity was formalized in the coming together of men of wealth, education and social prominence in the Malolos congress. To the Katipunan, this all gave the appearance of unity, not the experience of unity. As long as the gentry-revolutionaries thought in terms of maintaining vertical relationships with themselves at the top, the power of unity, of "coming together," was weak or absent.[72]

In the context of lower-class mobilization, we can see the value of early elections and a public school system, for these two "popular" instruments could be used by the state to counter and perhaps neutralize radical impulses. In trying to convince Sakay to surrender, Nacionalista leader Dominador Gomez explained that the Philippine Assembly had become the new "gate of kalayaan."[73] The promise to expand the electorate helped channel nationalist sentiment away from the embattled Katipunan to a state-sponsored electoral process, and public education satisfied a popular demand that was strongly felt among the lower classes. These two mechanisms doubtless had the potential to fulfill nationalist aspirations, but they more immediately served the colonial state–Filipino elite alliance, because the electoral process was already dominated by the Nacionalistas and mass education would inculcate the merits of "benevolent assimilation."

Tension between the reality and potential of colonial democracy echoed that between reform and revolution in the recent past. José Rizal and the ilustrados first articulated the distinctiveness of Philippine society to emergent Filipinos and the world; Andres Bonifacio and the Katipunan tried to bring it to fruition by declaring the nation's independence from Spain. The relationship between these facets of nationalism was charged with tension from the moment of Bonifacio's execution/murder. Historians have pointed out that by the time Emilio Aguinaldo returned from Hong Kong, this tension was starkly evident between the lower classes who had begun the revolution and the elites who belatedly joined it. Elite domination of the Malolos Republic, the early surrender of many of its leaders to the Americans, and the continuing pockets of resistance for the remainder of the decade confirmed that the nationalist movement had many faces.[74] The birth of the Filipino nation was not only "aborted" by U.S. colonialism, as many Filipinos feel today; it was already riven with class conflict. Tension between elites and masses would become a defining feature of Philippine political development, lending an "unfinished" quality to the political discourse of the revolution to the present day.[75]

The idiosyncratic nature of American colonial rule—looking forward to granting Filipinos some form of autonomy—nurtured the quest for a "Filipino nation." But its deradicalization aggravated the class divide. As politicians of the next generation explored ways to assert "Filipino interests" within the colonial state, they were haunted by the "fanatical sects" that continued to resist in the name of the Katipunan and Rizal. These groups painted nationalism with a broader pallette, a result of both the class and the conceptual divide between secular and millenarian understanding. There was no longer a single Filipino nationalism, but Filipino *nationalisms*, the meanings of which depended upon the group or individual articulating them.

It is important to recognize that the birth of the Philippines as an idea and a material reality was accomplished through both "reform" and "revolution"—not as mutually exclusive routes but as intertwined streams. Scholars in the Philippines tend to highlight the break between Propagandists and revolutionaries, thereby underlining the armed and radical character of the nationalist revolution against Spain. This tendency, we believe, has to do with postwar debates over the "true" legatees of the revolution—debates informed by the circumstances of the postcolonial republic (see chapter 7) and the Marcos dictatorship (chapter 8). Only by recognizing the simultaneous unity and contradiction of these two streams can we understand the passion and energy with which Filipino political leaders sought to take over the colonial state under the Americans, even if they were largely content to remain within the American embrace.

Millenarian movements began to fade as American colonial rule was consolidated and popular attention drawn toward elections, the Partido Nacionalista, and the ambitions of its leaders, Manuel L. Quezon and Sergio Osmeña. Yet sentiments of millenarianism and the inspiration of the Katipunan continued in many rural localities, particularly in areas where the struggles against Spain and the United States had been most intense. The Partido Nacionalista itself contained factions advocating "immediate independence"; they were quickly compromised by Quezon's and Osmeña's pragmatism. Such revolutionary residues would eventually find their way into secular organizations in the second decade of colonial rule, its followers finding commonality with trade union organizers, radical peasant leaders, and pre-Marxist socialist intellectuals.

NOTES

1. O. D. Corpuz, *The Roots of the Filipino Nation* (Quezon City: Aklahi Foundation, 1989), 1:475; Eliodoro Robles, *The Philippines in the Nineteenth Century* (Quezon City: Malaya Books, 1969), 13.
2. Corpuz, *Roots of the Filipino Nation*, 1:484.
3. Corpuz, *Roots of the Filipino Nation*, 1:476.
4. Corpuz, *Roots of the Filipino Nation*, 1:504–9.
5. Robles, *Philippines in the Nineteenth Century*, 197.
6. José Rizal, quoted in Cesar Adib Majul, *Mabini and the Philippine Revolution* (Quezon City: University of the Philippines Press, 1960), 125.
7. Mariano Ponce, quoted in John N. Schumacher, *The Propaganda Movement: The Creation of a Filipino Consciousness, The Making of the Revolution*, rev. ed. (Quezon City: Ateneo de Manila University Press, 1997), 179.
8. Schumacher, *The Propaganda Movement*, 28–29.
9. Quoted in Schumacher, *The Propaganda Movement*, 26. Emphasis added.
10. Nicanor Tiongson, *The Women of Malolos* (Quezon City: Ateneo de Manila University Press, 2004), 32–39.
11. Schumacher, *The Propaganda Movement*, 107.
12. Schumacher, *The Propaganda Movement*, 105–27.
13. Tiongson, *Women of Malolos*, 139, 146.
14. Benedict Anderson, *The Spectre of Comparisons: Nationalism, Southeast Asia, and the World* (London: Verso, 1998), 230.
15. Schumacher, *The Propaganda Movement*, 254–60, 281–94.
16. Apolinario Mabini, "Contestación a las Preguntas del General Wheeler" (Answers to the Questions of General Wheeler), *La Revolución Filipina*, 2:125, quoted in Majul, *Mabini and the Philippine Revolution*, 254–55.
17. Teodoro A. Agoncillo, *The Revolt of the Masses: The Story of Bonifacio and the Katipunan* (Quezon City: University of the Philippines Press, 1956), 48–57, 69–71.

18. Renato Constantino and Letizia R. Constantino, *The Philippines: A Past Revisited* (Quezon City: Tala Pub. Services, 1975), 131–32, 141–42.

19. Reynaldo Clemeña Ileto, *Pasyon and Revolution: Popular Movements in the Philippines, 1840–1910* (Quezon City: Ateneo de Manila University Press, 1989).

20. David R. Sturtevant, *Popular Uprisings in the Philippines, 1840–1940* (Ithaca, N.Y.: Cornell University Press, 1976), 262–63.

21. Reynaldo C. Ileto, "Bernardo Carpio: *Awit* and Revolution," in *Filipinos and Their Revolution: Event, Discourse, and Historiography* (Quezon City: Ateneo de Manila University Press, 1998), 1–27.

22. Agoncillo, *Revolt of the Masses*, 200–77.

23. Glenn Anthony May, *Battle for Batangas: A Philippine Province at War* (New Haven, Conn.: Yale University Press, 1993); Resil B. Mojares, *The War against the Americans: Resistance and Collaboration in Cebu, 1899–1906* (Quezon City: Ateneo de Manila University Press, 1999).

24. Constantino and Constantino, *The Philippines: A Past Revisited*, 201–3; Mojares, *The War against the Americans*.

25. Majul, *Mabini and the Philippine Revolution*, 170.

26. Majul, *Mabini and the Philippine Revolution*, 169–76.

27. Quoted in Teodoro A. Agoncillo, *Malolos: The Crisis of the Republic* (Quezon City: University of the Philippines Press, 1960), 251. See also Jose V. Abueva, "Philippine Ideologies and National Development," in *Government and Politics of the Philippines*, ed. Raul P. de Guzman and Mila A. Reforma (Singapore: Oxford University Press, 1988), 40.

28. E. J. Hobsbawm, *The Age of Empire, 1875–1914* (New York: Pantheon Books, 1987), 85–87.

29. Majul, *Mabini and the Philippine Revolution*, 177–81.

30. Martin Shefter, *Political Parties and the State: The American Historical Experience* (New Jersey: Princeton University Press, 1994); Kenneth Finegold, *Experts and Politicians: Reform Challenges to Machine Politics in New York, Cleveland, and Chicago* (Princeton, N.J.: Princeton University Press, 1995).

31. Stephen Skowronek, *Building a New American State: The Expansion of National Administrative Capacities, 1877–1920* (Cambridge: Cambridge University Press, 1982).

32. Angel Velasco Shaw and Luis Francia, eds., *Vestiges of War: The Philippine–American War and the Aftermath of an Imperial Dream, 1899–1999* (New York: New York University Press, 2002), 3–21, 134–62.

33. On the Philippine–American War, see Sentenaryo/Centennial, "The Philippine Revolution and the Philippine–American War," available at http://www.boondocksnet.com/centennial/war.html (last accessed November 13, 2004).

34. Reynaldo C. Ileto, "Hunger in Southern Tagalog," in *Filipinos and Their Revolution*, 99–116.

35. John Gates, "War-Related Deaths in the Philippines, 1898–1902," *Pacific Historical Review* 53 (1983): 367.

36. Ken De Bevoise, *Agents of Apocalypse: Epidemic Disease in the Colonial Philippines* (Princeton, N.J.: Princeton University Press, 1995).

37. Agoncillo, *Malolos*, 307.

38. Frank Golay, *Face of Empire: United States–Philippine Relations, 1898–1946* (Madison: University of Wisconsin, Center for Southeast Asian Studies, 1998), 93–94.

39. Golay, *Face of Empire*, 57.

40. Golay, *Face of Empire*, 121–22.

41. Jerome M. Mileur, "The Legacy of Reform: Progressive Government, Regressive Politics," in *Progressivism and the New Democracy,* ed. Sidney M. Milkis and Jerome M. Mileur (Amherst: University of Massachusetts Press, 1999), 265.

42. *Report of the Philippine Commission*, January 31, 1900 (Washington, D.C.: GPO, 1902–1916), 121.

43. Golay, *Face of Empire*, 138.

44. Onofre D. Corpuz, *The Bureaucracy in the Philippines* (Quezon City: Institute of Public Administration, University of the Philippines, 1957), 165–66.

45. Corpuz, *Bureaucracy in the Philippines*, 169, 183 (table 5), 195.

46. W. Cameron Forbes, *The Philippine Islands* (Cambridge, Mass.: Harvard University Press, 1945), 169, 171.

47. Forbes, *Philippine Islands*, 178, 175–76.

48. Andrew B. Gonzalez, *Language and Nationalism: The Philippine Experience Thus Far* (Quezon City: Ateneo de Manila University Press, 1980), 34.

49. Gonzalez, *Language and Nationalism*, 34–37, 27.

50. Forbes, *Philippine Islands*, 105, 111.

51. Jose N. Endriga, "The Friar Lands Settlement: Promise and Performance," *Philippine Journal of Public Administration* (October 1970): 397–413.

52. Sturtevant, *Popular Uprisings in the Philippines*, 55.

53. Harry Luton, "American Internal Revenue Policy in the Philippines to 1916," in *Compadre Colonialism: Studies on the Philippines under American Rule*, ed. Norman G. Owen (Ann Arbor: Center for South and Southeast Asian Studies, University of Michigan, 1971), 70–71.

54. Peter G. Gowing, *Mandate in Moroland: The American Government of Muslim Filipinos, 1899–1920* (Quezon City: Philippine Center for Advanced Studies, University of the Philippines, 1977), 160–63, 238–42.

55. Gerard A. Finin, "Regional Consciousness and Administrative Grids: Understanding the Role of Planning in the Philippines' Gran Cordillera Central" (Ph.D. diss., Cornell University, 1991); Patricio Abinales, *Making Mindanao: Cotabato and Davao in the Formation of the Philippine Nation-State* (Quezon City: Ateneo de Manila University Press, 2000).

56. "Report of the Governor of the Moro Province," in *Report of the Philippine Commission, 1907* (Washington, D.C.: Government Printing Office, 1908), 384.

57. Golay, *Face of Empire*, 115–16; Arturo G. Corpuz, *The Colonial Iron Horse: Railroads and Regional Development in the Philippines, 1875–1935* (Quezon City: University of the Philippines Press, 1999), 110–67.

58. Dean C. Worcester, quoted in Benito M. Vergara Jr., *Displaying Filipinos: Photography and Colonialism in Early Twentieth-Century Philippines* (Quezon City: University of the Philippines Press, 1995), 51.

59. Daniel F. Doeppers, "Evidence from the Grave: The Changing Social Composition of the Populations of Metropolitan Manila and Molo, Iloilo, during the Later Nineteenth Century," in *Population and History: The Demographic Origins of the Modern Philippines*, ed. Daniel F. Doeppers and Peter Xenos (Quezon City: Ateneo de Manila University Press, 1998), 266.

60. Donna J. Amoroso, "Inheriting the 'Moro Problem': Muslim Authority and Colonial Rule in British Malaya and the Philippines," in *The American Colonial State in the Philippines: Global Perspectives*, ed. Julian Go and Anne L. Foster (Durham, N.C.: Duke University Press, 2003).

61. "Report of the Governor of the Moro Province, 1908," in *Annual Report of the War Department* (Washington, D.C.: Government Printing Office, 1909), 3–4.

62. Earl Pomeroy, *The Territories and the United States, 1861–1890: Studies in Colonial Administration* (Seattle: University of Washington Press, 1947), 49–50.

63. Michael Cullinane, *Ilustrado Politics: Filipino Elite Responses to American Rule, 1898–1908* (Quezon City: Ateneo de Manila University Press, 2003), 157.

64. Luzviminda G. Tangcangco, "The Electoral System and Political Parties in the Philippines," in *Government and Politics of the Philippines*, ed. Raul P. de Guzman and Mila A. Reforma (New York: Oxford University Press, 1988), 81.

65. Glenn May, "Civic Ritual and Political Reality: Municipal Elections in the Late Nineteenth Century," in *Philippine Colonial Democracy*, ed. Ruby R. Paredes (Quezon City: Ateneo de Manila University Press, 1989), 13–36.

66. Quoted in Cullinane, *Ilustrado Politics*, 77.

67. Michael Cullinane, "Implementing the 'New Order': The Structure and Supervision of Local Government during the Taft Era," in Owen, *Compadre Colonialism*, 24.

68. Golay, *Face of Empire*, 143–44.

69. Ileto, *Pasyon and Revolution*, 170.

70. Sturtevant, *Popular Uprisings in the Philippines*, 109–38.

71. Ileto, *Pasyon and Revolution*, 240.

72. Ileto, *Pasyon and Revolution*, 183.

73. Ileto, *Pasyon and Revolution*, 194.

74. Constantino and Constantino, *The Philippines: A Past Revisited*, 174–236.

75. Reynaldo C. Ileto, "The 'Unfinished Revolution' in Political Discourse," in *Filipinos and Their Revolution*, 177–201.

Chapter Six

The Filipino Colonial State, 1902–1946

"POLITICS" AND THE PHILIPPINE ASSEMBLY

Nineteenth-century Spanish officials and ilustrados who thought about the problems of the Philippines thought about the state. The new twentieth-century governors, set on proving the superiority of American rule, thought about democracy. To be sure, these officials built state agencies for revenue generation, peace and order, health, education, and day-to-day administration of the colony. They also controlled them tightly, especially the Bureau of Education, which they considered central to the goal of creating a unified citizenry.

But equally important to this colonial regime was the speedy establishment of representative institutions from the municipal to the national level. The crucial element was "representation," a political norm at the core of American constitutional politics. In early twentieth-century America, "genuine representation" was thought to reside at the state, not federal, level. It was expressed through political parties that competed for seats in the U.S. Congress, where legislators deliberated national affairs and controlled the nation's purse strings. The institutions of purely national power—the presidency, federal armed forces, and federal bureaucracy, for example—had far less institutional strength than Congress or even the courts. Political parties fought hard to keep that power based in Congress, where it was deployed through patronage and appropriations; the Progressive movement tried to strengthen central state agencies and tame the party "machines." Their struggle was ongoing; both sides won victories and suffered defeats.

Many of the men sent to govern the Philippines were men "of courts and parties," a political orientation found in both major parties.[1] William Howard

Taft, the first governor-general, was a Republican judge from an Ohio political dynasty, and his successor, Luke E. Wright, was a Democrat, corporate lawyer, and former attorney general of Tennessee. President McKinley's instructions to the Philippine Commission in 1900 reflected the localist temperament: "In the distribution of powers . . . the presumption is always to be in favor of the smaller subdivision" (see box 6.1). As David Barrows, first director of the Bureau of Non-Christian Tribes and a Progressive, later wrote, "The American Commissioners had in view the American country as a model, and were impressed with the evils of 'centralization' and 'autocracy.'"[2]

A representative system was therefore built from the local level up. Municipal elections began in pacified areas in December 1901, followed by the Philippines' first polls for provincial governors in February 1902. It was an extremely restricted electorate of municipal elites that participated, but this was a crucial step in "the linking of municipal and provincial politics." For the latter now "had to look to the municipalities to obtain support for political positions" rather than rely on the central government for direction.[3] By mid-1903, 1,035 municipal governments and 31 provincial governments had been created. These led to the next phase of colonial consolidation—the 1907 election of representatives to the Philippine Assembly. Filipino elites quickly grasped the potential of this system, which reversed the Spanish effort to gather power at the center. To win a local, provincial, or assembly seat, an aspirant first deployed his local network of family, friends, and business associates. Party affiliation was also necessary, and as the Nacionalistas had quickly consolidated the ideological upper hand, membership in this party often ensured electoral victory. Finally, politically ambitious men sought the backing of an American *padrino* (patron), who could shepherd a favored client into the Philippine Assembly and introduce him to politicians from other provinces and American officials in the capital.

Some of this was familiar from the Spanish period, when a friar's blessing and principalia kin would help to win a gobernadorcillo seat. But at that time the process led no further, and the Filipinos were merely "puppets on the stage performing according a script" written by the friars.[4] The new regime introduced a political ladder to climb, making more politics worthwhile. In the Assembly, a politician gained power over the distribution of resources; at home, his network protected his local turf and served as trusted lieutenants: "brothers, uncles and cousins for the senior posts, and nephews for the junior ones."[5] The focus of state building therefore moved from the institutionalist concerns of the Malolos Congress to "politics"—the battle to capture the machinery of representation.

Box 6.1. "The Opportunity to Manage Their Own Local Affairs"

Excerpts from President William McKinley's instructions to the Taft Commission, April 7, 1900

"As long as the insurrection continues the military arm must necessarily be supreme. But there is no reason why steps should not be taken from time to time to inaugurate governments essentially popular in their form as fast as territory is held and controlled by our troops. . . .

"You will instruct the [new] Commission to proceed to the city of Manila, where they will make their principal office. . . . Without hampering them by too specific instructions, they should in general be enjoined, after making themselves familiar with the conditions and needs of the country, to devote their attention in the first instance to the establishment of municipal governments, in which the natives of the islands, both in the cities and in the rural communities, shall be afforded the opportunity to manage their own local affairs to the fullest extent of which they are capable, and subject to the least degree of supervision and control which a careful study of their capacities and observations of the workings of native control show to be consistent with the maintenance of law, order, and loyalty.

"The next subject in order of importance should be the organization of government in the larger administrative divisions corresponding to counties, departments, or provinces, in which the common interests of many or several municipalities falling within the same tribal lines, or the same natural geographical limits, may best be subserved by a common administration. . . .

"In the distribution of powers among the governments organized by the Commission, the presumption is always to be in favor of the smaller subdivision, so that all the powers which can properly be exercised by the municipal shall be vested in that government, and all the powers of a more general character which can be exercised by the departmental government shall be vested in that government, and so that . . . the central government . . . following the example of the distribution of powers between the States and the National Government of the United States, shall have no direct administration except of matters of purely general concern, and shall have only such supervision and control over local governments as may be necessary to secure and enforce faithful and efficient administration by local officers. . . .

"In all the forms of government and administrative provisions which they are authorized to prescribe, the Commission should bear in mind that the government which they are establishing is designed not for our satisfaction, or for the expression of our theoretical views, but for the happiness, peace, and prosperity of the people of the Philippine Islands, and the measures should be made to conform to their customs, their habits, and even their prejudices, to the fullest extent consistent with the accomplishment of the indispensable requisites of just and effective government.

"At the same time, the Commission should bear in mind, and the people of the Islands should be made plainly to understand, that there are certain great principles of government which have been made the basis of our governmental system which we deem essential to the rule of law and the maintenance of individual freedom, and of which they have, unfortunately, been denied the experience possessed by us; that there are also certain practical rules of government which we have found to be essential to the preservation of these great principles of liberty and law, and that these principles and these rules of government must be established and maintained in their islands for the sake of their liberty and happiness however much they may conflict with the customs or laws or procedures with which they are familiar."

—William H. McKinley, "Instructions to the Taft Commission through the Secretary of War," United States War Department, April 7, 1900, in *Annual Report of the War Department* (Washington, D.C.: Government Printing Office, 1909)

The Philippine Assembly—the central arena for locally based power—was important to state building in several ways. Historian Bonifacio Salamanca calls it "the matrix from which real Philippine autonomy evolved":

In the halls of the Manila ayuntamiento [city hall], where the Assembly's sessions were held, the members of the Filipino elite met face to face, probably for the first time, to deliberate freely on matters affecting the Philippines. As such, the Assembly was a useful instrument of political socialization, and, therefore, of nation building.[6]

Outside the Assembly, the socializing continued. Anderson observes that the legislators "went to the same receptions, attended the same churches, lived in the same residential areas, shopped in the same fashionable streets, had affairs with each other's wives, and arranged marriages between each other's children. They were for the first time forming a self-conscious *ruling* class."[7] This formation of a "national elite" out of the gathered local power-holders was another step in the realization of "the Philippines" as it is today.

The careers of the two most powerful politicians of the American period, Manuel Quezon and Sergio Osmeña, illustrate the shift from institutionalism to "politics." Quezon, from Tayabas province south of Manila, rose quickly from petty provincial bureaucrat in a small municipality to provincial governor. His own indomitable qualities were largely to thank (see box 6.2), but his friendship with American constabulary chief Harry Bandholtz set him on the path, playing a crucial role in his election as Tayabas representative to the Philippine Assembly.[8]

Sergio Osmeña was born to a prominent family in Cebu City. This origin and his education "provided him with the credentials for membership within the rather select group of ilustrados in Cebu" and allowed him to establish connections with prominent Americans and Filipinos there and in Manila. In 1904, Osmeña was appointed acting governor of Cebu province, and in 1906 he won election to the post with endorsements from Governor-General Cameron Forbes and ex-governor Taft. After consolidating his provincial network, Osmeña established alliances with "several like-minded fellow governors" to take control of the vital governors' convention. He then joined

---

Box 6.2.   The Qualities of Manuel Quezon

"[He] was ingratiating and charismatic, a brilliant orator and a consummate politician. He was audacious, resourceful, unencumbered by integrity, and capable of
shrewdly using his political strength to mold public opinion. His assessments of those
with whom he dealt were unerring. He manipulated where he could—Filipinos and
Americans alike—and used the electoral process to bludgeon those Filipinos who
challenged him. He equated political opposition with enmity and was ruthless in
dealing with influential Filipinos who were loyal to rival leaders or to abstract ideas
that incurred his ire. These qualities were moderated only by the transfer to himself
of the loyalty of Filipinos buffeted by his combativeness or their withdrawal from the
arena of insular politics. . . . The speed with which Quezon mastered congressional
procedures, the promptness with which he acquired proficiency in English, and the
sure political sense evident in his ready assimilation to congressional culture were
remarkable accomplishments."

—Frank Golay, *Face of Empire: United States–Philippine Relations, 1898–1946*
(Madison: University of Wisconsin, Center for Southeast Asian Studies, 1998), 166

---

the Partido Nacionalista and won election to the Philippine Assembly. Once
in the legislature, Osmeña and Quezon teamed up to lead the Nacionalistas.[9]
Osmeña was elected speaker and Quezon majority floor leader.

The two men were not content to dominate party and Assembly, however,
as long as key agencies remained in the firm grasp of the Americans. Barrows
noted that, the "evils of centralization" notwithstanding,

> ostensibly autonomous . . . [local] governments were never entrusted with
> important branches of the service or utilized by the insular authorities as local
> agents. Education, constabulary, forests, mines, lands and posts were commit-
> ted to the insular bureaus with headquarters in Manila and representatives in all
> parts of the islands.[10]

The tax system was also centralized, meaning that revenues flowed in the
direction of the Manila-based insular treasury. This allocation became institutionalized, with Manila receiving up to 65 percent of the revenues and the
provincial and municipal treasuries sharing the remaining portion.[11] Once
they understood that "the Assembly had been plastered onto a viable government," Filipino politicians concluded that "seizing power in that government
by burrowing from within was more promising than . . . radically changing
it through the legislative process."[12] And so they began to expand the power
of the legislature by encroaching on the power of the executive. Within a few
months of the Assembly's opening session, Filipino politicians were pushing the limits of American patience—passing laws beneficial to their own
interests, investigating the colonial budget, and criticizing policies of the

Philippine Commission, the executive body headed by the governor-general that was now a de facto upper house.[13]

In their early skirmishes, the Commission prevailed, as Taft used his veto power to override self-serving laws, defend executive appointments, and limit legislative spending. The Filipinos' relative inexperience also hampered them. But for every defeat, they learned a lesson. By the time Forbes became governor-general in 1909, Quezon and Osmeña were adept at combining legislative attack with "the game of favors and political back-scratching"—a game deeply familiar to their American mentors.[14]

The next step was to get a foot in the door of the executive office. Osmeña continued to strategize from the halls of the Assembly, while the more astute Quezon accepted the Assembly's nomination to be resident commissioner for the Philippines in the United States House of Representatives. In Washington, D.C., Quezon would lobby for both Philippine interests and his own with the congressmen who had decisive control over the future of Philippine affairs.

FILIPINIZATION

Tammany Hall in Manila

On the national level, the U.S. Republican and Democratic parties differed in their Philippine policies largely on the question of time: How long would close supervision continue, and when would full self-government be granted? Republicans, whose presidents McKinley, Theodore Roosevelt, and Taft administered the first decade of colonial rule, expected the process to be one of long duration (at least two generations in the case of the special provinces). Democrats wanted self-government to occur sooner. Woodrow Wilson's victory in the 1912 presidential election gave the Democratic party the chance to substitute its own vision.

In late 1912, Quezon returned to Manila with the new governor-general, Francis Burton Harrison, a New York Tammany Hall politician whose task was to implement the "Filipinization" of the colonial state. Quezon had lobbied hard for Harrison's appointment and was not disappointed. Upon taking office, Harrison immediately set the stage for a substantial shift in colonial personnel and power. One of his first orders was to curtail American executive power, especially in the oversight of provincial and local governments. To minimize opposition from American bureaucrats, he encouraged many to resign by cutting executive salaries.[15] Harrison then broadened Filipino power, giving the Nacionalistas a free hand in determining local and provincial appointments. He raised no objection when the Assembly claimed the right to compel executive officials to testify and submit documents. Nor did he oppose the Assembly's appropriation of the right to determine budgetary allocations.[16]

Harrison ended a decade of parallel state building in the Moro and Mountain provinces, implementing the transfer of authority from the U.S. Army to civilian Filipino officials. This effectively quashed the separatist intentions brewing in southern Mindanao, forcing Muslim datus, deprived of their American patrons, to seek accommodation with Filipino politicians. Quezon and Osmeña reciprocated by welcoming them into the Philippine Assembly, although executive power was vested in the newly created, Filipino-controlled Department of Mindanao and Sulu. Henceforth, Muslim elites became part of the political hierarchy, political brokers mediating between their communities and the Filipino colonial state. This inaugurated a long period of stability in the Muslim south.[17] In the Cordilleras, "highlanders" who received their initial education and training under the Americans readily formed a bloc in support of Filipinization.[18]

The impact of Harrison's policies on the colonial bureaucracy was swift. When he took office in 1913, "there were 2,623 Americans in the insular service, with 147 of them in major positions (assistant bureau chief or higher, judges, provincial governors, or lieutenant governors) . . . [while] there were only 859 Filipinos in insular service holding high office, and 1,080 in classified services." By 1919, "only 58 Americans were left holding higher offices and 702 in classified services (half of these were teachers). The proportion of Americans in the colonial state was reduced from 29 to 6 percent, with those in senior positions dropping from one-seventh to one-twentieth." Correspondingly, Filipinos in insular service holding high office numbered 6,363 and those in classified services had reached 12,047.[19]

In 1916, the U.S. Congress gave its stamp of approval to Filipinization with the Philippine Autonomy Act, commonly known as the Jones Law, which "placed in the hands of the people of the Philippines as large a control of their domestic affairs as can be given them." The law abolished the Philippine Commission and passed on its remaining legislative functions to the upper house of the new bicameral legislature.[20] Harrison then created the Council of State "to harmonize the executive and legislative departments."[21] The American governor-general's power was diminished by the mandate that all executive bureaus (except Public Instruction) be headed by Filipinos and that these agencies assist the legislature in crafting laws. Filipinos now had equal say in all aspects of policy making, budget preparation, and defining the functions of departments. Under this "hybrid Commission-Assembly government," the Nacionalistas dominated both houses of the legislature. Osmeña remained in the lower house, while Quezon became president of the new

Senate.[22] Harrison declared, "It will now never be so . . . for an executive to ride ruthlessly over the people he is sent here to govern, without due regard for their sentiments and due consideration of their wishes."[23]

Crony Capitalism circa the 1920s

While the legislature had its share of members representing landed interests from the late Spanish era, the majority were upwardly mobile men from relatively humble backgrounds. With their control of the colonial state vastly expanded, these leaders began to use it as an instrument of "primitive accumulation." There were two sources of largesse. First was the state itself. Through the "spoils" system, Filipino politicians distributed offices (and their corresponding budgetary allocations) to relatives and supporters. Political appointment of kin, allies, and cronies became standard practice, with entry into government assured by the backing of a powerful politician. In exchange, an appointee facilitated the business success of his patron and protected other members of his network within the bureaucracy.

The other path to material enrichment was the extension of the spoils system into the economy. Here the vehicles were state corporations established to promote colonial economic development. The Philippine National Bank (PNB), for example, created by the Assembly to finance sugar production and exportation, was taken over by Sergio Osmeña "in violation of every principle which prudence, intelligence and even honesty could dictate."[24] Osmeña used appointments to the PNB's offices to repay political debts, without regard for appointees' knowledge of the sugar industry or bank management. Almost immediately, the media began reporting on corruption inside the bank, and investigations revealed that Osmeña's appointees "authorized extravagant loans to companies in which they were themselves investors . . . [or] to finance personal consumption, instead of production or commerce."[25] The irregularities were so blatant that one Osmeña protégé, General Venancio Concepcion, was eventually jailed; even his patron could not help him.

Manuel Quezon controlled the Manila Railroad Company (MRC) and likewise used that state corporation as a source of employment for supporters in Manila and in the provinces reached by the company's lines. But Quezon never thoroughly "politicized" the MRC for his own benefit. To fill key management positions, Quezon hired professionals, most notably Jose N. Paez, the MRC's general manager. An engineer trained at the Swiss Federal University and New York's Cornell University, Paez represented a "new group of Filipino officials" who wanted to "establish a merit-based and non-political service in the islands." Paez ran the MRC up to the eve of World War II, making it one of the most successful state corporations of the colonial era.[26]

Combining corruption and competence would become a pattern among state leaders. Even Osmeña was not solely concerned with self-enrichment. Outside the PNB, he was described as an "achievement-oriented public official" who "built a track record as a 'modern,' 'rational' official replete with achievements in such areas as urban planning, fiscal management, public health, peace and order, and bureaucratic reform."[27] How does one account for this combination of achievement-oriented professionalism with abuse of the spoils system? Scholars of Philippine history and politics have not explored this question, understandably drawn to the abundant evidence of perfidy and dishonesty among Filipino leaders. But we find a tentative explanation in the regime of colonial accountability. While they certainly felt entitled to the spoils of office, Filipino officials were also compelled to prove their competence in order to move toward self-government. As the future leaders of the state, too, they wanted something left standing, if only so the robbery could continue. Thus Quezon hired a professional to run the MRC even as he turned the railway into his personal fiefdom, and Osmeña could be described as "the Philippines' first political technocrat."[28]

But accountability to the American executive was limited, both by the Jones Law and by the politics of nationalism. Osmeña disarmed American critics of the PNB scandal by labeling them "anti-Filipino" and used nationalism to justify putting Filipinos (his supporters) into leadership positions. Peter Stanley notes, "The centrality of the independence issue and the standing challenge of American control focused Filipinos' energies upon politics and made even the elementary pursuit of profit and gain a political act." Personal aggrandizement thus became synonymous with national interest, individual ambition with a sense of history: "Hence the paradox that the use of the bank to develop and sustain the economy through the elite appeared an economic means to a political end, self-determination, while control of the bank's credit policy through the majority party was in fact, for some, a political means to an economic end, personal profit."[29]

American officials were not the only critics of the dominant party. A prominent Visayan congressman, Vicente Sotto, was a vocal and relentless detractor of the hypocrisy of the Nacionalista leadership, especially on the issue of independence (see box 6.3). But Sotto "remained an individual voice" and "essentially powerless." Even when oppositionists united around the Democrata party, they gained no traction, becoming merely "a kind of ineffectual 'third party' to the bipolar competition between the Quezon and Osmeña factions of the Nacionalista Party."[30]

Box 6.3.   Vicente Sotto, Congressman, Second District of Cebu, 1922–1925

"Both in and outside Congress, [Vicente Sotto] was one of the most vocal critics of the 'independence missions' to the United States that Quezon and Osmeña dispatched almost yearly from 1919 to 1934. He criticized it as a waste of the people's money and as not worth its annual appropriation of one million pesos. . . . On 3 September 1923, together with representatives Claro M. Recto of Batangas and Alfonso Mendoza of Manila, Sotto asked Speaker Manuel Roxas to allow them to examine disbursements from the independence fund. When they were ignored by Roxas, they appealed to Governor-General Leonard Wood to order the Insular Auditor to examine the accounts of the Independence Commission. When Wood demurred, saying that unless charges of fraud were preferred he could not allow examination of the books, the Democratas staged a rally . . . where speeches were delivered charging that the Nacionalistas were squandering the independence funds and diverting them for personal and electoral purposes. They followed this up . . . with a mandamus petition with the Supreme Court to compel the opening of the books of account. The Supreme Court denied the petition. . . . Sotto charged Osmeña and Quezon with foisting a 'deception' on the Filipino people with their self-interested manipulation of the independence issue. He charged that the Nacionalista leaders were exploiting the issue to perpetuate themselves in power; that while Osmeña and Quezon were fiery in their independence demands at home, they were submissive and compliant in Washington; and that, in truth Osmeña and Quezon had no effective plan for the independence campaign but were handling it with an eye for how they could advance their political fortunes at home."

—Resil B. Mojares, *Vicente Sotto, the Maverick Senator*
(Cebu City: Cebuano Studies Center, 1992), 90–92

Restraining "Politics"

As we will see in succeeding chapters, active opposition from social forces with a stake in a society's development can often mitigate the plunder of state resources. In the colonial Philippines, the American business community might have been one such social force. Its location in strategic sectors of the colonial economy—power, telecommunications, and export agriculture—and its anti-Filipino sentiment qualified it to serve as a deterrent to crony capitalism.[31] But this sector was weakened by several factors. The U.S. Congress had limited land ownership by American enterprises to 1,000 hectares (approximately 2,500 acres) at the behest of domestic agriculture. When the Assembly later moved to block non-Filipino access to public land and vital economic activities such as interisland shipping, the American business community lacked the position from which to oppose it.[32]

With the exception of Standard Oil and the California Packing Company, many of these businesses had weak linkages with the American mainland.

Moreover, the opposition of U.S. sugar and tobacco interests prevented Philippine products from gaining further access to the American market. The Philippine Tariff Act of 1902 "provided only a 25 percent reduction in the tariff on goods coming from the Philippines—much lower than the 75 percent reduction which administrators in the Philippines called for." Anticorporate agitation by the Anti-Imperialist League, Americans' sense that the Philippines was "too far away . . . to make investment profitable," the greater attraction of the China market, and impending self-rule kept American business interest in the Philippines weak.[33] This left most of the Philippine economy in Filipino hands, notably those of the landed elite in agriculture and crony capitalists in the emergent industrial and service sectors.

American officials did not always surrender to the "politicization" of the colonial state. When Republican Warren Harding was elected president, he appointed Leonard Wood, former military governor of the Moro province, as governor-general (1921–1926). Wood tried to reassert executive power by trimming bloated budgets, rejecting political appointees, and vetoing legislation blatantly designed to benefit Filipino politicians. Wood, who was popular with the Muslims, also tried to reverse policies of the Harrison administration by transferring jurisdiction of Muslim areas to executive agencies still under American control, appointing American provincial officers to replace Filipinos, and assuring Muslims that Philippine independence was still far in the future. The latter, sensing a change in the political wind, endorsed these moves enthusiastically.[34] (See box 6.4.) Wood, in short, tried to strengthen the capacity of the central state, inspired by Progressive advances in empowering the U.S. federal government against local states and parties.[35]

Quezon and Osmeña fought Wood just as the two primary American political parties fought the Progressives. The two Philippine leaders ordered all Nacionalistas to resign their membership of executive agencies, refused to pass bills sponsored by Wood, and attempted to override bills he vetoed. They cut budget allocations to the governor-general's favorite projects, rejected his cabinet appointees, and accused him of abusing his executive power. Wood also became a useful symbol of the "anti-Filipino" American. His Filipino allies, who, according to one, supported him "in spite of his ideological position with respect to Philippine independence, because he was an honest and impartial administrator, aloof from local party politics, and had a sincere and zealous concern for good government," were damaged politically by association with him.[36] But Wood prevailed in these skirmishes because he had the support of the Republican administration in Washington, much as Spanish liberals could briefly impose reforms in the nineteenth century. The battle ended abruptly, however, when Wood died during a surgical procedure on August 7, 1926. IIis was the last attempt by American

Box 6.4. Muslims and the Colonial State: Transformations

1902: Datu

"[Datu Piang] is very shrewd, has brains and is self-made, being now quite wealthy and a power in the valley, he controls all of Dato Ali's influence over the [non-Muslim] tribes and adds to this his own brain. He is the only prominent Moro who seems to appreciate what the American invasion means and the business opportunities it brings with it. The Chinese blood in him makes him a shrewd businessman, and he has accumulated quite a fortune and is daily adding to it. He practically controls all the business of Cotabato, especially exports, through his own Chinese agents in that place; has complete control of the Moro productions; and working with the Chinese merchants makes it practically impossible for a white firm to enter into business in the Rio Grande [Pulangi River valley], even with much capital behind them."

—U.S. Army report, quoted in Jeremy Beckett, "The Defiant and the Compliant," in
Philippine Social History: Global Trade and Local Transformations, ed.
Alfred W. McCoy and Ed C. de Jesus (Quezon City:
Ateneo de Manila University Press, 1982), 401

1926: Embattled

"The American Army officers who governed us then were good men and just. They gave us assurance that they would protect us and not turn us over to those whom we do not trust. Whether these officers had the power to make those promises we do not know. But we trusted them. . . . But year after year, slowly, they have given the Christian Filipinos more power over us. Their laws are too complicated for us; the Moros need a simple government. Our own is more simple, ours are laws that have been handed down from father to son for many centuries. My sons have told me [about] one of the bills presented to Congress by Mr. Bacon of New York. They tell me that this is to separate Mindanao [and] Sulu from the rest of the Philippines. That would be better. Perhaps not the best solution but better than present conditions. Our hearts are heavy just now."

—"Interview with Datu Piang of Dulawan, 1926," Joseph Ralston Hayden Papers,
University of Michigan, Box 28-24

1931: Compromising

"I am reminded of a story about the Moros told me by Director Hidrosollo himself. The Director accompanied some Americans to Mindanao and on one occasion the Moro chieftains in their usual oratorical fashion told the Americans that they did not want the Christian Filipinos to rule them, and that they wanted the Americans to remain there. Later on when one of those Moro chiefs realized that Director Hidrosollo was there, he invited the Director to a private corner. When they were out of hearing of the Americans, the Moro datu said, 'Well, Director, don't mind what we said in our speeches. They are for American consumption. The real thing is that we are brothers. Christian Filipinos and Moros are of the same blood and race. So don't believe what I told them.' The Moros are unfortunately forced by circumstances to play this kind of politics."

—Maximo Manguiat Kalaw, "The Moro Bugaboo,"
Philippine Social Review (1931): 73–74

(continued)

> **1935: Integrating**
>
> "We do not like to be called 'Moros' because when we are called 'Moros' we feel we are not considered as part of the Filipino people. You also know that the name 'Moro' was given to us by the Spaniards because the Morocco had been under the rule of Spain [*sic*] like Mindanao and Sulu. So that I would like to request the members of this Convention that we prefer to be called 'Mohammedan Filipinos' and not 'Moros' because if we are called Moros we will be considered as enemies, for the name 'Moro' was given to us by the Spaniards because they failed to penetrate into the island of Mindanao."
>
> —Aluya Alonto, "Speech of Aluya Alonto on the Problem of Mindanao (interpreted from Moro to English by Datu Marigan Saramain Alonto), in *Proceedings of the Philippine Constitutional Convention, 1934–1935* (Manila: Bureau of Printing, 1935), 420

colonial officials to slow down Filipinization. His successors lost interest in strengthening the American-controlled executive once Washington decided to grant the Philippines independence.[37]

Amid their battles with American governors, Quezon and Osmeña fought each other for control of the legislature and the Nacionalistas—in other words, for eventual control of the state. One of their many skirmishes after government reorganization under the Jones Law involved Osmeña's proposal for a "quasi-parliamentary government." Osmeña wanted to serve as secretary of the interior while keeping his position as speaker of the Assembly. Holding both positions, he would "be in a strategic position to both encroach upon the American executive and withstand challenges from Filipino rivals." His strategy failed when Quezon, recognizing a maneuver to subordinate his role as Senate leader, refused to support the proposal. Here the question of institutional reform, always subject to political interests, was raised solely to pursue individual short-term advantage.

Quezon's favorite way to thwart Osmeña was to criticize him publicly for monopolizing power, offer to resign as Senate president, and orchestrate his own allies' rejection of his resignation. Quezon would reluctantly heed their pleas for the greater good.[38] Another tactic was to send Osmeña to Washington to negotiate with American presidents and congressional leaders over the terms of independence. In 1922, Quezon went a step further: He accused Osmeña of "authoritarianism" and split the Nacionalistas, creating his own Collectivista party for the upcoming elections.[39] His new, short-lived party won, but Quezon again worked closely with Osmeña against Wood's reassertion of executive prerogative. In this case, it was party structures that were subordinated to short-term political interest.

After Wood was gone, Filipino political leaders lobbied Washington to hasten self-government and Washington responded in March 1934 with the Tydings-McDuffie Act, also known as the Philippine Independence Act, which approved the creation of a transitional, ten-year Commonwealth of the Philippines, with independence scheduled for 1946, and a constitutional convention to prepare for both.[40] The act, together with a peasant uprising in provinces north of Manila, put an end to Nacionalista infighting, as Quezon and Osmeña reunited to control the drafting of the constitution. In the resulting 1935 Commonwealth Constitution, the existing executive–legislative configuration was retained, with a single-chamber National Assembly and a popularly elected president and vice president.

Popular Insurgency

The Nacionalistas claimed that their government was "of the people," but in reality, they paid little attention to landlessness, wages, and other problems of the rural and urban poor in the first two decades of colonial rule. The suffrage—limited to propertied and English- or Spanish-educated men—was widened in 1916 to include men literate in native languages, but the property qualification still excluded most rural Filipinos, who lived in conditions of economic and political dependence. "The people" were useful to threaten the Americans with demonstrations calling for immediate independence—a popular desire—but there was no need to mobilize the populace for elections. This changed when the 1935 Commonwealth Constitution removed property qualifications and a plebiscite two years later confirmed female suffrage. Literacy remained a qualification in this period, excluding about half the adult population.[41] But those who qualified for the suffrage were highly likely to register and vote. Filipinos now had de facto control of the colonial state, and independence was around the corner. Suddenly, "the people's" concerns became more prominent.

Before the Nacionalistas or other parties had considered how to cultivate a "mass base," insurgencies from below commanded the attention of the national elite. The second and third decades of colonial rule were punctuated by small millenarian movements led by "popes" promising to end landlord rule and deliver independence and rural prosperity. In northeastern Mindanao, Western Visayas, and central Luzon, such groups declared that the "time was at hand," attacked constabulary troops, and were easily repulsed.[42] The frequency and spread of these rural revolts worried the Americans, and their concern turned to alarm when new "secular movements" began to appear among the urban and rural poor, assisted by veterans of the Philippine Revolution and the Philippine–American War.

The surge in popular protest in the 1920s and 1930s was due as much to the inadequacy of the evolving state as to the poverty of the countryside and cities. According to David Sturtevant:

> Filipinization produced a political system directed by indigenous leaders, but failed to provide practical methods for contesting or transforming the landed elite's conventional economic values. . . . Mass education created literacy rates and aspiration levels well beyond the range normally associated with colonial milieus, but neglected to supply adequate routes for upward mobility. More disturbing still was the demographic outcome of efficient public-health programs. Between 1903 and 1939, the archipelago's population soared from seven to approximately sixteen million. Productivity and diversification, unfortunately, did not keep pace.[43]

To these were added the effects of the Great Depression, which "produced additional disequilibriums conducive to the generation of strident protest movements."[44]

In the 1930s, one movement most alarmed American and Filipino authorities because its organization spanned rural and urban areas. A disgruntled Quezon adherent, Benigno Ramos, built up a network of supporters in Manila and nearby provinces through his newspaper, *Sakdal* ("To accuse"), leading to the establishment of the Partido Sakdalista on October 29, 1933. The appeal of the Sakdalistas lay in their criticism of the Nacionalistas' "maladministration," combined with a comprehensive rural and urban political program. In contrast to the ten-year transitional commonwealth, the Sakdalistas demanded "complete and absolute independence." They called for the abolition of taxes; "equal or common" ownership of land; investigation of remaining friar estates and Church wealth accumulated "through dishonest means"; the formation of a Philippine army; the use of local languages in public schools; lawyers for poor defendants; lower pay for officials and increased pay for laborers, teachers, and policemen; and the "adoption of voting machines to prevent election frauds." Most disturbingly, they pierced the Nacionalistas' ideological armor, accusing them of being satisfied with American rule and insincere in their commitment to independence.[45]

The party's program attracted a variety of people—from peasants suffering onerous tenancy agreements and urban workers with low wages to urban and rural voters aggrieved by Nacionalista corruption and betrayed by its compromises with the United States. In the 1934 general election, the Sakdal party scored impressively: three seats in the House of Representatives, including one from Quezon's own province; the Marinduque subprovincial governorship; and municipal offices in Laguna, Bulacan,

Nueva Ecija, Rizal, and Cavite provinces. Most of these provinces surrounded Manila, where popular antipathy toward Quezon and his party was high. Colonial officials worried that the Sakdalistas' "Philippine-style populism" would coalesce with that of the fledgling Partido Komunista ng Pilipinas (Communist Party of the Philippines, or PKP), which had been established in 1930. The Communist cadres of the PKP were proving effective recruiters among the urban proletariat in Manila, organizing trade unions and drawing workers from the Nacionalista-controlled unions.[46] The opportunity to disarm this threat came when the Sakdals started to debate strategy—should the tiny number of Sakdal lawmakers participate in the politics of compromise in the legislature (where they wouldn't have much impact) or should the party turn to more militant action? The latter option was already attracting more peasant recruits and changing what Sturtevant calls "a bourgeois challenge to the *Nacionalista* oligarchy into a rampant patriotism of the millennial variety."[47]

Municipal officials began to restrict Sakdal political meetings in the provinces through police harassment, arrest, and denial of the right to assemble. The party responded with rallies and protests and rumors that "Independence will appear magically like the burst of a sunrise." On May 2, 1935, Sakdalistas engaged constabulary units in armed confrontation in several towns around Manila. The battles were all one-sided: Sakdalistas armed only with "clubs, bolos [machetes], sickles, daggers, rusting pistols and homemade guns" were no match for the rifles of the well-trained constabulary. By May 4, the uprising was over. More than a dozen Sakdalistas were killed or wounded, and hundreds were sentenced to prison terms of two to seventeen years. The provincial backbone of the party was broken. Ramos, who was in Japan at the time seeking international support, could only watch helplessly as his 68,000-strong party collapsed. (See box 6.5.)

In late 1935, elections for the commonwealth president, vice president, and National Assembly were held. The national electorate—largely untouched by Sakdal propaganda or organizing—had been alarmed by the revolt, a reaction that inspired the Nacionalista slogan "Quezon or Chaos." Numerous small parties and oppositionists united around aging revolutionary Emilio Aguinaldo, but he was more a symbol than a relevant politician. The Nacionalista party machine was vastly superior to its opponents, and 68 percent of Filipino voters chose Manuel Quezon for president. Conservative nationalism won this particular skirmish, although it confirmed the problem of disunity between the poor majority of the Filipino people and their compromising elite. With the advent of mass suffrage, it also posed a new question—elections or mass action?

Box 6.5. Excerpts from an Interview with Sakdal Leader Salud "Generala" Algabre

I. Her Early Life

Where and when were you born?

In Cabuyao, October 10, 1894.

What were your parents' occupations?

My mother was a seamstress. Father was a landowner. He managed extensive lands.

How extensive?

There were five warehouses—three large old buildings, and two smaller ones. The granary was big. . . .

How long had the land been owned by the family?

I do not know for certain. Grandmother told me that grandfather was a *capitan* [gobernadorcillo]. Only men with land became *capitanes*. The land must have belonged to them for a long time.

Did your father fight against the Spaniards?

Yes. In 1896–1897, in the War of the Katipunan. Father and grandfather were both soldiers. . . .

Did your father and grandfather fight the Americans?

They did not fight in 1898–1899. . . .

II. Her Grievances

When did you begin to consider the government as unjust to the people?

1930.

Why?

Because of the abuses against the people. The needs of the laborers were ignored. The leaders paid no attention to the people.

Before you became a Sakdal, were you a member of any other political group or party?

I was a *Nacionalista*. When I became disgusted with them, I joined the *Democratas* under old Sumulong.

Why were you disgusted? You said your family was well-to-do. Was there no property left?

None. It was all gone, even before I came of age. Father managed the lands. I did not bother about them. I was in Manila when it happened. The properties must have been sold. I do not know.

As tenants you were abused?

When we worked the land, we were cheated. The terms on the estate were 50–50. If the tenants harvested 1,000 tons, 500 were to go to the *proprietario* and 500 to the farmers. But we never got the agreed 50 per cent. We would get a mere 25 per cent, sometimes even less.

Did you share the 25 per cent?

We divided it among ourselves. But even then it amounted to less. They got all the disbursements back. All the expenses in planting were borne by us, even the land tax. We were very poor.

Then the basic problem was one of poverty or having enough to live?

Having enough, but without abuses.

Did you not protest?

Of course. But nothing happened. We even sent our case to Mr. Quezon and to Malacañang.

What happened?

Nothing.

It was poverty, then, and abuses which caused your discomfort?

No, it was more. There was a root cause behind everything. Nothing could solve our problems except independence, as the United States had promised. Freedom was the solution. From the time we were *Nacionalistas,* until we became *Democratas,* that was our goal. There was no other answer to the abuses and poverty. With independence the leaders would cease to be powerful. Instead, it would be the people who were powerful. The people would have their freedom. We would have our own lands; they would no longer be the monopoly of the *proprietarios* and of the government officials. As it was, we had nothing.

Your problem, in short, was poverty and power?

You might say that; that was our belief. Under independence, no one would be powerful, because the people would exercise power. . . .

III. Her Role in the Uprising

How and where was the uprising planned?

There was a meeting in our house on April 7, 1935. Only the local leaders were there. We talked of the rebellion and what each of us was to do. . . .

Were all the Sakdals in Laguna informed of the uprising?

No. Only key leaders in each town. They were to rally their followers when the time came to strike. Some important party members . . . were purposely kept in the dark. If they had known of the plot, it might have caused them trouble. Neither of the Sakdal congressmen favored violence. They were good men but somewhat passive.

What was the plan?

The people were to march to their municipal buildings, capture them, raise the Sakdal flag, and proclaim independence.

What kind of weapons did the Sakdals have?

Bolos, clubs, sickles, some shotguns, and a few revolvers.

In your plans, did it not occur to you that you would be fighting trained Constabulary soldiers equipped with rifles and, if necessary, with machine guns and cannons?

In my experience, the abused fellow does not care if there are cannons.

That might be, but behind the constables there was the power of America. Did you really think that you could achieve independence?

We had reason to believe the Constabulary and Philippine Scouts would join the uprising. We also believed other abused people would rebel when they learned of our action. If everyone joined the revolution we would have independence. . . .

Was there any fighting at the municipal building?

No. We entered the building—it was not locked—and ordered that the Sakdal flag be raised. . . .

Were there no officials or policemen at the municipal building?

The *presidente* was there and three policemen. The *presidente* asked if it would not be possible to stop the whole affair. We said no, it could not be stopped. "Very well," he said, "touch nothing, not even pencils and papers, and take nothing from the building." That is all there was to it.

What about the police?

They did nothing. One was even my uncle. . . .

(continued)

What about the incident with the Marines?

The Marines came up the highway from Los Baños. . . . The sergeant asked, "What's going on? Who are you? What do you want?" I said, "We are Sakdals! We want immediate, complete, and absolute independence." The sergeant said, "We don't know anything about any of this. I suggest you write to Congress. They have the answer to everything. Tell them what you want." I asked them for their side arms and the keys to the car. They gave me four .45s and the keys. I wrote them a receipt.

Did any of the men who were in the churchyard tell you how the firing began?

Governor Cailles and the constables spread out and advanced slowly down the street. The Governor called on the men to surrender. They refused. Governor Cailles gave the command, *"Fuego!* Attack!" That's what he said. Some fought back. Others ran away because they had no arms to fight with. . . .

Where did you go after the uprising failed?

No uprising fails. Each one is a step in the right direction. . . .

Where you captured?

I was not captured. I was taken to the authorities by my uncle. . . .

While you were in jail, were you questioned by any representative of Acting Governor General Hayden?

Yes, five Americans questioned me.

Were they in uniform? How did they treat you?

They wore civilian clothes. The man named Manley asked the questions. They treated me decently. They said they wanted to know why we had risen against the government; that I should feel free to talk, because they would not use what I said as evidence.

What did you tell them?

When he asked me what we wanted, I said, "Immediate, complete and absolute independence."

What did they say?

They agreed with me.

Where were you tried? What was your sentence?

There was a mass trial of Laguna Sakdals in Santa Cruz. . . . I was sentenced to the Women's Correctional in Mandaluyong, Rizal, for a term of six to ten years and fined P5,000. I was the only woman Sakdal to be imprisoned. I served one year, seven months, and three days. I was pardoned by President Quezon at the intercession of Vicente Sotto. . . .

This is a difficult question to answer, but how did you avoid becoming bitter? How did you remain a lady through that time in prison?

I was not bitter. I did what I thought was right. We lost and I was punished. The principles we fought for, and my faith in God, strengthened me. I also kept very busy. I learned everything I could about chickens. . . .

Are conditions better or worse now than they were then?

They are worse—far worse. All we are free to do now is talk.

After all you have been through and knowing the course of events, if you had it all to do again, would you do the same?

I am reluctant to say I will do something I cannot do. I am old. But I would do it again.

David Sturtevant, *Popular Uprisings in the Philippines, 1840–1940* (Ithaca, N.Y.. Cornell University Press, 1976), 288–99

THE COMMONWEALTH REPUBLIC OF THE PHILIPPINES

The Origins of Philippine Authoritarianism?

Quezon used the Sakdal uprising and the organizing activities of the PKP to justify the centralization of state power under his presidency. He blamed the uprising on the government's failure to address social problems and maintain autonomy from the demands of competing social forces. Claro M. Recto, a leading critic of Nacionalista corruption, agreed with Quezon on the question of centralization and gave voice to the expectation that the president "will not only know how to govern, but will actually govern, with a firm and steady hand, unembarrassed by vexatious interferences by other departments, or by unholy alliances with this and that social group."[48] Quezon, however, had perhaps older and more personal motives for creating a president-centered "partyless democracy."

After he spent almost twenty years engaged in "politics," the establishment of the commonwealth was a high point for Quezon. But it was not in his nature to accept limitations on his power, even if he and Osmeña (now vice president) spent years in the legislature trying to restrict the power of executive offices they now occupied. If he wanted to remain "on top," the dispensation of patronage and spoils would not be enough. It became equally important to wield and expand the powers of the presidency; the pretext of effective governance may have just been convenient. Quezon deftly used his powers like a carrot and stick to dominate the legislature, bribing representatives with state largesse and pressuring them with the veto. In June 1940, after a popular referendum amended the constitution to re-create a Senate and House of Representatives,[49] Quezon successfully fought to make senatorial constituencies nationwide in order to "uproot the new Senate from its regional base . . . [and] render it an extension of his executive authority."[50]

Quezon also appropriated and tightened control over such vital executive agencies as the Civil Service Bureau, the Bureau of the Budget, and the Bureau of Audit—critical instruments in the disbursal of patronage because they administered the flow of personnel and use of government monies.[51] Through control of the civil service, Quezon packed the upper echelons of all executive departments with loyalists. The Bureau of the Budget was useful in demonstrating that the commonwealth executive was as capable of "balancing the budget" as American governor-generals; in fact, accounting feats hid a deficit that rose from 11 million pesos in 1936 to 44 million in 1938.[52] Quezon also ordered the creation of a commonwealth army and ensured its loyalty to him by appointing officers he could trust and placing his American friend and business partner General Douglas MacArthur in command.

As president of the commonwealth, however, Quezon presided over a state built from the bottom up, local autonomy part of its foundational ideology. He therefore reached outward and downward to provincial, city, and municipal officials, and his firm control of the Nacionalista party gave him a nationwide structure through which to transmit policies and patronage. Joseph Hayden, American vice governor immediately before the Commonwealth period, wrote: "Governors, *presidentes* and the provincial representatives of the insular bureaus sought his approbation and feared his criticism. Other Governor-Generals sought to keep in personal touch with provincial affairs [but] they lacked the administrative staff which Mr. Quezon has developed." Hayden added, "No Governor-General ever disciplined half as many provincial governors as has President Quezon and large numbers of erring lesser local officials have been brought to book by him."[53]

Quezon was not always in reproachful mode, of course. He kept local officials happy by ordering the national legislature to create new cities and by supporting tax exemptions for coconut oil, a core industry of his rural supporters. Above all, he kept local elites close to him by devoting "90 percent" of his relationship with them to dispensing patronage. With support from below secure, he could undercut the opposition and pressure reluctant allies in the capital. With the support of governors and city and municipal mayors, Quezon could "topple most national figures who threatened him," while continuing to "manipulate his colonial superiors."[54]

The smooth running of these vertical and horizontal linkages was belied only by the Sakdalistas. Their revolt disrupted and exposed the incompleteness of the system, forcing Quezon to expand the circle of beneficiaries of "progressive conservatism."[55] He tinkered with tax laws to improve incomes, especially of the middle class, and proposed an ambitious program to address the economic problems of the poor. His "Social Justice" program would break up the landed estates and distribute them to cultivators, introduce social welfare measures such as the eight-hour working day and a minimum wage, expand the rights of workers and peasants (including the right to form unions) and their access to the courts, and create official resettlement programs to move families from densely populated areas to land-rich Mindanao.[56] All the reform measures submitted to the legislature passed—including the eight-hour day and the minimum wage—gaining Quezon some popular goodwill.[57] But nothing came of the proposal to break up the landed estates because of intense landlord opposition. The powerful presidency had found its limit; Quezon shelved the proposal and promised to hasten the settlement of Mindanao.[58] And the exploitative relationship of the countryside remained untouched, preserving the seeds of future revolts.

American officials watched with "discomfort . . . the erosion of democratic institutions and processes, the neglect of festering social problems and the waste of opportunities to prepare the new Philippine Republic for meaningful economic independence." But they supported Quezon because they saw no alternative. Fundamentally, the officials "were determined to avoid any confrontation with Quezon that might precipitate the overt reassertion of American sovereignty in the colony"[59]—an action that was untenable in part because of past failure to dominate Philippine politics and in part because the future was set. The U.S. Congress had already decided to grant Philippine independence.

Historian Alfred W. McCoy suggests that the lineage of dictatorship in the Philippines—see chapter 8 on the tenure of President Ferdinand Marcos—can be traced to the Commonwealth period and the presidency of Manuel Quezon. McCoy provides ample evidence for this thesis, citing the many times Quezon wielded dictatorial powers to push his political and economic agenda, remunerate his cronies, and crush his enemies.[60] Quezon himself offers confirmation with remarks like the following (which reveal one or two other traits as well):

> To tell the truth, gentlemen, I should like to continue being President of the Philippines if I were sure I would live 100 years. Have you ever known anyone who had voluntarily renounced power unless it was for a lady that, in his opinion was more important than power itself, or because of the threatening attitude of the people? Everybody likes power. It is the greatest urge of human nature. I like to exercise power.[61]

Yet this was more than simple kleptocracy and power grabbing. Quezon was indeed an autocrat, but he stood apart from his peers, including Osmeña, in seeing himself as a leader of what historian Peter Stanley calls a "nation in the making." He certainly coveted political power for his own ends, but also wanted Filipinos to see the office as *their* presidency, encouraging provincial audiences to see him differently than his American predecessors: "I'm a Filipino, so tell me the truth."[62] He personalized both the office and the nation. In exile during World War II, dying of tuberculosis in an upstate New York hospital and realizing that he would never return to the Philippines, he indulged a peculiar fantasy: "Look at that man," he indignantly referred to his own reflection in the mirror. "Why did God give him such a body when I am here struggling for my life? I am Manuel L. Quezon—I am the Filipino people—I am the Philippines."[63]

Such "megalomania" was not unique. The habit of autocrats identifying themselves with their country was quite pervasive at the time. In Soviet Russia, Josef Stalin was *Vozhd* (Leader or Boss) of the Russian people, while

Figure 6.1. Representation of the Philippine Commonwealth: Map, friars, conquistadores, U.S. flag and American eagle, Commonwealth seal and flag . . . and Manuel Quezon (courtesy of the Lopez Memorial Museum, Philippines)

Benito Mussolini fashioned himself a Roman emperor. National-conservative regimes dominated Japan, Finland, and Poland, and nationalist-fascist parties ruled Italy, Hungary, Spain, and Argentina. Quezon's "progressive conservatism" and "partyless democracy" were in tune with the era's "retreat of liberal political institutions."[64] But because he was "the first Filipino politician with the power to integrate all levels of politics into a single system," as McCoy ably puts it,[65] Quezon was also an original. He set the precedent for future leaders seeking to strengthen state power because there was no one else to emulate.

In what sense was Quezon Filipino—that is, a product of the unique confluence of state and social forces prevailing at a particular time in the history of this "nation in the making"? We suggest that the deeper origins of "Philippine-style centralization" lie in the transition from late Spanish to revolutionary to American leadership at the turn of the century, especially in the interaction of the new American state with emergent Philippine social forces. By basing political power at the local level and offering patronage to likely prospects, the U.S. colonial state introduced a measure of sociopolitical mobility that allowed a new elite to supplant the Manila-based ilustrados. But failing utterly to reform the land tenure and tax structure quite undercut this mobility and condemned the vast majority of Filipinos to the crushing inequities of the old regime. These structural definitions helped perpetuate older models of social hierarchy and encouraged the new elites to emulate old habits of capital accumulation, production, and consumption. Moreover, the strict division between political power and so-called key agencies of state—perhaps a consequence of the party–Progressive battles current in U.S. politics—encouraged a predatory attitude on the part of Filipino politicians.

The combination of political decentralization and centralized state capacity "produced" Manuel Quezon. He rose through the political half of the system, without the strong institutionalist orientation of the Malolos generation or of the American Progressives. Is it so surprising that when both halves of the state fell into his lap, his centralization of the state would be "political"—accomplished through political means and in pursuit of his own political power?

Social Changes on the Eve of World War II

The Sakdal revolt was an indication of the persistence of social problems from the late Spanish into the American colonial period. This does not mean that Philippine society was unchanged by the new colonizers. Public education, the teaching of English, a mass media, commercialization, and electoral politics profoundly altered social life. Rich mestizo families continued to prosper under American rule, their properties untouched and their children entering occupations aimed at enhancing status (medicine and the law) and promoting their economic interests (local and national politics). But a nascent urban "middle class" was also forming as state and market demanded economic specialization. New colleges offering diverse programs produced this urban white-collar workforce. By 1939, writes social demographer Daniel Doeppers, "Filipinos comprised almost 90 percent of all professionals in [Manila]."[66] The new professionals also included increasing numbers of women. Professions such as teaching, nursing, and pharmacology became common careers as both elite and middle-class families invested in their daughters' secondary and college education.

American values of individual achievement, commercialism, and populism spread at the expense of a marginalized Spanish cultural matrix. The middle class epitomized this profound change in Philippine culture, acting as the main agent of American consumer culture brought into Filipino homes via radio, imported magazines, and Hollywood movies.[67] Tony Joaquin, nephew of a preeminent Filipino writer, describes how his own family made this profound cultural shift:

> Leocadio Joaquin [Tony's grandfather], a dashing, quick-witted, articulate barrister trained under the Spanish legal system and the codigo civil [civil code], was fluent in Spanish, but being pragmatic as well, he was one of the first to learn English knowing that many younger lawyers were already becoming adept in the new language. Ping himself [Tony's father] had trained to become a classical pianist but he was drawn to the beat and the rhythms of jazz, the "low class music" that the Americanos had brought with them to the Philippines. For jazz, Ping abandoned his classical leanings. And so there were many who believed that he had, too easily, embraced the "music of the devil" and having done so, he no longer held much regard—not to mention respect—for the values and the attitudes of the past.[68]

On the maternal side, Joaquin's family was more attached to "socially established norms" and sent his mother to the Centro Escolar de Señoritas, where she "learned not only the basic skills of reading, writing, and arithmetic but also how to converse and write in Spanish and French, and to acquire genteel, social and domestic manners." She did not stop at this "finishing school," however, but continued her education at the U.S.-established, competitive, public University of the Philippines (established 1908), where she interacted with the brightest children of the middle class and the poor. She graduated with a degree in psychology and taught at a small college—"a feat rather unusual for any young middle class Filipino woman . . . of that day."[69] These were young people whose values and ambitions were much closer to middle-class Americans than to the ilustrados of the late Spanish period. As Joaquin notes, it wasn't yet a typical path, but it was trend-setting.

The political perspective of this middle class was visibly influenced more by Quezon and the Nacionalistas than by the older generation of revolutionary and ilustrado leaders. They accepted American colonial rule and Filipinization and saw themselves as "fiscalizers," young people who wanted government to work better. The more boisterous of these "reformers" organized the Young Philippines Party (YPP) on December 27, 1933, which called on "men and women of liberal tendencies to take a vigilant attitude towards public questions confronting the country and contribute in their humble way to the formation of a vigorous public opinion."[70] The YPP elected its president to the Constitutional Convention and worked with the Nacionalistas for "better governance." This was American-type civics at work.

Chinese residents of the Philippines, as noted in chapter 5, were once again marked as outsiders in this period. The Philippine Commission extended American exclusion laws to the Philippines, ending legal Chinese immigration until 1941, when the Commonwealth government allowed an annual quota of five hundred immigrants per nationality to come into the country. The immigration ban compelled Chinese men to marry within the community instead of traveling to the mainland and returning with a Chinese bride. As a result, the Chinese grew more cohesive yet and organized a unified association to lobby the state for their interests. But a protected U.S. market for Philippine exports favored Filipino elites and forced the Chinese to shift their attention back to domestic retail, where they dominated groceries and hardware. Not all Chinese families survived efforts of Filipino leaders to "nationalize" the economy; those who did spoke English, were Christian, had highly educated children, and maintained close contact with Americans and Filipinos.[71]

WORLD WAR II AND THE SECOND REPUBLIC

The Japanese launched an air raid on military facilities in the Philippines on December 8, 1941, within hours of their attack on Pearl Harbor. A hastily organized, ill-prepared Filipino–American force resisted the invading Japanese with exceptional bravery, but was defeated by the sheer military superiority of its opponent. General Douglas MacArthur retreated to Australia, vowing to return to liberate the Philippines. An ailing Manuel Quezon, Sergio Osmeña, and a number of their staff were ferried to Australia and hence to the United States to establish a government in exile. Meanwhile, the new colonial power set about consolidating rule of the colony. Japan's rhetoric justified the war as an expression of fraternal solidarity with Asian peoples seeking to end Western colonialism. The Japanese colonial regime in the Philippines invoked the nationalist themes of the Revolution and implemented programs to eliminate American influence in society. In its "Asia for the Asians," Japan continued to allow Filipinos to run the government, although they were more closely supervised than under the Commonwealth.

In 1943, the Japanese granted the Philippines independence and installed a "Second Republic."[72] We share the observation of many scholars that this "puppet regime" represented continuity with Quezon's Commonwealth, but note that the interregnum also served to turn the kaleidoscope, altering perspectives on collaboration and resistance and allowing suppressed nationalist visions to reemerge. Regionally, the Japanese invasion of Southeast Asia marked the beginning of the end of Western rule and emboldened anticolonial nationalist movements to push for independence. The Philippines defied this trend. Most Filipino leaders who collaborated with the Japanese did so for pragmatic reasons—the Americans had abandoned them—or in compliance with Quezon's directive to work with the invaders to prevent political and social breakdown. Comprising the majority of Filipino officials, these collaborators provided continuity between the deposed Commonwealth and the new Japanese-controlled regime.[73]

There was also a segment of the Filipino elite that hoped to restore the nationalism of the revolution aborted by the Americans and transformed by the likes of Quezon and Osmeña. They saw the new order as an opportunity to pursue alternative nationalist programs: teaching and writing in Filipino languages, restoring the Philippine Revolution to the national history books, and developing the perspective of the Philippines as part of Asia. José P. Laurel, president of the Second Republic, remained loyal to Quezon and justified his position on the grounds of deterring Japanese abuse of Filipinos and stabilizing the polity. But Laurel also defended the new order as an opportunity to revive long-suppressed "anti-imperialist" sentiments.

His justification of collaboration in nationalist terms was perfectly understandable. Laurel came from the province of Batangas, where some of the bloodiest fighting between American soldiers and Filipino revolutionaries had taken place and where pacification had been harsh. His family had actively supported the revolutionaries and were critical of U.S. rule even after joining the Nacionalistas and agreeing to play by the colonial rules. Laurel thus saw the Second Republic as a chance to fight for the principles of the Katipunan and the Malolos Republic. His was a minority view, however.[74] When the tide of war began to change, Laurel would be abandoned by colleagues more concerned with their own preservation once U.S. power was restored.

Figure 6.2.   Manila, 1941: Declared an open city to avert destruction by entering Japanese forces (courtesy of the Philippine National Historical Institute)

After defeat in its one major battle of the war—on the Bataan Peninsula northwest of Manila—the U.S. Armed Forces in the Far East (USAFFE) broke into various smaller "commands" and waged guerrilla war against the invaders. Some did so valiantly (the guerrilla commands in the southern Philippines), while others fought halfheartedly, content to await General MacArthur's return. Some commands turned their guns on each other, trying to control scarce resources and establish "turf" in the countryside. In Mindanao and the Visayas, inter-guerrilla rifts were endemic, prompting MacArthur to send an emissary to reconcile the rival forces. Many Filipino commanders of these groups would later convert them into the private armies that became a feature of postwar politics.[75]

The only sustained armed resistance against the Japanese came from the "people's army" of the PKP. The party's Hukbong Bayan laban sa Hapon (People's Anti-Japanese Army), or Hukbalahap, carved out "liberated zones" in several provinces north of Manila, harassing Japanese troops and mobilizing peasant communities to maintain economic activity on agricultural estates abandoned by landlords.[76] Like most Communist parties in Asia, the PKP toned down its radicalism in favor of a broad "anti-fascist" coalition against Japan. And many peasant fighters and Communist cadres believed that the returning American army would regard them as allies. But as the liberation of

Figure 6.3.   Refugees in Manila, 1945: The city was largely destroyed during its recapture (courtesy of the Philippine National Historical Institute)

the Philippines began in earnest, the American army, USAFFE guerrillas, and members of the Filipino elite saw the Hukbalahap's peasant organizing as an obstacle to the reclamation of landed estates. They would soon join forces to eliminate this radical wing of the anti-Japanese opposition.[77]

The U.S. military invaded the country in late 1944 and General MacArthur's forces advanced rapidly from their landing base in the central Philippines toward Manila. A brutal one-month battle to take Manila cost the lives of a thousand Americans, sixteen thousand Japanese, and tens of thousands of Filipinos. Eighty percent of Manila was destroyed, making it the second most damaged city in the war after Warsaw.[78] Osmeña returned to the Philippines to deal with the officials who had collaborated with the Japanese. But MacArthur had already taken sides on this issue, protecting collaborators who were his friends and business associates from prosecution.[79] While "war trials" were held in the immediate postwar period, no major political figure experienced any significant jail time. As Joel David Steinberg curtly put it: "The elite survived."[80]

NOTES

1. Stephen Skowronek, *Building a New American State: The Expansion of National Administrative Capacities, 1877–1920* (Cambridge: Cambridge University Press, 1982), 38–46.

2. David P. Barrows, *A Decade of American Government in the Philippines: 1903–1913* (New York: Yonkers, 1914), 17.

3. Michael Cullinane, *Ilustrado Politics: Filipino Elite Responses to American Rule, 1898–1908* (Quezon City: Ateneo de Manila University Press, 2003), 150.

4. Glenn May, "Civic Ritual and Political Reality: Municipal Elections in the Late Nineteenth Century," in *Philippine Colonial Democracy*, ed. Ruby R. Paredes (Quezon City: Ateneo de Manila University Press, 1989), 35; Cullinane, *Ilustrado Politics*, 159.

5. Benedict R. O'G. Anderson, "Cacique Democracy in the Philippines," in *The Spectre of Comparisons: Nationalism, Southeast Asia, and the World* (London: Verso, 1998), 203.

6. Bonifacio S. Salamanca, *The Filipino Reaction to American Rule, 1901–1913* (Quezon City: New Day Publishers, 1984), 52.

7. Anderson, *Spectre of Comparisons*, 202.

8. Michael Cullinane, "Manuel L. Quezon and Harry Bandholtz: The Origins of Special Relationship," *Bulletin of the American Historical Collection* 9 (January-March, 1981): 79–90.

9. Cullinane, *Ilustrado Politics*, 150–51, 205–44, 278–79.

10. Barrows, *Decade of American Government*, 17.

11. Harry Luton, "American Internal Revenue Policy in the Philippines to 1916," in *Compadre Colonialism: Studies on the Philippines under American Rule*, ed. Norman

G. Owen (Ann Arbor: Center for South and Southeast Asian Studies, University of Michigan, 1971), 70–71.

12. Frank Golay, *Face of Empire: United States–Philippine Relations, 1898–1946* (Madison: University of Wisconsin, Center for Southeast Asian Studies, 1998), 144.

13. Frank Jenista Jr., "Conflict in the Philippine Legislature: The Commission and the Assembly from 1907 to 1913," in Owen, *Compadre Colonialism*, 35–44.

14. Lewis E. Gleeck Jr., *The American Half-Century, 1898–1946*, rev. ed. (Quezon City: New Day Publishers, 1998), 124; Peter W. Stanley, *A Nation in the Making: The Philippines and the United States, 1899–1921* (Cambridge, Mass.: Harvard University Press, 1974), 172, 139–63; Golay, *Face of Empire*, 148–49, 151–52, 191–92.

15. Stanley, *Nation in the Making*, 206–8; Golay, *Face of Empire*, 181, 189.

16. Golay, *Face of Empire*, 180–81.

17. Patricio N. Abinales, *Making Mindanao: Cotabato and Davao in the Formation of the Philippine Nation-State* (Quezon City: Ateneo de Manila University Press, 2000), 30–40.

18. Gerard A. Finin, "Regional Consciousness and Administrative Grids: Understanding the Role of Planning in the Philippines' Gran Cordillera Central" (Ph.D. diss., Cornell University, 1991), 110–16.

19. Golay, *Face of Empire*, 176.

20. Aurora C. Catilo and Proserpina D. Tapales, "The Legislature," in *Government and Politics of the Philippines*, ed. Raul P. de Guzman and Mila A. Reforma (New York: Oxford University Press, 1988), 140.

21. Maximo Manguiat Kalaw, *The Development of Philippine Politics* (Manila: Oriental Commercial Co., 1926), 389.

22. Stanley, *Nation in the Making*, 174.

23. Francis Burton Harrison, quoted in Kalaw, *Development of Philippine Politics*, 363.

24. Golay, *Face of Empire*, 220.

25. Stanley, *Nation in the Making*, 236–37, 244.

26. Arturo G. Corpuz, *The Colonial Iron Horse: Railroads and Regional Development in the Philippines, 1875–1935* (Quezon City: University of the Philippines Press, 1999), 57–74. Quotation is on page 60.

27. Resil B. Mojares, "The Dream Goes On and On: Three Generations of the Osmeñas, 1906–1990," in *An Anarchy of Families: State and Family in the Philippines*, ed. Alfred W. McCoy (Madison: University of Wisconsin, Center for Southeast Asian Studies, 1993), 335.

28. Mojares, "The Dream Goes On and On," 335.

29. Stanley, *Nation in the Making*, 244–45.

30. Resil B. Mojares, *Vicente Sotto, the Maverick Senator* (Cebu: Cebuano Studies Center, 1992), 63–65, 77–88, 90–98, 110–14, 115–19, 121–33. Sotto later became a Commonwealth senator.

31. Theodore Friend III, "American Interests and Philippine Independence, 1929–1933," *Philippine Studies* 2, no. 4 (October 1963): 508–9.

32. Golay, *Face of Empire*, 208; Friend, "American Interests," 510.

33. Julian Go, "The Chains of Empire: State Building and 'Political Education' in Puerto Rico and the Philippines," in *The American Colonial State in the Philippines: Global Perspectives*, ed. Julian Go and Anne L. Foster (Durham and London: Duke University Press, 2003), 196.

34. Ralph Benjamin Thomas, "Muslim but Filipinos: The Integration of the Philippine Muslims, 1917–1946" (Ph.D. diss., University of Pennsylvania, 1971), 137–38.

35. Skowronek, *Building a New American State*, 91.

36. Claro M. Recto in Renato Constantino, *The Making of a Filipino: A Story of Colonial Politics* (Quezon City: Malaya Books, 1969), 50–51.

37. Samuel K. Tan, *The Critical Decade, 1921–1930* (Quezon City: University of the Philippines College of Social Sciences and Philosophy, 1993).

38. Golay, *Face of Empire*, 204–6.

39. Joseph Ralston Hayden, *The Philippines: A Study in National Development* (New York: Macmillan, 1942), 329–31.

40. Golay, *Face of Empire*, 237, 243–44, 249, 253, 262, 269, 289–94, 313–35.

41. Hayden, *The Philippines*, 204.

42. David Sturtevant, *Popular Uprisings in the Philippines, 1840–1940* (Ithaca, N.Y.: Cornell University Press, 1976), 149–92.

43. Sturtevant, *Popular Uprisings in the Philippines*, 216.

44. Sturtevant, *Popular Uprisings in the Philippines*, 216.

45. Sturtevant, *Popular Uprisings in the Philippines*, 223, 225.

46. On the rise and decline of the PKP, see Andrew James Richardson, "The Genesis of the Philippine Communist Party" (Ph.D. diss., School of Oriental and African Studies, University of London, 1984).

47. Sturtevant, *Popular Uprisings in the Philippines*, 228.

48. Quoted in Golay, *Face of Empire*, 354.

49. Hayden, *The Philippines*, 401–35.

50. Alfred W. McCoy, "Quezon's Commonwealth: The Emergence of Philippine Authoritarianism," in Paredes, *Philippine Colonial Democracy*, 120.

51. Hayden, *The Philippines*; Aruna Gopinath, *Manuel L. Quezon: The Tutelary Democrat* (Quezon City: New Day Publishers, 1987), 62–63.

52. Vicente Angel S. Ybiernas, "The Philippine Commonwealth Government: In Search of a Budgetary Surplus," *Philippine Studies* 15, no. 1 (2003): 122.

53. Hayden, *The Philippines*, 296–97.

54. McCoy, "Quezon's Commonwealth," 120.

55. Manuel Luis Quezon, *The Good Fight* (New York: D. Appleton-Century, 1946), 171.

56. Gopinath, *Manuel L. Quezon*, 76, 83, 93–95.

57. Gleeck, *The American Half-Century*, 404.

58. Francis Burton Harrison, *Origins of the Philippine Republic: Extracts from the Diaries and Records of Francis Burton Harrison*, ed. Michael P. Onorato (Ithaca, N.Y.: Southeast Asia Program, Cornell University, 1974), 115–16.

59. Golay, *Face of Empire*, 443.

60. McCoy, "Quezon's Commonwealth," 120.

61. Quoted in Gopinath, *Manuel L. Quezon*, 42.

62. Quezon, *Good Fight*, 164.

63. David Joel Steinberg, *Philippine Collaboration in World War II* (Manila: Solidaridad, 1967), 103. Quezon died on August 1, 1944.

64. Eric Hobsbawm, *The Age of Extremes: A History of the World, 1914–1991* (New York: Pantheon Books, 1994), 111–41.

65. McCoy, "Quezon's Commonwealth," 120.

66. Daniel F. Doeppers, *Manila, 1900–1941: Social Change in a Late Colonial Metropolis* (Quezon City: Ateneo de Manila University Press, 1984), 64.

67. Leonora Angeles, "Feminism and Nationalism: The Discourse on the Woman Question and Politics of the Women's Movement in the Philippines" (M.A. thesis, University of the Philippines, 1989), 88.

68. Tony Joaquin, *Simple Memories: A Memoir* (Pasig, The Philippines: Anvil Publishing, 2000), 16.

69. Joaquin, *Simple Memories*, 17–18.

70. Corazon Damo Santiago, *A Century of Activism* (Manila: Rex Book Store, 1972), 38.

71. Wong Kwok-Chu, *The Chinese in the Philippine Economy, 1898–1941* (Quezon City: Ateneo de Manila University Press, 1999), 59, 29.

72. Steinberg, *Philippine Collaboration*, 71–99.

73. Steinberg, *Philippine Collaboration*, 32–33.

74. Reynaldo Clemeña Ileto, "Laurel and the Struggles over Philippine History" (paper presented at the Asian Studies Conference–Japan, Tokyo, June 22–23, 2002).

75. Renato Constantino and Letizia Constantino, *The Philippines: The Continuing Past* (Quezon City: Foundation for Nationalist Studies, 1978), 136–37; Carlos P. Quirino, *Chick Parsons: Master Spy in the Philippines* (Quezon City: New Day Publishers, 1984), 68–212; Uldarico Baclagon, *Christian-Moslem Guerrillas in Mindanao* (Manila: Lord Avenue, 1988), 116–42.

76. Benedict Kerkvliet, *The Huk Rebellion: A Study of Peasant Revolt in the Philippines* (Los Angeles, Berkeley and London: University of California Press, 1979), 63–77.

77. Constantino and Constantino, *The Philippines: The Continuing Past*, 138–50.

78. Steinberg, *Philippine Collaboration*, 113–14.

79. Keith Thor Carlson, *The Twisted Road to Freedom: America's Granting of Independence to the Philippines* (Quezon City: University of the Philippines Press, 1995), 28–53.

80. Steinberg, *Philippine Collaboration*, 164.

Chapter Seven

All Politics Is Local, 1946–1964

THE REPUBLIC OF THE PHILIPPINES

In this chapter, we discuss the tenure of the first five postwar Philippine presidents: Manuel Roxas, Elpidio Quirino, Ramon Magsaysay, Carlos Garcia, and Diosdado Macapagal. These presidents committed themselves to a national economic development plan based on close ties with the United States. Having encountered lower-class insurgencies in the past, they promised to "liberate" the peasantry from bondage but stopped short of destroying landlord power. Instead, they attempted to expand agricultural productivity through technological inputs, credits, and social welfare programs. Opening up the largest land frontier in Mindanao also provided a safety valve for the volatile countryside.

All five presidents adhered to the democratic rituals established in the Commonwealth era, despite occasional attempts to subvert the rules of the game. They were also practitioners of patronage, but were enjoined to steer the newly independent country toward full "modernization." In the regional context of the Cold War—Communist victory in China, the politics of nonalignment in Southeast Asia, and expanding nationalist-Communist revolution in Indochina—they wanted to prove "American-style" democracy superior to its radical rivals. These pressures and the challenge of a domestic Communist rebellion demanded attention to effective governance. "Islands of state strength" began to appear inside the postcolonial Philippine state. At the same time, however, the institutional and social limits on state building became abundantly clear.

The End of "Partyless Democracy"

Perhaps the most dramatic political change in the postcolonial period was the unraveling of Manuel Quezon's project of strengthening the presidency. It began almost as soon as the United States reaffirmed Filipino control of political and economic power. Although most former officials of the "Second Republic" were back in the political arena within a year or two, new actors were also set to join the game. These new "local strongmen" were without the landed wealth of the older generation; their power derived from education and professional talent, black market speculation, or arms and networks they acquired as guerrilla leaders during the war.[1]

Ferdinand Marcos (of Ilocos Norte) and Salipada Pendatun (of Cotabato) are illustrative cases. Marcos and Pendatun were son and protégé, respectively, of colonial officials; they both earned degrees at the prestigious University of the Philippines College of Law, made their mark as lawyers, and joined the war. After independence, with their private armies and wartime prestige, they launched political careers in the legislature. Ramon Magsaysay (of Zambales province) did not complete his college education, but wartime exploits became his passport to provincial governorship and eventually the presidency.

Private armies were essential to these strongmen, because postwar economic difficulties and the limited resources available as they were entering politics meant vicious competition with equally ambitious rivals. But coercion was not enough: The most successful strongmen rose by establishing electoral and patronage alliances with older elites, families who had amassed their wealth and earned their political spurs during the American period. Many rising politicians therefore sought alliances with sugar barons like the Lopez family of Negros Oriental to win election to Congress and even the presidency. Together the allies had the money, connections, and force necessary to deliver votes from northern Luzon to frontier Mindanao. In Congress and the executive office, the new leaders worked to defend and promote local interests against attempts within the state or by reformist social forces to shift power away from the provinces and the localities to the central state. Eventually overcoming their limited political experience and carving out their own niches, some would challenge and overpower their old patrons.[2]

After the formal grant of independence in 1946, these factions of the postwar elite created a republic that was in important ways the antithesis of the Commonwealth. It put Congress on an equal footing with the presidency, restrained executive agencies by retaining the legislature's power to approve the national budget, and kept the military on a tight leash via congressional appointment and promotion. Four interrelated changes enabled this reversal: the marginalization of Quezon's allies; the end of virtual one-party rule; the expansion of the electorate by removal of the literacy qualification; and the subordination of state and party interests to the "scattered, particularistic" interests of political clans and family networks.[3]

The unraveling of state centralization began when those who shared the late president's idea of "constitutional dictatorship" were eased from power. José P. Laurel and his allies in the Second Republic had always been disliked by the United States for their anticolonial nationalism; when they were tried as "Japanese collaborators," the Americans remained cool, undermining their position within the Nacionalista party. Even President Sergio Osmeña (who had succeeded upon Quezon's death) was politically weakened by wartime exile and General Douglas MacArthur's patronage of other politicians. Moreover, in an attempt to win popular support, Osmeña associated himself with the Democratic Alliance, a coalition of radical Nacionalistas and the Partido Komunista ng Pilipinas (PKP). This drove away landed elites, who feared Osmeña would revive and implement Quezon's "Social Justice" program.[4]

The battle was first joined within the Nacionalista party over the issues of collaboration, distribution of war damage compensation, "back pay" for government employees, and peasant mobilization in response to violent attacks by the Philippine Constabulary and landlords' private armies. Leading the assault on "old guard" centralizers was Manuel Roxas, a prewar senator and favorite of Quezon and MacArthur. Roxas was joined by provincial leaders who did not want the return of a powerful central state under Osmeña and by the new strongmen whose immediate concern was consolidating their provincial power. An intrusive central state was neither to their liking nor in their interest. The Nacionalistas eventually split; Roxas and his allies established the Liberal party, and the first postwar election became a hotly contested two-party battle. Roxas was endorsed by MacArthur and Quezon's widow, thereby gaining a slight edge over the aging Osmeña, who was snubbed by the popular general. That Osmeña was defeated by a mere 203,000 votes suggests that many people still identified with the Nacionalistas and were suspicious of the new politicians.

Some observers welcomed the Liberal party victory as a "healthy development [that] tended to disperse the illusion of executive omnipotence."[5] Campaigning was intense, as suffrage had been universalized and it was through the parties that votes were mobilized. Carl Landé explains the interdependence of votes, money, favors, and office:

> Candidates for national offices need votes, which local leaders with their primary hold upon the loyalty of the rural electorate can deliver. Local leaders in turn need money to do favors for their followers, and this the candidate for high offices can supply. Local leaders also need a constant supply of public works

projects and services for their localities. Holders of high elective offices such as senators and congressmen . . . can affect the supply of projects and services.[6]

Block voting had been retained from the Commonwealth to ensure that voters were mobilized for the whole party slate, not for individual candidates. So although the parties were driven mainly by patronage, they also tried to project an identity—Nacionalistas as the party of Quezon, Liberals as the party of the new republic—especially in urban areas. For a brief period, the two-party system represented different interests and generations and competed for voters as organizations, not simply as loose associations dominated by individuals.

From the perspective of creating an effective central authority, however, the "healthy development" of two-party competition was a step backward. While some argue that, from the beginning, there was no fundamental programmatic difference between the parties, Nacionalistas who served with Quezon or in the Second Republic knew the value of a strong executive and the power of nationalism to motivate service to the common good. Claro M. Recto, Laurel, and Osmeña were still committed to centralizing the capacities of the state to strengthen the nation. The Liberals, in contrast, had little use for nationalism once the Philippines was independent. With Roxas's election, power reverted almost entirely to their local bases. Henceforth, those who sought to use the presidency to govern would have to work through elaborate patronage networks of politicians whose main concern was strengthening their own power, not assisting in the construction of an effective national authority.

A Fragile Economy

The impact of World War II on the Philippines was uneven: While most of the country was relatively untouched, Manila was devastated, and the success of communist guerrilla operations against the Japanese in provinces surrounding the capital profoundly altered their political makeup. Elsewhere, armed confrontation between Japanese and guerrilla forces had been minimal; the Japanese saw no reason to sustain the war effort in a country with less strategic value than Dutch Indonesia or British Malaya.

But the destruction of Manila, the displacement of landlord power in the adjoining provinces, and the disruption of plantation agriculture were enough to destabilize the new nation-state. The United States contributed to the problem when it demanded that the new government accept a "free trade" treaty heavily favoring the industrialized United States over the agrarian Philippines. The Bell Trade Act of 1946 accorded American entrepreneurs "parity" rights to land ownership, natural resource exploitation, and other business activities. Not surprisingly, nationalist scholars and activists have condemned this trade agreement; Amando Doronila points out that "it started the post-war economy on the narrow base of agricultural primary products," rather than encouraging industrialization or diversity of trade partners.[7] But criticism of its unequal provisions has come from liberal and conservative scholars as well. Economist Frank Golay, for example, wrote that the treaty included "a number of obnoxious infringements on Philippine sovereignty," including U.S. control of Philippine monetary and exchange policy.[8]

The United States also pressured the Philippine government to sign a Military Bases Agreement (1946) giving the United States the right to maintain military bases in the country for ninety-nine years and American military advisers a major role in the development of the Philippine military. Approval of these treaties was the condition for the release of $620 million in rehabilitation funds. Of this amount, $400 million was allocated for property damage compensation and only $120 million for the reconstruction of roads, highways, and harbors; the remaining $100 million would come as surplus military property. Faced with desperate problems of wartime recovery, the Philippine Congress approved the treaties, although only after Roxas ousted from Congress seven Democratic Alliance representatives and three anti-treaty Nacionalista senators on trumped-up charges of electoral fraud and terrorism. Because provisions of the Bell Trade Act contravened the Philippine Constitution, an amendment to the constitution was also passed and subjected to a national plebiscite. The electorate approved the amendment overwhelmingly, attesting to the continuing goodwill Filipinos felt for the United States.

Free trade and the disbursement of war-damage claims benefited only a small sector of the economy, mainly American-owned companies and Filipino exporters. Among those who drew cash from the rehabilitation funds were wealthy Filipino families with vast investments in land and commerce, some identified as collaborators with the Japanese or, in the case of one Spanish-Filipino tycoon, with European fascists. The landed elite—many were Roxas allies—profited from free trade as American market demand for primary commodities such as sugar, coconut oil, and hemp revived plantation production. And the sale of surplus military property simply became an opportunity for plunder. The Rehabilitation Finance Corporation, tasked to sell material worth 200 million pesos, turned over only 28 million pesos to the government after three years of operation. The rest was never accounted for.

Cronyism and the spoils system ensured that war funds were distributed to those closest to the regime. A vaguely defined American directive to release military "back pay" and related compensation to those who had not renounced their affiliation to USAFFE opened up a rich source of largesse to anti-Japanese guerrilla fighters—both genuine and fraudulent. (One of the latter was the young Congressman Ferdinand Marcos, who submitted false claims that he led the guerrilla force "Maharlika.") The Roxas government facilitated these payments because many of the claimants were affiliated with the new president and his Liberal party. Former Japanese collaborators–turned–Roxas supporters were also compensated for property damage; the regime assured the United States that speculation and hoarding of scarce goods during the war had fronted for supporting the guerrilla resistance. Worst of all, this money, which should have been invested in the production of goods and services needed for economic recovery, went largely toward the consumption of imported goods. (See box 7.1.)

The "unprecedented demand for imports" (over 1 billion pesos' worth by the end of 1948), pervasive corruption, and rampant overpricing precipitated a balance-of-payments crisis that led to capital flight, inflation, and 15 percent unemployment in an active workforce of 7.4 million Filipinos.[9] By 1949, the

---

Box 7.1.   Consumerism, or the Dissipation of Foreign Reserves

"A few representative items of the things we were starved for will suffice to remind everyone of the things that we have had to buy abroad, after conditions settled down a bit. Our working people were starved for the Piedmont cigarettes that they were smoking before the war; they were starved for the canned sardines and salmon and pineapple that they had come to like very much; and just to complete the picture, they were starved for just simple, plain good rice.

"Our middle class people were starved for the apples, grapes and oranges that were part of their daily diet before the war; they were starved for the Chesterfield and Lucky Strike cigarettes that they had missed for four years; they were starved for the five-tube and seven-tube radios with which they made life pleasant during the Commonwealth era; they were starved for the phonographs and phonograph records with which they enlivened many a dull evening during the time of peace.

"Our moneyed class were starved for the more expensive things. They were starved for the bacon and ham and Dutch butter which they had enjoyed on their tables before the war; they were starved for the limousines and sedans with which they cruised along Dewey Boulevard on warm evenings or on moonlight nights; they were starved for the grand pianos and the seven-cubic-foot refrigerators, for cabinet radio-phonographs, the woolen and Palm Beach clothes, the silk and linen dresses, the nylon stockings, and a hundred other luxuries that were part of their daily life before Pearl Harbor.

"Because of this profound and immense starvation, it was natural that as soon as money came into the hands of these different strata of people again, they began buying heavily all the things that they had been accustomed to, things that they needed and wanted, things that they enjoyed."

—Secretary of Finance Pio Pedrosa (1950), quoted in
Salvador P. Lopez, *Elpidio Quirino: The Judgement of History*
(Manila: Elpidio Quirino Foundation, 1990), 83–84

economy was on the brink of collapse, with international reserves at a critically low $260 million. By the end of the year, capital flight caused the reserves to decline by a further $75.4 million.[10] Urban unemployment spurred organized labor, and the Communist-controlled Congress of Labor Organizations demanded increased support for the poor and criticized the continuing influence of American and landlord forces in government. In the rural areas, peasant groups protested Roxas's ties with the landed elite. Aggravating the situation was the government's failure to set its own house in order: By late 1949, the payment of military wages remained irregular and the entire educational system suffered from lack of funds.[11] Nevertheless, no effort was made to resolve the difficulties of tax collection. The United States now recommended the adoption of direct taxation—the very reform it had shied away from when the responsible power—but the Roxas administration declined as well, lest it alienate its business and landlord allies and their representatives in Congress.

In April 1948, Roxas died suddenly of a heart attack, spreading fear that the Republic was on the brink of collapse; his vice president and successor, Elpidio Quirino, was seen as lacking the ability to deal with the economic crisis. Luckily for Quirino, U.S. president Harry S. Truman and his advisers were persuaded that free trade between two countries with unequal economic capacities would not promote Philippine economic development. Alarmed by the victory of Communist forces in China and the radicalization of Filipino peasants, they needed to arrest the Philippines' decline. With the approval of the U.S. president, the Philippine government implemented a series of "import and exchange controls" to stem capital drain.[12] But what was approved by the United States as an emergency measure presented an opportunity for Philippine economic planners to begin import substitution development.[13] Their goal was to stimulate industrial production by limiting imports and allowing local industry to grow in a protected market. To prevent unauthorized imports, the Central Bank controlled the country's dollar reserves and determined access to them. Industries that needed to import raw materials or capital inputs to produce for the domestic market had priority in dollar allocation. Firms seeking to import finished consumer goods qualified last or not at all. The United States promised $250 million in loans and credits and sent advisers to help in critical areas such as economic planning. This commitment came at a crucial time, for President Quirino's government faced a serious popular challenge in the PKP-led Huk uprising.

The Huk Rebellion

PKP rhetoric was radical and mimicked political calls emanating from Stalinist Russia, but Filipino Communists were actually inclined initially toward "legal struggle," that is, the mobilization of urban workers and peasants along constitutional lines. This reality did not prevent state authorities from attacking the party. As fervent anticommunists, government officials had always believed the PKP's real agenda was to seize state power. Quezon had harassed and imprisoned PKP leaders in the 1930s until the war led to a "popular front" against Japanese aggression. During the war, the PKP-led Hukbalahap distinguished itself as an effective guerrilla army, much like its Communist counterparts in Vietnam and China. But it did more: In areas north of Manila, after landed elites fled to the cities, the Hukbalahap became the de facto state and gave peasants a taste of local power. This brief experience with "popular democracy" did not escape the notice of the United States, whose anticommunism dovetailed with elites' efforts to recover power and control over the countryside.

State harassment and landlord reprisals increased popular resentment, and violence escalated between Hukbalahap units and private armies supported by the Philippine Constabulary and local police. Hukbalahap leaders tried to negotiate with the Americans, but their anti-Japanese achievements in the war had become irrelevant as anticommunism became the new U.S. priority. As a Communist-led organization, the Huks (pronounced HOOKS)—as they were popularly called—were now the enemy. At the same time, Roxas's exclusion of the PKP from constitutional politics forced its leaders to explore alternatives. When negotiations with President Quirino failed, the PKP decided on armed struggle. The anti-Japanese army was renamed the Hukbong Mapagpalaya ng Bayan (People's Liberation Army, or HMB), and a series of counteroffensives was launched against the government. By 1950, rumors circulated in Manila social circles that the Huks were just months away from capturing Malacañang, the presidential palace. (See box 7.2.)

The PKP leadership may have believed this, too—but it was wrong. The party overestimated both its own strength and the commitment of its peasant base. Its leaders assumed that experience under the Japanese, followed by government and landlord assaults after the war, had sufficiently radicalized the peasants. It turned out, however, that peasants had different notions about "socialism" and that their pragmatic "economistic" interests clashed with the PKP's ideologically "proletarian" perspective. Peasant support for the armed resistance was not resilient because it was not founded on a consistent belief in armed struggle to seize state power. Many joined the HMB to defend themselves from military reprisals, while others simply hoped to shock the government into implementing land reform. Moreover, PKP leaders failed to refine military coordination between the armed struggle in the countryside and the labor movement in the cities.[14]

Box 7.2.   Causes of the Huk Rebellion

"Last Sunday, through the medium of a Sunday pictorial magazine, the starving four million in this country were shown how the four hundred make merry.

"As I thumbed through the pages, noting the glitter and the lavishness of the two parties pictured, my mind went to the masses who invariably go hungry when crops fail or their fields are converted into battlefields; to the thousands who are unemployed; the millions who live in filth and squalor in ramshackle houses; the thousands who get sick and die for lack of medical attention.

"Given for one night only, such birthday parties as pictured in the magazine could, I surmise, feed the population of a barrio for a whole week.

"Of course, the rich and the powerful can claim they have a right to dispose of their money any way they see fit. But the trouble is they are not content with merely giving lavish parties; they also have to advertise the fact. Their enjoyment doesn't seem complete unless the whole country learns of their gay and reckless spending.

"Usually, these party-givers are the same people who bewail the lack of peace and order in the country. They don't understand why there are strikes and why the peasants take up arms in an effort to improve their lot."

—Armando J. Malay, *Manila Chronicle*, May 31, 1949

Meanwhile, American intervention led to major changes in the Armed Forces of the Philippines (AFP). Taking direct control of counterinsurgency operations, American officials and the Central Intelligence Agency (led by the infamous operative Edward Lansdale) used the Joint United States Military Advisory Group (JUSMAG) to introduce changes in AFP military organization and make it an effective counterinsurgency force. Improved training, better equipment, and military aid boosted morale and fighting performance. Public perception of the AFP changed for the better, too, when it captured the top members of the PKP Politburo.

To these two generally cited factors for the failure of the Huk rebellion, we should add the importance of migration to escape poverty and oppressive tenancy arrangements. In the first fifteen years of the postwar period, Filipinos from the densely populated northern and central islands moved in massive numbers to the southern "frontier" of Mindanao. The migration of more than a million people by 1960 was largely spontaneous and had little government support, but was surprisingly well organized and did not produce the volatility that often accompanies mass migration.[15] Utilizing family and village networks, migrants from Cebu and Bohol provinces in the Central Visayas and some Pampangos from central Luzon moved steadily into northern and eastern Mindanao. Migrants from northern Luzon settled in western Mindanao and those from Western Visayas settled in the southern

Figure 7.1. President Quirino (right, gesturing) displaying captured Huk leader Luis Taruc to the media (courtesy of the Lopez Memorial Museum, Philippines)

province of Cotabato. Migration resulted in more complex political networks reaching across geographical areas. Visayan or Ilocano politicians, for example, could no longer rely on their traditional "bailiwicks" alone and had to establish links with Visayan and Ilocano communities in the frontier zones. By the 1950s, northern and eastern Mindanao were already among the top ten vote-rich provinces of the country.

The wholesale migration of communities from Huk-influenced areas such as Pampanga and Bulacan indirectly aided government efforts to deprive guerrilla "fish" of their peasant "water." By easing pressure and stabilizing politically explosive regions, migration postponed class conflict for at least a generation. It was a phenomenon the AFP and CIA immediately appreciated, prompting them to add organized resettlement of surrendered Huk supporters and sympathizers to the counterinsurgency program. The Economic Development Corporation (EDCOR) project, which settled ex-Huks in Lanao del Sur and Cotabato, became a powerful propaganda tool of the state—it advertised an alternative to rebellion, the chance to own a piece of land, and a way out of poverty. With the surrender of leading HMB commanders by the middle of Quirino's term, the Huk rebellion ended.[16]

The Weak State

The Huks had been seen as a grave threat in part because the state was seen as completely ineffective under Roxas and Quirino. Corruption that began in the Roxas period reached serious proportions during the Quirino presidency. He himself was charged with extending favors to relatives and allies, with profligacy (for example, ownership of a golden chamber pot), and with tolerating corruption in Congress. (See box 7.3.)

Yet there was evidence of professional governance as well. The National Economic Council and the Budget Commission were "powerful tools to determine the course of economic development" under the new import substitution policy.[17] The Central Bank, which tightly supervised import licenses and American dollar allocation, helped stabilize the economy and created opportunities for domestic industries to grow; with American support, it withstood pressure from powerful sugar barons to gain unlimited access to the country's dollar reserves.[18] At the critical juncture when import controls needed to be implemented and defended, the bank's professional staff performed well.

Box 7.3.   Corruption

Senate President Jose Avelino, upon learning that President Quirino had approved an investigation into Avelino's alleged corruption, 1950

"Why did you have to order an investigation, honorable Mr. President? If you cannot permit abuses, you must at least tolerate them. What are we in power for? We are not hypocrites. Why should we pretend to be saints when in reality we are not? We are not angels. And besides, when we die we all go to hell. Anyway, it is preferable to go to hell where there are no investigations, no Secretary of Justice, no Secretary of Interior, to go after us."

President Garcia's executive secretary, Juan Pajo, 1958

"I was playing golf at Malacañang Park on the other side of the Pasig River across from the Palace. [A businessman] had come to see me about the approval of a barter license. I was new in my office then and I recommended that it be approved because in my opinion it was perfectly legal. As soon as the baggage compartment was opened, he pointed to a pile of paper bills amounting, according to him, to P50,000. 'That's for you,' the man said, 'for having recommended the approval of my firm's barter license.' The man was about to lift the box containing the money when I told him not to bother moving it because I was not interested in any part of his P50,000. When he realized that I meant what I said, he became apologetic. He must have been very embarrassed because he left in a hurry."

Lewis E. Gleeck Jr., *The Third Philippine Republic, 1946–1972* (Quezon City: New Day Publishers, 1993), 226–27

The import and exchange controls laid the foundation for a "viable manufacturing sector" that reduced economic dependence on imports. By the end of Quirino's term in 1954, the manufacture of goods for local consumption had expanded dramatically. Postwar Japanese reconstruction and the Korean War also stimulated a rise in exports, and Philippine products from timber to sugar to coconuts enjoyed favorable prices on the international market. Temporary cessation of legislative–executive battles allowed some new tax measures to pass, including higher corporate tax rates, which increased government revenues. When Quirino became president in 1948, annual tax revenue was 329 million pesos. By the end of his term, it had increased to 655 million pesos, leading to the first budget surplus since 1946.

There were limits to the efficacy of state reform, however. The government continued to resist American pressure to implement direct taxation, so the tax system remained regressive—heavily skewed against the middle class and poor, who paid a higher proportion of their income through indirect consumption taxes. Moreover, although domestic capitalism was strengthened and Americans complained about the Filipinos' "unfair advantage," U.S. firms actually benefited from the currency and import regime. Their subsidiaries—legally registered Philippine corporations or joint ventures with Filipino business partners—qualified for dollar allocation to import raw materials or semifinished products from the parent corporation. Others put up "packaging and assembly plants" in the Philippines, ostensibly to service the domestic market but essentially to qualify as dollar importers.[19]

Executive initiatives were also costly in terms of new opportunities for graft and corruption. The import and currency regime led to the emergence of "new cronies," businessmen whose close ties to state officials gave them easy access to dollar allocation and import privileges. A popular phrase of the day was "ten percenter"—an official who demanded 10 percent from importers and businessmen who sought a license to open an import substitution business. Quirino's success in stabilizing the economy was thus overshadowed by tales of corruption and "well-publicized large scale postwar scandals in the body politic," including some involving his own family.[20] Journalist Amando Doronila described the Quirino era as "represent[ing] the lowest ebb of central authority in relation to centrifugal forces and the autonomy of the State in relation to domestic forces seeking to influence public policy."[21] This image stuck with Quirino throughout his term, and when he ran for reelection in 1953, he was soundly beaten by his former defense secretary, Ramon Magsaysay.

REFORMING THE STATE THROUGH ELECTORAL POLITICS

"My Guy Magsaysay"

Magsaysay's candidacy was backed by professional military officers, the CIA, the Catholic Church, professional associations, and anticommunist labor and peasant associations, which formed the Magsaysay-for-President Movement, a well-oiled propaganda machine that promoted his image as a nontraditional politician. These forces also set up the National Movement for Free Elections (NAMFREL), an election watchdog that organized teams to guard against fraud and ensure fair vote counting. Magsaysay's image as a reformist dovetailed with middle-class anticommunism and the desire for stable, "clean and honest government" after the turbulent Roxas and Quirino eras. Magsaysay's background also enraptured the popular imagination—a mechanic, he was the first national leader from a provincial lower-class family and the first nonlawyer to aspire for the presidency. Finally, the AFP's successful counterinsurgency campaigns, which came under his watch as defense chief, enhanced his stature as a competent leader. The CIA and his supporters in the national and international media packaged these political assets to create the image of Magsaysay as a "man of the people." Quirino, tarred with corruption charges and portrayed as the quintessential traditional politician, was no match for Magsaysay.

In his first year in office, Magsaysay vigorously pursued reform. Personal popularity, American support, and majority control in both houses of Congress enabled him to pass: Republic Act 997, which increased the powers of the executive office; a law to improve management of the state budget; and a five-year national economic development plan to generate 1.7 million jobs. He recruited business executives to oversee economic projects and bolster the image of a professional, apolitical executive branch. Magsaysay also tapped the military for projects outside its normally authorized sphere of activities. AFP units played an active role in "civic action programs" to improve rural livelihoods and thwart Communist recruiters. Officers also ran certain executive offices, such as the Bureau of Customs and the Mindanao resettlement programs. This broke the enshrined tradition separating military from civilian work and used the army internally for the first time. But little opposition was heard from Congress or the media as long as the AFP was identified with its popular ex-boss and still basking in national and international commendation for its successful counterinsurgency war.

Magsaysay created another precedent with his effort to reach directly to rural communities through the Presidential Assistant for Community Development (PACD), an office that delivered government assistance to farmers. The

Figure 7.2. Ramon Magsaysay (in civilian clothing): A Cold War president who enjoyed strong U.S. military support (courtesy of the Lopez Memorial Museum, Philippines)

PACD was backed by a series of smaller, specialized presidential agencies that provided agricultural extension services to improve farmers' productivity and access to markets. Operating alongside these agencies were groups like the Philippine Rural Reconstruction Movement (PRRM) and the Philippine Rural Improvement Society (PRIS), the first nongovernmental organizations (NGOs) in the Philippines, set up by Magsaysay's private-sector supporters. American officials gave their full support to these projects by providing the PACD with start-up capital of $4.2 million and promising an additional $42.5 million to keep the program going.[22]

Magsaysay's network of presidential agencies and NGOs had not only economic objectives but also the political aim of popular mobilization independent of local "political bosses" and landed elites. Agencies like the PACD functioned as instruments for the executive branch to bypass local strongmen and deal directly with rural constituents. PACD's seven-thousand-strong workforce functioned as both "community development workers" and political officers promoting rural popular democracy. Magsaysay, who understood what dependence on patronage politics and backroom deals in Manila could do to a president, saw the PACD, its subsidiary agencies, its NGOs, and its American supporters as vital to setting up an electoral base independent of his party and its patronage network.

Francis Starner was correct to observe that Magsaysay's presidency signified the "gradual breaking down of the semiautonomous centers of local power, and a reorientation of these areas in the direction of the national government."[23] This was not new, but rather the return of a political habit last seen in the Commonwealth period—the "excessive personalization of the functions of the presidency."[24] Like Manuel Quezon, Magsaysay used his popularity to make administrative changes aimed at strengthening the central state *as well as* his own stature as leader. Yet he was different from his colonial predecessor in that he mobilized social forces directly. This set a precedent for future presidents who wanted to establish a direct link with the people. It was the first postwar image of Filipino populism.

In terms of strengthening the state, however, the personalized presidency has certain disadvantages. No matter how effective the presidential agencies may have been, their association with Magsaysay *personally* detracted from their ongoing value *institutionally* as instruments of executive power. Such initiatives tended to have useful lives coinciding with the term of their creator, although they lived on as sources of jobs and patronage, waiting to be reactivated. Second, the personalized and increasingly powerful presidency eventually stirred a congressional backlash. Magsaysay's use of the army, for example, did not directly threaten legislators, who still controlled military appointments and promotions, but it angered their local networks. Wherever the

AFP operated, it sidelined and overruled the local police, the instrument of social control wielded by local bosses and landlords. Their displeasure rather quickly found its way into the halls of Congress. When Magsaysay tried to pass the Land Reform Act of 1955, he exempted the huge estates of the sugar barons, and the legislature further weakened the act with amendments making it difficult for tenants to actually acquire land. Shortsighted American policy makers offered no help on this score. Sensing that the Communists had been thoroughly defeated, they eased their pressure on politicians to pursue land reform and recalled American advisers who proposed more radical measures for comprehensive land distribution.[25]

Before these problems had a chance to affect his popularity, Magsaysay was killed in a plane crash in May 1957. His vice president, Carlos P. Garcia, completed his term and then won his own presidential term.

A Patchwork State

Garcia lacked Magsaysay's charisma and was more at home with patronage politics than with Magsaysay's reformist allies. When the latter tried to challenge Garcia in 1957 by forming a third party, he relied on the Nacionalista party machine to defeat them. But Garcia was no Quirino—he was an "old line Nacionalista," admirer of Quezon, and legatee of the nationalism of José Laurel and Claro Recto. Having witnessed the impact of free trade and the dominant role of American economic interests in the postwar period, Garcia saw import controls as an opportunity to assert a Filipino presence in, if not control over, the economy—an issue important to his mentors Laurel and Recto as well. He therefore anchored his presidency in his "Filipino First" policy, the active promotion of the "Filipino business establishment." The policy drew protests from American, Chinese, and Chinese-Filipino business interests. The Chinese in particular regarded the policy's narrow interpretation of "Filipino" as a discriminatory ruse to eject them—as "aliens"—from the retail trade. The program was well received, of course, by their Filipino counterparts, who saw a chance to increase their share of dollar allocations under the import and currency control program.

Since the imposition of import controls, the economy had experienced 40.8 percent growth in manufacturing, 17.2 percent growth in agriculture, and 34.5 percent growth in mineral exploitation. Under Garcia's Filipino First policy, domestic industries numbered about five thousand in 1960; the Filipino share of new investments rose to 88 percent. It was now possible to talk of the Philippines having a "modest industrial base" and a more diversified economic elite.[26] Domestic consumer goods production and secondary industries (for example, cement and machine parts) increased the urban work-force and led to the dramatic expansion of urban centers, especially Manila and Cebu.

On the other hand, economic growth failed to improve social equity. Income distribution remained heavily skewed in favor of the rich. In 1957, the top 20 percent of Filipino families received 55 percent of total income while the lowest 20 percent received only 4.5 percent.[27] The middle class remained stable but failed to grow. Lower-class antagonism was kept in check only by the virtual disappearance of the radical Left, the moderating influence of reformist peasant and urban associations, and the continuing availability of land in Mindanao. The government, and the Catholic Church hierarchy that shared its anticommunism, headed off potential linkages between disgruntled lower classes and politicized intelligentsia through a systematic anticommunist inoculation campaign in schools and churches.[28]

If the Filipino First policy essentially benefited the elite, it also became contaminated by the spoils systems. Garcia's reliance on the Nacionalista machine and the support of local warlords and strongmen gave "business buccaneers" close to the president license to engage in "primitive accumulation." State corporations, such as the National Development Corporation, became havens of corruption, bribery, fraudulent transactions, and favoritism. Businesses which supported and subsidized Nacionalista political leaders were rewarded with easy access to dollar allocations and credits, import privileges, tax exemptions, and, if they faced bankruptcy, government bailouts. Garcia himself candidly admitted that when it came to cronyism, his presidency had become "a ship that has gathered a lot of barnacles along the way; I cannot shake them off. . . . [T]his was during the time of controls, when it was so easy to make anybody a millionaire; just give him a license and it's done."[29] By the end of his second year in office, Filipinos saw no difference between Garcia and Quirino in terms of corruption.

Again, the picture was not wholly grim. Certain agencies were able to maintain their autonomy from patronage interests. Under Miguel Cuaderno's leadership, for example, the Central Bank and Monetary Board fought a rearguard action to limit attempts by rent-seekers and others to eliminate import controls (see box 7.4). Cuaderno was able to rein in government spending, including attempts by Garcia himself to waste dollar reserves. As the *Philippine Free Press* reported:

> When the President got funny ideas on how to spend government money extravagantly for political purposes, Cuaderno put his foot down. When the politicians . . . bloated the national budget, Cuaderno . . . wielded the axe and cut the budget down to size. The Central Bank in Cuaderno's time imposed not just monetary but also fiscal discipline on the government.[30]

Box 7.4. An Island of State Strength

"Because of the widespread opposition to Central Bank Circular No. 79, which provided for additional restrictions on bank credit, President Garcia called a joint meeting of the Cabinet and members of the Monetary Board on board the Presidential yacht 'Sta. Maria' one evening.

"When I noticed that the purpose of the joint meeting was for the Cabinet to consider the wisdom of the issuance of said circular, I was constrained to perform the very delicate duty of explaining that the credit regulations adopted by the Monetary Board were not subject to review by the Cabinet. When one of the Cabinet members expressed doubt as to the validity of my statement for the reason that the members of the Monetary Board were Presidential appointees, I was compelled to explain that it was precisely the intention of Congress to give this body as much freedom of action as possible that the Charter of the Central Bank gave the majority of its members fixed terms of office.

"I felt that the remarks did not please the President and some members of the Cabinet, but it would be most unfortunate if any action taken by the Monetary Board in the discharge of its responsibility with respect to the maintenance of monetary stability could be reversed by the Cabinet. Since action of the Monetary Board in this connection is usually unpopular and politically unpalatable, central bank legislation since the advent of the managed currency system has tended to free the monetary authorities from extraneous control."

—Miguel Cuaderno Sr., *Problems of Economic Development: The Philippines, a Case Study* (Manila: Miguel Cuaderno Sr., 1964), 57–58

The mixture of plunder and professionalism made the state look like a quilt: Small patches of good governance adjoined larger patches of corruption and inefficiency. Unfortunately, as in the Quirino period, the latter overwhelmed the "islands of state strength." Scandals piled up—malversation of funds allotted to the National Marketing Corporation, favoritism in the disbursement of Japanese reparation funds, the privatization of public lands, the private use of government retirement accounts.[31]

With each exposé, Garcia's hold on power became more vulnerable. American, Chinese, and Chinese-Filipino businesses discriminated against by the Filipino First policy became more vocal. They were joined by Filipino commodity exporters who wanted to end tariff and currency controls and by middle-class associations dismayed by the return of "old corruption." These social forces were augmented by American businessmen, who had always regarded Filipino First as a ruse to introduce socialist-type economic programs and links with suspect regimes like Sukarno's Indonesia. Senior AFP officers, who had been marginalized by Garcia after running executive agencies under Magsaysay, began to plot a coup against the president—the first time Filipino military officers contemplated such a move. While it was nipped in the bud, the rumors alone destabilized Garcia's administration.[32] Meanwhile, opponents in Congress initiated impeachment proceedings.

Garcia ran for reelection in 1961, but was soundly defeated by his Liberal party rival, Diosdado Macapagal, who promised to open the economy to world trade, welcome back foreign investment, and improve state capacities to play a more meaningful role in economic development.

National Development

Macapagal was the first president to attempt national development planning. He established the Program Implementation Agency (PIA), an executive body charged with creating and implementing a comprehensive national economic development plan. The PIA was also meant to balance the National Economic Council, which under Garcia had ceased to function as an executive planning body as it fell under the control of politicians.[33] Macapagal insulated the PIA from "particularistic interests" by ensuring that its senior staff was apolitical and not easily swayed. He found able candidates for the job among a team of American-trained technocrats who shared his vision of an open economy, were rich enough not to be tempted by wealth, and were well liked by international agencies such as the International Monetary Fund and the World Bank.

The PIA was instrumental in implementing currency decontrol beginning in 1962, and agricultural exports received a temporary boost from the peso's devaluation. But the accompanying protective tariffs meant that the country still lacked a coherent development policy. The main beneficiaries of this situation were the family-owned conglomerates that were diversifying into new exports and industries. With "loyalties to family . . . stronger than to any single economic sector," these families needed access to "particularistic favors" more than they needed coherent policy.[34] However, they were now threatened by Macapagal's promise to go after "tax evaders" and "corrupt businessmen." He especially targeted the Lopez family—one of the country's richest, with interests in sugar, media, and power utilities. The battle fizzled as the Lopezes used their extensive patronage network in Congress to deflect Macapagal's attacks. Congress accused the president of "dictatorial tendencies" and refused to support his projects. Of the twenty-six "socioeconomic" bills Macapagal sent to Congress, only three became law. A land reform bill did pass, but it hardly resembled the original after the addition of more than two hundred amendments, including the exemption of lands devoted to real estate and the elimination of a tax to finance the reform.

Timely media exposés of government corruption sealed the fate of Macapagal's reform efforts. Stories of "conspicuous consumption" amid unremitting poverty, presidential vindictiveness toward enemies, policy implementation derailed by petty conflict, and growing nepotism undermined his presidency. Macapagal was forced to back down from his legislative agenda. His defeat soon brought to light other compromises. These included arrangements with certain senators not to disrupt their smuggling operations in exchange for votes, and "sweetheart deals" with American agricultural interests to rent public lands at bargain prices for banana and pineapple production. Most devastating was his dismissal of justice secretary Jose W. Diokno, whose investigation of illegal dealings between politicians and American businessman Harry Stonehill was heading dangerously close to the president's inner circle. The firing of Diokno was described by the *Philippine Free Press* as a "major setback in the administration's crusade against graft and corruption."[35]

Macapagal ended his term like Garcia—known more for the corruption permeating his administration than for his attempt to coordinate economic development. His rival in the 1965 presidential election, Ferdinand Marcos, pledged to do better in modernizing the country.

POSTWAR NATIONALISM

Debates over Filipino nationhood changed with independence. First, they shifted from dissatisfaction with American rule to criticism of military, economic, and cultural "neo-colonialism," as manifested in U.S. military bases, lopsided economic agreements, and the "Americanization" of Filipino culture and consciousness.[36] This postwar nationalist critique was articulated first by the PKP and upon its defeat was picked up by nationalists such as senators Laurel and Recto.[37] These politicians became the ideological spokesmen of the "nationalist business class" that supported Garcia's Filipino First policy and the inspiration for a small but vocal group of students at the University of the Philippines and the Laurel family–owned Lyceum College. Working together, the nationalist social forces achieved certain changes in Philippine–American relations, including a law limiting "alien" ownership and involvement in the economy and the renegotiation of the tenure of the military bases.[38]

The nationalists did not go unchallenged. Conservative social forces in government, the church, the media, and universities launched an aggressive campaign to silence the students, associate Recto's nationalism with communism, and expose corruption within the "nationalist class." The conservative counteroffensive worked against the politicians, but it failed to stamp out the nationalist resurgence on the campuses, which called for the Filipinization of private school curricula and staff and the teaching of José Rizal's novels (see box 7.5). By the early 1960s, nationalists at the University of the Philippines had survived McCarthy-style Communist witch-hunts, emerging stronger and better organized. In 1962, a group called the Student Cultural Association of the University of the Philippines drew national attention with its criticism of the Vietnam War and defense of the university's tradition of autonomy, now under attack by conservatives. Its leader was a young lecturer named Jose Maria Sison, who would go on to "reestablish" the Communist Party of the Philippines.[39]

Box 7.5.   Claro M. Recto, the Catholic Hierarchy, and the Rizal Law

"During the 1955 [senatorial] campaign, Recto was the target of a well-organized opposition by members of the Catholic hierarchy and its many organizations. They charged him with being a communist and an anti-Catholic. . . .

"Church displeasure with Recto increased during the controversy over the Rizal bill. He was the original author of the proposal to make Rizal's *Noli Me Tangere* and *El Filibusterismo* compulsory reading in all universities and colleges. . . . The measure immediately ran into determined opposition from the Catholic hierarchy. . . . Their argument was that the bill would violate the freedom of conscience and religion. The Catholic hierarchy even issued a pastoral letter detailing its objections to the bill and enjoining Catholics to oppose it. . . .

"A more organized campaign . . . was launched [by] the Catholic Action of Manila. This organization urged Filipino Catholics to write their congressmen and senators asking them to 'kill' the Rizal bill. During a symposium which this group organized, one of the speakers, Fr. Jesus Cavanna, introduced as an authority on Rizal, said that the novels belong to the past and it would be harmful to read them because they present a false picture of conditions in the country at that time. He described the *Noli Me Tangere* as 'an attack on the clergy' and alleged that the novel was not really patriotic because out of 333 pages, only 25 contained patriotic passages while 120 contained anti-Catholic statements. Another speaker, radio commentator Jesus Paredes, said that since some parts of the novels had been declared 'objectionable matter' by the hierarchy, Catholics had the right to refuse to read them so as not to 'endanger their salvation.' . . .

"In reply to a threat that Catholic schools would close should the Rizal bill pass, Recto went on record in favor of the nationalization of all schools. He contended that nationalization might be just the step needed to foster a movement for vibrant nationalism among Filipinos. He did not really believe the threat. 'They are making too much profit which they can ill-afford to give up,' he said.

"Finally, on May 12, the month-old controversy ended with unanimous approval of a substitute measure [that] accommodated the objections of the Catholic hierarchy. Though it still provided that the basic texts in the collegiate courses should be the unexpurgated editions of the two novels, it was now possible for students to be exempted from using the unexpurgated editions on grounds of religious belief. Opponents of the original Recto version jubilantly claimed a 'complete victory.' Proponents felt they had at least gained something."

—Renato Constantino and Letizia Constantino, *The Philippines: The Continuing Past* (Quezon City: Foundation for Nationalist Studies, 1978), 297–98

Another shift in postcolonial nationalism pertained to the place of Chinese in the new republic. Despite a long and intimate history between coastal southern China and the Philippines, independent Filipinos began to exhibit what Caroline Hau calls "a general amnesia, a forgetting of the centrality of the 'Chinese' and the Chinese mestizo in the history and everyday life of the nation-state."[40] Because the Chinese were well integrated into community life, state leaders—both nationalist and antinationalist—were forced to pass laws stipulating their "alien" origins in order to limit their participation in society and the economy. Hau notes that the Retail Trade Nationalization Act of 1954, passed to establish Filipino priority in obtaining business licenses, actually *exempts* "citizens and juridical entities of the United States." In the eyes of Filipino leaders, Chinese became "objects of distrust and censure because they supposedly pervert the 'true' value of citizenship." Their exclusion from the national community, however, did not prevent politicians from seeking them out for financial assistance. In scenes reminiscent of the Spanish era when top colonial and religious officials demanded bribes to allow Chinese entrepreneurs to conduct business, Filipino politicians tapped Chinese businessmen to enrich themselves or contribute to their electoral war chests.[41]

Relations between the majority and the other "outsider" group were less prominent in this period. There was no significant departure from Quezon's policy of acknowledging cultural and religious differences between Muslim Filipinos and the Christian majority, even while noting their shared "Malay heritage."[42] Neither were there substantive programs to strengthen the political assimilation of the Muslim communities into the nation-state. Filipino historians gave perfunctory recognition of the Muslims' distinct identity, but never added their "local history" to the national narrative.[43] Politicians acknowledged the backwardness and poverty of the Muslim areas, but did nothing to promote their development. While the military was preoccupied with the Huk threat, stability in the southern Philippines was entrusted to Muslim politicians, who became adept at playing the patronage games of Manila. They passed on responsibility for their constituents' welfare to local allies who ran their provinces like personal fiefdoms.[44] This indifference persisted through the terms of Roxas, Quirino, Magsaysay, Garcia, and Macapagal.

Not all Filipino-Chinese or Muslims were hurt by these policies during the first two decades of the Republic. The "nationalization law" had a silver lining for those Chinese businessmen, who, barred from the retail, rice, and corn industries, could afford to diversify into other growing sectors of the economy.[45] Their dynamic presence in manufacturing, banking, and the service sector eventually led to their resurrection as a major force in Philippine society. Unfortunately, this would only reinforce the association of ethnicity with capital.[46]

Muslim politicians with roots in the Quezon era continued their mutual accommodation with the central state as representatives of the Muslims in Manila and representatives of the central state in Mindanao. They employed a "traditional mask" of Muslim identity and datu leadership when they addressed the central state; this validated their claim to represent and defend the Muslims and reassured Manila leaders, who were "generally unfamiliar with and lacking access to the Muslim community." But when they returned to the province, they donned the "modern mask" of the Filipino politician, demonstrating their ability to "bring the benefits of the modern state to their constituents: from patronage funds to new programs and even the latest political gossip from the capital."[47] This position was tremendously advantageous, and from it they would dominate local politics until social tension on the closing frontier and a more aggressive national state began to undermine their authority.

POSTWAR DEMOCRACY

Those who study the Philippines generally argue that there was little structural discontinuity from the colonial to the postcolonial period despite the interregnum of World War II. We suggest here, however, that although "the elite survived," change did occur from the perspective of state formation. The Japanese occupation and the Second Republic broke the momentum toward state centralization that had begun under Manuel Quezon's presidency of the Commonwealth of the Philippines.

In the postwar period, virtual one-party rule gave way to two-party competition. The Nacionalista party faced ongoing challenges from the Liberal party, a breakaway faction that attracted many of the new "strongmen." These new elites drew their strength from Commonwealth-era education that facilitated their rise out of lower-class origins, from coercive resources amassed as guerrilla leaders during the war, and from American-dispensed patronage and reparations after the war. They had no prewar commitment to the national state, and the Liberal party generally reflected their localist orientation.

With the defeat of the PKP and its peasant army, however, there was no sustained pressure for the parties to become ideological or programmatic institutions. The reformist impulses that brought Magsaysay to power began to wane as even the "man of the people" adjusted his rhetoric and actions to accommodate the interests of a landlord-controlled Congress. Nationalism had been a powerful mobilizer in the recent past, but by the Garcia and Macapagal era, little distinguished the Nacionalistas from the Liberal party, as both were controlled by local interests. Since party affiliation came to have no value other than possession of a war chest and patronage network, party switching became habitual. Jose Maria Sison was certainly correct to remark that the two parties were the Pepsi and Coke of politics. Switching parties was always publicly justified by "principle," of course, but the emptiness of this rhetoric was obvious to all.

The preeminence of patronage and local interests also created a new relationship between the executive and legislative branches. In this period, the legislature was able to immobilize executive initiatives through either outright rejection or watered-down legislation. But most characteristic was the way dominant social forces—family clans, settler leaders, landed elites—eviscerated the implementation of state initiatives through infiltration and corruption. The more the executive tried to accomplish, the more deals were needed. The bigger the program, the more spoils to be distributed. The stricter the controls, the more opportunities for bribery. It didn't help that executive officeholders were themselves enmeshed in the networks, which were predicated on safeguarding wealth and social power—whether old or new, legally or illegally gained.

If political office is viewed primarily as an opportunity for enrichment, these networks, which delivered votes and total obedience from below, were ideal vehicles. But where local power-holders controlled their resources with weapons and private armies, or could simply withhold votes or switch allegiance, state actors were forced to think twice before imposing central control or demanding professional, efficient, and corruption-free governance. Magsaysay, for example, cleaned up and improved the fighting prowess of the AFP, but never used it to break up the private armies. By the mid-1960s, the stalemate of the first five presidential administrations had yielded a high level of public cynicism toward the state. Yet the sheer accumulation of development-oriented executive agencies had created a discernable *internal* constituency for "governance" that could potentially be activated, as would happen under the next president, Ferdinand Marcos.

NOTES

1. Amando Doronila, *The State, Economic Transformation, and Political Change in the Philippines, 1946–1972* (New York: Oxford University Press, 1992), 92.

2. Alfred W. McCoy, ed., *An Anarchy of Families: State and Family in the Philippines* (Madison: University of Wisconsin, Center for Southeast Asian Studies, 1993).

3. Steven Rood, "Decentralization, Democracy, and Development," in *The Philippines: New Directions in Domestic Policy and Foreign Relations*, ed. David G. Timberman (Singapore: Institute of Southeast Asian Studies, 1998), 114.

4. Hernando J. Abaya, *Betrayal in the Philippines* (New York: A. A. Wyn, 1946).

5. Frank Golay, *The Philippines: Public Policy and National Economic Development* (Ithaca, N.Y.: Cornell University Press, 1961), 18.

6. Carl H. Landé, *Leaders, Factions, and Parties: The Structure of Philippine Politics*, Southeast Asia Studies Monograph Series no. 6 (New Haven, Conn.: Yale University Press, 1964), 2.

7. Doronila, *The State*, 47.

8. Frank Golay, *Underdevelopment and Economic Nationalism in Southeast Asia* (Ithaca, N.Y.: Cornell University Press, 1969), 59.

9. Golay, *Underdevelopment,* 59; Vicente B. Valdepeñas Jr. and Germelino M. Bautista, *The Emergence of the Philippine Economy* (Manila: Papyrus Press, 1977), 182.

10. Renato Constantino and Letizia R. Constantino, *The Philippines: A Past Revisited* (Quezon City: Tala Pub. Services, 1975), 227.

11. Joseph Ralston Hayden, *The Philippines: A Study in National Development* (New York: Macmillan, 1942), 499.

12. Golay, *Underdevelopment*, 95.

13. Doronila, *The State*, 51–52.

14. Jesus B. Lava, *Memoirs of a Communist* (Pasig, The Philippines: Anvil Publishing, 2002), 147–77.

15. Frederick Wernstedt and Paul D. Simkins, "Migration and Settlement in Mindanao," *Journal of Asian Studies* (November 1965): 92–94.

16. Lava, *Memoirs of a Communist*, 253–78.

17. Doronila, *The State*, 54.

18. Paul D. Hutchcroft, *Booty Capitalism: The Politics of Banking in the Philippines* (Ithaca, N.Y.: Cornell University Press, 1998), 72–73.

19. Sylvia Maxfield and James Nolt, "Protectionism and the Internationalization of Capital: U.S. Sponsorship of Import Substitution Industrialization in the Philippines, Turkey, and Argentina," *International Studies Quarterly* 34 (1990): 49–81.

20. Golay, *Underdevelopment*, 77.

21. Doronila, *The State*, 95.

22. Paul M. Monk, *Truth and Power: Robert S. Hardie and Land Reform Debates in the Philippines, 1950–1987* (Clayton, Vic., Australia: Centre for Southeast Asian Studies, Monash University, 1990).

23. Frances Lucille Starner, *Magsaysay and the Philippine Peasantry: The Agrarian Impact on Philippine Politics, 1953–1956* (Berkeley: University of California Press, 1961), 22.

24. Doronila, *The State*, 97.

25. Monk, *Truth and Power*.

26. Renato Constantino and Letizia R. Constantino, *The Philippines: The Continuing Past* (Quezon City: Foundation for Nationalist Studies, 1978), 312.

27. Edita A. Tan, "Income Distribution in the Philippines," in *Philippine Economic Problems in Perspective*, ed. Jose Encarnacion Jr. et al. (Quezon City: Institute of Economic Development and Research, School of Economics, University of the Philippines, 1976), 218.

28. Mario V. Bolasco, *Points of Departure: Essays on Christianity, Power, and Social Change*, ed. Edicio de la Torre (Manila: St. Scholastica's College, 1994), 239–44.

29. Quoted in Lewis E. Gleeck Jr., *The Third Philippine Republic, 1946–1972* (Quezon City: New Day Publishers, 1993), 212.

30. *Philippine Free Press*, July 8, 1972, quoted in Gleeck, *Third Philippine Republic*, 242.

31. Gleeck, *Third Philippine Republic*, 227–37.

32. Alfred W. McCoy, *Closer than Brothers: Manhood at the Philippine Military Academy* (New Haven, Conn.: Yale University Press, 1999), 131–35.

33. Miguel Cuaderno Sr., *Problems of Economic Development: The Philippines, a Case Study* (Manila: Miguel Cuaderno Sr., 1964), 7, 48–49, 96–99.

34. Emmanuel S. De Dios and Paul Hutchcroft, "Political Economy," in *The Philippine Economy: Development, Policies, and Challenges*, ed. Arsenio M. Balisacan and Hal Hill (Quezon City: Ateneo de Manila University Press, 2003), 48.

35. *Philippine Free Press*, May 26, 1962.

36. Claro M. Recto, *The Recto Reader: Excerpts from the Speeches of Claro M. Recto*, ed. Renato Constantino (Manila: Recto Memorial Foundation, 1965).

37. Hernando J. Abaya, *The CLU Story: Fifty Years of Struggle for Civil Liberties* (Quezon City: New Day Publishers, 1987); Marites N. Sison and Yvonne T. Chua, *Armando J. Malay: A Guardian of Memory: The Life and Times of a Filipino Journalist and Activist* (Manila: Anvil Publishing, 2002), 103.

38. Renato Constantino, *The Making of a Filipino: A Story of Colonial Politics* (Quezon City: Malaya Books, 1969), 200–240.

39. Francisco Nemenzo, "An Irrepressible Revolution: The Decline and Resurgence of the Philippine Communist Movement," manuscript, November 13, 1984, 44–47.

40. Caroline S. Hau, *Necessary Fictions: Philippine Literature and the Nation, 1946–1980* (Quezon City: Ateneo de Manila University Press, 2000), 126.

41. Joseph L. Piang, "The Chinese and the Philippine Political Process," in *Philippine-Chinese Profile: Essays and Studies*, ed. Charles J. McCarthy. (Manila: Pagkakaisa sa Pag-unlad, 1974), 93–96.

42. Resident Commissioner of the Philippines to the U.S. Congress [Manuel Quezon], *The Filipino People* (October 1912): 5.

43. Alunan Glang, *Muslim Secession or Integration?* (Quezon City: R. P. Garcia, 1969).

44. Peter G. Gowing, *Muslim Filipinos: Heritage and Horizon* (Quezon City: New Day Publishers, 1979), 185–87.

45. Teresita Ang See, "The Chinese in the Philippine Political Process: From Retail Trade Nationalization to Retail Trade Liberalization," in *The Chinese in the Philippines: Problems and Perspectives* (Manila: Kaisa para sa Kaunlaran, 1997), 2:69–84.

46. See Caroline S. Hau, "'Who Will Save Us from the Law?' The Criminal State and the Illegal Alien in Post-1986 Philippines," in *Figures of Criminality in Indonesia, the Philippines, and Colonial Vietnam*, ed. Vicente L. Rafael (Ithaca, N.Y.: Cornell University, Southeast Asia Program, 1999), 128–51.

47. Patricio N. Abinales, *Making Mindanao: Cotabato and Davao in the Formation of the Philippine Nation-State* (Quezon City: Ateneo de Manila University Press, 2000), 188.

Chapter Eight

Marcos, 1965–1986

THE PRESIDENCY OF FERDINAND MARCOS

In the first two decades of the postwar republic, no Philippine president succeeded in winning reelection. This popular rebuke spoke to the ineffectiveness of presidential policies in the face of persistent economic problems, including inequality and uneven development. By the mid-1960s, the nation that prided itself on being the most "advanced" in the region faced new problems as well. Land planted to the traditional export crops, sugar and coconut, was expanding at the expense of rice land. This was in response to higher U.S. demand for Philippine sugar and the peso's devaluation following currency decontrol in 1962. But while the sugar bloc enjoyed high commodity prices, the cost of food staples increased, causing the real income of urban consumers to decline.[1] Neither did small rice farmers benefit; their plots were too small and their productivity stagnant because of underdeveloped rural infrastructure, insufficient access to credit, and inefficient agricultural services. As rice and corn production declined, the Philippines became a rice-importing country and the rural unemployed were pushed off the land.

But industry could not absorb the growing numbers seeking work in the cities. Manufacturing growth had slowed considerably. This was not because of decontrol—high tariffs had immediately been erected to protect domestic industry—but because import substitution industrialization (ISI) had inherent limitations as a development strategy. Early-stage industrialization depended on imported capital inputs, for which entrepreneurs had enjoyed privileged access to dollars—this had encouraged capital-intensive rather than labor-intensive production. Further, ISI promoted "light industry," which had a limited domestic market. These and other factors meant import substitution had run its course as a source of employment growth and stimulus to economic development. The entry of a new wave of unskilled, unorganized labor into the market therefore brought wages down, and these workers contributed to the formation of a new urban proletarian underclass.

"This Nation Can Be Great Again"

Ferdinand E. Marcos's defeat of Macapagal was accomplished by the usual pattern of elite interdependence—the help of Ilocano allies in consolidating his northern Luzon bailiwick, a tactical alliance with the Lopez sugar-media-energy dynasty, and a war chest of funds accumulated as a member of the Senate. On the campaign trail, Marcos promised that "this nation can be great again," that the days of corruption and inefficiency were over. By 1965, however, the idea of a new president turning things around was hardly believable. The corruption of the Garcia and Macapagal presidencies had nurtured public cynicism, and Marcos himself had been accused of corruption while in the Senate. Neither his candidacy nor his slogan inspired much optimism, although the candidate was youthful and his beauty-queen wife Imelda gave his campaign a touch of glamour.

To make his run for president, Marcos switched from the Liberal to the Nacionalista party, justifying his turn against erstwhile ally Macapagal by a commitment to fight corruption and reform the bankrupt political system. This tactic had first been used by Manuel Roxas when he split the Nacionalistas to run against Sergio Osmeña as a Liberal in 1946. Then Ramon Magsaysay switched parties to run against Elpidio Quirino, and it has since become a normal feature of national politics. At the time, however, because Congress was dominated by Liberals who were not pleased with Marcos's betrayal, it took him two years to gain a majority, despite his skill as a backroom dealer. Marcos thus began his presidential term in a position of some weakness.

But all was not bleak for the minority president. Marcos had a better grasp of two realities than most politicians. First was his recognition of the public's yearning for economic stability and its disgust with a Congress that passed fewer bills, made longer speeches, and paid itself higher salaries with each passing year.[2] Second was his appreciation of the existing resources and potentially vast powers of the office of the presidency. While Congress voted appropriations, only the president could release the funds on which congressional patronage depended, giving him leverage he would use to pass key legislation. Marcos then set out to do what Manuel Quezon had done a generation earlier—take advantage of public sentiment and the executive office to control Congress. The three instruments at his disposal were increased public spending, executive agencies staffed with "apolitical" technocrats, and use of the army to implement development programs. With these he sought to bypass Congress and exercise executive authority—his authority—directly.

Marcos's rural development strategy was to increase productivity on existing rice lands in order to make newly opened land, especially in the interior of Mindanao, available for foreign investment in the new export crops of bananas and pineapples. He therefore launched an ambitious rural infrastructure program funded by local and external borrowing and development aid. He built new irrigation systems, supported technological innovations, and began to upgrade existing road systems. He also pumped credit into the rural economy through the state-owned Land Bank. The rural strategy received a big boost when high-yielding rice varieties were introduced by the International Rice Research Institute at the University of the Philippines (UP). With high-yielding rice, irrigation, credit to purchase chemical inputs, and government crop purchase subsidizing the "green revolution," the return of rice self-sufficiency became a strong possibility. Not to neglect social development, Marcos upgraded rural education with the construction of "Marcos schoolhouses," prefab buildings designed for public elementary and secondary education. (These and other projects funded by U.S. aid obliged him to break a campaign promise not to involve the Philippines in the American war in Vietnam. Soon after he became president, a battalion of military engineers was sent to South Vietnam.)

Figure 8.1.   Ferdinand and Imelda Marcos: The president releasing *bangus* (milk fish) fry into a fishpond while the first lady (in gown) looks on (courtesy of the Lopez Memorial Museum, Philippines)

To lessen dependence on agricultural exports, Marcos pushed the 1967 Investment Incentives Act through Congress. This legislation encouraged investors of foreign capital to participate in domestic industrial development and to use the country as a base for export production. A few nationalist senators fought it, but the bill passed because the entry of foreign capital created opportunities for members of Congress and their allies, who were increasingly diversifying into business. But although passage of the act signaled the start of an export-oriented industrialization policy, tariff regulations protecting domestic industries such as food processing, tobacco, and retail were not removed.[3]

Marcos did encounter congressional resistance to his programs, of course. But he neutralized some legislative opponents with the selective release of public funds, while exercising his veto on bills such as one that would have limited his right to raise revenue through borrowing. Then, because Congress was more likely to approve a project than to implement it, Marcos deployed the executive agencies established by his predecessors. He revived Macapagal's Program Implementation Agency (PIA) and drew on American economic aid to reactivate Magsaysay's Presidential Assistant for Community Development (PACD); both extended the central state's presence into the countryside.[4] Most important, he filled these agencies with technocrats—economists, lawyers, finance and management specialists, and engineers—and granted them power to implement development programs.

Like Magsaysay, Marcos deployed the Armed Forces of the Philippines (AFP) in development projects, particularly in areas where civilian agencies lacked the resources to undertake projects themselves. Marcos regarded the AFP as a close and permanent "partner" in the pursuit of development and declared that "its manpower, material and equipment resources plus its organizational cohesiveness . . . should be exploited to the maximum . . . considering that the problem besetting the country is socioeconomic rather than military and that the resources available to solve this problem are scarce and limited."[5] This laid the groundwork for further military involvement in national and local administration and politics.

In his first-term initiatives—economic liberalization, pursuit of productivity gains over comprehensive land reform, and the use of executive and military agencies to shape society—we see continuity with past presidents. Neither did Marcos differ in the use of power to enrich himself, his clan, and his allies. In the patchwork state, cupidity coexists with national commitment, and self-interest overlaps "reasons of state." Marcos's first term, developmentalist though it was, exhibited the self-serving corruption of his predecessors. Increased government involvement in agriculture led to overpriced rice in times of shortage, and in the infrastructure program, officials took kickbacks from construction companies owned by Marcos supporters, who built roads with inferior materials.

But Marcos was able to deflect corruption charges. Perhaps because the label applied equally to congressional leaders and local politicians, Marcos was able to turn the tables on his accusers, insisting that corruption had become a system-wide problem. He had two further advantages: The green revolution helped the country attain rice self-sufficiency in 1968, and anti-Marcos forces were not yet mobilized in large numbers. Since early in the decade, both moderate and radical students had staged protests against anticommunist witch-hunts and curtailment of academic freedom, high tuition, incompetent faculty, and the U.S. war in Vietnam, while a sprinkling of trade unionists organized industrial strikes. But these two distinct movements, the former largely confined to Manila's college campuses, did not yet affect public debate.[6]

What undermined Marcos was the fact that economic progress could not be sustained. The government had borrowed heavily for development programs on the assumption that export earnings and other revenues would finance debt repayment. But export revenues did not improve as much as expected. Despite the promotion of new crops, almost 70 percent of export value in 1967–1971 was still generated by sugar, coconut, and forestry products. The rising cost of imports was not offset by the value of such a narrow export base, which was subject to the fluctuation of global commodity markets. In fact, the terms of trade of such commodities—the price of exports relative to the price of the country's imports—had been declining since the early 1960s.[7]

At the same time, other sources of government revenue went untapped. From 1959 to 1968, Congress passed no tax legislation at all, despite significant structural changes in the economy. Legislators representing sugar interests specifically rejected taxes on exports. As a result, indirect taxation still contributed up to three-quarters of tax revenues, and even the Omnibus Tax Law of 1969 did not address the basic need to increase the ratio of income tax to general tax revenue. The distorted tax structure, poor collection efforts, and loss of funds to corruption left the Philippine state with insufficient resources to pursue its development projects. Throughout the 1960s and 1970s, even as the Philippines received massive loans from the World Bank and commercial lenders, public spending would remain less than half that of other, more successful, developmentalist states such as Malaysia and South Korea.[8]

American development assistance declined in the late 1960s—from $190 million in 1968 to $144 million in 1969—and foreign investment plunged from $20 million to $8 million, as the international community became wary of corruption and inefficiency. During Marcos's first term, the government deficit more than doubled, reaching 1.13 billion pesos.[9] The president had lost much of his original panache and was confronted by growing criticism from political opponents and even the hitherto tolerant middle class. Public antipathy spiked in May 1967, when the military shot and killed members of a millenarian group marching to Malacañang Palace to demand "true justice, true equality and true freedom for the country."[10]

Nevertheless, in 1969 Ferdinand Marcos became the first Philippine president to win reelection. His victory came at an extremely high price to the country. As much as $50 million went into the Marcos campaign, much of it public funds. For example, money from the Rural Improvement Fund was distributed through the patronage network down to the level of barrio captain, especially in his opponent's home province of Cebu. As historian Resil Mojares explains: "The election was decided by the question of greater and lesser power. . . . Millions were disbursed for billboards and outdoor propaganda materials, print publicity, campaign gifts, and the virtual monopoly of radio and television time."[11] Defeated candidate Sergio Osmeña Jr., in a postelection protest filed with the Presidential Election Tribunal, "charged . . . maximum use by Marcos of the power of his office through organized terrorism, massive vote-buying, and rampant fraud."[12] It was the classic case of being out-gunned, out-gooned, and out-gold.

Reform or Radical Change?

Marcos's reelection plunged the country into crisis. The unprecedented government deficit of more than one billion pesos forced Marcos to float the currency in early 1970. From its peg at two pesos to the dollar, the peso dropped to six to the dollar. Inflation, which had been stable at about 4.5 percent through the 1960s, rose quickly.[13] A sense of unease spread in urban areas, as the middle class feared an economic tailspin. Social and political activism became much more urgent, and student protest on Manila's campuses grew in frequency and intensity.

Activism addressing national and social themes also emerged within the Catholic Church, whose political influence had grown with its anticommunist offensive of the 1950s. U.S. colonialism had left the Catholic hierarchy foreign, replacing Spanish clergy with American and European priests and nuns. The hierarchy also remained hostile to Philippine nationalism (notably in the Rizal bill debate), which it associated with the anticlericalism of the 1896 Revolution. It was only in the 1960s that the issue of Filipinization within the Church was finally addressed in conjunction with the call of Rome's Vatican II council to "indigenize" the postcolonial churches.[14] Activism was further encouraged in the 1960s and 1970s when popes John XXIII and Paul

Figure 8.2. Jeepney strike, 1970: Rising inflation drove up the cost of imported oil (courtesy of the Lopez Memorial Museum, Philippines)

VI directed Catholics to be concerned with social justice as well as spiritual salvation. Younger priests, nuns, and lay members became directly involved with peasants and workers through the Church-sponsored Federation for Free Farmers and the National Social Action Secretariats.

Meanwhile, after almost a decade of silence, the Partido Komunista ng Pilipinas (PKP) renewed organizing for "parliamentary struggle." With its peasant and worker base still recovering from the Huk debacle, the party recruited students at the UP and the Lyceum in Manila who were already attracted to Marxism. Jose Maria Sison's Kabataang Makabayan (KM, Nationalist Youth) became the most vocal and dynamic of the PKP's new front organizations. Claiming Claro Recto's nationalist lineage and expressing solidarity with Vietnam's war of liberation and Mao Tse-Tung's Great Proletarian Cultural Revolution, KM began to make its presence felt. (See box 8.1.)

Party seniors, still traumatized by the Huk defeat, feared attracting the attention of the state and did not welcome the shocking militancy of their juniors, who quoted from Mao's "Little Red Book" and incited peasants to rebel. Their elders tried to silence them, but the youth resisted. Then Sison wrote a critical evaluation of PKP history in which he indicted the older generation for having destroyed the party. This led to the young comrades' expulsion and their "reestablishment" of the party in 1968 as the Communist Party of the Philippines (CPP).

Figure 8.3.   Student picket at University of Santo Tomas, 1970: Foreign and antinationalist personnel still dominated the Church and its institutions (courtesy of the Lopez Memorial Museum, Philippines)

The ensuing battle for influence between the old and new parties was framed by the unpopularity of the Vietnam War, the attraction of Mao's "continuing revolution," and the rise of a youthful New Left in Western Europe and the United States. The international and regional context gave the CPP an edge over the older and deeply conservative PKP. The CPP was also buoyed by the proliferation of "national democratic" organizations in schools throughout Manila, by its capture of the nationally prominent UP student council, and by alliances with workers' unions and peasant organizations. CPP "legal organizations" also attracted moderate students who were essentially reformist. A newspaper columnist described the students' radicalization:

> First they were sure it was only the lack of student councils. Then they felt, having got the councils, that it must be the poor classrooms and the underpaid professors. Then came the discovery that something more fundamental was at stake: the congressional allowances, perhaps, or the dirty elections, or the Constitution, the President and his friends. But even that was no longer enough. It was the entire system—nothing less.[15]

Whether radical or moderate, the activist view might be summed up in the words of one: "Democracy should be for the whole population, not for

Box 8.1.   The Radicalization of Jose Maria Sison

"Our house and that of my cousins are the only two private structures sharing the area around the plaza with the Catholic church, the municipal building and the local public school. The generation of my parents spoke Spanish. Tenants came daily to deliver land rent, ask for seeds, do menial tasks around the house or plead for some special consideration.

"The best front seats in church belonged to the family. During the town fiesta, special seats of honor were reserved for us because the mayor was almost always a close relative and was dependent on the captive votes of tenants. Up to the early 1950s, I would witness political candidates coming to our house to beg for these votes. . . .

"From childhood onward, I was encouraged to study law and become a lawyer so as to be able to defend the family property, become a political leader and revive the fading feudal glory of the family. The family was already assailed by fears of continuing land fragmentation from one generation to another and by the vigorous postwar political rise of professionals coming from the rural bourgeoisie. . . ."

—Jose Maria Sison with Rainer Werning, *The Philippine Revolution: The Leader's View* (New York: Crane Russak, 1989), 3

* * * * *

"The youth today face two basic problems: US imperialism and feudalism. These two are the principal causes of poverty, unemployment, inadequate education, ill health, crime and immorality which afflict the entire nation and the youth. The youth do not only suffer with their people the iniquities of US imperialism and feudalism but are also the first ones to suffer them.

"It is the task of the Filipino youth to study carefully the large confrontation of forces between US imperialism and feudalism on one side and national democracy on the other side. To know the nature of this contradiction of forces is to know the dynamism and internal motion of our semicolonial and semifeudal society.

"For the youth to know so much is for them to act more effectively and cooperate more thoroughly on the side of progress. . . .

"This generation of Filipino youth is lucky to be at this point in history when US imperialism is fast weakening at all significant levels of conflict: that between capitalism and socialism; that between the capitalist class and the working class; and that between imperialism and national independence movements in Asia, Africa and Latin America."

—Jose Maria Sison, "Kabataang Makabayan Founding Speech, November 30, 1964," in *Twenty Speeches That Moved a Nation*, ed. Manuel L. Quezon III (Pasig, The Philippines: Anvil Publishing, 2002), 65–66

the elite alone." But the KM and its affiliate CPP organizations went further, believing that violence was justified in fighting "feudalism (exemplified by land tenancy, social injustice, the too wide a gap between the poor and the rich), fascism (or the use of armed might to suppress civil liberties), and imperialism (the continued existence of US bases in the Philippines, among other things)."[16] In the countryside, Sison teamed up with a dissatisfied young Huk commander, Bernabe Buscayno, through the mediation of anti-Marcos politicians Senator Benigno Aquino Jr. and Congressman Jose Yap.[17] Their meeting led to the formation in 1969 of the New People's Army (NPA), which began to receive young urban recruits ready to go to the mountains.

Soon after Marcos's reelection, the two forces clashed. On January 26, 1970, Marcos addressed Congress while activists from a whole range of worker, peasant, and student organizations massed outside. Exiting through the front door, Marcos and his wife were pelted with stones and confronted with placards and an effigy of a coffin symbolizing the death of democracy. Police and presidential security forces responded by beating students with truncheons. Four days later, another demonstration gathered at Malacañang, the presidential palace. This time, four students were killed, and public opinion seemed equally shocked by the radicalism of the youth and the authorities' brutality. These days of violence became known as the "First Quarter Storm" of 1970 and inaugurated a year of pitched street battles. The "FQS" swelled the ranks of the radicals and, along with Mao's call for revolution among youth worldwide, turned CPP cadres and their supporters into romantic heroes.[18] (See box 8.2.)

It was also a time of unabashed opportunism. Radical propaganda got a great boost when Marcos's discarded allies, notably the Lopez and Laurel families, sensing that he was faltering, announced their sympathy with "the revolution" and opened their media outlets to student radicals. The television stations and newspapers highlighted demonstrations portraying Marcos as a "puppet" of imperialism (the United States), feudalism (Filipino landlords), and bureaucrat capitalism ("the use of public agencies for the accumulation of private wealth").[19] Suddenly, a relatively small left-wing group became a major national player, thanks to the political opportunism of anti-Marcos elites. When Marcos warned of an unholy alliance between radicals and "oligarchs," therefore, he spoke the truth. But as more and more government corruption was exposed in a crisis economy, Marcos was clearly on the defensive.[20]

The intensification of political battles outside the state was paralleled by escalating institutional combat within. Congress had authorized a constitutional convention to update the 1935 Commonwealth Constitution, and the directly elected delegates included activists who sought to reshape the exercise of power. Anti-Marcos delegates also planned to prevent him (or any immediate family member) from seeking another term. In Congress, the opposition regained a majority after key Nacionalistas withdrew their support and a Communist bombing of a Liberal party rally in August 1971 was popularly attributed to Marcos. Public anger surged when the president suspended

Box 8.2. From Beatles to Barricades, 1969–1972

"Low-waist were the pants when the decade began, but by 1962 the fad was hi-waist (belt-line above the navel) and dropped crotch . . . worn with red shirts. Girls looked like astronauts in the pouf hairdos, and wore dresses with plunging backlines.

"The tunes of the early '60s were *Teen-Age Señorita, Sad Movies Make Me Cry, The Young Ones, More Than the Greatest Love, Yellow Bird High Up In Banana Tree* and *I Left My Heart In San Francisco*.

"The top dance was, of course, the twist. . . .

"The youth gang that was to make history—Jose Maria Sison's Kabataang Makabayan—exerted, on campuses, the strongest snob appeal of all. It was very Now and very Mod to be a KM, especially if you were moneyed and burgis. The KM apocalypses of the 1970s can be said to have sprung from the revolts against Squareville in the '60s of young fat cats. . . .

"The later '60s brought in the shirt-jac, the mini, the Beatle hair, the Twiggy haircut, the mau-mau and the mask-k-pops, expressions like '*Dehin goli*' and '*pogi*' [unbathed and handsome, respectively], the turtleneck T-shirt in apple-green worn with fancy necklaces and pendant, the skin-tight jeans, and the coming of the Age of Aquarius.

"In 1968 . . . we were singing *Hey Jude* and *Can't Take My Eyes Off of You*.

"We were singing a very different tune when the 1970s began. '*Makibaka!*' [Struggle!] became the cry of a January evening in 1970 when Marcos and Imelda emerged from the Congress opening to find themselves being booed, rushed and stoned by youth picketers. The storm of demos had burst that would rage the whole year. . . .

"The demonstrator created a life style too. Early in the year, when the nights were cold, he marched in turtleneck. His weapons were stone and placard. After the initial riots, the use of the Molotov cocktail and the pillbox became more prevalent, provoked by police firepower. The demo itself become stylized into various varieties: picket, long march, living theater, people's tribunal, parliament of the streets.

"The chants of the year were: 'Down with imperialism, feudalism, fascism!' and '*Makibaka, huwag matakot!*' [Dare to Struggle!] . . .

"What Filipinos never thought to see in their lifetime, they saw this year: street fighting at barricades. Almost no month in Manila when no streets emptied, no stores closed in a hurry, and no pavement became a battleground between the youth marching with red flags and placard and helmeted troops marching with truncheon and wicker shield.

"The man on the street came to learn what tear gas smells like. . . .

"By 1971, third term talk had become cold potatoes as the Marcoses vanished from public view. . . . The Manila of 1971 had become accustomed to patrols on the streets at night and checkpoints at certain corners. And to seeing barbed-wire barriers on Mendiola Bridge, which had become the most famous bridge in our modern history.

"The activist scene seemed to be moving toward a culmination when we woke up one September day in 1972 and learned in shock that dear Mr. Marcos had locked us all in under martial law."

—Nick Joaquin, *Manila, My Manila: A History for the Young*
(Manila: Republic of the Philippines, 1990), 329–34

Figure 8.4. Antiwar demonstration at the U.S. Embassy, 1972 (courtesy of the Lopez Memorial Museum, Philippines)

the writ of habeas corpus and again upon revelations that he and Imelda had bribed convention delegates to oppose the third-term ban.

Yet despite losing battles in the media, legislature, and constitutional convention, Marcos had the military firmly on his side. And while senior party leaders abandoned him, Marcos maintained good relations with local power brokers by refusing to prosecute strongmen accused of violence in the previous election. Finally, though some technocrats resigned in disappointment over corruption, others defended him as a farsighted leader. As his education minister paraphrased Marcos's sentiments later: "The first duty of government is to govern; and if a government cannot govern, it has no claim to either the physical obedience or the moral allegiance of the people. But the government that is weak cannot govern well, and worse, a weak government is a threat to liberty, for a government that cannot redress wrongs cannot protect rights."[21]

Support for a stronger state was echoed by American business interests. The typical commentary acknowledged constitutional democracy as an important cornerstone of Philippine politics, but considered the existing system to be "severely deficient." It called for a "strengthening of presidential authority [to] enable President Marcos to introduce needed stability" for a sound business environment.[22]

On September 23, 1972, invoking the Constitution, Marcos declared a state of emergency on the basis of a "rightist-leftist" plot to overthrow the government (see box 8.3). His announcement was preceded by the arrest of thousands of opponents and the disarming of private military forces, including that of his top rival, the popular Senator Aquino. The AFP raided and closed schools, religious establishments, newspapers, and radio and television stations. In Manila, both houses of Congress were shut and deliberations of the constitutional convention suspended. Marcos's secretary of information later declared that martial law would continue as long as the republic was in imminent danger. The U.S. government's immediate response to martial law was "complete silence," in Raymond Bonner's words, in contrast to the public misgivings expressed three weeks later when South Korea imposed a similar state of emergency. Bipartisan support for martial law emerged in the U.S. Congress, and the American media praised Marcos for his decisiveness. The *New York Times* called him "the symbol and the person of strength in a nation of uncertainty."[23]

THE "U.S.-MARCOS DICTATORSHIP"

Ferdinand Marcos's dictatorship—the greatest dominance of state over society the Philippines has seen—endured until 1986. In the first two sections below, we trace the centralized state's initial success and later decline, examining its mechanisms of control, economic programs, and degree of autonomy from class and sectoral interests. Then we turn to social forces, going back to highlight the resistance offered by a Muslim secessionist movement and the CPP-NPA. Finally, we bring state and social forces together to understand Marcos's fall from power.

Heyday

The declaration of martial law devastated Marcos's opponents. Overnight, the entire network of anti-Marcos forces had disappeared from the public arena. Politicians were jailed, their patronage machines adrift and private armies demobilized. Students, academics, journalists, businessmen, and labor and peasant organizers had also been arrested, and many who had escaped went underground with the CPP. This strained the limited resources and organizational capacity of the party, which took more than a year to absorb the recruits and restore internal order. The rest of Philippine society simply accepted the new order. This reaction, especially among weary and stressed urbanites, is not surprising. After almost three years of political conflict, martial law was to many a welcome respite. Others saw it as a way out of economic crisis. Popular acquiescence, a unified military, and American consent enabled Marcos to consolidate swiftly.[24]

Box 8.3. The Declaration of Martial Law

"Whereas, on the basis of carefully evaluated and verified information, it is definitely established that lawless elements who are moved by a common or similar ideological conviction, strategy and goal and enjoying the active moral and material support of a foreign power and being guided and directed by intensely devoted, well trained, determined and ruthless groups of men and seeking refuge under the protection of our constitutional liberties to promote and attain their ends, have entered into a conspiracy and have in fact joined and banded their resources and forces together for the prime purpose of, and in fact they have been and are actually staging, undertaking and waging an armed insurrection and rebellion against the Government of the Republic of the Philippines in order to forcibly seize political and state power in this country, overthrow the duly constituted government, and supplant our existing political, social, economic and legal order with an entirely new one whose form of government, whose system of laws, whose conception of God and religion, whose notion of individual rights and family relations, and whose political, social, economic, legal and moral precepts are based on the Marxist-Leninist-Maoist teaching and beliefs. . .

"Whereas, it is evident that there is throughout the land a state of anarchy and lawlessness, chaos and disorder, turmoil and destruction of a magnitude equivalent to an actual war between the forces of our duly constituted government and the New People's Army and their satellite organizations. . .

"Whereas, . . . there is also the equally serious disorder in Mindanao and Sulu resulting from the unsettled conflict between certain elements of the Christian and Muslim population of Mindanao and Sulu . . . and between our government troops, and certain lawless organizations such as the Mindanao Independence Movement. . .

"Whereas, the rebellion and armed action undertaken by these lawless elements of the communist and other armed aggrupations [sic] organized to overthrow the Republic of the Philippines by armed violence and force have assumed the magnitude of an actual state of war against our people and the Republic of the Philippines

"Now, therefore, I, Ferdinand Marcos, President of the Philippines, by virtue of the powers vested upon me by Article VII, Section 10, Paragraph (2) of the Constitution, do hereby place the entire Philippines . . . under martial law and, in my capacity as their commander-in-chief, do hereby command the armed forces of the Philippines, to maintain law and order throughout the Philippines, prevent or suppress all forms of lawless violence as well as any act of insurrection or rebellion and to enforce obedience to all the laws and to all decrees, orders and regulations promulgated by me personally or upon my direction."

Reprinted in *Dictatorship and Revolution: Roots of People's Power*, ed. Aurora Javate de Dios, Petronilo Bn. Daroy, and Lorna Kalaw-Tirol (Manila: Conspectus, 1988), 374–77

In January 1973, Marcos staged a "national referendum" to approve the new constitution. Completed by a reconvened convention minus jailed oppositionists, the 1973 Constitution called for a single-chamber National Assembly to be popularly elected and a president and prime minister to be elected by the assembly. In designating the president "symbolic head of State" and the prime minister "head of the government," the new constitution discarded

a government of balanced powers for a parliamentary system. A literacy requirement no longer restricted suffrage, but the constitution *required* "every
citizen qualified to vote to register and cast his vote."[25] A "transitory provision" also allowed Marcos a term extension as president.

Marcos's profession in law probably explains why he demanded constitutional justification for his actions, but he did not stop with the term extension.
He packed the Supreme Court with close associates and signed a decree making all *subsequent* executive decrees and orders "laws of the land," thereby ar-
rogating legislative power to himself. Later amendments (decreed by Marcos)
made him both president and prime minister and allowed him "to exercise
legislative powers until martial law shall have been lifted." During the course
of martial law rule, Marcos issued 1,941 presidential decrees, 1,331 letters of
instruction, and 896 executive orders, leaving his mark on practically every
important legal and juridical issue the country faced.[26]

With his new powers, Marcos moved easily from the original idea of martial law as an emergency response to crisis, to martial law as an instrument
for creating a "New Society." He was now in a position to craft a strong state
with two powerful centralizing agencies—a military empowered during his
first term and technocrats who shared his idea of national development.

The AFP detained Marcos's political enemies—an estimated thirty thousand were imprisoned by early 1975—and took over regional and local political networks on his behalf. Freed from legislative constraints and media
scrutiny, it began a brutal engagement in the southern Philippines with the
Moro National Liberation Front and launched major attacks against the CPP-
NPA (discussed below). Marcos expanded the AFP's power by integrating
municipal police forces and the Philippine Constabulary into the AFP hierarchy, and he gave it a bigger role in governance by assigning officers to run
hitherto civilian agencies. As a defender of the New Society and partner in
national development, the AFP received the largest single allocation of the
national budget. From 1972 to 1976, the military budget rose from 880 million to 4 billion pesos.[27]

Technocrats who believed in the "fundamental restructuring" of governance were given a free hand in expanding executive power (see box 8.4).[28]
The number of agencies directly under the Office of the President and within
the larger Executive Department doubled in five years; by 1981, it stood at
forty.[29] The budget process was also linked closely to economic planning
through two new "superagencies," the Planning, Programming, Budgeting
System and the Development Budget Coordinating Committee. With these
apolitical agencies backing him and the landlord-dominated legislature
eliminated, Marcos turned to the deep structural problems of the countryside.
Presidential Decree no. 2 declared the entire country subject to land reform

Box 8.4. Technocratic Evolution

"The ascendency of the Communist Party in Russia and the spread of Marxist theory and practice in the intellectual world, the big depression of the 1930s, the Keynesian Revolution in 1936 and the Roosevelt Administration's application of its prescription in the United States, the onset of World War II and the employment of professional economists in the planning of wartime mobilization and in the Office of Price Administration in the United States, the development of national accounting—all these combined to fashion a science and art of macro-economic management. Management and statecraft combined once again. The practitioners of the new, more rigorous science and art became known as the technocrats. . . .

". . . [R]eturning Filipinos, educated in the economic, financial accounting, management and legal disciplines in the US and Europe, took their places in academe, private business, the Central Bank and the government department and defined the track of technocratic evolution in the country from the early 1950s to the present.

"The technocrats were first concentrated in the new Central Bank of the Philippines. Governor Miguel Cuaderno recruited the earliest team of economists, finance, statistics and accounting specialists. He had Dr. Andres Castillo, author of the earliest economics textbook still in use in local colleges and universities. The Department of Economic Research, organized by Leonides Virata in 1949, became the premiere center of applied economic and statistical research and attracted the cream of local talent. He was succeeded by Dr. Horacio Lava, with Fanny Cortez Garcia and Benito Legarda as assistants. I myself joined in 1954 as an 'assistant economist.' . . .

"Economics departments at the University of the Philippines and in private universities such as de la Salle College and Ateneo de Manila were turning out increasing numbers of students who would move on to the United States and Europe to get their doctorates and come back in the 1960s. Likewise, an increasing number of Filipinos were getting their MBAs at Harvard, New York University, Wharton, Stanford, and other Ivy League schools in the US.

"These were the seeds and early beginnings of a movement. The establishment of the Program Implementation Agency (PIA) under President Macapagal in August 1962 assembled a large number of economists, finance and management specialists, lawyers and engineers for the planning, programming and monitoring of development projects. A critical mass of technocrats was first concentrated in the government. Out of here, came some of the principal technocrats that served in the Marcos government—Armand Fabella, Placido Mapa Jr., Vicente Paterno. From the University of the Philippines came Rafael Salas, Cesar Virata, O.D. Corpus, Jaime Laya.

"The movement gained tremendous momentum after Marcos declared Martial Law and abolished Congress. The technocrats had free rein and Marcos is quoted as saying that he would just lie back and let them run the government."

—Sixto K. Roxas, *Juetengate: The Parable of a Nation in Crisis*
(Makati City, The Philippines: Bancom Foundation, 2000), 86–87

and the peasantry henceforth free from bondage. Presidential Decree no. 27 announced the start of "Operation Land Transfer" on tenant-occupied holdings of more than seven hectares (17.5 acres) on rice and corn lands. Technocratic management successfully accomplished this first phase through a combination of legal compulsion and vastly improved delivery of support services to small farmers. Under the rice self-sufficiency program "Masagana '99" (Prosperity 1999), within two years, "634,000 [farmers] borrowed $87 million from 420 rural banks, 102 branches of the Philippine National Bank and 25 offices of the Agricultural Credit Administration" to purchase three-hectare (7.5-acre) plots and agricultural inputs.[30]

Another technocratic initiative was the creation of state corporations assigned to actively "interfere in various markets or to compete directly with the private sector" in "strategic sectors" such as oil and banking or where private sector participation was limited or halfhearted. By the mid-1970s, these corporations and their associated bureaucracies had established a dominant presence in oil production (Philippine National Oil Company), power (National Power Corporation and National Electrification Administration), mass transportation (Metro-Manila Transit Corporation), fertilizer production (National Fertilizer Corporation), and new investment (National Development Corporation). Government finance institutions and two state banks, the Philippine National Bank and the Development Bank of the Philippines, infused with fresh funds, became new sources of credit to complement the Central Bank.[31]

Guaranteeing the early success of martial law was the support of the U.S. government. Washington's foremost interest in the Philippines was no longer its success in practicing "American-style" democracy, but rather the two huge military bases north of Manila—Subic Bay Naval Base and Clark Air Base. The test of martial law was whether it could stabilize Philippine society and protect American economic and strategic interests. As a U.S. official told Bonner:

> Democracy is not the most important issue for U.S. foreign policy. . . . The most important thing is the U.S. national interest, our security interest, our economic interest. If the two coincide, fine. If every world leader were a Madison or a Jefferson, it would be great. But they aren't.[32]

American military assistance soared from $18.5 million in 1972 to $45.3 million the following year.[33] The transfer of war materiel and training assistance also increased, as both were needed in the AFP's war on Muslim separatists and Communist insurgents.[34] In fact, Marcos exploited these security concerns to ensure continuing American support. U.S. president Jimmy

Figure 8.5.   The Armed Forces of the Philippines deployed against Muslim separatists in the 1970s (courtesy of the Philippine National Historical Institute)

Carter's human rights–inflected foreign policy did not preclude Marcos from receiving $500 million in security assistance. The bases were simply too important to be sacrificed to human rights and Marcos knew this.[35]

Nevertheless, to imbue his dictatorship with constitutionalism, Marcos required the semblance of electoral politics. He replaced the empty shell of a two-party system with a single progovernment party: the Kilusang Bagong Lipunan (KBL, New Society Movement). The KBL brought together his national and local allies with former members of the opposition who chose to join him rather than retire. With parliament and the Supreme Court under control, Marcos held a series of referenda and plebiscites—mainly for international consumption—to demonstrate popular support for his New Society. In 1978, he even held "demonstration elections" at the local and legislative levels, allowing small opposition parties outside Manila to win certain city and provincial positions and a tiny number of seats in the National Assembly. But in Manila, Marcos used all his resources to defeat a badly funded, underexposed, but feisty coalition of leftists and anti-Marcos politicians led by the detained Aquino. Not surprisingly, the KBL-Manila slate, led by Imelda Marcos, won.

By various economic measures, the Philippine economy—along with state strength and Marcos's rule—reached a high point in the mid-1970s after twelve years of average annual GNP (gross national product) growth of 6 percent.[36] The green revolution produced unprecedented harvests, and land reform largely redistributed the country's rice and corn land to tenants. Rice producers' net revenue peaked in 1972 after rising an average of 2.85 percent annually for ten years. GNP per capita and labor productivity were still rising (they would peak in 1981 and 1983, respectively), as the government pursued manufacturing growth through foreign investment in "export-processing zones." This period also saw the expansion of the service and commercial sectors and the provision of some affordable urban housing through the New Society Sites and Services program.

In the export agriculture sector, the acreage devoted to sugar and coconut doubled, a development made possible by the increased productivity of rice land. Although the terms of trade still trended downward, global markets for these commodities are volatile, and in the mid-1970s, international prices for coconut oil, sugar, logs, and lumber spiked sharply. The result was a $110 million surplus in the balance of payments for 1974—the only such surplus in Philippine postwar history.

As suggested by the continuing reliance on export crops, however, the Philippines' economic future did not look bright. Manufacturing and the construction industry grew more quickly than agriculture, but the latter was still the dominant economic sector when Marcos fell from power in 1986, accounting for 71 percent of GDP (gross domestic product). Attesting to the failure of economic development under Marcos, economist James Boyce states, "The Philippine economy did not experience rapid structural change." Three aspects of Marcos's development program that might have appeared to be strengths in the 1970s were actually problematic: agrarian land reform, the construction boom, and the ability to borrow money to spur development.

Marcos could justifiably boast that he was the first to implement real agrarian reform, all but eliminating the dominance of landed elites in the country's rice production. But the shortcomings of his program also highlighted the socioeconomic, legal, and coercive power of the landlord class: Because non-rice lands were exempt, some landlords simply ordered their tenants to change crops. Also exempt was land worked by wage labor, so some evicted their tenant/sharecroppers in favor of hired workers. This increased the ranks of landless peasants, another category excluded from the program. Poor land title records and corruption also allowed the backdated division of legal ownership to bring holdings below the seven-hectare cutoff. Many other strategies were employed to simply prevent tenant participation in the program—from physical intimidation to cutting off access to irrigation.

In terms of lasting economic benefits, the results were disappointing. Tenants who participated received a fifteen-year leasehold—essentially a mortgage, not a land deed—and the terms of leasehold were not necessarily better than those of tenancy. Land reform also inadvertently promoted class differentiation *within* the peasantry: Consolidation of ownership by wealthier peasants was accomplished despite the prohibition on buying and selling Certicates of Land Transfer. The ostensible aim of land reform was to create more security for farmers, but these subversions and side effects actually increased the number of landless laborers, the most vulnerable of the rural poor. As Boyce observes: "The technocrats who formulated Philippine development strategy under President Marcos did not challenge the country's inegalitarian economic and political order."[37]

Another highly visible aspect of the Marcos development plan was publicly funded construction. The government's share of total construction expenditures rose from 21 percent during Marcos's first term to 40 percent in 1975 and 43 percent in 1980. Although the rural infrastructure element was essential, much of the expenditure went to showcase projects initiated by Imelda Marcos to highlight the "achievements" of the New Society. The San Juanico Bridge, for example, connected her home province of Leyte with neighboring Samar Island; the highly specialized Philippine Heart Center in Manila diverted funds from badly needed primary health care. The frenetic pace with which the Marcos government undertook construction projects led economists to consider the Philippines distinct in Southeast Asia for "the proliferation of government buildings, many of which are over-designed by Asian and developing country standards."[38]

Public spending in the Marcos years was funded by public debt. Philippine borrowing of vast sums despite only modest economic growth—a pattern begun in Marcos's first term—was underwritten by multilateral agencies like the World Bank and the International Monetary Fund. Aside from direct assistance, these two bodies encouraged commercial lenders and private investors to put faith in the stability and investment-friendly environment of the country since September 1972.[39] Borrowing did not abate even when oil-induced recession in the industrialized world lowered demand for Philippine exports, causing dollar reserves and the balance of payments to fall. Still public debt accumulated—from $2.6 billion in 1975 to $10.5 billion in 1980. International lending agencies now kept credit lines open for fear the economy would collapse, while private credit institutions were attracted by the high interest rates they could impose on the Marcos government. By 1983, total debt was about $25 billion and the Philippines was one of the ten most indebted countries in the developing world. Worse, according to economist Germelino Bautista, was the way the money was spent on

> bankrupt government entities [as well as] structures which by themselves were not income-generat[ing] (e.g., monuments, government buildings and bridges of love); which were auxiliary, if not plainly superfluous to the unarticulated economic structure (e.g., the oversized Bataan export processing zone and nuclear plant); or which merely enlarged existing industries that catered to a volatile market (e.g., sugar mills and hotels).[40]

Decline

The factors that enabled Marcos to consolidate his dictatorship were also factors in its decline. "Martial law," according to Paul Hutchcroft, "created many new opportunities for reform, but at the same time facilitated the capture of the state by new—and more centralized—regime interests. As Marcos's chief ideologue remarked, Marcos 'believed he could have a vision for society . . . and still loot it.'"[41] The export boom and external borrowings boosted GNP in the early years of martial law, but the benefits of economic growth were distributed disproportionately to the Marcos family, its immediate relatives, and close friends.

Presidential decrees and directives gave this group monopoly control of the sugar and coconut industries, the domestic market for cigarettes and beer, and other expropriated private enterprises throughout the economy. Sugarcane haciendas, for example, had been exempted from land reform to keep them intact for takeover. Eugenio H. Lopez, by all accounts the country's leading "sugar tycoon," was the brother of Marcos's former vice president, Fernando Lopez. In late 1972, Eugenio's eldest son was detained without charge, held hostage to the Marcoses' determination to bring the Lopez family down. According to the family's biographer, hoping to win his son's release, Eugenio Lopez eventually sold "the bulk of his fortune, estimated at $400 M, for about P10,000."[42] Imelda's brother took over the facilities of the Lopez newspaper *Manila Chronicle* and of ABS-CBN, its network of television and radio stations. Loyal crony Roberto Benedicto won full control of the sugar industry, operating it through two state agencies established to rationalize the industry in order to better compete on the U.S. and global markets.[43]

In contrast to sugarcane, coconut growing was a smallholder industry. To wrest profit from it, Marcos imposed a series of levies on coconut production. The proceeds were deposited in the United Coconut Planters' Bank (UCPB), ostensibly for the development of a coconut seed farm and other projects to benefit smallholders. UCPB then set about purchasing, by intimidation where necessary, 80 percent of the nation's coconut mills, where the industry's profit is generated. The resulting corporation, United Coconut Oil Mills (UNICOM), used its market power to set a very low purchase price for unprocessed coconuts, generating a higher-than-normal profit margin. Coconut farmers became increasingly impoverished—it is not surprising that the NPA grew quickly in coconut-producing regions of Bicol and Mindanao.[44] Meanwhile, UCPB's president, Marcos ally Eduardo Cojuangco (Benigno Aquino's cousin-in-law), used his access to over $1 billion of coconut levies to generate hundreds of millions of dollars in personal assets. He later bought controlling shares in the country's most profitable company, the San Miguel Beer Corporation.[45]

This consolidation of wealth and power within a segment of the country's elite eventually acquired the name "crony capitalism." It was capitalism based not on competition but on monopoly, special access, and brute force. Cronies had access to millions of dollars squeezed out of small producers and billions in loans and credits from government finance institutions—ultimately from foreign lenders. Corporations set up by cronies received preference in issuing import licenses, approving joint ventures with Japanese and American firms, and acting as agents for foreign corporations. The perks extended to bribes and "commissions" paid to members of the crony network. Marcos and his wife themselves demanded a standard "cut" on every business transaction. Crony capitalism, in the main, was also inefficient—assured of government support and monopoly control, most crony corporations did nothing to improve their business performance. The sugar, automotive, hotel and entertainment, and construction industries experienced growth, but soon faltered and fell into the red. Cojuangco was an exception, as was Lucio Tan. Instead of relying on Marcos's patronage, Tan used his monopoly control of cigarette production, pricing, and marketing to diversify into banking, airlines, and alcohol. Cojuangco and Tan are today two of the country's richest and most powerful men.

The plunder of the state for the benefit of family and cronies was premised on the constant availability of funds to loot. However, various internal and external forces combined to dry up the source of those funds. Successive oil price hikes raised the nation's oil import costs from $187 million in 1973, to $651 million in 1978, and to more than $2 billion in 1982. Oil prices pushed up the cost of other imports, especially petroleum-based agricultural inputs, while agricultural export values declined and the country's balance of payments deteriorated. Expensive short-term borrowing became necessary to service past debt, accounting for more than one-third of total debt after 1976.[46]

Economic deterioration pushed the government deeper into deficit spending, but Marcos had no appetite for scaling down development programs, reforming the regressive tax system, or ending subsidies for favored corporations. Crony capitalism precluded such reforms. But the crony companies began to collapse anyway and turned to Marcos for help. Between 1981 and 1983, government capital outlay shifted from infrastructure to "corporate equity investment," a euphemism for rescuing failing companies. Loans from government finance corporations were extended to the Marinduque Mining Company, 15 billion pesos in debt, and the Delta Motors Corporation, which had an outstanding loan of 2 billion pesos.[47] The government bailed out the Construction Development Corporation of the Philippines (CDCP), owned by Marcos golf buddy Rodolfo Cuenca. Marcos ordered the Public Estates Authority, created in 1977, to pay CDCP 1.5 billion pesos for reclaimed land in Manila Bay and to assume 1.5 billion pesos of CDCP's debts and loan obligations.[48] (Cuenca recently recalled martial law as an idyllic period of "discipline.")[49] And after the world price of sugar collapsed, leaving the industry with worthless mills and tons of unexportable sugar, government came to the rescue of Roberto Benedicto, absorbing losses of more than 14 billion pesos. But the closed plantations and mills left thousands unemployed, and with no recourse to subsistence farmland, many former sugar workers on Negros Island faced starvation.[50]

All signs—including the Marcos couple's conspicuous profligacy—pointed to a breakdown. By 1980, the real wages of skilled and unskilled workers in Manila had fallen to less than half their 1962 level; Marcos responded by discontinuing the Central Bank series that tracked wages. World Bank and UP economists watched unemployment rise from an estimated 14.7 percent in 1978 to more than 24 percent in 1982.[51] In the face of this situation, Filipinos looked for work overseas to support families at home. When Middle Eastern states began to use oil revenues to modernize their economies, the Philippines was one of their first sources of labor. Filipino workers in Saudi Arabia, Kuwait, and Dubai remitted $82 million to their families in 1975, rising to $384 million in 1978. These remittances were soon depended upon to prop up foreign exchange reserves and the balance of payments.

The state of the financial system, described by a businessman, reflected the intense anxiety of an economy falling apart:

> At the end of 1983, 53 banks and quasi-banks were on emergency loans or on overdraft from the Central Bank. Small thrift banks were in trouble for failure to remit tax collections or irregularities in recording deposits. Half of the rural banks had ceased operations. The Philippine National Bank and the Development Bank of the Philippines had accumulated large non-performing loans.[52]

With growing disenchantment on the part of local and foreign business, as well as strains in U.S.–Philippine relations, international lines of credit were finally cut, threatening the state's major financial institutions. Economic and political uncertainty affected manufacturing, causing the retrenchment or closure of many businesses. Urban discontent was on the rise, and the CPP broadened its urban base from college campuses to factories and the slum areas where the majority of unemployed and underemployed now lived.

This is what the New Society amounted to—an unsustainable redistribution of wealth upward by a president who brilliantly wielded the power of the state. Benedict Anderson observes that Marcos "pushed the destructive logic of the old order to its natural conclusion. In place of privatized 'security guards,' a single privatized National Constabulary; in place of personal armies, a personal Army; instead of pliable local judges, a client Supreme Court; instead of a myriad pocket and rotten boroughs, a pocket or rotten country, managed by cronies, hitmen, and flunkies."[53]

Resistance

If the military faced little initial resistance in most of the Philippines, this was not the case in southern Mindanao. There, uncontrolled migration into the 1960s eventually produced tension between Christian settlers and non-Christian minorities and Muslims. Without an effective land registration system, violent clashes over land ownership occurred frequently, and state infrastructure projects increased the feeling of encroachment. Datu-politicians who had represented the state to Muslims and delivered the Muslim vote to their Manila patrons through the 1950s lost their grip on power as Marcos brought the state directly to Mindanao. They also felt pressure from the upcoming generation of Muslim students returning from religious schools in

Egypt and Libya, where they had been influenced by Nasserite nationalism, or from the UP, where they had imbibed anti-American nationalism and radicalism. The young leaders saw the politicians' accommodation with Manila as out of touch and the Christian state as oppressive and determined to obliterate the Muslim "way of life." Separatism, or more correctly, Muslim nationalism, was first expressed in the Mindanao Independence Movement, founded in 1968, and thereafter local land clashes became infused with religious and nationalist overtones. By 1970, the province of Cotabato erupted into war. Marcos sent in the military, bypassed the old politicians, and in some cases neutralized their private armies.[54]

In 1972, the students and politicians allied to form the Moro National Liberation Front (MNLF), a vanguard movement to create a Bangsa Moro Republik (Moro National Republic) consisting of Mindanao, the Sulu archipelago, and Palawan Island (see box 8.5). With arms supplied by Libya, the remaining weapons stockpiles of the anti-Marcos politicians, and a training camp provided by Malaysia for its rebel army, the MNLF was instantly mobilized when martial law was declared. The AFP's attempt to confiscate "illegal" firearms in the provinces of Cotabato and Lanao del Sur sparked the initial confrontation between the two forces.

Within months, the entire region had become a battleground. The MNLF war (1973–1977) caused the death of more than thirteen thousand people and forced more than a million to flee their homes. At the war's height, the dictatorship spent about $1 million a day containing the rebellion.[55] U.S. military assistance did help defray the expense, but the war was still a massive financial and political drain on the dictatorship. It caused people in the Muslim provinces to equate the New Society with military rule and alienated Muslim states sympathetic to the rebels.

The MNLF, however, was unable to exploit Marcos's weakness due to its own internal problems. Its military leaders lacked combat experience and suffered major battlefield losses, while its political leaders split along ethnic lines (Tausug versus Maguindanao) over tactical issues. As the MNLF lost on the military front, its politician allies also began to defect, making separate peace pacts with Marcos and presenting themselves as a "moderate alternative" to the revolutionary Moro nationalists. Government overtures to Libya and the cooperation of conservative Arab states eventually led to negotiations and a de facto cease-fire in 1977. The MNLF was no match for Marcos diplomatically and the decline of Arab support made the continuation of conventional warfare impossible. The war degraded into skirmishes while the government and MNLF sat at the negotiating table. Eventually, the organization narrowed to a Tausug constituency, the ethnic group of its founder, former UP lecturer Nur Misuari. Curiously, the arc of MNLF power closely shadowed that of

Box 8.5. The Manifesto of the Moro National Liberation Front

Establishment of the Bangsa Moro Republik

We, the five million oppressed Bangsa Moro people, wishing to free ourselves from the terror, oppression and tyranny of Filipino colonialism which has caused us untold sufferings and miseries by criminally usurping our land, by threatening Islam through wholesale destruction and desecration of its places of worship and its Holy Book, and murdering our innocent brothers, sisters and folks in a genocidal campaign of terrifying magnitude,

Aspiring to have the sole prerogative of defending and chartering our own national destiny in accordance with our own free will in order to ensure our future and that of our children;

Have evolved an appropriate form of ideology with which the unity of our people has been firmly established and their national identity and character strengthened;

Having established the Moro National Liberation Front and its military arm, the Bangsa Moro Army, as our principal instrument for achieving our primary goals and objectives with the unanimous support of the great mass of our people; and finally

Being now in firm control of a great portion of our national homeland through successive and crushing victories of our Bangsa Moro Army in battle against the Armed Forces of the Philippines and the Marcos military dictatorship, hereby declare:

1. That henceforth the Bangsa Moro people and Revolution, having established their Bangsa Moro Republik, are throwing off all their political, economic and other bonds with the oppressive government of the Philippines under the dictatorial regime of President Ferdinand E. Marcos to secure a free and independent state for the Bangsa Moro people;
2. That we believe armed struggle is the only means by which we can achieve the complete freedom and independence of our people, since Marcos and his government will never dismantle the edifice of Philippine colonial rule in our national homeland of their own accord;
3. That the Moro National Liberation Front and its military arm, the Bangsa Moro Army, shall not agree to any form of settlement or accord short of achieving total freedom and independence for our oppressed Bangsa Moro people;
4. That the Revolution of the Bangsa Moro people is a revolution with a social conscience. As such it is committed to the principle of establishing a democratic system of government which shall never allow or tolerate any form of exploitation and oppression of any human being by another or of one nation by another;
5. That those Filipinos who may wish to remain in the Bangsa Moro national homeland even after independence shall be welcomed and entitled to equal rights and protection with all other citizens of the Bangsa Moro Republik, provided that they formally renounce their Filipino citizenship and wholeheartedly accept Bangsa Moro citizenship; their property rights shall be fully respected and the free exercise of their political, cultural and religious rights shall be guaranteed;
6. That the Bangsa Moro people and Revolution are committed to the preservation and growth of Islamic culture among our people, without prejudice to the development and growth of other religious and indigenous cultures in our homeland. . . . ;

Therefore, we hereby appeal to the conscience of all men everywhere and the sympathy of all the nations of the world to help accelerate the pace of our people's Revolution by formally and unequivocally recognizing and supporting our people's legitimate right to obtain our national freedom and independence. Such recognition and support must be concretised by accepting the Bangsa Moro Republik as one of the members of the family of independent and sovereign nations in the world and giving official recognition to the Moro National Liberation Front.

> Done in the Bangsa Moro Homeland, this 28th day of April 1974
> Signed: *Hajji Nur Misuari, Chairman, Central Committee,*
> *Moro National Liberation Front*

Reprinted in W. K. Che Man, *Muslim Separatism: The Moros of Southern Philippines and the Malays of Southern Thailand* (Quezon City: Ateneo de Manila University Press, 1974), 189–90

the dictatorship. By the time Marcos fell, the MNLF had lost its dynamism as well.[56]

The CPP, in contrast, increased in strength as Marcos declined. (The PKP surrendered in 1974.) After realizing the folly of establishing a single mountain base in Isabela province—à la Mao's Yenan region—in 1974 the CPP leadership ordered its cadres to create autonomous, regional, self-sustaining organizations across the archipelago. The policy of "centralized command, decentralized operations" gave cadres considerable leeway to experiment with tactics based on evaluation of their own areas. It also enabled the CPP to survive the loss of many of its original leaders to prison—including Sison—or death, because the regional bodies functioned as training grounds for successor leaders. By the end of 1976, CPP organizing teams were patiently building underground networks and forming NPA units on most major islands of the country.

The party experienced its fastest growth in areas where the military's presence led to human rights violations. As Sison had predicted, Marcos's "fascist rule" made him the movement's top recruiter. Students, labor organizers, and peasants detained without due process and tortured, whose houses were burned, who were brutalized, whose family members were killed on suspicion of being NPA supporters—all these found their way into "the movement." By the late 1970s, the CPP could confidently claim a guerrilla force of about fifteen thousand, roughly the same number of cadres, and a "mass base" of about a million. At the same time, the tactical advantage shifted to the NPA in its almost-daily skirmishes with the military, despite the AFP's superior arms and numbers. Both forces grew quickly in this period, but there was a fundamental difference in esprit de corps. According to Gregg Jones, "Despite a high rate of illiteracy, communist soldiers could explain why they were fighting and what they were fighting for. In contrast, most government soldiers were poor peasants or slum dwellers who enlisted in the government army not out of political conviction but because of economic deprivation."[57]

In the cities, the party consolidated control of important schools through aboveground organizations such as the League of Filipino Students and gathered the labor unions it controlled under the umbrella federation Kilusang Mayo Uno (May First Movement).[58] Party cadres also reached out to non-communists, making "anti-imperialist" alliances with the few remaining nationalist politicians, including Lorenzo Tañada and Jose W. Diokno. These senators had the credibility to publicize Marcos's human rights violations; the CPP could mobilize the *masa* (masses). At rallies in Manila or Cebu, the presence of foreign media both publicized the news abroad and averted bloody repression.

Another non-Communist community targeted by the CPP was the Catholic Church, its secular priests, and members of Catholic religious orders. In 1974, the Catholic Church hierarchy, essentially in sympathy with Marcos's anticommunism, declared a policy of "critical collaboration" with the government, reluctantly heeding the growing opposition within its rank and file. The Church's conciliatory stance toward Marcos allowed it institutional autonomy and the ability to continue its social projects, which were meant to ameliorate the condition of the poor and defend them against communism. But priests working in rural parishes and nuns leaving school-teaching for involvement in the "social apostolate" became radicalized by the dictatorship's impact on the poor, and the party sent its best student cadres to recruit them.[59] Church recruits eventually formed Christians for National Liberation, an underground party organization, and utilized Church "social action" programs to generate funds from abroad from private donor agencies dedicated to the same social issues. Church leaders were appalled by this radical infiltration, but could do little about it. To attack its own rank and file for following the official Church position on human rights and social justice would open the hierarchy to charges of supporting the dictatorship. A serious breach opened up within the Philippine Church.

The MNLF war and the successful revival of Filipino communism spurred a parallel effort by two nonradical anti-Marcos groups—the "social democrats" (leaders of the late-1960s moderate student groups) and what the CPP called "anti-Marcos reactionaries." The latter were politicians who had not prospered under martial law (through loss of patronage funds, for example) but were not open opponents of the regime. In the late 1970s, when Marcos reintroduced elections, these politicians discovered a way back into the limelight by calling for the "restoration of democracy." Both groups experimented with "armed resistance," engaging in minor urban guerrilla actions aiming (in the social democrats' case) to demonstrate Marcos's vulnerability or (for the politicians) to compel further opening of the system. The strategy failed and factionalized both movements. Most of the politicians and the more senior social democrats preferred to advocate "parliamentary politics"; the younger activists and the more anti-American politicians wanted to establish ties with the CPP.

The ability of these political forces to survive martial law and amass resources to fight Marcos suggests a limit to the "strong state," even one with enhanced military power and centralized governance. The AFP's war on separatism and communism drained the state of substantial human and financial resources. The MNLF's shift to guerrilla warfare and the CPP's decentralized "people's war" left the military bogged down and increasingly overextended. The spreading use of torture and extrajudicial execution eroded the military's image, created more recruits for the opposition, and helped human rights groups portray the regime as a brutal dictatorship rather than a benevolent autocracy. Marcos was vulnerable on this point once he played the human rights card dealt by President Carter in order to continue receiving U.S. military aid. "Human rights" became a potent symbol and mobilizing theme that attracted religious leaders, professional associations, and business elites troubled by the brutality in the countryside and increasingly in the cities.

It would be a mistake to conclude from this survey, however, that the dictatorship was rapidly waning in strength. Despite rising numbers of CPP members, social democrats, human rights activists, and anti-Marcos politicians, the president continued to dictate the political rhythm. He kept the opposition divided by allowing the moderates some provincial electoral victories, admitting some mistakes to the Catholic bishops, and maintaining a hard-line stance against the radicals. The CPP leadership also played a role by refusing to "hasten the struggle" or pool its resources in a united front that would give "parity" to the smaller opposition forces.

It was Marcos himself who radically changed the political landscape on August 21, 1983. On that day, ex-senator Benigno Aquino Jr., who had been in the United States since 1980, returned to the Philippines. As he deplaned, he was surrounded by a military escort and shot dead. (See box 8.6.)

Collapse

Aquino's assassination catalyzed the sequence of events leading to Marcos's downfall. The urban middle class and economic elites, deeply worried by

Box 8.6.   The Martyrdom of Benigno Aquino

The Prepared Statement of Benigno Aquino Jr., August 21, 1983

I have returned on my free will to join the ranks of those struggling to restore our rights and freedoms through non-violence.

I seek no confrontation. I only pray and will strive for a genuine national reconciliation founded on justice.

I am prepared for the worst, and have decided against the advice of my mother, my spiritual adviser, many of my tested friends and a few of my most valued political mentors.

A death sentence awaits me. Two more subversion charges, both calling for death penalties, have been filed since I left three years ago and are now pending with the courts.

I could have opted to seek political asylum in America, but I feel it is my duty, as it is the duty of every Filipino, to suffer with his people especially in time of crisis.

I have never sought nor have I been given any assurance, or promise of leniency from the regime. I return voluntarily armed only with a clear conscience and fortified in the faith that in the end justice will emerge triumphant. . . .

So as to leave no misunderstanding, I shall define my terms:

1. Six years ago, I was sentenced to die before a firing squad by a military tribunal whose jurisdiction I steadfastly refused to recognize. It is now time for the regime to decide. Order my execution or set me free. . . .
2. National reconciliation and unity can be achieved, but only with justice, including justice for our Muslim and Ifugao brothers. There can be no deal with a dictator. No compromise with dictatorship.
3. In a revolution, there can really be no victors, only victims. We do not have to destroy in order to build.
4. Subversion stems from economic, social and political causes and will not be solved by purely military solution. It can be curbed not with ever increasing repression but with a more equitable distribution of wealth, more democracy and more freedom.
5. For the economy, to get going again, the working man must be given his just and rightful share of his labor, and to the owners and managers must be restored the hope where there is much uncertainty if not despair.

On one of the long corridors of Harvard University are carved in granite the words of Archibald Macleish: "How shall freedom be defended? By arms when it is attacked by arms; by truth when it is attacked by lies; by democratic faith when it is attacked by authoritarian dogma. Always, and in the final act, by determination and faith."

I return from exile and to an uncertain future with only determination and faith to offer—faith in our people and faith in God.

Reprinted in Aurora Javate de Dios, Petronilo Bn. Daroy, and Lorna Kalaw-Tirol, eds., *Dictatorship and Revolution: Roots of People's Power* (Manila: Conspectus, 1988), 572–74

the economic crisis, were shocked into political involvement and opposition ranks swelled. Many business elites were particularly angered by the brazen nature of the assassination and frightened by the economic effect of the turmoil. The once-fractious elite opposition and the splintered social democrats reunited to exploit Marcos's fondness for constitutional cover. The staging of elections, even on a pro forma basis, allowed his opponents to open "democratic spaces" by challenging the regime at the local and parliamentary level in the 1984 elections. The CPP, on the other hand, suddenly found its rural-based "protracted people's war" outpaced by urban mass mobilizations, obliging its leadership to allow more "experimentation"—mini-uprisings in rural and urban areas, "tactical coalitions" with anti-Marcos elites and social democrats, and "tactical offensives" by the New People's Army. Finally, the Catholic Church hierarchy was pushed toward confronting the dictatorship as more priests, nuns, and lay leaders expressed their opposition in rallies and from the pulpit.

At the same time, Marcos was losing support from his institutional allies. The first to waver were the technocrats. Their dream of creating a managerial state and developing the Philippines into a full market economy withered as "the political logic of cronyism placed major obstacles in the path of serious reform."[60] Even attempts to fix the banking system or limit the damage of crony capitalism—with its huge unpaid loans, "white elephant" corporations, and monopolistic practices—met with strong resistance by Marcos's kin and allies. The tension between technocrats and cronies worsened with Marcos's rescue of the failing businesses and his refusal to control Madame Marcos's lavish spending. It was clear that the professional managers had lost their clout when an embattled Marcos narrowed his inner circle to his immediate family and most loyal military officers.[61] In any case, the technocrats' international credibility had faltered, and with it their use to the regime.[62] As protests against Marcos mounted, some broke ranks and left for the opposition, while others slowly distanced themselves from the president.

The most serious internal threat to Marcos came from within the military establishment. Middle-level officers were frustrated with corruption in the AFP and pervasive favoritism in its officer corps. Failure to contain the insurgencies, growing demoralization within the ranks, and the exposure of human rights violations were all interpreted by these officers as signs of the government's defeat in the political and propaganda war. They organized a group called RAM (Reform the AFP Movement), purportedly to push for military reforms but quietly to sound out other officers and military units about plans for a coup against the government.

For more than two years, political stalemate ensued between the weakened state and surging social forces. Marcos was embattled but still had enough allies to stay in power—particularly the United States under President Ronald Reagan, who was unequivocal in his support.[63] And although anti–martial law forces had grown in membership, influence, and coordination, they still represented widely different interests. As long as the "democratic opposition" was unable to commit to a common strategy against Marcos, it was also unable to seize the initiative.

Then Marcos, for reasons that are still unclear, decided to change the tempo, calling a "snap election" for February 1986 to determine whether he should continue as president or step down. His challenger was Corazon (Cory) Aquino, widow of Benigno, who was convinced to run by moderate and elite oppositionists and the Catholic Church. Huge segments of the leftist movement, along with hundreds of thousands of ordinary citizens politicized by her husband's assassination, joined the Aquino campaign. The CPP was unprepared for this sudden turn of events and in its irritation at losing the vanguard position, ordered its cadres and legal organizations to boycott the elections, which proved a costly mistake. Despite limited resources, incessant intimidation by Marcos supporters (including a number of assassinations), and massive cheating by the progovernment KBL on election day, Aquino clearly won and so claimed her victory. Marcos, however, thought otherwise and ordered parliament to declare him reelected. This move was quickly undermined when computer analysts at the Commission on Elections recognized "statistical anomalies" in the ballot count as evidence of manipulation and staged a televised walkout. Marcos was unfazed. The political situation had deteriorated to the point of open repression or unceremonious resignation.

RAM broke the tension by launching its coup in the early morning hours of February 22 (see box 8.7). But Marcos had prepared for this eventuality with an expanded presidential security command. The rebels' wide recruitment efforts within the military had also brought advance warning (though incomplete knowledge) to the Marcos loyalists. RAM's attempt to grab power failed. Together with their patrons, Defense Secretary Juan Ponce Enrile and AFP Vice Chief of Staff Fidel V. Ramos, the rebels retreated to await counterattack in Manila's two large military camps facing each other across the broad Epifanio de los Santos Avenue (Edsa). To their rescue, however, came the Aquino coalition and the Catholic Church, which called on its supporters to surround the camps along Edsa and protect the rebels.

Within a day more than one million people heeded the call, forming an unusual line of defense against marines flown in from Mindanao to defend

---

Box 8.7.   The Planned Timetable of the RAM Coup, February 1986

01:30   At "H-hour minus thirty," Colonel Honasan and twenty commandos cross the Pasig River in rubber rafts and, guided by allies in the palace guard, break into the sleeping quarters to arrest the President and First Lady.

02:00   At "H-hour," as commandos secure the palace, Lieutenant Colonel Kapunan's hundred-man strike team penetrates the security compound on the south bank, hurling smoke grenades to sow confusion and detonating bombs to kill General Ver.

02:20   With these explosions as signals, two motorized rebel columns, backed by ten light tanks, break through the gates of the security compound.

02:20   Posing as pro-Marcos reinforcements to enter the main palace gate, Major Saulito Aromin's Forty-ninth Infantry Battalion reinforces Honasan's commandos and secures the palace.

02:30   The operations officer of the Presidential Security Command, a rebel sympathizer, begins transmitting false orders to the eight pro-Marcos battalions in Manila, immobilizing them during these critical hours.

02:30   Simultaneously, Colonel Tito Legazpi captures Villamor Air Base and radios rebel units in outlying provinces to commandeer aircraft and depart immediately for Manila.

03:00   With the palace secured, [Defense Minister] Enrile issues "Proclamation Number One" establishing a revolutionary government.

Reprinted in Alfred W. McCoy, *Closer than Brothers: Manhood at the Philippine Military Academy* (New Haven, Conn.: Yale University Press, 1999), 237–38

---

the presidency. Inside the camps, the rebels waged a "radio war" of disinformation against Marcos, targeting military units taking a wait-and-see attitude. On February 24, the defection of air force officers and the entire Manila police force turned the tide—the rebels could now meet a counterattack should Marcos fire on "the people." U.S. president Ronald Reagan was finally convinced by his senior advisers to withdraw American support, and Marcos had no options left. Early in the morning of February 25, the dictator, his family, and his closest cronies left the presidential palace aboard two American helicopters. They were taken to Clark Air Base, transferred to a military jet, and flown to Hawaii. The same day, Corazon Aquino and her supporters proclaimed the victory of a bloodless "people power" revolution and agreed to an alliance with RAM and its supporters to form a provisional revolutionary government. With the self-appointed task of facilitating the transition from authoritarian to democratic constitutional government, Aquino was sworn in as president of the Philippines on February 25, 1986 (see box 8.8).

Box 8.8.   Proclamation No. 1 by President Corazon C. Aquino, February 25, 1986:

Sovereignty resides in the people and all government authority emanates from them.

On the basis of the people's mandate clearly manifested last February 7, I and Salvador H. Laurel are taking power in the name and by the will of the Filipino people as President and Vice President, respectively.

The people expect a reorganization of government. Merit will be rewarded. As a first step to restore public confidence I expect all appointed public officials to submit their courtesy resignations beginning with the members of the Supreme Court.

I pledge to do justice to the numerous victims of human rights violations.

Consistent with the demands of the sovereign people, we pledge a government dedicated to uphold truth and justice, morality and decency in government, freedom and democracy.

To help me run the government, I have issued Executive Order No. 1, dated February 25, 1986, appointing key cabinet ministers and creating certain task forces.

I ask our people not to relax but to be even more vigilant in this one moment of triumph. The Motherland cannot thank them enough. Yet, we all realize that more is required of each and every one of us to redeem our promises and prove to create a truly just society for our people.

This is just the beginning. The same spirit which animated our campaign, and has led to our triumph, will once more prevail, by the power of the people and by the grace of God.

Done in the City of Manila, this 25th of February in the year of Our Lord, nineteen hundred and eighty-six.
Corazon C. Aquino
President

Reprinted in Aurora Javate de Dios, Petronilo Bn. Daroy, and Lorna Kalaw-Tirol, eds., *Dictatorship and Revolution: Roots of People's Power* (Manila: Conspectus, 1988), 761

NOTES

1. James K. Boyce, *The Political Economy of Growth and Impoverishment in the Marcos Era* (Quezon City: Ateneo de Manila University Press, 1993), 7–8.

2. Robert B. Stauffer, *The Philippine Congress: Causes of Structural Change* (Beverly Hills, Calif.: Sage Publications, 1975).

3. Emmanuel S. De Dios and Paul Hutchcroft, "Political Economy," in *The Philippine Economy: Development, Policies, and Challenges*, ed. Arsenio M. Balisacan and Hal Hill (Quezon City: Ateneo de Manila University Press, 2003), 48.

4. Sixto K. Roxas, *Juetengate: The Parable of a Nation in Crisis* (Makati City, The Philippines: Bancom Foundation, 2000), 87.

5. Quoted in Felipe Miranda, "The Military," in *The Philippines after Marcos*, ed. R. J. May and Francisco Nemenzo (New York: St. Martin's Press, 1985), 94–95.

6. A. O. Flores, "Student Militance through the Years," *Sunday Times* (Manila) *Magazine*, February 22, 1970: 39.

7. Vicente B. Valdepeñas Jr. and Germelino M. Bautista, *The Emergence of the Philippine Economy* (Manila: Papyrus Press, 1977), 221–22; Boyce, *Political Economy of Growth*, 167.

8. Amando Doronila, *The State, Economic Transformation, and Political Change in the Philippines, 1946–1972* (New York: Oxford University Press, 1992), 142–43.

9. Efren Yambot, ed., *Philippine Almanac and Handbook of Facts* (Manila: Bustamante Press, 1975), 167.

10. Reynaldo Clemeña Ileto, *Pasyon and Revolution: Popular Movements in the Philippines, 1840–1910* (Quezon City: Ateneo de Manila University Press, 1979), 1.

11. Resil B. Mojares, *The Man Who Would Be President: Serging Osmeña and Philippine Politics* (Cebu: Maria Cacao Publishers, 1986), 142.

12. Mojares, *The Man Who Would Be President*, 142.

13. Romeo M. Bautista, "Inflation in the Philippines, 1955–1974," in *Philippine Economic Problems in Perspective*, ed. Jose Encarnacion Jr. et al. (Quezon City: University of the Philippines, School of Economics, Institute of Economic Development and Research, 1976), 178–79; Lim Yoon Lin, ed., *Trends in the Philippines: Proceedings and Background Paper* (Singapore: Singapore University Press, for ISEAS, 1972), 4.

14. Coeli M. Barry, "The Limits of Conservative Church Reformism in the Democratic Philippines," in *Religious Organizations and Democracy in Contemporary Asia*, ed. Tun-Jun Cheng and Deborah A. Brown (Armonk, N.Y.: M. E. Sharpe, forthcoming).

15. Carmen Guerrero-Nakpil, "The Shedding of Innocence," *Sunday Times* (Manila) *Magazine*, February 22, 1970: 7.

16. Rodolfo G. Tupas, "From the Reformists to the Revolutionaries: The Rebels on Campus," and Mila Astorga-Garcia, "Left to Right: The Student Activists," *Sunday Times* (Manila) *Magazine*, February 22, 1970: 11, 34.

17. Gregg Jones, *Red Revolution: Inside the Philippine Guerrilla Movement* (Boulder, Colo.: Westview Press, 1989), 27–30.

18. Jose F. Lacaba, *Days of Disquiet, Nights of Rage: The First Quarter Storm and Related Events* (Pasig, The Philippines: Anvil Publishing, 2003).

19. Walden Bello, David Kinley and Elaine Elinson, *Development Debacle: The World Bank in the Philippines* (San Francisco: Institute for Food and Development Policy/Philippine Solidarity Network, 1982), 81.

20. Petronilo Bn. Daroy, "On the Eve of Dictatorship and Revolution," in *Dictatorship and Revolution: Roots of People's Power*, ed. Aurora Javate de Dios et al. (Manila: Conspectus, 1988), 1–125.

21. Speech by Onofre D. Corpuz, education minister, to the Philippine Historical Association in 1973, quoted in Lewis E. Gleeck Jr., *President Marcos and the Philippine Political Culture* (Manila: L. E. Gleeck, 1987), 123.

22. Daniel B. Schirmer and Stephen Rosskamm Shalom, eds., *The Philippines Reader: A History of Colonialism, Neocolonialism, Dictatorship, and Resistance* (Boston: South End Press, 1978), 168.

23. Raymond Bonner, *Waltzing with a Dictator: The Marcoses and the Making of American Policy* (New York: Random House, 1987), 109–10.

24. Rigoberto Tiglao, "The Consolidation of the Dictatorship," in Javate de Dios et al., *Dictatorship and Revolution*, 26–69.

25. Republic of the Philippines, Constitutional Commission of 1986, "1935 and 1973 Philippine Constitutions," appendix B of *The Constitution of the Republic of the Philippines with Highlights of the 1986 Constitution and Appendices*, comp. NBSI Editorial Staff (Manila: National Book Store, 1986).

26. Froilan M. Bacungan, ed., *The Powers of the Philippine President* (Quezon City: University of the Philippines Law Center, 1983), 14, 97–98.

27. Carolina Hernandez, "The Extent of Civilian Control of the Military in the Philippines, 1946–1976" (Ph.D. diss., State University of New York at Buffalo, 1979).

28. On Marcos and the technocrats, see Roman Dubsky, *Technocracy and Development in the Philippines* (Quezon City: University of the Philippines Press, 1993), 74–99.

29. Alex B. Brillantes Jr. and Bienvenida M. Amarles-Ilago, *1898–1992: The Philippine Presidency* (Quezon City: University of the Philippines Press, 1994), 134.

30. Tiglao, "Consolidation of the Dictatorship," 36.

31. Emmanuel S. De Dios, ed., *An Analysis of the Philippine Economic Crisis: A Workshop Report* (Quezon City: University of the Philippines Press, 1984), 36–37.

32. Bonner, *Waltzing with a Dictator*, 132–33.

33. Walden Bello and Severina Rivera, "The Logistics of Repression," in *The Logistics of Repression and Other Essays*, ed. Walden Bello and Severina Rivera (Washington, D.C.: Friends of the Filipino People, 1977), 7.

34. Schirmer and Shalom, *The Philippines Reader*, 251–53.

35. Bonner, *Waltzing with a Dictator*, 210.

36. The following discussion is based on Boyce, *Political Economy of Growth*, chaps. 2, 4, and 6.

37. Boyce, *Political Economy of Growth*, 8.

38. De Dios, *An Analysis*, 11, 34.

39. Bello, Kinley and Elinson, *Development Debacle*; Robin Broad, *Unequal Alliance, 1979–1986: The World Bank, the International Monetary Fund, and the Philippines* (Berkeley: University of California Press, 1988), 94–102.

40. Germelino Bautista, "From Contradiction to Crisis: The Case of the Philippine Political Economy," in *Transnationalization, the State, and the People: The Philippine Experience*, ed. Randolf S. David et al. (Quezon City: United Nations University–University of the Philippines Third World Studies Center, 1984), 28.

41. Paul D. Hutchcroft, *Booty Capitalism: The Politics of Banking in the Philippines* (Ithaca, N.Y.: Cornell University Press, 1998), 111.

42. Raul Rodrigo, *Phoenix: The Saga of the Lopez Family*, vol. 1, *1800–1972* (Manila: Eugenio L½pez Foundation, 2000), 5.

43. Alfred W. McCoy, "In Extreme Unction: The Philippine Sugar Industry under Martial Law," in *Political Economy of Philippine Commodities*, ed. R. S. David (Quezon City: University of the Philippines, Third World Studies Program, 1983), 135–79.

44. Emmanuel S. De Dios, "The Erosion of the Dictatorship," in Javate de Dios et al., *Dictatorship and Revolution*, 99–100.

45. Rigoberto Tiglao, *The Philippine Coconut Industry: Looking into Coconuts: Export-Oriented Agricultural Growth* (Davao City, The Philippines: ARC Publications, 1981), 79–93; Boyce, *Political Economy of Growth*, 205–7.

46. De Dios, *An Analysis*, 14, 16.

47. De Dios, *An Analysis*, 39.

48. Sheila S. Coronel, ed., *Pork and Other Perks: Corruption and Governance in the Philippines* (Manila: Philippine Center for Investigative Journalism, 1998), 84.

49. In *Imelda*, a film by Ramona S. Diaz, produced by Jam Bondon, Annie Del Castillo, and Joji Ravina, 2004. Distributed by United International Pictures and Unico Entertainment.

50. Schirmer and Shalom, *The Philippines Reader*, 293–97.

51. Boyce, *Political Economy of Growth*, 27, 31.

52. Roxas, *Juetengate*, 42.

53. Benedict Anderson, "Cacique Democracy in the Philippines," in *Spectre of Comparisons: Nationalism, Southeast Asia, and the World* (London: Verso, 1998), 212–13.

54. Patricio N. Abinales, *Making Mindanao: Cotabato and Davao in the Formation of the Philippine Nation-State* (Quezon City: Ateneo de Manila University Press, 2000), chapter 8.

55. Peter G. Gowing and Robert D. McAmis, eds., *The Muslim Filipinos* (Manila: Solidaridad, 1974), 234–35.

56. Eric Gutierrez et al., *Rebels, Warlords, and Ulama: A Reader on Muslim Separatism and the War in Southern Philippines* (Quezon City: Institute for Popular Democracy, 2000).

57. Jones, *Red Revolution*, 225–26.

58. Lois West, *Militant Labor in the Philippines* (Philadelphia: Temple University Press, 1997), 44–71; Mark Thompson, *The Anti-Marcos Struggle: Personalistic Rule and Democratic Transition in the Philippines* (New Haven, Conn.: Yale University Press, 1995), 99–106.

59. Barry, "Limits of Conservative Church Reformism."

60. Hutchcroft, *Booty Capitalism*, 53.

61. Alfred W. McCoy, *Closer than Brothers: Manhood at the Philippine Military Academy* (New Haven, Conn.: Yale University Press, 1999), 224–30.

62. Hutchcroft, *Booty Capitalism*, 145.

63. "Mixed Legacy," editorial, *Philippine Daily Inquirer*, June 9, 2004.

Chapter Nine

Democratization, 1986–2004

STATE AND SOCIETY AFTER THE FALL

In 1989, a statue of Mary, Queen of Peace, was consecrated near the spot where marines loyal to the government had waited for orders facing the outer perimeter of the crowd during the 1986 uprising. Known as Our Lady of Edsa Shrine, it is a symbol of the "Edsa Revolution" that brought down a dictator. It has also become a natural place to rally against other threats to democracy. In the years following the Philippines' revolution, the country came to look like a trendsetter in popular democracy movements worldwide— the Palestinian intifada, 1987; Tiananmen Square, 1989; Rangoon, 1989; Warsaw, Prague, and Berlin, 1989; and the dissolution of the Soviet Union, 1991. Much public writing at the time discussed the phenomenon of "people power," giving the Philippines a special place in the wave of "democratization" taking place.

Within the Philippines, the Edsa Revolution was symbolic of the brotherhood and sisterhood of the nation. This was evident in the much-remarked-upon mingling of classes on Edsa Boulevard, the united action of church and society, businesses' donation of food to the ralliers, ralliers handing packets of rice through the gates to the rebels, and nationwide support for Corazon Aquino, the country's "Tita (Auntie) Cory." The Edsa Revolution represented a spiritual unity to rival the 1896 Revolution.

These memories of people power are true to the symbolic life of the nation, but we should also remember what people power was *not*, in the political sense. It was *not* an act of unmediated love of nation or a dissolving of social divisions. Filipinos came to Edsa as members of social forces opposing the dictatorship in varying degrees for varying lengths of time—as student activ-

230

ists, Catholics, business executives, or urban-poor leaders. People power was *not* the result of consensus among those social forces, for the revolution was sparked by mistakes made by Marcos (calling the election) and the action of one opposition force (RAM's coup). It did *not* include all the social forces opposing Marcos, for it had little relevance to the Muslims and represented a defeat of sorts for the Communist Party of the Philippines. Most importantly, as a fairly spontaneous mobilization, people power was *not* a sustainable political action, even as a form of revolutionary change.

The limits of people power would soon become evident as the constituent elements of the Edsa Revolution returned to politics during the presidency of Corazon Aquino (1986–1992). Each of the forces that helped bring Aquino to power was determined to find expression in her government's policies. Emmanuel De Dios and Paul Hutchcroft describe these forces as "the politicized and putsch-oriented factions of the military, the anti-Marcos financial and industrial elite, traditional politicians disenfranchised by the previous regime, the Catholic Church, the articulate urban middle classes, and a plethora of nongovernment and people's organizations representing the moderate to the radical Left."[1] Aquino's legacy would be determined by her stance vis-à-vis these forces, especially the military and the traditional economic elite (to which she belonged) on the right and reformists ranging from moderate to radical on the left. Her dilemma was how to deal with Marcos's devastation of the nation's economy while restoring full constitutional rule via this coalition of often antagonistic interests. Her political and policy choices would be dictated by contingency, habit, and ideological outlook.

Aquino's Legacy

President Aquino inherited an excessively centralized, thoroughly discredited state. The economy was in severe recession, forced by capital flight and the withdrawal of short-term loans "to contract by more than 15% in two consecutive years (1984–1986)."[2] This contraction wiped out more than a decade of growth in GDP per capita; the 1982 peak income would not be seen again for two decades.[3] Social indicators were no less discouraging. In 1985, two-thirds of families consumed less than the recommended minimum daily calorie intake, and 22 percent of preschool children experienced moderate to severe malnutrition.[4] Aquino inherited not only a state and economy in crisis but also a nation with a growing proportion of poor citizens.

Two immediate challenges presented themselves, both indications that though Marcos was gone, the forces he had nurtured were not. First, Marcos loyalists in the AFP attempted to overthrow the government in May 1986, and RAM followed in November with the first of several coup attempts. From a

Figure 9.1.   Philippine Marine praying before attack on RAM rebels (Boy Cabrido and the *Philippine Daily Inquirer*)

small military force of about fifty thousand dominated by a professional officer corps in the mid-1960s, the AFP had become a politicized and divided agency of 154,139 in late 1986.[5] In addition to the immediate impact on civil order, coup attempts made foreign investors wary and so affected the degree of international assistance the Philippines could expect to receive in its recovery effort. Second, Aquino faced the international debt inherited from the previous government, estimated at $27.2 billion in 1986.[6] Considering that much of it had been lost to fraud—part of the $10–15 billion sent to private bank accounts abroad—there was significant popular support for restructuring or even repudiating portions of the debt.[7] This, of course, was opposed by international financial institutions and other creditors who wanted the Philippines to honor its financial obligations.

Under pressure from coup attempts, the International Monetary Fund (IMF), the World Bank, and the United States, Aquino vetoed radical changes in economic policy and decided to honor the country's debt obligations "fully and unconditionally instead of declaring a selective moratorium to address the resource transfer issue." She also enrolled the Philippines in the recovery programs of the IMF and World Bank, which required meeting a series of reform targets to liberalize the economy—ending agricultural monopolies and favoritism in industrial projects, reducing tariffs, and lifting import controls.[8] Aquino's decision in favor of full debt repayment and IMF conditionality meant that technocrats rather than social reformists set the economic agenda in the new government. In fact, the technocracy's role in the post-Marcos period became stronger with the claim that economic development could succeed if freed from "cronies" and opposition from the protectionist domestic industrial sector.[9] Aquino also mended fences with the United States, assuring its leaders that the Philippines would honor the military bases and other security commitments. American support—via fighter-jet flyovers—proved critical during RAM's 1989 coup attempt, the one of seven launched against Aquino that came closest to succeeding.[10]

To strengthen her presidency and delegitimize military discontents, Aquino moved to restore democratic government as quickly as possible, promising a new constitution within one year. Shortly after taking office, she appointed a constitutional commission broadly representing her coalition, and in February 1987 a new constitution was submitted to popular referendum. The commission had debated presidential versus parliamentary government (deciding in favor of the former by one vote), modes of popular representation, local government autonomy, land reform, and the degree to which the economy should be open to foreign participation. The urgency of the task meant that only a basic framework was submitted and most details were left for the elected legislature to elaborate. At Aquino's urging and given the pressing need for stability, the new charter easily won public approval.

The 1987 Constitution reflected the diverse makeup of its drafters in the homage it paid to various elements of society—the family, women, labor, and the private and other "sectors" (such as the peasantry and cultural minorities).[11] It cautiously enshrined the goal of "a more equitable distribution of opportunities, income, and wealth," but clearly defined "the promotion of social justice" as the creation of "economic opportunities based on freedom of initiative and self-reliance." The same nod to social justice combined with the guarantee of private property is found in the section mandating agrarian land reform: "The State shall, by law, undertake an agrarian reform program founded on the right of farmers and regular farmworkers, who are landless, to own directly or collectively the lands they till. . . . To this end, the State shall encourage and undertake the just distribution of all agricultural lands . . . subject to the payment of just compensation."

Most fundamentally, the 1987 Constitution, which remains in effect today, restored the pre–martial law constitutional system consisting of a president and vice president, bicameral legislature, and independent Supreme Court. The president is limited to one six-year term, senators to two six-year terms; presidents, vice presidents, and senators are elected by popular vote in national at-large elections. (Voters may "split" their vote any way, including between presidential and vice presidential running mates.) Representatives are elected by legislative districts, with an additional unspecified number to be elected "through a party-list system of registered national, regional, and sectoral parties or organizations [representing] labor, peasant, urban poor, indigenous cultural communities, women, youth [etc.]."

The commission cut back the excess executive powers Marcos had accumulated, but left the president "control of all the executive departments, bureaus, and offices" and the right to appoint, subject to approval by a congressional Commission on Appointments, "the heads of the executive departments, ambassadors, other public ministers and consuls, or officers of the armed forces from the rank of colonel or naval captain." The president is commander-in-chief and retains limited power to suspend the writ of habeas corpus and place the country under martial law. However, should it be invoked, this state of affairs cannot exceed sixty days, a written report must be submitted to Congress within forty-eight hours, and Congress can revoke the president's order by a simple majority, such revocation not subject to presidential reversal or veto. As further protection against martial law tyranny, the Constitution stipulates that "the Supreme Court may review, in an appropriate proceeding filed by any citizen, the sufficiency of the factual basis of the proclamation of martial law or the suspension of the privilege of the writ of habeas corpus," and that "a state of martial law does not suspend the operation of the Constitution, nor supplant the functioning of the civil courts or legislative assemblies."

Legislation is the domain of Congress, but the president is permitted to introduce legislation through party allies in the legislative branch. In a document concerned predominantly with principles and institutions, the following section on the legislature is noteworthy: "Discretionary funds appropriated for a particular official shall be disbursed only for public purposes to be supported by appropriate vouchers and subject to such guidelines as may be prescribed by law." Such discretionary funds are commonly known as "pork barrel," and their reinstatement signaled the return of patronage politics.

The 1987 local and legislative elections that followed featured 90 percent voter turnout, but the restoration saw the return to power of many "dynastic" families that had controlled politics in the pre–martial law period (see box 9.1).[12] With past knowledge of the mechanics of traditional politics, the clans' legislative representatives quickly doused the reformist torch carried by Aquino's supporters on the left. The most bitterly fought battle was for comprehensive agrarian reform to end decades of rural exploitation and impoverishment. Landlord interests in the newly installed Congress effectively derailed this vital issue that had helped build broad support for Aquino on the moderate left, especially among the peasantry. The president, whose extended family owned vast sugar estates north of Manila, did little to defend her "centerpiece program."[13]

Figure 9.2.   Voter filling out a ballot on election day (Ric Rocamora)

Box 9.1.   Dynastic Politics

"In his twilight, when he had taken to God and the Sacred Scriptures, Ramon S. Durano Sr. used the Bible to explain why families play such a central role in Philippine politics. 'Of the 12 apostles,' he told journalists who visited his sprawling seaside home in Danao, Cebu, in 1986, 'five are first-degree cousins of Jesus. John the Baptist, who baptized him, was his second-degree cousin. The rest are either second-degree or half-cousins. Of the 12, the only one not related to Jesus by blood was Judas Iscariot who betrayed the Lord.'

"'Now,' he continued, 'don't tell me this dynasty of Marcos, or my dynasty and the dynasty of Dimaporo in Lanao are our invention. Jesus was the one who invented the dynasty.'

"This is a bit over the top, of course. But one cannot fault the man for being a firm believer in dynastic politics. As of last count, his extended clan had at least 25 members who have held public office since the 1890s, when his father Demetrio was *teniente* or municipal councilor of Danao."

— Sheila S. Coronel et al., *The Rulemakers: How the Wealthy and Well-born Dominate Congress* (Quezon City: Philippine Center for Investigative Journalism, 2004), 56

* * * * *

"The results of the 11 May 1987 elections show that out of 200 congressmen in the House of Representatives, 130 belong to so-called traditional political families while another 39 are relatives of these families. Only 31 have no electoral record prior to 1971 and are not directly related to these old dominant families. Of the 169 congressmen who are members of or are related to dominant families, 102 are identified with the pre-1986, anti-Marcos forces while 67 are from pro-Marcos parties or families. Despite a few nontraditional figures among the 24 elected members of the Senate, the cast is largely made up of persons belonging to prominent, pre-1972, political families."

— Resil B. Mojares, "The Dream Goes On and On: Three Generations of the Osmeñas, 1906–1990," in *An Anarchy of Families: State and Family in the Philippines*, ed. Alfred W. McCoy (Madison: University of Wisconsin, Center for Southeast Asian Studies, 1993), 312

Political pressure from the far left—the CPP—pushed Aquino further to the right and in the long run helped stabilize her government. The CPP had been marginalized by its decision to boycott elections in 1986, was split in its stance toward the new constitution and electoral politics, and struggled to recover momentum in radically changed circumstances. The far right—RAM— also played a role in the party's troubles, targeting CPP legal organizations for harassment and its leaders for assassination in hopes of fomenting labor and student unrest to usher in another coup. Embattled, the party began to search for spies within its ranks, resorting to torture and execution of its own (see box 9.2).[14] These growing problems forced the CPP into peace talks with the new government, but the party withdrew in February 1987 after government troops fired on demonstrating peasants. When the CPP renewed its war against the state, Aquino ordered counterinsurgency operations to resume as well. This won her the trust of military factions that had suspected her of pro-communist sentiment, including that of General Fidel V. Ramos, who later retired from the military to become her defense chief.[15]

Reformists and Trapos

Aquino's rightward drift did not extinguish people power, however. An important element of support for the new regime came from reformist nongovernmental organizations (NGOs) and people's organizations (POs). G. Sidney Silliman and Lela Garner Noble, in their study of democracy, civil society, and the Philippine state, define NGOs as "any voluntary organization that is independent of both the government and the private business sectors." POs, according to James Putzel, are "membership-based organizations, like farmer organizations, trade unions, women's organizations, community organizations, and cooperatives, which are set up primarily to promote the interest of their members."[16] In other words, the educated professionals and other staff of NGOs mediate with business and the state, raise funds, run social welfare programs, or otherwise advance the interests of the sectors, while POs directly represent them.

The experience of NGOs and POs under the dictatorship and their decisive intervention in Marcos's last years gave them unprecedented influence in Philippine government after his fall. A paper by a group of academic economists explains that the "outwardly, non-traditional, if not revolutionary origins of the Aquino Government . . . created a political climate in which the language of 'people empowerment,' 'democratization,' 'social justice and human rights,' and 'non-governmental organizations/people's organizations (NGOs/POs)' suddenly became mainstream."[17] Henceforth, policies could not be simply imposed from above; they must be presented to the legislature *and* to the social forces concerned, deliberated, revised, and sometimes rejected.[18] Any act of the executive office aimed at improving state efficiency that bypassed this consultative process would be tagged "autocratic" and provoke boisterous warnings of a slide back to authoritarianism.[19]

Aquino's commitment to "full democratic restoration" also meant the passage of Republic Act 7160, Local Government Code 1991, to reinvigorate local governance. As it was implemented over the next decade, it would devolve some of the powers of the national government to local and provincial governments, increase their share of revenue allotments, and give them the

Box 9.2. Torture inside the Communist Party of the Philippines

"My comrades called me Joey—it was my *koda*, my *nom de guerre*. I was 18 years old when I joined the revolutionary movement, 19 when I became a member of the Communist Party of the Philippines. It may be the idealism of youth, or just a deep down desire to make a difference. Whatever, I was an angry young man who wanted to change the world.

"Young as I was, I pursued my revolutionary task with creativity and appropriate fervor. I worked systematically at building the Party organization at the university, having the knack of getting the maintenance men and office secretaries to stay after office hours. We discussed such political stuff as rights and issues and such imperatives as revolution.

"Needless to say, it was dangerous, clandestine work. The threat to life and limb was omnipresent. While it was a dreaded notion, the prospect of being arrested and tortured by the enemy was an accepted reality. On the 25th of January 1986, it became so, though not exactly as I imagined.

"On that day, I was brought to a certain house on the pretext of computer training. Loud, piercing music greeted my ears upon entering the place. Thereupon I was ordered by men inside to drop to the floor. Next thing I knew, I was blindfolded and handcuffed. They brought me to another place and promptly the interrogation began.

"My captors said they were from the military. They arrested me because, as they claimed, I work with a rival military unit as a DPA (deep penetration agent) within the revolutionary movement. They said I was one of Colonel (Rolando) Abadilla's men, and I was responsible for the identification and subsequent death of one of their own infiltrators.

"For four days I was tortured. They put out their lighted cigarettes on my skin, laughing as they did. They hit me with a lead pipe, punched me, and threw water on my face when I was about to pass out. They did their own crude style of 'good-cop-bad-cop'—with one interrogator offering me cigarettes and food while pleading with me to 'cooperate,' and another beating me black and blue.

"As these were ostensibly military men, I tried to invoke the name of a top military official—one of my wedding sponsors. But this only enraged them further.

"One night, the interrogators complained about getting nowhere with me. Putting up a show of impatience, they hauled me inside a sack and brought me to a spot where I smelled freshly dug earth. I was thrown inside a shallow grave, and was told that I would be buried alive if I did not confess to being a DPA.

"Before I could decide what to do, their two-way radio crackled. They went back inside the house and left me in the grave. Later on I was brought back to the house.

"Inside, I overheard from their arguments that they did not know what to do with me. A bunch of confused, undecided men were deliberating whether I should continue living or not.

"After a while, my captors came out and surprised me. They told me they were just fooling around.

"Still, as a final test, I was to be released on the condition that I agree to be *their* agent. I readily agreed to this, without any intention of fulfilling it. I believed I had to consent to anything if I were to survive.

"Later, I was dropped off a certain place and given some transportation fare. Commuting home, I remember people staring at me, at my dark and sunken eyes, disheveled hair, ill-fitting clothes.

"When I got home some of my father's military friends were in the house. They immediately tried to trace the military units who might be responsible for my abduction. They came up with nothing.

"At this point, with my security at the mercy of the nameless, faceless men, I decided to get out of the country. My wife and I moved to Australia and continued our revolutionary tasks there.

"Those four days of torture left an indelible mark in my life. The beatings and cigarette burning were indescribably painful, but one single moment left the deepest scar. That was when my captors tricked me into divulging where my wife and I were staying.

"They taunted me to no end about how worthless a jerk I was to betray my own wife. If what they intended was to make a mockery of my dignity, to totally destroy my will, to break me completely, then they have succeeded.

"That single act has permanently marred my relationship with my wife, and eventually led to the breakdown of my marriage. It would torment me forever.

"What made it infinitely worse was the true identity of my tormentors, which was revealed to me years later. As it turned out, they were my own comrades in the revolutionary movement."

—"Testimony of Joey," in Robert Francis Garcia,
To Suffer Thy Comrades: How the Revolution Decimated Its Own
(Pasig, The Philippines: Anvil Publishing, 2001), 37–39

right to impose property taxes on state-owned or -controlled corporations in their localities.[20] NGOs and POs would find space for participation in governance in this arena as well (discussed below).

Even traditional politics did not revert completely back to "the good old days." Marcos's destruction of the Nacionalistas and Liberals ended the two-party system, and the splintering of his Kilusang Bagong Lipunan (KBL) in 1986 left no single organization with a nationwide network capable of dominating the political arena. Politicians were powerful within their realms (provinces, cities, and municipalities), but their ties to the national state were no longer coursed through a single patronage machine. Instead, a mélange of small political parties with constantly shifting memberships created short-lived, election-based alliances. It was some time before anything approximating a national party was reconstructed. Even then, the new organizations—Laban ng Demokratikong Pilipino (LDP, Struggle of the Democratic Filipino) and its breakaway group, the Lakas ng Bansa (Strength of the Nation, or Lakas)—were less the unified patronage parties of old than coalitions of factions and smaller parties kept tenuously together by patronage and pork barrel politics.

Sensing opportunity in this new political context, many "trapos" (traditional politicians) forged alliances with NGOs and POs, which agreed to the "tactical alliances" to expand their knowledge of "parliamentary struggle" and piggyback onto the trapo networks to build their own.[21] (See box 9.3.) The birth of election-driven coalitions—including "right-wing" politicians, "left-wing" NGOs, and influential personalities from national leaders to movie stars—has become a notable feature of post-Marcos politics. The objective of the coalitions is to capture the two top executive posts and as many legislative seats as possible. If successful, coalition members are apportioned state agencies and positions commensurate with their strength and contribution to the electoral campaign. They are then free to run their agencies according to their own policies and priorities.

Trapos often regard such offices as a source of spoils and proceed accordingly. But in agencies run by NGOs/POs and business and middle-class Aquino allies, governance agendas were pursued with professionalism and efficiency. Examples of "islands of state strength" that flourished under reformist supervision were the Finance Department and the Central Bank, which sought to shed their Marcos-era cronyism; the Department of Health, which pushed for a generic prescription drug program; and the Housing and Urban Development Coordinating Council, which successfully brokered with Congress and urban poor NGOs and POs to craft an urban land reform

---

Box 9.3. Portrait of the Post-Marcos Trapo

"On the one hand, Tomas Osmeña projected his competence in economic matters (employing, among others, Asian Institute of Management Dean Gaston Ortigas as campaign consultant). On the other hand, he cultivated the image of advocacy for urban-poor causes by means of such tactics as sleeping in the houses of campaign supporters in the city's depressed *barangays* [and] articulating 'urban-poor' planks in his platform. . . . Using personal contacts and links to local development agencies, his staff devised the 'People's Alternative' scenario, under which a group of private, voluntary organizations (PVOs) and nongovernmental organizations (NGOs) organized the Cebu Development Forum, which launched the People's Alternative project on 30 November 1987, just fifty days before the election. Ostensibly its purpose was to create an urban-poor agenda for the city government, lobbying for candidates' commitment to it, staging nonpartisan forums, and then openly endorsing the candidates 'who can best serve the cause of the urban poor.' It was an Osmeña scenario: top strategists in the Osmeña camp had direct links to the PVOs and NGOs involved, drew up the agenda, and directed the projects. On 11 January 1988, at a convention attended by four hundred delegates, Tomas Osmeña was declared the 'People's Choice.'"

—Resil B. Mojares, "The Dream Goes On and On:
Three Generations of the Osmeñas, 1906–1990," in *An Anarchy of Families:
State and Family in the Philippines,* ed. Alfred W. McCoy (Madison:
University of Wisconsin, Center for Southeast Asian Studies, 1993), 342–43

law beneficial to city slum dwellers.[22] The National Economic Development Authority (NEDA), which Marcos had created to conceptualize development programs, maintained its professionalism and became a notably active reformist agency run by a maverick economist who was a close Aquino ally.[23] The effectiveness of these "islands" often stopped at their shores, as they operated in a sea of agencies dominated by patronage forces and brutal strongmen. But in contrast to previous regimes, the honest managers were no longer limited to apolitical technocrats. The NGOs and POs brought the popular sectors into the state.

One sector that experienced unprecedented prominence in the political arena has earned less attention from scholars than most. We refer here to women, beginning with the election of the country's first female president. In the later years of the Marcos dictatorship, the democratic opposition was organized not simply along class lines or mobilized under the broad goal of "democracy"—feminists and leftists also spearheaded organization along gender lines. Behind the growth of "women's organizing" lay peasant women's defense of their communities from military abuses, middle-class concern about the spread of prostitution, the illegal trafficking in women that accompanied Filipinos' search for employment abroad, and union organizing in factories with female-dominated workforces.[24] Then, during the 1985–1986 election campaign, Marcos belittled Aquino as a presidential rival, driving hitherto apathetic middle-class and elite women into her camp, where they formed a boisterous and influential group that cemented support for her presidency in the "golden ghettos." Many of the professional women among them later served in her administration.[25]

Aquino was of course preceded by Imelda Marcos as a woman projecting authority on a national scale. But Mrs. Marcos made no attempt to mobilize other women; neither she nor her allies organized politically along gender lines. Her autocratic demeanor and narcissism precluded this and distinguished her from her democratic rival.[26] It is also commonly argued that Corazon Aquino is best understood as a member of a class (the landed elite) and of a family (the Aquino-Cojuangco political clan).[27] Her political decisions—especially on land reform—certainly reflect this. But it should not obscure the fact that during her restoration of democratic practices, women's participation in the public sphere expanded significantly. Aquino opened the doors of the state to women, and they have remained open since.

At the end of Aquino's presidency in 1992, an editorial writer captured the enormity of her task:

From the disarray of pillaged institutions and the insensitivity engendered by the wanton abuse of civil rights, she was expected to restore a democracy that would guarantee freedom from fear and want and ensure equal opportunity and prosperity through the broad consensus of a society compartmentalized by varied primal interests and degraded by political opportunism.[28]

Aquino's presidency was a mosaic of contradictory elements, wherein structural and political remnants from the authoritarian past abutted democratic practices exploited by reformists and trapos alike. This political reality had an element of strength in its weakness: It undercut attempts by right-wing forces to topple the new regime and curbed left-wing forces within and outside the governing coalition. Aquino eventually settled into a "middle ground" that she described as "a peaceful political transition . . . protected every step of the way by the military."[29] The middle ground was her political legacy—but it would also be a curse on her successors, for it dictated a delicate balance between strengthening state capacities and the need to assure a rightly skeptical public of the state's commitment to democracy.

ECONOMIC RECOVERY AND STATE REBUILDING

Between Recovery and Crisis

The long-term survival of electoral democracy in the Philippines ultimately depends on its ability to foster economic well-being. The downward economic spiral Aquino inherited from Marcos was halted by her decision to honor the country's financial obligations, dismantle import controls and monopolies that protected crony enterprises, and initiate trade reform. After some hesitation, foreign investment began to return, rising from $564 million in 1987 to $2.5 billion in 1992.[30] The value of exports doubled in the same period, reaching $8.8 billion.[31] Government spending on public works, education, and infrastructure grew, while "countryside development programs" were restored with the assistance of grants to NGOs and POs.[32]

But honoring the Marcos-era debt had disadvantages, too. Eighty percent of the country's foreign debt was held by the public sector, and during Aquino's term the government paid $3.5 billion per year—about 10 percent of the GDP—to service this debt.[33] The "foreign debt hemorrhage caused a huge drain on the budget and severely limited the government's options." Trying to stem the outflow through "heavy domestic borrowing" only increased the deficit and created a "vicious cycle": "large deficits pushed up interest rates, increased the internal debt-service requirements, and caused even larger deficits."[34] Domestic debt soared to $12.3 billion in 1990, and each year from 1987 to 1991, payments on foreign and domestic debt consumed between 40 and 50 percent of the national budget.[35]

Toward the end of her term, the deficit severely constrained Aquino's ability to address social welfare problems, infrastructure needs, and rehabilitation. Nature added to the country's travails when a major earthquake in 1990 was followed the next year by the volcanic eruption of Mount Pinatubo and devastating floods in the central Philippines. The 1991 Persian Gulf War reduced remittances from overseas Filipino workers, and the Senate declined to renew the military bases agreement with the United States, costing the treasury $480 million annually in rent.[36] In 1991 the economy entered a recession from which it did not emerge until 1994. If not for the $4 billion remitted by overseas Filipino workers (for whom Taiwan was a new destination) and the rise in foreign and domestic investment, a balance of payments and trade deficit might have destabilized Aquino's government.[37]

More fundamental problems of poverty and income disparity remained unaddressed. In the late Marcos period, 49.3 percent of Filipinos lived in poverty; this figure declined to 46.5 percent during Aquino's term, condemned by sociologist Walden Bello as "a marginal reduction."[38] Forty percent of the national income remained in the hands of the country's richest 10 percent while the poorest 30 percent shared only 10 percent.[39] In many countries, the seriousness of this economic situation would have dictated government intervention, but two factors precluded any such action in the restored Philippine democracy. First, Aquino's firm commitment to her particular interpretation of "democracy" and the public's lingering mistrust of state power made intervention undesirable. Second, the state was essentially bankrupt. This was due not only to the burden of debt repayment but also to lost revenue. While publicly professing support for Aquino, wealthy Filipinos were not so eager to do their civic duty: The individual income tax evasion rate rose from about 10 percent to more than 35 percent during her term (because income tax is withheld from the paychecks of wage earners, evasion is disproportionately committed by self-reporting professionals and businesspeople).[40]

In the absence of government welfare programs, NGOs and POs tried to fill the gap. In 1986, they received $3.38 billion in grants from the United States, Great Britain, Australia, Germany, and Japan. From 1987 to the early 1990s, the Canadian International Development Agency (CIDA) alone gave such organizations $30.5 million.[41] This tremendous flow of external funding sponsored many social welfare projects, but these could not replace comprehensive state efforts to alleviate poverty and correct income inequality. Further, NGOs and POs could not be present in every community, so the majority of the population was left to fend for itself during the second economic crisis in a decade. The return of democracy was a welcome development, but the new regime's ability to foster economic prosperity was found wanting.

A Declaration of State Strength

Nearing the end of her term, President Aquino endorsed Fidel Ramos as her successor. Like Aquino, Ramos campaigned with a coalition of NGOs and POs, local politicians, and business interests. He was particularly popular with Filipino and Chinese-Filipino businessmen for his "professionalism" and with a younger generation of forward-looking Filipinos who did not identify with the Marcos period.[42] Although he won by only a slim majority, Ramos began his term under favorable conditions: Budget-tightening measures and remittances from overseas Filipinos had stabilized the economy, and he was already well regarded by the middle class and by urban elites for his loyalty to Aquino and the constitution through the coup attempts.

Ramos began his term (1992–1998) with a vision of institutional and economic reform. In a major departure from the populist, antistate rhetoric of the Aquino administration, he offered

> a strategic framework for development which will be guided by a strong State. By a Strong State I mean one that can assert our country's strategic interests because it has relative autonomy over the influence of oligarchic groups. For the last 47 years, we have had a political system that has been too responsive to groups possessing wealth and power enough to bend the State to do their will. Such a political system has distorted our economy and rendered government ineffectual. This is the reason why the Philippines has lagged so far behind the East Asian Tigers.[43]

In contrast to the state under Marcos, Ramos pledged a "strong state" anchored in "people empowerment" and committed to "a policy environment" in which reformists could pursue their "economic, political, social, cultural, and spiritual aspirations."[44] In practical terms, this broad endorsement of the reform agenda was to be realized by implementing the 1991 Local Government Code and institutionalizing the "rainbow coalition" of traditional politicians, loyal military officers, business allies, and NGOs that supported his candidacy.[45]

Ramos's economic strategy was more detailed, consisting of a determined liberalization program geared to attract foreign investment and foster competitiveness; the accelerated privatization of state corporations; and the breakup of cartels and monopolies in the power, shipping, domestic air transport, telecommunications, banking, and oil industries. With the growing prevalence of free-trade agreements, Ramos felt the need to reposition the Philippine economy regionally and internationally—his declared goal was to turn the Philippines into an "economic cub" by 2000. In this context, Ramos and his "chief ideologue," Jose Almonte, used the term "strong state" to signal their intention to face down family conglomerates' control of key industries.[46]

Since Aquino's primary goals of political stabilization and institutional restoration had been met, Ramos meant to focus on rebuilding and reshaping the economy. The institutional reforms he pursued in the first four years of his term should therefore be seen as serving his economic goals. As Almonte told business leaders, "The paradox of market reforms is that they require capable states." Likewise, the devolution of responsibility to the local level, while consistent with "people empowerment," was also meant to trim the national bureaucracy and budget, allowing greater flexibility to pursue the national economic agenda.

Ramos represented only the third Philippine president to come into office with a strong vision of national economic development. Liberalization itself was not a new idea; it had been adopted briefly by Marcos in the early 1980s and was begun again by Aquino to meet IMF conditionality. But in 1992, with the triumph of market forces proclaimed worldwide, Ramos embraced liberalization more fully and started the country on an economic path that it followed until late 2003. Since Ramos was also the last president (as of this writing) to pursue an economic policy for a full six-year term, we will briefly survey the elements of his "strategic vision" in light of their continuing effect on the Philippine economy.

Trade liberalization involved lowering tariffs and lifting quantitative import restrictions on hundreds of goods (notably, not rice); removing capital controls to allow capital to flow unimpeded in and out of the country; and opening previously restricted sectors and industries to foreign ownership. These policies yielded some impressive results. Foreign investors were attracted, in rough order of importance, by the perception of increased political stability, improvements in infrastructure (especially electricity), the opening of energy and other sectors to foreign equity, tariff reductions, and tax incentives. Investment in "special economic zones" and industrial estates produced three hundred thousand new jobs and revived provincial economies around Manila, in central and northern Luzon, and in Cebu province.[47] Related to the growth of export zones was the emergence of electronics equipment (especially semiconductors) as the new dominant export, representing "the entire merchandise trade expansion in the 1990s or almost 70% of the merchandise exports of the country."[48] The inflow of foreign capital, export of new products, and moderate improvement in employment increased domestic demand, broadened the tax base, and improved the country's balance of payments.[49] Foreign direct investment, which flowed mostly into industry and banking, peaked in 1994, while GDP growth peaked at 5.8 percent in 1996 (this was the year before the Asian economic crisis, which will be addressed below).

Although growth was slower than in other Southeast Asian countries, it was seen as strong enough, in conjunction with pro-market policies, to indicate an economic turnaround.

Export-oriented industrialization did not continue to perform as expected, however. Instead of expanding its share of GDP and employment, the industrial sector—led by manufacturing—actually declined from 1990 to 2002, from 34.5 percent of GDP to 31.6 percent. Industry's share of employment—15–16 percent—has been virtually stable since 1970. Economists suggest a number of reasons for industry's failure to grow, including low levels of value added in electronics assembly and the appreciation of the peso in real terms until 1997, which dampened exports.[50] Whatever the reasons, the implications for continued market reforms are significant. Without expanding employment in manufacturing, the loss of jobs in formerly protected industries will result in unacceptably high unemployment and/or push more people into the burgeoning informal service sector in congested urban centers.

Economists Romeo Bautista and Gwendolyn Tecson maintain that a few years of trade policy reform alone cannot produce sustained growth, especially after the "heavily protectionist trade regime [that] was a major contributor to the country's economic disarray and income inequality for three decades in the postwar period."[51] But prominent globalization critic Walden Bello argues, to the contrary, that Philippine technocrats indiscriminately lowered tariffs hoping to replicate the 8–10 percent growth of other ASEAN countries, but fundamentally misread those nations' "selective liberalization." He points out that in Malaysia, Indonesia, and Thailand, as well as South Korea and Taiwan, "an activist state posture—manifested in industrial policy, protectionism, mercantilism, and intrusive regulation—was central in the drive to industrialize."[52] (Boxes 9.4 and 9.5 present excerpts of arguments by these scholars for and against liberalization.)

Privatization was the second pillar of Ramos's economic strategy. During the dictatorship, public enterprises had proliferated to more than three hundred companies, many of which were nonperforming due to plunder and mismanagement. After Marcos fell, the government took control of almost five hundred *more* companies "proved to have been illicitly acquired." The maintenance of these assets was a significant drain on the national accounts, not to mention a continuing enticement to corruption. When Ramos speeded up the sale of these two categories of firms, many of the latter were reacquired by their former owners (such as the Lopezes) or by former Marcos cronies (such as Lucio Tan, who purchased Philippine Airlines). It was harder to find buyers for unprofitable public corporations, but many were eventually acquired by a combination of local and foreign investors. The sale of some, such as Manila's Metropolitan Water and Sewerage System, have

---

Box 9.4. The Imperative of Competitiveness

"During the decade before the Asian crisis, Philippine economic growth had been less rapid than that of most other economies in the Asian region, investment flows among the lowest, and inflation rates among the highest. . . . The country's protracted history of import substitution hardly helped to provide the right environment for the emergence of a culture of world-class competitiveness among entrepreneurs and workers, so crucial in the present globalization era. A sense of urgency to become and remain competitive must be gained if industries and firms are to survive the cold, rough winds of international competition. For this a truly outward-oriented macro and microeconomic environment must be fostered—hence the need to sustain the drive toward liberalization and increasing openness to both trade and foreign investment.

"Due to its relatively higher labor costs, the Philippines has already begun to lose its comparative advantage in unskilled labor-intensive production to countries such as China, Vietnam, and Indonesia. Fortunately, its history of educating a relatively high proportion of its people, and the large pool of teachable workers still possessing the skill to speak—or at least comprehend—the English language give it some comparative edge in simple, semi-skilled labor-intensive goods in flexible manufacturing, such as back-end semiconductors and computer parts. However, such an advantage risks being a temporary one, given the rapid pace of development in the region. The Philippines must ensure—at the very least—that it *maintains* that edge through sustained investments in human capital. This implies continual investments in human resource development and skills training relevant to the needs of the market. Moreover, other complementary capital is required, such as investments in competitively-priced, good-quality infrastructure, power, transport, communications, and industrial locations. In addition, since the cost of doing business in the country is often raised unduly by poor governance, attention will have to be paid to minimizing, if not eradicating, corruption at all levels and to providing a better-quality public service."

—Romeo Bautista and Gwendolyn Tecson, "International Dimensions," in
The Philippine Economy: Development, Policies, and Challenges,
ed. Arsenio M. Balisacan and Hal Hill (Quezon City: Ateneo de
Manila University Press, 2003), 166

---

proved of lasting public controversy as they involve control of and profit-taking from a natural resource. Nevertheless, from 1987 to 1998, privatization earned the government almost 300 billion pesos, or $12 billion.[53] This revenue helped balance the budget and restore "both fiscal and monetary control, while the perennial problem of external balance that had been immediately due to the foreign debt hangover had been addressed—at least in the short term."[54] On the other hand, in restructuring the virtually insolvent Central Bank of the Philippines, which had losses of "close to 1.6% of the GDP in 1992," the national government absorbed its liabilities and injected 10 billion pesos of fresh capital into a leaner, renamed Bangko Sentral ng Pilipinas (BSP).[55]

Box 9.5. The Costs of Liberalization

"Over two decades of trade liberalization, beginning with the World Bank–IMF structural adjustment [beginning in 1981], had reduced the effective rate of protection for manufacturing from 44 percent to 20 percent. That had been achieved at the cost of multiple bankruptcies and massive job losses. The list of industrial casualties included paper products, textiles, ceramics, rubber products, furniture and fixtures, petrochemicals, beverage, wood, shoes, petroleum oils, clothing accessories, and leather goods. An indication of the comprehensive negative impact of unilateral liberalization was the decision of a government review committee constituted under Executive Order 241 [of 2003] to raise tariffs on 627 of 1,371 locally produced goods to provide relief to industries suffering from unfair competition from imports. One of the industries most severely affected by the tariff cuts, as well as the abuse of duty-free privileges, was the textile industry, which shrank from 200 firms in the 1970s to less than 10. [Outgoing finance secretary Isidro] Camacho's words were unambiguous: 'There's an uneven implementation of trade liberalization, which was to our disadvantage.' While consumers may have benefited from tariff cuts, 'it has killed so many industries. . . .'"

—Walden Bello et al., *The Anti-Development State: The Political Economy of Permanent Crisis in the Philippines* (Quezon City: University of the Philippines, Department of Sociology; Focus on the Global South, 2004), 25–26

Finally, Ramos's campaign against cartels and monopolies had mixed results. The most affected industry—telecommunications—may serve to illustrate. Through 1992, the Cojuangco-owned Philippine Long Distance Telephone (PLDT) company held a near-monopoly over the nation's local and long-distance telephone services and owned the only international "gateway," a very profitable position given the increasing number of Filipinos working abroad. According to Peter Krinks, "PLDT was making over P3 billion profit annually and had a net worth exceeding P13 billion ($547 million). [It owned] over 90 percent of the one million telephone lines, but there was a backlog of half a million applications for lines, and service was poor."[56] Ramos's determination to make the Philippines competitive for international investment made this industry his first target. In early 1993, despite opposition from some of the country's top business leaders, he ordered the creation of a "universally accessible and integrated national network." New investors (including some of his erstwhile critics) quickly entered the market. Within four years, thirteen companies, most with foreign partners, competed to provide local and long-distance, mobile, and international telephone service at significantly lower cost to consumers.

Nevertheless, "PLDT remained far ahead of its nearest rivals," and the industry was still dominated by the familiar family names—Ayala, Lopez, Gokongwei, Yuchengco. Today, as in other countries, the high capitalization costs of providing integrated voice, data, and Internet services are leading to industry reconcentration. Another measure of success, however, is public access to telephone lines, which has historically been very low and uneven. From 1996 to 2000, telephone lines per thousand people increased by almost 57 percent (to 40 per 1,000), but the lines are still disproportionately located in cities; most rural barangays do not have a single telephone line. On the other hand, the opening of the industry facilitated the widespread accessibility of mobile telephone service, which is more affordable and feasible for lower-income groups. Mobile service increased from 13.7 phones per thousand people in 1996 to 84.4 in 2000, a 516 percent increase.[57]

Ramos did less in terms of direct poverty alleviation measures. His 1994 Social Reform Agenda, for example, launched to support social welfare programs already in place at the provincial level, was not able to move forward because of lack of funds.[58] The government continued to proclaim that 20 percent of its expenditure went to "human priority projects," but in real terms spent only 16 percent, one-third of which came from international aid agencies.

Neither did he do much to address the increasingly woeful state of agriculture, despite "wide agreement in the development literature that sustained economic growth in heavily agricultural countries is not likely to be achieved without them first—or concurrently—developing their agricultural sectors." In the Philippines in 1995, crop, poultry, and livestock agriculture, together with fisheries and forestry, employed 43.5 percent of the labor force, but contributed only 21.4 percent of GDP. (In 2002, these had declined to 37 percent and 14.9 percent, respectively.) Most crucially, the rural sector is home to almost 70 percent of the nation's poor; according to Bautista and Tecson, this is a situation in which "rapid expansion of agricultural production can also lead to a significant improvement in income distribution."[59]

Agriculture had traditionally been a leading foreign exchange earner, but by the 1990s, agricultural imports outstripped exports. This was partly the result of decades of overlogging, forest degradation, and depletion of fish stock, a consequence of treating the country's "natural capital . . . as free, reproducible hence inexhaustible instruments for . . . resource extraction rather than conservation" and replenishment.[60] In export crop agriculture, coconut was still the leader, though declining. But sugar, after years of assured U.S. markets and little incentive to improve productivity, had declined to only 5 percent of export value. Banana exports had likewise leveled off due to overreliance on the Japanese market, where market opening gave consumers a wider choice of tropical fruits. Rising agricultural imports were due to a variety of factors: Inputs for the livestock and poultry industries (the only growing subsectors of agriculture) were cheaper to import than produce domestically. Rice and corn production also increasingly depended on imported pesticides, fertilizers, and farm machinery. Even some rice and corn was imported, as were fruit and cattle, as trade liberalization removed protection from more products.[61]

But economist Cristina David finds the sector's difficulties to be due less to domestic and foreign market pressures than to "weaknesses in the policy and institutional frameworks." Two examples will illustrate. First, the 1987 Comprehensive Agrarian Land Reform Program (CARP) was very slowly implemented due to high compensation costs and the unwillingness of the "landlord-dominated Congress" to fund it. Nevertheless, David argues that the greater problem was the law's prohibition on the sale of redistributed land in order to prevent reconcentration of ownership. Indeed, she suggests that "the economic cost of the malfunctioning of land markets due to restrictions on land ownership is probably greater than the direct benefits of land reform."[62]

> The threat of land reform in areas where implementation has not been completed [has] prevented land markets from functioning efficiently and discouraged long-term agricultural investment. This has also eroded the value of land as collateral, limiting the availability and/or raising the cost of agricultural investments. . . . [I]n the wake of the CARP legislation, the ability of poor landless workers to gain access to land through the established market [has] worsened significantly.[63]

Second, David argues that public spending in the agricultural sector has been misdirected and inadequate. Irrigation, research and development, and extension services were—and still are—underfunded, while roads meant for all-purpose use are built to low construction standards, lack adequate secondary arteries, and are not maintained.[64]

Germelino Bautista attributes much of the decline of agriculture since the 1970s to factors rarely accounted for in the economic literature, but which can also be traced to poor policy. Focusing on declining land quality, he singles out the downstream effects of deforestation and upland farming in logged-over areas: reduced stream flows, surface runoff and soil erosion, and silted-up irrigation works. How is the state dealing with the growing scarcity of water, as well as the nation's degraded irrigation infrastructure? Bautista finds a failure to "conceptually and programmatically link the lowland farm demand for water with its sources, . . . the absence of a headwater forest protection policy, . . . and lack of coordination among various government agencies." In the absence of national policy, both central agencies and local governments have resorted to short-term solutions and small-scale irrigation projects.[65]

In revenue collection, Ramos projected a cigar-chomping, hands-on image, but even here the "strong state" had some very weak spots. Tax reform—like the introduction of a value-added tax (VAT) to replace the more complicated sales tax—did raise revenue, but pervasive corruption in the Bureau of Internal Revenue and widespread evasion by business limited its effectiveness. Corporate tax evasion during Ramos's term was estimated at "between 53% and 63% for domestic sales taxes, and between 48% and 55% for import taxes." Meanwhile, "non-payment of taxes on salaries [was estimated] at between 24% and 43% and on professional income at between 65% and 83%." The failure of government to prosecute notorious tax evaders such as former Marcos crony Tan underscored state weakness and encouraged more evasion. Faced with "resistance," the government focused its attention on raising the contribution of income taxes.[66]

In the realm of governance, the country's local government units (LGUs) enthusiastically welcomed the implementation of the Local Government Code, which devolved the powers of several national agencies to the provincial, city, and town governments and increased their share of internal revenue taxes from 20 to 40 percent. The code applies to the following national services: "agricultural extension and research, social forestry, environmental management and pollution control, primary healthcare, hospital care, social welfare services, repair and maintenance of infrastructure facilities, water supply and communal irrigation, and land use planning."[67] We have already noted the "too localized" response to water problems, but this is a failure to be laid at the feet of national planners. In terms of local governance, many LGUs have successfully absorbed these agencies, thereby stimulating local economic development and reinforcing institutional reform and political stability. The participation of NGOs and POs in this process has been conspicuous and relates to yet another development—new leadership coalitions between sectoral representatives and the well-educated, policy-savvy sons and daughters of some traditional political clans (see box 9.6).[68] The most oft-cited success story of devolution combined with liberalization was the unprecedented growth in the mid-1990s of Cebu, the country's second major city, although the "Ceboom" also had negative social and ecological consequences.[69]

But administrative decentralization did not reduce overall government expenditure. The transfer of seventy thousand personnel from the national government merely shifted institutional "fat" to the LGUs, where the increased share of tax revenues and power to levy local taxes led to uneven management. According to political scientist Jorge Tigno, many LGUs were guilty of "illegal use of trust funds, unliquidated cash advances, cash shortages, and failure to conduct an annual physical survey of supplies and property." LGU deficit spending rose from 543 million pesos in 1992 to 2.09 billion pesos in 1998, while annual LGU unliquidated cash advances (public money spent

---

Box 9.6.   The Next Generation

"Criticisms of the longevity of so-called elite families and political dynasties miss an interesting generational shift that seems to be ongoing among the political elite. There is no doubt that many of today's politicians indeed belong to long-standing political families. Yet the sons and daughters are often quite different from the fathers. Lanao del Norte governor Abdullah Dimaporo is an American-educated sophisticate quite at home with technocratic modes of governance. He has his father Ali's mastery of Maranao culture and politics, but he balances that with an orientation toward development that goes well beyond the short-term thinking of the elder Dimaporo. Whereas some scholars think of this phenomenon as a cyclical one, accompanying the rise and decline of political families, I believe it is part of a long-term trend toward more development-oriented government officials.

"The fame of Ali Dimaporo as a warlord draws attention to the contrast between traditional and more modern politics and governance, but there are many similar, less famous examples. Governor Rene Relampagos and Vice-Governor Edgar Chatto of Bohol are in their thirties, the younger generation of political families, but they embrace organizational development for the provincial machinery, public-private sector partnership in investment planning, and public opinion polling to sound out their constituents on such hot-button issues as water diversion for the city of Cebu. Or there are examples like the terribly traditional municipal mayor in the interior of Capiz Province whose approach to getting a water system was to have a local beauty queen kiss a visiting senator. The mayor's son, however, is a provincial board member conversant in issues of sustainable development, environmental impact, and long-range planning."

—Steven Rood, "Decentralization, Democracy, and Development," in
The Philippines: New Directions in Domestic Policy and Foreign Relations, ed.
David G. Timberman (Singapore: Institute of Southeast Asian Studies, 1998), 125

---

for which no receipt has been produced) rose from 358 million to 2.3 billion pesos in the same period.[70] Failure to maximize local revenue collection and devise mechanisms to arrest overspending was a serious drawback in the implementation of decentralization. Instead of freeing the national government from its sole responsibility for raising the funds for economic development and local governance, decentralization created "heavier revenue obligations" as the "financial requirements of LGUs took away some room for fiscal flexibility on the national front."[71]

The worst offenders were the poorest provinces, especially those with majority Muslim populations that had been devastated by war. In 1996, Ramos signed a peace treaty with the Moro National Liberation Front and its leader, Nur Misuari, was elected third governor of the constitutionally mandated Autonomous Region in Muslim Mindanao (ARMM). In 1998 and 1999, the ARMM provinces of Tawi-Tawi, Basilan, and Sulu led the country in unliquidated cash advances. At the same time, ARRM received a hefty share of the internal revenue allocation, a good percentage of Department of Environment and Natural Resources collections, and other taxes, much of which was used to maintain a spoils system—the dispensing of offices to a politician's allies and supports. Sixty-six percent of the ARMM budget went to personnel services, "leaving only 14% and 20% for maintenance [and] operating expenses and capital outlay, respectively."[72] Ramos could not rein in ARMM's skewed spending without jeopardizing the MNLF agreement that kept the peace in the southern Philippines.

DEMOCRATIZATION AND THE CHINESE-FILIPINO COMMUNITY

During the 1990s, Chinese-Filipinos experienced a fundamental shift in their standing in Philippine society. After World War II, the state had refused to accept them as part of the national community, as reflected in their economic exclusion under Garcia's Filipino First policy. The state also made it exceedingly difficult for Chinese residents and their Philippine-born children to acquire citizenship in the early 1950s. Filipino politicians even turned naturalization into a source of booty, as immigration quotas assigned to congressmen were allocated to applicants for a "fee" of approximately five thousand pesos. Business license charges were sold for as much as fifty thousand pesos in the same period.[73] The response of the Chinese-Filipino community was to quietly support more sympathetic Filipino politicians via the Federation of Filipino-Chinese Chambers of Commerce and Industry. This body "established a 'war chest' for campaign contributions, arguing in 1954, that channeling campaign contributions through the Federation would create a buffer between the politicians and the rich Chinese as well as increase the political leverage of the community as a whole."[74]

It was not until the 1970s, when Ferdinand Marcos recognized the Chinese community's value as political allies, that naturalization laws were liberalized. Chinese-Filipino enterprises expanded tremendously during this period as the state made credit available to them and facilitated joint ventures.[75] The greatest beneficiaries, of course, were those businessmen who became Marcos cronies. The story of Lucio Tan illustrates the fundamental similarity of cronyism, regardless of ethnicity.

Lucio Tan was probably a Marcos associate even before 1972, when he owned a small cigarette factory in Ilocos (the home region of the president). But it was only with the declaration of martial law in that year that his meteoric ascent began. By 1980, thanks to extensive support from the Palace in gaining tax, customs, financing, and regulatory favors, his Fortune Tobacco Co. had become by far the country's largest maker of cigarettes. In return, Lucio Tan is said to have provided large contributions to Marcos and his New Society Movement, and cut the president into a large equity stake in his firms. Marcos also signed into law a cigarette tax code that had actually been written by Fortune Tobacco, and—as if writing the tax laws wasn't enough—Tan allegedly printed, with impunity, his own internal revenue stamps for use on cigarette packs.[76]

In 1984, as Marcos tried desperately to restore economic stability in the aftermath of the Aquino assassination, Chinese-Filipino businessmen and black market operators came to his rescue. They set up an underground "central bank" to regulate the peso–dollar exchange rate on the black market and help stabilize the currency at a time when it was under speculative attack. The same "Binondo Central Bank" (after the old Chinese district in Manila) facilitated the transfer of millions of dollars to private accounts in Hong Kong and London believed to be owned by Marcos and associates.[77]

With the exception of the Marcos cronies, whose corporations were temporarily sequestered by the new government, Corazon Aquino did not change the position of the state vis-à-vis the Chinese-Filipino community. Its economic presence continued to be highly visible, with Chinese-Filipino families holding a substantial or controlling interest in four large private banks, the textile industry, food and real estate, and manufacturing.[78] It was Ramos who assiduously sought Chinese-Filipino support when he ran for the presidency and subsequently expressed open and enthusiastic acknowledgment of their role in promoting "Philippines 2000." Ramos also made peace with Tan, easing state threats to prosecute him for tax evasion.[79]

In many ways, "the Chinese" ceased being outsiders and became full members of the Philippine nation in the 1990s. They now invoke "citizenship" in expressing their political preferences and promoting their interests.[80] Chinese-Filipino families are prominent in the society pages of newspapers, and their literature and other cultural works are eulogized in literary and artistic circles.[81] But as the *New York Times* also observed, their "highly visible role . . . in Philippine economic growth . . . made [Chinese-Filipinos] obvious targets of extraction."[82] A surge of bank robberies and kidnappings of wealthy Chinese-Filipino businessmen occurred in the mid-1990s, committed by criminal networks representing the flotsam of the Marcos years: former and active soldiers, policemen and anticommunist vigilantes, former NPA guerrillas, and armed units of the MNLF not benefiting from the peace agreement.[83]

Between 1993 and 1997, the number of victims ranged from 179 to 286 per year and the total yearly ransoms grew from $2.5 million to $10.4 million.[84] The Chinese community criticized the government for failing to protect it, and Ramos's critics publicly claimed that the "kidnappings have been engineered by police and military to raise funds for [the coming] elections."[85] As the profitability of kidnapping attracted more criminal groups, targets broadened to include Chinese children, Filipino businessmen and women, and middle-class Chinese and Filipino professionals.

Ramos's inability to curb this crime was a blemish on the image of a robust Philippines. Instead of a new economic tiger, Manila in 1997 was known as "Asia's kidnapping capital."[86] Ramos's admission that his government had failed to contain a crime that "lacerated Philippine civil society" reinforced public fear of the state's deteriorating effectiveness. While he promised to deal decisively with the problem in his remaining months in office, wealthy Chinese-Filipino families opted to send their children abroad and beefed up their private security forces. (See box 9.7.)

Box 9.7. Chinese-Filipinos and the State

"If our commonsensical distinctions between Chinese and Filipino have their origins in Spanish colonial policy and practice, much of the Chinese's present troubles with immigration and citizenship can be traced to the often contradictory American colonial policies, which lay the legal foundations for encouraging Chinese economic activities while depriving the Chinese of the means for political participation. Subsequent legal and economic nationalism during the Commonwealth and postwar years have been supplemented by an entire industry based on corruption and illegal immigration that has made it inordinately difficult for the Chinese to acquire citizenship. Recent laws, in fact, operate on the same extractive logic as that of kidnapping for ransom, since they offer permanent residency and amnesty for Chinese aliens at the cost of two hundred thousand pesos per head, all the time brandishing the threat of violence, illegality and deportation over the heads of those who cannot afford to pay the fee or those who fear, not without reason, that registering with the government will only mean future harassment. And if the only Chinese the state is interested in naturalizing is the rich Chinese, those who can afford to successfully acquire citizenship do not escape the harassment of repeated official inquiries into their immigration history and citizenship status. We need only think of the Yuyitung brothers of *Chinese Commercial News* to realize how easily a Chinese Filipino can be deported to a country he or she has never lived in on fabricated charges of subversion, notwithstanding the fact that the Yuyitungs advocated the assimilation of the Chinese into Philippine society. Since Chinese money (and not all of it freely given) has funded many a politician's election campaign, the sharp increase in the number of kidnapping cases in the closing of the Ramos presidency should provide some clues as to how and where the ransom money is being spent. In situations like these, it is difficult to tell whether the state is acting like a criminal, or whether the criminals act like the state."

—Caroline S. Hau, "Afterword," in *Intsik: An Anthology of Chinese Filipino Writing,* ed. Caroline S. Hau (Pasig, The Philippines: Anvil Publishing, 2000), 304–5

THE UNRAVELING OF "PHILIPPINES 2000"

Ramos's campaigns against vested interests in the economy were not all as successful as the partial breakup of the telecommunications monopoly. One notable failure was the banking industry, which staved off all but the limited entry of foreign financial institutions. And the decision of the government in 1995 to fix the currency exchange rate within a narrow band (around twenty-six pesos to the dollar) was probably due to the influence of Philippine banks eager to reenter the realm of international borrowing and domestic lending. Freedom from exchange rate risk combined with the lifting of capital controls resulted in a surge of foreign borrowing by banks and private corporations that financed construction in real estate, shopping malls, and golf courses—but little vital infrastructure.[87]

Similar exuberant borrowing was occurring in neighboring economies as U.S. portfolio funds fell in love with "emerging markets." The subsequent Asian stock market and real estate bubbles inevitably burst when currency speculators attacked the Thai baht in 1997, sparking an "Asian crisis" that afflicted the entire region with capital flight. Contagion led to a "sympathetic abandonment of the peso, leaving huge bankruptcies in banks and other corporations that had borrowed aggressively abroad."[88] The government tried to defend the peso, selling as much as $4.5 billion, but only managed to deplete foreign reserves before allowing the peso to float.[89] Domestic industries with heavy import requirements were hit hard, causing unemployment to rise from 7.7 percent to 10.6 percent in two years. Since the crisis, the sharply depreciated peso (in 2004, nearly fifty pesos to the dollar) has helped exports narrow the trade deficit, but foreign investment has not recovered.

Among the countries hit by the crisis—most with much stronger economies—the Philippines was noteworthy for its resilient weathering of the storm. Unlike Thailand and Indonesia, for example, the Philippines did not experience a general banking crisis; nor did it experience as sharp or prolonged negative GDP growth. Observers agree that a major reason for this was the Philippines' lower exposure to debt; an external debt moratorium had only been lifted in 1991 and other markets were more attractive to investors. Since less capital had flowed into the Philippines, there was less to flow out. Some economists also credit the Bangko Sentral with imposing strong capitalization requirements and regulatory oversight on the country's banks. And certainly of great help were the 1997 remittances of overseas Filipino workers, totaling $5.7 billion—the equivalent of 20 percent of export earnings.[90]

Another view of the Philippines' comparative success in 1997 and 1998 comes from political scientist Andrew MacIntyre, who compares decision making and policy management in Thailand, Malaysia, Indonesia, and the Phil-

Figure 9.3. Filipinos applying for work permits at the Philippine Overseas Employment Administration (courtesy of *Newsbreak*)

ippines, with special attention to their handling of the 1997 crisis. MacIntyre places the four countries on a scale ranging from highly centralized to highly fragmented decision making, based on the number of "veto players" whose support must be gained for a major policy decision. Describing what he terms a "power concentration paradox," MacIntyre finds that systems with either highly *centralized* decision making (one veto player) or highly *fragmented* decision making (four or more veto players) were not able to formulate credible and/or timely responses to the financial meltdown of 1997. For example, Indonesia fell at the extremely centralized end of the scale, with former President Suharto the only veto player. While Suharto could act quickly, his policy responses were characterized by "volatility and even arbitrariness." Thailand was at the other end of the scale; its executive branch alone contained six veto players, the parties in its coalition cabinet. While any policy that all six agreed upon would likely be credible and stable, they constituted too many actors to come to a timely response.[91]

MacIntyre found the Philippines to benefit from an institutional arrangement that limited veto players to three—the president, the House of Representatives, and the Senate, as those two bodies must reduce their individual interests to one position through a vote. The Philippines' 1997 policy test concerned the oil industry, which had been "heavily regulated and subsidized"

Chapter Nine

until its liberalization in February 1997 as part of a package of reforms on which IMF assistance was conditioned. But as the economic crisis caused the peso to fall and the price of oil to rise, public opposition to liberalization spiked. In late 1997, the Supreme Court responded to a constitutional challenge by striking down the oil deregulation law. This was a populist victory for Filipino consumers, but it jeopardized IMF assistance and credit for future oil purchases. For international investors, it called into question the Philippine government's ability to commit to a policy adjustment. Upcoming elections in May 1998 (including for the presidency) did not make a new deregulation law easy to accomplish, but through the much-maligned process of political and economic payoffs, a compromise bill was passed in time to meet IMF requirements. Unlike Thailand, the Philippine "framework of government" was found to be "functional—perhaps not optimal, but at least functional."[92]

This analysis points to what we may paraphrase as the "paradox of reform through patronage." Throughout Ramos's term, the success of national-level reform initiatives was due to some very old-fashioned—and costly—patronage bargaining with congressional leaders. The cost of pork barrel and other "discretionary" funds reached nearly $1 billion in 1997—allocations *on top of* the customary annual pork barrel allocation of 62.5 million pesos ($2.4 million) per member of Congress.[93] If this money had been spent on its targeted projects, it might not have incurred such public wrath, but Ramos's budget secretary admitted that about 45 percent of the supplementary Countryside Development Funds and Congressional Initiative Allocations ended up in legislators' pockets. Ramos later said that 20 percent of the government budget was "lost to corruption every year."[94]

The unpopularity of oil deregulation added to a wellspring of anger over liberalization—seen as benefiting elite businesses and middle-class consumers—and added to a string of political defeats. In 1995, Ramos had entered into an ad hoc alliance with the legislative opposition for the election season; this practical compromise alienated many of his NGO supporters, ending hopes of institutionalizing a left-to-right coalition and hurting Ramos's reform credentials. While the presence of reformists was conspicuous in state agencies concerned with social welfare and in alliance with more professional politicians at the provincial and city levels, clans and patronage were clearly still dominant in the conduct of local and national politics.[95] Even Ramos's own integrity was questioned, as when allies in his political party allegedly accepted two billion pesos from a company bidding for a Manila Bay reclamation project.[96]

Political tremors also came from a new quarter. In 1995, police authorities arrested one Abdul Hakim Murad, who confessed under torture to plans by an Islamic group to assassinate Pope John Paul II on a Manila visit and to plant bombs on American airlines flying out of the Philippines. Murad was extradited to the United States, but two armed Islamic groups soon made their presence felt in the southern Philippines. In April 1995, a band of kidnappers calling themselves the Abu Sayyaf Group attacked a small town in southwestern Mindanao, routed the police force, looted the town, and used a group of hostages to slow down pursuit by army units.[97] The Abu Sayyaf Group was originally organized by the Philippine military to use against the MNLF, but was cut loose during the mid-1990s peace negotiations. The group gained notoriety when its kidnapping sprees reached international tourist sites in Malaysia and the Philippines and when it set off bombs in Manila and Mindanao.

Two years later, another Islamic group signaled its intent to carry on the separatist war abandoned by the MNLF. The breakaway Moro Islamic Liberation Front (MILF) gave the media a glimpse of its firepower and mass base by staging a million-strong rally in central Mindanao. While it originally described itself as a moderate force that favored autonomy instead of separatism, the MILF declared itself compelled by government unresponsiveness and bias toward the MNLF to become more militant. The MILF's show of force and reports of its connection with Islamic groups in the Middle East unnerved the government—it was a glaring indication that peace was still an elusive goal in the country.[98] Ramos tried to deal with these threats by lobbying Congress for an antiterrorism bill, but he was rebuffed by his own allies and widely criticized by the public for resorting to Marcos-era tactics. He quickly backed down.

One final defeat was in store for this president. Ramos had long declared himself in favor of switching to a parliamentary system of government. Ostensibly quite separately, a "popular initiative" had been launched in 1996 to gather sufficient signatures for a constitutional convention to pursue charter change (dubbed "Cha-Cha" in the Philippine press). As the May 1998 presidential elections neared and the vice president, the populist ex–movie actor Joseph Estrada, seemed the likely winner, the business community and other proliberalization forces began to raise the alarm. If Estrada was unqualified to be president and no one else was as popular, wouldn't a late-term conversion to a parliamentary system allow Ramos to stay on or run again to become prime minister? Ramos himself was coy, but this attempt to evade the one-term limit triggered more outrage from social forces already critical of his economic policies. The Supreme Court's decision to stop the People's Initiative for Reform, Modernization, and Action (PIRMA) emboldened Ramos's critics. He was accused of threatening democracy and endangering individual freedoms with his antiterrorism bill and wanting to stay in power in violation of the constitution. Ramos's coalition collapsed as his NGO and PO allies abandoned him and his legislative allies distanced themselves; Corazon Aquino and the Catholic Church mobilized the middle-class anti-Marcos coalition and threatened to rally; business became fearful of the effect on the investment climate. Ramos was finally forced to repudiate PIRMA's campaign.[99]

Amid this disillusionment, Filipinos turned to Joseph Estrada for hope.

MOVIE STAR MILLENARIANISM

Estrada's nickname is "Erap," a reverse spelling of *pare* (pronounced PA-ray; buddy). The nickname aptly described the new president—a pal to ordinary folk, sharing the simplicity of their needs and aspirations and even their lifestyle. Erap's popularity was that of a street-smart leader who acquired power through guts, sheer determination, and hard work. President Ramon Magsaysay supposedly had this quality, but Estrada set himself apart with a mocking hostility toward the "hypocrisy of political discourse." Magsaysay may have been called the "man of the masses," but Erap actually *talked* like the masses and "translated the prerogatives of power into the language of the streets making them seem acceptable and normal." He is, to continue journalist Sheila Coronel's splendid description, "a charming rascal who expects to get away with his rascality."[100] Erap is any Filipino's (especially male Filipino's) pare.

Estrada's popularity did not spring from political charisma, however; he developed his strong lower-class following from his original institutional base in the movie industry. As a young actor, Estrada almost always played the popular role of defender of the oppressed. As he grew older and moved into politics, his movie career declined, but his fame did not. The reason was television. In the 1990s, television networks, which had achieved national coverage, aired his old movies and introduced him to a younger generation. Inspired by the American entertainment industry, Filipino networks also began to mix information and entertainment programming. Their first experiments were very profitable, and by the late 1990s, the top television conglomerates, ABS-CBN and GMA, had happily embraced "spicing up the news and public affairs programs by injecting the elements of entertainment—comedy, drama, showbiz intrigue, crime and the supernatural—to keep the viewers glued."[101]

The result was a leveling between news and everyday gossip that spread throughout the mass media. Soon there was little difference between the treatment of a free trade debate and a movie star's love affair. Politicians who sensed the growing importance of the new formula "turned to television to maintain a high profile or boost their flagging popularity."[102] At the same time, the marriage of news and entertainment turned newscasters into celebrities and entertainment figures into political pundits, as movie and television stars recognized their power to influence public opinion. As one business executive admitted: "A lot of your life is sometimes governed by what actors and actresses do. Maybe they're out there talking to people about moral standards which might be followed by your kid!"[103] The leap from moral to political was relatively easy. To the criticism that movie stars lacked the skill to be political leaders, many simply pointed to Corazon Aquino—the "mere housewife" who brought down a dictatorship and restored democracy.

In 1987, Estrada was one of two anti-Aquino candidates who won a seat in the Senate, where critics poked fun at his lack of contribution to the legislative process. But he turned many heads and gained the respect of nationalists with his vote against renewing the U.S. military bases agreement and his feature film in support of that cause. Having fused his movie and political personas, Estrada became a presidential candidate at an opportune time. He was not alone in appreciating the changing political climate: A bevy of movie and television celebrities, newscasters, singers, and basketball players also campaigned for provincial, city, and congressional seats in the 1998 and 2000 elections (see box 9.8).[104]

The movie star as politician was the face of Filipino populism in the 1990s. The new populists differed from older politicians in several ways. In contrast to Aquino's popularity—tempered by her elite lineage and anchored in moral rectitude—the new populists entertained crowds and lent pageantry to political life. "Media populism" or "movie star millenarianism" had an entirely different electoral base as well.[105] Aquino's and Magsaysay's support had transcended class lines, while the voters favoring Estrada and other media populists were overwhelmingly poor voters. Accordingly, Aquino and Magsaysay used broad, all-inclusive political themes, while Estrada was anti-elite in rhetoric. Finally, although neither type of populist displayed command of complex policy matters, the new populists personalized the state without seriously advancing *any* economic vision. Estrada simply assured the poor that, if elected, he would use the state to serve *their* needs instead of those of the rich or middle classes.[106]

Once he proclaimed his candidacy, however, Estrada attracted a coalition as ideologically broad as those that had backed Aquino and Ramos. On the conservative side, many joined on the basis of friendship, dislike of Ramos, or older allegiances. Estrada especially relied on financial assistance from former Marcos cronies Eduardo Cojuangco and Lucio Tan, as well as from

Box 9.8. Star-Studded Elections, 1998 and 2000

Name	Position Sought	Previous Occupation
Joseph Estrada	President	action star
Ramon Revilla	Senator	action star
Vicente Sotto	Senator	comedian
Robert Jaworski	Senator	basketball player
Noli de Castro[a]	Senator	TV anchor
Francis Pangilinan[a]	Senator	TV/radio host
Ted Failon[a]	Congressman	TV anchor
Teodoro Locsin Jr.[a]	Congressman	TV host
Gilbert Remulla[a]	Congressman	TV reporter
Ronald Estella[a]	Congressman	TV reporter
Ramon Revilla Jr.	Governor, Cavite	action star
Manuel Lapid	Governor, Pampanga	action star
Rio Diaz	Governor, Negros Occidental	TV host
Jun del Rosario[a]	Provincial Board Member	TV reporter
Rudy Fernandez	Mayor, Quezon City	action star
Herbert Bautista	Mayor, Quezon City	comedian
Rey Malonzo	Mayor, Kalookan City	action star
Joey Marquez	Mayor, Paranaque City	comedian
Jinggoy Estrada	Mayor, San Juan City	action star
Vilma Santos	Mayor, Lipa City	movie/TV star
Alfredo Lim[a]	Mayor, Manila	TV host
Edu Manzano	Vice Mayor, Makati City	action star
Concepcion Angeles	Vice Mayor, Quezon City	TV host
Philip Cezar	Vice Mayor, San Juan City	basketball player
Yoyoy Villame	Councilor, Las Pinas City	comedian/singer
Robert Ortega	Councilor, Manila	TV personality
Dingdong Avanzado	Councilor, Marikina City	singer
Sonny Parsons	Councilor, Marikina City	action star
Cita Astals	Councilor, Manila	comedian
Anjyo Yllana	Councilor, Paranaque City	comedian

[a] 2000 election. Luz Rimban, "Lights, Camera, Election," *I: The Investigative Reporting Magazine,* January–June 1998: 42; David Celdran, "The Cult of the Celebrity," *I: The Investigative Reporting Magazine,* January–March 2001: 31

the anti-Ramos Chinese-Filipino community. These wealthy donors compensated for Estrada's weak election machinery, enabling him to outspend his rivals. On the reformist side, two groups were unabashed in supporting Estrada's candidacy: academics and former Communists who admired his anti-bases vote. The former were eager to use Estrada to advance their own governance ideas, reasoning that he had "no mindset to change because he ha[d] no mindset."[107] The ex-Communists were drawn to Estrada's anti-elitism, believing that he "was really for the people."[108] A former CPP cadre explained his decision to join Estrada: "This is the alternative to . . . waiting for the new dawning of the new revolutionary elite."[109]

Estrada's campaign slogan was simple: "Erap para sa Mahihirap" (Erap for the poor). On election day, he won an unprecedented 46.4 percent of votes cast; his closest rival, House Speaker Jose de Venecia, received 17.1 percent.[110] After being sworn in as the country's thirteenth president, Estrada promised a government that would exercise transparency and professionalism, assured critics that he would disallow family involvement in his administration, and vowed to continue the economic reforms of the Ramos years.

The Erap Presidency

Despite his election day promises, in less than half a term in office, Estrada transformed the presidency from a respected symbol of the nation into a rogue's court of family members, "mistresses, bastard children, denizens of show-business, gambling partners, business partners both established and obscure," and late-night drinking buddies who made major decisions regarding affairs of state. Access to the president was everything following an executive order requiring presidential approval for all contracts in excess of 50 million pesos. Economist Emmanuel De Dios describes how "enfranchised deal-cutters competed over who would be first to interpose themselves between approving authorities and private contractors. The effect was something akin to a feeding frenzy, as members of this privileged swarm sought to secure niches for themselves."[111]

Corruption under Estrada was distinct in "the leveraging of government assets and authority to undertake deals that were ultimately mediated by the market."[112] Examples of such innovative, market-oriented corruption include the use of funds from government-controlled financial institutions to support corporate takeovers, to rescue ailing banks and corporations, and to buy into companies coveted by the president and his family. Estrada also used his influence to help a crony manipulate the stock exchange. To this should be added old cases such as Estrada's unabashed defense of the corporate interests of Cojuangco and Tan in the name of removing government interference from the private sector.[113]

Estrada's popularity dropped as stories of governance by "midnight cabinet" circulated. The stories were fueled by his bad relationship with the media, the failure of an anticorruption drive, and his administration's slow implementation of antipoverty programs. Critics began to refer to Estrada as the second coming of Ferdinand Marcos, especially after he forced a critical newspaper to shut down. Yet this was not entirely accurate. Most Estrada cronies were "engaged only in small or non-mainstream business," and the interests of his families (official and unofficial) were not in primary sectors. Estrada's corruption therefore lacked the devastating effect on the economy that Marcos's had had.[114] And although Estrada valued his friendships, he eventually heeded the critics, distanced himself from his cronies, and tried to act more presidential. And he did honor his promise to continue the market liberalization programs of his predecessor.

In 1999, Estrada sought to project decisiveness by ordering the destruction of Moro Islamic Liberation Front camps and the takeover of Jolo Island to destroy the Abu Sayyaf Group. He and the Congress approved the return of American military forces to the Philippines to train and advise the AFP in these campaigns.[115] To show his new commitment to governance, Estrada gave his cabinet secretaries autonomy to run their offices without interference, prompting the *Far Eastern Economic Review* to comment that he had metamorphosed into "a savvy politician [who] had found a way to get things done."[116] The performance of certain government agencies, some under the management of ex-leftists, popular activists, and academics, did offset the erratic leadership at the top. Despite limited funds and the surrounding corruption, the Department of Agrarian Reform, Bureau of Immigration, Civil Service Commission, and Bureau of Treasury performed credibly.[117]

These improvements received unlikely reinforcement from an economy that "sloughed off the 'sick man of Asia' label that had dogged [it] through-

Figure 9.4. AFP checkpoint on a road in Mindanao (Ric Rocamora)

out the 1980s."[118] Signs of recovery included 2.2 percent growth in GNP in the first quarter of 1999, agriculture's "turnaround real growth rate of 2.5 percent against a drop of 3.8 percent in the same quarter" of the previous year, and a $4 billion trade surplus following a 20 percent rise in exports led by computers and electronics.[119] The country's international reserves rose to nearly $15 billion, strengthened by a two-year IMF standby facility and bond financing in the international capital market.[120] But sustained growth was still threatened by a ballooning budget deficit of 132.5 billion pesos in 2000.[121]

These modest economic and governance improvements were outweighed by negatives. Estrada began to lose allies in the House, and Congress refused to pass the next series of reforms needed to sustain economic recovery. The political points won in early 2000 by taking a strong stand against Islamic rebels were wiped out by the military's lack of a decisive victory. Government coffers were also hurt by the war in Mindanao: Unofficial estimates ranged from $500,000 to $2.3 million daily, forcing budget officials to divert monies from other programs.[122]

Finally, accusations of government complicity in drug smuggling and illegal gambling led to Estrada's downfall. *Jueteng* (pronounced WHET-ting), an illegal lottery, is the centerpiece of the nation's thriving informal economy. Because millions of ordinary Filipinos regularly place a one-peso bet on a combination of numbers hoping for a four-hundred-peso winning, jueteng can net a local operator as much as 1.2 million pesos and provincial bosses about 4.8 million pesos monthly.[123] Its profitability spawned a complex, nationwide network of alliances between operators, politicians, and law enforcement agencies. Political campaigns and poorly paid military officers alike have come to depend on jueteng revenues.[124]

Because of its national span, any crack in jueteng's highly centralized and well-protected structure could have serious implications. In early October 2000, Ilocos Sur governor Jose Singson—a longtime Estrada crony, gambling partner, and drinking companion—revealed that he had personally delivered $8 million in illegal gambling money to the president over a twenty-one-month period, plus an additional $2.5 million as the president's "cut" of the tobacco excise taxes allotted to his province. Singson went public after Estrada allegedly tried to have him assassinated, although he had already decided to reveal all when he learned that the president planned to set up a bingo network to rival his jueteng organization.

With Singson's revelations, anti-Estrada forces coalesced to drive him from office. The alliance of conservative church and business sectors, "traditional" politicians from opposition parties, NGOs, middle-class associations, and different factions of the Left brought back memories of the Aquino years.

The CPP, learning its lesson from 1986, made sure its legal organizations acted with the anti-Estrada front. Of course, the president was not without his own supporters. The core of Estrada's alliance—former Marcos cronies, the movie industry, provincial and town officials grateful for hastily released internal revenue allocations, Christian fundamentalist groups whose leaders sought to evade Church control, and former Communists in government—remained steadfast behind him.

Initial skirmishes began when the House of Representatives passed the first articles of impeachment against Estrada, charging him with plunder, graft, and corruption. In early December 2000, the Senate, where Estrada controlled a majority, formed itself into a tribunal to deliberate the charges. Meanwhile, the jueteng exposé and impeachment plunged the economy into crisis. The peso had depreciated 22 percent from the start of the year, investments were down 20 percent, and the scandal-plagued stock market continued to sink. When pro-Estrada senators blocked prosecutors from revealing a critical piece of incriminating evidence, the battle moved to the streets. On January 16, 2001, anti-Estrada forces—one million strong—gathered at the Edsa Shrine. In a festive atmosphere, they vowed not to leave until Estrada resigned the presidency.

Figure 9.5.   Mobile phone–driven anti-Estrada protests (courtesy of the Philippine Center for Investigative Journalism)

The composition of "Edsa 2" ranged from core "veterans" of the 1986 Revolution to members of Couples for Christ and Iglesia ni Kristo, who did not hesitate to demand a role on the "coordinating committee." As expected, Estrada rebuffed the protestors, and his supporters staged their own show of force in a similarly large rally. The impasse was broken on January 20, when the AFP leadership withdrew its support and Estrada had to abandon the presidential palace.[125] Vice President Gloria Macapagal Arroyo was immediately sworn in as president and Edsa 2 was widely praised as "a massive exercise in direct democracy after the institutions of impeachment had failed."[126]

Edsa 2 versus Edsa 3 (Poor People's Power)

On April 25, 2001, the government arrested Joseph Estrada on charges of plunder, violation of the antigraft law, perjury, and illegal use of an alias. The perceived discourtesy of the arresting authorities angered the ex-president's supporters, who mobilized up to three million people at the Edsa Shrine, a gathering notable for including "no Church symbols [and] no Church personnel."[127] After four days of speeches and rallies, about three hundred thousand people broke away from the main group and marched on the presidential palace, where they fought a bloody street battle with police and military forces. Declaring a "state of rebellion," President Arroyo ordered a full military-police counterattack. By May 1, the "rebels" were in full retreat, with five killed and more than a hundred arrested. Edsa 2 groups declared victory over "the mob" with a "triumphant Mass" at the Edsa Shrine, symbolizing their recovery of the sacred site.[128]

While easily routed, "Edsa 3" had reverberations that shook the new government. State officials and anti-Estrada intellectuals insisted that the pro-Estrada mobilization was not an example of people power because its violence contradicted the peaceful nature of people power. But Arroyo supporters could not dismiss the importance of the class divide: Edsa 3 was predominantly a poor people's movement, while Edsa 2, despite the presence of pro-poor groups, was mainly urban middle class and elite in composition.[129] Portraying Edsa 3 participants as "a drug-crazed mob that was brought and made to do what they did by . . . leaders who were not there" did little to dispel this uncomfortable reality. While it was true that the violence was incited and funded by anti-Arroyo politicians, "poor people's power" was clearly a manifestation of lower-class grievances against the nation's comfortable classes.[130] Despite a decline in poverty in the late 1990s, the gap in quality of life and power between the classes was growing.[131] Emmanuel De Dios and Paul Hutchcroft explain Estrada's ouster in this context: "What for [Edsa 2 activists] was a step toward rational and impartial government, represents for

[Edsa 3 supporters] a return to a heartless dispensation and an affront to the already powerless."[132]

As a result of Edsa 3, the optimism that followed Edsa 2 was short-lived, replaced by apprehension and questioning of the value of people power as a political act. Even Estrada's critics had second thoughts about the wisdom of resorting to popular uprising. "People Power as a method of political change and of ousting leaders," wrote journalist Amando Doronila, "has made Filipino democracy volatile, unstable, and unpredictable. More dangerously, it has brought Philippine democracy to the edge of mob rule, even if exercised in the name of social change."[133]

Edsa 2 and Edsa 3 also saw a shift in the constellation of political forces that influenced the country's political direction. On the one hand, reformist NGOs and POs that supported Estrada's ouster were not united in their support of Arroyo. As the alliance that brought them together unraveled, they won fewer cabinet positions in the new administration, and in public discourse they were challenged for the right to represent "the people" by the more disciplined CPP (which had kept its legal fronts autonomous from the alliance). On the other hand, the new president was clearly beholden to military officers (active and retired) and traditional politicians. The former were directly or indirectly responsible for two of the country's four political transitions since 1986. AFP-watcher Glenda Gloria notes that the dependence of weak civilian governments on the military "puts regimes in a most vulnerable situation" and "the military's access to arms" affects appointments. An attempted coup in July 2003 (the Oakwood Mutiny) only increased this dependence.[134]

The resurrection of the traditional politician was exemplified by Governor Singson. While trapos had been active players in 1986 and did in fact dominate the Aquino and Ramos governments, their prominence was treated with some disdain and suspicion. Singson, in contrast, was proclaimed a hero. This admitted high-level operator in the illegal economy, this warlord who ruled his province with an iron fist, this quintessential backroom dealer, became the man of the hour—praised by fellow trapos, the new regime, the Catholic Church, and even some NGOs and POs. Those who raised the issue of his background were roundly shouted off the stage. Singson's apotheosis suggested that despite the rise of media populism, trapos and strongmen controlling patronage networks and votes would not be so easily disposed of.

DREAMING A "STRONG REPUBLIC"

Gloria Macapagal Arroyo—trained economist, daughter of President Diosdado Macapagal, and veteran politician—"became head of state not because she was the unanimous choice at EDSA 2 but simply because, as vice president, the constitution said she was next in line," a succession that was eventually approved by the Supreme Court.[135] Her careful handling of Estrada's detention and a publicity offensive portraying her as "pro-poor" partly defused lower-class anger, but it was only with the general elections of May 2001 that she achieved a majority in the legislature and the support of local officials. These did not come without a price, of course. Creating a congressional majority required compromise and the dispensing of pork barrel funds. These compromises alienated NGOs and POs, who accused her of pursuing her own political survival "at the expense of civil society and progressive forces."[136] The poor apparently had not forgiven her, either, electing Estrada's wife and his former police chief (Panfilo Lacson) to the Senate and several of his cronies to the House of Representatives. This meant that Arroyo's legislative agenda would encounter some resistance.

Economic recovery was more important than ever, and some positive signs followed the resolution of the political crisis. Pressure on the peso eased, and the decline in the GDP share of agriculture and industry was mitigated by real growth in the service sector, especially after Congress passed the Retail Trade Liberalization Act opening that subsector to foreign investment.[137] GDP growth bounced back to 4.4 percent in 2002 (after dropping to 3.0 percent in 2001). Remittances from overseas Filipino workers also picked up after a late-1990s plateau.[138] While the government still engaged in deficit spending, reduction targets were set and the ratio of spending to revenue collection fell. Spending cuts, unfortunately, left social welfare hanging in the balance. Poverty reached 40 percent (up from 31.8 percent in 1997), and social indicators such as education, health, and domestic unemployment and underemployment remained troubling.[139] Government's ability to deal with these social problems continued to be hampered by debt servicing, which consumed more than one-fourth of the national budget in 2002.

In any case, modest economic accomplishments were again overshadowed by continuing political turmoil. Despite lifting the death penalty moratorium for kidnappers, abductions continued unabated.[140] In June 2001, after the Abu Sayyaf Group kidnapped sixteen people from a central Philippine resort, senior military officers were accused of helping the group escape a besieged position in Basilan in exchange for a cash payment. This controversy led to exposés of corruption in the AFP's procurement system and its inability to deal with the Abu Sayyaf Group.[141] Other corruption investigations by independent journalists implicated senior government officials in the government insurance system, Department of Justice, and power and waste management sectors.[142]

To dispel the growing impression of weakness, Arroyo announced, in her July 2002 address to the nation, her goal of building a strong republic.[143] She followed up with a number of attempts to assert the state's regulatory power and put its own house in order. Government lawyers charged the Lopez family conglomerate with overpricing its electric power services and revoked (on the grounds of rigged bidding) a contract signed by the previous administration with a foreign firm to build and operate a new international airport terminal.[144] Arroyo also instituted "lifestyle checks" on government personnel, targeting bureaucrats in the notoriously corrupt Bureau of Internal Revenue (BIR) and Bureau of Customs, and ways were explored to minimize graft in these offices (see box 9.9).

Arroyo's anticorruption drives signaled her intent to make the state "autonomous of dominant classes and sectors, so that it represents the people's interests."[145] But these well-publicized actions backfired in some instances, only serving to highlight the real limitations of state capacity. BIR bureaucrats made clear their intention to stonewall reform by slowing collection efforts and appealing to patrons in Congress, while Arroyo's newly appointed BIR commissioner was sued by his own officers when he "tried to move them and uproot their patronage networks." After a bomb threat at his office, he resigned, and Arroyo backed away from overhauling the entire revenue collection system.[146] Court cases against the airport contractor and the Lopez family became bogged down in the judicial system, and the president did

Figure 9.6. "Police and Citizens: Shoulder to Shoulder for a Strong Republic" (Donna J. Amoroso)

little to speed them along. Her vacillation renewed criticisms that she "would rather have safe, if sticky, compromises"—classic trapo behavior.[147]

Critics on the left labeled her "strong republic" a ruse to bring back dictatorship. Continuing Estrada's policy against armed southern Islamists, Arroyo approved a "visiting forces agreement" with the United States in 2003 that allowed longer-term visits by American troops; this act arguably

---

Box 9.9. Improving Revenue Performance

"Since 1986, the government has embarked on tax policy reforms designed to simplify the country's tax structure. These tax reforms are focused on lowering rates and broadening the tax base. However, numerous tax exemptions and fiscal incentives provided under various laws have undermined the tax policy reforms. Clearly, there is a need to rationalize these tax exemptions and fiscal incentives in order to plug the tax leakage and make tax obligations transparent. Presumptive taxation for hard-to-tax groups such as professionals and small businesses can also reduce the discretionary power of both taxpayer and tax assessor and make tax calculations simpler and clearer. Tax simplification and elimination of special exemptions can help curb opportunities for corruption, reduce the compliance cost of honest tax payers, and increase the overall efficiency of the economy.

"An area where reforms could yield the highest return is in revenue administration, particularly institutional and administrative arrangements. A major proposal in this area is to grant the BIR some degree of autonomy and shield it from political interference. With greater autonomy, the BIR can have more flexibility in its human resources and budgetary decisions, allowing it to attract good people and manage human resources on the basis of skills and performance.

"Together with greater BIR autonomy, a system of internal and external checks should be strengthened. Strong and credible internal audit systems, covering financial, procedural and management functions, complemented by effective external audit provisions should be in place. As in other countries, perhaps it would help to create anti-corruption units within the bureau. The Commission on Audit should be given access to BIR to undertake its revenue audit function. Congress should also actively pursue its oversight of the BIR as mandated under the Tax Code of 1997.

"Civil society involvement in revenue oversight should also be promoted. A private-sector led Taxpayers Foundation can be organized to: (a) serve as a venue for taxpayers' complaints against unscrupulous BIR personnel, (b) file appropriate charges in court, (c) conduct continuing taxpayer education, and (d) assist small- and medium-scale taxpayers in their dealings with the BIR.

"Excessive contact between taxpayers and tax personnel opens opportunities for corruption, hence this should be minimized or avoided. Among the instruments that can be helpful in this regard are: (a) the use of third party information for tax assessment, (b) automation or computerization, and (c) privatization of selected functions of tax administration."

—Congressional Planning and Budget Office, "Special Study:
Getting Out of the Fiscal Bind," June 2002: 10.

skirted a constitutional provision banning the presence of foreign troops on Philippine territory. Soon after, U.S. troops began to assist the AFP in pursuing the Abu Sayyaf Group. While the collaboration was well received by most Filipinos, including those in Muslim Mindanao, in Manila it provoked intense criticism. And when she pledged support for the American "war on terror" in advance of the U.S. invasion of Iraq in 2003, critics ranging from the CPP to nationalist academics branded her a "puppet," exacerbating her strained relationship with reformists.[148]

The year 2002 ended with the news that government had overshot its budget deficit target by 71 percent because of poor tax collection.[149] A despondent Arroyo announced on December 30—the anniversary of Jose Rizal's execution—that she would not campaign for her own presidential term in the May 2004 election and would instead devote the remainder of her time in office to policy implementation free from "the influence and interference of narrow sectional interests."[150] Her decision not to run was received with warm public support, and her approval ratings began to rise.

The 2004 Election: Machine Politics versus Media Populism

Arroyo's critics and political opponents did not relent in their attacks, however, continuing to allege widespread corruption by the president, her family, and her allies.[151] By November 2003, acquiescing to pressure from allies and angered by attacks on her family, the president announced her decision to "defer" retirement and "offer [her]self to the electorate in 2004."[152] This reversal confirmed her critics' suspicions, but a clear alternative candidate and philosophy of governance was lacking. Four major candidates ran against Arroyo in 2004—Paul Roco, her popular former secretary of education; Panfilo Lacson, the "law and order" candidate with murder charges hanging over his head; Brother Eddie Villanueva of the Jesus Is Lord movement, who became the middle-class "protest" candidate when Roco dropped out for health reasons; and aging action-movie star and political novice Fernando Poe Jr., who emerged as the most serious challenger.[153]

It looked to be a contest between an incumbent's political machine and a media populist with no known political positions except friendship with the disgraced former president Joseph Estrada. As Poe took an early lead in the polls, business leaders, academics, and political commentators feared the worst, and reformist NGOs and POs became increasingly irrelevant to the contest. Many of the latter opted to support Arroyo without lobbying for the inclusion of their agenda into her platform. Those in Poe's camp did not even bother to fashion a sophisticated argument for him (as they had for Estrada), because their presence was hardly recognized by the candidate himself. The growing attractiveness of the party-list system and the CPP threat also dictated that reformists pay greater attention to contesting sectoral seats in Congress.[154] (CPP positions carry weight in national debates via a sympathetic national media, and its party-list organizations would succeed in electing all six of its candidates to the House of Representatives in 2004.)

Arroyo depended heavily on the electoral machinery of her coalition of political allies nationwide; Poe, who had no such machinery, used his movie star persona—the quiet hero—to attract voters. Both candidates chose news anchors–turned–senators (proven vote-getters) as their vice presidential running mates and took full advantage of relaxed election rules that allowed maximum use of all forms of media.[155] Oddly enough, Poe turned out to be the less effective campaigner. His personality (taciturn and humorless), political inexperience (leading to frequent upheavals in his campaign team), discomfort with the media (which he alternately shunned and snapped at), and near-total lack of policy articulation cost his initial lead in the polls.[156] Arroyo campaigned vigorously throughout the country, speaking the local language in her native Visayas and several other regions, reminding voters of the "avalanche of financial support and development projects" her government was providing, exercising political muscle on wavering local officials, and dispensing campaign funds to local candidates.[157] Her well-managed attack on Poe's inexperience and an agreement with the CPP to allow her party to campaign in NPA territory in exchange for supporting Communist party-list candidates also helped tilt the race in Arroyo's favor.[158]

President Gloria Macapagal Arroyo was elected by a margin of 1,123,576 votes out of roughly twenty-five million cast. A postelection analysis in the *Philippine Daily Inquirer* pointed to the Arroyo team's astute combination of old and new strategies, an indication that media populism would henceforth be a crucial part, but not the sole determinant, of electoral politics. According to writer Tony Bergonia, "The campaign strategy involved unbridled access to government resources, the hiring of an expert pollster, brilliant use of opinion surveys, a deal with a popular TV personality and innovations to tried and tested campaign devices." Bergonia points to how "the normal delivery of government services [was used] as a campaign tool without making it look like what it really was—an attempt to capture votes." For example, road maintenance in Metro Manila created 250,000 jobs by using labor-intensive rather than capital-intensive methods, and student loans were disbursed by the Student Assistance Fund for a Strong Republic. Bergonia's sources told him that "Ms. Arroyo's strategists found nothing irregular in the so-called governance projects since the state funds used had already been allotted and were not realigned from other existing projects."[159]

The campaign team engaged an in-house pollster to survey voter approval on key issues and "gauge to what extent voters would follow the endorsements of such figures and groups as Jaime Cardinal Sin, ex-President Corazon Aquino, the Iglesia ni Cristo and the Catholic group El Shaddai." (Pacts with the religious groups delivered many votes and continued to pay off when vote counting in the House of Representatives was subject to repeated delaying tactics and Arroyo's victory looked vulnerable to opposition protest. In early June the Catholic Bishops Conference of the Philippines endorsed the election and its results: Arroyo called it "an answer to her prayers.")[160] Bergonia emphasized the media popularity brought to the campaign by vice presidential candidate Noli de Castro (a new strategy) and, finally, alleged the preparation of a "very massive operation to commit fraud" if the local political machines failed to "get the votes and perform magic" (a very old strategy).[161] This allegation was vigorously denied by the president's office, though few Filipinos doubt the capacity of *any* successful politician to commit election fraud.

Arroyo's Challenge: Economic Governance

With her political coalition winning majorities in the Senate, House of Representatives, and provincial and municipal governments, Gloria Arroyo secured the opportunity to govern for six years unhampered by the taint of illegitimacy she faced while completing Estrada's term. Yet Arroyo's promise to create a "strong republic" will no doubt encounter bureaucratic opposition and resistance from Congress, which, although containing more reformist members, continues to be dominated by patronage politicians. Due to the manner of her election, Arroyo will herself remain beholden to these politicians, while reformists struggle to revive a mobilizing capacity to strengthen their bargaining power inside state institutions.

Her short- and medium-term priority will be the economy. In the July 2004 State of the Nation address, Arroyo labeled the budget deficit and tax collection the most pressing problems facing the nation. She called for business to "adopt an attitude of tax acceptance" and Congress to pass a package of tax laws to increase revenue by eighty billion pesos per year. To reduce spending, she promised to abolish thirty agencies under the Office of the President (in addition to the eighty already eliminated), attack corruption, eliminate redundant offices, and encourage early retirement.

Public reaction was swift, demanding first that government improve tax collection and rein in corrupt BIR officials before asking citizens to pay more taxes and, second, that Congress accept the reduction or elimination of the discretionary funds that fuel patronage—pork barrel—"the most visible symbols of corruption in government." As the country's leading newspaper editorialized: "So long as the pork barrel exists, any cost-saving campaign and any anti-corruption drive will be meaningless, and any new tax measure will be an undue imposition on the people."[162] (See box 9.10.)

The month following Arroyo's address, a group of prominent University of the Philippines economists expressed "doubt whether the President's message has been truly understood and internalized by the political elite and

---

Box 9.10. "The Unmistakable Stench of Institutionalized Corruption"

"The dust is beginning to settle on one of the most divisive, acrimonious and bitter electoral exercises this country has ever seen. . . . Those who voted for President Macapagal-Arroyo despite the three difficult years just past, did so in the hope that if she had a true mandate she would finally be able to steer the country toward a brighter future. Only a competent and well-meaning president with a clear mandate can possibly lead us through this difficult time when collective national sacrifice will have to be the rule of the day . . . before . . . economic recovery can even begin to emerge.

"Cognizant of this, many thinking Filipinos like me are ready to make sacrifices. But we must also see that our leaders, especially our legislators, are likewise willing to share in our collective sacrifice. So far however, other than jockeying for juicy committee chairmanships and fighting over offices, all we have heard from the majority of our honorable legislators is empty talk about 'burden sharing.' None of them has yet categorically announced that they are willing to make one of the biggest sacrifices of all: giving up part of their pork barrel.

"Depending on the source of information, each representative receives an estimated P70 to P100 million a year in pork barrel funds while a senator receives about P200 million a year. Multiply this by 236 representatives (party list excluded) and 23 senators and you arrive at the mind-boggling figure of P28 billion a year!

"This in itself is bad enough, particularly in the light of our alarming budget deficit and the dismal legislative output. . . . But things really get unbearable when one reads reliable investigative reports saying that as much as 45 percent of this amount ends up in the pockets of legislators.

"True or not, exaggerated or not, it cannot be denied that the term 'pork barrel' or the more palatable 'Countrywide Development Fund' carries with it the unmistakable stench of institutionalized corruption. . . .

"Cynicism, distrust of government and a general lack of hope are the predominant sentiments that weigh heavily on our people, enveloping our country in a thick, dark cloud. Unless the President and her men can break through this cloud, effective governance will be virtually impossible. The 'Pork Barrel Sacrifice,' painful though it may be, might just be the sword that can cut through this cloud. . . . Anything short of this sacrifice would send the disturbing message that it is 'business as usual' for our elected leaders. At this particular time in our nation's history, when we are being primed for higher taxes, higher utility rates, higher prices and tough times ahead, all for the sake of our country, 'business as usual' . . . should have absolutely no place in governance and will only spell disaster."

—Minguita Padilla, "Business as Usual?" commentary,
Philippine Daily Inquirer, July 29, 2004

public." The UP School of Economics report argued the imminence of a fiscal crisis and the superficiality and/or wrongheadedness of some solutions being discussed. This influential report was widely disseminated and set the agenda for public policy debate at the start of Arroyo's term.[163] It also made admirably explicit the often implicit contract between state and society in its discussion of causes and proposed solutions. As so often in the past, a crisis helped illuminate the state's relationship with the various forces both within it and in society at large.

The UP report first establishes the problem: At the end of 2003, the Philippine national government debt was 3.36 trillion pesos, or 78 percent of GDP. More important to the analysis, total public sector debt (explained below) exceeded 130 percent of GDP. Service on the debt, an automatic appropriation, consumed 27 percent of the year's national budget. All these numbers are trending upward, but the authors argue that yearly increases in the level of debt have not been caused by rising interest rates or higher government spending. In fact, even as government moved from mid-1990s balanced budgets to budget deficits, spending by its agencies "declined significantly . . . and is now at its lowest level in a decade." Such fiscal discipline was "not a sign of strength—rather one of despair." For, aside from debt servicing, "large chunks of the national budget are already pre-empted by salaries, maintenance and operating expenses, and the internal revenue allotment to local governments, leaving little room for infrastructure spending and other development needs."[164]

The authors acknowledge that 43 percent of the debt increase from 1997 to 2003 was caused by budget deficits and attribute these largely to "failure of the tax structure and bureaucracy." The success or failure of revenue collection is measured as a percentage of GDP; the Philippines' tax effort "fell from a high of 17 percent of GDP in 1997 to only 12.5 percent by 2003."[165] Including both tax and nontax revenue, the Philippines' tax effort was 19 percent of GDP; this was about the same as Thailand and better than Indonesia, but much weaker than Malaysia (23 percent) and Singapore (37 percent). The tax effort of developing countries as a whole averages 18 percent of GDP, while that of industrialized countries averages 31.2 percent.[166]

Naturally, corruption in the BIR and judicial failure to pursue "large tax evaders" contribute to falling revenue, but the report also points to "serious structural flaws" that can be laid more broadly at the feet of the executive, Congress, and taxpayers themselves:

> An inflexible and unresponsive tax structure, mortally weakened by the legislative failure to adjust specific taxes (e.g., taxes on petroleum, beverage, and tobacco); the excessive grant of incentives and exemptions (e.g., from the BOI [Board of Investments] and for special economic zones); the failure to provide

for administrative rules to plug revenue leakages (e.g., failure to ensure that final taxes on loans and deposits withheld by banks are actually remitted to the government); and an unabashed surrender to lobbying, as illustrated by the VAT [value-added tax] exemptions given by Congress to doctors, lawyers (and law firms!), and even show-business.[167]

The report attributes a further 37 percent of the debt increase to "non-budgetary accounts" and "assumed liabilities and lending to corporations." Such off-budget expenditures represent the difference between national government debt (generated by "activities involving regular branches and agencies") and total public debt. This difference stems from the operation and liabilities of government-owned or -controlled corporations such as the National Power Corporation (NPC), the Public Estates Authority (manager of public lands), and the bodies responsible for social security and public-sector employee insurance. The government is also involved in commercial banking and in manufacturing, real estate, and media companies. The accounts of these corporations are meant to be separate from the government's, but we have seen how, in the post-Marcos era of cleanup and restructuring (of the Central Bank, for example), government assumed the liabilities of many failed corporations.

This practice continues, especially where the delivery of vital public services such as power is concerned. When the NPC, for example, was unable to sell bonds abroad to cover operating losses, "the national government . . . bought the NPC debt paper, then proceeded to borrow abroad on its own account" to further finance this unprofitable institution. The report points out that unprofitability is not due solely to mismanagement but is often imposed by the government itself when "for political reasons, [it] decided to reduce power-rate charges." Whatever the cause, when government assumes corporate debt, "what ought to have been liabilities only of these corporations and the clients they serve become transformed into debts of the national government and of all Filipinos."[168]

Observers agree that the growing debt has had a tremendous negative impact on Philippine growth by restricting the ability of government to make strategic investments in its people (education) and economy (infrastructure). And the problem is self-perpetuating, "with successive credit downgrades raising the cost of borrowing." But the UP report argues that the trend is unsustainable for much longer and, further, that any of a number of external factors—higher global interest rates or falling overseas workers' remittances—could quickly result in debt default and a full-blown fiscal crisis marked by "sharp peso depreciation, most likely aggravated by capital flight, severely contract[ed] trade . . . a deep recession and unemployment." Nor, it argues, can the problem be solved by budget cuts "without provoking large dislocations and inviting social unrest" or be outgrown: "When has the economy

ever demonstrated the ability to achieve, much less sustain, GDP growth of
7–8 percent annually?" Corruption is not solely to blame and so its elimination would not comprise the whole solution; in any case, the authors question
"whether the time exists for such reforms in administration to play out before
the fiscal time bomb explodes."[169]

Instead, the UP report calls for a package of measures that spreads the
burden among the branches of the state, the private sector, and the general
public. These include (1) cutting nonbudgetary expenditures by half, forcing
government-owned and -controlled corporations to adopt sound business
practices, and retreating from "politicized price-setting"; (2) moving national
government expenditures from deficit to surplus by first optimizing existing laws—automatic updating of excise taxes and audits on self-reported
income—and later phasing in tax increases (VAT, petroleum) and new taxes
(car registration, new vehicles); (3) cutting local government unit (LGU)
allotments by a quarter, from 40 percent to 30 percent, which the president
is authorized to do for a three-year period by declaring an "unmanageable
public-sector deficit"; and (4) cutting pork by half and increasing government
credibility by using some of the savings on publicly visible infrastructure
projects, the rest on deficit reduction. Once the deficit has been stabilized,
the report recommends rationally downsizing government bureaucracy; completely replacing the revenue agencies; pursuing a new round of privatization; rationalizing and reducing future tax incentives; establishing "credible
regulatory bodies" to set power rates, transit fare, and tolls; and making LGU
revenue allotments "conditional on the quality of spending or as matching
grants to supplement new local revenues."[170]

The UP School of Economics recommendations are not beyond debate.
Another line of thought is represented by Walden Bello (of the NGO Focus
on the Global South) and Lidy Nacpil and Ana Marie Nemenzo (of the NGO
Freedom from Debt Coalition) in their rejoinder, "Overdue, Selective, Not
Daring Enough."[171] They take issue with the UP report's neglect of tariff
reduction as a cause of declining revenue, noting that the UP authors are all
supporters of trade liberalization. Bello and colleagues, who cite the depart-
ing remarks of former finance secretary Jose Isidro Camacho in support of
their position, back recent executive orders freezing or raising tariffs on
selected agricultural, fishery, and manufactured products and call for the accelerated reversal of liberalization throughout the economy.

Most fundamentally, these critics question why the UP economists do not
face the issue of foreign debt head-on. Since 1986, opinion has been growing
that Corazon Aquino erred in not attempting to restructure the debt at the very
time the Philippines, emerging from a larcenous dictatorship, was most likely

to win concessions from its creditors. In fact, some of the UP authors were among the early critics of the "model debtor" policy, by which "repaying the debt on the terms demanded by the creditors became the national economic priority, with development taking a backseat." Although in agreement with many of the UP-proposed measures, Bello and his coauthors believe that "never ending and rising payments to foreign creditors" are the major reason the Philippines is facing fiscal crisis. But where the UP report sees default on international debt as unthinkable, Bello, Nacpil, and Nemenzo point to Argentina, which, they argue, collapsed in 2002 due to its "good debtor" policy, after which it redirected its "resources . . . into investment rather than debt service." They want the Philippines to follow the example of the Argentine president, who offered his country's creditors 20 to 25 cents on the dollar and still received a new IMF loan: "To our creditors, many of whom have been paid many times over for the original sum lent us, we can say, loosen your terms to, say, 50 cents to the dollar now or you will get a bankruptcy that will drag you along with it."

But beyond its specific recommendations, which can and should be debated, the value of the UP report lies in its recognition that "modern government—in principle anyway—is based on a contract in which people agree to be taxed in exchange for protection, justice, infrastructure and services provided by the state." Violation of this contract has caused a "tacit but undeniable tax revolt by citizens appalled that taxes are used to support feckless, unresponsive government." The authors therefore put the onus on government to begin to fix the problem, but acknowledge that all state branches and social forces will have to show unprecedented unity: "Congress, the President, local governments, business, professionals, and people at large, all effectively possess some veto power over the outcome, since by refusing to cooperate, they could scuttle the package."[172]

The fiscal crisis faced by the Philippines in the early twenty-first century highlights a recurrent pattern that can be traced back to the mid-nineteenth century—the need to improve state capacity in order to cope with economic change. Then, too, the state faced dilemmas raised by globalization and the movement of international capital and then, too, sought to strengthen revenue collection and other primary functions. In the 1930s, when worsening agrarian relations led to peasant rebellion, the Commonwealth reinforced state capacity in the name of "social justice." The pattern recurred in the import-substitution phase of the postwar Republic, as well as on the eve of martial law. As the years passed, however, expectations of responsive government grew, reformist and radical social forces protested the skewed distribution of rewards, and the solution grew more complex.

NOTES

1. Emmanuel S. De Dios and Paul D. Hutchcroft, "Political Economy," in *The Philippine Economy: Development, Policies, and Challenges*, ed. Arsenio M. Balisacan and Hal Hill (Quezon City: Ateneo de Manila University Press, 2003), 50.

2. De Dios and Hutchcroft, "Political Economy," 50.

3. Germelino M. Bautista, "An Assessment of the Philippine Economy," *Kyoto Review of Southeast Asia* 4 (October 2003): 17, available at http://kyotoreview.cseas.kyoto-u.ac.jp/issue/issue3/index.html (last accessed October 14, 2004).

4. James K. Boyce, *The Political Economy of Growth and Impoverishment in the Marcos Era* (Quezon City: Ateneo de Manila University Press, 1993), 47, 50.

5. Felipe B. Miranda and Ruben Ciron, "Development and the Military in the Philippines: Military Perceptions in a Time of Continuing Crisis," in *Soldiers and Stability in Southeast Asia*, eds. J. Soedjatudjiwando and Yong Mun Cheong (Singapore: Institute of Southeast Asian Studies, 1988), 173.

6. Boyce, *The Political Economy of Growth and Impoverishment*, 3.

7. For more information, see Freedom from Debt Coalition, http://www.freedomfromdebtcoalition.org.

8. De Dios and Hutchcroft, "Political Economy," 53.

9. Teresa Encarnacion Tadem, "Filipino Neo-Liberalism before and after the Crisis," in *Hegemony, Technocracy, and Networks: Papers Presented at the Core University Program Workshop on Networks, Hegemony, and Technocracy*, ed. Takeshi Hamashita and Takashi Shiraishi (Kyoto: Center for Southeast Asian Studies, 2002), 445–500.

10. Alfred W. McCoy, *Closer than Brothers: Manhood at the Philippine Military Academy* (New Haven, Conn.: Yale University Press, 1999), 284–95.

11. All references are to *The Constitution of the Republic of the Philippines with Highlights of the 1986 Constitution and Appendices*, comp. NBSI Editorial Staff (Manila: National Book Store, 1986).

12. John T. Sidel, *Capital, Coercion, and Crime: Bossism in the Philippines* (California: Stanford University Press), 73-78, 113-15, 130-38.

13. Jose Magadia, *State–Society Dynamics: Policy Making in a Restored Democracy* (Quezon City: Ateneo de Manila University, 2003), 43–66.

14. Kathleen Weekley, *The Communist Party of the Philippines, 1968–1993: A Story of Its Theory and Practice* (Quezon City: University of the Philippines Press, 2001), 224–58; Marites Dañguilan Vitug, "Lean Alejandro: Activist-Thinker," in *Six Young Filipino Martyrs*, ed. Asuncion David Maramba (Pasig, The Philippines: Anvil Publishing, 1997), 34–36; and Robert Francis Garcia, *To Suffer Thy Comrades: How the Revolution Decimated Its Own* (Pasig, The Philippines: Anvil Publishing, 2001).

15. Glenda M. Gloria, *We Were Soldiers: Military Men in Politics and the Bureaucracy* (Quezon City: Friedrich-Ebert Stiftung, 2003), 35–36.

16. G. Sidney Silliman and Lela Garner Noble, eds., *Organizing for Democracy: NGOs, Civil Society, and the Philippine State* (Quezon City: Ateneo de Manila University Press, 1998), 6; James Putzel, "NGOs and Rural Poverty," in Silliman and Noble, *Organizing for Democracy*, 78.

17. Ateneo de Manila University, Department of Economics, "The Socio-Political Nature of the Aquino Government," in *The Aquino Presidency and Administration, 1986–1992: Contemporary Assessments and the Judgement of History*, ed. Jose V. Abueva and Emerlinda R. Roman (Quezon City: University of the Philippines Press, 1993), 29.

18. *State–Civil Society Relations in Policy Making*, ed. Marlon Wui and Glenda Lopez (Quezon City: University of the Philippines, Third World Studies Center, 1997).

19. *NGO and PO Policy Influence in Urban Land Reform Advocacy*, ed. Ana Maria Karaos et al. (Quezon City: Institute on Church and Social Issues, 1995).

20. Isidro D. Cariño, "Education, Culture, and Sports," in Abueva and Roman, *Aquino Presidency and Administration*, 146.

21. Jennifer Conroy Franco, *Elections and Democratization in the Philippines* (New York: Routledge, 2001).

22. On the Department of Finance, see Nick Joaquin, *Jaime Ongpin, the Enigma: A Profile of the Filipino as Manager* (Manila: J. V. Ongpin Institute of Business and Government, 1990). On the urban land reform law and the generic drug campaign, see Magadia, *State–Society Dynamics*, 93–112, 128–37.

23. Arsenio M. Balisacan and Hal Hill, "An Introduction to Key Issues," in Balisacan and Hill, *The Philippine Economy*, 19. On NEDA's reform-driven director, see Lorna Kalaw-Tirol, "Winnie Monsod: Thoroughbred Maverick," in *Public Lives, Private Lives* (Pasig, The Philippines: Anvil Publishing, 2000), 192–203.

24. Leonora Angeles, "Feminism and Nationalism: The Discourse on the Woman Question and Politics of the Women's Movement in the Philippines" (M.A. thesis, University of the Philippines, 1989), 187–92; Elizabeth Uy Eviota, *The Political Economy of Gender: Women and the Sexual Division of Labour in the Philippines* (London: Zed Books, 1992), 94–97; *Towards Feminist Consciousness: Filipino Mothers and Daughters Tell Their Story*, ed. Sylvia H. Guerrero (Quezon City: University of the Philippines, University Center for Women Studies, 1997), 75–144; Lynn M. Kwiatkowski, *Struggling with Development: The Politics of Hunger and Gender in the Philippines* (Quezon City: Ateneo de Manila University Press, 1999), 111–43; Lois West, *Militant Labor in the Philippines* (Philadelphia: Temple University Press, 1997), 72–92.

25. Angeles, "Feminism and Nationalism," 198–207.

26. On Imelda Marcos, see Katherine Ellison, *Imelda, Steel Butterfly of the Philippines* (New York: McGraw-Hill, 1998); and Beatriz Romualdez Francia, *Imelda and the Clans: A Story of the Philippines* (Manila: Solar Publishing, 1988).

27. Benedict Anderson, "Cacique Democracy in the Philippines," in *Spectre of Comparisons: Nationalism, Southeast Asia, and the World* (London: Verso, 1998), 192–93.

28. "Cory's Legacy," *Business World*, June 30, 1992, 6.

29. Corazon C. Aquino, "Reflections on Our Democracy," in Abueva and Roman, *Aquino Presidency and Administration*, 1.

30. Alasdair Bowie and Danny Unger, *The Politics of Open Economies: Indonesia, Malaysia, the Philippines, and Thailand* (Cambridge: Cambridge University Press, 1997), 121.

31. *Far Eastern Economic Review*, September 3, 1992.

32. "Cory's Legacy," 6.

33. Walden Bello et al., *The Anti-Development State: The Political Economy of Permanent Crisis in the Philippines* (Quezon City: University of the Philippines, Department of Sociology; Focus on the Global South, 2004), 14.

34. De Dios and Hutchcroft, "Political Economy," 53.

35. Emmanuel S. De Dios, "Philippine Economic Growth: Can It Last?" in *The Philippines: New Directions in Domestic Policy and Foreign Relations*, ed. David G. Timberman (Singapore: Institute of Southeast Asian Studies, 1998), 52; Bello et al., *The Anti-Development State*, 22.

36. Bowie and Unger, *Politics of Open Economies*, 121. On the military base negotiations, see Alfredo R. A. Bengzon with Raul Rodrigo, *A Matter of Honor: The Story of the 1990–1991 RP–US Bases Talks* (Manila: Anvil Publishing, 1997).

37. Ateneo de Manila University, Department of Economics, "Socio-Political Nature," in Abueva and Roman, *Aquino Presidency and Administration*, 31.

38. Bello et al., *The Anti-Development State*, 22.

39. Ateneo de Manila University, Department of Economics, "Socio-Political Nature," in Abueva and Roman, *Aquino Presidency and Administration*, 32.

40. Republic of the Philippines, Congressional Planning and Budget Office, "Special Study: Getting Out of the Fiscal Bind," June 2002: 8–9.

41. Jorge V. Tigno, "People Empowerment: Looking into NGOs, POs, and Selected Organizations," in *Democratization: Philippine Perspectives*, ed. Felipe Miranda (Quezon City: University of the Philippines Press, 1997), 121.

42. John Linantud, "Whither Guns, Goons, and Gold? The Decline of Factional Election Violence in the Philippines," *Contemporary Southeast Asia* 20, no. 3 (December 1998): 298–318.

43. State of the Nation Address, 1993, quoted in Joel Rocamora, *Breaking Through: The Struggle within the Communist Party of the Philippines* (Pasig, The Philippines: Anvil Publishing, 1994), 174.

44. Rocamora, *Breaking Through*, 18.

45. Patricio N. Abinales, "Coalition Politics in the Philippines," *Current History* 100, no. 645 (April 2001): 154–61.

46. De Dios and Hutchcroft, "Political Economy," 54–57.

47. Peter Krinks, *The Economy of the Philippines: Elites, Inequalities, and Economic Restructuring* (London: Routledge, 2002), 63–64, 78.

48. Bautista, "An Assessment of the Philippine Economy," 47.

49. Gerardo P. Sicat and Rahimaisa D. Abdula, "Public Finance," in Balisacan and Hill, *The Philippine Economy*, 120.

50. Bautista, "An Assessment of the Philippine Economy," 31, 47.

51. Romeo Bautista and Gwendolyn Tecson, "International Dimensions," in Balisacan and Hill, *The Philippine Economy*, 157–58.

52. Bello et al., *The Anti-Development State*, 17–18.

53. Krinks, *Economy of the Philippines*, 65–66.

54. De Dios, "Philippine Economic Growth," 55.

55. Sicat and Abdula, "Public Finance," 128–29.

56. Krinks, *Economy of the Philippines*, 210–14.

57. Asian Development Bank, "Philippines: PSA Quantitative Indicators," September 10, 2003, available at http://www.adb.org/Documents/Others/CQI/Philippines_qi.pdf (last accessed October 14, 2004); Krinks, *Economy of the Philippines*, 212.

58. Solita Collas Monsod, "The War against Poverty: A Status Report," in Timberman, *The Philippines: New Directions*, 95.

59. Quotations from Bautista and Tecson, "International Dimensions," 151. Figures from Bautista, "An Assessment of the Philippine Economy," 31.

60. Bautista, "An Assessment of the Philippine Economy," 49.

61. Cristina C. David, "Agriculture," in Balisacan and Hill, *The Philippine Economy*, 179–81, 196.

62. David, "Agriculture," 176.

63. David, "Agriculture," 210.

64. David, "Agriculture," 200, 204.

65. Bautista, "An Assessment of the Philippine Economy," 57–59.

66. Sicat and Abdula, "Public Finance," 134.

67. Jorge V. Tigno, "Economic Viability and Local Governance: The Political Economy of Decentralization in the Philippines," in *The Role of Governance in Asia,* ed. Yasutami Shimomura (Singapore: Institute of Southeast Asian Studies, 2003), 276–77.

68. Rodolfo A. G. Silvestre Jr., "The Magnificent Seven," *Newsbreak*, January 6/20, 2003: 24–26.

69. Lisa Law, "Cebu and *Ceboom*: Globalisation in a Philippine City," in *Pacific Rim Development: Integration and Globalisation in the Asia Pacific Economy*, ed. Peter Rimmer (Sydney: Allen and Unwin, 1997), 240–66.

70. Tigno, "Economic Viability and Local Governance," 283–85.

71. Sicat and Abdula, "Public Finance," 116.

72. Tigno, "Economic Viability and Local Governance," 285, 293.

73. Joseph L. Piang, "The Chinese and the Philippine Political Process," in *Philippine-Chinese Profile: Essays and Studies*, ed. Charles J. McCarthy (Manila: Pagkakaisa sa Pag-unlad, 1974), 93–96, 100.

74. Caroline S. Hau, "'Who Will Save Us from the Law?': The Criminal State and the Illegal Alien in Post-1986 Philippines," in *Figures of Criminality in Indonesia, the Philippines, and Colonial Vietnam*, ed. Vicente L. Rafael (Ithaca, N.Y.: Cornell University, Southeast Asia Program, 1999), 141 n. 42.

75. Temario C. Rivera, *Landlords and Capitalists: Class, Family, and State in Philippine Manufacturing* (Quezon City: University of the Philippines Press and Center for Integrative Development Studies, 1994), 64, 70, 99–106.

76. Paul D. Hutchcroft, *Booty Capitalism: The Politics of Banking in the Philippines* (Ithaca, N.Y.: Cornell University Press, 1998), 133–34.

77. Emmanuel S. De Dios, "The Erosion of the Dictatorship," in *Dictatorship and Revolution: Roots of People's Power*, ed. Aurora Javate de Dios et al. (Manila: Conspectus, 1988), 111–15.

78. Rivera, *Landlords and Capitalists*, 66–67.

79. Hutchcroft, *Booty Capitalism*, 212.

80. Hau, "'Who Will Save Us from the Law?'" 131–32.

81. See, for example, Caroline S. Hau, ed., *Intsik: An Anthology of Chinese Filipino Writings* (Pasig, The Philippines: Anvil Publishing, 2000).

82. *New York Times*, March 17, 1996: 3, quoted in Hau, "'Who Will Save Us from the Law?'" 129.

83. "Criminals and Gangsters," *I: The Investigative Reporting Magazine*, January–March 2003: 12–23.

84. "Kidnap Watch," *Asiaweek*, October 30, 1998.

85. Antonio Lopez, "When Will They Ever End?" *Asiaweek*, December 19, 1997, available at http://asiaweek.com/asiaweek/97/1219/nat1c.html (last accessed July 15, 2004).

86. Anthony Paul, "Philippines: Kidnapping Problem Spreads," *Fortune*, March 17, 1997.

87. De Dios and Hutchcroft, "Political Economy," 56–57; Bello et al., *The Anti-Development State*, 114.

88. De Dios and Hutchcroft, "Political Economy," 57. See also Krinks, *Economy of the Philippines*, 55.

89. *The State and the Market: Essays on a Socially Oriented Philippine Economy*, ed. Filomeno Santa Ana III (Quezon City: Ateneo de Manila University Press, 1998), 88.

90. Maria Socorro Gochoco-Bautista and Dante Canlas, "Monetary and Exchange Rate Policy," in Balisacan and Hill, *The Philippine Economy*, 90–91; Bautista and Tecson, "International Dimensions," 162–63.

91. Andrew J. MacIntyre, *The Power of Institutions: Political Architecture and Governance* (Ithaca, N.Y.: Cornell University Press, 2003), 31–32, 71.

92. MacIntyre, *Power of Institutions*, 76–79, 70.

93. *Pork and Other Perks: Corruption and Governance in the Philippines*, ed. Sheila Coronel (Manila: Philippine Center for Investigative Journalism, 1998), 13–14.

94. Fidel R. Ramos, "Good Governance against Corruption," keynote address at the Fletcher School of Law and Diplomacy Conference on Good Governance against Corruption, April 26, 2001, Tufts University, Medford, Mass.

95. Franco, *Elections and Democratization*, 201–83; Takeshi Kawanaka, *Power in a Philippine City* (Chiba, Japan: Institute of Developing Economies and Japan External Trade Organization, 2002); Eric U. Gutierrez, Ildefonso C. Torrente, and Noli G. Narca, *All in the Family: A Study of Elites and Power Relations in the Philippines*, ed. Noel T. Pangilinan (Quezon City: Institute for Popular Democracy, 1992); Jose F. Lacaba, ed., *Boss: Five Case Studies of Local Politics in the Philippines* (Manila: Philippine Center for Investigative Journalism and Institute for Popular Democracy, 1995).

96. Ellen Tordesillas and Sheila S. Coronel, "Scam," in *Pork and Other Perks,* ed. Sheila S. Coronel, 82–111.

94. See Marites Dañguilan Vitug and Glenda M. Gloria, *Under the Crescent Moon: Rebellion in Mindanao* (Quezon City: Ateneo Center for Social Policy and Public Affairs and the Institute for Popular Democracy, 2000), 192–205 on the Abu Sayyaf Group, and 222–29 on the Murad revelations.

98. Vitug and Gloria, *Under the Crescent Moon*, 111.

99. Miriam Go, "People Power Aborted," *Newsbreak*, September 1, 2003: 28–29.

100. Sheila Coronel, "The *Pare* Principle," *I: The Investigative Reporting Magazine*, October–December 1998: 7.

101. "The Empire Strikes Back," *I: The Investigative Reporting Magazine*, July–September 1996: 10–11.

102. Luz Rimban, "In and Out," *I: The Investigative Reporting Magazine*, October–December 1998: 13–16.

103. "The Empire Strikes Back," 10.

104. Luz Rimban, "Lights, Camera, Election," *I: The Investigative Reporting Magazine*, January–June 1998: 40–45.

105. The phrases were introduced by Sheila Coronel, executive director of the award-winning Philippine Center for Investigative Journalism.

106. Aprodicio Laquian and Eleanor Laquian, *Joseph Ejercito "Erap" Estrada, the Centennial President* (Vancouver, B.C.: University of Vancouver, Institute of Asian Research; Quezon City: University of the Philippines, College of Public Administration, 1998).

107. Sheila S. Coronel, "The Man Who Would Be President," *I: The Investigative Reporting Magazine*, April–June 1996: 9.

108. Rigoberto Tiglao, "The Philippines," *Far Eastern Economic Review Yearbook*, 1999: 185.

109. As quoted in Ben Reid, *Philippine Left: Political Crisis and Social Change* (Manila: *Journal of Contemporary Asia*, 2000), 75.

110. Figures from electionworld.org, "Elections around the World," at http://www.electionworld.org/philippines.htm (last accessed October 15, 2004).

111. Emmanuel S. De Dios, "Corruption and the Fall," in *Between Fires: Fifteen Perspectives on the Estrada Crisis*, ed. Amando Doronila (Pasig, The Philippines: Anvil Publishing, 2001), 47.

112. De Dios, "Corruption and the Fall," 49.

113. Sheila S. Coronel, ed., *Investigating Estrada: Millions, Mansions, and Mistresses: A Compilation of Investigative Reports* (Manila: Philippine Center for Investigative Journalism, 2001).

114. Sheila Coronel, "Erap and Families," *I: The Investigative Reporting Magazine*, July–September 2000: 5–10.

115. Mel C. Labrador, "The Philippines in 2000: In Search of a Silver Lining," *Asian Survey* 41, no. 1 (January/February 2001): 221.

116. *Far Eastern Economic Review,* April 15, 1999.

117. Patricio N. Abinales, "Governing the Philippines in the Early Twenty-First Century," in *States, Markets, and Societies after the Asian Crisis*, ed. Takashi Shiraishi and Patricio N. Abinales (Kyoto: Kyoto University Press, 2005).

118. Asia Society and the Asian Development Bank, "Financing Asian Development: Growing Opportunities in Asia's Debt Markets (Report of a Study Mission to the Philippines, Thailand and South Korea)," May 20–30, 1998.

119. *The 2000 Philippines Yearbook* (Manila: *Fukien Times*, 1999), 165.

120. "The Philippines," in *Asian Development Bank Outlook, 2000* (Manila: Asian Development Bank, 2000), 108.

121. Cayetano Paderanga et al., "The Erap Economy," in Doronila, *Between Fires,* 180–84, 188.

122. *Asiaweek Magazine,* June 2, 2000.

123. On jueteng revenues, see "Illegal Gambling Has a Grassroots Base," *Philippine Center for Investigative Journalism and Institute for Popular Democracy Reports,* December 4, 1995.

124. "Jueteng Is Embedded in Local Society and Culture," *Philippine Center for Investigative Journalism and Institute for Popular Democracy Reports,* December 4, 1995.

125. For a comprehensive account of the ouster of President Estrada, see Amando Doronila, *The Fall of Joseph Estrada: The Inside Story* (Pasig, The Philippines: Anvil Publishing, 2001).

126. Jose V. Abueva, "A Crisis of Political Leadership: From 'Electoral Democracy' to 'Substantive Democracy,'" in Doronila, *Between Fires,* 83.

127. Barry, "Limits of Conservative Church Reformism."

128. Manuel L. Quezon III, "The May Day Rebellion," *Philippine Free Press,* May 12, 2001.

129. Maria Cynthia Rose Banzon Bautista, "'The Revenge of the Elite on the Masses'?" in Doronila, *Between Fires,* 8–26.

130. Alex Magno, "The State of Rebellion Is Not a Proclamation—It's a Description of the Situation," *UP Forum* Online, May 2001, available at http://www.up.edu.ph/forum/2001/5/magno.html (last accessed October 15, 2004).

131. Arsenio M. Balisacan, "Did the Estrada Administration Benefit the Poor?" in Doronila, *Between Fires,* 101–2.

132. Emmanuel De Dios and Paul Hutchcroft, "Political Economy," in *The Philippine Economy: Development, Policies, and Challenges,* ed. Arsenio M. Balisacan and Hal Hill (Quezon City: Ateneo de Manila University Press, 2003), 65.

133. Doronila, *Fall of Joseph Estrada,* 256.

134. Glenda M. Gloria, *We Were Soldiers: Military Men in Politics and the Bureaucracy* (Quezon City: Friedrich-Ebert Stiftung, 2003), 34.

135. Maria Lourdes Mangahas, "The Transactional President," *I: The Investigative Reporting Magazine,* April–June 2001: 6–8.

136. Mangahas, "The Transactional President," 11.

137. Ma. Joy V. Abrenica and Gilberto M. Llanto, "Services," in Balisacan and Hill, *The Philippine Economy,* 256–57, 259.

138. Germelino M. Bautista, "An Assessment of the Philippine Economy," *Kyoto Review of Southeast Asia* 4 (October 2003): 18, 57, available at http://kyotoreview.cseas.kyoto-u.ac.jp/issue/issue3/index.html (last accessed October 14, 2004).

139. Mangahas, "The Transactional President," 7; Alejandro N. Herrin and Ernesto M. Pernia, "Population, Human Resources, and Employment," in Balisacan and Hill, *The Philippine Economy,* 283–309.

140. "No More Ransoms," *The Economist,* May 31, 2001. Anticrime groups reported an average of four kidnappings a week by early 2002.

141. Romeo Gacad, "Lamitan under Siege," and Ed Lingao, "Grease," *I: The Investigative Reporting Magazine,* July–September 2001: 26–30, 31–34, respectively.

142. On the power sector, see Luz Rimban, "In Haste, Government Approves Controversial IMPSA Deal," *I: The Investigative Reporting Magazine*, April 2–3, 2001. On the retirement services and Department of Justice, see Sheila Samonte-Pesayco, "Winning Winston," and Malou C. Mangahas, "The Politics of Justice," *I: The Investigative Reporting Magazine*, January–March 2002: 4 and 7–11, respectively. On government waste management, see Jet Damazo, "The Stink That Won't Go Away," *Newsbreak*, March 18, 2002: 20–21.

143. Gloria Macapagal Arroyo, "Towards a Strong Philippine Republic," State of the Nation address at the opening of the 2nd Regular Session of the 12th Congress, July 22, 2002.

144. Ricky Carandang, "Fraport Ups the Ante," *Newsbreak*, April 28, 2003: 30.

145. Rigoberto Tiglao, "Building a Strong Republic," *Newsbreak*, January 6–20, 2003: 13.

146. *Bangkok Post*, August 4, 2004, 4.

147. Sheila S. Coronel, "The Problem with Gloria," *I: The Investigative Reporting Magazine*, April–June 2003: 18.

148. Manny Mogato, "America's Agenda," *Newsbreak*, February 13, 2002: 7–9; Julie S. Alipala, "Mixed Signals from Sulu," *Newsbreak*, March 31, 2003: 8–10.

149. Emmanuel De Dios, "Alarm over the Deficit," *Newsbreak*, January 6–20, 2003: 6–7.

150. Rigoberto Tiglao, "Manifesto for a Strong Republic," manuscript, 2003: 2.

151. Miriam Grace A. Go, "Mike's Company," *Newsbreak*, September 15, 2003: 18–20, 21; Miriam Grace A. Go, "Ping's Coup," *Newsbreak*, September 15, 2003: 22–25.

152. Quoted in Concepcion Paez, "Run Gloria, Run," *Newsbreak*, November 10, 2003: 17.

153. Jo-Ann Q. Maglipon, "FPJ: The Man and the Myth," *Newsbreak*, December 22, 2003; Uro Q. de la Cruz, "The Myth of *Ang Panday*," *I: The Investigative Reporting Magazine*, October–December 2002: 10–13.

154. "The Party List," *Philippine Daily Inquirer*, June 6, 2004.

155. Glenda M. Gloria, "Lethal Weapon," *Newsbreak*, March 1, 2004: 11–20, 23.

156. Isagani de Castro Jr., "Preventing a Checkmate," *Newsbreak*, May 10, 2004: 9–11.

157. Aries Rufo, "Sibling Rivalry," *Newsbreak*, May 10, 2004: 14–15.

158. Loretta Ann P. Rosales, "The NPA as the New Mafia," *Newsbreak*, March 1, 2004: 24; Luz Rimban, "Strange Bedfellows," in Sheila S. Coronel et al., *The Rulemakers: How the Wealthy and Well-born Dominate Congress* (Manila: Philippine Center for Investigative Journalism, 2004), 218–26.

159. Tony Bergonia, "GMA Election Strategy: Blending Governance, Magic, Noli," *Philippine Daily Inquirer*, July 28, 2004.

160. Barry, "Limits of Conservative Church Reformism."

161. Bergonia, "GMA Election Strategy."

162. *Philippine Daily Inquirer*, July 28, 2004.

163. Emmanuel S. De Dios et al., "The Deepening Crisis: The Real Score on Deficits and the Public Debt" (Quezon City: University of the Philippines, School of

Economics, 2004), available at http://www.up.edu.ph/upse_on_fiscal_crisis/up%20 econ-the%20deepening%20crisis.pdf (last accessed November 15, 2004). Also published by the Philippine Center for Investigative Journalism (http://www.pcij.org) and the *Philippine Daily Inquirer*. All quotations are taken from the first source.

164. De Dios et al., "The Deepening Crisis," 4, 10.

165. De Dios et al., "The Deepening Crisis," 3, 5.

166. Gerardo P. Sicat and Rahimaisa D. Abdula, "Public Finance," in Balisacan and Hill, *The Philippine Economy*, 116–17.

167. De Dios et al., "The Deepening Crisis," 5.

168. De Dios et al., "The Deepening Crisis," 6, 7.

169. De Dios et al., "The Deepening Crisis," 2, 9, 11.

170. De Dios et al., "The Deepening Crisis," 24–25.

171. Walden Bello, Lidy Nacpil, and Ana Marie Nemenzo, "Overdue, Selective, Not Daring Enough," available at http://www.focusweb.org/philippines/html/article 284.html (last accessed November 15, 2004). See also Walden Bello, Herbert Docena, Marissa de Guzman, and Marylou Malig, *The Anti-Development State: The Political Economy of Permanent Crisis in the Philippines* (Quezon City: University of the Philippines, Department of Sociology; and Focus on the Global South, 2004).

172. De Dios et al., "The Deepening Crisis."

Chapter Ten

The Rise and Fall of "The Strong Republic"

"PEOPLE POWER FATIGUE"

A Jesuit priest who was once one of the leaders of the 1986 uprising warned that any repeat of people power to change regimes had become a major obstacle to national stability. Fr. Romeo Intengan argued that "[p]eople power practiced too often sends a message abroad that you're a very unstable country." He proposed that social forces should focus more on strengthening state institutions "so that even in an emergency they can take care of transitions more effectively than in the past."[1] Former president Fidel V. Ramos chimed in, asserting that "[p]eople power in [*sic*] the present time is not relevant anymore," because it had failed to inspire Filipino leaders to stop the country's economic slide. Ramos added that Filipinos "are tired of the political bickering [and] simply want to carry on with their lives and remain hopeful of a better future." Their main attention now was their livelihood, and they "worry most about high prices and unemployment."[2]

Sheila Coronel described 2006 as the year when "people power fatigue" became evident. She observed that the "replicability of the 1986 formula for ousting presidents—popular mobilization and the military's withdrawal of support from [an] unpopular head of state—was . . . now in serious doubt."[3] Coronel was proven right when activists tried to agitate supporters of former president Corazon Aquino, upon her death on August 1, 2009, to rekindle people power, failed. The tens of thousands who joined the funeral were not mouthing militant slogans but "sonorous shouts of gratitude to the former president for 'bringing back democracy.'"[4]

If some were blighted by "people power fatigue," others completely withdrew from politics. Corporate executives, academics, government officials,

---

Box 10.1. *Gawad Kalinga* and Class Consciousness

"Gawad Kalinga retains the same strong commitment to change through relational, personal transformation. Gawad Kalinga personnel informed me their priority is 'bridging the gap in relationships [in Philippine society] with 'care and share' (Interview 2010). The relationship gaps are principally those between the poor and the non-poor, although in fact it is clear that the non-poor participants highly value (and enjoy) the relationships they establish among themselves."

—Jane Hutchinson, "Housing the Poor in Metro Manila," Workshop run by Asia Research Centre, Murdoch University, The Elephant in the Room: Politics and the Development Problem, December 13–14, 2010, 104.

---

and media people who once were part of the "people power movement" now joined charity organizations where they could continue serving the poor. The most popular among these associations was *Gawad Kalinga* ("extending care") (GK), a charity group organized by a businessman whose vision was to provide as much material support to the poor. GK's biggest project was the construction of homes for the poor, and this was where the hitherto politicized advocates of people power found new meaning. Michael Pinches called this phenomenon a "discourse of class construction, through which [the middle classes] connect, but command and distance themselves from the *masa*." GK was now the middle class's new "vision of nation building through slum eradication."[5] The marches on the streets had given way to a Philippine version of Habitat for Humanity.

The poor had also turned their back on politics. Amando Doronila wrote that "Masa politics, or the rich-versus-poor theme, [was] not [anymore] the name of the game in 2010."[6] He points to the ouster and arrest of President Joseph Estrada, and the Arroyo government's aggressive response to Edsa 3 as having showed the poor how easy it was for the elites to violate the rules of the electoral game that it had set up in the first place after Marcos fell. Then the decision of the left-wing organizations to join the anti-Estrada coalition added to popular disenchantment. The sight of the vanguard of the proletariat marching side by side with the very bourgeois it promised to overthrow was an incomprehensible sight. Faced with a political process that was permeated with so much opportunism, poor Filipinos saw no more reason to be on the streets.[7]

Lisandro Claudio blamed the ideological battles between moderate and radical social forces over the proprietorship of "people power" as further weakening the slogan's mobilizing capacity. Then the Catholic Church—one of the winners of Edsa 1—claimed people power was a divine miracle to purge the concept of its reformist or radical substance. Thus the downfall of

Marcos was not the result of a popular uprising anymore—it was God inspiring people to go to Edsa and protect the rebels. Finally, memorializing people power through a museum for those who died fighting the dictatorship only hastened people power's evanescence. The *Bantayog ng mga Bayani* became the symbol of compromise between representatives of the Left and moderate forces on how to portray the anti-Marcos struggle, and the animosity these groups had toward each other was peppered over for the sake of the museum.[8]

People with Some Power

The decline of protests did not necessarily mean that political involvement had become passé. Filipinos still loved to vote, although the makeup of elections had changed significantly with the passage of Republic Act 6646 in 1987, which synchronized both local and national elections to maximize voters' participation. Another law, the 1995 Party-List Law (Republic Act 7941), allotted 20 percent of the seats in the House of Representatives to parties representing the poor and marginalized. Both laws gave civil society groups, reformist politicians, and the different left-wing forces the opportunity to join in the electoral game.[9]

Reformists had every reason to be optimistic about suffrage. Voter turnout was consistently high (80 to 85 percent).[10] Filipinos, however, went to the polls with a mixed bag of sentiments. Reformist aspirations appeared to mesh seamlessly with economic carpetbagger and personal or family obligations to candidates. There were those who voted for fear of violence and intimidation; others saw their voting as a form of showing silent disapproval of the powers-that-be.[11] Elections, in short, now embodied discrepant features: Their corrupt and politically instrumentalist currents coexisted and sometimes even blended with more progressive and ethically driven motivations.[12] They had become, as Filomeno Aguilar Jr. put it, "a time of tension between the sacred and the profane, the ideal and the expedient, of inversion but also of affirming social hierarchy, free but totally constrained, participatory from below yet engineered from the top and meaningful yet meaningless at the same time."[13]

The Filipina had become this capricious elector who defended democracy and avidly supported her beloved action hero or favorite patron. During elections, she obeyed her local warlord's wishes as to which candidate to write on her ballot, but she also inserted her favorite reformist's name to the list. Filipinos, according to Benedict Kerkvliet, had made elections "about legitimacy, fairness, and democratic processes, [and] to preserve or create some integrity and honesty in elections and to turn them into expressions of actual sentiments or evaluations of candidates and issues."[14] They likewise treated

---

Box 10.2.   The Paradox of Oligarchic Democracy

"Democracy in the Philippines is a paradox. It was the first country in the region to topple authoritarian rule. Signs of a vibrant democracy are extensive: high voter turnout, civic engagement, institutional arrangements that theoretically promote accountability and safeguard rights and liberties. Yet the flaws in the democratic process are also extensive: elite dominance, institutional weakness, and widespread abuse of public office, which suggest true representation is largely illusory."

—Bjorn Dressel, "The Philippines: How Much Real Democracy?" *International Political Science Review* 32, no. 5 (November 2011): 529.

---

these exercises as opportunities to earn some money by selling their votes to the candidate who made the highest bid for their ballots.

The Senate was the quintessential admixture of these political preferences. Since 1986, Filipinos elected actors and comedians, entrepreneurs, demagogues, and coup plotters alongside human rights advocates, economic and social reformists, and nationalists. Even supporters of and children of the Marcos family had been elected to various posts. The public accused some senators of being corrupt, praised others for their integrity and principles, and respected political pedigrees. The political combat inside the Senate preserved this diversity. Senators proposed blatantly interest-driven, reactionary, and frivolous laws in one session, then introduced the most progressive ordinances in the next one. While most of the laws passed were trivial—the renaming of streets after politicians or families was the most popular—some were also the most enlightened. The Senate debated and eventually got the president to sign one of the most stringent laws against domestic abuse in Asia and human trafficking.[15] An anti-rape law sent a once-powerful northern Mindanao congressman to a two-life jail term for raping a minor.[16] In 2010, women's rights were further advanced when a "Magna Carta for Women" (Republic Act 9710) passed after seven years of languishing at the committee level. Finally, a revised Family Code, while containing some conservative provisions that represent the powerful influence of the Roman Catholic Church (anti-divorce), included provisos that strongly protect the rights of the child.[17]

Taming Extra-Constitutionalist Politics

More importantly, the Senate functioned as a "tempering platform" where the radical was compelled to learn the art of negotiating with a conservative counterpart, and where the human rights advocate worked with the movie star or the demagogue to pass a bill or a resolution. A legislator with extremist views would never survive inside the legislature. The career of Senator Gregorio Honasan is a good example of the neutralizing powers of the legislative process. Thirty years ago Honasan and his comrades from the Reform the AFP Movement (RAM) almost succeeded in grabbing power twice. RAM admitted defeat and signed a peace agreement with President Fidel Ramos, then Honasan shifted strategy and ran for the Senate and won. RAM's network helped Honasan win, and Honasan won because voters preferred him—their Rambo—in the Senate than in the urban jungle, planning conspiracies against the government.[18]

This popular preference accounted partly for Honasan's parliamentary successes. A May 14, 2001, survey asked voters what they believed were the qualities of a senatorial candidate, and they listed and ranked the following answers: (1) intelligent and knowledgeable; (2) against anomalies in government; (3) approachable; (4) pro-poor; and (5) possessing integrity. Most were traits that could apply to a rightist, left-wing, or centrist politician. The attribute "relates well to others" was so broadly defined that it could apply to a patronage politician or a human rights advocate, while the phrase "has integrity" could mean a former military rebel or a nationalist and communist sympathizer.

Honasan was voted to the Senate because voters recognized his "integrity," charisma, alleged incorruptibility, and his ability to "relate well to others." Filipino voters gave Honasan the opportunity to recover politically but only in an arena of their own choosing. He placed ninth in his first electoral campaign, surprising even his critics. But a ninth-place finish in a twenty-four-slot Senate slate similarly suggested the ex-colonel had lost some of the charisma he had when he launched his coups. He was no longer a central political figure as he had been in the past; he had become just one voice of twenty-four, restrained by institutional norms.

Unschooled in the formalities of Senate procedures, and unfamiliar with the typical backroom deals that enabled laws to be passed, Honasan was lost in his first year as legislator. His contributions were modest and his participation in deliberations minimal. He recovered in his second year, and realized that for him to remain in the center of politics, he had to broaden his concerns. Henceforth, the proposed laws Honasan supported were those addressing social welfare, such as rent control, housing law, solid-waste management, and the highly contested Clean Air Act. The issue that elected him for the first time, defending military interests, took a backseat. Honasan was now just one of many co-sponsors of bills, but was content in sitting quietly on the sidelines.[19]

However, the state's policy toward other social forces operating outside of the state and refusing to play the electoral game was to destroy them. The government continued counterinsurgency operations against the Communist Party of the Philippines (CPP) to slow down the latter's recovery.[20] The Party's New People's Army (NPA) had returned to its 1978-level strength, especially in the northeastern and central parts of Mindanao Island where 1,500 guerrillas, had reestablished "five regional committees and 42 guerrilla fronts . . . launched 250 'tactical offensives,' seized more than 200 weapons and killed roughly 300 soldiers and police."[21] The towns and cities, however, were not able to keep pace with the armed struggle.[22] This imbalance in the development of its forces—fast in the countryside, slower in the cities— would be exploited by the military, and beginning in 2005, special military units began to assassinate top CPP cadres in the slower-developing "white areas."[23]

Of the total 801 victims of extrajudicial executions in 2006, 320 were suspected CPP cadres and activists; another 206 were abducted and never heard of again.[24] The impact was devastating. According to Nathan Quimpo, "[T]he participation of NGOs and POs in policymaking processes (*read: the legal organizing of CPP cadres*) was to some extent impaired, especially at the local level, by the unbridled extrajudicial killings of leftist activists and other human rights violations."[25] Despite the killings, the CPP did manage to get representatives in their party-list organizations into the House of Representatives. The once-despised strategy of "parliamentary struggle" now was the only option left for Party cadres to organize "above ground." Soon its Party leaders were urging urban cadres to give serious thought to electoral alliances with other social forces, including traditional politicians. In 2010, the CPP's legal organizations joined the Senate slate that included the son of the dictator, Ferdinand Marcos. It did badly in the elections, and when these organizations tried to reintroduce non-electoral "militant" mass actions, the voters demurred.[26]

Noncommunist progressive social forces were not doing well either. A 2002 Asian Development Bank briefing on civil society in the Philippines noted that while "government has always maintained some openness to civil society" since 1986, "the democratic space for CSOs [civil society organizations] has been expanded or constricted through the years depending on the inclinations of those in power."[27] Progressives, who let their naiveté get the best of them and joined the Arroyo government, realized how difficult it was to work for someone who had become a quintessential dispenser of patronage. It exposed their "limited usefulness" in quite stark terms.[28]

The recurring tension between these social forces and politicians accustomed to the "conventional" way of doing politics (compromises, patronage, and spoils) eventually unraveled, forcing these progressives to resign from the cabinet.[29] In other instances, according to Ben Reid, nongovernment organizations and political organizations were simply "double-crossed" by their elite allies, with "well-intentioned NGO personnel who previously adopted a critical stance toward neo-clientelism ultimately become absorbed by these relations." He mournfully concluded: "A deep cynicism now exists over the capacity of any civil-society organization to have substantive impacts on policy formation and implementation."[30] Strengthening state institutions by collaborating with politicians had only achieved "very modest gains."[31]

The electoral alliances these non-communist forces forged with politicians badly compromised the former. The fate of Akbayan, an alliance of ex-communists and social democrats, which took this route, was illustrative. In an appraisal of the party's poor performance in the 2007 legislative and local elections, the president Joel Rocamora admitted, "the party-list system had been successfully subverted by old political clans." He attributed this to the failure of the party to realize that "what was supposed to be a national contest had been broken into so many local contests," adding that "our party-list vote declined because we devoted too much attention to the 'national' party list (PL) campaign and not enough to local electoral contests." Akbayan was a victim of an ill-conceived "organizational strategy" that had a nationwide perspective but a "shallow . . . party structure."[32] Six years after arriving at this despondent conclusion, Akbayan repeated the same mistake, suggesting among other things that lessons about the regressive effects of cacique democracy on Progressive politics remained unlearned.[33]

Hardly mentioned was the fact that the community reach of progressive social forces was still circumscribed. In 2004, the Center for Civil Society Studies ruefully reported that only 1.9 percent of "economically active" Filipinos belong to civil society organizations (CSOs).[34] The seemingly sizable number of registered and non-registered CSOs listed by groups like the Asian Development Bank—between 249,000 to 497,000 registered and non-registered—often understated how insignificant progressive groups were to the lives of the majority of Filipinos.

State and Separatists

Arroyo reversed Estrada's "all-out war" against the MILF, formed a new peace panel, and asked the Malaysians to convince the MILF to return to the negotiating table.[35] The two sides renewed the talks despite attempts by the MILF's rival—the Moro National Liberation Front (MNLF)—to derail these with warnings of renewed war.[36] The government and the United States were also aware that the MILF hosted members of terrorist groups like Jemaah Islamiya (JI) and even provided them with military training.[37] This did not last long. The MILF's commitment to the peace process made it difficult to allow the JI to use its camps as bases to launch bombing operations. Moreover, the JI was beginning to unsettle "the delicate ethnic balance between Maguindanao and Maranao-dominated commands," and this worried the MILF leadership. The result was the expulsion of JI cadres from the MILF camps.[38]

The MILF even went one step further, keeping "away from operations related to Balikatan 02–01 for one or more of three reasons: its survival instinct, President Arroyo's resolve to engage it in negotiations, and American determination to keep the Philippine front in the anti-terror war small and manageable."[39] The two sides renewed peace negotiations in 2003 in Kuala Lumpur, and the MILF surprised everyone by formally seeking the U.S. government to co-mediate with Malaysia (see box 10.3).[40] The latter

---

Box 10.3. MILF Chairman Salamat Hashim's Letter to President George W. Bush

20 January 2003
His Excellency George W. Bush
President of the United States
The White House, Washington D.C.

Your Excellency:

In the name of the Moro Islamic Liberation Front (MILF), we send our profound and felicitous greetings of peace on behalf of the Bangsamoro People of our historic homeland in Mindanao, Sulu and Palawan.

The Bangsamoro People have always looked upon your country, the United States of America, and its people, with esteem as a great champion of freedom and democracy. The founding fathers of the American Nation as firm believers of "self-evident truths" and "inalienable rights" have become inspirations for the Moro Nation in our quest for the right to self-determination.

Your ambassador to the Philippines, His Excellency Francis J. Ricciardone, who recently addressed the Foreign Correspondents Association of the Philippines, raised the question of the US Government's desire to know "what they (MILF) want and how it's (the Problem) going to be resolved."

We take this opportunity to inform Your Excellency that the MILF is a national liberation organization, with leadership supported by the Bangsamoro People, and with legitimate political goal to pursue the right of the Moro Nation to determine their future and political status. As part of this process, we have an ongoing negotiation with the Government of the Republic of the Philippines to arrive at a negotiated political settlement of the Mindanao conflict and the Bangsamoro problem, through the mediation and tender of the good offices of the Government of Malaysia.

Your desire to be informed of the MILF goals remind us of the historic, legal and political relationship between the Moro Nation and the US Federal Government as borne out by documents, treaty relations and instruments. Your official policy, under President William McKinley's Instruction to the First Philippine Commission of

1900, treated the Moro Nation initially as a Dependent Nation similar to the North American Indian Nations under treaty relations with the US Federal Government. Subsequently, the Moro Nation was accorded the political status of a US protectorate under the Kiram-Bates Treaty of 1899, confirming the Treaty of 1878 between the Sultan of Sulu and Spain.

Your policy to consider the Philippines as an unincorporated territory of the United States paved the way for the US Government to administer affairs in the Moro territories under a separate political form of governance under the Moro Province from the rest of the Philippine Islands.

Your project to grant Philippine independence obliged the leaders of the Moro Nation to petition the US Congress to give us an option through a referendum to either by remaining as a territory to be administered by the US Government or granted separate independence fifty years from the grant of Philippine independence. Were it not for the outbreak of the Pacific War, the Moro Nation would have been granted trust territory status like any of the Pacific island states who are now independent or in free association with the United States of America.

On account of such circumstances, the Moro Nation was deprived of their inalienable right to self-determination, without waiving their plebiscitary consent. Prior to the grant of Philippine independence on July 4, 1946, American Congressional leaders foresaw that the inclusion of the Moro Nation within the Philippine Commonwealth would result in serious conflicts in Mindanao, Sulu and Palawan, arising from the inability of the Filipino leaders to govern the Moro people. This condition or states of affairs have continued to prevail to the present day.

In view of current global developments and regional security concerns in Southeast Asia, it is our desire to accelerate the just and peaceful negotiated settlement of the Mindanao conflict, particularly the present colonial situation in which the Bangsamoro people find themselves.

We are therefore appealing to the basic principle of American fairness and sense of justice to use your good offices in rectifying the error that (*sic*) continuous to negate and derogate the Bangsamoro People's fundamental right to seek decolonization under the United Nations General Assembly Resolution 1514 (XV) of 1960. For this purpose, we are amenable to inviting and giving you the opportunity to assist in resolving this predicament of the Bangsamoro People.

With assurances of our highest esteem and cordial regards.

Very truly yours,
Salamat Hashim
Chairman

Through: His Excellency Francis J. Ricciardone
United States Ambassador to the Philippines and Palau
US Embassy, Roxas Boulevard, Manila

—Jarius Bondoc, "MILF Letter to Bush Sped Up Settlement," *Philstar Global*, August 1, 2008, http://www.philstar.com/opinion/76398/milf-letter-bush-sped -settlement (last accessed March 29, 2016).

obliged, sending a team from the United States Institute for Peace to join the discussions. Brunei and Malaysia followed suit and sent monitoring teams to minimize hostilities in 2005.[41] Muslim civil society organizations assisted the teams in mediating between the MILF and the AFP in the field. These social forces also set up "zones of peace" all around the war zones.[42] Military encounters did continue despite the negotiations, but these were no longer battles between two political forces. They were mainly triggered by the clan wars (*rido*) where members of the military, the MILF, the MNLF, and those in the private armies of politicians mobilized and came together to defend their respective families.[43]

Why did the MILF, with its 12,000-strong armed force, cohesive organization, and loyal cadre core prefer to talk instead of responding in kind to government attacks, and why did an Islamic organization approach the United States—by then the most despised country in the Muslim world for its invasion of Iraq—to help in the negotiations? The obvious answer was also the most ironic. The MILF had a big army, but it was designed not for guerrilla warfare but for open, face-to-face battles against the military. This preference for conventional warfare was odd given that some of the MILF's leaders fought in the Afghan resistance against the Soviet Union. Back in the Philippines, they appeared to have forgotten how to engage in guerilla warfare.[44] When the armed movement did try its hand at conventional warfare, the AFP soundly defeated the rebel group. In a matter of days, its main camps were captured by government troops, and the MILF was forced to shift to guerrilla warfare. This did not last for long. Military encounters declined, and the MILF and the Philippine military retreated to the areas under their control. But in the case of the MILF, the areas where they were to return turned out to be constricted spaces that made it easy for the military to track its movements.

These were also not just a military handicap, for in confining itself to its own territory, the MILF's political naiveté and amateurism became apparent. It had never made any attempt to expand its support beyond its largely Maguindanao base. The Tausugs of the Sulu archipelago remained loyal to the MNLF, while the Maranaos, who inhabited the provinces north of the MILF's area, were inconsistent in their support for separatism. None of these groups came to the aid of the MILF in 2000. Neither could the MILF expect support from the traditional politicians who saw the armed group as a threat to their local power.[45]

The MILF likewise lacked the coalition-building talent at which the communists excelled during martial law. Non-Muslim indigenous communities (Lumad) continued to be distrustful of Muslims, as memories of their ancestors being traded as slaves and treated as culturally inferior were still strong in the minds of the younger generation. The MILF eventually acknowledged Lumad aspirations and took measures to bring them into the discussions. Its insistence, however, that the Lumad are a part of the Bangsamoro people meant that the tensions between the two minority groups would remain. Neither had the MILF reached out to the Christian communities for support and sympathy, despite the growing anti-Manila sentiments in these communities arising from a perception that Mindanao was just a milking cow of the republic, its wealth sucked out to the national capital with nothing received in return.

This failure at united front politics was apparent in 2008 when President Arroyo and the MILF tried to fast-track a Memorandum of Agreement on Ancestral Domain (MOA-AD). This unilateral move caused massive opposition among the Christian groups, backed by their legislators. When the Supreme Court declared the agreement illegal, the MILF suffered the consequences the most. On October 14, 2008, after the Supreme Court's declaration, one of the MILF's battle-tested units broke away from the organization. Calling themselves the Bangsamoro Islamic Freedom Fighters (BIFF), they attacked several coastal towns but were repelled by government troops working closely with Christian militias. The MILF withdrew from the talks, while the government panel dissolved after its head resigned.[46]

Finally, there was the shared fatality of age. When Maguindanao cadres formed the MILF in 1978 after breaking away from the MNLF, their average age was between thirty and thirty-five years old. By 2008 they were well into retirement age, their once-robust physiques steadily exhausted by the demands of the struggle. Many were reported to be unwell, and a good number were secretly wishing to end the struggle so they could spend their remaining days in pleasant retirement with their families. [47] This weariness extended down to the mass base, as the MILF's constituents began demanding that their communities be rehabilitated so they could return to their occupations. A cause of this popular demand was the envy over what international assistance had done to rehabilitate the communities under MNLF control.[48]

There was another actor who was now a major player in Muslim Mindanao politics: the United States (U.S.). Under Arroyo, U.S.-Philippine relations had begun to thaw since the Philippine Senate voted not to extend the military bases agreement between the two countries. On January 6, 1995, Philippine police thwarted a plan by Islamic terrorists to blow up eleven airlines over the Pacific with the arrest of one of the plotters in Manila.[49] Three years later, the two governments signed a visiting forces agreement (VFA) that set the guidelines on how Americans must operate in the Philippines.[50] Soon after, the *Balikatan* (shoulder-to-shoulder) joint military exercises involving 2,500 American soldiers working closely with 2,393 Filipino troops commenced on January 31 and ran through March 3.[51] On May 27, 2001, when the Abu Sayyaf held a group that included an American missionary couple, the United States offered intelligence assistance to the Philippine military. From that time on, American military personnel were visiting different parts of Muslim Mindanao.[52] In October, two dozen U.S. Special Forces personnel added Mindanao to their tour of duty, to help the AFP fight the Abu Sayyaf.[53]

American military assistance to the Philippines also grew. The State Department promised $19 million in military financing, ten times more than what the Philippines received in 2001 ($2 million). President Bush added another $10 million in Department of Defense goods and services, another $10 million for counterterrorism enforcement, and a bevy of military hardware—from attack helicopters to patrol boats and rifles.[54] The high point of this renewed relationship was the September 11, 2001, terrorist attack that destroyed the twin towers of the World Trade Center in New York. Arroyo joined President George W. Bush's "Coalition of the Willing" and sent a small contingent to Iraq.[55]

Filipinos remained strongly pro-American. As late as 2014, despite the global hostility toward the United States due to President Bush's disastrous invasion of Iraq, 92 percent of Filipinos still had a positive view of the United States (South Korea followed at 82 percent).[56] Muslims also strongly favored the United States for the assistance it had consistently given to their communities. The most-cited example was the success of the U.S. Agency for International Development (USAID) in reintegrating 28,000 MNLF fighters by giving them back their livelihood or helping them develop new ventures.[57]

STATE AND LOCAL POWER

As we pointed out in chapter 9, bossism was not always the means of governing at the local level. There were mayors who belonged to political families but who reached political adulthood during the two most critical periods of Philippine history—the radicalization of the 1960s and the fifteen years of martial law. On the one hand, they continued their families' way of ruling—combining patronage politics, opportunistic bargaining with other political clans, and often the use of private armies to win local power. On the other hand, they also could not ignore the post-Edsa social forces that were committed to expanding community empowerment, better infrastructure, tidier city surroundings, and more efficient social services. They therefore had to either work together with these civil society forces, nongovernment organizations, and left-wing and reformist groups or address the issues they were championing.

In the late twentieth and early twenty-first centuries, three mayors were repeatedly cited as examples of these kinds of politicians: Jesse Robredo of Naga City, Rodrigo Duterte of Davao City, and Bayani Fernando of Marikina. Robredo turned Naga City, a medium-size city south of Manila, into one of "the most improved cities in Asia" and returned it to its place as the top city in the Bicol Province.[58] He accomplished this via a sustained support of civil society groups that kept the politically dominant families of the region at bay.[59] Duterte successfully turned Davao City from a battleground between communists and the military into one of the safest cities in the country. He did this by crafting a broad coalition that brought to his city council left-wing social forces and scions of the local political clans, and using this legitimacy to conduct a brutal campaign directed at physically eliminating drug addicts and pushers in his city.[60] A journalist recently described him as "a Leftist but with a strongman tendencies."[61] The third mayor was Bayani Fernando, who turned Marikina City into one of the cleanest cities of metropolitan Manila. Fernando described himself as the quintessential populist-technocrat who promised to raise revenues and encouraged its citizens to exercise discipline and comply with city regulations.[62]

Yet, as was the case in the early post-Marcos period, these three officials remained the exceptions to the rule. Local clans retained their power, although they were not only reliving the glory days of their "feudal past" but had also adjusted to the "democratic transition." One of the new things they learned was the argot of international development assistance (human development index, social capital, capacity building, stakeholders, community welfare), and quietly appropriated these terms to further strengthen their power (see box 10.2). Some partnered with civil society forces and nongovernment organizations to purse a common social welfare agenda but were soon outstaging the latter by controlling access and use of livelihood funds from the government and international aid agencies.[63] Others proclaimed themselves defenders of "safe" (i.e., apolitical) issues like protecting the environment or creating the cultures of peace in war zones. At the end of the day, however, they remained satraps who reigned over their communities, often brutally, in the name of their families.

The Strong Republic Unravels

In short, little had changed in the relationship between local clans and bosses and the state in early twenty-first-century politics. President Arroyo used her presidential powers to influence politics outside of Manila through the judicious allotment of state funds and the appointment of local allies to executive positions.[64] She cut out the political middlemen, funneling government patronage funds directly to village captains and town and city mayors and concentrated her patronage on the Visayas, where she claimed a local connection based on her mother's side of the family.[65] This practice was "a justifiable act of political survival in a system that rewards, not party loyalty, but a politician's ability to ingratiate himself to an all-powerful, spoils-dispensing president."[66] Autocratic regional and local bosses and dynasties responded by switching their support to Arroyo in the House of Representatives and giving her a majority. Arroyo could now easily neutralize populist upsurges and defeat new military threats. She survived the 2005 impeachment against her "not because it was weak or baseless but because Malacanang dangled money, pork barrel projects, government positions and other juicy incentives which proved irresistible to the unscrupulous congressmen."[67]

Treasury officials estimated that the country lost $7.6 billion dollars from tax evasion in 2003 alone. The budget deficit only declined from $385 billion to $3.7 billion.[68] Arroyo was accused of alleged money laundering, bribery in connection with the rehabilitation of a nuclear power plant, overpricing road construction, extortion, allegedly being involved in a fertilizer fund scam to divert funds for election purposes, receiving kickback from a telecommunications deal with a Chinese company, and presiding over the mysterious disappearance of monies allocated for automated election counting machines.[69]

Yet Arroyo survived, and this was thanks to the local coalitions that supported her. This, however, ended in 2009. Her closest ally in Central Min-

---

Box 10.4. Local Power Unaltered

"From the perspective of foreign observers and Manila-based analysts, the national government appears to play a dominant role. To average Filipinos, though, government in every practical sense means *local* government. Virtually all government services are delivered through city, provincial and municipal authorities; local and regional administrators of national agencies are more closely connected to local officials than to their nominal chain of authority. A small number of tightly interconnected families, a structure of elite control that grew out of the colonial-era dominance of large landowners, dominate these local positions. Business interests and positions in government and the military have largely replaced control of land as the source of elite wealth. The cast of characters has changed in many regions, with old aristocrats displaced by politically connected upstarts. Yet the overall pattern of elite domination has not changed, and most municipal and provincial governments remain effectively controlled by either a single family or a narrow cast of competing elite factions."

—Steven Rogers, "Philippine Politics and the Rule of Law,"
Journal of Democracy 15, no. 4 (October 2004): 116.

danao was the Ampatuan family whose brutal grip over the region ensured the president the one million votes she needed to win the 2004 elections.[70] On November 23, 2009, Andal and his two sons presided over the killing of fifty-eight people who were part of an unarmed convoy escorting the wife of a rival from another powerful clan.[71] The wife was planning to register her husband at the regional office of the Commission on Elections and run against Zaldy Ampatuan, the incumbent chair of the Autonomous Region for Muslim Mindanao (ARMM). The Ampatuans and their men redirected the convoy to an isolated patch and systematically gunned down the passengers. Before they died, however, the victims were able to send text messages to their family and friends. The military sent a search mission to the area and found the bodies in the process of being dumped into a pit.[72] The Maguindanao massacre was the coup de grace that ended Arroyo's plans to extend her term.[73] Arroyo came under intense public criticism and was left with no choice but to order the army to arrest Ampatuan, his two sons, and more than a dozen relatives and bodyguards. She had to do this while acting like a Filipina Marie Antoinette: hosting an extremely expensive dinner for family and friends in an upscale New York City restaurant while a typhoon devastated thousands in metropolitan Manila and adjoining provinces.[74]

In 2005, foreign direct investments rose to $1.2 billion and overseas Filipinos remitted over $12 billion.[75] Growth continued in 2006, and the country exceeded growth projections when it rose to a high 7 percent.[76] This, however, slowed down in 2007 and 2008 but rebounded again after that. Despite these positive signs, the gap between the rich and the poor continued to widen.[77] These figures allowed Arroyo to boast that the country was on the road to recovery, and she began to hint again at extending her term.[78] Then the economy dropped from a 7.3 percent growth rate to about 2 percent.

Box 10.5.   The Violence of the Ampatuans

"The first option always of the Ampatuan in their political strategies was killing[. . . .] That is the first option[. . . .] Later on [. . .] when they became richer, then they had more tools. Money, influence and the option to kill receded. But it's always been in the background. The option to kill was always there before. So that is why Ampatuans' thinking was killing. Because that has always been the default. That's how they projected themselves: You get in our way, we kill you. And for those in the lower strata the option was always killing. So killing came naturally. If you were not armed, you did not have your own clan to protect yourself, you were just an ordinary guy, then the option was always default, was killing."

—As quoted by Peter Kreuzer, "Philippine Governance: Merging Politics and Crime," *Peace Research Institute, Frankfurt (PRIF) Report*, No. 93 (2009): 12.

On May 10, 2010, Filipinos elected Benigno Aquino III, the son of the late president Corazon Aquino, as the fifteenth president. He won by a big plurality (41.1 percent), with the second-highest votes going to—surprisingly—former president Joseph Estrada (29.2 percent).[79] Aquino's victory was a signal that reformists were now in a position to take over the levers of the state.[80]

NOTES

1. Von Totanes, "20 Filipinos, 20 years after People Power," *Philippine Center for Investigative Journalism I Report*, February 2, 2006, http://pcij.org/stories/romeo-j-intengan/ (last accessed March 3, 2016).

2. Ellen Tordesillas, "Fidel V. Ramos: 'The People Are Tired of Constant Bickering,'" *Philippine Center for Investigative Journalism I Report*, February 2, 2006, http://pcij.org/stories/fidel-v-ramos/ (last accessed January 30, 2016).

3. Sheila S. Coronel, "The Philippines in 2006: Democracy and Its Discontents," *Asian Survey* 47, no. 1 (January/February 2007): 207.

4. Patricio N. Abinales, "The Philippines in 2009: The Blustery Days of August," *Asian Survey* 50, no. 1 (January/February 2010): 219–20.

5. Michael Pinches, "The Making of Middle Class Civil Society in the Philippines," in *The Politics of Change in the Philippines*, ed. Yuko Kasuya and Nathan Gilbert Quimpo (Manila: Anvil, 2010): 305.

6. Amando Doronila, "Estrada Is Damaged Goods," *Philippine Daily Inquirer*, May 27, 2009, as quoted by Mark R. Thompson, "Populism and the Revival of Reform: Competing Political Narratives in the Philippines," *Contemporary Southeast Asia* 32, no. 1 (2010): 3.

7. Lisandro E. Claudio, "From Scandalous Politics to Public Scandal: Corruption, Media and the Collapse of the Estrada Regime in the Philippines," *Asian Politics and Polity* 6, no. 4 (2014): 539–54.

8. Lisandro Claudio, *Taming People Power: The EDSA Revolutions and Their Contradictions* (Quezon City. Ateneo de Manila University Press, 2013).

9. Julio Teehankee, "Electoral Politics in the Philippines," in *Electoral Politics in Southeast and East Asia*, ed. Aurel Croissant and John Marei (Germany: Friederich-Ebert-Stiftung, 2002): 188–94.

10. Bjorn Dressel, "The Philippines: How Much Real Democracy?" *International Political Science Review* 32 (2011): 533.

11. Jennifer Franco, *Campaigning for Democracy: Grassroots Citizenship Movements, Less-than-Democratic Elections and Regime Transition in the Philippines* (Quezon City: Institute for Popular Democracy, 2001).

12. Patricio N. Abinales, "The Enigma of the Popular Will," *I: The Investigative Reporting Magazine*, May 2004.

13. Filomeno V. Aguilar Jr., "Betting on Democracy: Electoral Ritual in the Philippine Presidential Campaign," in *Elections as Popular Culture in Asia*, ed. Chua Beng Huat (New York: Routledge, 2007): 72.

14. Benedict Kerkvliet, "Contested Meanings of Elections in the Philippines," in *The Politics of Elections in Southeast Asia*, ed. R. H. Taylor (New York: Cambridge University Press, 1996.): 163.

15. Philippine Commission on Women. "Philippine Initiatives to Eliminate VAW," http://www.pcw.gov.ph/focus-areas/violence-against-women/initiatives (last accessed March 3, 2016). Republic Act No. 9262. An Act Defining Violence Against Women and their Children, Providing for Protective Measures for Victims, Prescribing Penalties therefore, and for other purposes." The description of violence ranges from physical violence to "economic abuse." Section 25 (Public Crime), for example, allows complaints of abuse to be filed "by any citizen having personal knowledge of the circumstances involving the commission of the crime." Section 26 does not assign any criminal or civil liability of battered women "notwithstanding the absence of the elements for justifying circumstances of self-defense under the Revised Penal Code," and Section 28 allows battered mothers to retain custody of children.

16. "People of the Philippines, plaintiff-appellee, vs. Romeo G. Jalosjos, accused-appellant. G.R. Nos. 132875-76, November 16, 2011, http://sc.judiciary.gov.ph/jurisprudence/2001/nov2001/132875_76.htm (last accessed March 1, 2016).

17. Abinales, "The Philippines in 2009: The Blustery Days of August," 226.

18. Jennifer Conroy Franco, *Campaigning for Democracy: Grassroots Citizenship Movements, Less-than-Democratic Elections and Regime Transition in the Philippines* (Quezon City: Institute for Popular Democracy, 2001).

19. Contrast Honasan's Senate to that of a younger colleague—Antonio Trillanes, who had led a mutiny of junior officers against President Arroyo. See Nicole Curato, "The Road to Oakwood Is Paved with Good Intentions: The Oakwood Mutiny and the Politics of Recognition," *Philippine Sociological Review* 59 (2011): 23–48. Unlike Honasan, Trillanes was a very active member of the Senate. See Reynaldo Santos Jr. and Michael Bueza, "8 Things to Know about Antonio Trillanes IV," *Rappler*, February 26, 2016, http://www.rappler.com/newsbreak/iq/107961-fast-facts-antonio-trillanes-iv (last accessed April 1, 2016).

20. Coronel, "The Philippines in 2006," 179. At the start of 2005, with $20 million promised by Arroyo, the AFP intensified the implementation of the second phase of Operation Plan Freedom Watch (*Oplan Bantay Laya*) with a promise to end the insurgency in three years.

21. International Crisis Group. "The Communist Insurgency in the Philippines: Tactics and Talks," *Asia Report* No. 202, February 14, 2011, 10.

22. Dominique Caoutte, "Ups and Downs of a Contemporary Maoist Movement: Shifting Tactics, Moving Targets and (Un)orthodox Strategy, the Philippine Revolution in Perspective," in *Emancipatory Politics: A Critique*, ed. Stephan Feuchtwang and Alpa Shah (Open Anthropology Cooperative Press, 2015), http://openanthcoop.net/press/emancipatory-politics-a-critique/chapter-5/ (last accessed February 23, 2016).

23. William N. Holden, "Ashes from the Phoenix: State Terrorism and the Party-List Groups in the Philippines," *Contemporary Politics* 15, no. 4 (2009): 377–93.

24. Alliance for the Advancement of People's Rights (Karapatan), "State Terror and Martial Rule," *Karapatant Report on the Human Rights Situation 2006*, 5, http://www.karapatan.org/files/HRHRSIT2006.pdf (last accessed March 2, 2016).

25. Nathan Gilbert Quimpo, "Countries at the Crossroads 2011: Philippines," *Freedom House,* November 12, 2015, 4.

26. International Crisis Group, "The Communist Insurgency in the Philippines," 8.

27. Asian Development Bank, "Civil Society Briefs: The Philippines," http://www.adb.org/sites/default/files/publication/30174/csb-phi.pdf (last accessed March 12, 2016).

28. Asian Development Bank, "Civil Society Briefs: The Philippines," http://www.adb.org/sites/default/files/publication/30174/csb-phi.pdf (last accessed March 12, 2016).

29. Joel Rocamora, "Partisanship and Reform: The Making of a Presidential Campaign," in Kasuya and Quimpo, 86.

30. Ben Reid, "Development NGOs, Semiclientelism and the State in the Philippines: From 'Crossover' to Double-Crossed," *Kasarinlan* 23, no. 1 (2008): 6.

31. Nathan G. Quimpo, *Contested Democracy and the Left in the Philippines after Marcos* (Quezon City: Ateneo de Manila University Press, 2008), 126.

32. Joel Rocamora, "Learning New Ways of Being (Left), Akbayan—A New Left Party in the Philippines," as posted in *Mga Diskurso ni Doy Blog*, November 13, 2007, http://doycinco.blogspot.com/2007/11/learning-new-ways-of-being-left.html (last accessed February 13, 2017).

33. Patricio N. Abinales, "Progressives in Disarray: Risa Hontiveros' Loss," *Rappler*, August 22, 2015, http://www.rappler.com/thought-leaders/103382-part-1-progressives-disarray-risa-hontiveros-loss (last accessed March 9, 2016); and "Progressives in a Bind," *Rappler*, September 5, 2015, http://www.rappler.com/thought-leaders/104733-part-2-progressives-in-bind (last accessed March 9, 2016).

34. Yuko Kasuya, "Democratic Consolidation in the Philippines: Who Supports Extra-Constitutional Government Change?" in Kasuya and Quimpo, 111.

35. Mel Labrador, "The Philippines in 2001: High Drama, a New President and Setting the Stage for Recovery," *Asian Survey* 42, no. 1 (January/February 2002): 146.

36. Labrador, "The Philippines in 2001," 141–42.

37. International Crisis Group, "Southern Philippines Backgrounder: Terrorism and the Peace Process," *Asia Report* No. 8, July 13, 2004.

38. International Crisis Group, "Philippine Terrorism: The Role of Militant Islamic Converts," *Asia Report* No. 110, December 19, 2005, 15–16.

39. Michael T. Montesano, "The Philippines in 2002: Playing Politics, Facing Deficits, and Embracing Uncle Sam," *Asian Survey* 43, no. 1 (January/February 2003): 162.

40. Jarius Bondoc, "MILF Letter to Bush Sped Up Settlement," *PhilStar Global*, August 1, 2008, http://www.philstar.com/opinion/76398/milf-letter-bush-sped-settlement (last accessed March 29, 2016).

41. Temario C. Rivera, "The Philippines in 2004: New Mandate, Daunting Problems," *Asian Survey* 45, no. 1 (January/February 2005): 129–30.

42. *Philippine Human Development Report 2005,* 12.

43. Wilfredo M. Torres III, *Rido: Clan Feuding and Conflict Management in Mindanao* (Quezon City: Ateneo de Manila University Press, 2014).

44. Rudy Rodil, *Kalinaw Mindanao: The Story of the GRP-MNLF Peace Process* (Davao City: Alternate Forum for Research in Mindanao, 2006), 43.

45. Mark S. Williams, "Retrospect and Prospect of Magindanawn [*sic*] Leadership in Central Mindanao: Four Vantage Points," *Kyoto Review of Southeast Asia*, December 11, 2009, http://kyotoreview.org/issue-11/retrospect-and-prospect-of-magindanawn-leadership-in-central-mindanao-four-vantage-points/ (last accessed March 20, 2016).

46. Patricio N. Abinales, *Orthodoxy and History in the Muslim Mindanao Narrative* (Quezon City: Ateneo de Manila University Press, 2010), 119–53.

47. Roel Parentildeo, "Salamat Dead; Murad Takes Over," *Philstar Global*, August 6, 2003, http://www.philstar.com/headlines/216252/salamat-dead-murad-takes-over (last accessed March 31, 2016).

48. Patricio N. Abinales, "The End of War in the Southern Philippines," *Asian Ethnicity* 15, no. 3 (2014): 394–98.

49. "Terrorists Plotted to Blow Up 11 U.S. Jumbo Jets," *Los Angeles Times*, May 28, 1995, http://articles.baltimoresun.com/1995-05-28/news/1995148047_1_bojinka-philippines-plot (last accessed March 15, 2016).

50. U.S. Department of State, "Philippines, Defense: Status of Forces, Agreement Between the United States of America and the Philippines, Signed at Manila, February 10, 1998, and Agreement Between the United States of America and the Philippines, Signed at Manila, October 9, 1998," in Treaties and Other International Act Series 12931, http://www.state.gov/documents/organization/107852.pdf (last accessed March 24, 2016).

51. Maria Ressa, "The Philippines: War on Terror's Second Front," *CNN World*, April 16, 2002, http://articles.cnn.com/2002-04-16/world/phil.blair_1_abu-sayyaf-joint-military-exercises-martin-and-gracia-burnham?_s=PM:asiapcf (last accessed April 7, 2016); and Gregg K. Kakesako, "Hawaii Leads Joint War Games," *Honolulu Star Bulletin,* February 8, 2000, http://archives.starbulletin.com/2000/02/08/news/story3.html (last accessed March 3, 2016).

52. Rivera, "The Philippines in 2004," 132.

53. United States of America, *Congressional Record* V. 146, Pt. 8, June 13 to June 21, 2000, 10450.

54. Renato Cruz de Castro, "U.S. War on Terror in East Asia: The Perils of Preemptive Defense in Waging a War of the Third Kind," *Asian Affairs* 31, no. 1 (Winter 2005): 212–31.

55. Jason Sherman, "Philippines to See Boost in U.S. Military Financing," *Defense News*, November 5-11, 2001; Mel Labrador, "The Philippines in 2001," 142.

56. Bruce Stokes, "Which Countries Do Not Like America and Which Do," Pew Research Center, Fact Tank, July 15, 2014, http://www.pewresearch.org/fact-tank/2014/07/15/which-countries-dont-like-america-and-which-do/ (last accessed March 24, 2016).

57. USAID–Philippines, 1995, "USAID/Phil activities in Mindanao," http://pdf .usaid.gov/pdf_docs/Pdacf583.pdf (last accessed February 12, 2016); "Growth with Equity in Mindanao (GEM) Program, Vol. 1: Main Report," August 28, 1995– September 30, 2002, p. ix.

58. Robredo was so popular that a children's book was even written about him. See Yvette Fernandez, *Simply Jesse: The Story of Jesse Robredo* (Manila: Summit Publishing Co. Inc., 2013).

59. Bea Cupin, "The 'Ordinariness' of Jesse Robredo," *Rappler*, August 19, 2015, http://www.rappler.com/nation/103090-jesse-robredo-death-anniversary (last accessed January 12, 2016).

60. Human Rights Watch, "You Can Die Any Time: Death Squads Killings in Mindanao," June 4, 2009, https://www.hrw.org/report/2009/04/06/you-can-die-any -time/death-squad-killings-mindanao (last accessed January 2, 2016). Duterte's critics, however, accused the mayor of a fib, citing a Philippine National Police report that ranked Davao City as fourth among the cities with high crime rates. See "Davao is Number 4 on PNP's Worst PH Cities with Highest Crime Rate," *Politiko*, April 6, 2016, http://politics.com.ph/davao-is-number-4-on-pnps-worst-ph-cities-with -highest-crime-rate/ (last accessed April 1, 2016).

61. Pia Ranada, "Rody Duterte: The Man, the Mayor, the President," *Rappler*, June 29, 2016, http://www.rappler.com/newsbreak/in-depth/137583-rodrigo-duterte -philippine-president-profile (last accessed October 10, 2016).

62. Jet Damazo, "Bayani the Hero," *Newsbreak*, July 22, 2002, http:// archives.newsbreak-knowledge.ph/2002/07/22/bayani-the-hero/ (last accessed October 9, 2016); and Felyne Siao, "Because We Want to Make Marikina Even Better," *Rappler*, March 19, 2013, http://www.rappler.com/nation/politics/elections -2013/24107-because-we-want-to-make-marikina-even-better (last accessed March 2, 2016). Unlike Robredo, however, Fernando's family was one of the town's ruling families.

63. See, for example, "Development Partners, Province of Lanao del Norte: The Land of Beauty and Bounty," http://www.lanaodelnorte.gov.ph/Development -Partners/ngo.html (last accessed January 6, 2016).

64. Mark R. Thompson, "The Politics Philippine Presidents Make: Presidential-Style, Patronage-Based, or Regime Relational?" *Critical Asian Studies* 46, no. 3 (2014): 433–60. The presidency remains the most powerful agency of the state, crafted back in 1935. See Michael J. Montesano, "The Philippines in 2002," 161.

65. Patricio N. Abinales, "Weak State, Resilient President," *Southeast Asian Affairs 2008* (Singapore: Institute of Southeast Asian Studies, 2008): 293–312.

66. Florencio B. Abad, "The Case for Parliamentary Government," in *Towards a Federal Republic of the Philippines with a Parliamentary Government: A Reader*, ed. J. V. Abueva, R. M. Teves, G. C. Somena Jr., C. R. Carlos, and M. O. Mastura (Marikina City, The Philippines: Center for Social Policy and Governance, Kalayaan College, 2002).

67. Quimpo, "Countries at the Crossroads 2011," 4.

68. Montesano, "Philippines in 2002, 160; and Michael J. Montesano, "The Philippines in 2003: Troubles, None of Them New," *Asian Survey* 44, no. 1 (January/February 2003): 98.

69. Tetch Torres-Tupas, "Arroyo Cleared in P728M Fertilizer Fund Scam," *Philippine Daily Inquirer*, May 8, 2014, http://newsinfo.inquirer.net/600623/arroyo -cleared-in-p728m-fertilizer-fund-scam (last accessed March 15, 2016); Republic of the Philippines Senate Committee on Accountability of Public Officers and Investigations, "NBN-ZTE Executive Summary," November 11, 2009, https://www.senate .gov.ph/lisdata/1293411633!.pdf (last accessed March 24, 2016); Roel R. Landingin, "New Joint-Venture Rules Allow Little Oversight, More Abuse," Philippine Center for Investigative Journalism, July 2009, http://pcij.org/stories/2009/laiban2. html (last accessed February 5, 2016); and Mayen Jaymalin, "Comelec: Case vs. Mega Pacific Filed," *Philippine Star*, December 16, 2005, http://www.philstar.com/ headlines/312395/comelec-case-vs-mega-pacific-filed (last accessed March 24, 2016). See also Federico D. Pascual Jr., "Ramos, Estrada, Arroyo All Had a Hand in Impsa," *Philippine Star*, December 19, 2002, http://www.philstar.com/opinion/ 188449/ramos-estrada-arroyo-all-had-hand-impsa (last accessed March 1, 2016); Gil C. Cabacungan, "Road to Perdition: 13 Found Guilty in Overprice," *Philippine Daily Inquirer*, February 6, 2015, http://newsinfo.inquirer.net/670875/road-to-perdition -13-found-guilty-in-overprice (last accessed March 14, 2016); and Jet Damazo, "The Stink That Won't Go Away, *Kyoto Review of Southeast Asia* 2, October 2002 (Disaster and Rehabilitation), http://kyotoreview.org/issue-2-disaster-and-rehabilitation/ (last accessed March 15, 2016).

70. "Ampatuan Sr.'s Power Coincided with Arroyo's Victory in 2004," *Politiko*, http://politics.com.ph/ampatuan-srs-power-coincided-with-arroyos-victory-in-2004/ (last accessed December 12, 2015).

71. On the Ampatuans' penchant for violence, see "'They Own the People.' The Ampatuans, State-Backed Militias and Killings in the Southern Philippines" (New York: Human Rights Watch, November 2010): 10–65.

72. Matikas Santos, "Maguindanao Massacre: How It Happened," *Philippine Daily Inquirer*, November 21, 2014, http://www.inquirer.net/143183/maguindanao -massacre-how-it-happened (last accessed January 3, 2016).

73. International Crisis Group, "The Philippines: After the Maguindanao Massacre," *Asian Briefing* No. 98, December 21, 2009.

74. Patricio N. Abinales, "The Philippines in 2010: Blood, Ballots and Beyond," *Asian Survey* 51, no. 1 (January/February 2011): 163–64.

75. Coronel, "The Philippines in 2006," 181–82. Coronel, however, notes that the boom never trickled down to the poor.

76. Allen Hicken, "The Philippines in 2007: Ballots, Budgets, and Bribes," *Asian Survey* 48, no. 1 (January/December 2008): 79.

77. Allen Hicken, "The Philippines in 2008: Peace-Building, War-Fighting, and Crisis Management," *Asian Survey* 49, no. 1 (January/February 2008): 96.

78. Raissa Espinosa-Robles, "Arroyo's Charter Change Moves Copied from the Marcos Book," Philippine Center for Investigative Journalism, http://pcij.org/stories/

arroyos-charter-change-moves-copied-from-the-marcos-book/ (last accessed April 7, 2016).

79. Amando Doronila, "A Gracious Political Act," *Philippine Daily Inquirer*, May 11, 2010, http://opinion.inquirer.net/inquireropinion/view/20100511-269481/A -gracious-political-act (last accessed September 24, 2014).

80. Joel Rocamora, "People Power Is Alive and Well," *Third World Quarterly* 33, no. 2 (2012): 204.

Chapter Eleven

Cacique Democracy Personalized

ELECTIONS, "PEOPLE POWER," AND *DAANG MATUWID*

President Benigno Aquino III's supporters did not waste time in portraying his victory as yet another legatee of the "People Power" that his mother brought forth in 1986.[1] Conrado de Quiros wrote:

> People Power doesn't always have to take the form of massing in physical space to oust a nasty non-president, or an unsavory non-chief justice. It can always take the form of massing in cyberspace to bring the corrupt to heel. These days, with the interactive media having made instantaneous reaction possible, that is probably the more viable, or realizable, option. It can always take the form of an epic campaign to make people realize that taxes are their money. You're not going to be furious about corruption unless you see that it is stealing, or worse, that it is stealing your money. It can always take the form of not voting for the monstrously corrupt and their protectors.[2]

This revision of the idea of people power signaled the demise of this extra-constitutional-but-morally-legitimate-act that had, along with its "evil twin," the military coup, been one of the hallmarks of the post-Marcos period. Both had relinquished their places in the political arena to the only viable and most constitutional game in town—elections.

In his first months in office, Aquino immediately played to the peanut gallery. His first act was to ban the use of sirens by government officials—including him—when they travel across towns and cities. He followed this with an executive order creating a Truth Commission to investigate and prosecute corrupt officials. The creation of this special commission again

311

echoed President Corazon Aquino's establishment in 1986 of the Presidential Commission on Good Government to recover the billions plundered by the Marcos family. The first became policy, but the Supreme Court struck down the second as unconstitutional.³ This did not deter Aquino from pursuing his crusade to root out corruption, especially those perpetrated by former president Gloria Macapagal Arroyo and her allies.⁴

Aquino forced the resignation of Merceditas Gutierrez, who as ombudsman (state prosecutor) had failed to secure convictions for officials charged with corruption during Mrs. Arroyo's term. The lower house had already voted overwhelmingly to impeach Gutierrez, leaving her with no choice but to resign.⁵ Aquino's legislative allies successfully impeached Supreme Court Chief Justice Renato Corona, another known Arroyo associate. The Senate, acting as justices, found Corona guilty for a "betrayal of [the] public trust," after the latter refused to reveal how much he and his family were worth.⁶ To ensure the military's loyalty, Mrs. Arroyo had refused to interfere with affairs within the Armed Forces of the Philippines (AFP) by not signing the verdict of the military finance comptroller, General Carlos Garcia. Garcia was charged with the same crimes as the chief justice.⁷

On November 18, 2011, the government arrested Mrs. Arroyo and charged her with co-conspiring to rig the elections in the province of Maguindanao in May 2007. She had allegedly instructed Governor Zaldy Ampatuan of the Autonomous Region in Muslim Mindanao (ARMM) to ensure a "12-0 victory for the senatorial candidates of Team Unity," Mrs. Arroyo's party.⁸ She was released in July 2012 after posting a P1-million bail, but was rearrested three months later, this time on charges of plunder. She had allegedly misused government charity funds, taking out $9 million as "intelligence funds" to support allies running for legislative positions.⁹ Before her arrest, Mrs. Arroyo had successfully run for a seat in the House of Representative in 2010 (the first being José P. Laurel, who became president of the Japanese puppet republic, then won a Senate seat in 1951). She was reelected in 2013 despite being under hospital arrest, defeating an Aquino ally.¹⁰ Aquino had opposed any legal effort to either allow her to post bail or be on house arrest in light of her medical condition. To ensure that Mrs. Arroyo would be unable to keep in constant touch with her allies, the police denied her access to the Internet and cell phones in her hospital/prison cell.¹¹ As Mrs. Arroyo shriveled into political irrelevance—and certainly not helped along by her weakening physical condition—her allies either moved to the ruling party or drifted into the group of another opposition leader.

The detention of these three high officials boosted Aquino's image as a reformist determined to improve on state institutions and practices toward making governance transparent and government officials accountable.[12] These major corruption issues and the rise in the number of corruption cases filed by the ombudsman's office against "high-ranking officials" improved the country's international standing. The World Economic Forum's Global Competitiveness Report moved the Philippines from being the 87th among the 133 most corrupt countries in 2010 to 47th by the end of 2015. In the Transparency International Corruption Perception index, the Philippines rose from the 134th to the 95th spot on the list of 175 most corrupt countries worldwide (see table 11.1). In 2014, the European Chamber of Commerce president stated that "intensified integrity and less corruption in the Philippines" had led to "a clean and level playing field for all." At the end of 2015, the leaders of the influential Makati Business Club also praised the president for having "walked his talk."[13]

Yet, to many, this was only "modest progress," with the picture slightly grayer than what Aquino's political and business allies painted.[14] Mark Thompson observed that while he sent his opponents to jail, "Aquino has

Table 11.1. Philippine Corruption Rank
(out of 175 countries covered in 2015 Corruption Perceptions by Transparency International)*

Year	Rank (out of 175 countries)	Index (100 points)
2006	121	25
2007	131	25
2008	141	23
2009	139	24
2010	134	24
2011	129	26
2012	105	34
2013	94	36
2014	84	38
2015	95	35

Source: "Philippine Corruption Rank, 1995–2016," http://www.tradingeconomics.com/philippines/corruption-rank (accessed May 4, 2016).

*According to Transparency International's Corruption Perceptions, "a country or territory's rank indicates its position relative to the other countries and territories in the index." The "latest reported value for - Philippines Corruption Rank - plus previous releases, historical high and low, short-term forecast and long-term prediction, economic calendar, survey consensus, and news. Philippines Corruption Rank—actual data, historical chart, and calendar of releases—was last updated on May of 2016." *Source*: "Philippine Corruption Rank, 1995–2016." At the other end, a country or territory's score indicates the perceived level of public sector corruption on a scale of 0 (highly corrupt) to 100 (very clean). . . . The "latest reported value for - Philippines Corruption Index - plus previous releases, historical high and low, short-term forecast and long-term prediction, economic calendar, survey consensus, and news. Philippines Corruption Index—actual data, historical chart, and calendar of releases—was last updated on May of 2016." *Source*: Transparency International, "Philippine Corruption Rank, 1995–2016," http://www.tradingeconomics.com/philippines/corruption-rank (last accessed May 4, 2016).

been accused of shielding his allies in Congress by limiting the Commission on Audit (COA) investigations of the scandal to before he took office in 2010."[15] He also refused demands to prosecute some members of his cabinet.[16] The COA reported that Agriculture Secretary Proceso Alcala allegedly squandered "more than P14.4 billion in questionable projects" together with a provincial governor who had been sentenced to ten years by the anti-graft court.[17] Alcala is a member of Aquino's Liberal Party.[18]

Despite Aquino's reformist campaigns, the darker features of the political process prevailed. The Senate remained under the control of the opposition after Ferdinand Marcos Jr.; the dictator's former defense secretary, Juan Ponce Enrile; and coup plotter Gregorio Honasan were reelected in the 2009 midterm elections.[19] The House of Representatives also continued to be the domain of political dynasties. The list of families that lost the congressional elections in 2010 was far shorter than those of clans whose representatives have held on to their seats for a long time. Their "years of unbroken rule" and "cumulative years in power" ranged from twelve to eighteen years. This was replicated at the city and provincial level, where clans whose rise to power could be traced back to 1986; the families that preceded them had also kept a tight control over their localities.[20] Political families even took advantage of the party-list system to circumvent term limits. The most notorious example was the creation by the son of Mrs. Arroyo of a fictitious party representing "security guards, tricycle drivers, farmers and small businessmen" with an eye on a seat in the House of Representatives.[21] Ang Galing Pinoy (The Filipino Talent) did not last long; it was disqualified by the Commission on Elections (Comelec) two years after it was "formed" because it was unable "to meet the requirements for representing marginalized sectors in the House of Representatives."[22]

Ominous members of these clans also graced the House of Representatives—former First Lady Imelda Marcos; Luis "Chavit" Singson, one of the longest-living warlords in the country; Singson's son Ronald, who was languishing for a while in a Hong Kong prison after being caught with illegal drugs until his father rescued him; Romeo Jalosjos, a congressman who was convicted for rape and pardoned by Mrs. Arroyo; and Ruben Ecleo Jr., a cult leader found guilty for strangling his wife and dumping her body in a black garbage bag.[23]

Nothing changed in 2013. That year, according to Clarissa David, "there were 80 gubernatorial races. In 50 percent of those local elections the candidates for governor were all members of political dynasties, the race was dynast versus dynast. Another 11 percent of races were uncontested, only a political dynast was running. A shocking 61 percent of governorships in the country were locked in a dynastic trap."[24] In another essay, David, with coauthor E. F. Legara, wrote:

> With each election, more provinces end up ruled by dynasties. These families in provinces grow to occupy many more offices than in the previous election. From 2004 to 2013, the average dynasty share grew from 0.30 to 0.44, representing a 47 percent increase. Dynasties have taken root and grown since 2004 in much of Northern Luzon, Ilocos Norte, Cagayan, Apayao, and Isabela. The whole island of Samar starts out with a slight dynasty presence and ends up being occupied by a deeply entrenched set of families. Then of course there is the southwest—Maguindanao, Lanao del Sur, and Sulu.[25]

This "anarchy of families" persists as the defining locus of politics even in the Age of Aquino III.[26] The president may be a reformist at heart but, like his predecessors, he had to make peace and establish a working relationship with the clans. Once Aquino signaled his intentions, the families reciprocated by switching their allegiance to the new president. A few months after Aquino was sworn in, twenty-four representatives had joined his Liberal Party and supported his candidate for House speaker.[27] The incentive to switch parties was quite straightforward: Like the past president, Aquino had the executive office's rich trove of discretionary funds to offer to them. The same pattern also became immediately visible with the regime that followed Aquino's.

Pork as Governance

In 1922, as Filipinos had practically taken over colonial governance, the National Assembly passed the Public Works Act (Republic Act 3044), otherwise described by a columnist as the "first pork legislation."[28] Sixty-nine years later, President Corazon Aquino gave it its first formal name, the Countrywide Development Fund (CDF), and when Joseph Estrada became president he called it the Priority Development Assistance Fund (PDAF). The fund's role was to add on to a legislator's annual development allocation (P70 million for a congressman and P200 million for a senator), and as of 2014, PDAF had reached more than P27 billion pesos—"more than ten times the original amount of P2.3 billion in 1990."[29] The Office of the President also has its own President's Social Fund (PSF), which started at P1 billion but had risen to P5 billion under Aquino. Both funds are part of the national budget, and are supplemented by revenues coming from such agencies as the Philippine Gaming and Amusement Board (Pagcor), a state-owned gambling facility, and the state's share of the Malampaya Natural Gas Facility, a joint venture with two multinational oil companies in the South China Sea.[30]

These bountiful resources gave the presidency the tremendous leeway and institutional heft to win over, divide, or neutralize the legislature. They are the carrot at the end of a stick that would compel the Senate and the House of Representatives to compromise with the executive in order to pass laws or act over a resolution in unison (see box 11.1). When Mrs. Arroyo was facing impeachment charges and congressional investigations over alleged corrupt practices, for example, she increased the release of funds for "soft" and "hard" projects to a total of P79.88 billion (an average of P26.63 billion) between 2007 and 2009, and reportedly released an additional P69.92 billion in infrastructure funds to the Department of Public Works and Highways (DPWH). She then handed over P900 million to the Department of Agrarian reform and P2 billion to the Philippine National Police.[31] These monies stymied the investigations as they gave Mrs. Arroyo the edge: She "could choose who and how much to give each congressman or senator who explains why some have more than others in the [Commission on Audit] report."[32]

Box 11.1. The Regressive Effects of Pork

"The pork barrel system upsets the power-separation arrangement and distorts the presidential system in at least 3 ways. First, the power of the purse belongs to Congress as an institution. It does not belong to its members. What this power means is that only Congress can decide how public money is to be allocated. It does not, in any way, include giving House [of] Representatives members and senators the authority to use public money for purposes other than lawmaking.

"Second, the pork barrel system undermines the independence of both the Executive and Legislative branches because it promotes collusion and bends the principle of power separation. In this system, the Executive practically offers the Legislature money by way of the inclusion of the PDAF in its proposed budget. This offer itself speaks volumes because both branches very well know that administering development projects is outside the Legislature's mandate. The Legislature's acceptance of said offer by way of approving the inclusion of the PDAF in the General Appropriations Act (GAA) cements the collusion.

"Third, the pork barrel system creates a conflict-of-interest situation and compromises the oversight function of Congress. Oversight entails impartial and objective scrutiny of administrative performance. Obviously, Congress cannot exercise oversight on itself. There is something intrinsically wrong with a Congress approving allocation/giving money to itself for work that it is not mandated to perform. This practice might even be illegal under the 1987 Constitution which is very categorical on the separation of powers between the executive and the legislative branches."

—Carmel V. Abao, "Why Rationalize Bad Practice? Abolish Pork Barrel," *Rappler*, August 17, 2013, updated July 11, 2014, http://www.rappler.com/thought-leaders/36635-abolish-pork-barrel (accessed April 7, 2016).

It was not only inevitable that this largesse would be turned into a target object of plunder. In 1996, the *Philippine Daily Inquirer* ran an exposé on the extensive corruption surrounding the disbursement and expenditure of the CDF based on the testimonies of a whistleblower that detailed how "huge sums of government money . . . regularly went into the pockets of legislators in the form of kickbacks." The whistleblower was the late Congressman Romeo C. Candazo, who revealed that kickbacks were "SOP [standard operating procedure] among legislators and ranged from a low 19 percent to a high 52 percent of the cost of each project, which could be anything from dredging, rip rapping, asphalting, concreting and construction of school buildings."[33] Funds intended for medicines and textbooks were also stolen with impunity.

On August 28, 2013, Janet Lim Napoles, the alleged mastermind of the PDAF scam, surrendered to President Aquino and was charged, along with her husband, for the crimes of tax evasion and plunder.[34] The National Bureau of Investigation (NBI) and the Department of Justice (DoJ) also filed plunder charges against Senators Ramon Revilla Jr., Juan Ponce Enrile, Jinggoy Estrada, and five members of the House of Representatives for stealing

Table 11.2. Legislators Identified as Collaborators in the Napoles PDAF Scam

Legislator	Chamber	Amount Exposed (Pesos)
Ramon Revilla Jr.	Senate	P1.015 billion
Juan Ponce Enrile	Senate	641.65 million
Jinggoy Estrada	Senate	585 million
Rizalina Seachon-Lanete	House of Representatives (Masbate)	137.29 million
Ferdinand Marcos Jr.	Senate	100 million
Conrado Estrella III	House of Representatives (Abono Party-list)	97 million
Edgar L. Valdez	House of Representatives (Association of Philippine Electric Cooperatives Party-list)	85 million
Rodolfo Plaza	House of Representatives (Agusan del Sur)	81.5 million
Erwin Chiongbian	House of Representatives (Sarangani Province)	65.35 million
Samuel Dangwa	House of Representatives (Benguet Province)	62 million
Robert Raymund Estrella	House of Representatives (Abono Party-list)	41 million
Gregorio Honasan	Senate	15 million
Total		2.928 billion

Source: https://en.wikipedia.org/wiki/Priority_Development_Assistance_Fund_scam (accessed April 9 2016).

P2.928 billion from the national treasury with Napoles' collaboration (see table 11.2). The Philippine National Police (PNP) arrested Enrile, Estrada, and Revilla. Enrile was later granted bail for "health reasons," but once out was suddenly "revived" to renew his role as the head of the opposition bloc in the Senate. Revilla and Estrada have remained in jail. At the same time, the Supreme Court ruled that the PDAF was unconstitutional, thereby ending this rich source of spoils and shutting out everyone—if only temporarily—from continuously tapping into the funds.[35]

Isles of State Efficiency?

Aquino did make good his promise to improve government performance, and some state agencies and offices responded well. In July 2015, an MBC survey listed the top ten best-performing government agencies based on a "satisfactory rating" (see table 11.3). While it is possible that the ranking reflects the bias of the organization conducting the survey, it remains the case that these best-performing state agencies are associated with the economy. There is general consensus that the Philippines had undergone a remarkable turnaround in the last years of the Arroyo regime and throughout the term of

Table 11.3. Makati Business Club's Top Government Agencies (second semester 2015)

Rank/Year			Percentage Rating		
2014	*2015*	*Government Agency*	*Net Score*	*Satisfactory*	*Net Satisfactory*
1	1	Bangko Sentral ng Pilipinas	90.8	95.4	4.6
3	2	Philippine Economic Zone Authority	84.4	92.2	7.8
2	3	Department of Tourism	81.8	90.9	9.1
6	4	Department of Foreign Affairs	78.8	89.4	10.6
4	4	PAGASA	78.8	89.4	10.6
9	6	Department of Finance	72.7	86.4	13.6
18	7	Department of Trade and Industry	69.7	84.8	15.2
5	8	Securities and Exchange Commission	69.2	84.6	15.4
20	9	Board of Investments	68.3	84.1	15.9
19	10	Civil Service Commission	61.3	80.6	19.5

Source: BSP Best Performer in Gov't; OVP Worst—MBC Poll," *Rappler*, August 13, 2015, http://www.rappler.com/business/211-governance/102488-bsp-tops-makati-business-club-survey (accessed August 14, 2015).

Aquino. These notable agencies were associated with the economy, the only bright feature in the Philippines under Aquino as well as during the last years of Mrs. Arroyo's government. The value placed on them by the business elite was also consistent with how other social forces in the past interacted with similar state agencies. In contrast, the least-admired state agencies were those concerned with domestic affairs, and which spent a lot of government largesse to implement public projects.

The Bureau of Customs (BoC) was another state agency that showed a remarkable transformation from being a haven of corrupt practices into an islet of transparency and exemplary performance (see table 11.4). Aquino proudly pointed out that under new leadership it had made an earnest and serious effort to raise revenues by putting a stop to tax evasion. In late 2010 the BoC and the Bureau of Internal Revenue (BIR) filed cases of tax evasion and smuggling against twenty-six individuals.[36] In turn, the BoC showed that the reforms were working when cases against individual officials were successfully prosecuted: Gloria Kintanar, a businesswoman who sold consumer products,

Table 11.4. Makati Business Club's Least-Regarded Government Agencies (second semester 2015)

Rank/Year			Percentage Rating		
2014	*2015*	*Government Agency*	*Net Score*	*Satisfactory*	*Net Satisfactory*
46	55	Court of Appeals	−27.0	36.5	63.5
50	56	Department of Agrarian Reform	−32.2	33.9	66.1
58	57	Lower Court System	−35.5	32.3	67.7
NA	58	Metropolitan Waterworks and Sewerage System	−40.6	29.7	70.3
57	59	Philippine National Police	−41.0	29.5	70.5
NA	60	Energy Regulatory Commission	−42.4	26.8	71.2
60	61	Department of Agriculture	−46.7	26.7	73.3
55	62	Bureau of Customs	−55.6	22.2	77.8
55	63	Department of Transportation and Communications	−61.9	19.0	81.0
33	64	Office of the Vice President	−76.3	11.9	88.1

Source: BSP Best Performer in Gov't; OVP Worst—MBC poll," *Rappler*, August 14, 2015, http://www .rappler.com/business/211-governance/102488-bsp-tops-makati-business-club-survey (accessed August 14, 2015).

was sentenced to four years in prison for tax evasion. Heavy fines reaching P6 million were leveled at Rogelio Tan, proprietor of a parking management company; and business partners Angelito Reyes and Efren del Rosario, who owned a trading company and distributed welding equipment, were found guilty of tax evasion and made to pay P6.7 million.[37] By 2013, there were 140 cases of tax evasion, and the government was hoping to get back P44.27 billion from these tax evaders. Some 121 of these cases, however, were "pending in the Department of Justice," while 17 had been decided upon by the lower courts, with those charged challenging the decisions at the Court of Appeals. In Aquino's last year in office, the number of prosecutions had risen to 450.[38]

Opprobrium over the incompetence of the Aquino-appointed head of the Department of Transportation and Communications (DoTC) had become universal, especially after trains in the deteriorating Metro Rail Transit (MRT) system began to break down nearly every day. Manila was voted the "worst city to drive on Earth" by users of a road navigation application, and in April 2016, a five-hour power outage hit the "modern international terminal" of Manila's airport complex.[39] Aquino, however, refused to fire DoTC chief Joseph Emilio Abaya, insisting that—in the words of an ally—the latter "has done his best given the situation he is in."[40] The pressure would have an effect on the government for one reason: Abaya was the acting president of Aquino's Liberal Party, and it was unlikely that Aquino would abandon his "good soldier."[41]

Another close Aquino ally, Department of Social Welfare and Development (DSWD) secretary Corazon Soliman was also blamed for failing to explain to the COA the unliquidated P5.6 billion in conditional cash transfer (CCT) programs funds and P2.7 million worth of wasted food intended for victims of Typhoon Haiyan.[42] Soliman defended herself well against these accusations, bolstered by a firm refusal by Aquino to have her alleged incompetence investigated.[43]

Economic Asymmetries

The upbeat economic news during Aquino's presidency signaled that the gloom left by his predecessor was over. The gross domestic product (GDP) shot up from 1.1 percent in 2009 to a high 7.6 percent at the start of Aquino's term. This was the highest the GDP had risen since the 6.6 percent record of 2007, thanks mainly to high election spending, strong export earnings, and the $10.6-billion remittances of overseas Filipino workers (OFWs), up from $706 million in 2009. This did not last, however, and the GDP dropped down to 3.7 percent in 2011, but rose again to 7.2 percent in 2013, before settling down to 6.0 percent in 2014–2015. As of July 2016, the GDP had rebounded

Table 11.5.   Annual GDP Growth Rate, Philippines, 2001–2012

Year	GDP Growth Rate (%)
2001	2.9
2002	3.6
2003	5.0
2004	6.7
2005	4.8
2006	5.2
2007	6.6
2008	4.2
2009	1.1
2010	7.6
2011	3.9
2012	6.6
2013	7.2
2014	6.0
2015	6.6
2016 (July)	7.0

Source: "Trading Economics: Philippines GDP Annual Growth Rate," http://www.tradingeconomics.com/philippines/gdp-growth-annual (last accessed October 30, 2016).

back to 7.0 percent (see table 11.5).[44] All in all, throughout the Aquino years, GDP growth averaged 6.2 percent annually. The early surge had not been enough for the Philippines' credit rating and investment-grade ratings to rise and stabilize the economy. In 2013, when the GDP rose to 7.1 percent, the country became a lender and committed $1 billion to the International Monetary Fund (IMF) to help stabilize the European economies.[45] As foreign investments grew ($5.7 billion by late 2014, a 63 percent rise since 2013), pundits and businessmen were bullish that the country now stood on "strong economic record."[46]

Finally, unemployment and underemployment had also remarkably decreased since Aquino started his term. According to economist Emmanuel de Dios, "the average number of people who were either unemployed or underemployed [has gone down] by 170,000 than in 2014," while "the overall rate of labour underutilization (unemployed plus underemployed as a percentage of the labour force) has fallen from 24.6% in 2010 to 23% (in 2015)."[47] Thus, when he ended his term, the World Bank country director proudly declared that "[t]he Philippines is no longer the sick man of East Asia but the rising tiger."[48] In 2016, the World Economic Forum report upgraded the Philippines' "competitiveness" ranking from 85th in 2010–2011 to 47th in 2015–2016.[49]

Aquino's boast of presiding over the extraordinary turnaround of the economy had not gone unchallenged. Mrs. Arroyo reminded Filipinos that it was under her stewardship that the country had witnessed economic growth. In an essay that she wrote from her place of detention, she argued that when she ended her presidency in June 2010, she "was able to turn over to the next Administration a new Philippines with a 7.9 percent growth rate." She added:

> [G]rowth rate capped 38 quarters of uninterrupted economic growth despite escalating global oil and food prices, two world recessions, Central and West Asian wars, mega-storms and virulent global epidemics. Our country had just weathered with flying colors the worst planet-wide economic downturn since the Great Depression of 1930. As two-thirds of the world's economies contracted, we were one of the few that managed positive growth.[50]

Mrs. Arroyo's argument was sustained by the National Statistical Coordination Board (NSCB) report that hers was "the best average economic performance among [the presidents] that completed their respective terms."[51] She assailed her successor's "divisive politics," hinting that it had something to do with the decline of the growth rate to 3.9 percent by the end of 2011. Viewed from this particular time period, Mrs. Arroyo was on the mark in her analysis. The economy, however, rebounded in 2012 (6.6 percent), and this time Aquino could claim the reversal as a result of his own policies. Mrs. Arroyo's criticism fell by the wayside, although the arguments her essay raised continued to provide her supporters the economic figures with which to assail Aquino.[52]

The illicit sector remained a problem.[53] Global Financial Integrity (GFI), the American anti-graft watchdog, reported that in a span of fifty-two years (1960–2011), more than $277.6 billion entered the country illegally, while $132.9 billion was moved out. In a narrower time frame, the movement of money to and from the Philippines rose from $14.2 billion in 2009 to $22.9 billion in 2010 and a "record high" of $25.8 billion in 2011.[54] In the first ten years of the twenty-first century, the GFI report added, "25 percent of the value of all goods imported into the Philippines—or 1 out of every 4 dollars—goes unreported to customs officials." The government had "at least $19.3 billion since 1990 in tax revenue due to customs duties evasion through under-invoicing alone. Combined with an additional $3.7 billion in tax revenue lost through export underpricing, [the] government has lost at least $23 billion in customs revenue due to trade mis-invoicing since 1990."[55] This problem only became worse under Aquino (see table 11.6).[56]

The question, then, is whether these parallel growths had made an impact on the lives of Filipinos. The *Atlantic Monthly* has observed warily that "economic growth only looks great on paper." Jilliam Keenan notes:

> The slums of Manila and Cebu are as bleak as they always were, and on the ground, average Filipinos aren't feeling so optimistic. The economic boom

Table 11.6. Smuggling Estimates, 2005–2014 (US$B)

Year	Bureau of Customs Import Reports	Exporting Countries Import Reports (10% Freight/Insurance Cost Discounted)	Discrepancy (Smuggling Estimates)	Percentage of Smuggled Imports, according to Reporting Countries
2005	47.4	47.4	−0.1	−0.1
2006	51.5	52.7	1.2	2.2
2007	55.5	59.8	4.3	7.3
2008	60.4	67.8	7.4	10.9
2009	45.9	53.8	7.9	14.7
2010	60.2	71.8	11.6	16.1
2011	66.2	80.5	14.3	17.8
2012	67.9	87.4	19.6	23.4
2013	68.0	90.4	22.3	24.7
2014	71.0	97.6	26.6	27.3
Total 2010–2014	333.3	427.6	94.4	22.1

Source: Rigoberto Tiglao, "Smuggling Utterly out of Control under Aquino Regime: P4 Trillion in Last Five Years," *The Manila Times*, August 25, 2015, http://www.manilatimes.net/smuggling-utterly-out-of-control-under-aquino-regime-p4-trillion-in-last-five-years/212920/ (last accessed May 9, 2016).*

*Tiglao drew from the International Monetary Fund's Direction of Trade Statistics and the Department of Trade.

appears to have only benefited a tiny minority of elite families; meanwhile, a huge segment of citizens remain vulnerable to poverty, malnutrition, and other grim development indicators that belie the country's apparent growth. Despite the stated goal of President Aquino's Philippine Development Plan to oversee a period of "inclusive growth," income inequality in the Philippines continues to stand out.[57]

Growth had, instead, further widened the income gap. The rich had tripled their incomes from P630 billion in 2010 to P2.2 trillion in 2015—a 250 percent increase—as they consolidated or expanded their control of the banking, telecommunications, and property development sectors.[58] Within this small group of privileged Filipinos, presidential cronies are a fairly substantial presence, comprising 11.9 percent of the 14.7 percent of billionaires' wealth as per the GDP in 2014, and 11.3 percent of the 14.2 percent of billionaires' wealth that is part of the GDP in 2016. The Philippines occupied the fifth place in *The Economist*'s crony-capitalism global index in 2014, then rose to third, below Russia and Malaysia, in 2016.[59] In 2013, there were eleven Filipinos who were on the *Forbes* Billionaires List; in 2016, there were fourteen (see table 11.7).

At the other end, the poorest 20 percent of Filipinos own "less than 5 percent of the country's total income."[60] *The Economist*'s Intelligence Unit

Table 11.7. Filipinos on *Forbes* 2013 and 2016 Lists of World Billionaires (in billions of dollars)

Rank	Billionaire/Family	2010	2011	2012	2013	2016
68	Henry Sy and family	4.2	5.8	8	13.2	
248	Lucio Tan and family	1.7	2.3	3.5	5	4*
270	John Gokongwei, Jr.	—	—	—	—	5.1
345	Andrew Tan	1.2	2.2	2.1	3.95	3.1*
503	David Consunji and family	—	—	—	2.8	3.2*
554	George Ty and family	—	—	—	2.6	3.8*
722	Enrique Razon Jr.	—	—	—	—	2.5
736	Lucio and Susan Co	—	—	—	2	
931	Roberto Coyiuto Jr.	—	—	—	1.6	1.59*
1121	Lucio and Susan Tan	—	—	—	—	1.63
1031	Tony Tan Caktiong and family	—	—	—	1.4	3.2*
1367	Manuel Villar	—	—	—	—	1.33
1175	Andrew Gotianum and family	—	—	—	1.2	
1175	Roberto Ongpin	—	—	—	1.2	

*Tan went down to 380; George Ty rose to 421; David Consunji went down to 569; Andrew Tan went down to 569; Tony Tan Caktiong rose to 569; and Roberto Coyiuto Jr. went down to 1121.

Sources: "11 Filipinos among World Billionaires," *Rappler*, October 10, 2013, http://www.rappler.com/business/23058-11-filipinos-among-world- billionaires (accessed May 14, 2016); and Rosette Adel, "11 Filipinos Return to Forbes 2016 World Billionaire List," *PhilStar Global*, March 2, 2016, http://www.philstar.com/business/2016/03/02/1558717/11-filipinos-return-forbes-2016-world-billionaire-list (accessed 14 May 2016).

warned that the country "remain[s] marked by wide inequalities of income, and the disparity between the richest and the poorest will stay particularly acute." It concludes that "large numbers of Filipinos will continue to live in poverty."[61] Another way to discern the tremendous negative impact of this growing inequality would be in terms of the capacity to purchase commodities for a family's needs. Jose Ramon G. Albert and Arturo Martinez Jr. cite a 2014 study on family expenditures, which found that "[a]bout half (51 percent) of households that started in extreme (expenditure) poverty in 2003 moved up the expenditure ladder (in 2009), but 77 percent of households that started non-poor moved down the expenditure distribution."[62]

Neither has the middle class really grown. According to two economists at the Philippine Institute of Development Studies (PIDS): "Examining the 2006 and 2009 [Family Income and Expenditure Statistics], we find that the relative size of the middle class to all households slightly declined in 2009 to 15.8 percent [from 16.2 percent in 2006], and increased to 16.7 percent as of 2012. We find marginal changes in the relative sizes of the other income groups across the period 2006, 2009, and 2012." They concluded that these were "not statistically significant."[63] In short, there had been no dramatic movement in the middle- and lower-income groups.

When he assumed the presidency, Aquino promised to reduce poverty. His first measure was to expand the coverage of the CCT program begun by his predecessor. The CCT was a World Bank (WB) antipoverty project in which the government transfers money to a poor family so that they could avail themselves of social welfare services like medical checkups and vaccinations, and give their children access to public education.[64] The CCT funds are sourced from "sin taxes" (i.e., taxes on tobacco and alcohol) and thus hardly dent other sources of revenue needed by the national budget.[65] Four years into his term, Aquino announced that the CCT had cut poverty incidence from 27.9 percent in 2012 to 24.9 percent.[66] By 2016, the number of CCT beneficiaries rose from 786,523 in June 2010 to 4,377,562 million in December 2015.[67]

The WB backed up Aquino, attributing the success to the fact that 83 percent of the funds under its Pantawid Pamilyang Pilipino program (PPP, or Bridging Program for the Filipino Family) had reached out to 4.5 million households, up from 360,000 in 2008. This represented 40 percent of the poor and the vulnerable. The poverty rate, however, inched up to 25.8 percent in 2014 after a super typhoon hit the country, but had since remained unchanged. The final shape of the long-term impact of the CCT program,

---

Box 11.2. The Impact of CCT on the Philippine Poor

"'The CCT grants, on average, only account for about 11 percent of the income of the poorest recipient households,'" said World Bank Country Director Motoo Konishi. "'Yet, for poor and vulnerable households the grants are very important. Two rounds of rigorous impact evaluation show that they use the money to buy food, school uniforms and school supplies for their children.'

"The impact evaluation studies, according to Konishi, also show that CCT is delivering on its objectives: keeping poor children in school and healthy:

"Enrollment among poor elementary school children increased by 5 percentage points, while secondary education enrollment increased by 7 percentage points.

"The program increased prenatal and postnatal care by 10 percentage points and increased the delivery of babies in health facilities by skilled health professionals by 20 percentage points.

"Children benefited by receiving higher intake of vitamin A and iron supplementation by around 12 percentage points and by increased weight monitoring visits to health facilities by 18 percentage points."

—The World Bank. "Philippines: CCT Proven to Keep Poor Children Healthy and in School—World Bank," September 23, 2015, http://www.worldbank.org/en/news/press-release/2015/09/23/philippines-cct-proven-to-keep-poor-children-healthy-and-in-school (last accessed 28 April 2016).

however, is still not discernible as one looks at the horizon. In fact, problems persist: According to reports, 11.4 million Filipinos still considered themselves poor in the first quarter of 2015, and 7.9 million Filipinos described themselves as "food-poor."[68]

POLITICS AND ENDGAMES

Three major political controversies during Aquino's term somehow reflected the contradictory nature of his presidency. First, Congress finally passed a reproductive health (RH) law that now allows the government to provide free contraceptives, enables people to get reproductive health care from state hospitals, and instructs public schools to teach sex education.[69] The "RH bill" was first introduced in 1999 by a group of legislators from diverse backgrounds and of varying political positions, backed by academics, noncommunist left-wing parties, and women's groups. The Catholic Church put up a fervent and successful opposition to the bill and its subsequent revisions, with the backing of conservative political leaders in the legislature.[70]

The bill did not move forward until President Aquino's election and the assumption to the position of House Speaker by a pro–RH bill congressman. This time, the bill passed despite opposition from Aquino's very own allies in the Liberal Party who joined forces with the Catholic Church. On December 12, 2012, the lower assembly's version of the bill passed, with 133 ayes and 79 nays. The Senate voted on a similar version of the bill with thirteen senators voting yes and eight no, and a week later Aquino signed the Responsible Parenthood and Reproductive Health Act of 2012 (or Republic Act 10354) into law.[71] Outside the legislative building, civil society groups and women's associations kept the pressure on recalcitrant legislators and helped defend their allies in both houses.[72] Opponents continued to engage in delaying tactics to prevent the law's implementation by appealing to the Supreme Court, and when this failed, they limited the allocation of government funds for the programs.[73] The resistance, however, was futile.

Aquino achieved only partial success with the second issue: the quest for lasting peace in war-torn Muslim Mindanao. Once he took over as president, the Moro Islamic Liberation Front (MILF) immediately agreed to return to the negotiating table, and signaled that armed separatism was over.[74] Aquino's peace panel and the MILF went back to the drawing board and came up with "The Framework Agreement on the Bangsamoro," which both parties signed on October 15, 2012. These consisted of several "annexes" that addressed issues including the nature of the new autonomous body, its jurisdictions and relationship with the national government, and revenue and wealth sharing.

There was also an annex that outlined the disarming and demobilization process of the MILF.[75] This was a substantive agreement that has earned praise from national security scholars and the active support of Brunei, Indonesia, Japan, Malaysia, and the United States.[76]

The agreement, which was renamed the Bangsamoro Basic Law (BBL), was introduced as two separate but similar bills to the House of Representatives and the Senate. It was already facing opposition during the plenary debates in the lower house committee hearings in the Senate, when tragedy struck a police force in a Mindanao village. On January 25, 2015, a seventy-three-man Philippine National Police Special Action Force (PNP SAF) raided the village of Tukanalipao in Mamapasano town, Maguindanao province, to capture a Malaysian terrorist and bomb maker who had been given refuge by the Bangsamoro Islamic Freedom Fighters (BIFF). Oplan (Operation Plan) Exodus failed: The raiders killed Zulkifli Abdhir but found themselves clashing with a superior combined group of MILF, BIFF, and private militias operating in the area. The daylong battle led to the deaths of forty-four SAF members, eighteen MILF guerrillas, and five BIFF terrorists, and only an agreement between the MILF and army commanders of the area allowed for an extraction team to rescue the survivors.[77]

The "mis-encounter," as the government initially called it, was the most serious loss in the short history of the SAF, and caused widespread resentment among the ranks. Aquino did not help allay the anger when he preferred to visit a newly opened Japanese car assembly plant instead of being at the airport when the bodies of the slain policemen were flown in. Public outrage heightened when congressional investigations discovered that the local military commanders had not been informed of Oplan Exodus and were only belatedly brought into the picture after news of the battles filtered in. The hearings also validated criticism that the president relied more on friendship rather than professional advice when making critical decisions (PNP chief Alan Purisima was a close friend), which, in turn exacerbated the interorganizational tensions between the police and the military.[78]

As a result, the president's popularity ratings dropped 21 points, with the biggest dip in Mindanao and among the poor—the lowest since he became president in 2010.[79] His net satisfaction rating bounced back by a high 173 percent on the eve of his June 2015 State of the Nation address to Congress, and then went down again by +37 percent by the end of the year.[80] In April 2016, his net satisfaction was "downgraded" further to +27 percent from a December 2015 high of +32 percent.[81]

The most serious consequence of the Mamapasano massacre, however, was the suspension of the congressional hearings on the Bangsamoro Basic Law and the de facto failure of the government-MILF peace agreement. The chief MILF negotiator, Mohagher Iqbal, cited the anti-Muslim sentiments of many legislators and the prejudice of many Filipinos toward the MILF and Muslims in general as important factors in the derailment of the BBL. It was, however, the Mamapasano tragedy that was "almost the singular incident that spelled the disaster for the BBL."[82]

Civil society forces remained hopeful that once the furor blew over, Congress would go back to the business of approving BBL.[83] It was all false optimism. At the end of 2015, attention had shifted to the coming presidential elections. Aquino had also bounced back from his lowest grade, after Mamapasano, rising to a 49 percent rating in March 2015. His performance rating fell to 38 percent in November 2015, but rose to 52 percent by March 2016.[84] A series of international travels kept him out of the limelight, while the public shifted its attention to the charges of corruption leveled by the justice department on Vice President Binay and his family.[85]

On May 9, 2016, the Philippines held national elections, with the Comelec reporting that voter turnout was at 84 percent—7 percent higher than in the 2010 national election. Three days later, Rodrigo R. Duterte, mayor of Davao City in southern Philippines, had already received 38.5 percent of votes (15,878,662) cast in 95.65 percent of all precincts. Aquino's heir apparent, former Local Government Secretary Manuel Roxas II, lagged behind by six million votes. Analysts traced this to an electorate that had become "sick and tired of empty promises by mainstream politicians," and which has come to mistrust whatever government claimed, even if the information were true.[86]

Aquino, the national and world business communities, the WB and the IMF, and economists repeatedly claimed how much the country's economy had grown, but Filipinos experienced only slow incremental change in their incomes. The optimism that *The Economist* saw in the rise in incomes ($2,373 in 2011 to $2,873 in 2014) did not resonate with those working in the trenches.[87] Meanwhile, everyone continued to witness more families, including the Marcoses, getting richer. Government and multilateral agencies maintained that corruption in public works projects had diminished considerably, leading to more robust infrastructure development across the country. But citizens only saw breakdown everywhere: from the repeated disrepair of the MRT in the nation's capital, to the incompetent patchwork repairs of the country's ramshackle airports and run-down road networks. The promise to increase jobs that could lure back overseas Filipino workers had some potential, but only in the last months of Aquino's presidency.[88] Finally, Filipinos regarded Aquino as an honest leader, but their esteem did not extend to his senior officials, congressional allies, and business associates.

The fusion of these contradictions was Benigno Aquino III's legacy. The question, then, was whether the impious Duterte could break this impasse.

NOTES

1. Amando Doronila, "A Gracious Political Act," *Philippine Daily Inquirer*, May 11, 2010, http://opinion.inquirer.net/inquireropinion/view/20100511-269481/A -gracious-political-act (last accessed April 6, 2016).

2. Conrado de Quiros, "The Longer View," *Philippine Daily Inquirer*, March 29, 2012, http://opinion.inquirer.net/25809/the-longer-view (last accessed April 5, 2016).

3. Office of the President, Republic of the Philippines, "Executive Order No. 1, s. 2010, creating the Philippine Truth Commission of 2010," July 30, 2010, http://www.gov.ph/2010/07/30/executive-order-no-1-s-2010/ (last accessed May 14, 2016).

4. Renato Cruz de Castro, "The Philippines in 2011: Muddling Through a Year of Learning and Adjustment, *Asian Survey* 52, no. 1 (January/February 2012): 212.

5. "Merceditas Gutierrez Resigns as Ombudsman," *The Economist*, 31 May 2011, http://country.eiu.com/article.aspx?articleid=1628143747&Country=Philippi nes&topic=Politics&subtopic=Recent+developments&subsubtopic=The+political+ scene:+Merceditas+Gutierrez+resigns+as+ombudsman (last accessed April 7, 2016).

6. Twenty senators convicted Corona while three voted to acquit. See "Corona Found Guilty, Removed from Office," *Rappler*, May 29, 2012, http://www.rappler .com/nation/special-coverage/corona-trial/6099-corona-found-guilty (last accessed April 7, 2016).

7. Glenda Gloria, Aries Rufo, and Gemma Bagayaua-Mendoza, *The Enemy Within: An Inside Story On Military Corruption* (Quezon City: Public Trust Media Group, 2011): 144.

8. Gil C. Cabacungan, Jeannette I. Andrade, and Miko Morelos, "Gloria Arroyo Now under Arrest," *Philippine Daily Inquirer*, November 19, 2011, http://newsinfo .inquirer.net/96621/gloria-arroyo-now-under-arrest (last accessed April 7, 2016).

9. Floyd Whaley, "Philippines Ex-President Is Arrested in Hospital on New Charges," *New York Times*, October 4, 2012, http://www.nytimes.com/2012/10/05/ world/asia/philippines-ex-president-arrested-in-hospital-on-new-charges.html (last accessed April 7, 2016). This time Arroyo had to stay in a military hospital due to her condition, and cannot post bail because plunder is a non-bailable offense in the Philippines. See Barnaby Lo, "Philippines' Ex-Leader Arroyo Arrested, Again," *CBS News*, October 4, 2012, http://www.cbsnews.com/news/philippines-ex-leader-arroyo -arrested-again/ (last accessed April 7, 2016).

10. Johanna Camille Sisante, "Arroyo Wins Congress Seat in Pampanga," *GMA News Online*, May 12, 2010, http://www.gmanetwork.com/news/story/190811/news/ regions/arroyo-wins-congress-seat-in-pampanga (last accessed April 7, 2016). On her 2013 campaign see Barbara Mae Dacanay, "Marcos and Arroyo Win in Philippine Polls," *Gulf News Philippines*, May 14, 2013, http://gulfnews.com/news/asia/philip- pines/marcos-and-arroyo-win-in-philippine-polls-1.1183219 (last accessed April 7, 2016).

11. Jan Escosio, "No Cellphones, No Internet for Arroyo at Veteran's Hospi- tal Suite," *Philippine Daily Inquirer*, December 2, 2011, http://newsinfo.inquirer

.net/104293/no-cellphones-no-internet-for-arroyo-at-veterans-hospital-suite (last accessed April 9, 2016).

12. Nathan Gilbert Quimpo, "Can the Philippines' Wild Oligarchy Be Tamed?" in *Routledge Handbook of Southeast Asian Democratization*, ed. William Case (Oxon and New York, 2015): 345.

13. Danessa O. Rivera, "PHL Ranking in Global Corruption Perception Good for Business," *GMA News Online*, December 3, 2014, http://www.gmanetwork.com/news/story/390891/money/economy/phl-ranking-in-global-corruption-perception-good-for-business (last accessed May 5, 2016); and "Noy's Fight vs. Corruption Marks Modest Progress," *Philstar Global*, November 15, 2015, http://www.philstar.com/headlines/2015/11/15/1521970/noys-fight-vs-corruption-marks-modest-progress (last accessed May 9, 2016).

14. Oliver Teves, "Philippine Leader's Corruption Fight Marks Modest Progress," *CNS News*, November 14, 2015, http://www.cnsnews.com/news/article/philippine-leaders-corruption-fight-marks-modest-progress (last accessed May 9, 2016).

15. Mark R. Thompson, "Aquino's Reformism Hits a Dead End," *East Asia Forum*, September 30, 2014, http://www.eastasiaforum.org/2014/09/30/aquinos-reformism-hits-a-dead-end/ (last accessed April 4, 2016). His spokesperson either denied the bias, or promised to go against the president's allies. This was, however, quietly shelved as the country's attention shifted to the next crisis. "Palace: We Aren't Protecting Allies in Pork Scam," *Rappler*, May 17, 2014, http://www.rappler.com/nation/58256-palace-pork-barrel-allies (last accessed April 9, 2016).

16. Hannah L. Torregoza and Charissa M. Luci, "Senators, UNA Assail DOJ Decision to Set Aside 3rd Batch of Pork, Malampaya Charges," *Manila Bulletin* 1, May 2015, http://www.mb.com.ph/senators-una-assail-doj-decision-to-set-aside-3rd-batch-of-pork-malampaya-charges/ (last accessed April 9, 2016).

17. Marlon Ramos, "Department of Agriculture Squandered P14-B—COA," *Philippine Daily Inquirer*, April 22, 2015, http://newsinfo.inquirer.net/686964/department-of-agriculture-squandered-p14b-coa (last accessed May 8, 2016).

18. Randy K. Ortega, "Beleaguered Honrado Not Resigning," *Politiko*, 9 May 2016, http://politics.com.ph/beleaguered-honrado-not-resigning/ (last accessed May 8, 2016).

19. Douglas Bakshian, "Philippine Opposition Wins 6 of 10 Senate Seats in Mid-Term Election," *Voice of America* 1, November 2009, http://m.voanews.com/a/a-13-2007-06-voa28/348200.html (last accessed April 4, 2016).

20. Steven Rood, "Families, Not Political Parties Still Reign in the Philippines," *In Asia: Weekly Insights and Analysis* 22, May 2013, http://asiafoundation.org/in-asia/2013/05/22/families-not-political-parties-still-reign-in-the-philippines/ (last accessed April 7, 2016).

21. Fat Reyes, "Galing Pinoy," *Philippine Daily Inquirer*, October 30, 2012, http://newsinfo.inquirer.net/298524/comelec-disqualifies-mikey-arroyos-ang-galing-pinoy (last accessed April 7, 2016).

22. Reyes, "Galing Pinoy."

23. Supreme Court of the Republic of the Philippines, "People of the Philippines, plaintiff-appellee vs. Romeo G. Jalosjos, accused-appellant, Decision on

Criminal Case No. 96-1985," http://sc.judiciary.gov.ph/jurisprudence/2001/nov2001/132875_76.htm (last accessed April 7, 2016); Freddie G. Lazaro, "Singsons Preserve Political Mastery in Ilocos Sur," *Balita*, May 13, 2010, http://balita.ph/2010/05/13/singsons-preserve-political-mastery-in-ilocos-sur/ (last accessed March 12, 2016); Momar Visaya, "Rep. Ronald Singson: On Struggles and Second Chances," *Asian Journal*, February 7, 2015, http://asianjournal.com/immigration/rep-ronald-singson-on-struggles-and-second-chances/ (last accessed April 7, 2016); and Charisse Ursal, "Court Finds Rep. Ecleo Guilty of Killing Wife," *Philippine Daily Inquirer*, April 14, 2012, http://newsinfo.inquirer.net/176219/court-finds-rep-ecleo-guilty-of-killing-wife (last accessed April 7, 2016).

24. Clarissa David, "Limiting Political Dynasties Will Help the Poor," *Rappler*, August 19, 2015, http://www.rappler.com/thought-leaders/103088-limiting-political-dynasties- help-poor (last accessed April 8, 2016).

25. Clarissa C. David and E. F. Legara, "How Much of Our Country Will We Lose to Political Dynasties in 2016," *Rappler*, October 20, 2016, http://www.rappler.com/thought-leaders/109892-how-much-country-lose-political-dynasties-2016 (last accessed April 5, 2016).

26. The phrase "an anarchy of families" comes from the book of the same title. See Alfred W. McCoy, *An Anarchy of Families: State and Family in the Philippines* (Madison: University of Wisconsin Press, Center for Southeast Asian Studies, 1993).

27. Jess Diaz, "24 House Members Join Noy's Liberal Party," *Philstar Global*, June 26, 2010, http://www.philstar.com/headlines/587462/24-house-members-join-noys-liberal-party (last accessed April 7, 2016). The new speaker, Feliciano Belmonte, also announced that another twenty more congressmen will switch parties.

28. Static Marvin A. Tort, Opinion: "Time to End a Century of Pork," *Business World Online*, August 6, 2013, http://www.bworldonline.com/content.php?section=Opinion&title=Time-to-end-a-century-of-pork&id=74531 (last accessed April 7, 2016).

29. Tort, "Time to End a Century of Pork."

30. Amelyn Veloso, "Malampaya Fund (Part 1): Limits to Use of Multibillion Earnings," *CNN Philippines*, June 11, 2015; "Malampaya Fund (Part 2): Does It Exist Only on Paper?" *CNN Philippines*, June 5, 2015, http://cnnphilippines.com/investigative/2015/06/04/Malampaya-Fund-Part-2-Does-it-exist-only-on-paper.html (last accessed April 8, 2016); and "Malampaya Fund (Part 3): Is Government Losing Out on Deal?" *CNN Philippines*, June 5, 2015, http://cnnphilippines.com/investigative/2015/06/05/Malampaya-Fund-Part-3-Is-government-losing-out-on-deal.html (last accessed April 8, 2016). President Corazon Aquino signed the Service Contract 38 (SC38) on behalf of the government in 1990, which lay the foundation for the Malampaya Deep Water Gas-to-Power Project.

31. Jess Diaz, "Noy's Social Fund to Get P5B from Pagcor," *Philstar Global*, September 1, 2013, http://www.philstar.com/headlines/2013/09/01/1156851/noys-social-fund-get-p5-b-pagcor (last accessed April 7, 2016).

32. Gil C. Cabacungan, "Arroyo Chose Who, How Much PDAF to Give," *Philippine Daily Inquirer*, August 22, 2013, http://newsinfo.inquirer.net/471659/arroyo-chose-who-how-much-pdaf-to-give (last accessed April 8, 2016).

33. Leila Salaverria and Inquirer Research, "Candazo, First Whistle-Blower on Pork Barrel Scam, Dies; 61," *Philippine Daily Inquirer*, August 20, 2013, http://newsinfo.inquirer.net/469439/candazo-first-whistle-blower-on-pork-barrel-scam-dies-61 (last accessed April 5, 2016).

34. "Tax Evasion Case vs. Napoles, Husband," *Rappler*, September 26, 2103, http://www.rappler.com/nation/39875-tax-evasion-case-vs-napoles-husband (last accessed April 9, 2016).

35. Camille Diola, "SC Declares PDAF Unconstitutional," *Philstar Global*, November 19, 2013, http://www.philstar.com/headlines/2013/11/19/1258492/sc-declares-pdaf-unconstitutional (last accessed April 9, 2016).

36. "Aquino Prepares 26 Cases against Tax Evaders," *Philstar Global*, September 17, 2010, http://www.philstar.com/breaking-news/612557/aquino-prepares-26-cases-against-tax-evaders (last accessed April 9, 2016).

37. Rosemarie Francisco and Stuart Grudgings, "For Philippines Leader, It's War on Graft, Tax Evasion," *Reuters*, July 3, 2012, http://www.reuters.com/article/us-philippines-economy-aquino-idUSBRE86207320120703 (last accessed April 9, 2016).

38. "Tax Evasion Cases under Aquino Reach 140," *Rappler*, January 6, 2013, http://www.rappler.com/business/19226-tax-evasion-cases-under-aquino-reach-140 (last accessed April 10, 2016); and Katrina Mennen A. Valdez, "BIR Bags 2 More Convictions against Tax Evaders," *Interaksyon*, July 3, 2012, http://interaksyon.com/business/36437/bir-bags-2-more-convictions-against-tax-evaders (last accessed April 10, 2016). Of the 121 cases, 2 were dismissed.

39. "Editorial: Just Fire Him Already, Please," *Interaksyon*, April 7, 2016, http://interaksyon.com/article/126142/editorial—just-fire-him-already-please (last accessed May 9, 2016); Raul Dancel, "Manila's Messy Rapid Transit," *Singapore Strait Times*, August 8, 2015, http://www.straitstimes.com/opinion/manilas-messy-rapid-transit (last accessed May 9, 2016); "Philippines: Manila Voted Worst City to Drive on Earth," *BBC News*, October 2, 2015, http://www.bbc.com/news/blogs-news-from-elsewhere-34424367 (last accessed May 9, 2016); and Michael Bueza, "Power Outage Hits NAIA Terminal 3," *Rappler*, April 2, 2016, http://www.rappler.com/nation/128023-power-outage-naia-terminal-3 (last accessed May 9, 2016).

40. Gil Cabacungan, Miguel Camus, and Jerry E. Esplanada, "LP: Aquino, Party Backs DOTC Chief," *Philippine Daily Inquirer*, January 8, 2016, http://newsinfo.inquirer.net/753547/abaya-stays-amid-quit-calls (last accessed May 9, 2016).

41. Abaya was a graduate of West Point Academy. Carmela Fonbuena, "Jun Abaya: 'A Good Soldier,'" *Rappler*, September 19, 2012, http://www.rappler.com/nation/11522-jun-abaya-a-good-soldier (last accessed May 4, 2016); and Jarius Bondoc, "Abaya Caught in 3 Rail Controversies," *PhilStar Global*, September 11, 2015, http://www.philstar.com/opinion/2015/09/11/1498471/abaya-caught-3-rail-controversies (last accessed May 4, 2016).

42. Aries Joseph Hegina, "All the President's Men: 5 Officials Defended by Aquino," *Philippine Daily Inquirer*, September 12, 2014, http://newsinfo.inquirer.net/637569/all-the-presidents-men-5-officials-defended-by-aquino (last accessed May 9, 2016).

43. Aries Joseph Hegina, "Only P200M, Not P5B of CCT Funds Are Unliquidated by Philpost—DWSD, *Philippine Daily Inquirer*, September 3, 2014, http://newsinfo.inquirer.net/635115/only-p200-m-not-p5b-cct-funds-are-unliquidated-by -philpost-dswd (last accessed May 9, 2016); and Julie M. Aurelio, "Soliman: COA Report Didn't Have DSWCD Side," *Philippine Daily Inquirer*, December 27, 2014, http://newsinfo.inquirer.net/659657/everything-is-accounted-for-says-soliman (last accessed May 9, 2016).

44. Republic of the Philippines, "Achievements of the Aquino Administration, 2010–2016," http://www.gov.ph/featured/daang-matuwid/ (last accessed May 14, 2016).

45. Renato Cruz de Castro, "The Philippines in 2012: 'Easygoing, Do-Nothing' President Delivers," *Asian Survey* 53, no. 1 (January/February 2013): 112.

46. Laura Southgate, "The Legacy of Philippines [*sic*] President Benigno Aquino," *Global Risk Insights*, August 25, 2015, http://globalriskinsights.com/2015/08/the -legacy-of-philippines-president-benigno-aquino/ (last accessed March 31, 2016).

47. Emmanuel de Dios, "Dear Ben . . ." *Per Se*, July 24, 2015, http://www.econ .upd.edu.ph/perse/?p=4775 (last accessed June 21, 2016).

48. Edith Regalado and Aurea Calica, "Philippines Is Asia's Rising Tiger— World Bank," *PhilStar Global*, February 6, 2013, http://www.philstar.com/head lines/2013/02/06/905371/philippines-asias-rising-tiger-world-bank (last accessed May 14, 2016).

49. "Achievements of the Aquino Administration, 2010–2016."

50. Gloria Macapagal Arroyo, "Arroyo to Aquino: It's the Economy, Student!" *Rappler*, January 13, 2012, http://www.rappler.com/thought-leaders/829-arroyo-to -aquino-it-s-the-economy,-student (last accessed May 19, 2016).

51. Riza T. Olchondra, "Arroyo Has Best Growth in Full Term, Aquino Tops 1st Year Growth among Presidents," *Philippine Daily Inquirer*, January 28, 2013, http://business.inquirer.net/104813/arroyo-has-best-growth-in-full-term-aquino-tops-1st -year-growth-among-presidents-nscb (last accessed May 19, 2016).

52. Tony Lopez, "Economic Growth under Aquino," *The Standard*, February 3, 2016, http://www.thestandard.com.ph/opinion/columns/virtual-reality-by-tony -lopez/198354/economic-growth-under-aquino.html (last accessed May 19, 2016).

53. Alfred W. McCoy, *Policing America's Empire: The United States, the Philippines, and the Rise of the Surveillance State* (Madison: University of Wisconsin Press, 2009), 15–58.

54. Patrick Temple-West, "Smuggling, Fraud Cost Philippines $25.8 Billion in 2011, Study Says," *Reuters*, February 4, 2014, http://www.reuters.com/article/us -philippines-fraud-study-idUSBREA130DY20140204 (last accessed May 4, 2016).

55. Dev Kar and Brian LeBlanc, "Illicit Financial Flows to and from the Philippines: A Study in Dynamic Simulation, 1960–2011," Global Finance Integrity, February 2014, http://iff.gfintegrity.org/iff2013/Illicit_Financial_Flows_from _Developing_Countries_2002-2011-HighRes.pdf (last accessed May 14, 2016).

56. Rigoberto Tiglao, "Smuggling Utterly out of Control under Aquino Regime: P4 Trillion in Last Five Years," *Manila Times*, August 25, 2015, http://www .manilatimes.net/smuggling-utterly-out-of-control-under-aquino-regime-p4-trillion -in-last-five-years/212920/ (last accessed May 9, 2016).

57. Jilliam Keenan, "The Grim Reality behind the Philippines' Economic Growth," *Atlantic Monthly*, May 7, 2013, http://www.theatlantic.com/international/archive/2013/05/the-grim-reality-behind-the-philippines-economic-growth/275597/ (last accessed May 14, 2015).

58. "Poor miss out on Philippines' economic ascent while rich get richer," *South China Morning Post*, March 5, 2013, http://www.scmp.com/news/asia/article/1177297/poor-miss-out-philippines-economic-ascent-while-rich-get-richer (last accessed February 13, 2017).

59. "Our Crony-Capitalism Index: The Party Winds Down," *The Economist*, May 7, 2016, http://www.economist.com/news/international/21698239-across-world-politically-connected-tycoons-are-feeling-squeeze-party-winds (last accessed May 12, 2016).

60. Kabiling and Chacez, *Manila Bulletin*, August 5, 2015.

61. "Philippines: An Outlook for Key Emerging Asian Markets," *The Economist Intelligence Unit*, July 2015, 8, http://www.eiu.com/ (last accessed June 12, 2015).

62. Jose Ramon G. Albert and Arturo Martinez Jr., "Are Poverty and Inequality Changing?" *Rappler*, February 25, 2015, http://www.rappler.com/thought-leaders/84833-poverty-inequality-data (last accessed May 9, 2015).

63. Jose Ramon Albert, Raymond Gaspar, and M. J. Raymundo, "How Big Is the Middle Class? Is It Benefiting from Economic Growth?" *Rappler*, June 24, 2015, http://www.rappler.com/thought-leaders/97243-middle-class-economic-growth-philippines (last accessed July 7, 2015).

64. The World Bank, "Conditional Cash Transfers," http://web.worldbank.org/WBSITE/EXTERNAL/TOPICS/EXTSOCIALPROTECTION/EXTSAFETYNETS ANDTRANSFERS/0,,contentMDK:20615138~menuPK:282766~pagePK:148956~p iPK:216618~theSitePK:282761,00.html (last accessed April 1, 2015).

65. Eunju Kim and Jayoung Yoo, "Conditional Cash Transfer in the Philippines: How to Overcome Institutional Constraints for Implementing Social Protection," *Asia and Pacific Policy Studies* 2, no. 1, 2015: 79–82. If one were to include the sin tax, the overall budget did balloon to "almost 52 times larger (at P62.32 billion) when it first started in 2008" (P1.2 billion). See Kristine Angeli Sabillo, "Philippine Poverty after Five Years on Aquino's Watch," *Philippine Daily Inquirer*, July 26, 2015, http://newsinfo.inquirer.net/707857/philippine-poverty-after-five-years-on-aquinos-watch (last accessed March 7, 2015).

66. Ben O. de Vera, "Poverty Incidence Worsened in 2014: Gov't Blames Higher Food Prices, 'Yolanda' Impact," *Philippine Daily Inquirer*, March 5, 2015, http://business.inquirer.net/188011/poverty-incidence-worsened-in-2014 (last accessed March 7, 2015).

67. "Achievements of the Aquino Administration, 2010–2016."

68. Rafael Antonio, "11.4M Families Remain Poor, SWS Poll," *Philippine Daily Inquirer*, May 6, 2015, http://newsinfo.inquirer.net/689515/11-4m-families-remain-poor-sws-poll (last accessed May 11, 2015).

69. Carmela Fonbuena, "RH Law: The Long and Rough Road," *Rappler*, January 2, 2013, http://www.rappler.com/newsbreak/18730-rh-law-the-long-and-rough-road (last accessed May 1, 2015), and Karen Boncocan, "Aquino Signed

RH Bill into Law," *Philippine Daily Inquirer*, December 28, 2012, http://newsinfo
.inquirer.net/331395/gonzales-aquino-signed-rh-bill-into-law (last accessed May
1, 2015).

70. Carolina S. Ruiz Austria, "The Church, the State and Women's Bodies in the
Context of Religious Fundamentalism in the Philippines," *Reproductive Health Matters* 12, no. 24 (November 2004): 96–103.

71. Carmela Fonbuena, "RH Law: The Long and Rough Road."

72. Sharmila Parmanand, "Mapping the Paths to Philippine Reproductive Rights
Legislation: Signs of Progress amidst Obstacles," *Social Transformations* 2, no.1
(February 2014): 61–80.

73. Floyd Whaley, "Philippine Court Delays Law on Free Contraceptives for
Poor," *New York Times*, March 19, 2013, http://www.nytimes.com/2013/03/20/
world/asia/philippine-court-delays-free-contraceptives-law.html (last accessed May
12, 2016); and Marvin Sy, "Senators Slam RH Budget Cut," *PhilStar Global*, January
9, 2016, http://www.philstar.com/headlines/2016/01/09/1540764/senators-slam-rh
-budget-cut (last accessed May 12, 2016).

74. International Crisis Group, "The Philippines: The Collapse of Peace in Mindanao," *Asia Briefing* No. 83 (October 23, 2008): 2–15; International Crisis Group,
"The Philippines: Running in Place in Mindanao," *Asia Briefing* No. 88 (February
16, 2009): 1–9.

75. *Official Gazette*, "Document: The Draft Bangsamoro Basic Law: House Bill
No. 5811, Submitted to the Ad Hoc Committee on May 27, 2015, http://www.gov.
ph/2014/09/10/document-the-draft-bangsamoro-basic-law/ (last accessed May 13, 2016).

76. See, for example, the comments of Professor Zachary Abuza, "Philippines
2016: Governance, Growth, Development and Security, P1," https://www.youtube
.com/watch?v=b3-oj-_X_e4 (last accessed May 14, 2016).

77. "Timeline: Mamapasano Clash," *Rappler*, February 23, 2015, http://www
.rappler.com/nation/82827-timeline-mamasapano-clash (last accessed May 14, 2016).

78. Bea Cupin, "President Aquino and the Ghosts of Mamapasano," *Rappler*,
September 19, 2015, http://www.rappler.com/newsbreak/in-depth/106243-aquino
-truth-saf-mamasapano (last accessed May 14, 2016).

79. Carmela Fonbuena, "Aquino's Ratings Drop to Lowest since 2010," *Rappler*,
October 10, 2014, http://www.rappler.com/nation/63239-aquino-lowest-ratings (last
accessed May 14, 2016).

80. Camille Elemia, "Aquino Bounces Back, Net Satisfaction Rating Up 173%,"
Rappler, June 24, 2015, http://www.rappler.com/nation/96846-aquino-sws-satisfaction
-rating-high-june (last accessed May 15, 2016); and "Aquino Admin's Net Satisfaction
Rating Rises to 'Good' + 37 – SWS," *Rappler*, October 13, 2015, http://www.rappler
.com/nation/129887-sws-survey-aquino-public-satisfaction-q1-2016 (last accessed
May 16, 2016).

81. K. D. Suarez, "Aquino Net Satisfaction Rating Lowest since 2015—Poll,"
Rappler, April 18, 2016, http://www.rappler.com/nation/129887-sws-survey-aquino
-public-satisfaction-q1-2016 (last accessed May 14, 2016).

82. Albert F. Arcilla, "Revisiting Mamapasano: A Disaster for the BBL," *Business World Online*, January 24, 2016, http://www.bworldonline.com/content.php?s

ection=Nation&title=revisiting-mamasapano-a-disaster-for-the-bbl&id=122002 (last accessed May 12, 2016).

83. Teresa Jopson, "Making Peace with the Bangsamoro Basic Law," *East Asia Forum*, May 11, 2016, http://www.eastasiaforum.org/2016/05/11/making-peace -with-the-bangsamoro-basic-law/ (last accessed May 12, 2016).

84. Pulse Asia, "Trust Ratings of President Benigno S. Aquino III, October 2015 to March 2016," Philippines, April 2016.

85. In 2015, four months after Mamapasano, Aquino went to Malaysia (April 26–28), the United States and Canada (May 6–9), Japan (June 2–5), Malaysia (November 20–22), and France, Italy, and the Vatican (November 29–December 4). In 2016 he visited the United States again February 15–17). On Binay's corruption, see Chay F. Hofileña, "VP Binay Liable for Graft and Corruption—COA," *Rappler*, March 10, 2016, http://www.rappler.com/nation/125289-vp-binay-liable-graft-corruption-coa (last accessed May 14, 2016); and Anna Estanislao, "More Corruption Allegations vs. VP Binay," *CNN Philippines*, August 26, 2015, http://cnnphilippines .com/news/2015/08/26/More-corruption-allegations-vs-VP-Binay.html (last accessed May 14, 2016).

86. Argylll Cyrus B. Geducos, "Voter Turnout for 2016 Polls Is 84% Says Comelec," *Manila Bulletin*, May 10, 2016, http://www.mb.com.ph/voter-turnout-for -2016-polls-is-84-says-comelec/ (last accessed May 14, 2016). Duterte's victory was unusual because while he won overwhelmingly in only three regions, the votes in his favor in other provinces were high enough for him to win. Miriam Grace A. Go, "Despite Huge Margins, Duterte Sweeps Only 3 Regions," *Rappler*, May 12, 2016, http://www.rappler.com/nation/politics/elections/2016/132728-regional-winners -presidential-election (last accessed May 14, 2016).

87. "The Philippines: Fist of Iron," *The Economist,* 14 May 2016, http://www economist.com/news/briefing/21698684-new-strongman-president-may-prevent -philippines-becoming-economic-star-fist?cid1=cust%2Fednew%2Ft%2Fbl%2Fn%2 F20160512n%2Fowned%2Fn%2Fn%2Fnwl%2Fn%2Fn%2FNA%2Fn (last accessed May 16, 2016).

88. Floyd Whaley, "Rodrigo Duterte and Other Candidates Seeking to Lead Philippines Tap into Aquino Fatigue," *New York Times*, April 19, 2016, http://www .nytimes.com/2016/04/20/world/asia/philippines-presidential-election.html?smid=fb -nytimes&smtyp=cur&_r=0 (last accessed May 14, 2016).

Chapter Twelve

Neo-Authoritarianism?

THE LOCAL CAPTURES THE NATIONAL

This chapter is a brief overview of the first seven months of the presidency of Rodrigo Duterte. We suggest that Duterte represents a distillation of the major features of over one hundred years of state and society relationship, dating back to when the United States began to turn over colonial governance to Filipino leaders after the 1907 elections, to the Philippine Commonwealth, to today's "cacique democracy."[1] The observations we make here are provisional, given that by the time this new edition is published, President Duterte will just have completed his first year in office. However, we do believe there is ample evidence to make some assertions with confidence and offer them to readers for consideration.

Populism and the Violent Local Strongman

Julio Teehankee and Mark Thompson described Duterte's victory as "a major rupture in the liberal-democratic regime reestablished thirty years ago after the 'people power' revolution against the dictatorship of Ferdinand Marcos." They added that "Duterte brought to the national stage the vulgarity long characteristic of local political campaigning in the Philippines."[2] This description of the sixteenth president of the republic is only partly correct. While basic elements of liberal democracy are apparent—a free press, the ritual of elections, a political opposition—at its core, the Philippines political system is still the oligarchy that rose out of the ashes of the 1986 People Power Revolution. Oligarchs and their families still control the legislature and the provincial and city governments, and all the heads of states have come from one family or another. The Philippines never had a liberal-democratic regime.

Table 12.1.   The Dutertes Rule Davao

Duterte in Office	Position	Term
Rodrigo	Officer-in-charge, Davao City	May 2, 1986–November 27, 1987
	Mayor	February 2, 1988–March 19, 1998
	Member, House of Representatives	June 30, 1998–June 30, 2001
	Mayor	June 30, 2001–June 30, 2010
	Vice Mayor	June 30, 2010–June 30, 2013
	Mayor	June 30, 2013–June 30, 2016
Sara (eldest daughter)	Vice Mayor	June 30, 2007–June 30, 2010
	Mayor	June 30, 2010–June 30, 2013
	Mayor	June 30, 2016–present
Paolo (eldest son)	Vice Mayor	June 30, 2016–present

Duterte was cut in the mold of the provincial clans and strongmen. His family was one of three that ruled Davao for most of the second half of the twentieth century, adjusting seamlessly to the change in politics during the Marcos dictatorship and when constitutional democracy was restored in 1986, shifting political fidelities with very little effort and ingratiating itself to the new regime. In May 1986, President Corazon Aquino appointed Duterte as Davao City's officer-in-charge, and since then he and his family have not relinquished control over Davao City (see table 12.1). He boasts of the twenty-three years he served the city as mayor, but his extended reign was the result of Duterte and his children performing political musical chairs (Duterte was vice mayor to his daughter in 2010–2013).

Provincial clans like the Dutertes outlasted national leaders advocating for a centralized, stronger state, communists who wanted to overthrow the state, and popular forces that wanted to reform it. In fact, in the first quarter of the twenty-first century, dynasties continued to grow, with new ones emerging in the northern provinces of Luzon Island, and dominating the island of Samar in the central Philippines and the southwest part of Mindanao island (see table 12.2).[3] Some were offshoots of older clans while others were families who had come to rule provinces that no family dominated before. This trend, warned Ronald U. Mendoza and Miann Banaag, "signals a complete deterioration of inclusiveness in our democratic leadership selection—only the moneyed and those with the correct last name appear to enjoy the entitlement of leadership."[4]

Duterte is not only just another strongman from a provincial clan. He is also the legatee of a populist strain of this oligarchic system that emerges during periods of intense political crisis.[5] Three past heads of state were associated

Table 12.2. Dynastic Share of Elected Positions, 2007–2017 (percentage)

Positions	2007	2010	2013	2016
Governor	69.6	82.3	86.3	81.3
Percentage increase/decrease		12.7	3.97	−5
Vice Governor	62	70.9	75	81
Percentage increase/decrease		8.87	4.11	6.01
House of Representatives	75.3	78.7	75.3	77.5
Percentage increase/decrease		3.44	−3.46	2.25
Mayor	57.6	67.2	67.5	68.8
Percentage increase/decrease		9.6	0.3	1.3
Vice Mayor	40.6	51.2	52.6	56.9
Percentage increase/decrease		10.6	1.4	4.3

Source: Ronald U. Mendoza and Miann Banaag, "Under Decentralization: More Ampatuans Than Robredos," *Rappler*, November 26, 2016, http://www.rappler.com/thought-leaders/153682-decentralization-political-dynasties-ampatuan-robredo (last accessed November 27, 2016).

with this strain—Ramon Magsaysay, Corazon Aquino, and Joseph Estrada. In the 1950s, the threat of a communist offensive on Manila, and popular fears that corruption had reached alarming levels, prompted middle-class professional associations, church organizations, reformist politicians, and the U.S. Central Intelligence Agency to "sponsor" Magsaysay. This coalition used his war record as a World War II guerrilla fighter and his "humble" family background to market Magsaysay as the "people's president." He won handily against his opponent, Elpidio Quirino, who had been successfully tarred by this coalition as a corrupt incumbent. Thirty-three years later, Aquino led the "People Power Revolution" that ousted the Marcos dictatorship and sent the dying Marcos to exile in Hawaii. A coalition similar to Magsaysay's, consisting of old patronage politicians, professional groups, left-wing organizations, the business elites, and the Catholic Church backed up Aquino.

Estrada's populism was cut from a different cloth. The former movie star, city mayor, senator, and vice president was backed by local provincial and city officials, a segment of the illicit sector, and the lower classes and marginalized minorities who were inspired by his last-action-hero movies where he played the ill-educated but lovable corner thug who beat up opponents and won the (rich) woman's love. The elite, middle classes, and national politicians were on the other side of the barricades and opposed Estrada right at the onset. They were finally able to oust Estrada after a year in office, with the military leadership's help. Duterte tapped the same lower-class support as Estrada, but he did so by also portraying himself as the savior who will end criminality and corruption "in the name of the people." He also promised to continue the economic reforms his predecessors had started, promising an end to poverty and inequality.[6]

For a society where "all politics is local," his victory took this mantra a notch higher. This time the local had become national. Duterte repeatedly reminded critics that he tolerated people "call[ing] me names" when he was only a mere mayor, but they now had to tread water when attacking him, for "these dimwits forgot that I'm now a President and I represent a country."[7] This is a twenty-first-century version of the slogan "*l'etat c'est moi*" ("the State, it is I"), albeit expressed in the crude argot of local politics. He also brought to the palace the idiosyncrasies of local politics, many of which are anathema to the "proper" way of acting presidential.[8] He introduced the "[c] oarse language and outrageous statements" of local politics into the national arena, which politicians who assume national office are often reticent to express in public.[9] His crass "provincial mindset" displaced presidential urbanity, and he appropriated "respectable" symbols of the national office and personalized these in the way that strongmen have turned state offices into their private demesne.

What gives Duterte the heft he needs is the large percentage of Filipinos who believe that society needs to be cleansed of a drug scourge that has been destroying their communities. They have also accepted his claims of being anti-elite, pro-people, and even an anti-American socialist.[10] They identify with his portrait of the mayor from an island long neglected by Manila, and a leader who shares in the anti-elite and anti-American "politics of anger" of the poor.[11] Duterte has skillfully sustained this popular resentment against elites and criminals by repeatedly backing up his street-gutter bluster with the public shaming of political opponents and the use of deadly extra-constitutional measures. In another essay written on the eve of the elections, Teehankee and Thompson called then-candidate Duterte's rise as "potentially the *most serious crisis of Philippine democracy* since 'people power' overthrew the Marcos dictatorship 30 years ago." They warned of the dire consequences of the Davao mayor's "threats to implement the Davao model nationwide, killing criminals without asking questions and pushing aside democratic institutions and due process if they stand in the way."[12]

This prediction turned out to be prescient. Once elected, Duterte gave the Philippine National Police (PNP) carte blanche to go after and kill drug lords, pushers, and addicts. He vowed to kill a million addicts if need be, in the same way that Adolf Hitler killed millions of Jews.[13] He saw no reason why this campaign would not succeed: If he were able to nearly eliminate the drug problem in Davao City where he and his family ruled for twenty-three years, he could achieve a similar feat as president.[14] Duterte promised the police that he would protect them even from legal action, and police doubled their campaign. The extra-judicial killings proceeded in earnest, and by December 14, 2016, six months after Duterte was sworn in as president, 6,095 suspected drug addicts and pushers had already been killed by police special assassination teams and vigilantes.[15]

Duterte has ingratiated himself to the Armed Forces of the Philippines (AFP) by visiting its camps frequently, something his predecessors rarely did.[16] Most of his major speeches have been delivered in front of soldiers, and these included promises to extend to them the best the state could offer them and their families. He likewise gave the military the same promise he gave the police if it was sued for human rights violations. Glenda Gloria observed that his "speeches masterfully wove in the official and the personal as he addressed them both as their commander-in-chief and their caring, doting father."[17] Conspiracy theorists see these visits as groundwork for replacing the constitutional system with a more autocratic one, but others describe these visits as Duterte's way to win the hearts and minds of an institution whose personnel "have guns. . . . They're authorized to have guns which [are] tremendous power, coercive power."[18]

Adding to his popular support was the force of the electoral coalition behind Duterte. This alliance brought together political forces that on other occasions were fiercely opposed to one another, but agreed to set aside their differences to back a presidential candidate whose victory could be a windfall to their political ambitions. His coalition partners included patronage politicians and strongmen, the Communist Party of the Philippines (CPP), the 1.7 million-strong quasi-cult group *Iglesia ni Kristo* (Church of Christ), families of the late dictator Ferdinand Marcos, former Marcos cronies, Filipino-Chinese capital, and friends and close allies from his hometown Davao City. The usual internal dissensions that unsettled past similar alliances were not there anymore: Radicals and reactionaries have accepted their place at the presidential table and now act as one voice.[19]

There were political forces that supported Duterte not because it suited their political calculations; they joined because they strongly identified with his "principles." Business groups bought into his anti-corruption position and believed that he would eliminate drug-related criminality.[20] The CPP turned a blind eye to the fact that Duterte admired their most despised opponent, President Marcos, justifying its unprecedented political opportunism by pointing out how it shared the president's position against "American imperialism."[21] Under Duterte, the last and largest of the left-wing opposition has been co-opted into the ruling elite. Rounding out the list were supporters of the Marcos family, who saw in Duterte a partisan of a strong state like their late father. This was sufficient enough to agree to be in the same room as the communists. The ruling elite's ideology was thus the mélange of left-wing progressives, conservative entrepreneurs, and traditional politicians—all seeing parts of themselves in Duterte. In today's politics, there are no more "red colors" on the political spectrum, and the centrist "yellows"—forces associated with the 1986 People Power Revolution, have been tarred as representing the old corrupt order that the new president promises to destroy with the help of his legislative allies, the police, and the justice system, as well as the communists.[22]

Finally, there is the economy. Duterte's anti-American rants had weakened the Philippine peso's position vis-à-vis the U.S. dollar, with financial groups predicting that it would decline further in value and go past 50 pesos to one U.S. dollar. Global fund managers regard this as a warning not to "see the peso as a long-term strategic investment." Since August 2016, these managers have pulled over $600 million out of Philippine stocks, especially after Duterte announced he was "separating" the Philippines from the American security umbrella.[23] Overseas Filipino workers (OFWs) are worried, and the World Bank predicted that the Philippines is "likely to see the slowest remittance expansion in the past decade . . . reflecting a decline in overseas workers deployments."[24] Finance officials, however, counterargue that this dip is only a temporary glitch (and some blame "global markets" instead of Duterte for the decline).[25] They contend that the economy continues to expand, especially since OFW remittances will more than compensate for the withdrawal of global investments.[26] Indeed, the economy did grow another 7.1 percent from 2015, exceeding expectations that predicted a growth of only 6.4 percent by September 2016.[27] At the end of the year, the Asian Development Bank revised the projections to show a much higher GDP growth rate: 6.8 percent.[28]

Criticism of Duterte's harsh methods is now universal, with even international pop singers becoming visibly upset by the rise in the numbers of dead people.[29] The president, however, continues to ignore these because of the factors mentioned above. The question, however, is how long can he keep this combination of popular support, police allegiance, a working electoral coalition, and a still steady economy working to his advantage? For, as 2016 closed, foreboding signs have begun to show.

Ominous Future

Rodrigo Duterte has staked his presidency on the destruction of the drug plague. By the end of 2016, the initial signs suggest that his campaign had gained some headway. From July to November 2016, the crime rate had gone down by 31 percent compared to the same period in 2015, but reportage on murders had gone up by 51 percent, from 3,950 to 5,970.[30] Of the latter, 3,841 were "murdered outside police operations" and remain unsolved.[31] Yet, these are victories that reflect a clear class bias and are limited in breadth. The majority of those killed "were not drug lords, but either small-time dealers sell-

Box 12.1. Profile of a Victim of Extra-Judicial Killings: Polydrug User

a. Nature: Polydrug user
b. Mean age: 31 years old
c. Status: 49.13 percent single
d. Gender ratio: 14 men; 1 woman
e. Average monthly family income: $203.53 (P10,172)
f. Status of work: 53.20 percent unemployed
g. Residence: 43.89 percent urban areas
h. Education: 28.34 reached college
i. Extent of drug use: 6 years

—Mikas Matsuzawa and Patricia Viray, "Casualties of Rody's War," *Philippine Star*, September 19, 2016, http://newslab.philstar.com/war-on-drugs/poverty (last accessed December 21, 2016).

ing *shabu* (as methamphetamine is known locally) to raise themselves out of poverty, or light drug users who would occasionally scrape together enough money to buy a sachet of *shabu* to escape the misery of Manila's shanty towns." (see box 12.1).[32] Police and paid assassins have raided urban poor communities, executing "defiant" addicts or pushers. However, when it came to raiding the Golden Ghettos of Manila and middle-class "subdivisions," authorities have not deployed an iron hand. On the contrary, police deferred to leaders of these plush residential areas. No drugs had been "discovered," and no suspected addicts arrested or killed.[33]

Duterte admitted bias but insisted that "given that the poor outnumber the rich, the campaign could not afford to spare the underprivileged from arrests." He blamed the rich for using their immense resources to thwart the police but also excused the rich, saying that their addicts only consume "safe drugs" (cocaine, marijuana, heroin) and not *shabu* (the poor man's cocaine).[34] He waved a "narco list" to journalists, claiming there were 150 politicians, judges, and policemen in the list. By November 2016, only mayors had been assassinated by police, who claimed that these officials resisted arrest.[35] The hit teams have not killed a provincial governor nor a member of the legislature, and the president had only linked one senator with the drug trade. Duterte's charges against Senator Leila de Lima, however, arose from personal vindictiveness—he had never forgiven the senator for investigating the extra-judicial killings in Davao while she was secretary of justice and Duterte was city mayor.[36]

On December 11, 2016, an assassination team barged into the house of Domingo Manosca and killed him and his six-year-old son Francis.[37] The following day, the president bragged: "I killed about three of them . . . I don't know how many bullets from my gun went inside their bodies. It happened, and I cannot lie about it."[38] He received a standing ovation from his audience of business leaders, and the *Reuters* Facebook page had 62,000 views with 327 comments.[39] On December 13, the media reported that the total number of people killed from Duterte's drug war had reached 6,000.[40] Finally, on December 21, the poll group Social Weather Stations released the following responses to a survey of how Filipinos viewed extra-judicial killings. The highlights were as follows:

- 70 percent agreed that the government is serious about solving extra-judicial killings
- 69 percent considered extra-judicial killing a serious problem
- 85 percent were satisfied with administration's campaign against illegal drugs
- 88 percent agreed that the drug problem declined after Duterte assumed office
- 94 percent said that it is important that drug suspects are alive upon capture
- 78 percent worried "that they, or anyone they know, will be a victim of extra-judicial killing"[41]

NOTES

1. Benedict Anderson, "Cacique Democracy in the Philippines," in *The Spectre of Comparison: Nationalism, Southeast Asia and the World* (London and New York: Verso, 1998), 192–226.

2. Julio C. Teehankee and Mark R. Thompson, "The Vote in the Philippines: Electing a Strongman," *Journal of Democracy* 27, no. 4 (October 2016): 125–26.

3. Clarissa David and E. F. Legara, "How Much of Our Country Will We Lose to Political Dynasties in 2016, *Rappler*, October 20, 2015, http://www.rappler.com/thought-leaders/109892-how-much-country-lose-political-dynasties-2016 (last accessed December 19, 2016).

4. Ronald U. Mendoza and Miann Banaag, "Under Decentralization: More Ampatuans Than Robredos," *Rappler*, November 26, 2016, http://www.rappler.com/thought-leaders/153682-decentralization-political-dynasties-ampatuan-robredo (last accessed November 27, 2016).

5. On Duterte's populists origins, see Adrian Chen, "When a Populist Demagogue Takes Power," *The New Yorker*, November 21, 2016, http://www.newyorker.com/magazine/2016/11/21/when-a-populist-demagogue-takes-power (last accessed December 1, 2016).

6. Trisha Macas, "Duterte's Economic Team Reveals 10-Point Socioeconomic Agenda," *GMA News Online*, June 20, 2016, http://www.gmanetwork.com/news/story/570703/money/economy/duterte-s-economic-team-reveals-10-point-socioeconomic-agenda (last accessed December 28, 2016).

7. Marlon Ramos, "Duterte to UN: Stop I Am the President," *Philippine Daily Inquirer*, August 26, 2016, http://newsinfo.inquirer.net/810196/un-broke-protocol-in -issuing-statement-against-killings-duterte (last accessed December 8, 2016).

8. Duterte himself bragged, "My crowd was very limited. I'm a probinsyano. A Hillbilly style that's from the province and, I said, the only guys that I know would really be the Davaoeños." Rodrigo Roa Duterte, "Duterte Transcripts: Wallace Business Forum Dinner, 12 December 2016," *Mindanews*, December 14, 2016, http:// www.mindanews.com/duterte-files/2016/12/duterte-transcripts-wallace-business -forum-dinner-12-dec-2016/ (last accessed December 15, 2016).

9. Teehankee and Thompson, "The Vote in the Philippines: Electing a Strongman," 126.

10. Norman P. Aquino and Chris Blake, "Duterte's U.S. Rants Rooted in Battle against Manila's Elites," *Bloomberg*, November 30, 2016, https://www.bloomberg .com/news/articles/2016-11-30/duterte-s-anti-u-s-rants-rooted-in-battle-against -manila-elite (last accessed December 18, 2016).

11. Julio C. Teehankee and Mark R. Thompson, "Duterte and the Politics of Anger," *East Asia Forum*, May 8, 2016, http://www.eastasiaforum.org/2016/05/08/ duterte-and-the-politics-of-anger-in-the-philippines/ (last accessed December 18, 2016). On Duterte's anti-elitism, see also Carmel V. Abao, "Engaging Duterte, Engaging Ourselves," *Rappler*, November 4, 2016, http://www.rappler.com/thought -leaders/139850-engaging-duterte-engaging-ourselves (last accessed December 18, 2016).

12. Julio C. Teehankee and Mark R. Thompson, "The Neo-Authoritarian Threat in the Philippines," *New Mandala*, April 29, 2016, http://www.newmandala.org/ the-neo-authoritarian-threat-in-the-philippines/ (last accessed December 19, 2016). Thompson penned another version of this piece in another journal. See Mark R. Thompson, "The Specter of Neo-Authoritarianism in the Philippines," *Current History: A Journal of Contemporary World Affairs* 16, no. 782, (September 2016): 220.

13. Lean Daval et al., "Duterte Cites Hitler, Wants to Kill Millions of Addicts," *Al Jazeera*, September 29, 2016, http://www.aljazeera.com/news/2016/09/duterte -cites-hitler-kill-millions-addicts-160930043443768.html (last accessed December 14, 2016).

14. Bruce Alpert, "Philippines' Duterte Promises to Cut Crime, Corruption," *Voice of America*, May 18, 2016, http://learningenglish.voanews.com/a/philippine-duterte -promises-cut-crime-corruption/3334494.html (last accessed October 30, 2016).

15. "Duterte's War on Drugs: The First 6 Months," *Rappler*, 2016, http://www .rappler.com/newsbreak/rich-media/rodrigo-duterte-war-on-drugs-2016 (last accessed December 14, 2016). While 2,102 of these casualties were killed during police operations, 3,993 died through extra-judicial/vigilante-style killing. To underscore the gravity of these killings, the online newsmagazine *Rappler* compared these to Filipinos killed during martial law (3,240 from 1972–1981); those who died in the World Trade Center in 9/11 (2,977); and Thailand's own war on drugs in 2003 (2,500).

16. Pia Ranada, "Duterte's Military Camp Hopping: Way to Soldier's Hearts," *Rappler*, July 31, 2016, http://www.rappler.com/newsbreak/in-depth/141443-duterte -military-camp-hopping-soldiers-loyalty (last accessed December 14, 2016). Even

President Ferdinand Marcos, the first president to appreciate the political value of the military as a prop to his power, did not frequent military camps in the same way Duterte has done.

17. Pia Ranada, "Why Has Duterte Visited 14 Military Camps in Less Than a Month?" *Rappler*, August 20, 2016, http://www.rappler.com/newsbreak/in-depth/143584-duterte-military-camp-visits-analysis (last accessed December 10, 2016).

18. Ranada, "Why Has Duterte Visited 14 Military Camps in Less Than a Month?"

19. Walden Bello, "The Left Under Duterte," *Jacobin*, June 29, 2016, https://www.jacobinmag.com/2016/06/walden-bello-philippines-duterte-dignidad-coalition-akbayan/ (last accessed December 10, 2016); Kristine Felisse Mangunay, "INC Backs Duterte, Marcos," *Philippine Daily Inquirer*, May 5, 2016, http://newsinfo.inquirer.net/783270/inc-backs-duterte-marcos (last accessed December 1, 2016); Paterno Esmaquel II, "Duterte Donor Imee Marcos Not in His SOCE," *Rappler*, October 11, 2016, http://www.rappler.com/nation/politics/elections/2016/148841-duterte-imee-marcos-campaign-contributor-soce (last accessed December 12, 2016); and Michael Bueza, "Who's Who in Duterte's Poll Contributors List," *Rappler*, December 9, 2016, http://www.rappler.com/newsbreak/iq/155060-duterte-contributors-list-2016-presidential-elections (last accessed December 13, 2016).

20. Kenneth Lim, "Duterte Backed by Filipino Businessmen, Warns Corrupt Officials to 'Stop It' and Declares Open Season on Criminals," *Inquisitr*, June 23, 2016, http://www.inquisitr.com/3236008/duterte-backed-by-filipino-businessmen-warns-corrupt-officials-to-stop-it-and-declares-open-season-on-criminals/ (last accessed December 10, 2016).

21. Trevor Moss, "Behind Duterte's Break with the U.S., a Lifetime of Resentment," *Wall Street Journal*, October 21, 2016, http://www.wsj.com/articles/behind-philippine-leaders-break-with-the-u-s-a-lifetime-of-resentment-1477061118 (last accessed December 21, 2016).

22. Trisha Macas, "Duterte to 'Yellows': Reds Will Kill You if You Oust Me," *GMA News Online*, December 14, 2016, http://www.gmanetwork.com/news/story/592393/news/nation/duterte-to-yellows-reds-will-kill-you-if-you-oust-me (last accessed December 19, 2016). See also Leila B. Salavarria, "Duterte: Only the Yellows Are Against Me," *Philippine Daily Inquirer*, December 7, 2016, http://newsinfo.inquirer.net/851635/duterte-only-the-yellows-are-against-me (last accessed December 19, 2016).

23. Lilian Karunungan, "Duterte's Talked the Peso to Its Lowest in Seven Years," *Bloomberg*, November 1, 2016, https://www.bloomberg.com/news/articles/2016-11-01/duterte-seen-talking-peso-beyond-50-level-reached-in-2008-crisis (last accessed December 25, 2016).

24. Ben O. de Vera, "Growth in OFW Remittances in 2016 Seen Slowest in 10 Years," *Philippine Daily Inquirer*, October 8, 2016, https://business.inquirer.net/216240/growth-in-ofw-remittances-in-2016-seen-slowest-in-10-years/ (last accessed December 25, 2016).

25. Giovanni Nilles and Prinz Magtulis, "Rody Not to Blame for Weaker Peso," *Philstar Global*, September 28, 2016, http://www.philstar.com/headlines/2016/09/28/1628223/rody-not-blame-weaker-peso (last accessed December 25, 2016).

26. Dana Sioson, "Duterte's First 100 Days: A Progress Report on the Economy, War on Drugs," *Asia Journal*, October 8, 2016, http://asianjournal.com/news/dutertes-first-100-days-a-progress-report-on-the-economy-war-on-drugs/ (last accessed December 28, 2016).

27. Siegfrid Alegado and Cecila Yap, "Philippines Posts Strongest Economic Growth in Asia," *Bloomberg*, November 16, 2016, https://www.bloomberg.com/news/articles/2016-11-17/philippine-growth-quickens-to-7-1-on-duterte-s-spending-spree (last accessed December 16, 2016).

28. "ADB Upgrades PH Growth Forecast for 2016, 2017," *Rappler*, December 13, 2016, http://www.rappler.com/business/155409-adb-upgrades-philippines-growth-forecast-2016-2017 (last accessed December 21, 2016). The bank attributed this growth to the rise in public and private investments, "partly supported by election-related spending ahead of the national polls in May."

29. "James Taylor Cancels Philippines Concert over Rodrigo Duterte's Drug War Killings," *The Guardian*, December 21, 2016, https://www.theguardian.com/world/2016/dec/21/james-taylor-cancels-philippines-show-rodrigo-duterte-drug-war-killings (last accessed December 25, 2016).

30. "PNP: Crime Rate Down, But Murder Rate Up," *ABS-CBN News*, December 19, 2016, http://news.abs-cbn.com/news/12/19/16/pnp-crime-rate-down-but-murder-rate-up (last accessed December 22, 2016).

31. Kimberly Jane Tan, "More Than 5,800 Killed Amid War on Drugs: PNP," *ABS-CBN News*, December 6, 2016, http://news.abs-cbn.com/news/12/06/16/more-than-5800-killed-amid-war-on-drugs-pnp (last accessed December 23, 2016). See also Daniel Berehulak, "They Are Slaughtering Us Like Animals: Inside President Rodrigo Duterte's Brutal Antidrug Campaign in the Philippines, Our Photojournalist Documented 57 Homicide Victims over 35 Days," *New York Times*, December 7, 2016, http://www.nytimes.com/interactive/2016/12/07/world/asia/rodrigo-duterte-philippines-drugs-killings.html (last accessed December 22, 2016).

32. David Sim, "Is Duterte's War on Drugs Really a War on the Poor?" *International Business Times*, October 14, 2016, http://www.ibtimes.co.uk/dutertes-war-drugs-really-war-poor-graphic-images-1586262 (last accessed December 21, 2016). Sim adds that those who were killed "may not have been involved in drugs at all—they may simply have made a few powerful enemies who wanted them out of the way. Whether they were guilty or not may never be known."

33. Annelle Tayao-Juego, "Cops Unable to Take Antidrug Drive to Rich Makati City Villages," *Philippine Daily Inquirer*, July 22, 2016, http://newsinfo.inquirer.net/798065/cops-unable-to-take-antidrug-drive-to-rich-makati-city-villages (last accessed December 21, 2016).

34. Alex Ho, "Duterte Explains: Why the Rich Are Beyond Reach of Drug War," *CNN Philippines*, August 25, 2016, http://cnnphilippines.com/news/2016/08/24/Duterte-why-rich-beyond-reach-drug-war.html (last accessed December 21, 2016). This official line was abandoned a month later with the chief of the police declaring, "We do not discriminate." "'We Do Not Discriminate': Rich, Poor Are All Targets in Drug War, Philippine Police Chief Says." *South China Morning Post*, September 5, 2016, http://www.scmp.com/news/asia/southeast-asia/article/2015190/we-do

-not-discriminate-rich-poor-are-all-targets-drug-war (last accessed December 21, 2016).

35. "The Duterte List: Judges, Mayors, Police Officials Linked to Drugs," *Rappler*, August 7, 2016, http://www.rappler.com/nation/142210-duterte-list-lgu-police-officials-linked-drugs (last accessed December 21, 2016); and Arianne Merez, "Duterte's Narco List Has More Than 5,000 Gov't Officials," *ABS-CBN News*, November 27, 2016, http://news.abs-cbn.com/news/11/27/16/dutertes-narco-list-has-more-than-5000-govt-officials (last accessed December 21, 2016). On the mayors who were killed, see Katerina Francisco, "'Drug' Mayors Surrender to PNP Chief," *Rappler*, August 5, 2016, http://www.rappler.com/nation/142062-mayors-surrender-pnp-chief (last accessed December 21, 2016); Euan McKirdy, "Philippines Mayor, Bodyguards Killed in Shootout," *CNN*, October 28, 2016, http://www.cnn.com/2016/10/28/asia/philippines-mayor-killed/ (last accessed December 21, 2016); Carlo Agamon, Chris V. Panganiban, Edwin Fernandez, and Williamor Magbanua, "End of the Road for Mayor on Drug List, 9 Others," *Philippine Daily Inquirer*, October 29, 2016, http://newsinfo.inquirer.net/835698/end-of-the-road-for-mayor-on-drug-list-9-others (last accessed December 21, 2016).

36. *Rappler* has a list of articles its journalists have written about the De Lima-Duterte conflict. See "Duterte vs. De Lima—Previous Articles," *Rappler*, http://www.rappler.com/previous-articles?filterMeta=Duterte+vs+De+Lima (last accessed December 22, 2016).

37. Will Ripley and Jay Croft, "Philippines Drug War's Wide Net Claims 6-Year Old Shot Dead in His Sleep," *CNN World*, December 16, 2016, http://www.cnn.com/2016/12/15/world/philippines-duterte-killings/ (last accessed December 23, 2016).

38. "Philippines: Duterte Confirms He Personally Killed Three Men," *BBC News*, December 16, 2016, http://www.bbc.com/news/world-asia-38337746 (last accessed December 23, 2016). Duterte added: "And I go around in Davao on a motorcycle, with a big bike around, and I would just patrol the streets looking for trouble also. I was looking for an encounter so I could kill."

39. Erin Hale, "Why Rodrigo Duterte May Not Be as Popular in the Philippines as He Thinks," *Forbes*, December 16, 2016, http://www.forbes.com/sites/erinhale/2016/12/16/why-rodrigo-duterte-may-not-be-as-popular-in-the-philippines-as-he-thinks/ (last accessed December 23, 2016).

40. Ted Regencia and Mohsin Ali, "Philippines: Death Toll in Duterte's War on Drugs," *Al Jazeera*, December 15, 2016, http://www.aljazeera.com/indepth/interactive/2016/08/philippines-death-toll-duterte-war-drugs-160825115400719.html (last accessed December 23, 2016). The *Philippine Daily Inquirer* has a "kill list" that it regularly updates. See "The Kill List," *Philippine Daily Inquirer*, July 7, 2016, http://newsinfo.inquirer.net/794598/kill-list-drugs-duterte (last accessed December 23, 2016).

41. Social Weather Station, "Extent of Worry That Someone from One's Family Will Be a Victim of Extra-Judicial Killing or EJK," Fourth Quarter Survey, December 3-6, 2016, http://www.sws.org.ph/swsmain/artcldisppage/?artcsyscode=ART-20161219110734 (last accessed December 23, 2016). The survey interviewed 1,500 adults (eighteen years and older), broken into 600 in Luzon island, 300 in metropolitan Manila, the Visayas islands, and Mindanao island.

Glossary

Term	Meaning and source[a]
alcalde mayor	Spanish provincial governor (Sp.)
anito	Divinity; image or figure representing the divinity (Tag.)
anting-anting	Amulet that confers spiritual power or protection (Tag.)
baja de la campana	Under the church bells (Sp.)
barangay	Boatload of kin and dependencies led by a datu; a 30- to 100-household settlement; village or city district (Tag.)
barrio	Village (Sp.)
bayan	Nation, country, people (Tag.)
baylan	Spirit ritualist (Vis.)
burgis	Bourgeoisie; bourgeois (Fr.)
cabecera	Large town with church and resident friar (Sp.)
cabeza de barangay	Barangay chief, usually a former datu (Sp.)
cacique	Local political boss (Sp. of Latin American origin)
carabao	Water buffalo (Vis.)
catalonan	Spirit ritualist (Tag.)
cédula personal	Paper carried by persons subject to the tribute serving as identification (Sp.)
conquista espiritual	Spiritual conquest (Sp.)
contribución industrial	Tax on earnings (Sp.)
convento	Friar's residence (Sp.)
cortes de madera	Polo duty felling timber and shipbuilding (Sp.)

criollo	Creole; Spaniard born in the Philippines or America (Sp.)
datu	Title for a leader of a small settlement; "big man" (Philippine and other Austronesian languages)
daulat	Spiritual power of a sultan; sovereignty (Mal.)
diwata	Divinity; image or figure representing the divinity (Vis.)
encomienda	Right granted by Spanish king to collect tribute and draft labor within a defined area and responsibility to provide protection and spiritual instruction (Sp.)
esclavo	Slave (Sp.)
gobernadorcillo	"Little governor"; indio official above the cabeza de barangay (Sp.)
hacienda	Landed estate (Sp.)
ilustrado	Enlightened one (Sp.)
imam	Muslim prayer leader (Ar.)
indio	Native (Sp.)
inquilino	Renter-lessor of friar lands (Sp.)
jihad	"Struggle" or "striving"; in political sense, must be defensive or to right a wrong (Ar.)
jueteng	An illegal lottery (Hok.)
kalayaan	Freedom, independence (Tag.)
lamang lupa	Land spirit (Tag.)
maginoo	Hereditary datu class (Tag.)
maharlika	Hereditary warrior class (Tag.)
mandala	Network of personal loyalty among leaders, centered on a "man of prowess"; a form of early Southeast Asian polity (Sans.)
masa	Masses; the people (Eng.)
mestizo	Offspring of Chinese and indio, or Spanish and indio (Sp.)
naturale	Native (Sp.)
pacto de retroventa	"Agreement of repurchase"; land mortgage (Sp.)
padrino	Patron (Sp.)
panglima	District official below datu (Mal.)
parián	District where Chinese were required to reside (Hok.)
pasyon (Pasyon)	Play based on the life of Christ (a particular play) (Sp.)
peninsulare	Spaniard born in Spain (Sp.)

plaza mayor	Open square in a cabecera (Sp.)
poblacíon	Town smaller than a cabecera (Sp.)
polos y servicios	Forty days' labor per year owed to the Spanish colonial state (Sp.)
principalia	Local elite under Spanish rule comprised of current and past officials, ex-datus, and wealthy Chinese mestizos (Sp.)
rajah	Hindu-Malay title for ruler (Sans.)
reconquista	Reconquest (Sp.)
reducción	Resettlement of native population from scattered settlements into cabeceras and visitas for conversion to Christianity and collection of tribute (Sp.)
remontado	One who returns to the mountains (Sp.)
sangley	Chinese merchant (Hok.)
sayyid	Descendant of the Prophet (Ar.)
sitio	Hamlet (Sp.)
sultan	Islamic title for ruler (Ar.)
tao, tawo	Common people (Tag., Vis.)
timawa	Hereditary warrior class (Tag., Vis.)
trapo	"Dishrag"; traditional politician (Fil.)
vandala	Forced sale (Sp.)
visita	Outlying settlement with a chapel (Sp.)

[a] Etymological sources:

Ar.	Arabic
Eng.	English
Fil.	Filipino
Fr.	French
Hok.	Hokkien
Mal.	Malay
Sans.	Sanskrit
Sp.	Spanish
Tag.	Tagalog
Vis.	Visayan

Bibliography

BOOKS AND ARTICLES

Abad, Florencio B. "The Case for Parliamentary Government." In *Towards a Federal Republic of the Philippines with a Parliamentary Government: A Reader*, ed. J. V. Abueva, R. M. Teves, G. C. Somena Jr., C. R. Carlos, and M. O. Mastura. Marikina City, The Philippines: Center for Social Policy and Governance, Kalayaan College, 2002.

Abao, Carmel V. "Engaging Duterte, Engaging Ourselves." *Rappler*, November 4, 2016. Available at http://www.rappler.com/thought-leaders/139850-engaging-duterte-engaging-ourselves (last accessed December 18, 2016).

———. "Why Rationalize Bad Practice? Abolish Pork Barrel." *Rappler*, August 17, 2013, updated July 11, 2014. Available at http://www.rappler.com/thought-leaders/36635-abolish-pork-barrel (accessed April 7, 2016).

Abaya, Hernando J. *Betrayal in the Philippines*. New York: A. A. Wyn, 1946.

———. *The CLU Story: Fifty Years of Struggle for Civil Liberties*. Quezon City: New Day Publishers, 1987.

Abinales, Patricio N. "Coalition Politics in the Philippines." *Current History* (April 2001).

———. "The End of War in the Southern Philippines," *Asian Ethnicity* 15, no. 3, 2014.

———. "The Enigma of the Popular Will." *I: The Investigative Reporting Magazine*, January–June 2004.

———. "Governing the Philippines in the Early Twenty-First Century." In *States, Markets and Societies after the Asian Crisis*, ed. Takashi Shiraishi and Patricio N. Abinales. Kyoto: Kyoto University Press, 2005.

———. *Making Mindanao: Cotabato and Davao in the Formation of the Philippine Nation-State*. Quezon City: Ateneo de Manila University Press, 2000.

———. *Orthodoxy and History in the Muslim Mindanao Narrative*. Quezon City: Ateneo de Manila University Press, 2010.

————. "The Philippines in 2009: The Blustery Days of August," *Asian Survey* 50, no. 1, (January/February 2010): 219–20.

————. "The Philippines in 2010: Blood, Ballots and Beyond," *Asian Survey* 51, no. 1, (January/February 2011), 163–64.

————. "Progressives in a Bind." *Rappler*, September 5, 2015. Available at http:// www.rappler.com/thought-leaders/104733-part-2-progressives-in-bind (last accessed March 9, 2016).

————. "Progressives in Disarray: Risa Hontiveros' Loss." *Rappler*, August 22, 2015. Available at http://www.rappler.com/thought-leaders/103382-part-1-progressives-disarray-risa-hontiveros-loss (last accessed March 9, 2016).

————. "Weak State, Resilient President," *Southeast Asian Affairs 2008*. Singapore: Institute of Southeast Asian Studies, 293–312.

Abrenica, Ma. Joy V., and Gilberto M. Llanto. "Services." In *The Philippine Economy: Development, Policies, and Challenges*, ed. Arsenio M. Balisacan and Hal Hill, 254–82. Quezon City: Ateneo de Manila University Press, 2003.

Abueva, Jose V. "A Crisis of Political Leadership: From 'Electoral Democracy' to 'Substantive Democracy.'" In *Between Fires: Fifteen Perspectives on the Estrada Crisis*, ed. Amando Doronila, 78–79. Pasig, The Philippines: Anvil Publishing, 2001.

————. "Philippine Ideologies and National Development." In *Government and Politics of the Philippines*, ed. Raul P. de Guzman and Mila A. Reforma, 18–74. Singapore: Oxford University Press, 1988.

————. ed. *Towards a Federal Republic of the Philippines with a Parliamentary Government: A Reader*. Marikina City, The Philippines: Center for Social Policy and Governance, Kalayaan College, 2002.

Abueva, Jose V., and Emerlinda R. Roman, eds. *The Aquino Presidency and Administration, 1986–1992: Contemporary Assessments and the Judgement of History*. Quezon City: University of the Philippines Press, 1993.

Abuza, Zachary. "Philippines 2016: Governance, Growth, Development and Security, P1." Available at https://www.youtube.com/watch?v=b3-oj-_X_e4 (last accessed May 14, 2016).

Adel, Rosette. "11 Filipinos Return to Forbes 2016 World Billionaire List." *PhilStar Global*, March 2, 2016. Available at http://www.philstar.com/business/2016/ 03/02/1558717/11-filipinos-return-forbes-2016-world-billionaire-list (accessed May 14, 2016).

Agamon, Carlo, Chris V. Panganiban, Edwin Fernandez, and Williamor Magbanua. "End of the Road for Mayor on Drug List, 9 Others," *Philippine Daily Inquirer*, October 29, 2016. Available at http://newsinfo.inquirer.net/835698/end-of-the -road-for-mayor-on-drug-list-9-others (last accessed December 21, 2016).

Agoncillo, Teodoro A. *Malolos: The Crisis of the Republic*. Quezon City: University of the Philippines Press, 1960.

————. *The Revolt of the Masses: The Story of Bonifacio and the Katipunan*. Quezon City: University of the Philippines Press, 1956.

Aguilar, Filomeno V., Jr. "Betting on Democracy: Electoral Ritual in the Philippine Presidential Campaign." In *Elections as Popular Culture in Asia*, ed. Chua Beng Huat. New York: Routledge, 2007.

——. *Clash of Spirits: The History of Power and Sugar Planter Hegemony on a Visayan Island.* Honolulu: University of Hawai'i Press, 1998.

Albert, Jose Ramon G., and Arturo Martinez Jr. "Are Poverty and Inequality Changing?" *Rappler*, February 25, 2015. Available at http://www.rappler.com/thought-leaders/84833-poverty-inequality-data (last accessed May 9, 2015).

Albert, Jose Ramon, Raymond Gaspar, and M. J. Raymundo. "How Big Is the Middle Class? Is It Benefiting from Economic Growth?" *Rappler*, June 24, 2015. Available at http://www.rappler.com/thought-leaders/97243-middle-class-economic-growth-philippines (last accessed July 7, 2015).

Alegado, Siegfried, and Cecilia Yap. "Philippines Posts Strongest Economic Growth in Asia." *Bloomberg*, November 16, 2016. Available at https://www.bloomberg.com/news/articles/2016-11-17/philippine-growth-quickens-to-7-1-on-duterte-s-spending-spree (last accessed December 16, 2016).

Alliance for the Advancement of People's Rights (Karapatan). "State Terror and Martial Rule," *Karapatant Report on the Human Rights Situation 2006.* Available at http://www.karapatan.org/files/HRHRSIT2006.pdf (last accessed March 2, 2016).

Alonso, Luis. "Financing the Empire: The Nature of the Tax System in the Philippines, 1565–1804." *Philippine Studies* 51, no. 1 (2003): 63–95.

Alonto, Aluya. "Speech of Aluya Alonto on the Problem of Mindanao (interpreted from Moro to English by Datu Marigan Saramain Alonto)." In *Proceedings of the Philippine Constitutional Convention, 1934–1935.* Manila: Bureau of Printing, 1935.

Alpert, Bruce. "Philippines' Duterte Promises to Cut Crime, Corruption," *Voice of America*, May 18, 2016. Available at http://learningenglish.voanews.com/a/philippine-duterte-promises-cut-crime-corruption/3334494.html (last accessed October 30, 2016).

Amoroso, Donna J. "Inheriting the 'Moro Problem': Muslim Authority and Colonial Rule in British Malaya and the Philippines." In *The American Colonial State in the Philippines: Global Perspectives*, ed. Julian Go and Anne L. Foster, 118–47. Durham, NC: Duke University Press, 2003.

"Ampatuan Sr.'s Power Coincided with Arroyo's Victory in 2004." *Politiko*, 2004. Available at http://politics.com.ph/ampatuan-srs-power-coincided-with-arroyos-victory-in-2004/ (last accessed December 12, 2015).

Andaya, Barbara Watson, ed. *Other Pasts: Women, Gender, and History in Early Modern Southeast Asia.* Honolulu: Center for Southeast Asian Studies, University of Hawai'i at Manoa, 2000.

Anderson, Benedict. "Cacique Democracy in the Philippines." In *The Spectre of Comparison: Nationalism, Southeast Asia and the World*, 192–226. London and New York: Verso, 1998.

——. "Elections and Participation in Three Southeast Asian Countries." In *The Politics of Elections in Southeast Asia*, ed. R. H. Taylor. New York: Cambridge University Press, 1996, 12–22.

——. "Old State, New Society: Indonesia's New Order in Comparative Historical Perspective." In Benedict R. O'G. Anderson, *Language and Power: Exploring*

Political Cultures in Indonesia, 94–120. Ithaca, NY: Cornell University Press, 1990.

——. *The Spectre of Comparisons: Nationalism, Southeast Asia, and the World.* London: Verso, 1998.

Angeles, Leonora. "Feminism and Nationalism: The Discourse on the Woman Question and Politics of the Women's Movement in the Philippines." M.A. thesis, University of the Philippines, 1989.

Antonio, Rafael. "11.4m Families Remain Poor, SWS Poll." *Philippine Daily Inquirer*, May 6, 2015. Available at http://newsinfo.inquirer.net/689515/11-4m -families-remain-poor-sws-poll (last accessed May 11, 2015).

Aquino, Corazon C. "Reflections on Our Democracy." In *The Aquino Presidency and Administration, 1986–1992: Contemporary Assessments and the Judgement of History*, ed. Jose V. Abueva and Emerlinda R. Roman, 1–3. Quezon City: University of the Philippines Press, 1993.

Aquino Norman P., and Chris Blake. "Duterte's U.S. Rants Rooted in Battle against Manila's Elites." *Bloomberg*, November 30, 2016. Available at https://www .bloomberg.com/news/articles/2016-11-30/duterte-s-anti-u-s-rants-rooted-in -battle-against-manila-elite (last accessed December 18, 2016).

"Aquino Prepares 26 Cases against Tax Evaders." *Philstar Global*, September 17, 2010. Available at http://www.philstar.com/breaking-news/612557/aquino -prepares-26-cases-against-tax-evaders (last accessed April 9, 2016).

Arcilla, Albert F. "Revisiting Mamapasano: A Disaster for the BBL." *Business World Online*, January 24, 2016. Available at http://www.bworldonline.com/content.php ?section=Nation&title=revisiting-mamasapano-a-disaster-for-the-bbl&id=122002 (last accessed May 12, 2016).

Arcilla, Jose S., ed. *Kasaysayan: The Story of the Filipino People.* Vol. 3, *The Spanish Conquest.* Manila: Asia Publishing Co., 1998.

Arroyo, Gloria Macapagal. "Arroyo to Aquino: It's the Economy, Student!" *Rappler*, January 13, 2012. Available at http://www.rappler.com/thought-leaders/829 -arroyo-to-aquino-it-s-the-economy,-student (last accessed May 19, 2016).

——. "Towards a Strong Philippine Republic." State of the Nation address at the opening of the 2nd Regular Session of the 12th Congress, July 22, 2002.

Asia Society and the Asian Development Bank. "Financing Asian Development: Growing Opportunities in Asia's Debt Markets (Report of a Study Mission to the Philippines, Thailand and South Korea)." Special Reports, May 20–30, 1998. Available at http://www.asiasociety.org/special_reports/financing.html (last accessed October 14, 2004).

Asian Development Bank. "Civil Society Briefs: The Philippines." 2016. Available at http://www.adb.org/sites/default/files/publication/30174/csb-phi.pdf (last accessed March 12, 2016).

——. *Economic Trends and Prospects in Asia: Southeast Asia.* Manila: Asian Development Bank, 2004.

——. *Key Indicators of Developing Asian and Pacific Countries 2002.* Manila: Asian Development Bank, 2002. Available at http://www.adb.org/Documents/ Books/Key_Indicators/2002/ (last accessed November 26, 2004).

———. "Philippines: PSA Quantitative Indicators." September 10, 2003. Available at http://www.adb.org/Documents/Others/CQI/Philippines_qi.pdf (last accessed October 14, 2004).

Astorga-Garcia, Mila. "Left to Right: The Student Activists." *Sunday Times* (Manila) *Magazine*, February 22, 1970: 33.

Ateneo de Manila University. Department of Economics. "The Socio-Political Nature of the Aquino Government." In *The Aquino Presidency and Administration, 1986–1992: Contemporary Assessments and the Judgement of History*, ed. Jose V. Abueva and Emerlinda R. Roman, 29–32. Quezon City: University of the Philippines Press, 1993.

Aurelio, Julie M. "Soliman: COA Report Didn't Have DSWCD Side." *Philippine Daily Inquirer*, December 27, 2014. Available at http://newsinfo.inquirer.net/659657/everything-is-accounted-for-says-soliman (last accessed May 9, 2016).

Baclagon, Uldarico. *Christian-Moslem Guerrillas in Mindanao*. Manila: Lord Avenue, 1988.

Bacungan, Froilan M., ed. *The Powers of the Philippine President*. Quezon City: University of the Philippines Law Center, 1983.

Bakshian, Douglas. "Philippine Opposition Wins 6 of 10 Senate Seats in Mid-Term Election." *Voice of America* 1, November 2009. Available at http://m.voanews.com/a/a-13-2007-06-voa28/348200.html (last accessed April 4, 2016).

Balisacan, Arsenio M. "Did the Estrada Administration Benefit the Poor?" In *Between Fires: Fifteen Perspectives on the Estrada Crisis*, ed. Amando Doronila, 98–112. Pasig, The Philippines: Anvil Publishing, 2001.

Balisacan, Arsenio M., and Hal Hill, eds. *The Philippine Economy: Development, Policies, and Challenges*. Quezon City: Ateneo de Manila University Press, 2003.

Barrows, David P. *A Decade of American Government in the Philippines: 1903–1913*. New York: Yonkers, 1914.

Barry, Coeli M. "The Limits of Conservative Church Reformism in the Democratic Philippines." In *Religious Organizations and Democracy in Contemporary Asia*, ed. Tun-Jun Cheng and Deborah A. Brown. Armonk, NY: M. E. Sharpe, 2006.

Bautista, Germelino M. "An Assessment of the Philippine Economy." *Kyoto Review of Southeast Asia* 4 (October 2003). Available at http://kyotoreview.cseas.kyoto-u.ac.jp/issue/issue3/index.html (last accessed October 14, 2004).

———. "From Contradiction to Crisis: The Case of the Philippine Political Economy." In *Transnationalization, the State, and the People: The Philippine Experience*, ed. Randolf S. David et al., 2:1–36. Quezon City: University of the Philippines, Third World Studies Center, 1984.

Bautista, Maria Cynthia Rose Banzon. "'The Revenge of the Elite on the Masses'?" In *Between Fires: Fifteen Perspectives on the Estrada Crisis*, ed. Amando Doronila, 8–26. Pasig, The Philippines: Anvil Publishing, 2001.

Bautista, Romeo M. "Inflation in the Philippines, 1955–1974." In *Philippine Economic Problems in Perspective*, ed. Jose Encarnacion Jr. et al., 178–213. Quezon City: University of the Philippines, School of Economics, Institute of Economic Development and Research, 1976.

Bautista, Romeo, and Gwendolyn Tecson. "International Dimensions." In *The Philippine Economy: Development, Policies, and Challenges*, ed. Arsenio M. Balisacan and Hal Hill, 136–74. Quezon City: Ateneo de Manila University Press, 2003.

Beckett, Jeremy. "The Defiant and the Compliant." In *Philippine Social History: Global Trade and Local Transformations*, ed. Alfred W. McCoy and Ed C. de Jesus, 391–414. Quezon City: Ateneo de Manila University Press, 1982.

Bello, Walden. "The Left Under Duterte." *Jacobin*, June 29, 2016. Available at https://www.jacobinmag.com/2016/06/walden-bello-philippines-duterte-dignidad-coalition-akbayan/ (last accessed December 10, 2016).

Bello, Walden, Herbert Docena, Marissa de Guzman, and Marylou Malig. *The Anti-Development State: The Political Economy of Permanent Crisis in the Philippines*. Quezon City: University of the Philippines, Department of Sociology; and Focus on the Global South, 2004.

Bello, Walden, David Kinley, and Elaine Elinson. *Development Debacle: The World Bank in the Philippines*. San Francisco: Institute for Food and Development Policy/ Philippine Solidarity Network, 1982.

Bello, Walden, Lidy Nacpil, and Ana Marie Nemenzo. "Overdue, Selective, Not Daring Enough." *Business World Online*, August 28, 2004. Available at http://www.focusweb.org/philippines/html/article284.html (last accessed October 10, 2004).

Bello, Walden, and Severina Rivera. "The Logistics of Repression." In *The Logistics of Repression and Other Essays*, ed. Walden Bello and Severina Rivera, 7–27. Washington, DC: Friends of the Filipino People, 1977.

Bengzon, Alfredo R. A., with Raul Rodrigo. *A Matter of Honor: The Story of the 1990–1991 RP–US Bases Talks*. Manila: Anvil Publishing, 1997.

Berehulak, Daniel. "They Are Slaughtering Us Like Animals: Inside President Rodrigo Duterte's Brutal Antidrug Campaign in the Philippines, Our Photojournalist Documented 57 Homicide Victims over 35 Days." *New York Times*, December 7, 2016. Available at http://www.nytimes.com/interactive/2016/12/07/world/asia/rodrigo-duterte-philippines-drugs-killings.html (last accessed December 22, 2016).

Bergonia, Tony. "GMA Election Strategy: Blending Governance, Magic, Noli." *Philippine Daily Inquirer*, July 28, 2004.

Bolasco, Mario V. *Points of Departure: Essays on Christianity, Power, and Social Change*, ed. Edicio de la Torre. Manila: St. Scholastica's College, 1994.

Boncocan, Karen. "Aquino Signed RH Bill into Law." *Philippine Daily Inquirer*, December 28, 2012. Available at http://newsinfo.inquirer.net/331395/gonzales-aquino-signed-rh-bill-into-law (last accessed May 1, 2015).

Bondoc, Jarius. "Abaya Caught in 3 Rail Controversies." *PhilStar Global*, September 11, 2015. Available at http://www.philstar.com/opinion/2015/09/11/1498471/abaya-caught-3-rail-controversies (last accessed May 4, 2016).

———. "MILF Letter to Bush Sped Up Settlement." *PhilStar Global*, August 1, 2008. Available at http://www.philstar.com/opinion/76398/milf-letter-bush-sped-settlement (last accessed March 29, 2016).

Bonner, Raymond. *Waltzing with a Dictator: The Marcoses and the Making of American Policy*. New York: Random House, 1987.

Boudreau, Vincent. *Grass Roots and Cadre in the Protest Movement*. Quezon City: Ateneo de Manila University Press, 2001.

Bowie, Alasdair, and Danny Unger. *The Politics of Open Economies: Indonesia, Malaysia, the Philippines, and Thailand*. Cambridge: Cambridge University Press, 1997.

Boyce, James K. *The Political Economy of Growth and Impoverishment in the Marcos Era*. Quezon City: Ateneo de Manila University Press, 1993.

Brewer, Carolyn. "From Animist 'Priestess' to Catholic Priest: The Re/gendering of Religious Roles in the Philippines, 1521–1685." In *Other Pasts: Women, Gender, and History in Early Modern Southeast Asia*, ed. Barbara Watson Andaya, 69–86. Honolulu: Center for Southeast Asian Studies, University of Hawai'i at Manoa, 2000.

Brillantes, Alex B., Jr., and Bienvenida M. Amarles-Ilago. *1898–1992: The Philippine Presidency*. Quezon City: University of the Philippines, 1994.

British Broadcasting Corporation. "Philippines: Duterte Confirms He Personally Killed Three Men." *BBC News*, December 16, 2016. Available at http://www.bbc.com/news/world-asia-38337746 (last accessed December 23, 2016).

Broad, Robin. *Unequal Alliance, 1979–1986: The World Bank, the International Monetary Fund, and the Philippines*. Berkeley: University of California Press, 1988.

Bueza, Michael. "Power Outage Hits NAIA Terminal 3." *Rappler*, April 2, 2016. Available at http://www.rappler.com/nation/128023-power-outage-naia-terminal-3 (last accessed May 9, 2016).

———. "Who's Who in Duterte's Poll Contributors List." *Rappler*, December 9, 2016. Available at http://www.rappler.com/newsbreak/iq/155060-duterte-contributors-list-2016-presidential-elections (last accessed December 13, 2016).

Cabacungan, Gil C. "Arroyo Chose Who, How Much PDAF to Give." *Philippine Daily Inquirer*, August 22, 2013. Available at http://newsinfo.inquirer.net/471659/arroyo-chose-who-how-much-pdaf-to-give (last accessed April 8, 2016).

———. "Road to Perdition: 13 Found Guilty in Overprice." *Philippine Daily Inquirer*, February 6, 2015. Available at http://newsinfo.inquirer.net/670875/road-to-perdition-13-found-guilty-in-overprice (last accessed March 14, 2016).

Cabacungan, Gil C., Jeannette I. Andrade, and Miko Morelos. "Gloria Arroyo Now under Arrest." *Philippine Daily Inquirer*, November 19, 2011. Available at http://newsinfo.inquirer.net/96621/gloria-arroyo-now-under-arrest (last accessed April 7, 2016).

Cabacungan, Gil, Miguel Camus, and Jerry E. Esplanada. "LP: Aquino, Party Backs DOTC Chief." *Philippine Daily Inquirer*, January 8, 2016. Available at http://newsinfo.inquirer.net/753547/abaya-stays-amid-quit-calls (last accessed May 9, 2016).

Cannell, Fenella. *Power and Intimacy in the Christian Philippines*. Quezon City: Ateneo de Manila University Press, 1999.

Caoili, Manuel A. *The Origins of Metropolitan Manila: A Political and Social Analysis*. Quezon City: University of the Philippines Press, 1999.

Caoutte, Dominique. "Ups and Downs of a Contemporary Maoist Movement: Shifting Tactics, Moving Targets and (Un)orthodox Strategy, the Philippine Revolution in Perspective." In *Emancipatory Politics: A Critique*, ed. Stephan Feuchtwang and Alpa Shah. Open Anthropology Cooperative Press, 2015. Available at http://openanthcoop.net/press/emancipatory-politics-a-critique/chapter-5/ (last accessed February 23, 2016).

Cariño, Isidro D. "Education, Culture, and Sports." In *The Aquino Presidency and Administration, 1986–1992: Contemporary Assessments and the Judgement of History*, ed. Jose V. Abueva and Emerlinda R. Roman, 223–24. Quezon City: University of the Philippines Press, 1993.

Carlson, Keith Thor. *The Twisted Road to Freedom: America's Granting of Independence to the Philippines*. Quezon City: University of the Philippines Press, 1995.

Castro, Isagani de, Jr. "Preventing a Checkmate." *Newsbreak*, May 10, 2004: 9–11.

Catilo, Aurora C., and Proserpina D. Tapales. "The Legislature." In *Government and Politics of the Philippines*, ed. Raul P. de Guzman and Mila A. Reforma. Singapore: Oxford University Press, 1988.

Caucus of Development NGOs. *Civil Society: Creative Responses to the Challenge of Globalization, 3–5 September 1996 Proceedings*. Quezon City: Center for Alternative Development Initiatives, 1998.

Celdran, David. "The Cult of the Celebrity." *I: The Investigative Reporting Magazine*, January–March 2001: 28–31.

Chen, Adrian. "When a Populist Demagogue Takes Power." *The New Yorker*, November 21, 2016. Available at http://www.newyorker.com/magazine/2016/11/21/when-a-populist-demagogue-takes-power (last accessed December 1, 2016).

Ch'en Ching-ho. *The Chinese Community in the Sixteenth-Century Philippines*. Tokyo: Centre for East Asian Cultural Studies, 1968.

Chirot, Daniel, and Anthony Reid, eds. *Essential Outsiders: Chinese and Jews in the Modern Transformation of Southeast Asia and Central Europe*. Seattle: University of Washington Press, 1997.

Chua, Yvonne T. *Robbed: An Investigation of Corruption in Philippine Education*. Manila: Philippine Center for Investigative Journalism, 1999.

Claudio, Lisandro. "From Scandalous Politics to Public Scandal: Corruption, Media and the Collapse of the Estrada Regime in the Philippines." *Asian Politics and Polity* 6, no. 4 (2014): 539–54.

———. *Taming People Power: The EDSA Revolutions and Their Contradictions*. Quezon City: Ateneo de Manila University Press, 2013.

Constantino, Renato. *The Making of a Filipino: A Story of Colonial Politics*. Quezon City: Malaya Books, 1969.

Constantino, Renato, and Letizia R. Constantino. *The Philippines: A Past Revisited*. Quezon City: Tala Pub. Services, 1975.

———. *The Philippines: The Continuing Past*. Quezon City: Foundation for Nationalist Studies, 1978.

Coronel, Sheila S. "Erap and Families." *I: The Investigative Reporting Magazine*, July–September 2000: 5–10.

———. "The Man Who Would Be President." *I: The Investigative Reporting Magazine*, April–June 1996: 6–11.

———. "The *Pare* Principle." *I: The Investigative Reporting Magazine*, October–December 1998: 6–12.

———. "The Philippines in 2006: Democracy and Its Discontents." *Asian Survey* 47, no. 1, (January/February 2007): 207.

———. "The Problem with Gloria." *I: The Investigative Reporting Magazine*, April–June 2003: 15–20.

Coronel, Sheila S., ed. *Betrayals of the Public Trust: Investigative Reports on Corruption*. Manila: Philippine Center for Investigative Journalism, 2000.

———. *Investigating Estrada: Millions, Mansions, and Mistresses: A Compilation of Investigative Reports*. Manila: Philippine Center for Investigative Journalism, 2001.

———. *Pork and Other Perks: Corruption and Governance in the Philippines*. Manila: Philippine Center for Investigative Journalism, 1998.

Coronel, Sheila S., Yvonne T. Chua, Luz Rimban, and Booma Cruz. *The Rulemakers: How the Wealthy and Well-born Dominate Congress*. Manila: Philippine Center for Investigative Journalism, 2004.

Corotan, Gemma Luz. "The Meteoric Rise of Hilarion Ramiro." *Philippine Star*, November 9–10, 1995.

———. "The NFA: Tailor-made for Corruption." *Today*, September 11, 1995. Available at http://www.tag.org.ph/investigativereports/archive11/archive11.4.htm (last accessed October 4, 2004).

Corpuz, Arturo G. *The Colonial Iron Horse: Railroads and Regional Development in the Philippines, 1875–1935*. Quezon City: University of the Philippines Press, 1999.

Corpuz, Onofre D. *The Bureaucracy in the Philippines*. Quezon City: Institute of Public Administration, University of the Philippines, 1957.

———. [O. D. Corpuz.] *An Economic History of the Philippines*. Quezon City: University of the Philippines Press, 1997.

———. *Education and Socioeconomic Change in the Philippines, 1870–1960s*. Quezon City: University of the Philippines Press, 1967.

———. [O. D. Corpuz.] *The Roots of the Filipino Nation*. 2 vols. Quezon City: Aklahi Foundation, 1989.

Cortes, Rosario Mendoza, Celestina Puyal Boncan, and Ricardo Trota Jose. *The Filipino Saga: History as Social Change*. Quezon City: New Day Publishers, 2000.

Costa, Horacio de la. *Readings in Philippine History: Selected Historical Texts Presented with a Commentary by H. de la Costa*. Makati City, The Philippines: Bookmark, 1992.

"Criminals, Inc." *I: The Investigative Reporting Magazine*, January–March 2003: 12–23.

Cuaderno, Miguel, Sr. *Problems of Economic Development: The Philippines, a Case Study*. Manila: Miguel Cuaderno Sr., 1964.

Cullinane, Michael. "Accounting for Souls: Ecclesiastical Sources for the Study of Philippine Demographic History." In *Population and History: The Demographic*

Origins of the Modern Philippines, ed. Daniel F. Doeppers and Peter Xenos, 281–346. Quezon City: Ateneo de Manila University Press, 1998.

———. "The Changing Nature of the Cebu Urban Elite in the Nineteenth Century." In *Philippine Social History: Global Trade and Local Transformations*, ed. Alfred W. McCoy and Ed C. de Jesus, 251–96. Quezon City: Ateneo de Manila University Press, 1982.

———. *Ilustrado Politics: Filipino Elite Responses to American Rule, 1898–1908*. Quezon City: Ateneo de Manila University Press, 2003.

———. "Implementing the 'New Order': The Structure and Supervision of Local Government under the Taft Era." In *Compadre Colonialism: Studies on the Philippines under American Rule*, ed. Norman Owen, 9–34. Ann Arbor: Center for South and Southeast Asian Studies, University of Michigan, 1971.

Cupin, Bea. "The 'Ordinariness' of Jesse Robredo." *Rappler*, August 19, 2015. Available at http://www.rappler.com/nation/103090-jesse-robredo-death-anniversary (last accessed January 12, 2016).

———. "President Aquino and the Ghosts of Mamapasano." *Rappler*, September 19, 2015. Available at http://www.rappler.com/newsbreak/in-depth/106243-aquino-truth-saf-mamasapano (last accessed May 14, 2016).

Curato, Nicole. "The Road to Oakwood Is Paved with Good Intentions: The Oakwood Mutiny and the Politics of Recognition." *Philippine Sociological Review* 59 (2011): 23–48.

Dacanay, Barbara Mae. "Marcos and Arroyo Win in Philippine Polls." *Gulf News Philippines*, May 14, 2013. Available at http://gulfnews.com/news/asia/philippines/marcos-and-arroyo-win-in-philippine-polls-1.1183219 (last accessed April 7, 2016).

Dalpino, Catharin E. "Challenges for a Post-Election Philippines: Issues for U.S. Policy." Washington, DC: Council on Foreign Relations, Center for Preventive Action, 2004.

Damazo, Jet. "Bayani the Hero." *Newsbreak*, July 22, 2002. Available at http://archives.newsbreak-knowledge.ph/2002/07/22/bayani-the-hero/ (last accessed October 9, 2016).

———. "The Stink That Won't Go Away." *Newsbreak*, March 18, 2002: 20–21.

Dancel, Raul. "Manila's Messy Rapid Transit." *Singapore Strait Times*, August 8, 2015. Available at http://www.straitstimes.com/opinion/manilas-messy-rapid-transit (last accessed May 9, 2016).

Daroy, Petronilo Bn. "On the Eve of Dictatorship and Revolution." In *Dictatorship and Revolution: Roots of People's Power*, ed. Aurora Javate de Dios et al., 1–125. Manila: Conspectus, 1988.

Daval, Lean et al. "Duterte Cites Hitler, Wants to Kill Millions of Addicts." *Al Jazeera*, September 29, 2016. Available at http://www.aljazeera.com/news/2016/09/duterte-cites-hitler-kill-millions-addicts-160930043443768.html (last accessed December 14, 2016).

"Davao Is Number 4 on PNP's Worst PH Cities with Highest Crime Rate." *Politiko*, April 6, 2016. Available at http://politics.com.ph/davao-is-number-4-on-pnps-worst-ph-cities-with-highest-crime-rate/ (last accessed April 1, 2016).

David, Clarissa. "Limiting Political Dynasties Will Help the Poor." *Rappler*, August 19, 2015. Available at http://www.rappler.com/thought-leaders/103088-limiting-political-dynasties- help-poor (last accessed April 8, 2016).

David, Clarissa, and E. F. Legara. "How Much of Our Country Will We Lose to Political Dynasties in 2016. *Rappler*, October 20, 2016. Available at http://www.rappler.com/thought-leaders/109892-how-much-country-lose-political-dynasties-2016 (last accessed December 19, 2016).

David, Cristina C. "Agriculture." In *The Philippine Economy: Development, Policies, and Challenges*, ed. Arsenio M. Balisacan and Hal Hill, 175–218. Quezon City: Ateneo de Manila University Press, 2003.

David, Karina C. "The Philippine Experience in Scaling-Up." In *Making a Difference: NGOs and Development in a Changing World*, ed. Michael Edwards and David Hulme, 137–47. London: Earthscan Publications, 1992.

David, Randolf S. "The Decline of Political Parties." *Philippine Daily Inquirer*, May 2, 2004.

David, Randolf S., Germelino Bautista, Elpidio Santa Romana, Karina Constantino-David, Edmundo Garcia, Alexander M. Magno, Teresa Encarnacion, and Patricio N. Abinales. *Transnationalization, the State, and the People: The Philippine Experience.* 2 vols. Quezon City: University of the Philippines, Third World Studies Center, 1985.

De Bevoise, Ken. *Agents of Apocalypse: Epidemic Disease in the Colonial Philippines*. Princeton, NJ: Princeton University Press, 1995.

De Castro, Renato Cruz. "The Philippines in 2011: Muddling Through a Year of Learning and Adjustment. *Asian Survey* 52, no. 1 (January/February 2012): 212.

———. "The Philippines in 2012: 'Easygoing, Do-Nothing' President Delivers." *Asian Survey* 53, no. 1 (January/February 2013): 112.

———. "U.S. War on Terror in East Asia: The Perils of Preemptive Defense in Waging a War of the Third Kind." *Asian Affairs* 31, no. 1 (Winter 2005): 212–31.

De Dios, Emmanuel S. "Corruption and the Fall." In *Between Fires: Fifteen Perspectives on the Estrada Crisis*, ed. Amando Doronila, 43–61. Pasig, The Philippines: Anvil Publishing, 2001.

———. "Dear Ben . . ." *Per Se*, July 24, 2015. Available at http://www.econ.upd.edu.ph/perse/?p=4775 (last accessed June 21, 2016).

———. "The Erosion of the Dictatorship." In *Dictatorship and Revolution: Roots of People's Power*, ed. Aurora Javate de Dios et al., 70–131. Manila: Conspectus, 1988.

———. "Philippine Economic Growth: Can It Last?" In *The Philippines: New Directions in Domestic Policy and Foreign Relations*, ed. David G. Timberman, 49–84. Singapore: Institute of Southeast Asian Studies, 1998.

De Dios, Emmanuel S., ed. *An Analysis of the Philippine Economic Crisis: A Workshop Report.* Quezon City: University of the Philippines Press, 1984.

De Dios, Emmanuel S., Benjamin E. Diokno, Emmanuel F. Esguerra, Raul V. Fabella, Ma. Socorro Gochoco-Bautista, Felipe M. Medalla, Solita C. Monsod, Ernesto M. Pernia, Renato E. Reside Jr., Gerardo P. Sicat, and Edita A. Tan. "The Deepening Crisis: The Real Score on Deficits and the Public Debt." Quezon City: University of the Philippines, School of Economics, 2004. Available at http://www.up.edu.ph/

upse_on_fiscal_crisis/up%20econ-the%20deepening%20crisis.pdf (last accessed September 18, 2004).

De Dios, Emmanuel S., and Paul Hutchcroft. "Political Economy." In *The Philippine Economy: Development, Policies, and Challenges*, ed. Arsenio M. Balisacan and Hal Hill, 45–73. Quezon City: Ateneo de Manila University Press, 2003.

De la Cruz, Uro Q. "The Myth of Ang Panday." *I: The Investigative Reporting Magazine*, October–December 2002: 10–13.

De Quiros, Conrado. "The Longer View." *Philippine Daily Inquirer*, March 29, 2012, Available at http://opinion.inquirer.net/25809/the-longer-view (last accessed April 5, 2016).

De Vera, Ben O. "Growth in OFW Remittances in 2016 Seen Slowest in 10 Years." *Philippine Daily Inquirer*, October 8, 2106. Available at https://business.inquirer .net/216240/growth-in-ofw-remittances-in-2016-seen-slowest-in-10-years/ (last accessed December 25, 2016).

———. "Poverty Incidence Worsened in 2014: Gov't Blames Higher Food Prices, 'Yolanda' Impact." *Philippine Daily Inquirer*, March 5, 2015. Available at http:// business.inquirer.net/188011/poverty-incidence-worsened-in-2014 (last accessed March 7, 2015).

Diaz, Jess. "24 House Members Join Noy's Liberal Party." *Philstar Global*, June 26, 2010. Available at http://www.philstar.com/headlines/587462/24-house-members -join-noys-liberal-party (last accessed April 7, 2016).

———. "Noy's Social Fund to Get P5B from Pagcor." *Philstar Global*, September 1, 2013. Available at http://www.philstar.com/headlines/2013/09/01/1156851/noys -social-fund-get-p5-b-pagcor (last accessed April 7, 2016).

Diola, Camille. "SC Declares PDAF Unconstitutional." *Philstar Global*, November 19, 2013. Available at http://www.philstar.com/headlines/2013/11/19/1258492/ sc-declares-pdaf-unconstitutional (last accessed April 9, 2016).

Doeppers, Daniel F. "Evidence from the Grave: The Changing Social Composition of the Populations of Metropolitan Manila and Molo, Iloilo, during the Later Nineteenth Century." In *Population and History: The Demographic Origins of the Modern Bibliography 319 Philippines*, ed. Daniel F. Doeppers and Peter Xenos, 265–77. Quezon City: Ateneo de Manila University Press, 1998.

———. *Manila, 1900–1941: Social Change in a Late Colonial Metropolis.* Quezon City: Ateneo de Manila University Press, 1984.

———. "Migration to Manila: Changing Gender Representation, Migration Field, and Urban Structure." In *Population and History: The Demographic Origins of the Modern Philippines*, ed. Daniel F. Doeppers and Peter Xenos, 137–79. Quezon City: Ateneo de Manila University Press, 1998.

Doeppers, Daniel F., and Peter Xenos. "A Demographic Frame for Philippine History." In *Population and History: The Demographic Origins of the Modern Philippines*, ed. Daniel F. Doeppers and Peter Xenos, 3–16. Quezon City: Ateneo de Manila University Press, 1998.

Doronila, Amando. "A Gracious Political Act." *Philippine Daily Inquirer*, May 11, 2010. Available at http://opinion.inquirer.net/inquireropinion/view/20100511 269481/A-gracious-political-act (last accessed September 24, 2014).

———. *The Fall of Joseph Estrada: The Inside Story*. Pasig, The Philippines: Anvil Publishing, 2001.

———. *The State, Economic Transformation, and Political Change in the Philippines, 1946–1972*. New York: Oxford University Press, 1992.

Doronila, Amando, ed. *Between Fires: Fifteen Perspectives on the Estrada Crisis*. Pasig, The Philippines: Anvil Publishing, 2001.

Dressel, Bjorn. "The Philippines: How Much Real Democracy?" *International Political Science Review* 32, no. 5 (November 2011): 529–45.

Dubsky, Roman. *Technocracy and Development in the Philippines*. Quezon City: University of the Philippines Press, 1993.

Duterte, Rodrigo Roa. "Duterte Transcripts: Wallace Business Forum Dinner, 12 December 2016." *Mindanews*, December 14, 2016. Available at http://www.mindanews.com/duterte-files/2016/12/duterte-transcripts-wallace-business-forum-dinner-12-dec-2016/ (last accessed December 15, 2016).

"Editorial: Just Fire Him Already, Please." *Interaksyon*, April 7, 2016. Available at http://interaksyon.com/article/126142/editorial—just-fire-him-already-please (last accessed May 9, 2016).

Elemia, Camille. "Aquino Bounces Back, Net Satisfaction Rating Up 173%." *Rappler*, June 24, 2015. Available at http://www.rappler.com/nation/96846-aquino-sws-satisfaction-rating-high-june (last accessed May 15, 2016).

Ellison, Katherine. *Imelda, Steel Butterfly of the Philippines*. New York: McGraw-Hill, 1998.

"The Empire Strikes Back." *I: The Investigative Reporting Magazine*, July–September 1996: 10–11.

Endriga, Jose N. "The Friar Lands Settlement: Promise and Performance." *Philippine Journal of Public Administration* (October 1970): 397–413.

Escosio, Jan. "No Cellphones, No Internet for Arroyo at Veteran's Hospital Suite." *Philippine Daily Inquirer*, December 2, 2011. Available at http://newsinfo.inquirer.net/104293/no-cellphones-no-internet-for-arroyo-at-veterans-hospital-suite (last accessed April 9, 2016).

Esmaquel, Paterno, II. "Duterte Donor Imee Marcos Not in His SOCE." *Rappler*, October 11, 2016. Available at http://www.rappler.com/nation/politics/elections/2016/148841-duterte-imee-marcos-campaign-contributor-soce (last accessed December 12, 2016).

Espinosa-Robles, Raissa. "Arroyo's Charter Change Moves Copied from the Marcos Book." Philippine Center for Investigative Journalism, 2016. Available at http://pcij.org/stories/arroyos-charter-change-moves-copied-from-the-marcos-book/ (last accessed April 7, 2016).

Estanislao, Anna. "More Corruption Allegations vs. VP Binay." *CNN Philippines*, August 26, 2015. Available at http://cnnphilippines.com/news/2015/08/26/More-corruption-allegations-vs-VP-Binay.html (last accessed May 14, 2016).

Eviota, Elizabeth Uy. *The Political Economy of Gender: Women and the Sexual Division of Labour in the Philippines*. London: Zed Books, 1992.

Fernandez, Yvette. *Simply Jesse: The Story of Jesse Robredo*. Manila: Summit Publishing Co. Inc., 2013.

Finegold, Kenneth. *Experts and Politicians: Reform Challenges to Machine Politics in New York, Cleveland, and Chicago.* Princeton, NJ: Princeton University Press, 1995.

Finegold, Kenneth, and Theda Skocpol. "State Capacity and Economic Intervention in the Early New Deal." *Political Science Quarterly* 97 (1982): 255–78.

Finin, Gerard A. "Regional Consciousness and Administrative Grids: Understanding the Role of Planning in the Philippines' Gran Cordillera Central." PhD diss., Cornell University, 1991.

Flores, A. O. "Student Militance through the Years." *Sunday Times* (Manila) *Magazine*, February 22, 1970: 38.

Fonbuena, Carmela. "Aquino's Ratings Drop to Lowest since 2010." *Rappler*, October 10, 2014. Available at http://www.rappler.com/nation/63239-aquino-lowest -ratings (last accessed May 14, 2016).

———. "Jun Abaya: 'A Good Soldier.'" *Rappler*, September 19, 2012. Available at http://www.rappler.com/nation/11522-jun-abaya-a-good-soldier (last accessed May 4, 2016).

———. "RH Law: The Long and Rough Road." *Rappler*, January 2, 2013. Available at http://www.rappler.com/newsbreak/18730-rh-law-the-long-and-rough-road (last accessed May 1, 2015).

Forbes, W. Cameron. *The Philippine Islands.* Cambridge, MA: Harvard University Press, 1945.

Francia, Beatriz Romualdez. *Imelda and the Clans: A Story of the Philippines.* Manila: Solar Publishing, 1988.

Francisco, Katerina. "'Drug' Mayors Surrender to PNP Chief." *Rappler*, August 5, 2016. Available at http://www.rappler.com/nation/142062-mayors-surrender-pnp -chief (last accessed December 21, 2016).

Francisco, Rosemarie, and Stuart Grudgings. "For Philippines Leader, It's War on Graft, Tax Evasion." *Reuters*, July 3, 2012. Available at http://www.reuters.com/ article/us-philippines-economy-aquino-idUSBRE86207320120703 (last accessed April 9, 2016).

Franco, Jennifer Conroy. *Campaigning for Democracy: Grassroots Citizenship Movements, Less-than-Democratic Elections and Regime Transition in the Philippines.* Quezon City: Institute for Popular Democracy, 2001.

———. *Elections and Democratization in the Philippines.* New York: Routledge, 2001.

Friend, Theodore, III. "American Interests and Philippine Independence, 1929– 1933." *Philippine Studies* 2, no. 4 (October 1963): 505–23.

Gacad, Romeo. "Lamitan under Siege." *I: The Investigative Reporting Magazine*, July–September 2001: 26–30.

Garcia, Robert Francis. *To Suffer Thy Comrades: How the Revolution Decimated Its Own.* Pasig, The Philippines: Anvil Publishing, 2001.

Gates, John. "War-Related Deaths in the Philippines, 1898–1902." *Pacific Historical Review* 53 (1983): 367–78.

Geducos, Argylll Cyrus B. "Voter Turnout for 2016 Polls Is 84% Says Comelec." *Manila Bulletin*, May 10, 2016. Available at http://www.mb.com.ph/voter-turnout for 2016-polls-is-84-says-comelec/ (last accessed May 14, 2016).

Glang, Alunan. *Muslim Secession or Integration?* Quezon City: R. P. Garcia, 1969.

Gleeck, Lewis E., Jr. *The American Half-Century, 1898–1946*. Rev. ed. Quezon City: New Day Publishers, 1998.

———. *President Marcos and the Philippine Political Culture*. Manila: L. E. Gleeck, 1987.

———. *The Third Philippine Republic, 1946–1972*. Quezon City: New Day Publishers, 1993.

Gloria, Glenda M. "Bouncing Back." *Newsbreak*, April 1, 2002: 8–10.

———. *We Were Soldiers: Military Men in Politics and the Bureaucracy*. Quezon City: Friedrich-Ebert Stiftung, 2003.

Gloria, Glenda, Aries Rufo, and Gemma Bagayaua-Mendoza. *The Enemy Within: An Inside Story On Military Corruption*. Quezon City: Public Trust Media Group, 2011, 144.

Go, Miriam. "People Power Aborted." *Newsbreak*, September 1, 2003: 28–29.

Go, Miriam Grace A. "Despite Huge Margins, Duterte Sweeps Only 3 Regions." *Rappler*, May 12, 2016. Available at http://www.rappler.com/nation/politics/elections/2016/132728-regional-winners-presidential-election (last accessed May 14, 2016).

Gochoco-Bautista, Maria Socorro, and Dante Canlas. "Monetary and Exchange Rate Policy." In *The Philippine Economy: Development, Policies, and Challenges*, ed. Arsenio M. Balisacan and Hal Hill, 77–105. Quezon City: Ateneo de Manila University Press, 2003.

Golay, Frank. *Face of Empire: United States–Philippine Relations, 1898–1946*. Madison: University of Wisconsin, Center for Southeast Asian Studies, 1998.

———. *The Philippines: Public Policy and National Economic Development*. Ithaca, NY: Cornell University Press, 1961.

———. *Underdevelopment and Economic Nationalism in Southeast Asia*. Ithaca, NY: Cornell University Press, 1969.

Gonzalez, Andrew B. *Language and Nationalism: The Philippine Experience Thus Far*. Quezon City: Ateneo de Manila University Press, 1980.

Gopinath, Aruna. *Manuel L. Quezon: The Tutelary Democrat*. Quezon City: New Day Publishers, 1987.

Gowing, Peter G. *Mandate in Moroland: The American Government of Muslim Filipinos, 1899–1920*. Quezon City: Philippine Center for Advanced Studies, University of the Philippines, 1977.

———. *Muslim Filipinos: Heritage and Horizon*. Quezon City: New Day Publishers, 1979.

Gowing, Peter G., and Robert D. McAmis, eds. *The Muslim Filipinos*. Manila: Solidaridad, 1974.

Growth with Equity in Mindanao. GEM Program—Main Report, August 28, 1995–September 30, 2002.

The Guardian. 2016. "James Taylor Cancels Philippines Concert over Rodrigo Duterte's Drug War Killings." December 21, 2016. Available at https://www.theguardian.com/world/2016/dec/21/james-taylor-cancels-philippines-show-rodrigo-duterte-drug-war-killings (last accessed December 25, 2016).

Guerrero, Leon Maria. *The First Filipino: A Biography of José Rizal*. Pasig, The Philippines: Anvil Publishing, 1998.

Guerrero, Sylvia H., ed. *Towards Feminist Consciousness: Filipino Mothers and Daughters Tell Their Story*. Quezon City: University of the Philippines, University Center for Women Studies, 1997.

Guerrero-Nakpil, Carmen. "The Shedding of Innocence." *Sunday Times* (Manila) *Magazine*, February 22, 1970: 9.

Gutierrez, Eric, Aijaz Ahmad, Francisco L. Gonzales, Eliseo R. Mercado, Joel Rocamora, Marites Dañguilan Vitug, and Abdulwahal Guialal. *Rebels, Warlords, and Ulama: A Reader on Muslim Separatism and the War in Southern Philippines*. Quezon City: Institute for Popular Democracy, 2000.

Gutierrez, Eric U., Ildefonso C. Torrente, and Noli G. Narca. *All in the Family: A Study of Elites and Power Relations in the Philippines*, ed. Noel T. Pangilinan. Quezon City: Institute for Popular Democracy, 1992.

Guzman, Odine de. "Overseas Filipino Workers, Labor Circulation in Southeast Asia, and the (Mis)management of Overseas Migration Programs." *Kyoto Review of Southeast Asia* 4 (October 2003). Available at http://kyotoreview.cseas.kyoto-u.ac.jp/issue/issue3/index.html (last accessed October 15, 2004).

Hale, Erin. "Why Rodrigo Duterte May Not Be as Popular in the Philippines as He Thinks." *Forbes*, December 16, 2016. Available at http://www.forbes.com/sites/erinhale/2016/12/16/why-rodrigo-duterte-may-not-be-as-popular-in-the-philippines-as-he-thinks/ (last accessed December 23, 2016).

Harper, T. N. *The End of Empire and the Making of Malaya*. Cambridge: Cambridge University Press, 1999.

Harrison, Francis Burton. *Origins of the Philippine Republic: Extracts from the Diaries and Records of Francis Burton Harrison*, ed. Michael P. Onorato. Ithaca, NY: Cornell University, Southeast Asia Program, 1974.

Hau, Caroline S. "'Who Will Save Us from the Law?' The Criminal State and the Illegal Alien in Post-1986 Philippines." In *Figures of Criminality in Indonesia, the Philippines, and Colonial Vietnam*, ed. Vicente L. Rafael, 128–51. Ithaca, NY: Cornell University, Southeast Asia Program, 1999.

Hau, Caroline S., ed. *Intsik: An Anthology of Chinese Filipino Writings*. Pasig, The Philippines: Anvil Publishing, 2000.

———. *Necessary Fictions: Philippine Literature and the Nation, 1946–1980*. Quezon City: Ateneo de Manila University Press, 2000.

Hayden, Joseph Ralston. *The Philippines: A Study in National Development*. New York: Macmillan, 1942.

Hefner, Robert W. "Civil Society and Democracy." *Journal: Civnet's Journal for Civil Society* 2, no. 3 (May/June 1998).

Hegina, Aries Joseph. "All the President's Men: 5 Officials Defended by Aquino." *Philippine Daily Inquirer*, September 12, 2014. Available at http://newsinfo.inquirer.net/637569/all-the-presidents-men-5-officials-defended-by-aquino (last accessed May 9, 2016).

———. "Only P200M, Not P5B of CCT Funds Are Unliquidated by Philpost— DWSD. *Philippine Daily Inquirer*, September 3, 2014. Available at http://

newsinfo.inquirer.net/635115/only-p200-m-not-p5b-cct-funds-are-unliquidated
-by-philpost-dswd (last accessed May 9, 2016).

Herrin, Alejandro N. "Consensus Lack Marks RP Population Policy." *Philippine Star*, August 23, 2003.

Herrin, Alejandro N., and Ernesto M. Pernia. "Population, Human Resources, and Employment." In *The Philippine Economy: Development, Policies, and Challenges*, ed. Arsenio M. Balisacan and Hal Hill, 283–309. Quezon City: Ateneo de Manila University Press, 2003.

Hicken, Allen. "The Philippines in 2007: Ballots, Budgets, and Bribes," *Asian Survey* 48, no. 1 (January/December 2008).

———. "The Philippines in 2008: Peace-building, War-fighting, and Crisis Management," *Asian Survey* 49, no. 1 (January/February 2009).

Hilhorst, Dorothea. *The Real World of NGOs: Discourses, Diversity, and Development*. Quezon City: Ateneo de Manila University Press, 2003.

Ho, Alex. "Duterte Explains: Why the Rich Are Beyond Reach of Drug War." *CNN Philippines*, August 25, 2016. Available at http://cnnphilippines.com/news/2016/08/24/Duterte-why-rich-beyond-reach-drug-war.html (last accessed December 21, 2016).

Hobsbawm, Eric. [E. J. Hobsbawm.] *The Age of Empire, 1875–1914*. New York: Pantheon Books, 1987.

———. *The Age of Extremes: A History of the World, 1914–1991*. New York: Pantheon Books, 1994.

———. *The Age of Revolution, 1789–1848*. New York: Vintage Books, 1996.

Hofileña, Chay F. "VP Binay Liable for Graft and Corruption—COA." *Rappler*, March 10, 2016. Available at http://www.rappler.com/nation/125289-vp-binay
-liable-graft-corruption-coa (last accessed May 14, 2016).

Holden, William N. "Ashes from the Phoenix: State Terrorism and the Party-List Groups in the Philippines." *Contemporary Politics* 15, no. 4 (2009): 377–93.

Human Rights Watch. "'They Own the People.' The Ampatuans, State-Backed Militias and Killings in the Southern Philippines." New York. November 2010.

———. "You Can Die Any Time: Death Squads Killings in Mindanao." June 4, 2009. Available at https://www.hrw.org/report/2009/04/06/you-can-die-any-time/death
-squad-killings-mindanao (last accessed January 2, 2016).

Hutchcroft, Paul D. *Booty Capitalism: The Politics of Banking in the Philippines*. Ithaca, NY: Cornell University Press, 1998.

Hutchcroft, Paul D., and Joel Rocamora. "Strong Demands and Weak Institutions: The Origins and Evolution of the Democratic Deficit in the Philippines." *Journal of East Asian Studies* 3, no. 2 (Spring 2003): 259–92.

Hutchinson, Jane. "Housing the Poor in Metro Manila." Workshop run by Asia Research Centre, Murdoch University, The Elephant in the Room: Politics and the Development Problem, December 13–14, 2010, 104.

Ileto, Reynaldo Clemeña. [Reynaldo C. Ileto.] *Filipinos and Their Revolution: Event, Discourse, and Historiography*. Quezon City: Ateneo de Manila University Press, 1998.

————. "Laurel and the Struggles over Philippine History." Paper presented at the Asian Studies Conference–Japan, Tokyo, June 22–23, 2002.

————. *Pasyon and Revolution: Popular Movements in the Philippines, 1840–1910.* Quezon City: Ateneo de Manila University Press, 1989.

"Illegal Gambling Has a Grassroots Base." Philippine Center for Investigative Journalism and Institute for Popular Democracy Reports, December 4, 1995: 6–7.

Ilocos Sur. The Heritage Province of Ilocos Sur: Official Website of the Province of Ilocos Sur. Available at http://www.ilocossur.gov.ph/index.php?option=com_content&view=article&id=78&Ite mid=190 (last accessed February 23, 2016).

International Crisis Group. "The Communist Insurgency in the Philippines: Tactics and Talks." *Asia Report* No. 202, February 14, 2011.

————. "Philippine Terrorism: The Role of Militant Islamic Converts." *Asia Report* No. 110, December 19, 2005.

————. "The Philippines: After the Maguindanao Massacre." *Asian Briefing* No. 98, December 21, 2009.

————. "The Philippines: The Collapse of Peace in Mindanao." *Asia Briefing* No. 83 (October 23, 2008): 2–15.

————. "The Philippines: Running in Place in Mindanao." *Asia Briefing* No. 88 (February 16, 2009): 1–9.

————. "Southern Philippines Backgrounder: Terrorism and the Peace Process." *Asia Report* No. 8, July 13, 2004. Available at http://www.crisisweb.org/home/index.cfm?id=2863&1=1 (last accessed October 15, 2004).

"Interview with Datu Piang of Dulawan, 1926." Joseph Ralston Hayden Papers. University of Michigan, Box 28-24.

Javate de Dios, Aurora, Petronilo Bn. Daroy, and Lorna Kalaw-Tirol, eds. *Dictatorship and Revolution: Roots of People's Power.* Manila: Conspectus, 1988.

Javellana, Rene B. "The Colonial Townscape." In *Kasaysayan: The Story of the Filipino People.* Vol. 3, *The Spanish Conquest*, ed. Jose S. Arcilla, 66–83. Manila: Asia Publishing Co., 1998.

Javier, Kristian. "OFT remittances seen to reach 'all-time high' $28B in 2016," *PhilStar Global*, December 21, 2016. Available at http://www.philstar.com/business/2016/12/21/1655597/ofw-remittances-seen-reach-all-time-high-28b-2016 (last accessed March 17, 2017).

Jaymalin, Mayen. "Comelec: Case vs. Mega Pacific Filed." *Philippine Star*, December 16, 2005. Available at http://www.philstar.com/headlines/312395/comelec-case-vs-mega-pacific-filed (last accessed May 24, 2016).

Jenista, Frank, Jr. "Conflict in the Philippine Legislature: The Commission and the Assembly from 1907 to 1913." In *Compadre Colonialism: Studies on the Philippines under American Rule*, ed. Norman G. Owen, 35–44. Ann Arbor: Center for South and Southeast Asian Studies, University of Michigan, 1971.

Jesus, Ed [Edilberto] C. de. "Control and Compromise in the Cagayan Valley." In *Philippine Social History: Global Trade and Local Transformations*, ed. Alfred W. McCoy and Ed C. de Jesus, 21–37. Quezon City: Ateneo de Manila University Press, 1982.

Joaquin, Nick. *Jaime Ongpin, the Enigma: A Profile of the Filipino as Manager.* Manila: J. V. Ongpin Institute of Business and Government, 1990.

———. *Manila, My Manila: A History for the Young.* Manila: Republic of the Philippines, 1990.

Joaquin, Tony. *Simple Memories: A Memoir.* Pasig, The Philippines: Anvil Publishing, 2000.

Jocano, F. Landa, ed. *The Philippines at the Spanish Contact: Some Major Accounts of Early Filipino Society and Culture.* Manila: MCS Enterprises, 1975.

Jones, Gregg. *Red Revolution: Inside the Philippine Guerrilla Movement.* Boulder, CO: Westview Press, 1989.

Jopson, Teresa. "Making Peace with the Bangsamoro Basic Law." *East Asia Forum,* May 11, 2016. Available at http://www.eastasiaforum.org/2016/05/11/making -peace-with-the-bangsamoro-basic-law/ (last accessed May 12, 2016).

"Jueteng Is Embedded in Local Society and Culture." Philippine Center for Investigative Journalism and Institute for Popular Democracy Reports, December 4, 1995: 8–11.

Junker, Laura Lee. *Raiding, Trading, and Feasting: The Political Economy of Philippine Chiefdoms.* Honolulu: University of Hawai'i Press, 1999.

K. [Kadir] Che Man, W. *Muslim Separatism: The Moros of Southern Philippines and the Malays of Southern Thailand.* Quezon City: Ateneo de Manila University Press, 1974.

Kakesako, Gregg K. "Hawaii Leads Joint War Games." *Honolulu Star Bulletin,* February 8, 2000. Available at http://archives.starbulletin.com/2000/02/08/news/ story3.html (last accessed March 3, 2016).

Kalaw, Maximo Manguiat. *The Development of Philippine Politics.* Manila: Oriental Commercial Co., 1926.

———. "The Moro Bugaboo." *Philippine Social Review* (1931).

Kalaw, Teodoro M. *The Philippine Revolution.* Kawilihan: Jorge B. Vargas Filipiniana Foundation, 1969.

Kalaw-Tirol, Lorna. "Winnie Monsod: Thoroughbred Maverick." In *Public Lives, Private Lives.* Pasig, The Philippines: Anvil Publishing, 2000.

Kar, Dev, and Brian LeBlanc. "Illicit Financial Flows to and from the Philippines: A Study in Dynamic Simulation, 1960–2011." Global Finance Integrity, February 2014. Available at http://iff.gfintegrity.org/iff2013/Illicit_Financial_Flows_ from_Developing_Countries_2002-2011-HighRes.pdf (last accessed May 14, 2016).

Karaos, Ana Maria et al., eds. *NGO and PO Policy Influence in Urban Land Reform Advocacy.* Quezon City: Institute on Church and Social Issues, 1995.

Karunungan, Lilian. "Duterte's Talked the Peso to Its Lowest in Seven Years." *Bloomberg,* November 1, 2016. Available at https://www.bloomberg.com/news/ articles/2016-11-01/duterte-seen-talking-peso-beyond-50-level-reached-in -2008-crisis (last accessed December 25, 2016).

Kawanaka, Takeshi. *Power in a Philippine City.* Chiba, Japan: Institute of Developing Economies and Japan External Trade Organization, 2002.

Keenan, Jilliam. "The Grim Reality behind the Philippines' Economic Growth." *Atlantic Monthly*, May 7, 2013. Available at http://www.theatlantic.com/international/archive/2013/05/the-grim-reality-behind-the-philippines-economic-growth/275597/ (last accessed May 14, 2015).

Kerkvliet, Benedict J. Tria. "Contested Meanings of Elections in the Philippines." In *The Politics of Elections in Southeast Asia*, ed. R. H. Taylor, 136–63. New York: Cambridge University Press, 1996.

Kim, Eunju, and Jayoung Yoo. "Conditional Cash Transfer in the Philippines: How to Overcome Institutional Constraints for Implementing Social Protection." *Asia and Pacific Policy Studies* 2, no. 1, 2015: 79–82.

Krinks, Peter. *The Economy of the Philippines: Elites, Inequalities, and Economic Restructuring*. London: Routledge, 2002.

Kwiatkowski, Lynn M. *Struggling with Development: The Politics of Hunger and Gender in the Philippines*. Quezon City: Ateneo de Manila University Press, 1999.

Labrador, Mel C. "The Philippines in 2000: In Search of a Silver Lining." *Asian Survey* 41, no. 1 (January/February 2001).

———. "The Philippines in 2001: High Drama, a New President and Setting the Stage for Recovery," *Asian Survey* 42, no. 1 (January/February 2002).

Lacaba, Jose F. *Days of Disquiet, Nights of Rage: The First Quarter Storm and Related Events*. Pasig, The Philippines: Anvil Publishing, 2003.

Lacaba, Jose F., ed. *Boss: Five Case Studies of Local Politics in the Philippines*. Manila: Philippine Center for Investigative Journalism and Institute for Popular Democracy, 1995.

Lanao, Provincial Government of. n.d. "Development Partners, Province of Lanao del Norte: The Land of Beauty and Bounty." Available at http://www.lanaodelnorte.gov.ph/Development-Partners/ngo.html (last accessed February 23, 2016).

Landé, Carl H. *Leaders, Factions, and Parties: The Structure of Philippine Politics*. Southeast Asia Studies Monograph Series no. 6. New Haven, CT: Yale University, 1964.

Landingin, Roel R. "New Joint-Venture Rules Allow Little Oversight, More Abuse." Philippine Center for Investigative Journalism, July 2009. Available at http://pcij.org/stories/2009/laiban2.html (last accessed February 5, 2016).

Laquian, Aprodicio, and Eleanor Laquian. *Joseph Ejercito "Erap" Estrada, the Centennial President*. Vancouver, BC: University of Vancouver, Institute of Asian Research; Quezon City: University of the Philippines, College of Public Administration, 1998.

Lava, Jesus B. *Memoirs of a Communist*. Pasig, The Philippines: Anvil Publishing, 2002.

Law, Lisa. "Cebu and *Ceboom*: Globalisation in a Philippine City." In *Pacific Rim Development: Integration and Globalisation in the Asia Pacific Economy*, ed. Peter Rimmer, 240–66. Sydney: Allen and Unwin, 1997.

Lazaro, Freddie G. "Singsons Preserve Political Mastery in Ilocos Sur." *Balita*, May 13, 2010. Available at http://balita.ph/2010/05/13/singsons-preserve-political-mastery-in-ilocos- sur/ (last accessed March 12, 2016).

Legarda, Benito J. *After the Galleons: Foreign Trade, Economic Change, and Entrepreneurship in the Nineteenth-Century Philippines*. Quezon City: Ateneo de Manila University Press, 1999.

Leonen, Mike. "Big Time Corruption in a Small Power Plant." Philippine Center for Investigative Journalism, 2001. Available at http://pcij.org/stories/print/power2.html (last accessed February 23, 2016).

Lim, Kenneth. "Duterte Backed by Filipino Businessmen, Warns Corrupt Officials to 'Stop It' and Declares Open Season on Criminals." *Inquisitr*, June 23, 2016. Available at http://www.inquisitr.com/3236008/duterte-backed-by-filipino-businessmen-warns-corrupt-officials-to-stop-it-and-declares-open-season-on-criminals/ (last accessed December 10, 2016).

Lim Yoon Lin, ed. *Trends in the Philippines: Proceedings and Background Paper*. Singapore: Singapore University Press, for the Institute of Southeast Asian Studies, 1972.

Linantud, John. "Whither Guns, Goons, and Gold? The Decline of Factional Election Violence in the Philippines." *Contemporary Southeast Asia* 20, no. 3 (December 1998): 298–318.

Lingao, Ed. "Grease." *I: The Investigative Reporting Magazine*, July–September 2001: 31–34.

Lo, Barnaby. "Philippines' Ex-Leader Arroyo Arrested, Again." *CBS News*, October 4, 2012. Available at http://www.cbsnews.com/news/philippines-ex-leader-arroyo-arrested-again/ (last accessed April 7, 2016).

Lopez, Antonio. "When Will They Ever End?" *Asiaweek*, December 19, 1997. Available at http://asiaweek.com/asiaweek/97/1219/nat1c.html (last accessed July 15, 2003).

Lopez, Tony. "Economic Growth under Aquino." *The Standard*, February 3, 2016. Available at http://www.thestandard.com.ph/opinion/columns/virtual-reality-by-tony-lopez/198354/economic-growth-under-aquino.html (last accessed May 19, 2016).

Lopez, Salvador P. *Elpidio Quirino: The Judgement of History*. Manila: Elpidio Quirino Foundation, 1990.

Los Angeles Times. "Terrorists Plotted to Blow Up 11 U.S. Jumbo Jets." May 28, 1995. Available at http://articles.baltimoresun.com/1995-05-28/news/1995148047_1_bojinka-philippines-plot (last accessed March 15, 2016).

Lotilla, Raphael Perpetuo M., ed. *The Philippine National Territory: A Collection of Related Documents*. Quezon City: Institute of International Legal Studies, University of the Philippines Law Center and Foreign Service Institute, Department of Foreign Affairs, 1995.

Luton, Harry. "American Internal Revenue Policy in the Philippines to 1916." In *Compadre Colonialism: Studies on the Philippines under American Rule*, ed. Norman G. Owen, 65–80. Ann Arbor: Center for South and Southeast Asian Studies, University of Michigan, 1971.

Macariag, Mynardo. "Arroyo Pushes for End to US-Style Government." *Bangkok Post*, August 2, 2004.

Macas, Trisha. "Duterte's Economic Team Reveals 10-Point Socioeconomic Agenda." *GMA News Online*, June 20, 2016. Available at http://www.gmanetwork.com/

news/story/570703/money/economy/duterte-s-economic-team-reveals-10-point
-socioeconomic-agenda (last accessed December 28, 2016).

———. "Duterte to 'Yellows': Reds Will Kill You If You Oust Me," *GMA News Online*, December 14, 2016. Available at http://www.gmanetwork.com/news/story/592393/news/nation/duterte-to-yellows-reds-will-kill-you-if-you-oust-me (last accessed December 19, 2016).

MacIntyre, Andrew J. *The Power of Institutions: Political Architecture and Governance*. Ithaca, NY: Cornell University Press, 2003.

Magadia, Jose. *State–Society Dynamics: Policy Making in a Restored Democracy*. Quezon City: Ateneo de Manila University, 2003.

Magno, Alex. "The State of Rebellion Is Not a Proclamation—It's a Description of the Situation." *UP Forum Online*, May 2001. Available at http://www.up.edu.ph/forum/2001/5/magno.html (last accessed October 15, 2004).

Majul, Cesar Adib. *Mabini and the Philippine Revolution*. Quezon City: University of the Philippines Press, 1960.

———. *Muslims in the Philippines*. 2nd ed. Quezon City: University of the Philippines Press, 1973.

Mangahas, Malou C. "The Politics of Justice." *I: The Investigative Reporting Magazine*, January–March 2002: 7–11.

Mangahas, Maria Lourdes. "The Transactional President." *I: The Investigative Reporting Magazine*, April–June 2001: 6–11.

Mangunay, Kristine Felisse. "INC Backs Duterte, Marcos." *Philippine Daily Inquirer*, May 5, 2016. Available at http://newsinfo.inquirer.net/783270/inc-backs-duterte-marcos (last accessed December 1, 2016).

Marr, David G. *Vietnamese Tradition on Trial, 1920–1945*. Berkeley: University of California Press, 1981.

Matsuzawa, Mikas, and Patricia Viray. "Casualties of Rody's War." *Philippine Star*, September 19, 2016. Available at http://newslab.philstar.com/war-on-drugs/poverty (last accessed December 21, 2016).

Maxfield, Sylvia, and James Nolt. "Protectionism and the Internationalization of Capital: U.S. Sponsorship of Import Substitution Industrialization in the Philippines, Turkey, and Argentina." *International Studies Quarterly* 34 (1990): 49–81.

May, Glenn Anthony. *Battle for Batangas: A Philippine Province at War*. New Haven, CT: Yale University Press, 1993.

———. "Civic Ritual and Political Reality: Municipal Elections in the Late Nineteenth Century." In *Philippine Colonial Democracy*, ed. Ruby R. Paredes, 13–40. Quezon City: Ateneo de Manila University Press, 1989.

May, R. J., and Francisco Nemenzo, eds. *The Philippines after Marcos*. New York: St. Martin's Press, 1985.

McCoy, Alfred W. "A Queen Dies Slowly: The Rise and Decline of Iloilo City." In *Philippine Social History: Global Trade and Local Transformations*, ed. Alfred W. McCoy and Ed C. de Jesus, 297–358. Quezon City: Ateneo de Manila University Press, 1982.

———. *Closer than Brothers: Manhood at the Philippine Military Academy*. New Haven, CT: Yale University Press, 1999.

———. "In Extreme Unction: The Philippine Sugar Industry under Martial Law." In *Political Economy of Philippine Commodities*, ed. R. S. David, 135–80. Quezon City: Third World Studies Program, 1983.

———. *Policing America's Empire: The United States, the Philippines, and the Rise of the Surveillance State*. Madison: University of Wisconsin Press, 2009, 15–58.

———. "Quezon's Commonwealth: The Emergence of Philippine Authoritarianism." In *Philippine Colonial Democracy*, ed. Ruby R. Paredes, 114–60. Quezon City: Ateneo de Manila University Press, 1989.

———. "The Social History of an Archipelago: Introduction." In *Philippine Social History: Global Trade and Local Transformations*, ed. Alfred W. McCoy and Ed C. de Jesus, 1–18. Quezon City: Ateneo de Manila University Press, 1982.

McCoy, Alfred W., ed. *An Anarchy of Families: State and Family in the Philippines*. Madison: University of Wisconsin, Center for Southeast Asian Studies, 1993.

McCoy, Alfred W., and Ed C. de Jesus, eds. *Philippine Social History: Global Trade and Local Transformations*. Quezon City: Ateneo de Manila University Press, 1982.

McKenna, Thomas M. *Muslim Rulers and Rebels: Everyday Politics and Armed Separatism in the Southern Philippines*. Berkeley: University of California Press, 1998.

McKinley, William H. "Instructions to the Taft Commission through the Secretary of War." United States War Department, April 7, 1900. In *Annual Report of the War Department*. Washington, DC: Government Printing Office, 1909.

McKirdy, Euan. "Philippines Mayor, Bodyguards Killed in Shootout." *CNN*, October 28, 2016. Available at http://www.cnn.com/2016/10/28/asia/philippines-mayor -killed/ (last accessed December 21, 2016).

McLennan, Marshall S. "Changing Human Ecology on the Central Luzon Plain: Nueva Ecija, 1705–1939." In *Philippine Social History: Global Trade and Local Transformations*, ed. Alfred W. McCoy and Ed C. de Jesus, 57–90. Quezon City: Ateneo de Manila University Press, 1982.

Mendoza, Ronald U., and Miann Banaag. "Under Decentralization: More Ampatuans Than Robredos," *Rappler*, November 26, 2016. Available at http://www.rappler .com/thought-leaders/153682-decentralization-political-dynasties-ampatuan -robredo (last accessed November 27, 2106).

"Merceditas Gutierrez Resigns as Ombudsman." *The Economist*, 31 May 2011. Available at http://country.eiu.com/article.aspx?articleid=1628143747&Country =Philippines&topic=Politics&subtopic=Recent+developments&subsubtopic=The +political+scene:+Merceditas+Gutierrez+resigns+as+ombudsman (last accessed April 7, 2016).

Merez, Arianne. "Duterte's Narco List Has More Than 5,000 Gov't Officials." *ABS-CBN News*, November 27, 2016. Available at http://news.abs-cbn.com/ news/11/27/16/dutertes-narco-list-has-more-than-5000-govt-officials (last ac- cessed December 21, 2016).

Migdal, Joel S. "The State in Society: An Approach to Struggles for Domination." In *State Power and Social Forces: Domination and Transformation in the Third World*, ed. Joel S. Migdal, Atul Kohli, and Vivienne Shue, 7–34. Cambridge: Cambridge University Press, 1994.

Migdal, Joel S., Atul Kohli, and Vivienne Shue, eds. *State Power and Social Forces: Domination and Transformation in the Third World*. Cambridge: Cambridge University Press. 1994.

Mileur, Jerome M. "The Legacy of Reform: Progressive Government, Regressive Politics." In *Progressivism and the New Democracy*, ed. Sidney M. Milkis and Jerome M. Mileur, 259–87. Amherst: University of Massachusetts Press, 1999.

Miranda, Felipe. "The Military." In *The Philippines after Marcos*, ed. R. J. May and Francisco Nemenzo, 90–109. New York: St. Martin's Press, 1985.

Miranda, Felipe B., and Ruben Ciron. "Development and the Military in the Philippines: Military Perceptions in a Time of Continuing Crisis." In *Soldiers and Stability in Southeast Asia*, ed. J. Soedjatudjiwando and Yong Mun Cheong, 163–212. Singapore: Institute of Southeast Asian Studies, 1988.

Mojares, Resil B. "The Dream Goes On and On: Three Generations of the Osmeñas, 1906–1990." In *An Anarchy of Families: State and Family in the Philippines*, ed. Alfred W. McCoy, 311–46. Madison: University of Wisconsin, Center for Southeast Asian Studies, 1993.

——. *The Man Who Would Be President: Sergio Osmeña and Philippine Politics.* Cebu: Maria Cacao Publishers, 1986.

——. *Vicente Sotto, the Maverick Senator.* Cebu City: Cebuano Studies Center, 1992.

——. *The War against the Americans: Resistance and Collaboration in Cebu, 1899–1906.* Quezon City: Ateneo de Manila University Press, 1999.

Monk, Paul M. *Truth and Power: Robert S. Hardie and Land Reform Debates in the Philippines, 1950–1987.* Clayton, Vic., Australia: Centre for Southeast Asian Studies, Monash University, 1990.

Monsod, Solita Collas. "The War against Poverty: A Status Report." In *The Philippines: New Directions in Domestic Policy and Foreign Relations*, ed. David G. Timberman, 85–110. Singapore: Institute of Southeast Asian Studies, 1998.

Montesano, Michael J. "The Philippines in 2002: Playing Politics, Facing Deficits, and Embracing Uncle Sam." *Asian Survey* 43, no. 1 (January/February 2003): 156–66.

——. "The Philippines in 2003: Troubles, None of Them New." *Asian Survey* 44, no. 1 (January/February 2004): 93–101.

Moss, Trevor. "Behind Duterte's Break with the U.S., a Lifetime of Resentment." *Wall Street Journal*, October 21, 2016. Available at http://www.wsj.com/articles/behind-philippine-leaders-break-with-the-u-s-a-lifetime-of-resentment-1477061118 (last accessed December 21, 2016).

Nemenzo, Francisco. "An Irrepressible Revolution: The Decline and Resurgence of the Philippine Communist Movement." Manuscript, Cornell University, November 13, 1984.

Newsom, Linda. "Old World Diseases in Early Colonial Philippines and Spanish America." In *Population and History: The Demographic Origins of Modern Philippines*, ed. Daniel F. Doeppers and Peter Xenos, 17–36. Quezon City: Ateneo de Manila University Press, 1998.

Nilles, Giovanni, and Prinz Magtulis. "Rody Not to Blame for Weaker Peso." *Philstar Global*, September 28, 2016. Available at http://www.philstar.com/headlines/2016/09/28/1628223/rody-not-blame-weaker-peso (last accessed December 25, 2016).

"No More Ransoms." *The Economist*, May 31, 2001.

"Noy's Fight vs. Corruption Marks Modest Progress." *Philstar Global*, November 15, 2015. Available at http://www.philstar.com/headlines/2015/11/15/1521970/noys-fight-vs-corruption-marks-modest-progress (last accessed May 9, 2016).

Office of the President, Republic of the Philippines. "Executive Order No. 1, s. 2010, creating the Philippine Truth Commission of 2010." July 30, 2010. Available at http://www.gov.ph/2010/07/30/executive-order-no-1-s-2010/ (last accessed May 14, 2016).

Official Gazette. "Document: The Draft Bangsamoro Basic Law: House Bill No. 5811, Submitted to the Ad Hoc Committee on May 27, 2015. Available at http://www.gov.ph/2014/09/10/document-the-draft-bangsamoro-basic-law/ (last accessed May 13, 2016).

Olchondra, Riza T. "Arroyo Has Best Growth in Full Term, Aquino Tops 1st Year Growth among Presidents." *Philippine Daily Inquirer*, January 28, 2013. Available at http://business.inquirer.net/104813/arroyo-has-best-growth-in-full-term-aquino-tops-1st-year-growth-among-presidents-nscb (last accessed May 19, 2016).

Ortega, Randy K. "Beleaguered Honrado Not Resigning." *Politiko*, 9 May 2016. Available at http://politics.com.ph/beleaguered-honrado-not-resigning/ (last accessed May 8, 2016).

"Our Crony-Capitalism Index: The Party Winds Down." *The Economist*, May 7, 2016. Available at http://www.economist.com/news/international/21698239-across-world-politically-connected-tycoons-are-feeling-squeeze-party-winds (last accessed May 12, 2016).

Owen, Norman G., ed. *Compadre Colonialism: Studies on the Philippines under American Rule*. Ann Arbor: Center for South and Southeast Asian Studies, University of Michigan, 1971.

Paderanga, Cayetano, Cristine Atienza, Ferdinand Co, and Flora Belle Villarante. "The Erap Economy." In *Between Fires: Fifteen Perspectives on the Estrada Crisis*, ed. Amando Doronila, 180–99. Pasig, The Philippines: Anvil Publishing, 2001.

Padilla, Minguita. "Business as Usual?" Commentary. *Philippine Daily Inquirer*, July 29, 2004.

Paez, Concepcion. "Run Gloria, Run." *Newsbreak*, November 10, 2003: 14–17.

Pangilinan, Francis. "Why Manila Left Iraq Early." *Far Eastern Economic Review*, July 29, 2004: 24.

Paredes, Ruby R., ed. *Philippine Colonial Democracy*. Quezon City: Ateneo de Manila University Press, 1989.

Parentildeo, Roel. "Salamat Dead; Murad Takes Over." *Philstar Global*, August 6, 2003. Available at http://www.philstar.com/headlines/216252/salamat-dead -murad-takes-over (last accessed March 31, 2016).

Parmanand, Sharmila. "Mapping the Paths to Philippine Reproductive Rights Legislation: Signs of Progress amidst Obstacles." *Social Transformations* 2, no.1 (February 2014): 61–80.

"The Party List." *Philippine Daily Inquirer*, June 6, 2004.

Pascual, Federico D., Jr. "Ramos, Estrada, Arroyo All Had a Hand in Impsa." *Philippine Star*, December 19, 2002. Available at http://www.philstar.com/ opinion/188449/ramos-estrada-arroyo-all-had-hand-impsa (last accessed March 1, 2016).

Patanñe, E. P. *The Philippines in the Sixth to Sixteenth Centuries*. Manila: LSA Press, 1996.

Paul, Anthony. "Philippines: Kidnapping Problem Spreads." *Fortune*, March 17, 1997.

"The People of the Philippines, plaintiff-appellee vs. Romeo G. Jalosjos, accused-appellant. G.R. Nos. 132875-76, November 16, 2011. Available at http:// sc.judiciary.gov.ph/jurisprudence/2001/nov2001/132875_76.htm (last accessed March 1, 2016).

Pernia, Ernesto M. "Population: Does It Matter? Revisiting an Old Issue." *Philippine Star*, August 16, 2003.

Philippine Center for Investigative Journalism. "Charter Change Moves Copied from the Marcos Book." May 2, 2006. Available at http://pcij.org/stories/arroyos -charter-change-moves-copied-from-the-marcos-book/ (last accessed April 7, 2016).

Philippine Civil Society and International Solidarity Partners: Strengthening Local and Global Advocacy Initiatives: Conference Proceedings. Quezon City: Bayanihan International Solidarity Conference, 2001.

Philippine Daily Inquirer. "The Kill List." July 7, 2016, Available at http://newsinfo .inquirer.net/794598/kill-list-drugs-duterte (last accessed December 23, 2016).

Philippine Democracy Agenda. Diliman, The Philippines: Third World Studies Center, 1997.

Philippine Human Development Report. Human Development Network. Manila, 2005.

Philippine Statistics Authority. "Poverty incidence among Filipinos registered at 21.6 in 2015—PSA," October 27, 2016. Available at https://psa.gov.ph/poverty-press -releases (last accessed March 17, 2017).

———. "Labor force survey," 2017. Available at https://psa.gov/ph/poverty-press -releases (last accessed March 17, 2017).

"Philippines: Manila Voted Worst City to Drive on Earth." *BBC News*, October 2, 2015. Available at http://www.bbc.com/news/blogs-news-from-elsewhere -34424367 (last accessed May 9, 2016).

"Philippines: An Outlook for Key Emerging Asian Markets." *The Economist Intelligence Unit*, July 2015, 8. Available at http://www.eiu.com/ (last accessed June 12, 2015).

"Philippines: Pyrrhic Victory and Abysmal Defeat." *Asia Times Online*, July 13, 2000.

"The Philippines GDP and Economic Data," *Global Finance*, March 26, 2017. Available at https://www.gfmag.com/global-data/country-data/the-philippines-gdp-country-report (last accessed March 17, 2017).

Piang, Joseph L. "The Chinese and the Philippine Political Process." In *Philippine Chinese Profile: Essays and Studies*, ed. Charles J. McCarthy, 87–106. Manila: Pagkakaisa sa Pag-unlad, 1974.

Pinches, Michael. "The Making of Middle Class Civil Society in the Philippines." In *The Politics of Change in the Philippines*, ed. Yuko Kasuya and Nathan Gilbert Quimpo. Manila: Anvil, 2010.

"PNP: Crime Rate Down, But Murder Rate Up." *ABS-CBN News*, December 19, 2016. Available at http://news.abs-cbn.com/news/12/19/16/pnp-crime-rate-down -but-murder-rate-up (last accessed December 22, 2016).

Pomeroy, Earl. *The Territories and the United States, 1861–1890: Studies in Colonial Administration*. Seattle: University of Washington Press, 1947.

"Poor miss out on Philippines' economic ascent while rich get richer," *South China Morning Post*, March 5, 2013, http://www.scmp.com/news/asia/article/1177297/ poor-miss-out-philippines-economic-ascent-while-rich-get-richer (last accessed February 13, 2017).

Pulse Asia. "Trust Ratings of President Benigno S. Aquino III, October 2015 to March 2016." Philippines, April 2016.

Putzel, James. "NGOs and Rural Poverty." In *Organizing for Democracy: NGOs, Civil Society, and the Philippine State*, ed. G. Sidney Silliman and Lela Garner Noble, 77–112. Honolulu: University of Hawai'i Press; Quezon City: Ateneo de Manila University Press, 1998.

Quezon, Manuel L., III. "The Origins of Celebrity Politics." *Philippine Daily Inquirer*, February 9, 2004.

Quezon, Manuel Luis. *The Good Fight*. New York: D. Appleton-Century, 1946.

Quimpo. Nathan G. "Can the Philippines' Wild Oligarchy Be Tamed?" In *Routledge Handbook of Southeast Asian Democratization*, ed. William Case, 345. Oxon and New York, 2015.

———. *Contested Democracy and the Left in the Philippines after Marcos*. Quezon City: Ateneo de Manila University Press, 2009.

———. "Countries at the Crossroads 2011: Philippines," *Freedom House*, November 12, 2015, 1–24.

Quirino, Carlos P. *Chick Parsons: Master Spy in the Philippines*. Quezon City: New Day Publishers, 1984.

Rafael, Vicente. *Contracting Colonialism: Translation and Christian Conversion in Tagalog Society under Early Spanish Rule*. Ithaca, NY: Cornell University Press, 1988.

Ramos, Fidel R. "Good Governance against Corruption." Keynote address at the Fletcher School of Law and Diplomacy Conference on Good Governance against Corruption, April 26, 2001, Tufts University, Medford, Mass.

Ramos, Marlon. "Department of Agriculture Squandered P14-B—COA." *Philippine Daily Inquirer*, April 22, 2015. Available at http://newsinfo.inquirer.net/686964/ department-of-agriculture-squandered-p14b-coa (last accessed May 8, 2016).

———. "Duterte to UN: Stop I Am the President." *Philippine Daily Inquirer*, August 26, 2016. Available at http://newsinfo.inquirer.net/810196/un-broke-protocol-in -issuing-statement-against-killings-duterte (last accessed December 8, 2016).

Ranada, Pia. "Duterte's Military Camp Hopping: Way to Soldier's Hearts." *Rappler*, July 31, 2016. Available at http://www.rappler.com/newsbreak/in-depth/141443 -duterte-military-camp-hopping-soldiers-loyalty (last accessed December 14, 2016).

———. "Rody Duterte: The Man, the Mayor, the President." *Rappler*, June 29, 2016. Available at http://www.rappler.com/newsbreak/in-depth/137583-rodrigo-duterte -philippine-president-profile (last accessed October 10, 2016).

———. "Why Has Duterte Visited 14 Military Camps in Less Than a Month?" *Rappler*, August 20, 2016. Available at http://www.rappler.com/newsbreak/in -depth/143584-duterte-military-camp-visits-analysis (last accessed December 10, 2016).

Rappler. "11 Filipinos among World Billionaires." *Rappler*, October 10, 2013. Available at http://www.rappler.com/business/23058-11-filipinos-among-world -billionaires (accessed May 14, 2016).

———. ADB Upgrades PH Growth Forecast for 2016, 2017." December 13, 2016. Available at http://www.rappler.com/business/155409-adb-upgrades-philippines -growth-forecast-2016-2017 (last accessed December 21, 2016).

———. "Aquino Admin's Net Satisfaction Rating Rises to 'Good' + 37 – SWS." *Rappler*, October 13, 2015. Available at http://www.rappler.com/nation/129887-sws -survey-aquino-public-satisfaction-q1-2016 (last accessed May 16, 2016).

———. BSP Best Performer in Gov't; OVP Worst—MBC Poll." August 13, 2015. Available at http://www.rappler.com/business/211-governance/102488-bsp-tops -makati-business-club-survey (accessed August 14, 2015).

———. "Corona Found Guilty, Removed from Office." May 29, 2012. Available at http://www.rappler.com/nation/special-coverage/corona-trial/6099-corona-found -guilty (last accessed April 7, 2016).

———. "Duterte's War on Drugs: The First 6 Months." 2016. Available at http:// www.rappler.com/newsbreak/rich-media/rodrigo-duterte-war-on-drugs-2016 (last accessed December 14, 2016).

———. "The Duterte List: Judges, Mayors, Police Officials Linked to Drugs," August 7, 2016. Available at http://www.rappler.com/nation/142210-duterte-list-lgu -police-officials-linked-drugs (last accessed December 21, 2016).

———. "Duterte vs. De Lima—Previous Articles." Available at http://www.rappler .com/previous-articles?filterMeta=Duterte+vs+De+Lima (last accessed December 22, 2016).

———. "Palace: We Aren't Protecting Allies in Pork Scam." May 17, 2014. Available at http://www.rappler.com/nation/58256-palace-pork-barrel-allies (last accessed April 9, 2016).

———. "Tax Evasion Cases under Aquino Reach 140." January 6, 2013. Available at http://www.rappler.com/business/19226-tax-evasion-cases-under-aquino -reach-140 (last accessed April 10, 2016).

———. "Tax Evasion Case vs. Napoles, Husband." September 26, 2103. Available at http://www.rappler.com/nation/39875-tax-evasion-case-vs-napoles-husband (last accessed April 9, 2016).

———. "Timeline: Mamapasano Clash." February 23, 2015. Available at http://www.rappler.com/nation/82827-timeline-mamasapano-clash (last accessed May 14, 2016).

Raslan, Karin. "How outsourcing transformed the Philippine middle class," *This Week in Asia*, December 29, 2016. Available at http://www.scmp.com/week-asia/business/article/2057901/how-outsourcing-transformed-philippine-middle-class (last accessed March 17, 2017).

Rasul, Amina. "Poverty and Armed Conflict in Mindanao." In *Muslim Perspective on the Mindanao Conflict: The Road to Peace and Reconciliation*, ed. Amina Rasul, 123–46. Makati City, The Philippines: Asian Institute of Management, 2003.

Recto, Claro M. *The Recto Reader: Excerpts from the Speeches of Claro M. Recto*, ed. Renato Constantino. Manila: Recto Memorial Foundation, 1965.

Reed, Robert Ronald. *Colonial Manila: The Context of Hispanic Urbanism and Process of Morphogenesis*. Berkeley: University of California Press, 1978.

———. *Hispanic Urbanism in the Philippines: A Study of the Impact of Church and State*. Manila: University of Manila, 1967.

Regalado, Edith, and Aurea Calica. "Philippines Is Asia's Rising Tiger—World Bank." *PhilStar Global*, February 6, 2013. Available at http://www.philstar.com/headlines/2013/02/06/905371/philippines-asias-rising-tiger-world-bank (last accessed May 14, 2016).

Regencia, Ted, and Mohsin Ali. "Philippines: Death Toll in Duterte's War on Drugs." *Al Jazeera*, December 15, 2016. Available at http://www.aljazeera.com/indepth/interactive/2016/08/philippines-death-toll-duterte-war-drugs-160825115400719.html (last accessed December 23, 2016).

Reid, Anthony. "Islamization and Christianization in Southeast Asia: The Critical Phase, 1550–1650." In *Southeast Asia in the Early Modern Era: Trade, Power, and Belief*, ed. Anthony Reid, 151–79. Ithaca, NY: Cornell University Press, 1993, 328.

———. *Southeast Asia in the Age of Commerce, 1450–1680*. Vol. 2, *Expansion and Crisis*. New Haven, CT: Yale University Press, 1993.

Reid, Ben. "Development NGOs, Semiclientelism and the State in the Philippines: From 'Crossover' to Double-Crossed." *Kasarinlan* 23, no. 1 (2008): 4–42.

———. *Philippine Left: Political Crisis and Social Change*. Manila: *Journal of Contemporary Asia*, 2000.

"Report of the Governor of the Moro Province." In *Report of the Philippine Commission, 1907*. Washington, DC: Government Printing Office, 1908.

"Report of the Governor of the Moro Province, 1908." In *Annual Report of the War Department*. Washington, DC: Government Printing Office, 1909.

Report of the Philippine Commission. January 31, 1900. Washington, DC: Government Printing Office, 1900.

Republic of the Philippines. "Achievements of the Aquino Administration, 2010–2016." Available at http://www.gov.ph/featured/daang-matuwid/ (last accessed May 14, 2016).

———. Congressional Planning and Budget Office. "Special Study: Getting Out of the Fiscal Bind." June 2002: 1–11. Available at http://www.geocities.com/cpbo_hor/specialstudies/fbind.pdf (last accessed January 31, 2004).

———. Constitutional Commission of 1986. *The Constitution of the Republic of the Philippines with Highlights of the 1986 Constitution and Appendices*, comp. NBSI Editorial Staff. Manila: National Book Store, 1986.

———. "A Guide to the Election of Party-List Representatives through the Party List System." Republic Act no. 7941. 1998.

———. Philippine Commission on Women. "Philippine Initiatives to Eliminate VAW." Republic Act No. 9262. Available at http://www.pcw.gov.ph/focus-areas/violence-against-women/initiatives (last accessed March 3, 2016).

———. Philippine Overseas Employment Administration. *Selected Statistics*, 1992.

———. Senate Committee on Accountability of Public Officers and Investigations, "NBN-ZTE Executive Summary," November 11, 2009. Available at https://www.senate.gov.ph/lisdata/1293411633!.pdf (last accessed March 24, 2016).

Resident Commissioner of the Philippines to the U.S. Congress. *The Filipino People*, October 1912.

Ressa, Maria. "The Philippines: War on Terror's Second Front." *CNN World*, April 16, 2002. Available at http://articles.cnn.com/2002-04-16/world/phil.blair_1_abu-sayyaf-joint-military-exercises-martin-and-gracia-burnham?_s=PM:asiapcf (last accessed April 7, 2016).

Reyes, Fat. "Galing Pinoy." *Philippine Daily Inquirer*, October 30, 2012. Available at http://newsinfo.inquirer.net/298524/comelec-disqualifies-mikey-arroyos-ang-galing-pinoy (last accessed April 7, 2016).

Richardson, Andrew James. "The Genesis of the Philippine Communist Party." PhD diss., School of Oriental and African Studies, University of London, 1984.

Ricklefs, M. C. *A History of Modern Indonesia*. London: Macmillan, 1981.

Rimando, Lala. "Voting Away from Home." *Newsbreak*, May 10, 2004: 12–13.

Rimban, Luz. "In and Out." *I: The Investigative Reporting Magazine*, October–December 1998: 13–16.

———. "Lights, Camera, Election." *I: The Investigative Reporting Magazine*, January–June 1998: 40–45.

———. "Power Play on Paper." *I: The Investigative Reporting Magazine*, April 2001: 45–48.

———. "Strange Bedfellows." In Sheila S. Coronel et al., *The Rulemakers: How the Wealthy and Well-born Dominate Congress*, 218–29. Manila: Philippine Center for Investigative Journalism, 2004.

Ripley, Will, and Jay Croft. "Philippines Drug War's Wide Net Claims 6-Year Old Shot Dead in His Sleep," *CNN World*, December 16, 2016. Available at http://www.cnn.com/2016/12/15/world/philippines-duterte-killings/ (last accessed December 23, 2016).

Rivera, Danessa O. "PHL Ranking in Global Corruption Perception Good for Business." *GMA News Online*, December 3, 2014. Available at http://www.gmanetwork.com/news/story/390891/money/economy/phl-ranking-in-global-corruption-perception-good-for-business (last accessed May 5, 2016).

Rivera, Temario C. *Landlords and Capitalists: Class, Family, and State in Philippine Manufacturing*. Quezon City: University of the Philippines Press and Center for Integrative Development Studies, 1994.

———. "The Philippines in 2004: New Mandate, Daunting Problems." *Asian Survey* 45, no. 1 (January/February 2005): 127–33.

Rizal, José. *El Filibusterismo*. Trans. Ma. Soledad Lacson-Locsin; ed. Raul L. Locsin. Makati City, The Philippines: Bookmark, 1997.

———. *Noli Me Tangere*. Trans. Ma. Soledad Lacson-Locsin; ed. Raul L. Locsin. Makati City, The Philippines: Bookmark, 1996.

Robles, Eliodoro. *The Philippines in the Nineteenth Century*. Quezon City: Malaya Books, 1969.

Rocamora, Joel. *Breaking Through: The Struggle within the Communist Party of the Philippines*. Pasig, The Philippines: Anvil Publishing, 1994.

———. "Learning New Ways of Being (Left), Akbayan—A New Left Party in the Philippines." As posted in *Mga Diskurso ni Doy Blog*. November 13, 2007. Available at http://doycinco.blogspot.com/2007/11/learning-new-ways-of-being-left.html (last accessed February 13, 2017).

———. "Partisanship and Reform: The Making of a Presidential Campaign." In *The Politics of Change in the Philippines*, ed. Yuko Kasuya and Nathan Gilbert Quimpo. Manila, The Philippines: Anvil, 2010, 73–89.

———. "People Power Is Alive and Well." *Third World Quarterly* 33, no. 2 (2012): 201–4.

———. "Political Parties in Constitutional Reform." Available at the Institute for Popular Democracy website, http://www.ipd.ph/features/july_2003/political_parties.html (last accessed October 15, 2004).

Rodil, Rudy. *Kalinaw Mindanao: The Story of the GRP-MNLF Peace Process*. Davao City: Alternate Forum for Research in Mindanao, 2006.

Rodrigo, Raul. *Phoenix: The Saga of the Lopez Family*. Vol. 1, *1800–1972*. Manila: Eugenio Lopez Foundation, 2000.

Rogers, Steven. "Philippine Politics and the Rule of Law." *Journal of Democracy* 15, no. 4 (October 2004): 116.

Rood, Steven. "Decentralization, Democracy, and Development." In *The Philippines: New Directions in Domestic Policy and Foreign Relations*, ed. David G. Timberman, 111–36. Singapore: Institute of Southeast Asian Studies, 1998.

———. "Elections as Complicated and Important Events in the Philippines." In *How Asia Votes*, ed. John Fuh-sheng Hsieh and David Newman. New York: Chatham House, 2002.

———. "Families, Not Political Parties Still Reign in the Philippines." *In Asia: Weekly Insights and Analysis* 22, May 2013. Available at http://asiafoundation.org/in-asia/2013/05/22/families-not-political-parties-still-reign-in-the-philippines/ (last accessed April 7, 2016).

Rosales, Loretta Ann P. "The NPA as the New Mafia." *Newsbreak*, March 1, 2004: 24.

Roth, Dennis Morrow. "Church Lands in the Agrarian History of the Tagalog Regions." In *Philippine Social History: Global Trade and Local Transformations*, ed.

Alfred W. McCoy and Ed C. de Jesus, 131–53. Quezon City: Ateneo de Manila University Press, 1982.

Roxas, Sixto K. *Juetengate: The Parable of a Nation in Crisis.* Makati City, The Philippines: Bancom Foundation, 2000.

Rueschemeyer, Dietrich, Evelyne Huber Stephens, and John D. Stephens. *Capitalist Development and Democracy.* Chicago: University of Chicago Press, 1992.

Rufo, Aries. "Sibling Rivalry." *Newsbreak*, May 10, 2004: 14–15.

Ruiz Austria, Carolina S. "The Church, the State and Women's Bodies in the Context of Religious Fundamentalism in the Philippines." *Reproductive Health Matters* 12, no. 24 (November 2004): 96–103.

Sabillo, Kristine Angeli. "Philippine Poverty after Five Years on Aquino's Watch." *Philippine Daily Inquirer*, July 26, 2015. Available at http://newsinfo.inquirer .net/707857/philippine-poverty-after-five-years-on-aquinos-watch (last accessed March 7, 2015).

Salamanca, Bonifacio S. *The Filipino Reaction to American Rule, 1901–1913.* Quezon City: New Day Publishers, 1984.

Salavarria, Leila B. "Duterte: Only the Yellows Are Against Me." *Philippine Daily Inquirer*, December 7, 2016. Available at http://newsinfo.inquirer.net/851635/ duterte-only-the-yellows-are-against-me (last accessed December 19, 2016).

Salaverria, Leila, and Inquirer Research. "Candazo, First Whistle-Blower on Pork Barrel Scam, Dies; 61." *Philippine Daily Inquirer*, August 20, 2013. Available at http://newsinfo.inquirer.net/469439/candazo-first-whistle-blower-on-pork-barrel -scam-dies-61 (last accessed April 5, 2016).

Salazar, Zeus A. *The Malayan Connection: Ang Pilipinas sa Dunia Melayu.* Lunsod Quezon, The Philippines: Palimbagan ng Lahi, 1998.

Samonte-Pesayco, Sheila. "Winning Winston." *I: The Investigative Reporting Magazine*, January–March 2002: 4.

Santa Ana, Filomeno, III, ed. *The State and the Market: Essays on a Socially Oriented Philippine Economy.* Quezon City: Ateneo de Manila University Press, 1998.

Santiago, Corazon Damo. *A Century of Activism.* Manila: Rex Book Store, 1972.

Santos, Matikas. "Maguindanao Massacre: How It Happened." *Philippine Daily Inquirer*, November 21, 2014. Available at http://www.inquirer.net/143183/ maguindanao-massacre-how-it-happened (last accessed January 3, 2016).

Santos, Reynaldo, Jr., and Michael Bueza. "8 Things to Know about Antonio Trillanes IV." *Rappler*, February 26, 2016. Available at http://www.rappler.com/ newsbreak/iq/107961-fast-facts-antonio-trillanes-iv (last accessed April 1, 2016).

Schirmer, Daniel B., and Stephen Rosskamm Shalom, eds. *The Philippines Reader: A History of Colonialism, Neocolonialism, Dictatorship, and Resistance.* Boston: South End Press, 1978.

Schivelbusch, Wolfgang. *Tastes of Paradise: A Social History of Spices, Stimulants, and Intoxicants.* Trans. David Jacobson. New York: Vintage Books, 1993.

Schumacher, John N. *The Propaganda Movement, 1880–1895: The Creation of a Filipino Consciousness, the Making of the Revolution.* Quezon City: Ateneo de Manila University Press, 1997.

———. *Readings in Philippine Church History*. 2nd ed. Quezon City: Loyola School of Theology, Ateneo de Manila University, 1987.

Schurz, William Lytle. *The Manila Galleon*. Manila: Historical Conservation Society, 1985.

Scott, William Henry. *Barangay: Sixteenth-Century Philippine Culture and Society*. Manila: Ateneo de Manila University Press, 1994.

———. *Looking for the Prehispanic Filipino and Other Essays in Philippine History*. Quezon City: New Day Publishers, 1992.

———. *Prehispanic Source Materials for the Study of Philippine History*. Rev. ed. Quezon City: New Day Publishers, 1984.

See, Teresita Ang. "The Chinese in the Philippine Political Process: From Retail Trade Nationalization to Retail Trade Liberalization." In *The Chinese in the Philippines: Problems and Perspectives*, ed. Teresita Ang See, 2:69–92. Manila: Kaisa para sa Kaunlaran, 1997.

Sentenaryo/Centennial. "The Philippine Revolution and the Philippine–American War." Available at http://www.boondocksnet.com/centennial/war.html (last accessed October 15, 2004).

Serrano, Isagani R. *On Civil Society*. Quezon City: Philippine Rural Reconstruction Movement, 1993.

Shaw, Angel Velasco, and Luis Francia, eds. *Vestiges of War: The Philippine–American War and the Aftermath of an Imperial Dream, 1899–1999*. New York: New York University Press, 2002.

Shefter, Martin. *Political Parties and the State: The American Historical Experience*. Princeton, NJ: Princeton University Press, 1994.

Sherman, Jason. "Philippines to See Boost in U.S. Military Financing." *Defense News*, November 5–11, 2001. n.p.

Siao, Felyne. "Because We Want to Make Marikina Even Better." *Rappler*, March 19, 2013. Available at http://www.rappler.com/nation/politics/elections-2013/24107-because-we-want-to-make-marikina-even-better (last accessed March 2, 2016).

Sicat, Gerardo P., and Rahimaisa D. Abdula. "Public Finance." In *The Philippine Economy: Development, Policies, and Challenges*, ed. Arsenio M. Balisacan and Hal Hill, 106–35. Quezon City: Ateneo de Manila University Press, 2003.

Sidel, John T. *Capital, Coercion, and Crime: Bossism in the Philippines*. Stanford, CA: Stanford University Press, 1999.

Silliman, G. Sidney, and Lela Garner Noble, eds. *Organizing for Democracy: NGOs, Civil Society, and the Philippine State*. Honolulu: University of Hawai'i Press; Quezon City: Ateneo de Manila University Press, 1998.

Silvestre, Rodolfo A. G., Jr. "The Magnificent Seven." *Newsbreak*, January 6/20, 2003: 24–26.

Sim, David. "Is Duterte's War on Drugs Really a War on the Poor?" *International Business Times*, October 14, 2016. Available at http://www.ibtimes.co.uk/dutertes-war-drugs-really-war-poor-graphic-images-1586262 (last accessed December 21, 2016).

Sioson, Dana. "Duterte's First 100 Days: A Progress Report on the Economy, War on Drugs." *Asia Journal*, October 8, 2016. Available at http://asianjournal.com/news/

dutertes-first-100-days-a-progress-report-on-the-economy-war-on-drugs/ (last accessed December 28, 2016).

Sisante, Johanna Camille. "Arroyo Wins Congress Seat in Pampanga." *GMA News Online*, May 12, 2010. Available at http://www.gmanetwork.com/news/story/190811/news/regions/arroyo-wins-congress-seat-in-pampanga (last accessed April 7, 2016).

Sison, Jose Maria. "Kabataang Makabayan Founding Speech, November 30, 1964." In *Twenty Speeches That Moved a Nation*, ed. Manuel L. Quezon III, 63–66. Pasig, The Philippines: Anvil Publishing, 2002.

Sison, Jose Maria, with Rainer Werning. *The Philippine Revolution: The Leader's View*. New York: Crane Russak, 1989.

Sison, Marites N., and Yvonne T. Chua. *Armando J. Malay: A Guardian of Memory: The Life and Times of a Filipino Journalist and Activist*. Manila: Anvil Publishing, 2002.

Skowronek, Stephen. *Building a New American State: The Expansion of National Administrative Capacities, 1877–1920*. Cambridge: Cambridge University Press, 1982.

Social Weather Station. "Extent of Worry That Someone from One's Family Will Be a Victim of Extra-Judicial Killing or EJK." Fourth Quarter Survey, December 3–6, 2016. Available at http://www.sws.org.ph/swsmain/artcldisppage/?artcsyscode=ART-20161219110734 (last accessed December 23, 2016).

Somers Heidhues, Mary. *Southeast Asia: A Concise History*. New York: Thames and Hudson, 2001.

Southgate, Laura. "The Legacy of Philippines [*sic*] President Benigno Aquino." *Global Risk Insights*, August 25, 2015. Available at http://globalriskinsights.com/2015/08/the-legacy-of-philippines-president-benigno-aquino/ (last accessed March 31, 2016).

Stanley, Peter W. *A Nation in the Making: The Philippines and the United States, 1899–1921*. Cambridge, MA: Harvard University Press, 1974.

Starner, Frances Lucille. *Magsaysay and the Philippine Peasantry: The Agrarian Impact on Philippine Politics, 1953–1956*. Berkeley: University of California Press, 1961.

Stauffer, Robert B. *The Philippine Congress: Causes of Structural Change*. Beverly Hills, CA: Sage Publications, 1975.

Steinberg, David Joel. *Philippine Collaboration in World War II*. Manila: Solidaridad, 1967.

Stokes, Bruce. "Which Countries Do Not Like America and Which Do." Pew Research Center, Fact Tank, July 15, 2014. Available at http://www.pewresearch.org/fact-tank/2014/07/15/which-countries-dont-like-america-and-which-do/ (last accessed March 24, 2016).

Sturtevant, David R. *Popular Uprisings in the Philippines, 1840–1940*. Ithaca, NY: Cornell University Press, 1976.

Suarez, K. D. "Aquino Net Satisfaction Rating Lowest since 2015—Poll." *Rappler*, April 18, 2016. Available at http://www.rappler.com/nation/129887-sws-survey-aquino-public-satisfaction-q1-2016 (last accessed May 14, 2016).

Supreme Court of the Republic of the Philippines. "People of the Philippines, plaintiff-appellee vs. Romeo G. Jalosjos, accused-appellant, Decision on Criminal Case No. 96-1985." Available at http://sc.judiciary.gov.ph/jurisprudence/2001/nov2001/132875_76.htm (last accessed April 7, 2016).

Sy, Marvin. "Senators Slam RH Budget Cut." *PhilStar Global*, January 9, 2016. Available at http://www.philstar.com/headlines/2016/01/09/1540764/senators-slam-rh-budget-cut (last accessed May 12, 2016).

Tadem, Teresa Encarnacion. "Filipino Neo-Liberalism before and after the Crisis." In *Hegemony, Technocracy, and Networks: Papers Presented at the Core University Program Workshop on Networks, Hegemony, and Technocracy*, ed. Takeshi Hamashita and Takashi Shiraishi. Kyoto: Center for Southeast Asian Studies, 2002.

Tan, Kimberly Jane. "More Than 5,800 Killed Amid War on Drugs: PNP," *ABS-CBN News*, December 6, 2016. Available at http://news.abs-cbn.com/news/12/06/16/more-than-5800-killed-amid-war-on-drugs-pnp (last accessed December 23, 2016).

Tan, Samuel K. *The Critical Decade, 1921–1930*. Quezon City: University of the Philippines, College of Social Sciences and Philosophy, 1993.

Tangcangco, Luzviminda G. "The Electoral System and Political Parties in the Philippines." In *Government and Politics of the Philippines*, ed. Raul P. de Guzman and Mila A. Reforma, 77–112. Singapore: Oxford University Press, 1988.

Tayao-Juego, Annelle. "Cops Unable to Take Antidrug Drive to Rich Makati City Villages." *Philippine Daily Inquirer*, July 22, 2016. Available at http://newsinfo.inquirer.net/798065/cops-unable-to-take-antidrug-drive-to-rich-makati-city-villages (last accessed December 21, 2016).

Taylor, R. H., ed. *The Politics of Elections in Southeast Asia*. New York: Cambridge University Press, 1996.

Teehankee, Julio. "Electoral Politics in the Philippines." In *Electoral Politics in Southeast and East Asia*, ed. Aurel Croissant and John Marei. Germany: Friederich-Ebert-Stiftung, 2002: 188–94.

Teehankee Julio C., and Thompson, Mark R. "Duterte and the Politics of Anger." *East Asia Forum*, May 8, 2016. Available at http://www.eastasiaforum.org/2016/05/08/duterte-and-the-politics-of-anger-in-the-philippines/ (last accessed December 18, 2016).

———. The Neo-Authoritarian Threat in the Philippines." *New Mandala*, April 29, 2016. Available at http://www.newmandala.org/the-neo-authoritarian-threat-in-the-philippines/ (last accessed December 19, 2016).

———. "The Vote in the Philippines: Electing a Strongman." *Journal of Democracy* 27, no. 4 (October 2016): 125–26.

Temple-West, Patrick. "Smuggling, Fraud Cost Philippines $25.8 Billion in 2011, Study Says." *Reuters*, February 4, 2014. Available at http://www.reuters.com/article/us-philippines-fraud-study-idUSBREA130DY20140204 (last accessed May 4, 2016).

Teves, Oliver. "Philippine Leader's Corruption Fight Marks Modest Progress." *CNS News*, November 14, 2015. Available at http://www.cnsnews.com/news/article/philippine-leaders-corruption-fight-marks-modest-progress (last accessed May 9, 2016).

Thomas, Ralph Benjamin. "Muslim but Filipinos: The Integration of the Philippine Muslims, 1917–1946." PhD diss., University of Pennsylvania, 1971.

Thompson, Mark R. *The Anti-Marcos Struggle: Personalistic Rule and Democratic Transition in the Philippines*. New Haven, CT: Yale University Press, 1995.

———. "Aquino's Reformism Hits a Dead End." *East Asia Forum*, September 30, 2014. Available at http://www.eastasiaforum.org/2014/09/30/aquinos-reformism-hits-a-dead-end/ (last accessed April 4, 2016).

———. "The Politics Philippine Presidents Make: Presidential-Style, Patronage-Based, or Regime Relational?" *Critical Asian Studies* 46, no. 3 (2014): 433–60.

———. "Populism and the Revival of Reform: Competing Political Narratives in the Philippines." *Contemporary Southeast Asia* 32, no. 1 (2010): 1–28.

———. "The Specter of Neo-Authoritarianism in the Philippines." *Current History: A Journal of Contemporary World Affairs* 16, no. 782 (September 2016): 220.

Tiglao, Rigoberto. "The Consolidation of the Dictatorship." In *Dictatorship and Revolution: Roots of People's Power*, ed. Aurora Javate de Dios et al., 26–69. Manila: Conspectus, 1988.

———. "Manifesto for a Strong Republic." Manuscript, the Center for Southeast Asian Studies, 2003.

———. *The Philippine Coconut Industry: Looking into Coconuts: Export-Oriented Agricultural Growth*. Davao City, The Philippines: ARC Publications, 1981.

———. "Smuggling Utterly out of Control under Aquino Regime: P4 Trillion in Last Five Years." *Manila Times*, August 25, 2015. Available at http://www.manilatimes.net/smuggling-utterly-out-of-control-under-aquino-regime-p4-trillion-in-last-five-years/212920/ (last accessed May 9, 2016).

Tigno, Jorge V. "Economic Viability and Local Governance: The Political Economy of Decentralization in the Philippines." In *The Role of Governance in Asia*, ed. Yasutami Shimomura, 253–312. Singapore: Institute of Southeast Asian Studies, 2003.

Timberman, David G., ed. *The Philippines: New Directions in Domestic Policy and Foreign Relations*. Singapore: Institute of Southeast Asian Studies, 1998.

Tiongson, Nicanor. *The Women of Malolos*. Quezon City: Ateneo de Manila University Press, 2004.

Tordesillas, Ellen. "Fidel V. Ramos: 'The People Are Tired of Constant Bickering.'" *Philippine Center for Investigative Journalism I Report*, February 2, 2006. Available at http://pcij.org/stories/fidel-v-ramos/ (last accessed January 30, 2016).

Torregoza, Hannah L., and Charissa M. Luci. "Senators, UNA Assail DOJ Decision to Set Aside 3rd Batch of Pork, Malampaya Charges." *Manila Bulletin* 1, May 2015. Available at http://www.mb.com.ph/senators-una-assail-doj-decision-to-set-aside-3rd-batch-of-pork-malampaya-charges/ (last accessed April 9, 2016).

Torres, Wilfredo M., III. *Rido: Clan Feuding and Conflict Management in Mindanao*. Quezon City: Ateneo de Manila University Press, 2014.

Torres-Tupas, Tetch. "Arroyo Cleared in P728M Fertilizer Fund Scam." *Philippine Daily Inquirer*, May 8, 2014. Available at http://newsinfo.inquirer.net/600623/arroyo-cleared-in-p728m-fertilizer-fund-scam (last accessed March 15, 2016).

Torrevillas, Domini M. "A Stronger No-No to Artificial Contraception." *Philippine Star*, August 5, 2003.

Tort, Static Marvin A. Opinion: "Time to End a Century of Pork." *Business World Online*, August 6, 2013. Available at http://www.bworldonline.com/content .php?section=Opinion&title=Time-to-end-a-century-of-pork&id=74531 (last accessed April 7, 2016).

Totanes, Von. "20 Filipinos, 20 Years after People Power." Philippine Center for Investigative Journalism *I Report*, February 2, 2006. Available at http://pcij.org/stories/romeo-j-intengan/ (last accessed March 3, 2016).

Tracy, Nicholas. *Manila Ransomed: The British Assault on Manila in the Seven Years War*. Exeter, Devon, England: University of Exeter Press, 1995.

Tupas, Rodolfo G. "From the Reformists to the Revolutionaries: The Rebels on Campus." *Sunday Times* (Manila) *Magazine*, February 22, 1970: 12–15.

United Nations Food and Agriculture Organization. *The State of the World's Forests*. New York: UNFAO, 2003.

United States of America. *Congressional Record* V. 146, Pt. 8, June 13 to June 21, 2000, 10450.

U.S. Agency for International Development–Philippines. 1995. "USAID/Phil Activities in Mindanao." Available at http://pdf.usaid.gov/pdf_docs/Pdacf583.pdf (last accessed February 12, 2016).

U.S. Central Intelligence Agency. *The World Factbook 2002: Philippines*. Washington, DC: Government Printing Office, 2002. Available at http://www.cia.gov/cia/publications/factbook/geos/rp.html (last accessed October 15, 2004).

U.S. Department of State. "Philippines, Defense: Status of Forces, Agreement Between the United States of America and the Philippines, Signed at Manila, February 10, 1998, and Agreement Between the United States of America and the Philippines, Signed at Manila, October 9, 1998." In Treaties and Other International Act Series 12931. Available at http://www.state.gov/documents/organization/107852 .pdf (last accessed March 24, 2016).

Valdepeñas, Vicente B., Jr., and Germelino M. Bautista. *The Emergence of the Philippine Economy*. Manila: Papyrus Press, 1977.

Valdez, Katrina Mennen A. "BIR Bags 2 More Convictions against Tax Evaders." *Interaksyon*, July 3, 2012. Available at http://interaksyon.com/business/36437/bir-bags-2-more-convictions-against-tax-evaders (last accessed April 10, 2016).

Veloso, Amelyn. "Malampaya Fund (Part 1): Limits to Use of Multibillion Earnings." *CNN Philippines*, June 11, 2015.

———. "Malampaya Fund (Part 2): Does It Exist Only on Paper?" *CNN Philippines*, June 5, 2015. Available at http://cnnphilippines.com/investigative/2015/06/04/Malampaya-Fund-Part-2-Does-it-exist-only-on-paper.html (last accessed April 8, 2016).

———. "Malampaya Fund (Part 3): Is Government Losing Out on Deal?" *CNN Philippines*, June 5, 2015. Available at http://cnnphilippines.com/investigative/2015/06/05/Malampaya-Fund-Part-3-Is-government- losing-out-on-deal.html (last accessed April 8, 2016).

Vergara, Benito M., Jr. *Displaying Filipinos: Photography and Colonialism in Early Twentieth-Century Philippines*. Quezon City: University of the Philippines Press, 1995.

Visaya, Momar. "Rep. Ronald Singson: On Struggles and Second Chances." *Asian Journal*, February 7, 2015. Available at http://asianjournal.com/immigration/rep -ronald-singson-on-struggles-and-second-chances/ (last accessed April 7, 2016).

Vitug, Marites Dañguilan. "Lean Alejandro: Activist-Thinker." In *Six Young Filipino Martyrs*, ed. Asuncion David Maramba, 1–39. Pasig, The Philippines: Anvil Publishing, 1997.

Vitug, Marites Dañguilan, and Glenda M. Gloria. *Under the Crescent Moon: Rebellion in Mindanao*. Quezon City: Ateneo Center for Social Policy and Public Affairs and the Institute for Popular Democracy, 2000.

"'We Do Not Discriminate': Rich, Poor Are All Targets in Drug War, Philippine Police Chief Says." *South China Morning Post*, September 5, 2016. Available at http://www.scmp.com/news/asia/southeast-asia/article/2015190/we-do-not -discriminate-rich-poor-are-all-targets-drug-war (last accessed December 21, 2016).

Weekley, Kathleen. *The Communist Party of the Philippines, 1968–1993: A Story of Its Theory and Practice*. Quezon City: University of the Philippines Press, 2001.

Wernstedt, Frederick, and Paul D. Simkins. "Migration and Settlement in Mindanao." *Journal of Asian Studies* 25 (November 1965): 83–103.

West, Lois. *Militant Labor in the Philippines*. Philadelphia: Temple University Press, 1997.

Whaley, Floyd. "Philippine Court Delays Law on Free Contraceptives for Poor." *New York Times*, March 19, 2013. Available at http://www.nytimes.com/2013/03/20/ world/asia/philippine-court-delays-free-contraceptives-law.html (last accessed May 12, 2016).

———. "Philippines Ex-President Is Arrested in Hospital on New Charges." *New York Times*, October 4, 2012. Available at http://www.nytimes.com/2012/10/05/ world/asia/philippines-ex-president-arrested-in-hospital-on-new-charges.html (last accessed April 7, 2016). Wickberg, Edgar. *The Chinese in Philippine Life, 1850–1898*. New Haven, CT: Yale University Press, 1965.

Williams, Mark S. "Retrospect and Prospect of Magindanawn (*sic*) Leadership in Central Mindanao: Four Vantage Points." *Kyoto Review of Southeast Asia*, December 11, 2009. Available at http://kyotoreview.org/issue-11/retrospect-and -prospect-of-magindanawn-leadership-in-central-mindanao-four-vantage-points/ (last accessed March 20, 2016).

Wolters, O. W. *History, Culture, and Region in Southeast Asian Perspectives*. Rev. ed. Ithaca, NY: Cornell Southeast Asia Program, in cooperation with the Institute of Southeast Asian Studies, Singapore, 1999.

Wong Kwok-Chu. *The Chinese in the Philippine Economy, 1898–1941*. Quezon City: Ateneo de Manila University Press, 1999.

The World Bank. "Conditional Cash Transfers." Available at http://web.worldbank .org/WBSITE/EXTERNAL/TOPICS/EXTSOCIALPROTECTION/EXTSAFETY NETSANDTRANSFERS/0,,contentMDK:20615138~menuPK:282766~pagePK: 148956~piPK:216618~theSitePK:282761,00.html (last accessed April 1, 2015).

———. "Philippines: CCT Proven to Keep Poor Children Healthy and in School—World Bank." September 23, 2015. Available at http://www.worldbank.org/en/news/press-release/2015/09/23/philippines-cct-proven-to-keep-poor-children-healthy-and-in-school (last accessed 28 April 2016).

Wui, Marlon, and Glenda Lopez, eds. *State–Civil Society Relations in Policy Making.* Quezon City: University of the Philippines, Third World Studies Center, 1997.

Ybiernas, Vicente Angel S. "The Philippine Commonwealth Government: In Search of a Budgetary Surplus." *Philippine Studies* 15, no. 1 (2003): 96–124.

Young, Crawford. *The African Colonial State in Comparative Perspective.* New Haven, CT: Yale University Press, 1994.

Zaide, Gregorio. *Philippine Political and Cultural History.* Rev. ed. Manila: Philippine Education Co., 1957.

NEWSPAPERS, NEWSMAGAZINES, AND WIRE SERVICES

ABS-CBN News
Agence France Press (AFP)
Al Jazeera
Asia Journal
Asia Pacific Bulletin
Asiaweek
Balita
Bloomberg
British Broadcasting Corporation (BBC)
Business World
CNN
CNN Philippines
The Economist
Far Eastern Economic Review (FEER)
Far Eastern Economic Review Yearbook
The Filipino People
Forbes Magazine
Fortune
GMA News Online
I: The Investigative Reporting Magazine
Inquisitr
International Business Times
The International Herald Tribune (IHT)
Institute for Popular Democracy Reports
Interpress Service
The Guardian
The Honolulu Star Bulletin
The Los Angeles Times

The Manila Bulletin
The Manila Chronicle
The Manila Times
Mindanews
New Mandala
Newsbreak
The New York Times
The New Yorker
Panorama Magazine
PhilStar Global
The Philippine Center for Investigative Journalism
The Philippine Daily Inquirer (PDI)
The Philippine Daily Inquirer–Visayas
The Philippine Free Press
The Philippine Post
The Philippine Star
The Philippine Yearbook
The Telegraph
Politiko
Rappler
South China Morning Post
The Sunday Times (Manila) *Magazine*
Time
Voice of America
Wall Street Journal

WEBSITES

Akbayan party, http://www.akbayan.org
Asia Times Online, http://www.atimes.com
Business World Online, http://www.bworld.com.ph
CyberDyaryo, http://www.cyberdyaryo.com
The Election World Organization, http://www.electionworld.org/philippines.htm
Jacobin, https://www.jacobinmag.com
Kyoto Review of Southeast Asia, http://kyotoreview.cseas.kyoto-u.ac.jp
Mindanews, http://www.mindanews.com
New Mandala, http://www.newmandala.org
Pew Research Center, http://www.pewresearch.org
The Philippine Census, www.census.gov.ph/
Philippine Center for Investigative Journalism, http://www.pcij.org
Philippine Center for Investigative Journalism *Public Eye*, http://www.pcij.org/imag/
    PublicEye
Politiko, http;//politics.com ph/
Rappler, http://www.rappler.com

Republic of the Philippines, National Statistical Coordination Board, http://www
.nscb .gov.ph/activestats/psgc/listprov.asp
Sanlakas party, http://www.geocities.com/sanlakasonline
Social Weather Station, http://www.sws.org.ph/swsmain/home/
The University of the Philippines Forum, http://www.up.edu.ph/forum

Index

75, 86–87, 98–99, 102, 171;
peninsulares (Iberian peninsula-
born), 86, 103, 106, 108; sojourners
and migrants, 79–80, 86
Spanish America, 47, 50, 55, 61–62, 67,
70–71, 75, 86
Spanish language, 47, 92–93, 95, 104,
107, 108, 110, 121, 201
Spanish mestizos, 98, 99
Spanish-American War, 113
special economic zones, 245
spoils system, 141–42, 153, 171, 240,
253
Srivijaya, 25–26, 34, 36, 38, 41, 43
Standard Oil, 143
Stanford University, 208
Stanley, Peter, 93, 142, 155
Starner, Francis, 181
state, attributes of, 6–8
Steinberg, Joel David, 163
Stonehill, Harry, 186
Strait of Malacca. *See* Malacca, Strait of
strong state, 204, 244
Strong Republic, 1, 268, 271, 273
Student Cultural Association of the
University of the Philippines
(SCAUP), 187
Sturtevant, David, 60, 81, 148, 150–52
Subic Bay Naval Base, 209
Suez Canal, 80
Suharto, 257
Sukarno, 184
Sulu, 10, 140, 145–46, 252, 298, 315;
Islam in, 43–46, 52, 95, 146, 217; in
maritime trade, 35, 41, 62, 69–70,
71, 95
Sulu sultanate, 44–45, 50, 69–70,
95–96, 97, 297
Sumatra, 25, 35, 44
Sumulong, Juan, 150
Swiss Federal University, 141
Sy, Henry, 324

Taft, William Howard, 118–19, 122,
134–35, 137, 139

Tagalog language, 11, 20, 27–28, 47,
50, 88, 110, 121
Tagalog provinces, 30, 78–80, 113
Tagalog(s), 27, 36, 50, 78–80
Taiwan, 243, 246
Tammany Hall, xviii, 139
Tan, Andrew, 324
Tan, Lucio, 215, 246, 251, 253–54, 261,
263, 324; and Susan Tan, 324
Tan Caktiong, Tony, 324
Tan, Rogelio, 320
Tañada, Lorenzo, 220
Tanjay archaeological site, 32, 36
tao, 30
Tausug(s), 45, 50, 217, 298
Tawi-Tawi, 252
taxation and revenue-generation, 16,
102, 104, 106, 109, 118, 122–23,
134, 138, 154, 157, 183, 185, 197,
215–16, 239, 243, 245, 253, 254,
271, 274, 276, 278–79; *cédula
personal* (head tax), 77, 91, 92,
107, 123; consumption tax, 178,
278; *contribucion industrial*, 91;
corporate taxation, 173, 178; *cortes
de madera*, 62, 63; customs, 62, 75,
80, 82, 88; direct taxation, 173, 178;
improving tax collection, 84, 89,
185, 245, 251; labor service, 30–31,
44, 53, 55, 57, 62–64, 67; land tax,
82, 150; legislative resistance to tax
legislation, 197; *polos y servicios*,
62, 85, 89; *repartimiento*, 63;
tax effort; tax evasion, 216, 243,
251, 254; tax farms, 76; tobacco
monopoly, 76–77, 82–84, 98; tribute,
23, 29–30, 32–35, 43–44, 48–49, 53,
55, 57–58, 61–62, 64–65, 67–68, 70,
77, 78, 80, 85–86, 89–91, 97; value
added tax (VAT), 250–51, 277-78;
vandala, 61
Tayabas province, 137
technocracy, 142,185, 194, 196, 204,
207, 208, 209, 212, 223
Tecson, Gwendolyn, 246, 247, 249

About the Authors

Patricio N. Abinales is professor in the School of Pacific and Asian Studies at the University of Hawai'i at Mānoa.

Donna J. Amoroso (1960–2011) was associate professor at the National Graduate Institute for Policy Studies, Tokyo, editor of the *Kyoto Review of Southeast Asia* at the Center for Southeast Asian Studies at Kyoto University.

STATE AND SOCIETY IN EAST ASIA

Series Editor: Elizabeth J. Perry